Fun and educational Places to go With Kids

"After buying this book, our family decided that we would devote one day of the weekend to a family outing. We have used the book to select our destinations, and our copy has post-it notes all over it, marking future destinations. We use it as our road map to fun! Recently, the Lakewood Rotary Club hosted a delegation of children from Japan for a one week visit. I made great use of the book to plan the itinerary for their visit. I would never have known about the Japanese American National Museum in Little Tokyo without the book, which was a big hit with our guests. Thanks for putting all this great information into one handy book!"

Lisa Rapp

President, Lakewood Rotary Club
and mother of two children

"Over 20 copies of <u>Fun and Educational Places to go With Kids</u> are continually checked out in the Orange County Public Library System; we can't keep them on the shelves! Children's librarians feel confident referring parents to this title. It's perfect for planning local inexpensive family outings."

Elke Faraci

Senior Administrative Librarian
Orange County Public Library System

"I could go on and on about this well-written book and the brilliance of the author. Suffice it to say, it is fun to read and an excellent guide for kids (like my husband and me) of all ages."

Jan Gallagher   *An unsolicited comment from a grandmother of seven, who also happens to be the author's mom!*

"I would like two copies of your book. One for me, a grandmother, and one for my son and family. Your column is informative and written with excitement, interest, and a sensitivity for children and parents. Thank you for sharing all your experiences and research so that we too may share these wholesome and educational fun times with our families."

J.G.   *Mother and grandmother*

"Susan Peterson's book <u>Fun and Educational Places to go with Kids</u> has been a great addition to our children's bookstore. Its extensive collection of family outings makes it a great resource for our customers. It is well organized, making it easy to find wonderful local outings to fit everyone's taste and budget. It has been a big seller, and we recommend it highly."

Ane & David Miller

Through a Child's Eyes (bookstore)
Downey

P9-CCL-286

Fün *and educational* Places to go With Kids

in Southern California

A comprehensive guide through Los Angeles, Orange, Riverside, San Bernardino, San Diego, and Ventura Counties, plus Big Bear and Palm Springs!

By Susan Peterson

Fun Places Publishing, California

Published by Fun Places Publishing
P.O. Box 376
Lakewood, California 90714-0376
(562) 867-5223

Distributed by Sunbelt Publications
(800) 626-6579

ISBN 0-9646737-2-X

Printed in the United States of America.

First Edition - May, 1995
Second Edition - May, 1996
Third Edition - May, 1997

ACKNOWLEDGMENTS

A book is _never_ put together alone! I especially want to thank:

My husband, Lance, who is also my best friend and partner. His computer skills have turned my ideas and typing into a readable format; his love, prayers, and encouragement have kept me going. Thank you, honey - you are God's greatest gift to me;

My three boys (who are the only kids I know that sometimes ask, "Can we please stay home?"):
Kellan (age 10), whose brilliant mind conceived the title;
Bryce (age 7), whose artistic ability is displayed on the cover; and
Terrell (age 5), who is the last jewel in my crown;

My parents, Jan and Joe Gallagher. From my mother, I inherited a love of travel and adventure, and the desire to do things well; from my father, I inherited organizational skills and the ability to get up early in the morning to get something accomplished;

My in-laws, Joyce, Pete, and Lerri Peterson, who have blessed us with consistent support, encouragement, and love;

My sister and one of my best friends, Beth Davidson, who helped me develop this idea, listened to my whining (I catch it from my kids), and just loves me;

My sister, Sandy Krupinsky, who has been excited for me about all the good things;

My best friend, Renee McKenzie, my "earth mother" who kept me focused, prayed for me, gave me support, and often watched my little darlings so I could do some serious writing about fun places;

My wonderful editors, without whom this book would be rife with ~~eros!~~ ~~erors!~~ oops, errors! How humbling it is to hand something you've poured your heart and time into writing to someone else to read; how much more humbling to get back those precious writings with lots of red marks! Some of my favorite comments include "I have no idea what you mean."; "Invest in a dictionary."; and "Huh???" Thank you all for taking time out of your busy schedules to read, edit, and gently (and sometimes sarcastically) redirect my writing efforts: Pauline Hirabayashi, Mary Kettles, Cathy Martinez, Gary Robertson, and Eileen Verosko. A special thanks goes to a treasured friend, mentor, and editor - my 95-year-old grandmother (who still runs circles around me) - Dora (Dee-Dee) Demme; and

All of the people associated with places mentioned in this book that were so willing to talk with me, send me information, and enable my family to come and visit.

Thank you, THANK YOU, **THANK YOU**!!

TABLE OF CONTENTS

INTRODUCTION and LEGEND EXPLANATION

In this world there are specifically fun places to go with kids, and there are places we go and bring our kids, anyhow. I think going shopping is great, but while I'm looking at clothes, my boys think it's fun to climb in the clothing racks and maybe even pull off a ticket or two to bring home as "prizes." This is not a fun family outing.

I've tried to do the weeding for you so that anywhere you choose to go in this guidebook, whether it's an all-day outing or just for an hour, would be an enjoyable time for you and your child. Some places are obvious choices; some are places you might have simply forgotten about; some are hidden treasures; and some are new attractions.

The book is set up by category; under each category, counties are listed alphabetically; and under each county, attractions are listed alphabetically. It contains a Calendar section, for annual events; an Ideas/Resources section, for general ideas of where else to go and for harder-to-find resources; and three indexes for easier cross-referencing - an Alphabetical Index, an Index by City, and an Index by Price. Tip: Look for discount coupons for main attractions in hotel lobbies and city visitors centers. Also, if you belong to AAA ask if admission to the attraction you're visiting is discounted for members, as there are often unadvertised special rates. Note: Names of places in all capital letters, used in a description (e.g. DISNEYLAND), are separately listed attractions in the book.

Next to most of the places described are symbols, meant to be at-a-glance guidelines. The **sun** indicates the average amount of time needed to see this attraction. You might decide you need more or less time - this is just a guideline. The **dollar signs and exclamation mark** are price guidelines. They incorporate *the entrance cost for one adult, a 10-year-old child, and the parking fee,* if there is one. If you have more than one child, or one who gets in for free, your cost will vary. **"Ages"** stands for recommended ages. It is meant to be an aid to help you decide if an attraction is appropriate and/or meaningful for your child. You know your child best. Some of the age restrictions, however, are designated by the place you are visiting.

☀ =	15 minutes to 1 hour	!	=	FREE!
☀ =	1½ hours to half a day	!/$	=	FREE, but bring spending money.
☀ =	all day	$	=	1¢ - $5
		$$	=	$5.01 - $10
		$$$	=	$10.01 - $20
		$$$$	=	$20.01 - $40
		$$$$$	=	over $40

P.S. My use of the word "he" or "him" in referring to a child in the book is meant to be generic, not political.

NEVER LEAVE HOME WITHOUT THESE ESSENTIALS

1) **SNACKS**: Always carry snacks and a water bottle with you and/or in the car. Listening to a child whine because he is hungry or thirsty can drive any sane parent over the edge. (And kids will not stop this endearing behavior until they actually get their food or drink!)

2) **MAP**: I would be lost without it! Invest in a street-finder map such as "The Thomas Guide" or "Rand McNally Streetfinder."

3) **TISSUES AND/OR WIPES**: For obvious reasons.

4) **QUARTERS**: A few quarters tucked away can come in handy for phone calls, those snacks I told you to pack but you forgot, metered parking, or arcade games. Tip: Put your quarters in a container in the car and hide it, or at least keep it of your child's reach.

5) **TOYS/BOOKS/GAMES**: Keeping little fingers busy helps keep little hands out of trouble. (Check out "Educational Toys, Books, and Games" under IDEAS/RESOURCES.)

6) **TAPES**: Audio tapes can get kids singing instead of fussing. (And if kids cry really loud, just turn up the volume of the tape even louder!) We've found story tapes to be a real blessing, too. (See "Audio Tapes" under IDEAS/RESOURCES.)

7) **FIRST AID KIT**: Fill it with the essentials including band aids, ointment, adhesive tape, scissors, an ice pack, Benedryl®, disposable gloves, and aspirin (both children's and adults').

8) **ROADSIDE EMERGENCY KIT**: This kit should contain jumper cables (know how to use them!), flares, a flashlight, batteries, extra drinking water, tools, matches, etc.

9) **JACKET**: Pack a light jacket or sweater for the unexpected change in weather or change of plans. (A change of clothes, too, for little ones who don't always make it to the bathroom in time could save your outing from being cut short.)

10) **BLANKET**: We mainly use ours for picnics, but it doubles in the program as an "I'm cold" helper and other emergencies.

11) **FANNY PACK**: Even if your kids are still in the diaper/stroller stage, a fanny pack is great for keeping your hands free to either help your children or grab them before they dart away.

12) **SUNSCREEN**: With our weather, we almost always need it.

13) **CAMERA AND FILM**: Capture those precious moments in a snap!

14) **A SENSE OF HUMOR!**

MISCELLANEOUS TIDBITS

1. **MATCHING OUTFITS -** Dress your kids in the same shirt (no, I don't mean one big shirt), or at least shirts of the same color (orange and red are bright choices) when you go on an outing. I thought this would look silly, but while we do get stares and comments, I can find my kids at just a glance.

2. **EXPECTATIONS -**
    A. Be Aware - Simply because you have a fun outing planned, whether it's going to the "happiest place on earth" or just an hour of play, please don't expect your child to necessarily enjoy every moment of it. Know and expect that your child will probably fuss about something, or seemingly nothing. Beware of the fun-stealers - tiredness and hunger. Visit places before or after nap time, and always bring food, even if you just ate.
    B. Be Prepared - Call ahead and make sure the place you want to visit is open, especially if there is something that you particularly want to see; check off your list of essentials; set realistic expectations for all participants; be flexible; and go for it!
    C. Family Mottos - We no longer promise our kids that we'll take them on an outing. A promise, as any parent knows, cannot be broken; it is an absolute. A plan, however, can be altered, depending on weather, circumstance, and/or attitude! One of our family mottos is, "It's a plan, not a promise." Another one is, "Oh well." Feel free to use either or both as the situation warrants.

SOME IDEAS TO EXTEND THE MAGIC OF YOUR OUTING

1. **CAMERA** - Buy your child an inexpensive 35mm camera (even a disposable one) and let him document the fun you have together. Keep ticket stubs and brochures. Have your older child keep a journal of his travels; where he went, when, and what he liked best. Give younger children duplicate pictures (or ones that aren't going in the family album) so everyone can put together their own album. Use craft scissors with patterned blades for creative cutting. Have kids use acid-free construction paper and stickers for decorations. Coming up with captions can be lots of fun - and funny! Spending this time together is a great way to extend a trip and continue making special memories. Note: Photo albums with magnetic pages will discolor your pictures eventually, but ones that use acid-free paper will not. See "Photo Albums" under the IDEAS/RESOURCES section in back of the book.

2. **COLLECTIONS** - Collect key chains, patches, pencils, or something inexpensive from each place you go and display them. One resourceful mom suggested collecting patches and sewing them on a quilt for each child. I bought colored flannel sheets and thin batting, doubled the sheets, and then "quilted" them. I sewed on the patches as we got them. My kids love their "travel blankets."

3. **EDUCATION** - Spend some time doing a little (or a lot) of research about a particular place (or time period) before you visit. It will make your outing more meaningful and make a lasting impression upon your child. Think of your field trip as curriculum supplement! You can call the attraction to get a brochure about it, use an encyclopedia to look up pertinent information, or do some research on-line on the web. Other educational activities to enhance your outing include:
   A) Read Stories - If you're going apple picking, for instance, read stories that have something to do with apples like Johnny Appleseed, William Tell, Snow White, Adam and Eve, Sir Isaac Newton, and specifically, "The Giving Tree" by Shel Silverstein or "Ten Apples on Top" by Theo. LeSieg.
   B) Theme Books - There are thematic study books for almost every subject written. (Teacher Created Materials, Inc., P.O. Box 1040, Huntington Beach, CA 92647, has over fifty thematic unit study books available.) Each book includes lessons and projects that incorporate math, arts and crafts, history, science, language arts, and cooking, into a study about one particular subject (i.e. weather, birds, the human body, holidays, etc.).

C) Spelling Words - Give your child a spelling list pertaining to the attraction you are visiting.

D) Map - Have older children use the map to track your way to your outing - this is an invaluable skill, especially if they learn to do it correctly!

E) Flash Cards - Take pictures of the places you go. Put the picture on a piece of construction paper and write the facts about the attraction on the back. "Laminate" it with contact paper. Use the cards as flash cards. Tip: If you're not a picture taker, buy postcards instead.

F) Bingo - Get duplicate pictures made of the places you go. Make bingo boards and cards. If the kids get a match, however, they have to tell you at least one fact about the place before they can put their chip on the board.

These are just a few ideas - I'm sure you'll come up with many of your own!

4. **YOUR IDEAS -**

ROAD GAMES

"Are we almost there yet?" and "I'm bored!" (along with "I have to go to the bathroom!") are common cries from children (and adults) who are traveling. Tapes, books, toys, and snacks all help to keep kids entertained; so do car games. Here are just a few of our favorites with brief explanations on how to play:

FOR THE YOUNGER SET:

MISSING LETTER ABC SONG - Sing the ABC song, leaving out a letter. See if your child can figure out what letter is missing. Now let your child sing (or say) the alphabet, leaving out a letter. Suggest correct (and incorrect) letters and see if your child agrees with you on what letter is missing. (Tip: Know your alphabet!)

MISSING NUMBER GAME - Count up to a certain number and stop. See if your child can figure out what number comes next. Now let your child do the counting. See if he/she agrees with what you say the next number should be.

COLOR CAR GAME - Look out the window for just red cars (or just blue or just green, etc.). Each time your child sees a red car, he/she can shout "red!" (or "blue!" or "green!", etc.) Together, count the number of cars of a particular color you see on your trip. Your child can eagerly share at night, "Daddy, we had a fifteen-red-car day!" A variation of this game is to count a particular type of car; VW Bugs is the popular choice for our family.

ABC WORD GAME - A is for apple; B is for bear; etc. Encourage your child to figure out words that start with each letter of the alphabet.

FOR OLDER CHILDREN:

ALPHABET SIGN GAME - Each person, or team, looks for a word outside the car (i.e. billboards, freeway signs, bumper stickers, etc.) that begins with each letter of the alphabet. When the words are found, the person, or team, shouts it out. The words must be found in order, starting with the letter A. Since words beginning with a Q, X, or Z are hard to find (unless you're near a Quality Inn, X-Ray machine, or a Zoo), players may find these particular letters used in any word. Again, the word can only be used in alphabetical sequence. A word on a sign, billboard, etc., can only be used once, by one player or team member. Other players must find their word in another sign, billboard, etc. The first one to get through the alphabet wins! Warning #1: Try to verify that the word has been seen by more than just the player who shouted it out, or learn to trust each other. Warning #2: From personal experience: If the driver is competitive and wants to play, make sure he/she keeps his/her eyes on the road!

ALPHABET WORD GAME - This is a variation on the above game. Instead of finding words that begin with each letter of the alphabet, each player must look outside the car and describe his surroundings using letters of the alphabet, in sequential order. This game can be played fast and gets creative, depending on the quick-thinking skills of the people playing. Example: Someone who is on the letter D might look at the land and see dirt; a person looking for an S might say soil; someone else who is on the letter G might say ground. All are correct. Players may use the same point of reference as long as the exact same word is not used. Whoever gets through the alphabet first wins.

GHOST - (Or whatever title you choose.) The object of this game is to add one letter per turn and be in the process of spelling a word, without actually spelling out a word. Players take turns adding letters until someone either spells a word, or can't think of another letter to add without spelling a word. A player may try to bluff and add a letter that doesn't seem like it spells a word. If he gets challenged by someone asking what he is spelling, he must come up with a legitimate word. If he doesn't, he loses the round. (If he does have a word, however, than the challenger loses that round.) Whoever spells a word or can't think of a letter to add, gets a G. The second time he loses a round, he gets an H, etc. Whoever earns G-H-O-S-T (i.e. loses 5 rounds) is eliminated from the game. Example: Player 1 says the letter "B." Player 2 adds the letter "E." (Words must be at least 3 letters long to count as a word.) Player 3 says "T." Player 3 gets a G, or whatever letter-round he is on. He loses the round even if his intent was to spell the word "better, " because "bet" is a word.

WORD SCRAMBLE - Make sure players have a piece of paper and a writing implement (i.e. a pencil or crayon). Using a word on a sign or billboard, or using the name of the place you are visiting, see how many other words players can make. To spice up the game, and add stress, set a time limit. Whoever has the most words wins. A variation is that letters are worth points: 2 letter words are worth 2 points, 3 letter words are worth 5 points, 4 letter words are worth 8 points, etc. The player with the most points wins. (Although a player may have fewer words, he/she could win the game by being long-worded.) Note: This game can be played for only a brief period of time by players who are prone to motion sickness.

<u>FOR ALL AGES:</u>
BINGO - This is the only game that you have to prepare for ahead of time. Make up bingo-type cards for each child. Cards for younger children can have pictures of things kids would typically see on their drive (although this depends on where you are traveling, of course): a blue car, McDonalds, a cow, a pine tree, etc. Cards for older children can have pictures, signs, license plates, and/or words that they would typically see on their drive: exit, stop, a traffic light, curvy road ahead, etc. Use magazines, newspapers, etc., and glue the pictures and words onto posterboard, one card per child. Tip: Have your kids help you prepare the cards as it's a fun project. Use raisins (or M&Ms) as

markers and when your child has bingo (or has seen a certain number of objects on his card), he can eat his reward. For those parents who intend to use the bingo boards more than once, "laminate" them with contact paper. Put small pieces of velcro on a part of each picture or sign on the card and make (non-edible) markers that have the other part of velcro on them. (This will keep markers from sliding off the cards during sudden turns!) Keep the cards and markers together in a plastic baggy (in the car).

20 QUESTIONS - This time honored game has many variations. (Our version is usually called 40 Questions.) The basic rules are for one player to think of a well-known person, or at least someone well-known to your children, and for other players to ask questions about the person to try to find out his/her identity. Only yes or no answers can be given. Whoever discovers the mystery person, in 20 questions or less, wins. Tip: Encourage players to ask general questions first to narrow down the field. (Inevitably, my youngest one's first question is, "Is it George Washington?") Teach them to ask, for instance: "Is it a man?"; "Is he alive?"; "Is he real?"; "Is he a cartoon?"; "Is he on T.V.?"; "Is he/she an historical figure?"; "Is it someone I know personally?" You get the picture. For a variation of the game, let mystery be an object instead of a person.

3 THINGS IN COMMON - This is a great thinking game that is easily adaptable for kids of all ages. One person names 3 words (or things) that have something in common. Everyone else takes turns guessing what that something is. Examples for younger children: #1) sky, ocean, grandpa's eyes (or whomever). Answer: Things that are blue. #2) stop sign, fire truck, Santa's suit. Answer: Things that are red. Examples for older kids and adults: #1) house, butter, horse. Answer: Things that have the word fly at the end of them. #2) chain, missing, sausage. Answer: Things that can end with the word link. #3) tiger, nurse, sand. Answer: Kinds of sharks. My favorite example is the one my middle child came up with: #4) lion, Jesus, Budweiser. Answer: They are all kings! (Who says kids aren't affected by commercials?)

I'M GOING ON A PICNIC. . . - This game tests a player's abilities to remember things and remember them in order. Player 1 starts with the words, "I'm going on a picnic" and then adds a one word item that he will bring. The next player starts with the same phrase, repeats player 1's item, and then adds another item, and so on. Play continues until one of the players can't remember the list of things, in order, to bring on a picnic. Example: Player 1 says, "I'm going on a picnic and I am going to bring a ball." Player 2 says, "I'm going on a picnic and I'm going to bring a ball and a kite." Variations of the game include adding items in alphabetical order or adding items beginning with the same letter.

PLEASE be aware that although the facts recorded in this book are accurate and current as of May, 1997:

- HOURS CHANGE!
- EXHIBITS ROTATE!
- ADMISSION COSTS ARE RAISED WITHOUT FANFARE!
- PLACES CLOSE, EITHER TEMPORARILY OR PERMANENTLY!

To avoid any unexpected (and unpleasant) surprises:

Always, ALWAYS, ALWAYS
CALL BEFORE YOU GO TO AN
ATTRACTION!!!

AMUSEMENT PARKS

Webster's definition of amusement is: "To cause to laugh or smile; entertainment; a pleasant diversion." So, from roller coasters to waterslides - have fun!

Tip: If you *really* enjoy a particular amusement park, look into getting season passes. Also, many parks offer discounts on admission after 3pm or 4pm.

MONSOON LAGOON

(310) 643-6130   *$$$$*

2410 Marine Avenue, Redondo Beach

(GOING N., EXIT SAN DIEGO FWY [405] N. ON HAWTHORNE BLVD., L. ON MARINE. GOING S. ON 405, EXIT E. ON ROSECRANS, R. ON INGLEWOOD, R. ON MARINE.)

This small (three-acre) water park is located next to MALIBU CASTLE miniature golf. Monsoon Lagoon has four waterslides. One, although it is good for all ages, does have a dark tunnel at the end of the ride which may be scary for younger children. My favorite slide is Big Splash. Hold on to your inner tube on this ride because you go around some pretty sharp turns. This is as close to river rafting as we'll get in Redondo Beach!

The younger set can splash around in Lazy Lagoon. This three-foot-deep wading pool has a waterfall, pint-size slides, a small geyser, and a little island in the middle. Another, bigger slide, ends into the pool with a splash.

Drier activities include a play structure, a moon bounce, a small beach area (bring buckets and shovels), a sand volleyball court, and large grassy areas for sun-bathing, resting, or picnicking. If you bring your own food in, you must rent a picnic table for $2 for the morning or afternoon, or $4 for the day. You may purchase food from the snack bar. The price for a Birthday Bash, which includes a slice of pizza, a soft drink, an ice-cream cone, plus a free return pass for each party attendee, is only $1 over the regular child's admission price, plus one adult is admitted for free. You need a minimum of six children for your party, and reservations are required.

Hours: Open mid-April through mid-June on weekends only from 10am - 6pm. Open mid-June through Labor Day daily from 10am - 7pm.

Admission: $10.50 for all ages; $7 for parents who are accompanying children 11 years and under. After 3pm, admission is $7 for all ages.

Ages: 1½ years and up.

RAGING WATERS

(909) 592-6453   *$$$$$*

111 Raging Water Drive, San Dimas

(TAKE SAN BERNARDINO FWY [10] OR ORANGE FWY [57] TO THE 210 FWY, EXIT AT RAGING WATERS DR.)

What a cool place to be on a hot day! Raging Waters is out*rage*ous with its fifty acres of chutes, white-water rapids, slides, drops, enclosed tubes (which make these slides dark and scary), a wave pool, lagoon areas, and sandy beaches. The rides run the gamut from the ultimate in daredevil (plunge headfirst on High Extreme - a 600-foot ride off a 100-foot tower) to a peaceful river raft ride in only three feet of water.

The younger set reigns at Kids Kingdom. They enjoy splashing around in this water area designed just for them. It has a big water play structure to climb on that shoots out water, plus tyke-size water slides and a tire swing. Elementary-school-aged kids have their own, fantastic, separate, activity pool with slides, a ropes course, and Splash Island. The "Island" is a five-story treehouse with slides, water cannons, and a huge bucket on top that spills over gallons of water.

Life vests are available at no extra charge. A picnic area is available just outside the main entrance gate. Outside food is not allowed inside, but there are many food outlets throughout the park. Hot tip: Wear water shoes, or sandals, because the walkways get very hot.

Hours: Open mid-April through May, and Labor Day through October on weekends only from 10:30am - 6pm. Open Memorial Day through June, Mon. - Fri., 10:30 - 6pm; Sat. - Sun., 10am - 7pm. Open July through August, Mon. - Fri., 10am - 9pm; Sat. - Sun., 9:30am - 9pm.

Admission: $21.99 for 48" and taller; $12.99 for under 48"; children 2 years and under are free. After 5pm, prices are $12.99 for 48" and taller; $9.99 for under 48". Purchase season passes by May and save $! Parking is $5.

Ages: 1½ years and up.

SIX FLAGS HURRICANE HARBOR   ☼

(818) 367-5965 or (805) 255-4111   *$$$$*

Magic Mountain Parkway, Valencia

(EXIT THE GOLDEN STATE FWY [5] W. ON MAGIC MOUNTAIN PKY. IT'S RIGHT NEXT TO MAGIC MOUNTAIN.)

Pirates and lost tropical islands are the themes creatively integrated throughout every attraction in this twenty-two-acre water park. Older kids enjoy the swashbuckling thrill of the vertical drops, enclosed tube rides, and a combination of the two in the tallest enclosed speed slide this side of the Mississippi. The wave pool is a hit for those practicing surfing techniques. The five-person raft ride is fun without being too scary, and the lazy, looping river ride in only three feet of water is great for everyone in the family.

Relax in the lounge chairs while the younger children play in a shallow pool with mini-slides, cement aquatic creatures, and a wonderful water play structure. The next harbor over is great for elementary-school-aged mateys to get wet and play on board the "floating" pirate ship. The adult activity pool has a net set up for water volleyball and, of course, it also has a few slides. Sand volleyball is available, too.

Tube rentals run between $6 and $8, although tubes are included in some of the rides. Food is available to purchase inside the Harbor as outside food is not allowed in. Hot tip: Wear water shoes, or sandals, as the walkways get very hot. Note: The Harbor shares the same parking lot as Magic Mountain.

Hours: Open May and September on weekends only from 10am - 6pm. Open daily June through Labor Day from 10am - 6pm, or so.

Admission: $18 for adults; $11 for seniors and kids under 48"; children 2 years and under are free. Combo tickets for Hurricane Harbor and Magic Mountain are $49 for adults; $28 for kids under 48"; children 2 years and under are free. Parking is $6.

Ages: 1½ years and up.

SIX FLAGS MAGIC MOUNTAIN   ☼
(818) 367-5965 or (805) 255-4111   *$$$$$*
Magic Mountain Parkway, Valencia
(EXIT GOLDEN STATE FWY [5] W. ON MAGIC MOUNTAIN PKY.)

If your children are thrill seekers and/or roller-coaster fanatics, action-packed Magic Mountain is the place for them. The roller coasters range from the classic, wooden Colossus to the feet-dangling, hairpin turns of Batman the Ride to the vertical drops, loops, and sheer speed of Superman. Magic Mountain has forty-three rides and attractions, mostly geared for kids 8 years and older.

Some of our highlights here include Yosemite Sam Sierra Falls (a raft ride through tubes, ending in water), the Log Ride, Jet Stream, bumper cars, and a visit to Pirate's Cove. The Sky Tower is a "must-do" for all ages because it affords a 360-degree view of the park and the surrounding area. Bugs Bunny World is ideal for the younger and shorter crowd (under 54"). The ten rides here include race cars, mini-prop planes, a roller coaster (of course) and, my children's favorite, the Tweety Bird Cage ride, which is a ride in an oversized bird cage.

Magic Mountain has entertainment such as live music, stunt shows, water shows, and interactive shows for younger kids like Bugs Bunny in Rabbit Hood. Cyclone Bay is towards the back of the park, where specialty shops are the specialty. Bayshore Candy is an especially sweet stop as kids can watch fudge, caramel apples, and all sorts of mouth-watering delights being made before their very eyes.

If it's real food that you're hankering for, try Mooseburger Lodge. The waiters and waitresses sing, a moose talks, and the dessert, chocolate "moose," is served in an edible chocolate shell.

Wear walking shoes because although there are lots of grassy, shady areas to rest, Magic Mountain is large and hilly. Be on the lookout for Looney Tunes characters throughout the park. (If you want wet, summertime fun, check out SIX FLAGS HURRICANE HARBOR, right next door to Magic Mountain.)

Hours: Open April through October daily from 10am - 6pm. Call for extended summer hours. Open the rest of the year weekends and holidays only from 10am - 6pm.

Admission: $34 for adults; $20 for seniors; $17 for kids 48" and under; children 2 years and under are free. Parking is $6. Combo tickets for Magic Mountain and Hurricane Harbor are $49 for adults; $28 for kids 48" and under; children 2 years and under are free.

Ages: 1½ years and up.

UNIVERSAL STUDIOS   ☼
(818) 508-9600 $$$$$
Universal Center Drive, Universal City
(EXIT HOLLYWOOD FWY [101] E. ON UNIVERSAL CENTER DR.)

This huge, unique, Hollywood-themed amusement park is really one of the world's biggest and busiest motion picture and television studios. Personal advice is to go on the forty-five-minute, guided tram tour first, as lines get long later on. The tour takes you behind the scenes, through several of Hollywood's original and most famous backlots. Along the way, some of the elaborate special effects that you'll encounter are: A confrontation with King Kong; the shark from "Jaws"; Earthquake - The Big One, where buildings collapse and a run-away big-rig crashes within inches of you, followed by fire and a flood coming toward you; and more disasters, like the Collapsing Bridge and the Flash Flood. Some of it gets a bit overwhelming for younger kids.

Want to go Back to the Future? Be prepared for an intense, jolting, simulated experience through the Ice Ages, into the mouth of a Tyrannosaurus Rex, and to the year 2015.

Down on the lower lot, kids can fly on a bike with E.T. and visit his planet. (This ride is best described as Disneyland's "It's A Small World" meets a world of E.T.'s.) Enter through the gates of Jurassic Park as you river raft through the primordial forest. What starts off as peaceful ride ends up as a very wet, terrifying, face-to-face encounter with bellowing dinosaurs! Follow this ride with Backdraft, where you literally feel the heat of the hottest attraction here. (You'll dry off from the Jurassic waters.) The sound stage becomes a fiery furnace, ablaze with ruptured fuel lines and melting metal. On the other hand, Waterworld is the coolest production here with explosive stunts and special effects that will blow you out of the water. In the sound stage show of Cinemagic, you can watch or take part in some of the special effects created for big and small screens. Lovers of Lucy can visit the heart-shaped facility and "walk through" her career, with the aid of photos, videos, sets, and memorabilia.

As Universal Studios is synonymous with quality productions, so the live shows are entertaining and, of course, highlighted with special effects. Some of the current shows include the Animal Actors Show, the Beetlejuice Review, and the Wild, Wild, Wild West Stunt Show, which is a funny western farce employing great stunts. (Get there early to watch the Charlie Chaplin character interact with the crowd.) The interactive Totally Nickelodeon show is totally fun. Based on

Nickelodeon shows, a few audience members are invited to compete on teams doing some very silly games and activities. The ultimate prize? Getting slimed! Some shows are seasonal and performed on weekends and holidays only.

There are many unique shops at Universal, too. Universal Ranch is tops on our list because kids can dig through a bin of rocks and fill up a small pouch for only $3.

Dine at some of the special restaurants inside the Studios such as Victoria Station, the restaurant in a train, or try Mel's Diner, a 1950's-style eatery that's just outside the gate. Get an early start for your adventure at Universal Studios, and don't forget to bring your camera for some wonderful photo opportunities.

If you're interested in "edutainment" ask about the Universal Studios Hollywood Course of Study Program. Fourth through twelfth grade students are introduced to a variety of subjects on a field trip here, including dinosaurs, sound effects, careers in advertising and entertainment. Other programs include assemblies at Universal, for seventh through twelfth graders, where speakers and live performances address important issues facing today's youth. Kids can then spend the remainder of the day at Universal Studios. Call (800) 959-9688 for more information on these programs.

Check out the adjacent UNIVERSAL CITYWALK for unusual shopping and dining experiences.

Hours: Open daily 9am - 7pm, the majority of the year. During the peak summer season, it's open daily 7am - 11pm. Call to find out the hours for the day of your visit. Tours in Spanish are available Sat. and Sun. Closed Thanksgiving and Christmas.

Admission: $36 for adults; $29 for seniors; $26 for ages 3 - 11; children 2 years and under are free. (Certain discounts available through AAA.) Parking is $6. Season passes are a great buy - $62 for adults; $53 for seniors; $49 for kids. Passes allow you priority tram boarding and complimentary parking.

Ages: 3 years and up.

ADVENTURE CITY   ☀
(714) 827-7469   *$$$*
10120 S. Beach Boulevard, Stanton
(EXIT ARTESIA FWY [91] S. ON BEACH BLVD. IT'S 2 MILES S. OF KNOTT'S BERRY FARM IN THE HOBBY CITY COMPLEX.)

My family travels a lot and one of our favorite cities to visit is Adventure City. This clean, two-acre little theme park, located in the HOBBY CITY complex, is perfect for younger children. The colorful, city scene facades throughout resemble storybook illustrations. The nine rides, designed to accommodate parents, too, include a wonderful train ride around the "city," a roller coaster, an airplane ride, and a bus with wheels that goes 'round and 'round. Kids can have a really hot time dressing up in full fireman apparel before (or after) they "drive" around on the 9-1-1 vehicle ride.

Adventure City also offers do-it-yourself face painting, a few video and arcade games, plus terrific, interactive, educational puppet shows at the theater. After the show, the puppeteers come out and allow kids to try their hand at puppeteering. Classes in puppeteering are also available. Thomas the Tank play area has a huge wooden train set that encourages toddlers' imaginations to go full steam ahead. A small petting zoo has goats, sheep, chickens, bunnies, and a llama.

The food is good and reasonably priced. Note: You may not bring your own food inside, but there is a small picnic area just outside the gates. Come and spend a delightful day in this city!

Hours: Open in the summer Mon. - Fri., 10am - 5pm; Sat. - Sun., 11am - 7pm. Open the rest of the year Fri., 10am - 5pm; Sat. - Sun., 11am - 7pm. Hours are subject to change.

Admission: Prices for ages 1 year and up are $3.95, which includes admission, puppet shows, face painting, Thomas the Tank area, and entrance to the petting farm; $9.95 includes all of the above, plus unlimited rides. Children under 1 year are free. Individual rides are $1.25 for all ages.

Ages: 1½ - 10 years old.

DISNEYLAND   ☼
(714) 999-4565 $$$$$
1313 Harbor Boulevard, Anaheim
(EXIT SANTA ANA FWY [5] S. ON HARBOR BLVD. OR EXIT GARDEN GROVE FWY [22] N. ON HARBOR BLVD.)

The world famous "Happiest Place on Earth" amusement park has so many things to do, see, and ride on that entire books are written about it. The following description is just a brief overview.

The park is "divided" into different sections, each section favoring a particular theme. The following attractions are just *some* of the highlights in these various areas: •Fantasyland is located inside the castle "walls." It features It's a Small World, Mr. Toad's Wild Ride, Alice in Wonderland, etc., and is definitely geared for the younger set, though some rides may be scary for them. •Mickey's Toontown is put together at crazy, cartoonish angles. Meet Mickey in "person" at his house in here. Kids enjoy the rides, with Roger Rabbit being one of the most popular, as well as just running all around this toddler-friendly town. •Frontierland features Tom Sawyer's Island, which is great for kids who like to climb on rocks. •New Orleans Square boasts of Pirates of the Caribbean. Yo ho, yo ho, with its catchy music and cannons "blasting" under a nighttime setting, it's a pirate's life for me. •Critter Country has an un*bear*ably funny show starring country bears. Splash Mountain (a wet roller coaster ride) is also in here. •Adventureland has the thrilling

Raiders of the Lost Ark roller coaster ride. You'll encounter snakes and other dangers and because it has different routes, you'll "never" encounter the same ride twice. •Tomorrowland takes you through the darkness of outer space in Space Mountain, and also into the wonders of the sea in the Submarine Ride. Coming in Spring of '98, look for Innovations, an interactive exhibit demonstrating the latest in home and office technology; a high-speed rocket ride (in place of the People Mover); and a new show, "Honey, I Shrunk the Audience."

The themed parades and shows are truly memorable. They are usually based on Disney's latest animation films. Fantasmic is a nighttime show (weekends only, usually shown at 9pm and 10:30pm) where good battles evil while mystical waters and laser storms flash from the dark in a thunderous symphony. Summer nights (actually May through September) bring a magic of their own to the Magic Kingdom. A spectacular fireworks display is shot off nightly (9:38pm) and a Light Magic show (replacing the Main Street Electrical Parade) is illuminating to behold! Call for a complete list of show information and times.

Main Street, U.S.A. is perfect for all your mini (and Mickey) shopping needs. Your child's favorite Disney characters are strolling all around the park, so keep your eyes open and your camera ready. Tip: Quite a few of the characters are gathered at Town Square when Disneyland opens in the morning. Come spend at least a day at the "Magic Kingdom"!

Hours: Open daily in the summer from 8am - 1am. The rest of the year it's open Mon. - Thurs., 9:30am - 6pm; Fri. - Sat., 9am - midnight; Sun., 10am - 10pm. Hours do fluctuate, so call before you visit.

Admission: A magical day costs $36 for adults; $32 for seniors; $26 for ages 3 - 11; children 2 years and under are free. Parking costs $6 per vehicle. Ask about 2 or 3 day passes. Several times throughout the year Southern California residents are offered a substantial discount on admission.

Ages: All

KNOTT'S BERRY FARM   ☼
(714) 220-5200 $$$$$
8039 Beach Boulevard, Buena Park
(EXIT ARTESIA FWY [91] S. ON BEACH BLVD.)

The atmosphere of the Old West is re-created throughout most of California's original theme park. The Old West Ghost Town has a humorous Wild West Stunt Show, an old-fashioned Stagecoach ride, lots of stores with a Western motif, and usually some cowboys hanging around. Indian Trails has tepees to go in, Indian crafts to see, and a terrific show with Native American dancers.

Fiesta Village has rides and shops with a Mexican theme. Adventure Fountain features Jaguar, a 2,700-foot long roller coaster!

Check out Windjammer, a duel track racing roller coaster at the Boardwalk area. Zap and get zapped with laser tag, a fast-moving action game which costs $5 per person to play. One of the most popular rides at Knott's is Kingdom of the Dinosaurs (guess why?), though it's a bit dark and scary for younger kids. Beware - Roaring Rapids **will** get you wet. There are roller coasters, bumper cars, and many other amusement park rides and attractions at Knott's. Camp Snoopy is ideal for kids from 2 to 7 years old. It has a ball pit, a petting zoo, a Snoopy bounce, and lots of kiddie rides.

There are also "hidden" parts to Knott's Berry Farm. For instance, in front of Roaring Rapids is a small, but terrific, Ranger Station. Inside, kids can see and hold a variety of insects and arachnids, such as a giant millipede and hissing cockroach. They can also pet a snake and touch animal pelts. The Edison Room in Camp Snoopy is a great first exposure to the science of how things work, utilizing magnets, generators, etc. A lot can be learned about the Old West and Native American life styles by talking to some of the costumed employees, visiting the old-fashioned schoolroom, and using some of the stores as mini-museums. There are many terrific educational tours available through Knott's education department. Learn about our early American heritage, pan for gold, explore Indian Trails with an Indian guide, learn about energy in motion, go on a natural history adventure, and much more! Call (714) 220-5244 for information on field trips.

In addition to Knott's Berry Farm's rides and attractions, there are twenty-six shops; delicious restaurants, including the famous Mrs. Knott's Chicken Dinner Restaurant; the Good Time Theater where major entertainers, including Snoopy, perform; and a full-size reproduction of INDEPENDENCE HALL. (See INDEPENDENCE HALL for a description.)

Hours: Open in the summer, Sun. - Thurs., 9am - 11pm; Fri. - Sat., 9am - midnight. The rest of the year it's open Mon. - Fri., 10am - 6pm; Sat., 10am - 10pm; Sun., 10am - 7pm. Hours may vary. Closed Christmas.

Admission: $31.95 for adults; $23.95 for seniors and ages 3 - 11; children 2 years and under are free. (Certain discounts available through AAA.) Parking is $6.

Ages: All

WILD RIVERS WATERPARK ☼
(714) 768-WILD (9453) *$$$$$*
8770 Irvine Center Drive, Irvine
(EXIT SAN DIEGO FWY [405] S. ON IRVINE CENTER DR.)

This park's all wet with twenty acres of over forty water rides and attractions! The mild to wild rides include a relaxing river raft ride, vertical drops, completely enclosed slides (i.e. dark and scary), wave pools (one has "real-sized" waves), shooting the rapids, and the opportunity to go belly-sliding down Surf Hill.

Younger kids have their own terrific water play area at Pygmy Pond. It has a climbing structure that shoots out water, a gorilla swing, just-their-size slides, and kiddie tube rides. Tunnel Town offers both wet and dry fun with twisting and turning tunnels to crawl through.

Two pools just for swimming are also here: One is three-and-a-half-feet deep, while the other is a bit deeper and it has a water basketball area. All of this, and plenty of sun-bathing opportunities, makes Wild Rivers a fantastic beach alternative.

Picnic areas are available outside the park, as no outside food may be brought in. Locker rentals are $4, and additional tube rentals are available. Hot tip: Wear water shoes, or sandals, as the cement walkways get very hot.

Hours: Open May through mid-June and mid-September through the beginning of October on weekends only from 11am - 5pm. Open daily mid-June through mid-September from 10am - 8pm.

Admission: $19.95 for adults; $9.95 for seniors; $12.95 for spectators; $15.95 for ages 3 - 9; children 2 years and under are free. After 4pm, admission is only $9.95 for all ages. Parking is $4.

Ages: 1½ years and up.

CASTLE AMUSEMENT PARK ☼
(909) 785-4140 $$$
3500 Polk Street, Riverside
(EXIT RIVERSIDE FWY [91] N. ON LA SIERRA AVE., R. ON DIANA ST., L. ON POLK ST. IT'S BETWEEN THE GALLERIA AT TYLER AND LA SIERRA AVE., AND VISIBLE FROM THE FREEWAY.)

Castle Amusement Park has a lot of action packed into only twenty-five acres. The compactness of the park makes it easy to walk all around. It has four scenic and challenging eighteen-hole miniature golf courses; a three-level arcade with over 400 video games and games of skill (plus a redemption center); and over thirty rides and attractions! The rides include the log ride, a huge carousel, roller coasters, a Ferris wheel, train rides, pony rides, Nascar go-karts, etc. There are plenty of "big kids" rides, as well as delightful kiddie rides. The atmosphere here reminds me of Coney Island in that the flashy rides are interspersed with carnival-type games.

The massive BIG TOP FOOD 'N' FUN RESTAURANT looks like a circus Big Top, complete with a large circus elephant statue outside. Pizza tops the list of food, but chicken nuggets, burgers, hot dogs, and salads are available, too. There are more arcade games in here, and shows are occasionally performed on stage to keep kids entertained while eating.

Castle Park also offers educational tours. For example, on the half-hour Pizza Tour kids see how pizza is made and learn how it fits into the four basic food groups. Then, they get to eat some! $2.50 per person includes the tour, a slice of pizza, and a soft drink. Special events and package deals are on-going here, so call for a schedule and more information.

Hours: Miniature golf and the arcade area are open Sun. - Thurs.,10am - 10pm; Fri. - Sat., 10am - midnight. The ride park is open Fri., 6pm - 10pm; Sat. - Sun., noon - midnight. (Summer hours and holidays the entire park is open extended hours.) Big Top Restaurant is open daily from 11am - midnight.

Admission: There is no admission fee. Miniature golf is $5 for adults; $3.75 for seniors and children 11 years and under. The log ride and pony rides are $2 each. Nascar go karts are $4. Ride tickets are 50¢ each; $9 for 22; $16 for 50; $25 for 100. Rides require between two - five tickets, depending on the age of the rider. (Children 10 years and under need fewer tickets.) Parking is free before noon; $2 after noon.

Ages: All

FANTASY FOREST AT SANTA'S VILLAGE   ☼

(909) 337-2481   *$$$$*

Highway 18, Sky Forest

(TAKE RIVERSIDE FWY [91] N.E. UNTIL IT TURNS INTO THE SAN BERNARDINO FWY [215]. STAY TO THE RIGHT AND TAKE THE 259/30 FWYS. STAY ON THE 30, THEN EXIT N. ON WATERMAN AVE. WATERMAN TURNS INTO HIGHWAY 18. FANTASY FOREST IS APPROXIMATELY 2 MILES PAST THE LAKE ARROWHEAD TURNOFF.)

Surrounded by the beauty of the San Bernardino Mountains is Fantasy Forest at Santa's Village. This fantasy-themed amusement park incorporates fairy tales, Santa Claus, and childhood delights with its twenty-five rides and attractions. Some of our favorite rides include the antique car ride, Christmas tree ride, bobsled ride, Ferris wheel, miniature train ride, bumper bugs (cars), and pony ride. The Forest also features a petting zoo, interactive puppet shows, a scrumptious bakery, and other wonderful stores for eating and shopping.

Ho-ho-ho! You can visit Santa Claus, and Dasher, Dancer, and rest of his reindeer here, too, although only until March 1, 1998. Then, Fantasy Forest is shutting down, because Santa is moving back to the North Pole.

Hours: Open June - August and November - December daily from 10am - 5pm. (Closed Christmas.) Open weekends only September, October, January, and February from 10am - 5pm.

Admission: $12 for ages 3 and up; $8.50 for seniors; children 2 years and under are free. Parking is $3.

Ages: 2 - 11 years.

PHARAOH'S LOST KINGDOM   ☼

(909) 335- PARK (7275) $$$$

California Street, Redlands
*(EXIT SAN BERNARDINO FWY [10] N. ON CALIFORNIA ST. IT'S THE FIRST PYRAMID
OFF THE FWY.)*

Mummies (and daddies) looking for a place to keep their kids
royally entertained, have found it at Pharaoh's Lost Kingdom. Enter
through the Sphinx into the world of arcade, video, and virtual reality
games. The lower level has a huge children's soft play area with ball
pits, slides, tubes, and obstacle courses. On the upper level, take your
best shot in Later Tag. With over 5,000 square feet of darkness,
mazes, tunnels, and opponents just waiting to zap you, the twelve-
minute game is action-packed. And all this is only the tip of the pyramid!

Outside, the Race Car Complex offers three different tracks -
Grand Prix, kiddie, and banked Indy speed track; some height
restrictions apply. Travel to ancient and exotic lands via the four nine-
hole miniature golf courses. Bumper boats are another great family
attraction. For an adrenaline rush, dare to try Sky Coaster, a harnessed
"ride" that lets you fly and swing from over 100-feet high - $19.95;
height and age restrictions apply. The thirteen amusement rides,
geared for young kids and old kids (i.e. adults), include a Ferris wheel,
carousel, tilt-a-whirl, mini motorboats etc.

We found a lot of fun at Pharaoh's Lost Kingdom waterpark. Climb
up the tower and go down the multiple open and enclosed slides; enjoy
a blissful raft ride in three feet of water on the Endless River; and body
or board surf at the Riptide wave machine. Younger children have their
own wading pool with a big water play structure and slides. Another
activity pool, for elementary-school-aged kids, has a water volleyball
area and a challenging ropes course over hard foam mummies and
tiles. A beach and a sand volleyball court are also here. King Tut never
had it so good!

Hours: Open daily at 9am. Closing times vary by season.

Admission: There are several price options here: A - $3.75 for a
single attraction of your choice: kid's indoor playground,
one-round of nine-hole miniature golf, bumper boats, or
kid's cars; B - $4.95 for a single attraction of your choice:
grand prix car ride, Indy car ride, laser tag, or 15 tickets
to the amusement park (each ride requires an average of
3 tickets); C - $24.95 for adults, $14.95 for ages 2 - 11 for
an unlimited pass to dry activities (not the water park); D
- $12.95 for adults, $9.95 for ages 2 - 11 for all day play
at the water park (tubes rentals, lockers, etc. are an
additional fee); E - $18.95 for adults; $12.95 for ages 2 -
11 for unlimited water park, unlimited amusement park,
plus 3 other attractions (choose an additional 2
attractions if the water park is not open); and F - $29.95
for adults, $19.95 for ages 2 - 11 for unlimited use of

everything in the park (except video and arcade games). Ask about season passes. Parking is $3.

Ages: 2 years and up.

BIG RIVER COUNTRY WATER PARK ☼

(760) 742-1921   *$$$*

Rt. 76 and Segnme Oaks Road, on the La Jolla Indian Reservation, Pauma Valley

(EXIT ESCONDIDO FWY [15] E. ON ROUTE 76 AND UP ABOUT 25 MOUNTAIN MILES, R. ON SEGNME OAKS RD.)

The woods along Route 76 hold a refreshing summer treat - a small water park! The park has five slipping, zipping, dipping slides; some that gently twist and some drop straight down! Younger children have their own large shallow pool area with slides, water play structures, and floating foam animals. The setting is attractive with shady trees, picnic areas (you can even bring your own food inside), volleyball courts, plus a general store, a full-service snack bar, showers, and lockers. Look up an adjacent attraction, LA JOLLA INDIAN RESERVATION CAMPGROUND / Tubing on San Luis Rey River.

Hours: Open on weekends from mid-May - mid-June, and September, 10am - 6pm; open daily mid-June, July and August from 10am - 7pm.

Admission: $11.99 for 48" and over; $7.99 for under 48."

Ages: 2 years and up.

FRASIER'S FRONTIER ☼

(619) 390-3440   *$$$$*

14011 Ridge Hill Road, El Cajon

(EXIT 8 FWY S. ON LAKE JENNINGS RD., WHICH TURNS INTO RIDGE HILL RD. AS IT TURNS R. IT IS LOCATED NEXT TO RIVER CANYON RACEWAY.)

Howdy partners! This western-themed family amusement center offers twelve carnival rides, six of them geared just for younger cowpokes. Enjoy the Little Dipper roller coaster, Tilt-A-Whirl, bumper cars, mini-airplanes, train, Ferris Wheel, etc. Kids can also just have fun on either of the two playgrounds, which have large wooden play structures, swings, etc. During the summer, two pools are available for your swimming pleasure. One is an adult-sized pool with lounge chairs, lockers, changing areas, etc., while the other is a gated, kiddie wading pool. Another great way to cool off during the hot summer days is to slide down the 500-foot waterslide! Frasier's Frontier also has grassy areas, plenty of shady oak trees, and picnic tables spread throughout. (My kids liked the picnic area with covered wagons the best.) You are welcome to bring in your own food, although no glass containers are allowed.

Hours: The park is open mid-March through mid-May and September through October on weekends from 10am - 6pm. It is open daily in the summer from 10am - 6pm. It is closed November through March. The pools and waterslide are open seasonally.

Admission: $6.50 for adults; $4 for seniors; $8.50 for ages 3 - 12 years; children 2 years and under are free. Admission includes entrance to the park and play areas, and unlimited rides. Weekday fees for the pools and unlimited waterslide rides is an additional $4.50 per person; weekend fees are $5 for 7 rides down the slide, plus usage of the pool.

Ages: 2 - 12 years.

LEGOLAND CARLSBAD, INC.   ☼
(760) 438-LEGO (5346)   *n/a*

Palomar Airport Road, Carlsbad˜

(EXIT SAN DIEGO FWY [5] E. ON PALOMAR AIRPORT RD. IT WILL BE LOCATED NEXT TO THE FLOWER FIELDS.)

Unfortunately, this park is not scheduled to open until 1999! But, because I hope this book will still be in circulation then, I wanted to let you know about it! There are two other Legolands in existence; one in Denmark and one in England. As the Carlsbad Legoland is modeled after them, the following information is a combination of what they've already done overseas and the projections for this particular Legoland.

This huge and unique park will offer several amusement rides, such as cars that look like Lego™ pieces; attractions such as Miniland where thirty million Legos™ will be used in replicating famous buildings; shows with audience participation; themed restaurants; and of course plenty of hands-on areas for building your own masterpiece. Even the conceptual drawing of the park looks incredible with its beautiful landscaping; bridges over lakes and lagoons; a Duplo™ village; Funtown; Imagination Center; and lots more. We can't wait 'til it opens!

Hours: To be announced

Admission: To be announced

Ages: 2 years and up. (Are you ever to old to play with Legos™?)

THE WAVE   ☽
(760) 940-WAVE (9283) $$$

161 Recreation Drive, Vista

(EXIT 78 FWY N.E. ON BROADWAY, L. ON RECREATION DR.)

Catch a wave at The Wave, on the "Flow Rider" wave machine. Swoosh on down the four waterslides here - two are enclosed, and two are convertible-style (no tops). (Some height restrictions apply.) Slip 'n slide down the fifth slide, which is short and slopes gently, and ends into "Crazy River," a ring of water that encircles the slide and lounge area. For those 41" and under, there is also a small children's water play area with a few slides and climbing apparatus with water spouting out. The large rectangular pool is used for lessons and the swim team, and is open to the public during Wave hours. There are a limited amount of picnic tables, plus a few grassy areas to lay out your towels. Lockers, double inner tubes, life vests, and shade pavilions are available for a small fee. (Usage of single inner tubes and body boards are included in your admission price.) Outside food is not allowed in, but there is a full-service snack bar here. Have big time fun at this small water park!

Hours: Open the end of May through the beginning of June, and the month of September on weekends and holidays from 11am - 5pm. Open the beginning of June through Labor Day daily from 10:30am - 6pm.

Admission: $8.75 for ages 7 to 59 years; $6.25 for ages 3 - 6 and seniors; children 2 years and under are free. Spectators pay the full admission price, but if their wristbands are dry when they leave, they will receive a $6 refund.

Ages: 1½ years and up.

WHITE WATER CANYON   ☼
(619) H2O - PARK (426-7275) $$$$$
2052 Otay Valley Road, Chula Vista
(FROM SAN DIEGO FWY [5], EXIT E. ON MAIN ST., WHICH TURNS INTO OTAY VALLEY RD. FROM JACOB DEKEMA FWY [805], EXIT W. ON OTAY VALLEY RD., ABOUT 2 MILES.)

The wild, wild West was never so wild, wild and wet! San Diego's liquid gold - White Water Canyon water park - is set in a re-created, western gold mining town, circa 1890. The park is spread over thirty-two acres, and although the landscaping is beautiful, the kids come here in herds because of the sixteen water slides: six inner-tube slides, six body slides, and four speed slides. Rip the curl in the wave pool, where waves can reach up to three-and-a-half-feet high. This huge pool can hold hundreds of swimmers and surfer "wanna-be's" at one time. Fort White Water is a four-story, interactive water family play structure with water cannons to shoot, cargo nets to crawl and climb on, and a floating lily-pad bridge aross the pool. (Going across on the lily pads is more challenging than it looks.) A large toddler play area has mini slides and a climbing structure in shallow waters. Still Water River is a restful, inner tube ride where you float along a continous river.

White Water Canyon also features a softball field, sand volleyball courts, a game arcade area, lockers, and showers. If you get hungry, walk along Main Street, with its western facades, and choose from three full-service eateries, or snack from one of the scattered "stands" throughout the park. Two picnic areas are also available. So, suit up, saddle up, and mosey on over to this western-themed water park, where you're expectations for a fun time will surely pan out. Hot tip: Wear water shoes, or sandals, as the cement pathways can get hot.

Hours: Open weekends only, May through mid-June, from 10am - 6pm; open mid-June through Labor Day, daily from 10am - 6pm.

Admission: $20.99 for 48" and taller; $13.99 for seniors; $14.99 for kids under 48"; children 2 years and under are free. Parking is $4.

Ages: 2 years and up.

ARTS AND CRAFTS

Children have creative urges. Art classes are offered in a dizzying array of places, and at fluctuating times (and prices). Most of the places listed here are stores that assist your young artists in developing their talents - move over Monet! Note: Museums are also great resources for arts and crafts workshops.

A.R.K. STUDIO AND GALLERY

(562) 438-3335   !/$$$$$

2218 E. 4th Street, Long Beach.
(EXIT SAN DIEGO FWY [405] S. ON CHERRY AVE., L. ON 4TH ST.)

A.R.K. stands for Artists Reaching Kids. This funky-looking storefront studio and gallery offers ways for kids to learn and express themselves artistically via painting, sculpture, ceramics, acting, dancing, storytelling, and writing! Classes, geared for children 7 years and up, are offered for visual arts and performing arts. The gallery displays rotate to show either art work done by kids, or art work that would be of interest to kids. For instance, one month the Long Beach Unified School District had a showing of students' masterpieces. The gallery was packed with kids checking out what other kids had created. Call for a schedule of exhibitions and class times - encourage your budding artist to blossom!

Going along with the art theme, a few buildings down from A.R.K. is a store called Artscape. This retail store specializes in local adult artists' sculptures, paintings, jewelry, etc. One of our favorite items is a lamp made from corner pieces of metal pipe. Your kids can get some great ideas here on how to turn some commonly-found objects into "artjects."

Hours: The A.R.K. Gallery is open Wed. - Sat., noon - 6pm; Sun., 1pm - 5pm. Class times vary.

Admission: The gallery is free. Prices for classes usually start at $65 for a twice a week, eight-week course that is two-and-a-half hours long, each session.

Ages: 6 years and up.

BARNSDALL ART PARK / JUNIOR ART CENTER

(213) 485-4474   !/$$$

4814 Hollywood Boulevard, Los Angeles
(EXIT HOLLYWOOD FWY [101] E. ON HOLLYWOOD BLVD.)

This art center is a hub of activity that offers three ways to inspire and stimulate your child's artistic talents: (1) On-going classes for ages 3 - 17 that range from film making and animation to drawing and pottery; (2) Sunday Open Sunday (yes, this is the real name of it), which is offered thirty-five Sundays a year at various art sites and locations throughout the Los Angeles area. These free, two-hour workshops are eclectic in what is demonstrated and produced - collages, paintings, cardboard houses, jewelry, masks, etc., but all are a lot of fun; and (3) A small children's gallery featuring rotating exhibits, such as art work produced by kids, or by illustrators of children's books.

The art park also has the famed Hollyhock House designed by Frank Lloyd Wright. Unlike most house tours, the emphasis is almost entirely on the architecture, not on the few furnishings inside the house.

Hours: Call for class and event information.

Admission: Free to the small gallery and Sunday Open Sunday.
Class fees range from $18 - $36.
Ages: 3 years and up.

COLOR ME MINE (Encino)
(818) 784-0400

$$$$

16101 Ventura Boulevard, Encino Place, Encino
(EXIT VENTURA FWY (101) S. ON HASKELL AVE., R. ON VENTURA BLVD.)

See COLOR ME MINE (Long Beach) for a description.
Ages: 4 years and up.

COLOR ME MINE (Long Beach)
(562) 433-4177

$$$$

5269 E. 2nd Street, Long Beach
(TAKE SAN GABRIEL RIVER FWY [605] TO THE END, W. ON GARDEN GROVE FWY
[22], EXIT S. ON STUDEBAKER, GO TO THE END, R. ON WESTMINSTER, WHICH TURNS
INTO 2ND ST.)

Do your kids have an artistic flair? (Or think they do?) Color Me
Mine is a delightful and cozy paint-your-own ceramic store. Encourage
kids to express themselves by first choosing a ceramic piece, and then
their palette. White dinosaurs, dolphins, mugs, plates, and more will be
transformed into vibrant works of art that will be treasured forever, or at
least a long time. My boys were so intent on their artistry that time just
flew by. Warning: This recreational activity can become quite addicting!
Pieces are glazed, fired, and ready to be picked up in a day or two.
Hours: Open Sun. - Thurs., 11am - 10pm; Fri. - Sat., 11am -
11pm.
Admission: Prices for mugs and vases start at $6. There is a $7 an
hour fee charged, per painter, plus a flat fee (usually $3)
for glazing.
Ages: 4 years and up.

COLOR ME MINE (Santa Monica)
(310) 393-0069

$$$$

1109 Montana Avenue, Santa Monica
(EXIT SAN DIEGO FWY [405] W. ON WILSHIRE BLVD., R. ON 14TH ST., L. ON
MONTANA AVE.)

See COLOR ME MINE (Long Beach) for a description.
Ages: 4 years and up.

KAR-LAN'S KRAFTS
(805) 251-7924

$$$$

17743 Sierra Highway, Canyon Country
(EXIT GOLDEN STATE FWY [5] N. ON ANTELOPE VALLEY FWY [14], N. ON VIA
PRINCESSA, R. ON SIERRA HWY.)

Kids kan kultivate their kreativity at Kar-Lan's Krafts. Both plastercraft and ceramics are available here to paint and glaze at this roomy and well-lighted krafts store. This is a wonderful way to spend an hour or so together!

Hours: Open Tues. - Fri., 10:30am - 6pm (open Wed. and Thurs. until 9pm); Sat., 11am - 5pm.

Admission: Prices start at $2 for a piece of unfinished art, plus $5 a day for paint and brushes. Firing costs extra, depending on the size of the piece.

Ages: 4 years and up.

KID'S ART (La Canada)
(818) 248-2483   *$$$$$*

2400 Foothill Boulevard, La Canada
(TAKE THE GLENDALE FWY [2] N. TO THE END, TURN L. ON FOOTHILL BLVD. OR, EXIT FOOTHILL FWY. [210] N. ON OCEAN VIEW BLVD., L. ON FOOTHILL BLVD.)

See KID'S ART (Tarzana) for a description.

KID'S ART (Northridge)
(818) 248-2483   *$$$$$*

19524 Nordhoff Street, #4, Northridge
(EXIT SAN DIEGO FWY [405] W. ON NORDHOFF ST. OR, EXIT SIMI VALLEY/ SAN FERNANDO VALLEY FWY [118] S. ON RESEDA BLVD., R. ON NORDHOFF ST.)

See KID'S ART (Tarzana) for a description.

KID'S ART (Pasadena)
(818) 248-2483   *$$$$$*

300 S. Raymond Avenue, Suite 10, Pasadena
(TAKE PASADENA FWY [110] N. TO THE END, TURNS INTO ARROYO PKY., L. ON CALIFORNIA, R. ON RAYMOND. GOING W. ON FOOTHILL FWY [210], EXIT S. ON FAIR OAKS, L. ON COLORADO, R. ON RAYMOND. GOING E. ON VENTURA FWY [134], EXIT E. ON COLORADO, R. ON RAYMOND.)

See KID'S ART (Tarzana) for a description.

KID'S ART (Tarzana)
(818) 996-1822   *$$$$$*

19642 - B Ventura Boulevard, Tarzana
(EXIT VENTURA FWY [101] S. ON RESEDA BLVD., R. ON VENTURA BLVD. IT'S ON THE CORNER OF SHIRLEY AND VENTURA.)

This small, wonderful classroom is a great setting for teaching kids realistic fine art skills using mediums such as drawing, painting, charcoal, pastel, and water color. Subject matter covered includes still life, landscape, animals, cartooning, and more. Each class has one instructor per eight students, so there is plenty of individualized instruction. The room has an intimate feel with kid-size easels, and kid-level shelves all around that have stuffed animals, vases with flowers, and other objects to inspire your young artist. Week-long summer workshops are also offered in clay, animation, etc.

Hours: Classes are given after school and on Saturdays.

Admission: Classes vary in cost. A one-hour class, once a week for four weeks, costs $56. There is also a $15 first-time registration fee, plus a drawing course material fee of $10.

Ages: 5 years and up.

KID'S ART (Valencia)
(805) 260-1774   *$$$$$*

25856 Tournament Rd., Valencia
(EXIT GOLDEN STATE FWY [5] E. ON MCBEAN PKWY., R. ON TOURNAMENT RD.)

See KID'S ART (Tarzana) for a description.

KID'S PAINT PLACE
(909) 699-4941   *$$$*

27540 Inez Road, Temecula
(EXIT TEMECULA VALLEY FWY [15] ON RANCHO CALIFORNIA RD., L. ON INEZ, R. TOWN CENTER. IT'S IN THE TARGET SHOPPING CENTER, ACROSS FROM THE PET CENTER.)

As the title suggests, this place is for kids. (Parents can paint if they promise to behave themselves.) Most of the store contains plaster items to paint, and there are specific shelves designated for younger children. Usage of the paints and brushes are included in the price of the item.

Hours: Open Mon. - Sat.,10:30 - 6pm; Sun., noon - 5pm. Closed holidays.

Admission: Magnets start at $3.25. An average price for an item (including paint and time) is $7.

Ages: 4 years and up.

MUDD BEACH (Manhattan Beach)
(310) 318-2242   *$$$$*

1113 Manhattan Avenue, Manhattan Beach
(GOING S. ON SAN DIEGO FWY [405], EXIT S. ON INGLEWOOD AVE., R. ON MANHATTAN BLVD. OR, GOING N. ON 405, EXIT N. ON HAWTHORNE BLVD., L. ON MANHATTAN BLVD. ONCE ON MANHATTAN BLVD., TAKE IT ALMOST TO THE END AND TURN L. ON MANHATTAN AVE.)

Help mold your children's artistic talents by signing them up for a class that includes working with clay. Or, get your children fired-up about art by encouraging them to paint some of the wonderful ceramic pieces here. Choose from a wide variety of animal figures, picture frames, children's tea sets, etc. With over fifty colors of paint, and a bright cheerful atmosphere, your kids will have a great time at Mudd Beach.

A gallery of retail art is here to lend inspiration. Some of the unique pieces for sale include mosaic mirrors and tables, candles, hand blown glass, etc.

Hours: Open Sun. - Mon., 11am - 8pm; Tues. - Thurs., 11am - 9pm; Fri. - Sat., 10am - 9pm.

Admission: Ceramic pieces start at about $3, plus $5.50 an hour per painter, and a $2 firing fee per piece.

Ages: 4 years and up.

MUDD BEACH (Pasadena)   ☼
(818) 449-4050 $$$$

148 West Colorado Boulevard, Pasadena
(BETWEEN DE LACEY AND PASADENA AVE.)

See MUDD BEACH (Manhattan Beach) for a description.

Ages: 4 years and up.

PAINT & FUN   ☼
(818) 708-2152 $$$

19458 Ventura Boulevard, Tarzana
(EXIT VENTURA FWY [101] S. ON RESEDA BLVD., R. ON VENTURA BLVD. IT'S ON THE CORNER OF SHIRLEY AND VENTURA.)

With a paintbrush in one hand and a plaster or ceramic ornament, statue, or part of a place setting in the other hand, plus paints in all the colors of the rainbow to choose from, your child is in his/her own little art heaven. The set-up is smartly arranged, as ceramics are on shelves on one wall, while tables with paint are against the opposite wall - less opportunity for broken pieces! T-shirt painting is also available. Paint & Fun is great place to make special gifts, or to have a birthday party.

Hours: Open daily from 10am - 6pm.

Admission: The cost for a plaster work of art starts at $3; ceramic starts at about $12; T-shirt painting begins at $12. There is no per hour fee charge, and paints, etc., are included in the price of your piece.

Ages: 4 years and up.

PAINT PALACE   ☼
(818) 541-1875 $$$

3600 Ocean View Boulevard, #4, Glendale
(FROM FOOTHILL FWY [210], EXIT S. ON OCEAN VIEW BLVD. GOING N. ON GLENDALE FWY [2], EXIT W. ON VERDUGO BLVD, L. ON OCEAN VIEW BLVD.)

This paint-your-own studio offers plaster figurines, magnets, frames, holiday decorations, sports items, etc., for your child's painting enjoyment. Smocks, paints, brushes, and inspiration are all provided. Note: The pieces generally do not last as long as glazed ceramic items, but they cost less and kids enjoy coming here just for the fun of creating.

Hours: Open Wed. - Mon. from 11am - 6pm.

Admission: Prices range from $3 - $20, with the average piece costing $7. (Paints and studio time are included in the item price.)

Ages: 4 years and up.

A PERSONAL TOUCH $\quad$ ☼

(714) 693-8777 $\qquad$ *$$$$*

5655 East La Palma Avenue, Suite 125, Anaheim

(EXIT RIVERSIDE FWY [91], N. ON IMPERIAL HWY, L. ON LA PALMA AVE.)

Come to this inviting store to make a keepsake that has a personal touch. There are several ceramic pieces to choose from, such as animal figurines, plates, trinket boxes, sports balls (i.e. baseballs, footballs, etc.), mugs, and tiles for hand or footprints. Paints, brushes, and studio time is included in the hourly fee. Kids love expressing themselves in this creative fashion (and it is so much better than watching TV!).

Hours: Open Mon., noon - 9pm; Tues. - Sat., 11am - 9pm; Sun., noon - 5pm.

Admission: The price of your ceramic item, plus $6 per hour for adults; $4 per hour for children 12 years and under. $2 - $5 for glazing and firing, depending on the size of the piece.

Ages: 4 years and up.

ARTMAKER $\quad$

(562) 596-8896 $\qquad$ *$$*

12371 Seal Beach Boulevard, Seal Beach

(EXIT SAN DIEGO FWY [405] N. ON SEAL BEACH BLVD. IT'S IN ROSSMOOR SHOPPING CENTER.)

Are your kids crafty? (I mean that question in the artistic sense.) Whether your answer is "yes" or "no," they will thoroughly enjoy their visit to the Artmaker. Each arts and crafts session features a special project or two, with only general instructions given so that imaginations have free reign. Recycled and everyday materials such as newspaper, egg cartons, glitter, glue, ribbons, buttons, paints, and milk jugs, become party hats, bird feeders, banners, etc. A snack is provided for your starving artists, and a bubble machine is turned on to entertain those who are done early. (Did you know that if you wet your hands, you can catch and hold a bubble?)

The Artmaker is decorated with children's creations, lending inspiration to your artists. Parents, you can assist your younger kids, or just relax as staff is on hand to help out. As an added bonus, when your child is done crafting, you may just leave without having to clean up the inevitable mess! The Artmaker has become a favorite place for my kids to come and create. Tip: This is a great place for a birthday party!

Hours: Classes are offered at varying times throughout the week, including mornings for Mommy/Daddy and Me, after school for older children, and every Sat. from 1pm - 2pm. Call for a schedule, and for adult class information, too.

Admission: One-hour classes are $8 per artist. Other classes start at $10 per artist.

Ages: 1½ years and up, depending on the class.

CERAMIC CREATIONS

(714) 458-7067 $$$$

24000 Alicia Parkway, Mission Viejo
(EXIT SAN DIEGO FWY [5] N.E. ON ALICIA PKWY.)

Come visit Ceramic Creations and let your creative juices flow! Choose from vases, mugs, Disney figurines, bowls, etc., and paint it with your special flare. My kids sometimes choose very interesting color combinations, but that is part of what makes their piece so special. Your item will be ready to be picked up in a day or two.

Hours: Open Mon. - Tues., 11am - 6pm; Wed. - Sat., 10am - 9pm; Sun., 10am - 6pm.

Admission: The price of your item, plus $4 per hour per painter, which includes paint, brushes, glazing, and firing.

Ages: 4 years and up.

CERAMIC ROSE

(714) 539-2732 $$$$

10552 Stanford Avenue, Garden Grove
(EXIT THE GARDEN GROVE FWY [22], N. ON BROOKHURST ST., R. ON STANFORD AVE.)

A rose is a rose is a rose, unless it's a Ceramic Rose. Your young artists' talent will blossom as they choose from a variety of bisque pieces to paint, creating their own design. The flat fee includes paints, studio time, glazing, and firing.

Hours: Open Mon., Tues., and Thurs., 10am - 9pm; Wed, Fri., and Sat., 10am - 6pm.

Admission: $5 per painter, plus the price of a ceramic piece.

Ages: 5 years and up.

IRVINE FINE ART CENTER

(714) 724-6880   !/$$$

14321 Yale Avenue, Irvine
(EXIT SANTA ANA FWY [5] S. ON CULVER, L. ON WALNUT, L. ON YALE. IT'S IN HERITAGE PARK.)

Various monthly exhibits display art work and photography by students, and/or local artists. The Center also hosts numerous art classes such as watercolor, drawing, calligraphy, etc. Two of the on-going classes are listed below:

The **Arts Club** is an after-school, drop-in program, geared for kids 5 - 11 years. This structured, class-like setting provides a great opportunity for kids to be creative using a variety of materials like clay, papier-mache, paints, etc. It is also a wonderful environment for making new friends. Supervision, materials, and fun are all provided.

The **Teen Open Studio** is a ceramics class for high schoolers, ages 13 - 18. An instructor is available for assistance and all materials are provided. (Also see HERITAGE PARK [Irvine].)

Hours: Tour through the Center, Mon. - Thurs., 9am - 9pm; Fri., 9am - 5pm; Sat., 9am - 3pm; Sun., 1pm - 5pm. Arts Club is offered Mon., Tues., and Thurs., 3pm - 6pm; Wed., 2pm - 6pm. Fri. from 3pm - 5:30pm is Children's Open Studio with a slightly different format and emphasis than the Arts Club. Teen Open Studio is offered Tues. and Thurs. from 4pm - 6pm. (Days are subject to change.)

Admission: The Center is free. Arts Club is $11 per child, per visit, or purchase a multiple-day pass and save money. Children's Open Studio is $9 per visit. Teen Open Studio is $5 per visit.

Ages: 5 - 11 years - Arts Club; 13 - 18 years - Teen Open Studio.

PAINT 'N PLATES
(714) 509-6115   *$$$$*

4213 Campus Drive, Irvine
(EXIT SAN DIEGO FWY [405], S.W. ON CULVER DR., R. ON CAMPUS DR. IT'S IN UNIVERSITY CENTER, ACROSS FROM U.C. IRVINE)

The first hard choice here is what to paint. Adults tend to go for platters, mugs, vases, canisters, etc., while kids usually choose dolphin or kitty figurines, frames, or popcorn bowls. Next, you need to decide if you want to make a free-hand design, use a stencil or two, paint it all one color, etc. Then, you have to decide what colors you want. Whew! Nothing like a relaxing time with your kids! Actually, painting a ceramic piece is a great activity, and one that everyone in my family enjoys.

Hours: Open Sun. - Tues., noon - 7pm; Wed. - Thurs., 11am - 9pm; Fri. - Sat., 11am - 10pm. The store stays open later in the summer.

Admission: $5 an hour per painter, plus the price of the item you're painting. Glazing is $3 per item.

Ages: 5 years and up.

PLAY IN THE MUD   ☼
(714) 680-4367 $$$$
418 W. Commonwealth Avenue, Fullerton
(EXIT RIVERSIDE FWY [91] N. ON HARBOR BLVD., L. ON COMMONWEALTH AVE.)

Looking for a great place for your children to be creative and not mess up your house? You've found it, at Play In the Mud. Kids can choose from dinosaur and dolphin figurines, mugs, plates, frames, tiles, and more at this paint-your-own ceramic store. After they've chosen their piece, they can paint it 'til their hearts are content using a myriad of colors and stencils. It will be glazed and fired and ready for pick up in a day or two. Their works of art make great gifts! Play In the Mud also offers special workshops for children for making beads, tin tiles, and mosaic tiles. Call for a current schedule.

Hours: Open Tues., Wed., and Fri., 3pm - 9pm; Thurs., and Sat., noon - 5pm. Call for extended summer hours.

Admission: The cost of your item, plus a $7 flat fee, which includes unlimited time and usage of paints, etc. $3 firing fee for adults; children 12 years and under get their item fired for free.

Ages: 4 years and up.

ARTOPIA   ☼
(619) 283-1653 $$$$
4224 Adams Avenue, Kensington
(GOING S. ON ESCONDIDO FWY [15], EXIT E. ON ADAMS (AT THE END OF THE ESCONDIDO FWY). GOING S. ON JACOB DEKEMA FWY [805], EXIT W. ON MADISON, R. ON 30TH ST., R. ON ADAMS. GOING N. ON 805, EXIT E. ON EL CAJON BLVD., L, ON WILSON AVE., R. ON MEADE AVE., L. ON WILSON AVE., R. ON ADAMS.)

Do your kids have that glazed look in their eyes? Then bring them to Artopia where they can pick out any piece of unfinished ceramic to paint, glaze, and fire. Choose from a wide assortment such as dinnerware, vases, figurines, etc. Creative kids (and adults) can literally sit for hours, designing and painting masterpieces. I, on the other hand, rely on others' ideas, and stencils. Either way, it is a great activity, and the finished product is always a special keepsake.

Hours: Open Tues. - Fri., noon - 8pm; Sat., 9am - 6pm; Sun., noon - 6pm.

Admission: The price of your piece (between $2 - $30), plus $5.50 per hour which includes paints, glazing, and firing.

Ages: 4 years and up.

CERAMICAFE   ☼
(619) 231-7991 $$$$
860 5th Avenue in the Gaslamp Quarter, San Diego

(GOING S. ON SAN DIEGO FWY [5], EXIT W. ON ASH ST., L. ON 6ᵀᴴ AVE., R. ON MARKET, L. ON 5ᵀᴴ AVE. GOING N. ON 5, EXIT S. ON 6ᵀᴴ AVE., R. ON MARKET, L. ON 5ᵀᴴ AVE. IT'S ONE BLOCK AWAY FROM HORTON PLAZA.)

"You've got a style all your own" can be taken several different ways. At the Ceramicafe, your children can develop a style all their own by choosing a mug, plate, figurine, picture frame, etc. to design and paint any way they want. What fun! This classy paint-your-own ceramic studio is located in the historic and romantic Gaslamp Quarter, so explore some of the unique stores before or after your time here.

Hours: Open Mon. - Thurs., 2pm - 10pm; Fri. - Sat., noon - midnight; Sun., noon - 8pm.

Admission: The cost of your item, ranging from $5 - $45, plus a $6 an hour fee that includes paints, glazing, and firing.

Ages: 5 years and up.

IT'S YOU

(714) 673-5969 $$$$

2919 East Coast Highway, Corona Del Mar
(TAKE THE SAN DIEGO FWY [405] OR THE COSTA MESA FWY [55] TO THE CORONA DEL MAR FWY [73], WHICH TURNS INTO MACARTHUR BLVD. EXIT MACARTHUR BLVD. S. ON EAST COAST HWY.)

Bowls, mugs, figurines, jewelry boxes, frames, etc., are just a few of the ceramic pieces available at It's You. Choose one item, and with paints and stencils galore to use, let your creative side take over, or at least have fun making something you can take home. This is a great activity for kids (and adults), who will treasure what they've made.

Hours: Open Mon. - Sat., 10am - 9pm; Sun., 10am - 6pm.

Admission: $6 per hour per painter - the clock doesn't start ticking until you actually start painting. Items cost between $2 - $40; glazing and firing cost between $1 - $5, depending on the size of your item.

Ages: 5 years and up.

PAINT, GLAZE, AND FIRE!

(760) 633-2254 $$$$

937 1ˢᵗ Street, Suite 109, Encinitas
(EXIT SAN DIEGO FWY [5] W. ON ENCINITAS BLVD., L. ON 1ˢᵗ ST. BY LUMBERYARD NEXT TO THE SHERIFF'S STATION.)

Ready, set, go, to Paint, Glaze, and Fire! This fun paint-your-own ceramic store offers lots of items to choose from such as plates, bowls, flower pots, goblets, salt & pepper shakers, animal figurines, and more. Kids will have a field day picking out colors and thinking of ways to design their chosen piece. Warning: This recreational activity can become habit forming! Finished masterpieces may be picked up in a day or two, after they've been glazed and fired.

Hours: Open Mon. - Sat., 10am - 7pm; Sun., 11am - 7pm.

Admission: $2 - $24 per piece, plus $6 per hour which includes paints, glazing and firing. (You only pay for the first two hours - after that there is no charge for your time.)

Ages: 4 years and up.

BEACHES

Beaches are a "shore" bet for a day of fun in the sun. Along with sand and water play, in-line skating, and/or biking, some beaches have playgrounds, picnic tables, and waveless waters making them particularly younger-kid friendly. This section includes just a few suggestions of where to go beaching.

Tip: If you and your family are Orange County beach bunnies, consider purchasing a $50 parking pass. For an additional $25, will also receive a pass for the Orange County Regional Parks. For more information, call (714) 661-7013.

CABRILLO BEACH   ☀

(310) 548-7562 $$

3720 Stephen M White Drive, San Pedro

(EXIT HARBOR FWY [110] TO THE END, L. ON GAFFEY ST., L. ON 9ᵀᴴ ST., R. ON PACIFIC AVE., ALMOST TO THE END, L. ON 36ᵀᴴ ST., WHICH TURNS INTO STEPHEN M WHITE DR.)

See CABRILLO MARINE AQUARIUM under ZOOS AND ANIMALS, as this terrific aquarium is adjacent to the beach (and is free!). The beach has a gated entrance, wonderful sandy stretches, a playground, and rock jetties to climb out on.

Hours: Open daily 6am - 10pm
Admission: $6.50 per vehicle.
Ages: All

LEO CARRILLO STATE BEACH   ☼

(805) 986-8591 - state beach; (818) 880-0350 - camping; $$
(800) 444-7275 - Destinet for camping reservations.

36000 Pacific Coast Highway, Malibu

(EXIT VENTURA FWY [101] S. ON WESTLAKE BLVD. [HWY 23], WHICH TURNS INTO MULHOLLAND HWY., WHICH TURNS INTO DECKER RD. GO TO THE END, AND TURN R. ON PACIFIC COAST HWY.)

Leo Carrillo combines the best of everything I enjoy about the beach - a beautiful, sandy beach; good swimming and surfing; sea caves to carefully explore; tidepools; a playground; lifeguards; coves; and nature trails. Camping near the beach (campsites are a five minute walk from the beach) makes this one of our favorite campgrounds. Each campsite has a fire pit and picnic table. Pack a sweater!

Hours: Open daily 7am - dusk.
Admission: $6 per vehicle. Camping starts at $17 a night, Sun. -
             Thurs.; $18, Fri. - Sat. Each campsite can have up to 8
             people and 2 vehicles.
Ages: All

MARINA BEACH or "MOTHERS BEACH"   ☀

5839 Appian Way, Long Beach $

(TAKE SAN GABRIEL RIVER FWY [605] TO END, W. ON GARDEN GROVE FWY [22], EXIT S. ON STUDEBAKER, GO TO THE END, R. ON WESTMINSTER, R. ON APPIAN WAY. IT'S ACROSS FROM THE LONG BEACH MARINA.)

This beach is aptly nicknamed because it is a mother-child hang out. There are waveless waters in this lagoon-type setting, lifeguards, a nice grassy playground, and barbecues.

Admission: Bring either lots of quarters for parking (25¢ for each half
             hour), or get here early to park on the street for free.
Ages: All

SEASIDE LAGOON

(310) 318-0681

200 Portofino Way, Redondo Beach.
(EXIT SAN DIEGO FWY [405] S. ON WESTERN, R. ON 190ᵀᴴ ST., WHICH TURNS INTO ANITA ST., WHICH THEN TURNS INTO HERONDO ST., L. ON HARBOR DR. IT'S ON THE S.W. CORNER OF HARBOR DR. AND PORTOFINO WAY.)

Have a swimmingly good time at the Seaside Lagoon. This large, saltwater lagoon is heated by a nearby steam generating plant, so the average water temperature is seventy-five degrees. Warm waveless waters, plus a lifeguard, make it an ideal swimming spot for little ones. There is also a beach, playground, snack bar (sponsored by Ruby's), barbecues, picnic tables, and volleyball courts.

Hours: The Lagoon is open daily Memorial Day through Labor Day from 10am - 5:45pm. It is open in September on weekends only from 10am - 5:45pm.

Admission: $3 for adults; $2 for ages 2 - 17.

Ages: All

ALISO BEACH

(714) 661-7013

31131 Pacific Coast Highway, Laguna Beach
(EXIT SAN DIEGO FWY [5] S. ON LAGUNA FWY, WHICH TURNS INTO LAGUNA CYN., L. ON PACIFIC COAST HIGHWAY. OR, EXIT SAN DIEGO FWY [5], S. ON CROWN VALLEY PKY., R. ON P.C.H.)

This beautiful, cove-like beach has a small playground, plus barbecues, picnic tables, and a short pier.

Hours: Open daily 7am - 10pm.

Admission: Metered parking is 75¢ an hour (or a parking pass).

Ages: All

BOLSA CHICA STATE BEACH

(714) 846-3460

Pacific Coast Highway, Huntington Beach
(GOING S. ON SAN DIEGO FWY [405], EXIT S. ON BOLSA CHICA ST., R. ON WARNER AVE., L. ON PACIFIC COAST HIGHWAY. GOING N. ON 405, EXIT E. ON WARNER AVE., L. ON P.C.H.)

There are six miles of beach here that are ideal for families because of the picnic areas (campfires are allowed), outdoor showers, five snack bars, and beach rentals. Year round camping in self-contained vehicles is allowed, but there are no hook ups. No tent camping is allowed.

Hours: Open daily 6am - 9pm.

Admission: $6 per vehicle. Camping is $17 Sun. - Thurs., $18 on Fri. - Sat.

Ages: All

CORONA DEL MAR BEACH and TIDEPOOL TOURS ☼
(714) 644-3044 $$
On Poppy Avenue and Ocean Avenue, Corona Del Mar
(TAKE THE SAN DIEGO FWY [405] OR THE COSTA MESA FWY [55] TO THE CORONA
DEL MAR FWY [73] WHICH TURNS INTO MACARTHUR BLVD., S. ON EAST COAST
HIGHWAY, R. ON POPPY AVE.)

Come for a few hours of tidepool exploration, then spend the rest of the day playing at the beach! Tidepools are a rich natural resource, and a fascinating way for kids to learn about marine life. After giving a short lecture, guides are helpful in pointing out interesting animal and plant life. Groups larger than ten need to make a reservation. The tidepools are adjacent to the public beach of Little Corona, so you are welcome to come visit them on your own, or to sign up for a tour. Just a short drive away is the big beach of Corona Del Mar.

Hours: Open daily sunrise to sunset.
Admission: $6 per vehicle for regular day use. Tours are $25 per group, which includes parking fees.
Ages: 3 years and up.

CRYSTAL COVE STATE PARK BEACH ☼
(714) 494-3539 $$
Between Laguna Beach and Newport Beach on East Coast Highway.
(TAKE THE SAN DIEGO FWY [405] OR THE COSTA MESA FWY [55] TO THE CORONA
DEL MAR FWY [73], WHICH TURNS INTO MACARTHUR BLVD. EXIT MACARTHUR BLVD.
S. ON EAST COAST HIGHWAY. A GATED ENTRANCE IS JUST OPPOSITE NEWPORT
COAST DR.)

See CRYSTAL COVE STATE PARK under GREAT OUTDOORS for details.

Hours: Open daily from 6am - sunset.
Admission: $6 per vehicle.
Ages: All

DANA POINT HARBOR or "BABY BEACH" ☼
Dana Point Harbor Drive, Dana Point   !
(EXIT SAN DIEGO FWY [5] S.W. ON CAMINO LAS RAMBLAS, WHICH TURNS INTO
PACIFIC COAST HIGHWAY, N. ON P.C.H., L. ON ST. OF THE GREEN LANTERN, L. ON
COVE RD. IT'S AT THE BOTTOM OF COVE RD.)

"Baby Beach" offers picnic tables, barbecues, free parking, and showers. Lifeguards oversee the waveless waters.
Admission: Free
Ages: All

DOHENY STATE BEACH PARK ☼
(714) 496-6172 $
25300 Dana Point Harbor Drive,

(EXIT SAN DIEGO FWY [5] S.W. ON CAMINO LAS RAMBLAS, WHICH TURNS INTO PACIFIC COAST HIGHWAY, N. ON P.C.H., L. ON DOHENY STATE BEACH PKY.)

Doheny State Beach Park is big and absolutely gorgeous. The park is divided into three parts. The northern area (also accessible by metered parking off Puerto Place) is for day use. It is five acres of grassy, landscaped picnic area, with barbecue grills and fire rings along the beach. The rocky area is ideal for tidepool exploration during low tide. Since Dana Point Harbor is right next door, this is also a perfect spot to watch the boats sail in and out.

The central section, south of the San Juan Creek, is a campground with 121 sites. Farther south is another day use area with fire rings, beach volleyball, and showers. Throughout the entire stretch of the park are sandy beaches and beckoning ocean waves!

A small Interpretative Center is to your left as you go through the entrance gates. It contains a simulated tidepool (not a touch tank), with sea stars and leopard sharks. The mural-covered wall has wood shells that ask questions like, "Do all sharks kill?" (Lift the shell tab for the answer.) There are also a few aquariums, plus taxidermied animals, fossils, and skeletons of a fox, raptor, and whale.

Hours: The park is open daily from 6am - 6pm. Summer hours may be longer. The Interpretative Center is usually open Fri. - Mon. Call for hours.

Admission: $5 per vehicle for day use. Admission to the Interpretative Center, when it is open, is free. Mon. - Fri. camping prices range from $17 a night for an inland site to $22 a night for a beachfront site; weekends are $1 more per site.

Ages: All

MAIN BEACH / HEISLER PARK ☼

(714) 497-0716 $

Cliff Drive & Myrtle Street, Laguna Beach

(FROM SAN DIEGO FWY [5], TAKE LAGUNA FWY S., WHICH TURNS INTO LAGUNA CANYON RD. [133]. BEFORE THE END, TAKE CLIFF DR. TO THE R. AND FOLLOW IT TO THE BEACH. EXIT LAGUNA CANYON RD. [133] S. ON PACIFIC COAST HIGHWAY [1] FOR MAIN BEACH.)

I mention this park and beach together because they are on either side of Highway 133. Both are incredibly popular (i.e. crowded) and noted for their unparalleled views of the ocean. The water is clear, and the horizon seems to go on forever.

Some activities available at Heisler Park are lawn bowling, shuffleboard, and a paved path for biking or skating. Main Beach offers a grass play area along with basketball courts, volleyball courts, and a small playground. This is a terrific place for beaching it and for swimming. Good luck finding a parking spot!

Hours: Both are open daily sunrise to sunset.

Admission: Free. Most parking is metered.

Ages: All

NEWPORT DUNES RESORT MARINA   ☼
(714) 729-3863 $
1131 Backbay Drive, Newport Beach
(TAKE NEWPORT FWY [55] S.W. TO END, TURNS INTO NEWPORT BLVD., L. ON W.
COAST HWY., L. ON JAMBOREE RD., L. ON BACKBAY DR. OR FROM CORONA DEL
MAR FWY [73], EXIT S.W. ON JAMBOREE R., R. ON BACKBAY DR. BEFORE E. COAST
HWY.)

Toddlers to teens will enjoy the enclosed acres of clean beach
here, along with a waveless lagoon and a myriad of boating activities.
There is a large fiberglass, stationary whale (nicknamed Moe B. Dunes)
in the water for kids to swim out to, and one on the beach. The
playground equipment includes a pirate ship to climb aboard - ahoy
mateys!

Remember the joys of collecting seashells? Newport Dunes is one
of the rare beaches around that still has shells. (Shellmaker Island is
adjacent to the resort marina.)

If you forget to bring food, have no fear of a growling tummy as a
grocery store and cafe are inside the gates, just around the corner from
the beach. Another amenity that Newport Dunes offers is indoor
showers, across from the beach. RESORT WATER SPORTS rentals is
located in the park for your kayaking, pedalboat, windsurfing, etc.,
needs.

Overnight camping is available here and there are plenty of RV
hook-ups. Although tent camping is allowed, stakes are not. The
surroundings are pretty; activities for campers are offered such as
crafts, ice cream socials, and special movie showings; and the Dunes
has a swimming pool. What more could you want out of life? This local
resort is my kind of "roughing it" vacation!

Hours: Open daily from 8am - 10pm.
Admission: $5 per vehicle. Camping prices range from $25 - $45 a
night.
Ages: All

SEAL BEACH   ☼
Main Street, Seal Beach   !
(EXIT SAN DIEGO FWY [405] S. ON SEAL BEACH BLVD., R. ON PACIFIC COAST
HIGHWAY, L. ON MAIN ST.)

This beach has lifeguards, great swimming, and a playground. My
kids love to gather the crabs crawling along the pier wall and put them
in buckets. (We let them go before we go home.) Take a walk on the
pier as the coastline view is terrific. There is also a Ruby's (40's diner)
at the end of the pier. Directly across the street from the beach is Main
Street, which is lined with unique shops and restaurants.

Admission: Park along the street, or pay a $5 entrance fee for the
parking lot.

Ages: All

CHILDREN'S POOL BEACH ☾

At the foot of Jenner Street, La Jolla !
(EXIT SAN DIEGO FWY [5] W. ON LA JOLLA VILLAGE DR., L. ON TORREY PINES RD., R. ON PROSPECT PL., WHICH TURNS INTO PROSPECT ST. LEAVE THE CAR AT THE S. END OF PROSPECT ST., OR PARK ANYWHERE YOU CAN.)

One of the most popular family beaches around is Children's Pool Beach, aptly named because the ocean water is partially enclosed by a seawall in a pool-type swimming hole. Everything here is to ensure a great day at the beach - sand, water, a cave to explore, tidepools, lifeguards, and rocks to climb on. The rocks along the breakwater have a sturdy guard rail. Just past the northeast green lawns is the La Jolla Underwater Park, which is a haven for divers and snorkelers.

Hours: Open daily
Admission: Free
Ages: All

LA JOLLA SHORES BEACH ☼

La Vereda, La Jolla $
(EXIT SAN DIEGO FWY [5] W. ON LA JOLLA VILLAGE DR., L. ON TORREY PINES RD., R. ON CALLE DE LA PLATA, L. ON AVENIDA DE LA PLAYA, R. ON LA VEREDA.)

This beach comes fully loaded for a full day of fun! The nearly two-mile stretch of beach offers year-round lifeguard service, rest rooms, showers (a parents' essentials), and a few playgrounds for the kids, complete with swing sets and climbing apparatus. Enjoy your time at the beach, and maybe even incorporate a drive around picturesque La Jolla.

Hours: Open daily
Admission: Free - good luck with parking.
Ages: All

SILVER STRAND STATE BEACH / CORONADO BEACH ☾

Coronado !
(EXIT SAN DIEGO FWY [5] W. ON 75 AND CROSS OVER THE CORONADO BRIDGE, L. ON ORANGE AVE. FOR CORONADO BEACH, TURN R. AT R H DANA PL., WHICH TURNS INTO OCEAN BLVD. FOR SILVER STRAND STATE BEACH, STAY ON ORANGE AS IT TURNS INTO SILVER STRAND BLVD. THE TOLL IS $1 TO CORONADO AND THE RETURN TRIP IS FREE. IF YOU ARE CAR POOLING, CROSS THE BRIDGE USING THE RIGHT LANE, AT NO CHARGE.)

One of the longest strips (seven miles) of beautiful white sandy beach, is the Silver Strand State Beach. Part of the beach is Coronado Beach, situated in front of the famous HOTEL DEL CORONADO. A terrific bike path also begins near the hotel. The waters are warm and the surf isn't too intense, which is good for younger children. There are picnic areas and lots of room to throw footballs and Frisbees.

Hours: Open daily
Ages: All

EDIBLE ADVENTURES

To market, or a restaurant,
  or maybe high tea,
We'll go together,
  my child and me;
Or maybe we'll stop
  for an ice-cream cone,
Or go apple picking,
  and then head for home.

BENIHANA OF TOKYO

Anaheim - (714) 774-4940; Beverly Hills - (213) 655-7311; City $$$$ of Industry - (818) 912-8784; Encino - (818) 788-7121; Marina Del Rey - (310) 821-0888; Newport Beach - (714) 955-0822; San Diego - (619) 298-4666; Torrance - (310) 316-7777

Enjoy the "show" and the food. This restaurant features hibachi style cooking, which is done right in front your child's eyes. Knives flash as the food is chopped up seemingly in mid-air, and on the frying table - all done with lightning speed. (This is the "show" part.) Tell your kids not to try this at home. Although my kids are not normally prone to trying new foods, they eat here because the way that the food is prepared makes it seem intriguing!

The atmosphere is unique, and the food is delicious, ranging from chicken to seafood to steak. Lunch prices range from $7.50 - $11; dinners from $15 - $22. Outside many Benihanas are a koi pond and traditional Japanese arched bridge.

   Hours: Open for lunch and diner.
Admission: Priced above.
    Ages: 5 years and up.

BULLWINKLE'S RESTAURANT

El Cajon - (619) 593-1155; Fountain Valley (ironically, there are $$$ no fountain shows at this location) - (714) 841-6469; Upland - (909) 946-9555; Vista - (760) 945-9474

Fa*moose* Bullwinkle's Restaurants are adjacent to FAMILY FUN CENTERS in the city's listed above. Eating here is always a highlight for my kids. This woodsy-themed, family-oriented restaurant has great food at delicious prices. Menu selections include pizza ($10.95 for a medium-size), ribs ($7.45, and it comes with a biscuit), a sixteen-piece chicken meal ($19.95, it comes with eight biscuits), salads, and more. Kids' meals average $2.79 for a choice of chicken nuggets, a hot dog, ribs(!), or a hamburger, plus it comes with fries, a drink, and ice cream. Most of the restaurants have entertainment such as Rocky and Bullwinkle cartoons on the T.V. monitors; a small stage where the electronic figures of Rocky and Bullwinkle come out and tell jokes; and a water show where fountain waters "dance" to the music and spotlights that change color. Come here to eat, and then play at the Family Fun Centers, because your kids won't let you go home without doing so. Food and fun - what more could you want?!

   Hours: Open Sun. - Thurs., 11am - 10pm; Fri., 11am - 11pm;
             Sat., 10am - 11pm.
    Ages: All

CHUCK E. CHEESE

Check your yellow pages for a local listing. $$$

This is a popular place for young kids as there are kiddie rides, and video and arcade games, as well as the all-important prize redemption center. Many facilities also have play areas with tubes, slides, and ball pits. Chuck E. Cheese, the costumed rat mascot, is usually walking around giving hugs and high fives. He also performs several stage shows throughout the day.

Every child's favorite food is served here - pizza! A salad bar is available, too. Note: This place is always a bit loud, but especially so on weekends when crowds descend upon it.

    Hours: Usually open during the week from 10am - 9pm; on the weekends from 10am - 11pm. Call for a particular location's hours.

Admission: Free admission, but count on spending money on pizza and tokens.

    Ages: 2 - 11 years.

FARMER'S MARKETS

Many cities host a weekly Farmer's Market. These markets usually consist of open-air (outside) booths set up for customers to purchase fresh fruits and produce, bakery goods, meats, and more - taste the difference! Freshly-cut flowers are often available, too. Indulge yourself while educating your kids about farming! Please call your local city hall to see if there is a Farmer's Market near you. Here is just a few of the cities that I know of that host a market: Calabasas, Coronado, Costa Mesa, Long Beach, Mission Valley, Oceanside (with llama rides!), Pacific Beach, Palm Springs, Riverside, Tustin, and Woodland Hills.

THE OLD SPAGHETTI FACTORY ☀

Call for one nearest you.   *$$$*

These elegant "factories" have posh, velvet seats in a variety of colors. The overhead fabric lamps are from a more genteel era. The old world antiques and the dark, rich furniture exudes a quiet, classy atmosphere. Yet, the restaurants are also very kid-friendly. Each Old Spaghetti Factory has a train or trolley car that is a highlight to eat in. The franchised restaurants differ only in regional decor. For instance, the one in Riverside, a citrus city, has orange crate labels on the walls.

The food is fine fare, such as spaghetti (what a surprise!) with wonderful variety of sauces to choose from, and pastas such as lasagna, tortellini, and ravioli. Prices range from $3.50 to $7.50. Kids' meals cost between $2.95 - $3.75.

    Hours: Open Mon. - Thurs., 11:30am - 3pm and 5pm - 10pm; Fri., 11:30am - 3pm and 5pm - 10:30pm; Sat. - Sun., noon - 10pm.

Admission: Priced above.

    Ages: 4 years and up.

PLANET HOLLYWOOD

Beverly Hills - (310) 275-7828; San Diego - (619) 702-7827;   *$$$$*
Santa Ana - (714) 434-7827

Beverly Hills - 9560 Wilshire Boulevard: San Diego - 197 Horton Plaza;
Santa Ana - 1641 W. Sunflower, at South Coast Plaza.

There are several Planet Hollywoods throughout Southern
California (and the rest of the world.) This very Hollywood restaurant
literally has the hand prints of co-owners Demi Moore, Arnold
Schwarzenegger, Bruce Willis, and Sly Stallone all over it. Film and
television memorabilia abound such as costumes, parts of sets, and
photographs. Just a few of the featured items at the Beverly Hills
location, for instance, are the original Batman costume, an astronaut
costume from Apollo 13, and the carousel horse ridden in Mary
Poppins. The memorabilia is definitely a main attraction at Planet
Hollywood. The food is California cuisine, which really encompasses
everything - pizza, pasta, burgers, ribs, chicken, salads, etc. Prices
range from $6.95 - $16. The kid's menu offers pizza, cheeseburgers,
and delicious chicken - $6.95 - $9.95.

Hours: Open daily 11am - 11:30pm.
Ages: 4 years and up.

RUBY'S

From San Diego to Santa Barbara!   *$$$$*

These 1940's-style diners are good food fun and have a terrific
atmosphere for kids. It has readily become one of our favorite places to
eat. Old-fashioned-looking jukeboxes that play your favorite oldies; red
vinyl booths and bar stools; and the kind of attentive service that all but
disappeared years ago, are some of Ruby's trademarks. Since the
restaurants are franchised, each one is slightly different in decor (some
have trains going around on tracks overhead) and in their choice of
menu items. Most breakfast choices include a omelettes ($4.89),
waffles ($3.79), etc. Lunch and dinner foods include a great selection of
burgers (beef, turkey, veggie, or chicken) for an average cost of $5.
They also offer salads, sandwiches, soups, and delicious concoctions
from the soda fountain. Kids' meals range from $2.99 - $3.79 for a
choice of a grilled cheese sandwich, corn dog, hamburger, chicken
fingers, etc. Meals also include fries, a small drink, and a kid-size ice
cream cone! Note: You'll find Ruby's at the end of several Southern
California piers; kind of like a pot of gold.

Hours: Open daily for breakfast, lunch, and dinner.
Admission: Priced above.
Ages: 2½ years and up.

COUNTRY STAR

(818) 762-3939   *$$$$*

1000 Universal Center Drive Universal CityWalk, Suite 195, Universal
City

(EXIT HOLLYWOOD FWY [101] N. AT UNIVERSAL CENTER DR. IT'S NEXT TO UNIVERSAL STUDIOS AND CITYWALK.)

The entrance to this restaurant is the shape of a huge, old-time jukebox, but there is nothing dated about County Star. Its investors include Reba McEntire, Vince Gill, and Wynonna. Y'all look down as you enter through the cave-like hallway and you'll see videos of the latest country stars at your feet. Then again, there are video screens everywhere, showcasing your favorite singers from waaay back to the hottest, current stars. The showy decor includes walls lined with guitars, boots, glitzy costumes, and photos, plus a motorcycle spinning on a pedestal in the center of the main room.

Good-old American food is served here, like fried chicken ($12.95), ribs ($13.95 for big beef ribs), steaks (filet mignon, $17.95), and burgers ($7.95), plus sandwiches, like club and barbecue beef ($8.95). Kids, ages 9 and under, have their choice of a hot dog, burger, grilled cheese sandwich, or spaghetti, plus fries, drink, and a hot fudge sundae for only $4.95. Boy howdy, delightful food and "down-home" singing make Country Star an entertaining dining experience.

Hours: Open Mon. - Fri., 11am - 10pm; Sat. - Sun., 11am - 11pm.
Admission: Priced above.
Ages: 4 years and up.

DC3 RESTAURANT   ☼
(310) 399-2323 $$$$
2800 Donald Douglas Loop North, Santa Monica
(EXIT SANTA MONICA FWY [10] S. ON BUNDY DR., R. ON OCEAN PARK BLVD., L. ON 28TH ST. IT'S JUST N. OF THE SANTA MONICA AIRPORT, AND ADJACENT TO THE MUSEUM OF FLYING.)

Come to DC3 Restaurant for an uplifting dining experience. This art-deco restaurant is stylish, and has a great view of the planes landing and taking off. It is very dear to my heart, though, because of the Jr. Jet kid's program. Kids eat pizza or spaghetti, plus a salad and ice cream for $7 per child. Then a licensed child care professional will care for them as they go play in the MUSEUM OF FLYING, which is an elevator ride down from the restaurant. (See MUSEUM OF FLYING to know all the wonderful things it has for children to do.) Do you realize what this means? You can enjoy uninterrupted, adult conversation while your kids are having a great time! Adult meals range from $18.95 to $26 for your choice of steak, ribs, seafood, etc.

Hours: The Jr. Jet program is offered Tues. - Sat. from 6pm - 9pm. (Don't forget to pick up your little darlings by 9pm.) Reservations are needed by 2pm of the day you are dining. The restaurant is open Sun. for brunch from 11am - 2:30pm; dinner 5pm - 7:30pm; Mon., 11:30am - 2:30pm; Tues. - Fri., 11:30am - 2:30pm and 6pm - 9pm or so; Sat., 6pm - 10pm, or so.

Admission: Priced above.
    Ages: The Jr. Jet program is for ages 3 - 13 years.

DIVE!   ☀

(310) 788-DIVE (3483)   *$$$*

10250 Santa Monica Boulevard, Century City, the Century City Shopping Center.
(EXIT SAN DIEGO FWY [405] N.E. ON SANTA MONICA BLVD.)

    Dive! is not just a place to eat, but an underwater experience. You'll hear the kids say, "How cool!" as soon as they enter through the hatch door of the submarine-shaped restaurant. Inside the entrance, to your left, is a periscope that pokes through the roof so kids can actually see what's going on outside. (The tantalizing buttons in this area are safe to push.) The rest of the interior also replicates a submarine, albeit a more colorful one than are normally found on the seas. It has port hole windows with bubbles in them. Adding to the submerged feeling, video screens on the walls show actual underwater footage of stingrays, sharks, and other fish, plus a few shots of backyard pools and Jacuzzis. Music also helps set the mood with tunes like "Yellow Submarine," etc.

    The elevator resembles a submarine locker room. Upstairs, a mini-submarine goes around on a track overhead. Even the bathrooms are nautically themed. (Come on - you've got kids - you know they check these things out!)

    The food is great. Sub-Starters menu choices include special fries ($2.95), with a choice of seven dips. Sub-stantial salads go from $4.95 for a house salad to $11.95 for a grilled lemon basil chicken breast salad. Dive! also serves pasta, burgers, ribs, and fish. There is a delicious variety of submarine sandwiches at an average cost of $7.95. The kid's menu, with entrees around $5.95, will bait your youngsters' appetites. The desserts taste incredible and are generous in portion so, as their motto "Never DIVE! alone" suggests, share one with a friend.

    Hours: Open Sun. - Thurs., 11:30am - 10pm; Fri. - Sat.,
                11:30am - 11pm.
    Ages: 4 years and up.

FARMERS MARKET   ☼

(213) 933-9211   *!/$$*

6333 W. 3ʳᵈ Street, Los Angeles
(EXIT SANTA MONICA FWY [10] N. ON FAIRFAX AVE. TO 3ᴿᴰ ST. IT'S ON THE "CORNER.")

    This unique outdoor market, originally founded in 1934, is an eclectic mixture of more than sixty fresh food and produce vendors, and over twenty kitchens that make and sell all sorts of homemade domestic and international favorites. The market can be crowded, but it is a fun place to shop or enjoy lunch. Patrons can order their favorite ethnic food and eat at an outdoor table. Kids love stopping by

Littlejohn's English Toffee House stall to watch (and sample) mouth-watering candy being made. They can also see peanuts steadily pouring into a large machine behind glass at Magee's House of Nuts, being churned around to make very fresh-tasting peanut butter. Across the way from the main marketplace, more than sixty-five retail stores offer unique clothing items and specialty gifts.

Hours: Open in the summer Mon. - Sat., 9am - 7pm; Sun., 10am - 6pm. The rest of the year the market is open Mon. - Sat., 9am - 6:30pm; Sun., 10am - 5pm. Closed major holidays.

Admission: Free

Ages: 2½ years and up.

FRILLS

(818) 303-3201

504 South Myrtle Avenue, Monrovia

(EXIT SAN GABRIEL RIVER FWY [605] N. ON MYRTLE AVE.)

Entering through the doors of Frills is like taking a step back in time. The front Victorian boutique sells vintage clothing and a variety of hats, plus gift items like cards and unusual buttons.

The back part of Frills is a tea room. If you feel inappropriately attired, choose a feather boa and/or a glamorous hat from the dress-up trunk. What fun! The room is decorated with lacy tablecloths, old-fashioned clothing and hats, and tea sets that are for sale. There are over forty types of tea to choose from, with cinnamon vanilla and cherry being the two most popular with the younger set. Order a meal fit for a king with King's Tea which includes a hearty meat pie or sausage roll, a variety of tea sandwiches, fresh fruit, dessert, and of course, tea - $11.50. Children's Tea, with a peanut butter sandwich, shortbread, fresh fruit, and tea costs $7. Other teas (meals) fit for a peasant, princess, or queen are available and all are served with fresh-baked bread and delicious dessert. Ask about their special children's programs.

Hours: Open Tues. - Sat., 11am - 4pm; Fri., 11am - 7:30pm.

Admission: Prices range from $7 - $11.50.

Ages: 4 years and up.

GRAND CENTRAL MARKET

(213) 624-2378

317 S. Broadway Street, Los Angeles

(EXIT VENTURA FWY [101] R. ON SPRING ST., R. ON 3RD ST., THEN A QUICK L. ON HILL. THE PARKING STRUCTURE IS BETWEEN 3RD ST. AND HILL ST.)

This is a fun, aromatic, cultural experience for kids who are used to shopping at grocery stores. There are over forty stalls inside this covered structure that sell everything from exotic fruits and vegetables, to octopus and pigs' heads. There are also meat stalls, restaurants, and a bakery. Stop here to shop, and/or eat on your on your way to visit other fun and educational places.

Hours: Open Mon. - Sat., 9am - 6pm; Sun., 10am - 5:30pm.
Admission: Parking is $1 for every fifteen minutes; $8 maximum. Parking is free for ninety minutes if you purchase merchandise worth $15 or more.
Ages: 3 years and up.

JOHNNY REB'S SOUTHERN SMOKEHOUSE

(562) 866-6455   *$$$*

16639 Bellflower Boulevard, Bellflower
(EXIT ARTESIA FWY [91] N. ON BELLFLOWER BLVD.)

This restaurant serves up southern hospitality as well as good southern cookin'. The immediate attraction is the bowl of peanuts because peanuts shells are to be thrown on the floor. (My floor looks like this too, sometimes. The only difference is that kids are allowed to do it here.) A breakfast of eggs, pancakes, or french toast ranges from $3 - $6. The lunch menu is the same as the dinner menu, only the portions are smaller, so the prices are lower. Food choices include chicken fried steak, catfish, all sorts of ribs, etc. Dinner prices range from $7 - $14. Tip: Kids eat for free from a selected menu of mini-burgers, chicken fingers, etc., on Wednesday nights. Note: Another, smaller Johnny Reb's is located at 4663 Long Beach Blvd. in Long Beach, (562) 423-7327.

Hours: Open Sun. - Thurs., 7am - 9pm; Fri. - Sat., 7am - 10pm.
Ages: 2 years and up.

OLIVIA'S DOLL HOUSE and TEA ROOM (Newhall)

(805) 222-7331   *$$$$$*

22700 Lyons Avenue, Newhall
(EXIT GOLDEN STATE FWY [5] E. ON LYONS AVE.)

This small, Victorian house is beautifully decorated with flowers and lace - a little girl's dream come true. Young ladies can dress up in gowns and jewelry; have their hair, make-up, and nails done; and enjoy hors d'oeuvres, finger sandwiches, and dessert. (Forget about little girls - this sounds like a mom's dream come true!) Parties are given by reservation only.

Hours: Open for parties by reservation.
Admission: Parties start at $225 and include cake and party favors.
Ages: 4 years and up.

OLIVIA'S DOLL HOUSE and TEA ROOM (West Hollywood)

(310) 273-6631   *$$$$$*

8804 Rosewood Avenue, West Hollywood

(EXIT SANTA MONICA FWY [10] N. ON ROBERTSON BLVD., L. ON ROSEWOOD AVE. OR, EXIT SAN DIEGO FWY [405] E. ON SANTA MONICA BLVD, R. ON ROBERTSON BLVD., R. ON ROSEWOOD AVE.)

See OLIVIA'S DOLL HOUSE and TEA ROOM (Newhall) for a description.

Hours: Open for parties by reservation.
Admission: Parties start at $225 and include cake an party favors.
Ages: 4 years and up.

PETER PIPER PIZZA (Los Angeles)

(213) 773-5502 $$$

6207 Atlantic, Los Angeles
(GOING N. ON THE 710 FWY, EXIT L. ON FLORENCE, R. ON ATLANTIC. IT'S ON THE CORNER OF ATLANTIC AND GAGE.)

This huge, fun-filled pizza place is very similar to Chuck E. Cheese. Obviously the main food offered here is pizza, but chicken wings and a salad bar are also available. For entertainment, there are ball pits, arcade games (there is a lot of skee ball at the Pacoima one), and a merry-go-round that is free (yea!). The mascot, a green-spotted purple dinosaur, comes on stage a few times throughout the day to put on a show. The kids love coming here - just cover your ears to block out the din. And yes, of course, they do birthday parties!

Hours: Open Mon. - Thurs., 11am - 9pm; Fri. - Sat., 11am - 11pm; Sun., 11am - 10pm.
Ages: 1½ years and up.

PETER PIPER PIZZA (Pacoima)

(818) 899-4848 $$$

13200 Osborne Street, Pacoima
(EXIT THE GOLDEN STATE FWY [5] E. ON OSBORNE. IT'S ON THE CORNER OR OSBORNE AND LAUREL CANYON.)

See PETER PIPER PIZZA (Los Angeles) for a description.

Hours: Mon. - Thurs., 11am - 9pm, Fri. - Sat., 11am - 11pm; Sun., 11am - 10pm.
Ages: 1½ years and up.

SHOGUN

(818) 351-8945 $$$$

470 N. Halstead Street, Pasadena
(EXIT FOOTHILL FWY [210] N. ON ROSEMEAD BLVD. IT'S ON THE CORNER OF ROSEMEAD BLVD. AND HALSTEAD ST.)

This Japanese-style restaurant has built-in tabletop grills where chefs prepare the food with rapid slicing and dicing movements (and "cool" tricks) in front of your eyes. (See BENIHANA, as it is a similar type of restaurant.) The "entertainment" is great and the food is delicious. Kids get a real kick out of the presentation, and are more likely to try "new" foods now that they've seen the unique way it's been prepared. Chicken, seafood, and steak are some of the menu selections. Lunch ranges from $8 - $10; dinners from $11 - $26. Kids' meals usually run between $6.95 to $8.95. (Kids are served the same foods as adults, just smaller portions.)

Hours: Open Mon. - Fri., 11:30am - 2pm and 5pm - 10pm; Sat., 5pm - 10:30pm; Sun., 4:30pm - 9:30pm.

Ages: 4 years and up.

ALICE'S BREAKFAST IN THE PARK   ☼

(714) 848-0690 $$

6622 Lakeview Drive, Huntington Beach
(EXIT THE 405 E. ON WARNER AVE., R. ON EDWARDS ST., L. ON CENTRAL PARK DR. IT'S THE RED BUILDING AT THE END OF THE PARKING LOT IN HUNTINGTON CENTRAL PARK.)

Everyone knows that breakfast is the most important meal of the day, so why not start your day at Alice's Breakfast in the Park?! The red barn-like building has a small dining room filled with antiques, giving it a homey atmosphere. Or, eat outside at the patio tables by the lake's edge. This is a delightful treat, especially for kids who don't always like to sit down throughout a meal. Watch out for the ducks and other birds that are usually hanging around, hoping for a handout.

Mmmmm - fresh baked bread or buns are served at all of Alice's breakfasts and lunches. Try an "outrageously delicious" cinnamon roll - at $2, it's big enough for a meal. Breakfast averages $4.25 for two eggs, home fries, and fruit. The menu offers a wonderful variety of other breakfast favorites, too. The lunch menu includes large sandwiches (average $4.50), salads, burgers, chili, etc. Kids' meals range from $1.75 - $3.50 - fries and a drink cost an additional $1.25.

The restaurant is located in HUNTINGTON CENTRAL PARK, so after your meal - go play! (Also see SHIPLEY'S NATURE CENTER.)

Hours: Open daily 7am - 1:30pm.

Ages: All

BEST OF FRIENDS TEA ROOM   ☼

(714) 633-4710 $$$$

1051 North Meads, Ridgeline Country Club, Orange
(EXIT COSTA MESA FWY [55] E. ON KATELLA, WHICH TURNS INTO VILLA PARK, THEN SANTIAGO CANYON RD., R. ON ORANGE PARK BLVD., L. ON MEADS.)

It's time to play dress-up, and share a cup of tea with a special child in your life. The price can include tea, scones, soup, sandwiches, fruit, and dessert, served in Victorian surroundings. Reservations are required. Call for various children's teas like Teddy Bear Tea, Alice in Wonderland Tea, and special holiday teas.

Hours: Tea is served Fri. - Mon., at 10am for breakfast and 1pm
              for high tea.
Admission: $15 for adults; $12 for children 7 years and under.
Ages: 5 years and up.

CAPISTRANO DEPOT
(714) 488-7600 $$$

26701 Verdugo Street, San Juan Capistrano
(EXIT SAN DIEGO FWY [5] W. ON ORTEGA HWY., L. ON CAMINO CAPISTRANO, QUICK R. ON VERDUGO ST.)

My family enjoys eating at unique locations. The Capistrano Depot
is inside a red brick railroad station originally built in 1894; it's fun to
look around here. You actually eat in stationary, antique railcars. The
old-fashioned ambiance and the surroundings of the historic Los Rios
District makes eating here an adventure. Menu choices range from
soups ($2.95 a cup) and salads ($8.50 for oriental chicken) to
barbequed pork sandwich ($8.50), pasta (average $9), and roast prime
beef ($17.95). Tip: Take a train trip here. Amtrack is right next "door" to
the Depot. (Also see JONES MINI FARM, MISSION SAN JUAN
CAPISTRANO, and ORANGE COUNTY MUSEUM OF NATURAL
HISTORY for other things to do and see in this immediate vicinity.)

Hours: Open daily for lunch and dinner.
Admission: See prices above.
Ages: 4 years and up.

COUNTRY ROCK CAFE - Family Day
(714) 455-1881 $$$

23822 Mercury Road, Lake Forest
(EXIT SAN DIEGO FWY [5] N.E. ON LAKE FOREST RD., R. ON ROCKFIELD. IT'S ON THE CORNER OF ROCKFIELD AND MERCURY, IN THE SHOPPING CENTER.)

Bring your achy breaky heart and your cowboy boots, and have
some family fun at the Country Rock Cafe. Cacti, bales of hay, saddles,
and great country murals decorate the inside and outside of the Cafe.
The music is constant so you might as well learn to country line dance
with lessons that are given hourly, or just join the people on the dance
floor. Good grub is available here, too. A kid's meal hot dog, corn dog,
or hamburger, plus fries and a drink are $2.50. Adult meals average
$5.75 for a burger, although sodas are $1.75 (and you will get thirsty
with all that dancing). Self-labeled "the best family entertainment
around," this is a great way to spend some "down-home" time together!
Yee-ha!

Hours: The Country Rock Cafe hosts Family Day every Sunday
              from 2pm - 7pm.
Admission: Family Day prices are $5 for adults, $3 for ages 2 - 10.
              Entry prices for adults at other times are $5.
Ages: 5 years and up.

EMERALD FOREST RESTAURANT BAR AND GRILL ☀
(714) 723-5000 $$$
309 Palm Street, Newport Beach
(TAKE COSTA MESA FWY [55] TO THE END, WHICH TURNS INTO NEWPORT BLVD.,
WHICH TURNS INTO BALBOA BLVD., L. ON PALM ST. THE RESTAURANT IS RIGHT BY
BALBOA ISLAND FERRY.)

It's a jungle out there. Well, actually, it's a jungle in here, too. Enjoy a dining safari in a rainforest setting with trees on the walls that reach to the ceiling, a few small waterfalls that end in a small pond (watch out for the [pretend] alligator!), and fish tanks. Look out the windows for a nice view of Newport Bay. Choose from a variety of food, including sandwiches, burgers, seafood, chicken pasta, Mexican food, etc. Adult meals cost between $7 - $15 for lunch or dinner. The children's menu includes a choice of Grill-A-Burger (or Gorilla Burger), fish and chips, grilled cheese sandwich, etc., plus fries for about $4. Beverages are extra. (See BALBOA FUN ZONE for close by activities and attractions.)

    Hours: Open daily 11am - 11pm.
    Ages: All

GOOFY'S KITCHEN ☽
(714) 778-6600 $$$$
1150 W. Cerritos Ave., at the Disneyland Hotel, Anaheim
(GOING S. ON SANTA ANA FWY [5], EXIT W. ON BALL RD., L. ON WEST ST., R. ON
CERRITOS. GOING N. ON 5, EXIT W. ON KATELLA, R. ON WEST ST., L. ON CERRITOS.
IT'S ON THE W. SIDE OF DISNEYLAND, ACROSS THE STREET.)

For a special, Disney-style meal, come to Goofy's Kitchen for an all-you-can eat breakfast/brunch or dinner buffet. Not only are the walls decorated with Disney cartoons, but your children's favorite characters come by the tables for a hug. We were visited by Pluto, Minnie Mouse, Chip (or was it Dale?), John Smith, Miko and, of course, Goofy. Kids even eat a bite or two in between hopping up to touch the costumed characters. Remember to bring your camera!

The dinner buffet costs $17.50 for adults, $8.50 for kids 4 - 12 years; $3 for children 3 years and under. We stuffed ourselves with prime rib, ham, chicken, seafood, side dishes, fruit, salad, and scrumptious desserts. (The way my family suffers just to be able to share with you!) The kids have their own food bar that offers familiar favorites like macaroni and cheese, mini-hotdogs, spaghetti, and chicken strips. The breakfast buffet, with equally delicious offerings, costs $13.75 for adults, $8.25 for kids 4 - 12; $3 for children 3 years and under.

Goofy's Kitchen offers good food in a fun, family atmosphere. Make your outing even more of a treat by coming early, or staying after mealtime to walk around and enjoy the hotel grounds. (See DISNEYLAND HOTEL for details.)

    Hours: Open daily for breakfast 7am - 11:30am. Open daily for
                dinner 5pm - 9pm.

Admission: Parking at the hotel is $1 every half hour for the first two hours; $2 an hour for the next four hours; and $15 for the day. Validation at Goofy's Kitchen will save you a few dollars.

Ages: 1½ years and up.

MARY POPPINS PRACTICALLY PERFECT TEA ☼
(714) 956-6755   *$$$$*

1717 South West Street, Anaheim

(GOING S., EXIT SANTA ANA FWY [5] W. ON BALL RD., L. ON WEST ST. GOING N., EXIT 5 FWY, W. ON KATELLA, R. ON WEST ST. IT'S ON THE 2ND FLOOR OF THE DISNEYLAND PACIFIC HOTEL, BY THE DISNEYLAND HOTEL.)

Just a spoonful of sugar . . . plus lots of good food, and your child will have the (tea) time of her/his life! Mary Poppins is your hostess, dispensing food, good cheer, and an occasional song throughout your hour-and-a-half tea. Kids will have a supercalifragilisticexpialidocious experience as they eat, dress up in hats (top hats for boys) and boas, and even take pictures with Mary Poppins. (Bring your camera!) Breakfast includes pastries, scones with jam, scrambled eggs, fresh fruit, and Mickey Mouse pancakes and waffles. The afternoon menu includes finger sandwiches for adults, such as shrimp and apple, turkey and mango, ham and Provolone, and cream cheese and sun-dried tomatoes. The children's sandwich platter consists of peanut butter and jelly, ham and cheese, and tuna salad sandwiches. Your choice of beverage, plus a delicious dessert, make this tea time very sweet, indeed.

Hours: Breakfast tea is served Sat. at 10am. Afternoon tea is served Sat. and Sun. at 12:30pm and 3pm.

Admission: $18.50 for adults; $12.50 for children 12 years and under.

Ages: 3 years and up.

MCDONALD'S (with a train theme) ☀
(714) 521-2303   *$$*

7861 Beach Boulevard, Buena Park

(EXIT ARTESIA FWY [91] S. ON BEACH BLVD. IT'S JUST N. OF KNOTT'S BERRY FARM.)

We've nicknamed this "Train McDonald's" because the center of the eating area has a large model train exhibit with seating available all around it. Kids (and adults) are enthralled as the train goes around the mountains and through the tunnels. Tracks and a train also run overhead.

This McDonald's also offers McThriller, a simulated jolting ride that allows you to experience white water rafting, downhill skiing at breakneck speed, and four other simulations. The cost is $2.50 for adults; $1.50 for kids. Children must be at least 42" tall. There are also arcade games.

Admission: Happy meal prices.
Ages: All

PLAZA GARIBALDI DINNER THEATER

(714) 758-9014 $$$$

1490 S. Anaheim Boulevard, Anaheim
(GOING S. ON SANTA ANA FWY [5], EXIT E. ON BALL RD., R. ON ANAHEIM BLVD.
GOING N. ON 5, EXIT E. ON KATELLA, R. ON ANAHEIM BLVD.)

Experience the finest Mexican entertainment and cuisine this side
of the border. Your two-hour dinner/show features a variety of acts
such as Mariachis, singers, folkloric dancers, cowboy ropers, tango
dancers, etc. The fiesta atmosphere, authentic costumes, and colorful
decor enhance your visit here. Adults can choose from numerous
entrees, ranging from traditional Mexican fare to seafood. Kids can
choose from hamburger with fries, carne asada, or chicken with rice.
(Beverages are extra.) Sunday brunches, at 1pm and 3pm, are all-you-
can eat buffets that come with champagne. Ole!
Hours: Seatings are Thurs. - Sat. at 8pm and 10pm; Sun., 1pm,
3pm, 7pm, 9pm, and 11pm.
Admission: $16.95 for adults; $8.95 for children 10 years and under.
The price includes dinner and the show.
Ages: 4 years and up.

POFOLKS

(714) 521-8955 $$$

7701 Beach Boulevard, Buena Park
(EXIT ARTESIA FWY [91] S. ON BEACH BLVD.)

For home-style cooking and a nice family atmosphere, PoFolks is a
great place to come. The walls are decorated with pictures, toll-
paintings, and other things that make it look homey. A model train is
running on tracks overhead and there are a few table games to keep
kids entertained. Menu choices include soup ($2.49), salads ($5.29 for
chef's), chicken, ribs, fish, and home-style dinners like pot roast ($7.99)
and country ham steak ($7.99). The kid's menu has chicken, fish, a
burger, corn dog, or grilled cheese sandwich for $2.79. Tip:
McDonald's, just down the street, has a free magazine called
"Welcome" that almost always contains discount coupons for PoFolks.
Hours: Open Sun. - Thurs., 7am - 9pm; Fri. - Sat., 7am - 10pm.
Ages: All

RITZ-CARLTON HOTEL TEA

(714) 240-2000 $$$$

1 Ritz-Carlton Drive, Dana Point
(EXIT SAN DIEGO FWY [5] R. ON ALICIA PKY. TO THE END, R. ON CROWN VALLEY TO
THE END, L. ON PACIFIC COAST HWY, R. AT RITZ-CARLTON DR. [SECOND LIGHT ON
THE R.])

The Ritz-Carlton is an incredibly classy hotel. Celebrate your child with a special afternoon of tea in an elegant room that overlooks the ocean. Choose from either Light Tea, with a delectable variety of pastries and tea ($16.50 per person); Pacific Tea or Traditional Tea, with pastries and scrumptious finger sandwiches, or pastries and a fruit platter ($21 per person); or the Royal Tea, with champagne or a non-alcoholic cocktail, tea, finger sandwiches, pastries, and strawberries and cream ($28.50 per person). Come early or stay a bit afterwards to explore the gracious hotel and beautiful grounds. Teddy Bear Teas, for families, are offered on selected days in December and include a marionette show. Call for times and details.

Hours: Tea is served Mon. - Fri. every half hour between 2pm - 4pm; Sat. - Sun. at 2pm and 4:30pm. Call to make reservations.

Admission: Priced above.

Ages: 5 years and up.

SPAGHETTI STATION

(714) 956-3250

$$$

999 W. Ball Road, Anaheim

(GOING S. ON SANTA ANA FWY [5], EXIT BALL RD. IT'S ON THE CORNER OF THE OFF RAMP AND BALL RD. GOING N. ON 5, EXIT N. ON HARBOR BLVD., L. ON BALL RD.)

For a taste of the Old West, come eat at Spaghetti Station. The lobby area has a stuffed mountain lion and deer, Butch Cassidy's saddle, wooden Indians, and cowboys statues. Either before or after your meal take a "tour" through the rustic restaurant. There is a lot of terrific Western memorabilia in glass cases in the rooms such as lanterns, cowboy boots, woman's lace-up shoes, saddles, musical instruments, guns, arrowheads, tomahawks, arrows, plus statues of bulls, cowboys, and stagecoaches. Upstairs is a game room for older kids.

Each room has a stone fireplace in a house-like setting. The menu has fun facts about the gold rush and other important Western dates and happenings. Food choices include spaghetti, fixed with a wide variety of sauces, plus ribs, chicken, Cowboy Pizza, salad, etc. Prices range from $5.95 to $13.95. The kid's menu offers up Pony Pizza, spaghetti, and chicken. Although there is a bar here, the restaurant part is great for your little cowhands.

Hours: Open Mon. - Fri., 11am - 10pm; Sat., noon - 11pm; Sun., noon - 10pm.

Ages: 2 years and up.

VILLA PARK PHARMACY

(714) 998-3030

!/$

17821 Santiago Boulevard, Villa Park

(GOING S. ON COSTA MESA FWY [55], EXIT E. ON LINCOLN, R. ON SANTIAGO (RIGHT AFTER THE FWY). GOING N. ON 55, EXIT E. ON NOHL RANCH RD., R. ON SANTIAGO.)

Chocolate phosphates, sorbet, dot candy - if these things bring back fond memories, or just make you hungry, head to the Villa Park Pharmacy, where old-fashioned fun is not out of date. The soda fountain is right out of the 1800's, with an old marble counter-top and brass bar stools, plus ornate ceiling tiles and ceiling fans. There are booths in here, too. Sip a Green River, or another specialty juice, or just have an ice-cream cone.

The candy "store" has big glass display cases, just like in an old-time general store. The cases are filled with a delicious variety of candy. Sometimes creamy fudge or caramel apples are being made on the nearby counter-top.

The rest of the store is a wonderful blend of antique fixtures and modern products. For instance, a 1938 ticket agent's booth is now used to sell lotto tickets, while an old-fashioned Post Office in the back is still used as a real Post Office. The store also carries a full line of cards, books, videos, cosmetics, and gifts. And yes, there is a pharmacy here, too.

Hours: Open Mon. - Sat., 9am - 7pm; Sun., 11am - 5pm.
Admission: Free, but bring spending money.
Ages: 2 years and up.

WATSON DRUGS and SODA FOUNTAIN
(714) 532-6315 - pharmacy; (714) 633-1050 - restaurant   *$$*
116 E. Chapman Avenue, Orange
(EXIT COSTA MESA FWY [55] W. ON CHAPMAN AVE.)

Watson Drugs and Soda Fountain, built in 1899, has the distinction of being the oldest drugstore in Orange County. Located in the wonderful shopping center of Old Town, it is a great place to stop for a meal, or just a treat. Part of Watson Drugs is a pharmacy/gift shop. Look up at the eclectic, old-fashioned items on the overhead shelves.

The other half is a retro 40's diner, with a big jukebox, red vinyl seats, and lots of memorabilia, such as old license plates, on the walls. Breakfast, such as omelets, pancakes, or french toast costs, on the average, $4.25. Lunch, like chicken salad, roast beef, burgers, and tuna melts costs, on the average, $4.75. Dinner, such as steak, fish, or chicken costs, on the average, $7.75. The kid's menu includes a choice of a hot dog, tuna fish sandwich, or grilled cheese sandwich for $2.95. Let's not forget the most important food item - dessert! Ice cream floats, sundaes, shakes, etc., are yours for the asking (and the paying). Eat inside and enjoy the ambiance, or choose one of the tables outside, and watch the world go by.

Hours: Open daily from 6:30am - 9pm.
Ages: 2 years and up.

BIG TOP FOOD -N- FUN RESTAURANT

(909) 785-4141

$$$

3500 Polk Street, Riverside

(EXIT RIVERSIDE FWY [91] N. ON LA SIERRA AVE., R. ON MAGNOLIA AVE., R. ON POLK ST. IT'S ADJACENT TO CASTLE AMUSEMENT PARK.)

For big time fun, come eat at Big Top Restaurant! The restaurant resembles a circus big top, complete with a lifelike statue of a circus elephant outside. Inside, it feels like a circus, too. (Then, again, meal time at our house always feels like a circus what with balancing plates of food, kids acting clownish, etc.) Red and white are the predominant colors. Overhead are stuffed animals in acrobatic poses.

The food is good, with pizza being the featured item - $11.75 for a medium, two topping pizza. A salad bar, burgers, hot dogs, sandwiches, soup, and chicken are also available. Kids love to be entertained at meal time (any time!), so the Big Top bear mascot occasionally appears on stage for a short show. There are a few kiddie rides, and a small arcade room with "G-rated" games, plus a redemption center. See CASTLE AMUSEMENT PARK for a description of the adjacent park.

Hours: Open Mon. - Thurs., 11am - 8pm; Fri. - Sun., 11am - 9:30pm.

Ages: 2 years and up.

TOM'S FARMS

(909) 277- 9992

!/$

Temescal Canyon Road, Corona

(EXIT RIVERSIDE FWY [91] S. ON THE 15 FWY, R. ON TEMESCAL CANYON RD., PAST THE FAST FOOD RESTAURANTS AT THE CORNER.)

Tom's Farms consists of five separate buildings, each one selling different products. The front building has farm fresh produce, dried fruit, nuts, and candies. This is a delicious stop. The Bird's Nest is unusual with various birds, cages, and related bird items for sale. The small restaurant, Tom's Hamburgers, offers large portions. Tasty hamburgers start at $3.75. Kids have their choice of a corn dog, grilled cheese sandwich, or a burger, plus fries and a drink for $2.75. An outside eating area is set up around a small pond that has black swans. Beyond the pond are a few penned farm animals to pet. The wine and cheese store also offers baked goods. On weekends only (although not during the month of January) a few craft booths are set up here, too. Grab a snack or eat a meal at this "farm" with a folksy ambiance.

Hours: Open in the summer daily from 8am - 8pm; open the rest of the year daily from 8am - 6pm.

Admission: Free

Ages: All

APPLE PICKING - OAK GLEN   ☼
(909) 797-6833 $$
Oak Glen Road, Oak Glen
(TAKE THE RIVERSIDE FWY [91] TO THE SAN BERNARDINO FWY [10] E., L. ON THE
YUCAIPA EXIT, L. ONTO OAK GLEN RD. IN ABOUT 6 MILES, YOU'LL SEE THE SIGN,
"WELCOME TO SCENIC OAK GLEN." ORCHARDS AND SHOPS DOT THE LONG AND
WINDING ROAD.)

Your *delicious* journey into Oak Glen takes you through a town that is ripe with fun things to do. Several orchards offer U-Pic, which means you pick your own apples, and sometimes raspberries, blackberries, and pears. Most orchards also have wonderful country stores with all sorts of apple concoctions and apple-related items for sale.

Here are a few of our favorites stops:

Parrish Pioneer Ranch, (909) 797-1753: The Ranch has a picnic area, U-Pic apples, a few gift shops, and a restaurant. Llamas, goats, and deer are in pens by the parking lot. Open daily 9am to 6pm. The shops are open daily 10am to 6pm.

Los Rios Rancho, (909) 797-1005: This Rancho has a store, a delicious bakery, an orchard with U-Pic fruit, plus pony rides ($2 around the track), and a half-hour hay ride ($3.50 for adults, $2.50 for children). The rides are usually available only on weekends during the harvest season, and by reservations at other times. Los Rios also offers a crop of educational programs. Take your choice of three-hour tours from a packing house/cider mill tour, which explores the relationship between farming and the environment and includes grading apples, pressing cider, caramel apples, taste testing, etc.; a pioneer tour, in which kids relive a day in the life of a pioneer, including butter making and tasting; and several nature programs including hiking, collecting and studying samples from a pond, and/or studying Native American lifestyles. Tours are $3.75 per person. A large, grassy area for picnicking comprises the front lawn of Los Rios. The Rancho is open January through August, Wednesday through Friday, 10am to 5pm; Saturday through Sunday, 9am to 5pm; open September through December daily from 9am to 5pm. Tours are by appointment only.

Riley's Log Cabin Farm, (909) 797-4061: This orchard not only offers seasonal U-Pic apples and berries, but there is weekend entertainment here, including "Johnny Appleseed" playing his fiddle. The farm offers a bountiful harvest of year-round group tours that can include a colonial or farm Bible study; participating in frontier skills like chopping wood and making candles, soap, or rope; building a log cabin; learning old-fashioned dances such as the minuet and/or square dancing; grinding corn and baking Johnny cakes; and making and drinking apple cider. Tour options range from two - six hours and cost between $5 and $10 per person. Riley's also hosts Civil War Reenactments a few times a year, as well as other special events.

Riley's Farm and Orchard, (909) 790-2364: Neighboring in-laws own this Riley's farm that also has a U-Pic, a general store, and tours for groups of twenty or more. Each tour includes a tractor-drawn hayride, making and drinking cider (this is a fascinating process), eating hot-dipped caramel apples (a personal favorite), and your choice of buttermaking, candlemaking, doing farm chores, and/or access to the petting farm. $5 per person for the two-hour tour is a great deal! Call to make reservations.

Oak Tree Village, (909) 797-4020: Located in the center of Oak Glen is the Village; a wonderful place to shop, play, and eat. Kids enjoy walking on the trail through the small animal park (50¢). Penned deer, sheep, a llama, goats, and birds are in here, plus a lot of squirrels that are running around freely. On the weekends only, kids can fish at the small Trout Pond ($2.50 per pound, poles, and bait provided), take a pony ride, and/or pan for gold. Up the walkway is Mountain Town, a store with a small cave-like museum that displays taxidermied wildlife (25¢). Along the perimeter of the museum are mini-stores that display merchandise tempting to young shoppers.

Although weekends (especially in October) can be crowded, some orchards will only let you pick apples then, so get an early start on your day's adventure! Call the orchards to find out when your favorite type of apple will be ripe. Tip: Buy an apple-recipe book, as kids get a little carried away with the joy of picking apples! Note: Oak Glen is beautiful in the spring, when the apple trees are in bloom.

Hours: Apple-picking season goes from September through November, with most U-Pics open on the weekends only. Stores and other activities are usually open year round.

Admission: Pay for U-Pic fruit by the pound. See Los Rios and both Rileys for tour prices.

Ages: All ages for most activities; 5 years and up for the educational tours.

BATES NUT FARM

(760) 749-3333   !/$

15954 Woods Valley Road, Valley Center

(FROM ESCONDIDO FWY [15] EXIT E. ON OLD CASTLE RD. WHICH TURNS INTO LILAC RD., R. ON VALLEY CENTER RD., E. ON WOODS VALLEY RD.)

Is your family a little nutty? Then join nuts from all over the world at the Bates Nut Farm. This eight-acre farm features a store with rows and rows of nuts (almonds, cashews, walnuts, etc.), dried fruits, and candies. Kids enjoy watching (and smelling) fresh peanut butter being made in the machines that are at eye level. The Farmer's Daughter gift boutique sells books, dolls, collectibles, country crafts, and more. Outside, kids enjoy the small animal farm with ducks, geese, sheep, and goats to feed and pet. There are picnic tables and shade trees on the grounds, too. Tours of the Bates Nut Farm that show and tell a more in depth look at the growing and processing of nuts are also available, with advanced reservations. Call about the many seasonal events held here, such as the pumpkin patch, choose n' cut Christmas trees, and arts and crafts fairs. You've got *nutin'* to lose by coming here for a visit!

Hours: Open daily 8am - 5pm.
Admission: Free, unless you purchase something.
Ages: All

CORVETTE DINER

(619) 542-1001 $$$

3946 5ʰ Avenue, Hillcrest

(Exit Cabrillo Fwy [63] E. on Washington St., L. on 5ᵀᴴ Ave., L. on University St., L. on 5ᵀᴴ Ave. (One way streets). Or, exit Cabrillo Fwy [163] W. on University St., R. on 5ᵀᴴ Ave., which is a one-way street. Valet park or circle around the block for self parking.)

This 50's style diner is really hopping and bebopping! The music played from the deejay's booth; the license plates, neon signs, and hub cabs that decorate the walls; the old gas pumps; the Bazooka bubble gum displays; and the red Corvette (parked inside) all add to the "happening" atmosphere of the restaurant. The rest of the decor incorporates black and white checked tiles with blue marbleized vinyl booths. Waiting for a table here can be more fun than usual as you sit on a bench made from the fins of a '59 Cadillac. On Tuesday and Wednesday evenings, from 6:30pm to 9:30pm, be entertained by "Magic Mike," who plies his tricks of the trade and jokes at your table. (Ask him to show your children how to magically stretch their arms.)

The food here is great! A Hawaii 5-O burger (burger with pineapple) or a Philly steak sandwich is $5.95. Other food choices include fish tacos, grilled Reuben, etc. Or try ribs, meatloaf, blackened chicken pasta, salads, etc. Desserts are delectable. They range from Green Rivers to peppermint smoothies to Snickers Pie to Death by Chocolate Cake. Kids' meals are $4.25 for their choice of spaghetti, burger, corn dog, grilled cheese sandwich, or chicken fingers, plus fries, a soft drink, and an ice cream bar. Was life really this good in the fifties?!

Hours: Open Sun. - Thurs., 11am - 11pm; Fri. - Sat., 11am - midnight.
Ages: All

EDEN CREEK ORCHARD

(760) 765-2102 $

1052 Julian Orchards Drive, Julian

(From San Diego Fwy [5] or Escondido Fwy [15], take 78 Fwy E. to Julian. 78 is Washington St. in Julian. From the 8 Fwy, take 79 N. to Julian, at 78 Jct. turn L. on Main St. Take Main St. N. out of town; it turns into Farmer, turn R. at Wynola Rd., which turns into Julian Orchards Dr. It is 2 miles N. of town.)

This bed and breakfast is open year round, although its biggest kid-draw is the U-Pic apple orchards. Apple picking season runs from

September through November, depending on the crop. At Eden Creek Orchard, children can pick and choose Golden Delicious, Macintosh, Red Delicious, and/or Jonathons. A picnic area is also here, so bring a lunch.

Hours: Usually open September through November, apple picking is available on weekends from 10am - 6pm. Groups can make appointments to come during the week.

Admission: Current price of apples.

Ages: All

EL TORITO FAMILY NIGHT

(619) 562-3434 (Alakazam Entertainment)

$$$

8910 Villa La Jolla Drive, La Jolla

(EXIT SAN DIEGO FWY [5] W. ON LA JOLLA VILLAGE DR., L. ON VILLA LA JOLLA DR.)

For good food and family entertainment, dine at El Torito in La Jolla. What makes this El Torito so special? Once a week P. J. Pineapple the Clown appears to either make balloon animals for kids or to paint your child's face - all for free. As an added bonus, for every adult meal purchased, one of your children eats for free. Now that's family value! Call to make sure P.J. is still appearing here.

Hours: Family Night is every Wednesday from 6:30pm - 8:30pm.

Admission: The cost of a meal, or two.

Ages: All

HORTON GRAND HOTEL / IDA BAILEY'S RESTAURANT

(619) 544-1886

$$$$

311 Island Avenue, San Diego

(GOING S. ON SAN DIEGO FWY [5], EXIT W. ON IMPERIAL AVE., R. ON 12TH AVE., L. ON ISLAND AVE. GOING N. ON 5, EXIT AT "J" ST., CONTINUE STRAIGHT OFF THE OFF RAMP AND TURN L. AT ISLAND.)

Put on the lace gloves, extend your pinky, and enjoy a delicious afternoon tea at this Victorian-style hotel. Afternoon Tea consist of petit fours, finger sandwiches, scrumptious scones, cake, and an assortment of teas. High Tea is a bit more formal and also includes sherry, a sausage roll, and truffle. As this hotel is in the heart of the historic Gaslamp District, take a stroll around before or after your tea to soak in the district's ambiance. There are many unique stores, so both window shoppers and "real" shoppers will be appeased.

Hours: Teas are served Tues. - Sat. from 2:30pm - 5pm.

Admission: $9.95 per person

Ages: 5 years and up.

HOTEL DEL CORONADO - TEA TIME

(800) HOTEL DEL (468-3533) $$$$

1500 Orange Avenue, Coronado

(EXIT SAN DIEGO FWY [5] W. ON 75 AND CROSS OVER THE CORONADO BRIDGE, L. ON ORANGE AVE. THE TOLL IS $1 TO CORONADO AND THE RETURN TRIP IS FREE. IF YOU ARE CAR POOLING, CROSS THE BRIDGE USING THE RIGHT LANE, AT NO CHARGE.)

   This hotel is the creme-de-la-creme of hotels (personal opinion), and tea time here is a true taste of elegance. (You must make some time before or after your tea to explore this incredible hotel and its grounds!) Teas consist of bay shrimp and celery salad on puff pastry; triple-layered cucumber, and cream cheese and watercress sandwiches; New York sirloin carpaccio on ciabatta toast; brie with apple and grape slices decorated with walnuts; smoked salmon with dill on rye bread (it's amazing what kids will try in an etiquettely correct atmosphere); an assortment of delectable pastries; and a variety of teas, of course. (Also see HOTEL DEL CORONADO.)

   Hours: Tea is served Sundays at noon, 12:30pm, 2pm, 2:30pm and 3:30pm.

   Admission: $14.95 includes the food described above. $21.95 also includes champagne, Belgium truffles, and a chocolate dipped strawberry. Parking in the hotel lot costs $2.50 per hour; street parking is free.

   Ages: 5 years and up.

KOOKY'S DINER

(619) 294-2926 $$$

1425 Frazee Road, Mission Valley

(EXIT CABRILLO FWY [163] E. ON FRIARS RD., L. ON FRAZEE. IT'S ON THE CORNER, IN THE SHOPPING CENTER.)

   This 50's art deco diner features black and white checked tiles, red vinyl booths, a huge mural of an old-fashioned drive-in, an "antique" jukebox, and lots of photographs of famous stars from this era (i.e. James Dean, Elvis Presley, etc.). The main feature, though, is waitresses on skates, or "skatetresses." (My youngest child was slightly disappointed, however, that the busboys didn't wear skates, too!) My kids watched our "skatetress" carefully as the meal was served, to see if she would fall. She didn't.

   The menu is extensive, from "Egg-Sullivan" Show breakfast foods to the "Platters" of dinner fare. $8.95 gets you a full meal of meat, mashed potatoes or fries, vegetable soup or salad, and bread. Hamburgers, taco salads, sandwiches, roast beef, chicken, etc., cost around $5.95 each. A "Sundae, Sundae, So Good to Me" costs $1.85. The Little Boppers menu offers hamburgers, hot dogs, spaghetti, chicken fingers, etc. Prices range from $1.95 - $3.25. The fourth Saturday of every month is Cruise Night at Kooky's. Vintage cars cruise by, a deejay plays 50's music, and there are contests and giveaways.

   Hours: Open 24 hours

Admission: Family Nights are Mon. - Thurs., when one child eats for free with the purchase of an adult entree.
Ages: All

MCDONALDS FAMILY NIGHT

(619) 562-3434 (Alakazam Entertainment)

$$

8876 Cuyamaca Street, Santee

(GOING N. ON SAN VICENTE FWY [67], EXIT W. ON PROSPECT AVE., R. ON CUYAMACA ST. GOING S. ON 67, EXIT W. ON WOODSIDE AVE., TURNS INTO MISSION GORGE RD. GOING E. ON FWY 52, GO TO THE END, GO E. ON MISSION GORGE RD. IT'S LOCATED ON THE CROSS STREETS OF CUYAMACA ST. AND MISSION GORGE RD.)

McDonalds is always a popular place to eat, but this particular one features P. J. Pineapple the Clown every Tuesday night. On the outdoor Play Place, P. J. entertains kids (for free) by either creating balloon animals or by face painting. In addition to this fun family event, for every parent's combo meal purchased, one of your children will receive an all-American meal for free! (i.e. The all-American meal is a happy meal without the toy.) Gotta love those golden arches! Tip: P. J. has been appearing here for almost year, but please call the above phone number to make sure she is still "on."

Hours: This Family Night is offered every Tuesday from 4pm - 8pm.
Admission: The cost of a meal, or two.
Ages: All

SEAU'S, THE RESTAURANT

(619) 291-SEAUS (7328)

$$$

1640 Camino Del Rio North, #1376, in the Mission Valley Shopping Center, San Diego

(GOING E. ON MISSION VALLEY FWY [8], EXIT N. ON MISSION CENTER RD., R. ON CAMINO DEL RIO RD. GOING W. ON 8, EXIT AT CAMINO DEL RIO RD., TURN R. IT'S NEXT TO ROBINSONS-MAY.)

San Diego Charger's All-Pro linebacker, Junior Seau, has opened a two-story restaurant for the good sports in your family to enjoy. Notice how the outside of the restaurant resembles a coliseum. The inside decor is equally eye-catching with a huge mural of Junior Seau, model sports figures in action poses, and signed sports paraphernalia all around such as surfboards, football helmets, baseballs, bats, jerseys, hockey sticks, etc. Suspended T.V. monitors show sporting events, and the huge main screen shows the sports channel. (What a surprise!) Music instead of commentary is heard, which is good as parents don't need to constantly admonish children to be quiet.

The black table tops have football plays drawn on them, but don't try to erase them even though it looks like they were done in chalk - they weren't. (We saw others try to do this, too!) Our kids enjoyed watching the pizza maker toss pizzas, and cook them in the wood-burning stove. Sometimes the simplest entertainment is the best kind.

The food goes the whole nine yards - everything we ate was scrumptious. Menu choices run the gamut from burgers ($6.95) and pizza ($9.95) to rib-eyed steak ($13.95) and lobster ravioli ($11.95). The kids meals are Junior (Seau) size, ranging from $3.55 (choice of hot dog, pizza, or burger) to $6.55 (jr. shrimp). They come with fries, fresh homemade ice cream, and a beverage in a small take home sports bottle. Ah, to be 12 years old (or younger) again!

Hours: Open Sun. - Thurs., 11am - 10pm; Fri. - Sat., 11am - midnight.
Admission: Priced above.
Ages: All

U.S. GRANT HOTEL

(619) 232-3121 $$$$

326 Broadway, San Diego
(GOING S. ON SAN DIEGO FWY [5], EXIT W. ON ASH ST., L. ON 4TH, R. ON
BROADWAY. GOING N. ON 5, EXIT S. ON 6TH AVE., R. ON BROADWAY.)

Old time elegance permeates tea time in the Grant Hotel lobby. Amid crystal chandeliers, polished mahogany furniture, and beautiful floral arrangements, little girls and boys transform into young ladies and gentlemen, respectively. Savor an assortment of finger sandwiches, scones with fresh cream and preserves, crumpets and pastries, and a fine selection of teas. (If your children don't care for tea, just request hot chocolate, or juice, for them.) What a delightful treat!

Hours: Tea is served Tues., - Sat. from 3pm - 6pm.
Admission: $12 per person
Ages: 5 years and up

WESTGATE HOTEL

(619) 557-3650 $$$

1055 2nd Avenue, San Diego
(GOING S. ON SAN DIEGO FWY [5], EXIT W. ON ASH ST., L. ON 4TH AVE., R. ON
BROADWAY, R. ON 2ND AVE. GOING N. ON 5, EXIT S. ON 6TH AVE., R. ON BROADWAY,
R. ON 2ND AVE.)

Fashioned after an anteroom at Versailles, children will feel like royalty as they sip their tea and nibble on finger sandwiches, petit fours, and scones topped with preserves, honey, seasonal berries, or Grand Marnier cream. Reservations are requested. (I wanted to write that the food is lip-smacking good, but the refined atmosphere here dictates a more decorous choice of words.) The luxurious surroundings include a Steinway piano, rich tapestries, gilded mirrors, and crystal chandeliers.

Hours: Tea is served Mon. - Sat. from 2:30pm - 5pm. Piano music starts at 3pm.

Admission: $12 for adults and $8 for ages 3 - 8 years from the above set menu; or various prices for order a la cart.
Ages: 5 years and up.

OLIVIA'S DOLL HOUSE and TEA ROOM (Thousand ☼ Oaks)

(805) 381-1553   *$$$$$*

1321 E. Thousand Oaks, #110, Thousand Oaks
(EXIT VENTURA FWY [101] N. ON THOUSAND OAKS)

See OLIVIA'S DOLL HOUSE and TEA ROOM (Newhall) for a description.
Hours: Open for parties by reservation.
Admission: Parties start at $225 and include cake and party favors.
Ages: 4 years and up.

FAMILY PAY AND PLAY

The family that plays together, stays together! Indoor play areas, outdoor miniature golf courses, rock climbing centers, laser tag arenas, etc., are great places to go to spend some special bonding time.

DISCOVERY ZONE

Check your yellow pages for a local listing. $$

   This giant, wonderfully safe, fun, inside play environment is made
for children to run around 'til their hearts are content! It reminds me of
three or four McDonald's Play Places™ put together under one roof.
There are colorful plastic tubes to go through (think kid-size gerbil runs)
that interconnect, creating maze-like tunnels. Other fun features include
foam-padded obstacle courses, ball pits, bounces, and slides. Each
Discovery Zone differs slightly in the additional activities offered, such
as a bungee cord room, or a small trampoline. There is a separate play
area for toddlers that has the same activities, just scaled down in size.

   With usually just one entrance in and out of the play area, it's
possible to just sit, *zone* out, and watch your child; or bring knee pads
and join in the fun. There are also token-taking games and a full-
service snack bar. Note: Socks are required.

Hours: Most Discovery Zones are open Mon. - Fri., 10am - 8pm
              (Fridays until 9); Sat., 9am - 9pm; Sun., 10am - 8pm.
Admission: $5.99 for ages 3 - 12; $3.99 for children 2 years and
              under. Adults play for free with a paid child's admission.
              (Certain discounts are available through AAA.)
Ages: 1½ - 12 years.

ARROYO MINIATURE GOLF

(213) 255-1506 $

1055 Lohman Lane, South Pasadena
*(GOING S. ON GOLDEN STATE FWY [5], EXIT S. ON ORANGE GROVE, R. ON MISSION.
GO STRAIGHT PAST ARROYO ONTO STONEY DR. GOING N. ON PASADENA FWY [110],
EXIT N. ON MARMION WAY, R. ON PASADENA, L. ON ARROYO, L. ON STONEY DR.
FROM MISSION ST., STONEY DR. WINDS AROUND TO THE (BIG) ARROYO GOLF
COURSE.)*

   This miniature golf course, adjacent to the real golf course, is very
simple (i.e. no fancy castles, etc.), hence the inexpensive price. For the
price, practice, and fun of it, why not bring the kids and come play a
couple of rounds?!

Hours: Open daily from 7am - 10pm.
Admission: $1.50 per person per round.
Ages: 3 years and up.

CASTLE PARK (Hollywood)

(818) 765-4000 $$$

12400 Vanowen Street, Hollywood
*(GOING N. ON HOLLYWOOD FWY [170], EXIT W. ON VICTORY, R. ON WHITSETT, R.
ON VANOWEN. GOING S. ON 170, EXIT W. ON SHERMAN WAY, L. ON WHITSETT, L.
ON VANOWEN.)*

   This big castle offers your family choices of entertainment, with two
miniature golf courses - $5.50 for adults, $4.50 for kids under 13

years; **go kart** racing - $3.50 for a four-minute ride (drivers must be at least 54" tall); **batting cages**; and a slew of video and arcade games.

Hours: Open Sun. - Thurs., 10am - 10pm; Fri. - Sat., 10am - midnight.

Admission: Attractions are individually priced above.

Ages: 4 years and up.

FUN FACTORY

(805) 250-8540

27125 Sierra Hwy #302, Canyon Country

(EXIT GOLDEN STATE FWY [5] N. ON ANTELOPE VALLEY FWY [14], N. ON VIA PRINCESSA, R. ON SIERRA HWY. IT'S IN A SHOPPING MALL.)

This small indoor soft playground offers slides, ball pits, tubes, mazes, and a mini-zip line! The area for children 7 years and under features similar things to do, just on a smaller scale. It also has a bounce floor. This factory definitely produces fun. A full-service snack bar offers pizza, hot dogs, and more. Note: Socks are required.

Hours: Open Sun. - Mon., 11am - 7pm; Tues. - Wed., 11am - 8pm; Thurs. - Sat., 11am - 9pm.

Admission: $4.75 for ages 2 - 12; $4.25 for 12 - 24 months. Adults play for free with a paid child's admission. Ask about the Factory's occasional specials, when admission is only $3.50. Also inquire about other passes and discounts for a group of ten or more kids.

Ages: 2 - 10 years.

GO KART WORLD

(562) 834-3800

21830 Recreation Road, Carson

(EXIT SAN DIEGO FWY [405] E. ON CARSON, TAKE AN IMMEDIATE R. ON RECREATION RD.)

Kids 54" and taller can drive slick track cars - $3.50 for four minutes (about twenty laps). A mini-Indy track is available for kids 45" and taller at $3.50 a ride. The electric oval kiddie track is $2 for a three-minute ride for children between 3 - 6 years. To ride the turbo cars, you must be 18 years old, have photo ID, and a release form. (Sounds safe to me!) - $3.50 for three minutes.

Hours: Open daily from 11:30am - 11pm.

Admission: Individually priced above.

Ages: 6 years and up.

GOLFLAND ARCADE

(818) 444-5163

1181 N. Durfee Avenue, South El Monte

(EXIT POMONA FWY [60] S. AT PECK AVE., R. ON DURFEE.)

What course of action will you take? Choose from four, well-kept miniature golf courses with lots of fun holes. The arcade area is clean and has games, such as air hockey, as well as video games. Tip: McDonald's is only a few buildings away.

Hours: Open Sun. - Thurs., 10am - 11pm; Fri. - Sat., 10am - 1am.

Admission: Miniature golf is $5 for adults; $3 for ages 7 - 12; $2 for children 6 years and under.

Ages: 4 years and up.

GOLF 'N STUFF - FAMILY FUN CENTER (Norwalk)   ☼

(562) 863-8338   *$$$*

10555 E. Firestone Boulevard, Norwalk
(Exit LONG BEACH FWY [605] E. ON FIRESTONE.)

This big family fun center offers several different ways to have fun, with three courses of **miniature golf** - $5.50 for adults, children 5 years and under are free; plus **Li'l Indy, bumper boats,** and **bumper car** rides - $3.75 per ride, or five rides for $10. Yes, there are also arcade games to be played. This can keep you and the kids busy for hours - just bring lots of quarters!

Hours: Open Sun. - Thurs., 10am - 11pm; Fri. - Sat., 10am - 1am; open in the summer an hour later at night.

Admission: Attractions are individually priced above or buy an all-park pass for $13.50 per person that entitles you to a round of miniature golf, 4 rides, and 4 tokens.

Ages: 4 years and up.

LASER MANIA   ☀

(562) 496-1128   *$$$*

2420 E. Carson Street, Lakewood
(Exit LONG BEACH FWY [710] E. ON DEL AMO BLVD., R. ON CHERRY AVE., L. ON CARSON ST.)

The swirling fog; the pulse-pounding music; the projected pictures on the wall of rockets blasting or fires blazing; the mazes engulfed in darkness - welcome to Laser Mania! The almost floor-to-ceiling maze walls have holes to poke your gun through or to peek out to see if the "enemy" is approaching. Two teams of up to twenty people can play this exciting game. It entails using a laser gun to zap your opponents, or your opponent's goal, to score points. Each game lasts twelve, intense minutes. Private party rooms are available. Other adjacent attractions include a skating rink, a bowling alley, and an arcade and video center.

Hours: Open during the school year Mon. - Thurs., 3pm - 10pm; Fri., 3pm - midnight; Sat., 10am - midnight; Sun., 10am - 10pm. Summer hours are different in that Mon. - Fri. it usually opens at noon.

Admission: One game is $6; two games are $10; three games are
$14. Group rates (for ten or more people) start off at $5 a
game.

Ages: 5 years and up.

LASER STORM (Torrance)

(310) 373-8470 *$$*

22535 Hawthorne Boulevard, Torrance

(GOING S. ON SAN DIEGO FWY [405], EXIT S. ON HAWTHORNE BLVD. GOING N. ON 405, EXIT W. ON SEPULVEDA BLVD., L. ON HAWTHORNE BLVD.)

Laser tag is taking kids by storm! Power up your laser gun as
teams compete against each other and "shoot" it out. Take cover
behind neon-colored partitions, with gak splats, as an opponent aims at
you. Or, use the partitions as cover to stealthily sneak up on someone.
The ten-minute games are action-packed, and all the running around
can literally take your breath away!

Hours: Open Mon. - Thurs., 3pm - 10pm; Fri., 3pm - midnight;
Sat., 10am - midnight; Sun., 10am - 10pm. It is open for
extended hours in the summer.

Admission: $3.25 per game, Mon. - Thurs.; $4.25, Fri. - Sun.

Ages: 5 years and up.

MALIBU CASTLE

(310) 643-5167 *$$$*

2410 Marine Avenue, Redondo Beach

(EXIT SAN DIEGO FWY [405] N. ON HAWTHORNE, L. ON MARINE. OR, EXIT 405 E. ON ROSECRANS, R. ON INGLEWOOD, R. ON MARINE.)

Hold court at Malibu castle as your little subjects play either one of
the two wonderful **miniature golf** courses here. There are video and
arcade games inside the castle walls, and **batting cages** just outside.
(Malibu Castle is located right next door to MONSOON LAGOON.)

Hours: Open Mon. - Thurs., 11am- 10pm; Fri. - Sat., 10am -
midnight; Sun., 10am - 10pm.

Admission: Miniature golf is $5.95 a round for adults; $2.95 for
seniors; $4.95 for children 13 years and under.

Ages: 4 years and up.

MOUNTASIA

(805) 253-4FUN (4386) *$$$*

21516 Golden Triangle Road, Santa Clarita

(EXIT GOLDEN STATE FWY [5] E. ON VALENCIA BLVD. WHICH TURNS INTO SOLEDAD CANYON RD., R. ON GOLDEN OAK RD., L. ON GOLDEN TRIANGLE RD.)

Mountasia offers mountains of fun for your family! Play either one
of two **miniature golf** courses that feature a cascading waterfall. (Note:
The zebra course has a hole that goes under the waterfall, inside a

cave.) - $5.95 for adults; $4.95 for ages 4 - 12; children 3 years and under are free. Zip around the race track in **go karts** - $4 for a single car; $4.50 for a double car. There are height and age restrictions. Try to avoid getting wet (or go for it) in the **bumper boats** - $4 a ride; a passenger can ride for free. Height and age restrictions apply. Kids at least 48" tall and 6 years old can improve their batting average at the **batting cages**.

Inside, skate around the **RollArena** with light and music shows (ask about their roller hockey games) - $5.50 a session. (Sessions run from opening to 5pm, and 5pm to closing.) Skate rentals are $2. Family-oriented video and arcade games, a redemption center, and an Express McDonald's are located inside, too.

Hours: Open Mon - Thurs., 11am - 10pm; Fri., 11am - midnight; Sat. 10am - midnight; Sun. - 10am - 10pm.

Admission: Attractions are individually priced above.

Ages: 4 years and up.

MULLIGAN FAMILY FUN CENTER (Torrance)

(310) 325-3950   *$$$*

1351 Sepulveda Boulevard, Torrance
(EXIT HARBOR FWY [110] W. ON SEPULVEDA PAST NORMANDIE. IT'S ON THE R. LOOK FOR THE SIGN, AS IT IS EASY TO MISS.)

This center features **batting cages** - $1 for twenty pitches (you can also buy time, by reservation only); two wonderful **miniature golf** courses - $5.50 for adults, $4 for seniors and kids ages 4 - 10; children 3 years and under play for free; **Slic Track** racing - $3.50 for five minutes (height restrictions apply); a Jungle Gym **play area** with tubes, slides, and ball pits just for children under 60" - $4 for unlimited time; and the ever-present arcade games.

Hours: Open Mon.- Fri., noon - 10pm; Sat. - Sun., 10am - 10pm.

Admission: Attractions are individually priced above.

Ages: 2 years through 60" for the play area; 4 years and up for miniature golf.

PEPE'S KARTLAND

(818) 892-9309   *$$*

8300 Hayvenhurst Place, North Hills
(EXIT SAN DIEGO FWY [405] W. ON ROSCOE BLVD., R. ON HAYVENHURST AVE., L. ON HAYVENHURST PL.)

Kids at least 4'2" and 7 years old can race around the curvy, asphalt track for an exhilarating, six-minute ride.

Hours: Open Mon. - Thurs., 3pm - 10pm; Fri., 3pm - 11pm; Sat., noon - 11pm; Sun., noon - 10pm.

Admission: $4 a ride or purchase a family pass of 16 rides for $40.

Ages: 7 years and up.

Q-ZAR (Valencia)

(909) 364-1055 - call the Q-ZAR in Chino for the Valencia phone $$$
number. (They were just opening at this time I went to press.
23460 Cinema Drive #C, Valencia
(EXIT GOLDEN STATE FWY [5] E. ON VALENCIA BLVD., R. ON CINEMA DR.)

    See Q-ZAR (Chino) for a description.

    Hours: Open Sun. - Thurs., 10am - midnight; Fri. - Sat., 10am - 1am.

Admission: $7 a game.

    Ages: 5 years and up.

RACE CITY

(310) 523-4630 $$
777 West 190th Street, Gardena
(TAKE ARTESIA FWY [91] W. TO END, L. ON VERMONT, L. ON 190TH. OR, EXIT SAN DIEGO FWY [405] AT VERMONT / 190TH, L. ON 190TH.)

    Go kart drivers on this seven-turn, slick-track (meaning the car can spin out) must be at least 4'6" tall. A kiddie track, which is a small oval track for ages 6 - 10, is also available.

    Hours: Open daily from 11:30am - 11pm.

Admission: A four-minute ride costs $3.50

    Ages: 6 years and up.

THE ROCK GYM

(562) 983-5500 $$$$
600 Long Beach Boulevard, Long Beach
(EXIT SAN DIEGO FWY [405] S. ON LONG BEACH BLVD.)

    Go rock climbing at the beach, Long Beach, that is. The Rock Gym is one of Southern California's largest indoor rock climbing facilities. The huge lead climbing roof, unique bouldering tunnel, and walls jutting out at various angles prove a fitting challenge for your young athletes, and for those who are not so athletic. Both seasoned climbers and those new to the sport will experience a sense of accomplishment as they conquer the rocky obstacles and terrain. The staff is on hand to harness, belay, and encourage climbers. Classes are offered where you can learn to belay your kids (and others). The multi-colored rocks, embedded in the realistic-looking granite walls, are marked so they can be used as trail guides, though the routes are changed every few months to stimulate your mind and body. So, if you're feeling caught between a rock and a hard place, come to the Rock Gym for safe, fun exercise for the whole family! Ask about the variety of classes and programs offered.

    Hours: Kids' climbs are held on Sat. from 1pm - 3pm, and include equipment, instruction, and a belayer.

Admission: Kids' climbs are $20 a child. An introduction to belaying for kids 12 years and up is $45, which also includes a week pass to the gym.

Ages: 5 years and up.

ROCKREATION (Los Angeles)

(310) 207-7199 $$$$

11866 La Grange Avenue, Los Angeles
(EXIT SAN DIEGO FWY [405] W. ON OLYMPIC AVE., N. ON BUNDY, R. ON LA GRANGE.)

See ROCKREATION (Costa Mesa) for a description.

Hours: The gym is open Mon. and Wed., 11am - 10pm; Tues. and Thurs., 6am - 10pm; Fri., 11am - 8pm; Sat., Sun., 9am - 7pm. Kids' Climb, for ages 5 - 15, is offered Wed., 4pm - 6pm; Fri., 6pm - 8pm; Sat., 10am - noon and 3pm - 5pm.

Admission: Call for adults prices, depending on what equipment you might. Kids Climb is $15 per participant. Reservations are needed.

Ages: 5 years and up.

SHERMAN OAKS CASTLE PARK

(818) 756-9459 $$

4989 Sepulveda Blvd., Sherman Oaks
(EXIT VENTURA FWY [101] N. ON SEPULVEDA.)

This Castle Park offers royal fun for the whole family. There are three majestic **miniature golf** courses to putt around on, nine **batting cages,** over 100 arcade games, a redemption center, and a snack bar. Kids must be 8 years old, or at least 4'6", to play in the batting cages.

Hours: Open Sun. - Thurs., 10am - 11pm; Fri. - Sat., 10am - midnight.

Admission: Miniature golf is $5.50 for the first round for adults; $4.50 for children 12 years and under. Pay only $1 a round for early bird specials on Sat. and Sun. morning from 10am - 11am.

Ages: 4 years and up.

ULTRAZONE (Alhambra)

(818) 282-6178 $$$

231 East Main Street, Alhambra
(EXIT SAN BERNARDINO FWY [10] N. ON GARFIELD AVE., R. ON MAIN ST.)

See ULTRAZONE (San Diego) for a description.

Hours: Open Mon. - Thurs., 3pm - 10pm; Fri., 3pm - midnight;
Sat., 10am - midnight; Sun., 10am - 10pm. Summer
hours are Sun. - Thurs., 10am - 10pm; Fri. - Sat., 10am -
midnight.

Admission: $7 a game

Ages: 5 years and up.

ULTRAZONE (Sherman Oaks)

(818) 789-6620   *$$$*

14622 Ventura Boulevard, Suite 208, Sherman Oaks

*(EXIT VENTURA FWY [101] S. ON VAN NUYS BLVD., R. ON VENTURA BLVD. IT'S ON
THE S. SIDE OF THE STREET, UPSTAIRS.)*

It's almost pitch black. You're going through mazes and tunnels
trying to find your way to the enemy's base before your enemy finds
you. Suddenly, ZAP - you get hit! You realize you've lost your power
and now you have to recharge. Where *is* the recharging site? After
getting lost several times you find it, and now your infrared sighting
helps spy one of "them"! You fire, hit, and score one for your team!

Ultrazone, with over 5,000 square feet of excitement, is the ultimate
in laser tag. You carry your own equipment - a headset, pack, and laser
gun (which weighs about five pounds, total) - and play with up to thirty
people, or three teams. After a ten-minute briefing, you'll play for fifteen
intense minutes. The first game will wear you out, but it's just practice.
Now, you've got a handle on how the game is played, so go for a
second round. Or, just play some video games and grab a bite to eat
from the snack bar.

Laser tag - there is fun to be had with a game this rad!

Hours: Open during the school year, Wed. - Thurs., 3pm - 10pm;
Fri., noon - midnight; Sat., 10am - midnight; Sun., 10am -
10pm. Summer hours are Mon. - Thurs., 11am - 10pm;
Fri., 11am - 1am; Sat., 10am - 1am; Sun., 10am - 10pm.

Admission: Games are $7 each. Role playing and advanced access
membership is also available.

Ages: 5 years and up, or not afraid of the dark.

VIRTUAL WORLD (Old Pasadena)

(818) 577-9896   *$$$*

One Colorado, 35 Hugus Alley, Suite 200, Old Pasadena

*(TAKE PASADENA FWY [110] N. TO THE END, TURNS INTO ARROYO PKY., L. ON
COLORADO. GOING W. ON FOOTHILL FWY [210], EXIT S. ON FAIR OAKS. GOING E.
ON VENTURA FWY [134], EXIT E. ON COLORADO. ONE COLORADO IS BETWEEN
COLORADO, FAIR OAKS, UNION, AND DE LACEY. VIRTUAL WORD IS ABOVE THE AMC
THEATERS.)*

See VIRTUAL WORLD (Orange County) for the description.

Hours: Open Mon. - Thurs., noon - 10pm; Fri. - Sat., 10am -
midnight; Sun., 10am - 10pm.

Admission: $7 Mon. - Fri. before 5pm; $8 Mon. - Thurs. after 5pm; $9
Fri. after 5pm and Sat. - Sun., and holidays.
Ages: 6 years and up.

BALBOA FUN ZONE   ☀
(714) 673-0408   !/$$
Main St., Balboa Peninsula, Newport Beach
*(TAKE COSTA MESA FWY [55] TO THE END, WHICH TURNS INTO NEWPORT BLVD.,
WHICH TURNS INTO BALBOA BLVD., L. ON MAIN ST.)*

This strip called the Fun Zone is across the road from the pier. (See
BALBOA PIER.) The carousel, Ferris wheel, bumper cars, and scary
dark ride (that's its real name) are the main attractions here. Rides
require one to two tickets, and tickets are $1 each. Arcade games, a
clown bounce for younger children, and Laser Force (laser tag) are also
here. May the Force be with you as you try to zap your opponents in
this game of laser tag. The darkened room has bright, florescent
markings giving it an other-world, funky feel. Ten minutes of action-
packed play costs $5. Craft activities in the Zone include making spin
art pictures, filling stretch-neck bottles with multi-colored sand, etc.

Kids also enjoy walking around, shopping, or eating a famous
Balboa Island ice-cream bar. If you're looking for physical activity, bike
rentals are available at Oceanfront Wheelworks, (714) 723-6510 at 105
Main Street. Rentals are $5 for the first hour for children's bikes, and
$12 for tandems, plus they have in-line skates, etc. Parasailing, (714)
673-1693, is $45 for ten minutes of air time and an hour boat trip. (See
TRANSPORTATION for harbor cruises launched from this immediate
area.)

Take the historic Balboa ferry which runs daily from 6:30am to
midnight (longer on the weekends) to Balboa Island. For only 35¢ for
ages 12 and up, 15¢ for ages 5 - 11, children 4 years and under ride for
free, and $1 for car and driver, it's a fun, affordable way to get to the
island, and kids love this mini-adventure. Once on the man-made
island, there is not a lot for kids to do, but enjoy a walk along the paved
pathway along the beach.

Hours: Stores and attractions along the Balboa Fun Zone are
usually open Mon. - Thurs., noon - 8pm; Fri., noon -
10pm; Sat., 11am - 10pm; Sun., 11am - 8pm. Most
parking along the street is metered.
Admission: Attractions are individually priced above.
Ages: All

CAMELOT   ☀
(714) 630-3340   !/$$$
3200 Carpenter Avenue, Anaheim
*(EXIT RIVERSIDE FWY [91] N. ON KRAEMER/GLASSELL, R. ON LA PALMA, R. ON
SHEPARD, L. ON CARPENTER. IT'S NEXT DOOR TO FAMILY FUN CENTER
(ANAHEIM).)*

This huge castle has dragons, knights in shining armor, and anything else your prince or princess might consider fun decor. Choose from five **miniature golf** courses - $5 for adults, $4.25 for ages 5 - 12, children 4 years and under are free with a paid adult; Putt's the Dragon **Playground**, which has balls, slides, ziplines, etc., for kids 2½ years through 58" - $3 per hour, $1 for each additional hour; four **waterslides** (usually open from May - September) - $4 for ten rides, $6 for twenty rides, and $7 for an all-day rides pass; over 300 video and arcade games; and the mandatory snack bar, serving pizza and Dryer's ice cream!

Hours: Open in the summer Sun. - Thurs., 10am - midnight; Fri. - Sat., 10am - 1am. The rest of the year it's open Sun. - Thurs., 10am - 11pm; Fri - Sat., 10am - midnight.

Admission: Attractions are individually priced above.

Ages: 2½ years and up.

FAMILY FUN CENTER (Anaheim)   ☼

(714) 630-7212 $$$$

1041 N. Shepard, Anaheim

(EXIT ARTESIA FWY [91] N. ON KRAEMER/GLASSELL, R. ON LA PALMA, R. ON SHEPARD. IT'S NEXT DOOR TO CAMELOT, MINIATURE GOLF.)

This is a fun center, but bring your money because fun costs. The many attractions here include **bumper boats** - $3.50 for kids over 44", $1.50 for kids under 44"; **batting cages**; **go-karts** - $4 for a five-minute ride (children must be at least 57" to drive); **Nascars** - $4.50 a drive (height restrictions apply); **battle boats,** which is like riding in a surfaced submarine while shooting balls at your "enemy" in the next boat - $4; and an **outdoor roller-skating rink** - $3 before 5pm, and $4 after 5pm. Skate rentals are $1 extra. The giant **maze craze** is amazing. Walk through and try to find your way out. To play the challenging maze game purchase a card, punch the time clock, and try to find the eight numbers hidden throughout the maze - they could even be up at any of the four towers! The game costs $4 per player. Tip: Keep younger children with you.

Big Top Fun Zone has eleven carnival rides, including a Ferris wheel, a yo-yo swing, and five kiddie rides. Each ride requires two to five tickets, and tickets are 50¢ each. An all-rides pass is $6.99 per person. Arcade games and a snack bar are available, too.

Hours: Big Top Fun Zone is open during the school year, Fri., noon - 10pm; Sat. - Sun., 11am - 11pm. It is open daily during the summer. The rest of the attractions are open Sun. - Thurs., 11am - 10pm; Fri. - Sat., 11am - midnight. Family Fun is open extended hours during the summer.

Admission: Attractions are individually priced above or buy an all-day pass for unlimited fun (excluding the batting cages) - $17.50 over 57"; $13.50 for kids 57" and under.

Ages: 2 years and up.

FAMILY FUN CENTER (Fountain Valley)
(714) 842-1011   *$$$$*

16800 Magnolia Street, Fountain Valley
(EXIT SAN DIEGO FWY [405] S. ON MAGNOLIA.)

Family Fun Center is fun for the whole family. The attractions here include **miniature golf** - $5.50 for adults, $3.50 for kids 12 years and under; **bumper boats** - $3.75 for a six-minute ride, and kids must be at least 44" to ride by themselves (children under 44" can ride with an adult); **batting cages** - eighteen pitches for $1; and **go karts** - $4 for a five-minute ride, and kids must be at least 57" to drive by themselves, $1.75 for additional passengers. The **Kiddie Big Top** has carnival rides such as Ferris wheels and spinning cups, geared for ages 7 and under. Each ride takes three - five tickets and tickets are 50¢ each, or purchase twenty-four tickets for $6; forty-four tickets for $10.

See BULLWINKLE'S RESTAURANT, which is adjacent to Family Fun.

Hours: Miniature golf is open Sun. - Thurs., 9am - 10pm; Fri. - Sat., 9am - midnight. Batting cages are open Mon. - Thurs., noon - 9pm; Fri. - Sun., 9am - 11pm. Go karts are open daily from 2pm - 10pm. The Kiddie Big Top is open Mon. - Fri., noon - 10pm; Sat. - Sun. 9am - 10pm. Family Fun attractions are open extended hours during the summer.

Admission: Attractions are individually priced above or, on weekends only, buy an all-day pass (excluding go karts) for $16.95 for 57" and taller; $12.95 for under 57".

Ages: 2 years and up.

FIGHTER TOWN, U.S.A.
(714) 855-8802   *$$$$*

20521 Teresita Way, Lake Forest
(EXIT SANTA ANA FWY [5] N.E. ON LAKE FOREST, GO 4 MILES, TURN R. ON REGENCY., L. ON TERESITA WAY. THE NEXT L. IS THE PARKING LOT.)

For older kids aiming to be Top Guns, these twelve flight simulators are the next best thing to actually being in the air. Offering different flying perceptions, some cockpits have twenty-seven inch monitors while others have fifteen-foot wall projections. The cockpits are realistic with fully functional avionic control panels, heads-up displays, and hands-on stick and throttle controls. Choose from single seat, dual seat, motion, or non-motion simulators.

After you're suited up in flight gear, you'll watch a fifteen-minute briefing video on the basics of flying, followed by a briefing on the particulars of your cockpit. Enjoy your half-hour flight as you compete in dog fights against computer-generated opponents or against a buddy in the next plane. You can also participate in a multi-craft air strike mission. You'll be in constant contact with the control tower.

For those who remain grounded, an Officer's Club is available with snacks and drinks to purchase. Monitors in here show what the pilots are experiencing, or take a look from the observation deck, which oversees the darkened pilot's room.

Reservations for a weekend flight must be made two weeks in advance; reservations for a weekday flight, one week. Ask about squadron and wing training, and about aviation youth camps.

Hours: Open Mon. - Thurs., 11am - 9pm; Fri., 11am - 11pm; Sat., 9am - 11pm; Sun., 9am - 7pm.

Admission: The cost for a flight cost ranges from $23.99 to $59.99, depending on the type of cockpit you choose. Kids under 12 years must "fly" with an adult, but there is no additional cost for them.

Ages: 10 years and up; 12 years and up can fly solo.

FUN DAZZLE

(714) 544-0222

$$

2802 El Camino Real, Tustin

(EXIT SANTA ANA FWY [5] N. ON JAMBOREE, L. ON EL CAMINO REAL. IT'S IN THE TUSTIN MARKETPLACE NEXT TO HOME DEPOT AND TOYS R US.)

Kids will be dazzled by this huge, indoor playground that has tubes, ropes, and obstacle courses! It's a terrific place to let them burn off some of that excess energy they always have, while playing in a safe and fun environment. Note: Socks are required. Toddlers, 3½ years and under, have a few of their own special play areas with ball pits, tubes, and slides. You need to be a bit active here, too, as there is not any one spot from which you can see the entire kid's play area.

Every two hours or so a craft project is available for kids to participate in. The projects can include finger painting, face painting, or a holiday-themed craft to take home. The activity center here also offers quieter activities such as working on computers and reading books. When you've worked up an appetite, grab a bite to eat at the full-service snack bar that serves pizza, salads, and sandwiches.

Fun Dazzle has a drop-off program where a state-certified child care worker watches over your beloved. It's a win/win situation as your child has a great time playing, and you have a great time doing whatever you want! Call to find out about enrollment.

Hours: Open Mon. - Wed., 10am - 7pm; Thurs. - Sat., 10am - 8pm; Sun., 11am - 6pm.

Admission: $5.95 per child; adults play for free with a paid child's admission.

Ages: 1½ - 12 years.

GOLF 'N STUFF - FAMILY FUN CENTER (Anaheim)   ☼
(714) 778-4100 $$$

1656 S. Harbor Boulevard, Anaheim
(EXIT SANTA ANA FWY [5] S. ON HARBOR, OR GARDEN GROVE FWY [22] N. ON HARBOR. IT'S ACROSS THE WAY FROM DISNEYLAND.)

Come, *par*take in some family fun, and play at the deluxe miniature golf courses here - $5.50 a round for adults; children 4 years and under play for free. There are plenty of arcade games available here, too.

Hours: Open Sun. - Thurs., 9am - 10pm; Fri. - Sat., 9am - midnight.
Admission: Priced above.
Ages: 4 years and up.

LASER QUEST   ☼
(714) 449-0555 $$$

229 East Orangethorpe Avenue, Fullerton
(EXIT RIVERSIDE FWY [91] N. ON HARBOR BLVD., R. ON ORANGETHORPE AVE.)

This large arena, with gothic decor, sets the stage for an exciting game of laser tag. Armed with laser guns, and vests with target lights, enter the multi-level maze. Amid the strobe lights, partitions, and loud music, race against the clock to "tag" the opposing team members and score. The ten-minute games are fast-paced, and leave you either tired or fired up to play another round! The lounge has video games.

Hours: Open Mon. - Thurs., 6pm - 10pm; Fri., 4pm - midnight; Sat., noon - midnight; Sun., noon - 10pm. It is open extended hours in the summer.
Admission: $7 per game
Ages: 5 years and up.

PALACE PARK   ☼
(714) 559-8336 $$$$

3405 Michelson Drive, Irvine
(EXIT SAN DIEGO FWY [405] S. ON CULVER DR., R. ON MICHELSON. OR, EXIT SAN DIEGO FWY [405] S. ON JAMBOREE, L. ON MICHELSON.)

This pink palace, which can be seen from the freeway, is definitely a kid's kingdom. There is an almost overwhelming amount of video and arcade games, or, to quote my boys, "Wow!" There is also a ticket redemption center and an Express McDonald's Restaurant. The **simulator** ride offers different adventures for $4 each. "Riders" must be at least 42" tall. Also inside the castle walls are activities for the younger set, such as kiddie arcade games; **Palace Playland**, which is a two-tiered play area with soft-play mazes, ball pits, tunnels, and slides - $3.50 for all-day play for kids 12 years and under; and **Palace Bouncer**, a castle bounce - $1 for kids under 60".

Outside, are three **miniature golf** courses at $5.50 a round for adults, children 4 years and under are free. Splash Island **bumper boats** are $3.50 a ride, $1 for additional riders, with riders being over 44" tall. I allowed my 10-year old to steer the boat and he did so gleefully - right under the fountain's waters. Oh, the joy of spending time together! The **Slick car race track** is $5 a ride, $1 for additional riders. Drivers must be 60" or taller and riders must be over 44" tall. **Go-carts,** where drivers can be minimum 44" tall, are $3.75 per ride, $1 for additional riders. **Batting cages** are here, too. In **Laser Storm**, you and your at least 5-year-old child (personal recommendation) enter a darkened, maze-like room with walls that are three-feet high and lit by fluorescent markings. For ten minutes you'll engage in laser tag, which entails alternately safeguarding your base while shooting at the players on the opposing team. It's a blast. The cost is $5 per game.

If the urge strikes, next door is the Irvine Recreation Center with plenty of bowling lanes.

Hours: Open Sun. - Thurs., 10am - 11pm; Fri. - Sat., 10am - 1am.

Admission: Attractions are individually priced above or purchase a pass of three attractions and $2 worth of tokens for $12; or four attractions and $4 worth of tokens for $15.

Ages: 2 years and up.

PLANET KIDS (Fountain Valley)   ☼
(714) 378-8733 $$
18081 Magnolia St., Fountain Valley
(GOING S. ON SAN DIEGO FWY [405], EXIT S. ON MAGNOLIA ST. GOING N. ON 405, EXIT N. ON EUCLID ST., L. ON TALBERT AVE., L. ON MAGNOLIA. IT'S ON THE CORNER OF MAGNOLIA AND TALBERT.)

See PLANET KIDS (Laguna Hills) for a description.

PLANET KIDS (Laguna Hills)   ☼
(714) 831-3500 $$
26538 Moulton Parkway, Laguna Hills
(EXIT SAN DIEGO FWY [5] S.W. ON LA PAZ RD., R. ON MOULTON PKY. IT'S IN A SHOPPING CENTER.)

Bring your earthling offspring to Planet Kids for indoor fun that is out of this world! Adventure Crater is the main play structure, where kids will run orbits around you. It has a wooden walkway all around, padded slides, tube slides, and a ball pit. Go through the tunnel under crater rock and peek out the windows into a desert diorama.

The Globe Theater has costumes and karaoke for your budding star. It also shows continuously running (mostly Disney) movies. Nintendo games are featured in the Galactic Games room - no tokens needed. Mission Control is a space-like shuttle room, with quite a few computers programmed with educational games that intrigue ages 5 -

95 years old. In the Eclipse room, "pictures" are taken against a photo-sensitive wall when the strobe-like light flashes. Take a family portrait.

You'll hear the "music" (i.e. loud noises) long before you actually enter the Lunar Tunes room. For band member "wannabes," or for kids who like to play with drums and other instruments, this is the place to be. A floor piano has keys that light up when stepped (or jumped) on (as in the movie "Big"). Another cosmic component in here is the individual rooms. One contains electric drums; another has a synthesizer; a third has complete stereo and karaoke equipment.

The Tot Spot, designed for kids five years and under, has a complete little beach area and a climbing play structure with a ball pit and soft foam animals. It also has a mini-schoolhouse room with toys, books, and a computer.

The snack bar has food ranging from pizza and soft pretzels to chef salad and baked potatoes. If you have places to go and things to do (and want to do it ten times faster without your kids), check into the Blast-Off program. It enables parents to enroll their children, ages 5 - 13, to stay here for up to four hours of supervised play. Note: Socks are required in all play areas.

Hours: Open Mon. - Thurs., 11am - 7pm; Fri., 11am - 9pm; Sat., 10am - 9pm; Sun., 10am - 7pm.

Admission: $5.95 for ages 1 - 3; $7.95 for ages 4 - 13. Adults play for free with a paid child's admission.

Ages: 1½ - 13 years.

PLANET KIDS (Orange)   ☽

(714) 288-4090 $$

1536 E. Katella Avenue, Orange
(EXIT COSTA MESA FWY [55] E. ON KATELLA AVE.)

See PLANET KIDS (Laguna Hills) for a description.

ROCKREATION (Costa Mesa)   ☽

(714) 556-ROCK (7625) $$$$

1300 Logan Avenue, Costa Mesa
(EXIT SAN DIEGO FWY [405] S. ON FAIRVIEW RD., R. ON BAKER ST., L. ON MCCLINTOCK WY., R. ON LOGAN AVE.)

Get the kids geared up - it's time to *rock* and roll at Rockreation! This huge indoor warehouse/rock climbing gym is a great place for beginners to learn climbing techniques in a safe and controlled environment. It also provides enough rocky terrain for serious climbers to train. The multi-colored rocks of various shapes and sizes jut out from the twenty-seven-foot geometrical walls for handholds and footholds, offering over 150 different climbing routes. Some of the walls are straight up and down, others have slight inclines, while still others have very challenging angles and overhangs. Belayers, those who hold the rope so if you slip you don't fall, are provided at the kids' climbs (and for adults who need a partner). Even if you were to hit rock bottom (which you won't), it's "carpeted" with black foam padding. Kids warm up using a short practice wall. Although my boys were a bit intimidated at first, by the end of our time here, they were really climbing the walls - all the way to the top. Enroll your child in a summer camp or one of the year-round classes offered for various levels and ages. Come hang out with your kids here, or better yet, tell them to go climb a rock! Also see ROCKREATION (Los Angeles).

Hours: The gym is open Mon. - Thur., 11am - 10pm; Fri., 11am - 8pm; Sat. - Sun., 9am - 7pm. Kids Climb, for ages 6 - 12, is offered Tues., 6pm - 8pm and Sat., 3pm - 5pm.

Admission: $15 per person for the day. $15 per participant for the Kids Climb. Reservations are needed.

Ages: Depending on your child's agility - 5 years and up.

SOUTHLAND HILLS GOLFLAND AND PIZZA

(714) 895-4550 $$

12611 Beach Boulevard, Stanton

(EXIT SANTA ANA FWY [5] S. ON BEACH. OR, EXIT GARDEN GROVE FWY [22] N. ON BEACH.)

*For*etunately for miniature golf lovers, Southland Hills has two great courses enhanced by a windmill, pagoda, a fort, etc. - $5.50 for adults; $3.50 for seniors; $4.50 for ages 11 and under. There are also video arcades, a redemption center, and a snack bar that serves pizza, etc. Monday night, after 5pm, is family night, when everyone can play miniature golf for only $3.50 a round.

Hours: Sun. - Thurs., 10am - 11pm; Fri. - Sat., 10am - midnight.

Admission: Prices are listed above.

Ages: 4 years and up.

VIRTUAL WORLD (Newport Beach)

(714) 646-2495 $$$

1785 Newport Boulevard, Suite 219, Newport Beach

(TAKE THE COSTA MESA FWY [55] TO THE END, WHICH TURNS INTO NEWPORT BLVD. IT'S LOCATED IN THE MALL, AT TRIANGLE SQUARE.)

Has anyone ever told you that you're in a world of your own? Well, you virtually are at Virtual World. In this comfortable setting, you'll sit in your own partially-enclosed booth while joining other pilots in inter-dimensional travel.

After a briefing on how to navigate, you'll be interacting with others on your ten-minute journey to and on other worlds - expect the unexpected. Some of the programs offered are "Battletech," with a slogan of "no guts, no galaxy," and "Red Planet," where you race your vehicle through the canals of Mars. This is a stimulating simulating experience.

Afterward, you can view your adventure from this world's instant replay machines, get a pilot's log (printed record), and share war stories with other real humans over refreshments and snacks in the lounge.

Hours: Open Mon. - Thurs., 11am - 11pm; Fri. - Sat., 10am - 1pm; Sun., 10am - 11pm.

Admission: $7 Mon. - Fri. before 5pm; $8 Mon. - Thurs. after 5pm; $9 Fri. after 5pm and Sat. - Sun. and holidays.

Ages: 8 years and up.

ADAMS KART TRACK

(909) 686-3826 $$$$

5292 Bell Avenue, Riverside

(EXIT POMONA FWY [60] N. ON MARKET. IT'S ON THE CORNER OF 24TH ST. AND MARKET.)

The main track, which is six-tenths of a mile of turns, twists, and straight track, is a great introduction to real racing. This race track school offers classes for kart racing, available for kids 5 years and up. Call for a class schedule.

Hours: The track is open daily 10am - 5pm.

Admission: Bring your own kart for the main track - $20 a day for non-members; $17 for members; $15 for an extra passenger; $7 for spectators. Classes start at $125 for four hours of instruction and racing.

Ages: 5 years and up.

FIREWORKS FAMILY FUN

(909) 222-4777 $$$

12125 Day Street, Moreno Valley

(EXIT MORENO VALLEY FWY [60] N. ON DAY ST. IT'S IN THE CANYON SWINGS PLAZA.)

Make sparks fly at Fireworks Family Fun! The two *tee*rific, nine-hole **miniature golf** courses are $3.25 for adults, $2.75 for ages 6 - 12, children 5 years and under are free (additional games are $1). **Go karts** are $3.50 for a five-minute ride with a 57" height requirement to drive; $1 for an additional passenger. **Bumper boats** are $3 a ride with a 47" height requirement for drivers; $1 for an additional passenger. Enter the dark and foggy room to play **Laser Tag.** $5 will buy you eight minutes of adrenaline pumping fun; shooting laser guns at your opponents while trying to avoid getting hit! What fun center could call itself complete without a myriad of arcade games to entice your kids?! Fireworks has 10,000 square feet of such games (i.e. a lot!).

Hours: Open Sun. - Thurs., 11am - 10pm; Fri. - Sat., 10am - midnight.

Admission: Attractions are individually priced above. Ask if their specials are still on - $10 to play one of each attraction; $14.95 for two of each attraction; $25 for a family of 5 to play one of each attraction (Monday nights only).

Ages: 4 years and up.

FAMILY FUN CENTER (Upland)
(909) 985-1313   *$$$$*

1500 West 7ᵗʰ Street, Upland
(*EXIT THE SAN BERNARDINO FWY [10] N. AT EITHER CENTRAL OR MOUNTAIN. YOU CAN SEE IT FROM THE FREEWAY.*)

Upland Family Fun Center offers fun for everyone in your family! This giant fun center has four, themed **miniature golf** courses. Two of them are indoors, so rainy days won't put a damper on your swing. Prices are $5.50 a round for adults, $3.50 for children 12 years and under. Take a spin on a **go kart** at $4 a ride (no sandals allowed), but drivers must be over 57", $1.50 for an additional passenger under this height. **Bumperboats** are always fun - $3.50 for kids over 44", $1.50 for riders under this height. There are eight **kiddie rides** here, including a Ferris wheel, roller coaster, mini-airplanes, moonbounce, and soft play area. Each ride or attraction costs three to five tickets. Tickets cost $6 for a book of twenty-four; $10 for a book of forty-four; and $20 for a book of 104. Kids can also practice for the big league at the **batting cages,** or play at the over 100 video and arcade games.

If you've worked up an appetite, BULLWINKLE'S FAMILY RESTAURANT - (909) 946-9555 - is right next door. Your choice of hamburgers, pizza, chicken, or ribs is served in a fun atmosphere, where there are more arcade games to play. (There is no escape from them.) See BULLWINKLE'S for more information.

Hours: Miniature golf and the arcades are open Mon. - Fri. from 10am - 11pm. The other attractions are open Mon. - Fri., noon - 9pm. All attractions are open Sat. - Sun. from 10am - 11pm. Family Fun is open extended hours during the summer.

Admission: Attractions are individually priced above or purchase an all-day pass which includes unlimited use of everything, except the arcade games; $16.95 for 57" and taller; $12.95 for under 57." The pass is only offered on Frid. after 5pm and all day Sat., Sun., and holidays during the school year; although it is available daily during the summer.

Ages: 3 years and up.

FIESTA VILLAGE
(909) 824-1111   *$$$*
1405 E. Washington Street, Colton

(EXIT SAN BERNARDINO FWY [215] E. ON WASHINGTON.)

Come party at Fiesta Village! There are two Western-motif **miniature golf** courses - $4.50 for adults, $3.75 for children 12 years and under; **go karts**, where drivers must be at least 53" tall - $4 for a five-minute ride; **batting cages**; and three **waterslides** with a lounging area for spectators - $5 for an all-day pass for ages 4 years and up. (There is no pool here, just slides.) Wild and crazy kids can jump on a **trampoline** attached to a bungee-type harness (for doing flips) - $4 for three minutes. Video arcades and a snack bar are also here.

The Great Gatsby restaurant is adjacent to Fiesta Village, offering pizza, salads, sandwiches, and ice-cream. If you're in the mood to play, there are video and arcade games, air hockey, and a pool table.

Hours: Miniature golf, go-karts, and the batting cages are open year round, Sun. - Thurs., 10am - 10pm; Fri. - Sat., 10am - 11pm. The trampoline is open daily in the summer. Call for hours the rest of the year. The waterslides are open weekends in May and September from 11am - 5pm, and daily in the summer. Call for hours.

Admission: Attractions priced above.

Ages: 4 years and up.

MULLIGAN FAMILY FUN CENTER (Murrieta)　☼

(909) 696-9696　　　　　　　　　　　　　　　　　　$$$$

24950 Madison Avenue, Murrieta

(EXIT TEMECULA VALLEY FWY [15] W. ON MURRIETA HOT SPRINGS RD., R. ON MADISON AVE.)

Calling all ranch hands: Git along to Mulligan Family Fun Center for some family fun! This western-themed miniature golf center has two impressive **miniature golf** courses. (You can see the red rock boulders, small western buildings, and stagecoaches when you're heading southbound on the I-15.) A round of golf costs $5.50 for 11 years and up; $4 for 10 years and under. Other attractions include **batting cages**; **bumper boats** - $3.50 for the driver, $1.50 for passengers; and **go-karts** - $4 for drivers, $1.50 for passengers. Complete your day (or night) on the town by coming in the spacious "town hall," which is done up right fine. (First, look at all the fun props outside, like cowboy mannequins literally hanging around.) Inside, the old west motif continues with a jail and kid's saloon (cafe). There are also plenty of modern-day shoot out games (i.e. arcade and video games).

Hours: Open Sun. - Thurs., 10am - 10pm; Fri. - Sat., 10am - 11pm. Closed Thanksgiving and Christmas.

Admission: Attractions are individually priced above. Unlimited all-day passes are available Mon. - Thurs. for $18 for 44" and up; $13 for kids under 44".

Ages: 3 years and up.

Q-ZAR (Chino)   ☀
(909) 364-1055   *$$$*

5479 Philadelphia Street, Chino
(EXIT POMONA FWY [60] N. ON S. CENTRAL AVE., R. ON PHILADELPHIA ST.)

The noise level from the action at the video games is the first thing I noticed about Q-Zar. Next, we were briefed on how to play Q-Zar laser tag. Tip: Listen carefully! Although there is the usual set up of two teams playing against each other, and points scored by "shooting" the lights on your opponents vests, gun, or home base, there are also some intricacies of this particular game. For instance, you are given so many shots (and lives) before you must re-energize your gun; after you've been hit your gun tells you it is deactivated, and you cannot hit your opponents for a few seconds; and when your gun is recharging, you can be hit, but temporarily can't retaliate. It gets a bit confusing, but in the heat of the battle, you just run around like crazy anyhow! Q-Zar is definitely ultra high-tech and wildly fun. Games are fifteen minutes long, yet in this massive (4,500 square feet) flourescent-lit arena, it seems a whole lot longer. Run, duck, hide, point, and shoot - it's time for laser tag!

Hours: Open Sun. - Thurs., 10am - midnight; Fri. - Sat., 10am - 1am.
Admission: $7 a game.
Ages: 5 years and up.

SCANDIA AMUSEMENT PARK   ☼
(909) 390-3092   *$$$$*

1155 S. Wanamaker Avenue, Ontario
(EXIT ONTARIO FWY [15] W. ON JURUPA, R. ON ROCKEFELLER, R. ON WANAMAKER.)

Vikings might have come to this country just to play at this amusement park! Well, maybe not, but it is a lot of fun and very well kept up. Attractions include two **miniature golf** courses at $5.75 for adults, while children 5 years and under play for free; **batting cages; amusement rides** for big kids such as a roller coaster, bumper boats, and scrambler; and rides for little kids such as a small semi-truck ride around a track, a carousel, and a slide. Tickets cost $1 each; $8.95 for twelve tickets. Children's rides require one to three tickets; adult rides require three to six tickets. Arcade games and a snack bar are here, too.

Hours: Open in the summer, Mon. - Fri., 10am - midnight; Sat. - Sun., 10am - 1am. Open the rest of the year, Mon. - Fri., 10am - 10pm; Sat. - Sun., 10am - midnight.
Admission: Attractions are individually priced above or purchase an unlimited pass (excluding arcade games) - $17.95 for 54" and above; $12.95 for kids under 54". Inquire about weekday specials.
Ages: 3 years and up.

SCANDIA FAMILY FUN CENTER
(760) 241-4007   *$$$*

12627 Mariposa Road, Victorville
(EXIT I-15 E. ON BEAR VALLEY RD.)

Enjoy some high-desert fun at Scandia Family Fun Center. There are two themed, **miniature golf** courses, with castles, bridges, and other small buildings that add interest - $5.95 for adults, children 5 years and under play for free; **go-karts** and **bumper boats** - $3.95 per ride (there are height restrictions); and **batting cages**. A full-service snack bar, arcade and video games, and prize redemption center are also here for your enjoyment.

Hours: Open Sun. - Thurs., 10am - 11pm; Fri. - Sat., 10am - midnight.

Admission: Attractions are individually priced above. Or, buy a pass for $10.95 per person that allows you to play on each attraction once, plus receive 5 tokens. An unlimited pass is $15.95 per person.

Ages: 4 years and up.

BELMONT PARK / PIRATE'S COVE
(619) 491-2988 - general information; (619) 488-1549 -   *$$$*
amusement rides; (619) 539- 7474 - Pirate's Cove;
(619) 488-3110 - The Plunge

West Mission Bay Drive and West Mission Boulevard, San Diego
(EXIT SAN DIEGO FWY [5] W. ON SEA WORLD DR. AND FOLLOW THE SIGNS TO W. MISSION BAY DR.)

Shops and restaurants encircle the ten or so **amusement rides** at Belmont Park. In the center, is the Giant Dipper Roller Coaster which doesn't have any loops, but has plenty of ups and downs! A replica of the Looff Liberty wooden carousel has horses as well as an ostrich, giraffe, and tiger to ride on. Other amusement rides include Bumper Cars (drivers must be 52"), a Tilt-A-Whirl, and five kiddie rides such as Baja Buggies, Thunder Boats, Submarines, and the Sea Serpent. Rides require between two to five tickets, with tickets costing 75¢ each, or $19.95 for forty-five tickets. For those with a strong stomach, Orbitron, the contraption that spins you head over heels and around and around, is also available at $4 a "ride." Jumpstart your heart with Trampoline Thing, where you can safely do flips because you're harnessed in - $4 per jumping session. Steer remote-controlled boats around a nifty little harbor, complete with mini docks and houses. Kid-friendly attractions around the perimeter of the rides include virtual reality at Cyber Station; movies at The Venturer Theater; arcade and video games at either Family Arcade or Prime Time; and Pirate's Cove.

Two buildings, with wonderful pirate murals, comprise **Pirate's Cove**, an indoor family playland for kids twelve years and under. One building has air hockey, a few video games, and kiddie rides.

Downstairs, is an underground cave-like tunnel that connects the two Cove buildings. This second building, with costumed ppirate mannequins, is where most of the swashbuckling action takes place. Here are the ball pits, soft play areas, obstacle courses, big plastic tunnels and tubes, that your mateys dream of! There is also a separate area for younger buccaneers to pillage, I mean play on. Socks are required at Pirate's Cove. Admission is $6.50 for ages 3 to 12; $4.50 for children 2 years and under; and two parents can play for free for each paying child. Note: If you come play here for just the last hour, admission is $3 per child.

While at Belmont Park, take the plunge at **The Plunge**. This large indoor swimming pool boasts a beautiful underwater/whale mural, painted by renown marine artist, Wyland. The enclosed pool, kept at 83 degrees, is surrounded by huge windows looking out on palm trees, suggesting a tropical atmosphere. Swim sessions are $2.50 for adults; $2.25 for seniors and children 6 months to 17 years. The pool is located on the other side of the movie theater.

Too nice a day to go swimming inside? Go for a dip outside, as the ocean is just a few steps away. The surf and sand, and bike trail on the beach are "shore" to help make your day at the park a good one!

Hours: The stores and restaurants are open daily, usually from 10am - 6pm. Pirate's Cove and most of the rides are open Mon. - Thurs., 11am - 7pm; Fri. - Sun., 11am - 8pm. Call first as hours fluctuate. The Plunge is open daily to the public with swim sessions held at various times.

Admission: Attractions are priced above. During the week, unlimited kiddie rides, plus entrance to Pirate's Cove, is only $7.95 a child. (Call to make sure this deal is still being offered.)

Ages: All

BOARDWALK ☼
(619) 449-7800 $

1286 Fletcher Parkway, El Cajon
(GOING E. ON 8 FWY, EXIT N. ON JOHNSON AVE., L. ON FLETCHER PKY. GOING W. ON 8, GO N. ON SAN VICENTE FWY [67] AND THEN IMMEDIATELY EXIT W. ON BROADWAY, WHICH TURNS INTO FLETCHER PKY. GOING S. ON 67, EXIT W. ON FLETCHER PKY.)

This Boardwalk is not made of boards, nor is it by the seaside; it is a large indoor amusement center for kids. It's clean with brightly colored games and rides that elicited several, "This is FUN!" comments from my kids. The main attractions are the **carousel** (three tokens), **castle bounce** (three tokens), **bumper cars** (six tokens), and **soft play gym** (eight tokens). This two-story play area, for kids 60" and under, has balls pits, a mini zip line, slides, and obstacle courses, plus tubes to crawl through. Each token costs 25¢. An all day/all play activity pass is the way to go, as it's only $3.95. There are numerous arcade and video games here, as well as fifty free and 5¢ games. The full-service snack bar offers salads, pizza, pasta, etc. Kids meals are $1.99, and include a choice of corn dog, chicken nuggets, or pizza, plus fries and a drink. If you feel like scoring more fun, strike out to Parkway Bowl, the connecting bowling alley.

Hours: Open Sun. - Thurs., 11am - midnight; Fri. - Sat., 11am - 1am.

Admission: Attractions are individually priced above. An unlimited play pass is $3.95.

Ages: 1½ years - 12.

FAMILY FUN CENTER (El Cajon) ☽

(619) 593-1155   *$$$$*

1155 Graves Avenue, El Cajon

(FROM 8 FWY, GO N. ON SAN VICENTE FWY [67] AND THEN IMMEDIATELY EXIT AT BROADWAY. AT THE END OF OFF RAMP, TURN L. ON GRAVES AVE.)

Come to this Family Fun Center to play for just an hour or have fun all day. Green fees pay for two rounds at any of the three nine-hole, themed **miniature golf** courses. Choose Memory Lane (fairy tale motif), Iron Horse (western), and/or Lost Crusade (Egyptian) - $5.50 for adults; $4.50 for kids 12 years and under. Other attractions include **bumper boats** - $3.50 for adults; $1.50 for passengers (height restrictions apply); **go-karts** - $4 for adults; $1.50 for passengers (height restrictions apply); **batting cages**; and the **Kid's County Fair**. The latter is comprised of six rides such as a roller coaster, train ride, Ferris wheel, mini-planes, etc. Each ride costs $1.50, or purchase a book of twenty-four tickets for $6, or forty-four tickets for $10. The two-story arcade and video game building is attractively set up. Try simulator rides such as skiing the slopes with the Alpine Racer, or jet skiing on Wave Runner. Upstairs is a nickel arcade area.

Bullwinkle's Restaurant is also at this fun center and eating here is always a highlight. (See BULLWINKLE'S RESTAURANT for more tasty details.) Food and fun - what more could you want?!

Hours: Kid's County Fair is open Mon. - Fri., noon - 8pm; Sat. - Sun., 10am - 8pm. Other attractions are open Mon. - Thurs., 11am - 10pm; Fri., 11am - 10pm; Sat. - Sun., 10am - 10pm. Hours fluctuate, so please call before you come.

Admission: Attractions are individually priced above, or buy a pass for $10 that includes 18 holes of miniature golf, 1 ride on the bumper boat or 10 tokens, 1 ride on the go-kart or $3 worth of County Fair tickets, and 4 game tokens or a turn at the batting cages, plus a discount on Bullwinkle's food. An unlimited pass is $16.95 for 60" and taller; $13.50 for kids under 60." The pass can be purchased only on Fri. after 4pm, and all day Sat. and Sun. during the school year; or, daily during the summer.

Ages: 2½ years and up.

FAMILY FUN CENTER (Escondido)   ☼

(760) 741-1326   *$$$$*

830 Dan Way, Escondido
(EXIT ESCONDIDO FWY [15], E. ON HWY 78, S. ON CENTRE CITY PKY., R. ON
MISSION AVE., R. ON DAN WAY.)

   This Family Fun Center, just one in a chain of several, is packed with fun activities. The three **miniature golf** courses offer interesting embellishments such as a double-headed dragon, a castle, a windmill, fountains, and miniature housing structures - $5.50 for adults; $3.50 for kids 12 years and under. The **Giant Maze** is an amazing (and confusing) game to play. Purchase a game card, punch the time clock, and then walk/run through the maze, which has four towers and numerous partitions. The object is to find all eight numbers and four letters on your card that are hidden throughout the maze. Verify your findings by using the special hole punch. Average game time is half an hour. A game card costs $3.25 per person. The seven rides in **Kiddieland** include a moon bounce, kiddie swing, rocket ship, Ferris wheel, and mini airplanes. Each ride takes four to six tickets costing $6 for twenty-four tickets, $10 for forty-four. Other attractions here are the **batting cages**; **go-karts** - $4 per driver (height restrictions apply), $1.50 for passengers under 44"; **bumper boats** - $3.25 (height restrictions apply), $1.50 for passengers under 44"; and video and arcade games. A full-service snack bar is available to take care of the inevitable hunger pangs that kids get when they know food is nearby. If you haven't had enough of kids running around, Chuck E. Cheese is right next door!

Hours: Kiddieland is open Sun. - Thurs., 11am - 6pm; Fri., 11am - 8pm; Sat., 11am - 8pm. The rest of the attractions are open Sun. - Thurs., 11am - 10pm; Fri., 11am - 11pm; Sat., 10am - 11pm.

Admission: Attractions are individually priced above. All day/all play passes (not including batting cages and video and arcade games) are $15.95 for 57" and taller; $12.50 for kids under 57". During the school year, the passes can be purchased Fri. after 4pm, or all day Sat., Sun., and major holidays. They can be purchased daily during the summer.

Ages: 2 years and up for Kiddieland; 4 years and up for most of the other attractions.

FAMILY FUN CENTER (Vista)   ☼

(760) 945-9474   *$$$$*

1525 West Vista Way, Vista
(EXIT 78 FWY N. ON EMERALD AVE., R. ON W. VISTA WAY.)

This Family Fun Center really has it all! If you're in a mutinous mood, play the **miniature golf** course with a pirate ship and fountains. If you're feeling rather noble, play King Arthur's course with its huge (relatively speaking) castles and dungeons and bridge over water. Golf prices are $5.50 for adults; $3.50 for kids 12 years and under. **Laser Runner** is an every man/woman/child for himself laser tag game played inside an inflatable battleship bounce. There are soft obstacles to hide behind (or jump on) and even small rooms to run around in. The game is action-packed, sweaty, and fun. The cost is $3.75 for a five-minute game, and children must be 5 years old to play. **Kidopolis** is a huge, four-story soft-play area with slides, obstacle courses, ball pits, tubes and tunnels. This major gerbil run was a major hit with my boys. The cost is $4.95 for kids who must be under 60"; two adults can play for free with each paid child's admission. Other attractions here include **batting cages; go karts** - $4 for drivers, (height restrictions apply), $1.50 for passengers; and **bumper boats** - $3.50 a ride, (height restrictions apply), $1.50 for passengers.

The noisy, but attractive, main two-story building houses numerous video and arcade games. Upstairs is a nickel arcade section. Bullwinkle's Restaurant is also here serving up its tasty family fare, along with a fun atmosphere. Rocky and Bullwinkle cartoons play on the television monitors and a spotlight flashes colored lights on a fountain in front of the stage while the water "dances" to the music. (See BULLWINKLE'S RESTAURANT for more information.)

Hours: Kidopolis is open Mon. - Fri., noon - 8pm; Sat. - Sun., 10am - 8pm. The other attractions are open Mon. - Fri., 11am - 9:30pm; Sat. - Sun., 10am - 10:30pm.

Admission: Attractions are individually priced above. Purchase a Super Saver, which is your choice of playing almost every attraction once - $12, or get an unlimited pass for $16.95 for 57" and over; $13.50 for 57" and under. The unlimited passes are only available on the weekends during school months; daily during the summer.

Ages: 2 years and up.

FAMILY FUN CENTER (San Diego)   ☼

(619) 560-7342 $$$$

6999 Clairemont Mesa Boulevard, San Diego
(EXIT JACOB DEKEMA FWY [805]. E. ON CLAIREMONT MESA BLVD.)

So much fun can be had at just one place! Choose from two themed **miniature golf** courses: Storybook Land with a castle, Cinderella's pumpkin, the shoe from the old woman who lived in one, etc., or Western Town with a bank, jail, storefront facades, a livery stable, and wagons - $5.50 for adults, $3.50 for seniors and children 12 years and under. Other attractions include **go karts** - $4 for a five-minute ride, $1.50 for a passenger (height restrictions apply); **Naskarts**

- $4.50 per ride (height restrictions apply); **bumper boats** - $3.50 per driver, $1.50 per passenger; **batting cages**; and **Lazer Runner**. This last game is laser tag played inside an inflated, spaceship-looking big bounce. With six to eight players, it's every kid (or adults) for himself/herself. Although this game is played with the usual laser tag equipment of a vest with flashing lights and a laser gun, running around inside a bounce (with obstacles, even!), adds a whole new element of fun. Five minutes of sweaty fun costs $3.75 per person, and players must be at least 5 years old. The **Fun Zone** has seven rides, including teacups, a Ferris wheel, a train ride, a swing, and a fire engine that goes in the air and around and around. Rides cost $2 each, or take between four to seven tickets at a cost of $7 for 28 tickets, or $10 for 44. Of course there is a video and arcade game area and a prize redemption center. There is also a separate section for less violent kiddie video games. For those making every nickel count, a special video arcade area has games to play for only 5¢. Fa*moose* Bullwinkle's food is on hand, although it is purchased at a snack bar, not at the usual sit-down restaurant. Ask about group rates and how good grades can translate into free tokens. Bring nickels, quarters, and dollar bills and enjoy your day (or night) here!

Hours: The Fun Zone is open daily in the summer from 10am - 10pm; it is open during the school year, Fri. - Sat., 10am - 11pm; Sun., 10am - 9pm. The rest of the attractions are open year round, Mon. - Thurs., 11am -midnight; Fri., 11am - 1am; Sat., 9am - 1am; Sun., 9am - midnight.

Admission: Attractions are individually priced above. An unlimited pass (except for video and arcade games) costs $17.50 for 57" and over; $13.50 for under 57."

Ages: 2 years and up.

FUN-4-ALL   ☼
(619) 427-1473   *$$$*
950 Industrial Boulevard, Chula Vista
(EXIT SAN DIEGO FWY [5] E. ON "L" ST., S. ON INDUSTRIAL BLVD.)

This small, family amusement park offers an older, well-used **miniature golf** course (with a nautical theme) - $4.50 for adults, $3.50 for kids 12 years and under; a fun **bumper boat** ride around a few islands - $3.50 per person; **go-karts** - $3.50 (height restrictions apply); and **batting cages.** There are also several video and arcade games inside the main building, and a full service snack bar.

Hours: Open Sun. - Thurs., 9am - 10pm; Fri. - Sat., 9am - midnight.

Admission: Attractions are individually priced above.

Ages: 4 years and up.

HIDDEN VALLEY PAINTBALL

(760) 737-8870   *$$$$$*

Lake Wohlford Road, Escondido

(EXIT ESCONDIDO FWY [15] E. ON R. VIA RANCHO PKY, WHICH TURNS INTO BEAR VALLEY, R. VALLEY CENTER PARKWAY, R. ON LAKE WOHLFORD RD. ABOUT 2.2 MILES TO THE TOP OF ROAD. THE INDOOR AREA IS AT 15TH ST. AND BROADWAY ST., DOWNTOWN SAN DIEGO.)

Armed with a semi-automatic paint gun and dressed in mask, goggles, and layers of clothing (to reduce the somewhat painful impact of the paintballs), you are now ready to play the wildly exhilarating and intense game of paintball. Teams are pitted against while running around the 100-acre outside playing area where hills, valleys, and trees are used for both offensive and defensive tactical maneuvers. Bring good running shoes, a water bottle, and most of all - stamina.

Although it doesn't have the same acreage or terrain, Hidden Valley also has an indoor paintball arena. The barriers, muted lighting, and thrill of the chase still make the game very exciting. This playing area is more accessible for corporate warriors and kids with pent-up, after-school energy.

Hours: The outdoor field is open weekends only from 8am - 4pm. (It is open during the week for groups of 20 or more people, with reservations.) The indoor arena is open Wed. - Fri., 2pm - 10pm; Sat. - Sun., noon - 11pm.

Admission: $45 for all-day play includes camouflage clothing, a semi-automatic marker, full face and head protection, all-day supply for air for gun, 200 paintballs, and lunch (pizza and a drink).

Ages: 10 years and up.

LASER STORM (Pacific Beach)

(619) 483-2081   *$$*

1321 Garnet Avenue, Pacific Beach

(GOING N. ON SAN DIEGO FWY [5], EXIT W. ON BALBOA/GARNET OR GOING S. ON 5, EXIT AT MISSION BAY DR, R. ON GARNET. STAY TO THE RIGHT ON GARNET.)

See ROLLERSKATE AND LASER STORM for a description of Laser Storm, laser tag.

Hours: Open Mon. - Thurs., 3pm - 10pm; Fri., 3pm - midnight; Sat., 10am - midnight; Sun., 10am - 10pm. Call for extended summer hours.

Admission: $3 per game, Mon. - Thurs.; $4 per game, Fri. - Sun.

Ages: 5 years and up.

MALIBU GRAND PRIX

(619) 566-4121 (619) 566-4121   *$$$*

8606 Miramar Road, San Diego

(EXIT JACOB DEKEMA FWY [805] E. ON MIRAMAR RD. OR EXIT ESCONDIDO FWY [15] W. ON MIRAMAR RD.)

For racing fanatics or for beginners; Malibu Grand Prix is a grand place to practice race car driving skills. A video arcade area keeps drivers occupied until it's their time to hit the road.

Hours: Open Mon. - Thurs., noon - 9pm; Fri., 11am - midnight; Sat., 10am - midnight; Sun. 10am - 9pm.

Admission: $2.95 for a one time license fee (includes 1 lap). Mini Virage and Virage cars are $2.95 for 1 lap; $19.75 for 11 laps. Grand Virage $3.95 for 1 lap; $19.95 for 10 laps. Ask about reduced prices offered Mon. - Fri., 5pm - 6pm.

Ages: Mini Virage drivers must be 54." Virage and Grand Virage drivers must have a valid drivers license, or have a learners permit and be accompanied by a parent.

RIVER CANYON RACEWAY

(619) 390-4907

$$

14011 Ridge Hill Road, El Cajon

(EXIT 8 FWY S. ON LAKE JENNINGS RD., WHICH TURNS INTO RIDGE HILL RD. AS IT TURNS R. IT IS LOCATED NEXT TO FRASIER'S FRONTIER.)

Rev your engines, and race around this oval go-kart slick track - just for the fun of it!

Hours: Open Tues. - Thurs., 3pm - 10pm; Fri. - Sat., 3pm - midnight; Sun., 3pm - 10pm.

Admission: $4 for a 5 minute ride.

Ages: 56" and taller.

ROLLERSKATE AND LASER STORM

(619) 562-3791

$$

9365 Mission Gorge Road, Santee

(GOING N. ON SAN VICENTE FWY [67], EXIT W. ON PROSPECT AVE., R. ON CUYAMACA ST., L. ON MISSION GORGE RD. GOING S. ON 67, EXIT W. ON WOODSIDE AVE., WHICH TURNS INTO MISSION GORGE RD. GOING E. ON FWY 52, GO TO THE END, GO E. ON MISSION GORGE RD. BEHIND JACK-IN-THE-BOX)

Take two opposing teams, arm them with vests and laser phasers, let them loose in a darkened arena with neon-colored partitions, and let the games begin! A dividing line separates the teams. When you shoot the "enemy," you deactivate their phaser. They have to go to the energy pod and reactivate it to get back into the game. Of course, if you get hit, you must do the same thing. A scoreboard keeps track of which team is ahead, and which team ultimately wins. Each exciting game lasts for about ten minutes. But just like potato chips, it's hard to stop at just one (game).

Roller skating is a separate activity from laser tag. Call for skate sessions.

Hours: Laser Storm doors are open Tues., 6pm - 9pm; Wed. - Thurs., 6pm - 10pm; Fri., 6pm - midnight; Sat., 10:30am - midnight; Sun., 1pm - 7pm. Call for extended summer hours. Call for skate sessions.

Admission: Laser Storm costs $3.50 for the first game; $2.50 for the second game. Skate sessions are $4 per participant; in-line skate rentals are an additional $3.

Ages: 5 years and up.

SOLID ROCK   ☼

(619) 299-1124   *$$$$*

2074 Hancock Street, San Diego

(GOING S. ON SAN DIEGO FWY [5] EXIT AT OLD TOWN AVE., OFF THE OFF RAMP ONTO HANCOCK ST. GOING N. ON 5 EXIT AT MOORE ST., L. ON OLD TOWN AVE, L. ON HANCOCK ST.)

Experience the thrill and physical challenge (i.e. you'll get sweaty) of rock climbing in a safe, indoor, controlled atmosphere. Novice climbers can learn the basic skills and importance of a well-placed foot and/or hand, while experienced climbers will enjoy the opportunity to continue training by sharpening their skills. This is a great sport to introduce kids to for at least three reasons: It builds confidence, physical fitness, and strategic thinking. (All this just by rock climbing - and we thought school was important!) Staff members are experienced climbers and are always around to instruct, belay, and encourage.

Multi-colored stones mark various routes on the walls, overhangs, and the bouldering cave. Although a child might be tentative at first, by the end of the first session, he/she is usually literally climbing the walls, and having a great time doing it. So, if you're looking for a creative way to channel your child's excess energy, turn off the cartoons and come *rock* and roll on Saturday mornings! Note: Kid's Climb is open to all ages, however, parents of climbers 8 years and under are required to stay and work with their children.

Hours: Kids Climb hours are Sat., 9am - 1pm; Sun., 3pm - 7pm. They are welcome to climb here at other times, but they will need an adult who can belay them. Solid Rock is open Mon. - Fri., 11am - 10pm; Sat., 9am - 9pm; Sun., 11am - 7pm.

Admission: Kids Climb is $15 for non-members, $10 for members. It includes 4 hours of climbing, staff supervision, and all rental equipment. The Rock costs $10, Mon. - Fri. before 5pm; $12, Mon. - Fri. between 5pm - 10pm, all day Sat., or all day Sun. Full package rentals - shoes, harness, and chalk bag is $6. Kids 12 years and under cost $8 a day, plus $3 for a harness (they need to wear tennis shoes).

Ages: 4 years and up.

SURF AND TURF   ☼
(619) 481-0363 $$

15555 Jimmy Durante Boulevard, Del Mar
(EXIT SAN DIEGO FWY [5] W. ON VIA DE LA VALLE, L. ON JIMMY DURANTE BLVD.)

Next to this driving range are two eighteen-hole, miniature golf
courses. The courses are not as elaborately embellished as others we
have played at, but there are enough mini structures, and twists and
turns, to keep them interesting and fun. Note: Older kids might want to
try out a bigger back swing at the driving range.

Hours: Open daily 7am - 9pm.
Admission: $4 for ages 3 and up - for as many rounds as you want to
            play.
Ages: 4 years and up.

ULTRAZONE (San Diego)   ☀
(619) 221-0100 $$$

3146 Sports Arena Boulevard, San Diego
(GOING W., EXIT OCEAN BEACH FWY [8] BEFORE THE END S. ON MIDWAY DR. /
MISSION BAY DR., L. ON SPORTS ARENA BLVD.)

Come play laser tag - the tag of the future! Put on your vest, pick
up your laser gun, and for fifteen minutes you'll play hard and fast.
Laser tag is action-packed, and the thrill of the chase really gets your
adrenaline pumping! This Ultrazone, with its dark cave-like setting, is
themed "Underground City." The multi-level "city," or playing arena, is
huge. Run up and down ramps; seek cover behind floor-to-ceiling walls;
duck into a partly-hidden doorway; and zap your opponents. Tip: The
best time for younger kids to play is weekday afternoons and early
evenings, or during the day on weekends. Older kids come out here in
hordes at nighttime.

Hours: Open Mon. - Thurs., 4pm - 11pm; Fri., 2pm - 2am; Sat.,
            11am - 2am; Sun., 10am - 11pm. Summer hours are
            Sun. - Thurs., 10am - 10pm; Fri. - Sat., 10am - midnight.
Admission: $6.50 a game. Sat. and Sun. until 2pm is Kids Zone -
            reduced prices for kids 11 years and under.
Ages: 6 years and up.

VERTICAL HOLD   ☼
(619) 586-7572 $$$$

9580 Distribution Avenue, San Diego
(EXIT JACOB DEKEMA FWY [805] E. ON MIRAMAR RD., L. ON DISTRIBUTION AVE. OR
EXIT ESCONDIDO FWY [15] W. ON MIRAMAR RD., R. ON DISTRIBUTION AVE.)

Indoor rock climbing is rapidly becoming one of the fastest growing
indoor sports in America. This physically challenging and mentally
stimulating activity is a great way to redirect a child growing up in our
couch potato/video game society. Vertical Hold has over 150 routes
that are changed every few months. Climb vertical walls (of course!),

overhangs, and chimney routes, or try your hand (and feet) at bouldering. At this particular rock climbing center, you need to bring your own belayer. (i.e. The person who stays on the ground attached to your rope so if you should slip or fall, you won't fall far.) So, in order for your child to climb or participate in the Kid's Climb, you or someone you bring with you, must be a certified belayer. Call about signing up for a belaying class, as well as a climbing class. Don't just crawl out from under a rock - go climb it!

Hours: Open Mon. - Fri., 11:30am - 10pm; Sat., 10am - 10pm; Sun., 10am - 8pm. Kids Climb is any three-hour time period on the weekends. Kids are welcome to climb at any other time, too, at the regular rate.

Admission: There are various fee structures to choose from: For those with their own equipment - $10 a day; $80 for 10 visits; or $50 for 10 visits at lunchtime (between 11:30am - 1:30pm). Otherwise, it's $20 a day (adults or children) with equipment rental of a harness, rope, shoes, and chalk included in this price. Weekend Kids Climb is $12 per child, which includes equipment rental.

Ages: 5 years and up.

VIRTUAL WORLD (San Diego)

(619) 294-9200 $$$

7510 Hazard Center Drive, San Diego

(EXIT CABRILLO FWY [163] E. ON FRYERS RD., R. ON FRAZEE, R. ON HAZARD CENTER DR. IT IS IN THE HAZARD CENTER COMPLEX, NEAR THE DOUBLETREE HOTEL, NEXT TO GAME EMPIRE.)

This Battletech software, with its awesome graphics and sounds, can best be described as "fast, furious, and extreme." You've, virtually, never played a game so intense as the one you'll engage in at this Virtual World. Please see VIRTUAL WORLD, (Newport Beach), for a more in-depth description.

Hours: Open Mon. - Thurs., noon - 10pm; Fri. - Sat., 10am - midnight; Sun., 10am - 10pm.

Admission: Games are $8, Mon. - Thurs., and Fri. until 5pm, and Sun. after 5pm; $9.50, Fri. after 5pm through Sun. before 5pm.

Ages: 8 years and up.

VISTA ENTERTAINMENT CENTER

(760) 941-1032 $$

435 West Vista Way, Vista

(EXIT 78 FWY, N. ON MELROSE DR., R. ON W. VISTA WY.)

(Laser) lights! Action! Laser Storm is a quick, action-packed game of laser tag. The arena is designed with cardboard hanging partitions painted with neon-colored "gak" splats. There are no solid walls to hide behind, so you need to be constantly on your guard and ready to fire. The ten-minute games, played nearly in the dark, are played by shooting laser guns at the opposite team members' vests and/or at their base, to score points. When you are hit (not "if" because you will get hit), you'll be unable to shoot for just a few seconds while you are being recharged. Laser Storm might not be as elaborately set-up as other laser tag places, but it is less expensive and a lot of fun!

Score more fun when you bowl in the lanes just outside the Laser Storm doors. The Entertainment Center has a large bowling alley, a small video games room, a full-service snack bar, and a nice-sized nursery/childcare room.

> **Hours:** Laser Storm is open Mon. - Tues. and Thurs., 6pm - 10pm; Wed., 7pm - 9pm; Fri., 6pm - midnight; Sat., noon - midnight; Sun., noon - 10pm. Call for open bowling times.
>
> **Admission:** Call for a schedule of prices for Laser Storm. Costs vary from $1 per game on Dollarmania nights to $3 per game to $10 for a whole night of fun called "Fire Til' You Tire."
>
> **Ages:** 5 years and up.

WILD WOODY'S ADVENTURES IN PAINTBALL   ☼

(760) 941-0230 - reservations; (760) 765-1820 - field $$$$$

Highway 78, Julian

(ON HWY 78, HEAD 5 MILES EAST PAST THE TOWN OF JULIAN. THE FIELD IS ON THE LEFT HAND SIDE.)

A simple explanation of paintball is that two opposing teams compete at a game of capture the flag. Add paintballs, however, a paintball gun (or marker), camouflage clothing, goggles, face mask, adrenaline, and 140 acres of shaded forest and hilly terrain, and this simple description takes on a whole new meaning. This intense game of hunter and the hunted is played while your heart is beating wildly, both from exhilaration and physical exertion. If you are hit with a paintball (splat), you are out of the game. A game is won when a player successfully returns the opponent's flag to his own team's flag station. Games usually last about twenty minutes, so six to ten games can be played in any given day. All games are refereed to insure player safety, and fair play. Tip: Wear pants, shoes with traction, and multiple layers of clothing to pad the sting of getting hit.

> **Hours:** Open Mon. - Fri. for group play only; open Sat. - Sun. to the public, 8am - 4:30pm.
>
> **Admission:** $25 - $40 depending on the type of equipment you want; a pistol, face mask, and goggles cost $25; a semi-automatic rifle is $20; two hundred paintballs are $10, etc.
>
> **Ages:** 12 - 17 year olds can play with prior arrangement; children as young as 10 years old can play at kids events and special games.

CLUB DISNEY   ☼
(805) 777-8000 $$$

120 South Westlake Boulevard, Thousand Oaks
(EXIT VENTURA FWY [101], N. ON WESTLAKE BLVD. IT'S ON CORNER OF WESTLAKE
BLVD. AND THOUSAND OAKS BLVD. IN A LARGE SHOPPING CENTER THAT HAS MANY
GREAT STORES SUCH AS BRISTOL FARMS, BORDERS, PIER ONE, ETC.)

"Disney" is synonymous with "family fun." Club Disney, the first of
its kind to open in a nationwide chain, lives up to the high expectations
and quality we associate with the Disney name. This inside play site
has several different rooms, activities, and entertainment, as well as a
lot of character appeal. Younger children can "plant" plastic carrots in
the holes in Rabbit's garden, crawl through a log, or cuddle up with
stuffed Tiggers for a honey of a storytime in Pooh's Corner. Goofy's
game area offers no-tokens-needed games such as Duck-a-Puck,
which is air hockey with Mighty Duck figures popping up to block your
shot, and a giant maze game that takes two people to control the board
and play. The Jungle Climber is a green-leaf carpeted, multi-level
climbing structure that kids can climb up, then use the slides to come
down. Mickey's Circus is a toddlers' area with soft play blocks, a small
merry-go-round, and a circus train to climb aboard. Applaudeville
Theater features your children dancing with Mickey and Donald,
interacting in a very animated story time, or starring in a fashion show.
The Mouse Pad has sixteen computer stations with educational games
that will challenge ages 3 - 103. Animation Alley has two real flatbed
editing tables used in post production animation. Turn the wheel slowly
to look at the cartoons one frame at a time, or spin it faster and it's like
looking through a flip book. Kids can also use toy figures and
computers to make their own stop motion animation film. Character
Creations offers half-hour art classes. It gives children (and adults) the
opportunity to actually learn about art as well as make their own
*mouse*terpiece! A small mirrored maze room has Cruella DeVille's and
the kidnappers' voices hounding kids at every turn. A few kids got
scared, but most enjoyed the attraction.

Merlin's Magic Chamber, where Merlin performs magic shows
throughout the day, is upstairs, as is a small room for adults - the Chat
Hat. Relax on a couch in here or surf the Internet. The Wizard's Lab,
which is a mini science station, is also upstairs. Kids can look in
carnival-type distortion mirrors; use a voice changer to sound like
anything from a chipmunk to Darth Vader; pump air to make colorful
balls move through clear tubes; make shadows on a photosensitive
wall; etc.

Club Disney also offers delicious Mickey-Mouse-shaped food in
their Club Cafe. The menu includes personal pizzas for $3.75; a bagel
with cream cheese for $1.25; chicken strips with dip and fries for $3.50;
and a to-die-for raspberry streusel for $2.75. Remember, you must
wear socks to play inside the second happiest place on earth. And yes,
of course, there is a gift shop!

Hours: Tues. - Thurs., 10am - 7pm; Fri., 10am - 9pm; Sat., 9am - 9pm; Sun., 9am - 7pm.

Admission: $8 per person for ages 2 years and up. Adults must be accompanied by a child.

Ages: 1 - 14 years old.

GOLF 'N STUFF   ☼

(805) 644-7132   *$$$*

5555 Walker Drive, Ventura

(EXIT VENTURA FWY [101] N. ON VICTORIA AVE., TAKE A QUICK L. ON WALKER ST. THE GOLF 'N STUFF SIGN IS VISIBLE FROM THE 101 FREEWAY.)

If you and the kids are in the mood for a little golf 'n stuff, here's the place for you. There are two **miniature golf** courses to putt around on at $5.50 per round for adults; $4.50 for seniors; children 5 years and under play for free. **Indy cars** have a height requirement of 52", while **bumper cars** and **water boats** both have height requirements of 48". The cost per ride is $3.75, or a five-ride deal for $10. Inside, are arcade games and a snack bar.

Hours: Open Sun. - Thurs., 10am - 11pm; Fri. - Sat., 10am - 1am.

Admission: Attractions are individually priced above or buy a pass that includes 4 rides, a round of miniature golf, and 4 arcade tokens for $13.50 per person.

Ages: 4 years and up.

GREAT OUTDOORS

or **Botanical Gardens, Nature Centers, and Parks**

Contrary to popular belief, Southern California cities consist not only of concrete buildings, but also of the great outdoors. So, come and explore the natural beauty of city life, and take a hike (with your kids)!

Tip: Passes to Orange County Regional Parks are available for $50 a year. For an additional $25, you will also receive a pass that is good at most Orange County beaches. Call any Orange County Regional Park for more information.

NURSERY NATURE WALKS
(310) 364-3591 $

From Los Angeles through Ventura Counties.

   Nursery Nature Walks provide guided walking tours for families and groups with babies, toddlers, and children up to 10 years old. With over sixty locations throughout the Los Angeles and Ventura Counties, you're almost guaranteed to find a walk at a park near you. Some of the hikes are very easy, while others are longer and more strenuous. The tour guides usually encourage strollers, and they gear the exploratory walk specifically towards kids. This is a tremendous opportunity for young children to be exposed to the beauty of nature, and to learn to respect the environment at a tender age.

   Bring your camera, sunscreen, and snacks, and enjoy the pitter patter of little feet next to yours on the nature trails!

   Hours: The nature walks are given almost daily at various
                  locations, and usually start at 10am.
   Admission: $5 per family. Some parks also have parking fees.
   Ages: Birth up to 10 years.

FORT TEJON STATE HISTORIC PARK
(805) 248-6692   !/$$

Fort Tejon Road, Old Fort Tejon
(76 MILES NORTHWEST OF LOS ANGELES, ABOUT 25 S. OF BAKERSFIELD, ON THE
WEST SIDE OF GOLDEN STATE FWY [5].)

   A long time ago, battles were fought, and the U.S. Dragoons were garrisoned at this fort. A good portion of the fort is still intact today. Come and explore the long, barracks building, walk through the officers' quarters that hold displays from war time, and pretend to shoot the cannons at unseen enemies. There is plenty of room for picnicking, and a few trails for hiking. I highly recommend coming here when Living History Days and/or Civil War Reenactments are presented. Living History Days activities include adobe brick making, playing old-fashioned games, participating in chores from days of yore, etc. Watch battle skirmishes and see demonstrations of weapons at the Civil War Reenactments. Guided tours of the fort are given in between battles. Come see history in action!

   Hours: The fort is usually open daily from 9am - 5pm. Living
                  History Days and Civil War Reenactments are held a few
                  times during the year. Call for dates and times.
   Admission: Free to the fort. Special programs cost $5 for adults; $3
                  for ages 6 - 12; children 5 years and under are free.
   Ages: 3 years and up.

APOLLO PARK
William Barnes Avenue, Lancaster   !

(Exit Antelope Valley Fwy [14] W. at Ave. G, R. on William Barnes Ave. (across from 50ᵀᴴ St. West), past the General Fox Airfield, into the park.)

This *space*cious park has three man-made lakes, named after the astronauts from Apollo XI: Lake Aldrin, Lake Armstrong, and Lake Collins. The lakes are stocked with trout, and while there is not a fee for fishing, you do need a California state fishing license if you are over 16 years of age. The park, though surrounded by the desert, is picturesque with shade trees and bridges over portions of water, plus plenty of run-around room. A small playground is also here. My kids were intrigued by the glass-cased, well-built mock-up of a command module. The placard describes the dedication of the park to the Apollo program. (Don't you love sneaking in a history lesson?) Tip: Bring bread to feed the (very friendly) ducks and geese. This ritual alone took us over half an hour!

Hours: Open daily from dawn to dusk.
Admission: Free
Ages: All

CASTAIC LAKE RECREATION AREA

(805) 257-4050 - lake information; (805) 257-2049 - boat rentals

Ridgeroute Road and Lake Hughes, Castaic

(Exit Golden State Fwy [5] E. on Lake Hughes. It's about 7 miles N. of Magic Mountain.)

There are so many ways to play in the great outdoors at the massive (8,000 acres) Castaic Lake Recreation Area. The lake and lagoon are stocked with trout and bass. A California state license is needed if you're over 16 years old. All kinds of boating activities are available. A lifeguarded swimming area at the lagoon (available seasonally), picnicking, and playgrounds can all be found in the park. The scenery is beautiful with shade and pine trees, plenty of grassy areas, and of course, the lake. Nature trails, for both hiking and biking, are as short as one mile and as long as seven miles. The trails range from an easy stroll to rugged hikes. (Maps are available.) Come spend the night in sites reserved for RV and tent camping. However long you choose to visit, come escape to Castaic Lake for all your recreational desires!

Hours: Open daily sunrise to sunset.
Admission: $6 per vehicle. Camping starts at $12 a night. At fourteen-foot aluminum, nine-horse-power boat rents for $28 for the first two hours, $8 an hour after that.
Ages: All

CHARLES WILSON PARK

2100 Crenshaw Boulevard, Torrance

(FROM SAN DIEGO FWY [405], EXIT S. ON CRENSHAW BLVD. GOING S. ON HARBOR FWY [110], EXIT W. ON CARSON ST., L. ON CRENSHAW BLVD. GOING N. ON 110, EXIT AT 220TH, L. ON FIGUROA ST., L. ON CARSON ST., L. ON CRENSHAW BLVD.)

This large, elongated park has a delightful playground for younger children, several baseball diamonds, grassy "fields," gently rolling hills lined with shade trees, stroller-friendly pathways crisscrossing throughout the park, and a small, pool-sized fountain in the middle. A hockey rink is also available to use, by reservation. On the first and third Sundays of each month, the Southern California Live Steamers Club offers free rides on their scale trains.

Hours: The park is open daily sunrise to sunset. Train rides are offered on the first and third Sunday from 11am - 3pm.

Admission: Free

Ages: All

CHATSWORTH PARK

(818) 341-6595

22360 Devonshire (South) or 22300 Chatsworth (North), Chatsworth
(EXIT SIMI VALLEY/SAN FERNANDO VALLEY FWY [118] S. ON TOPANGA CANYON BLVD., R. ON DEVONSHIRE FOR THE SOUTH PARK, OR R. ON CHATSWORTH FOR THE NORTH PARK.)

There are two Chatsworth parks, a north and a south. The north park has shade trees, baseball diamonds with stadium lights, a play area, a basketball and volleyball court, and some pathways to explore.

My family is partial, however, to Chatsworth Park South. It has two tennis courts, a basketball court, a playground, open grassy areas, a community center building that offers lots of activities (including a wheelchair hockey league), a small natural stream running through the park, and picnic tables. Best of all, it has several hiking trails around the perimeter of the park with our favorite ones leading up to, through, and on top of the surrounding rocks! I love climbing rocks and my kids share this passion, so we think this park is "boulderdacious"!

At the southern end of the south park, at 10385 Shadow Oak Drive, is the Chatsworth Museum, or historic Hill-Palmer House. Take a tour through here while visiting the park. It is open the first Sunday of every month from 1pm to 4pm, and admission is free.

Hours: The parks are open daily sunrise to sunset.

Admission: Free

Ages: All

CHESEBRO CANYON

(818) 597-9192

Chesebro Road, Agoura Hills
(GOING E. ON VENTURA FWY [101], EXIT AT AGOURA RD., L. ON PALO COMADO CANYON RD., R. ON CHESEBRO. GOING W. ON 101, EXIT N. ON CHESEBRO RD.)

Hike on the numerous trails here to go through canyons, grasslands, and riparian areas. The road most traveled is the one immediately accessible, the Chesebro Canyon Trail. The hike starts off moderately easy along a streambed and through a valley of oak trees. A picnic area is about a mile-and-a-half from the parking lot. Stop here, or continue and the hike gets a bit more strenuous. You'll reach Sulphur Springs (almost another two miles), where the smell of rotten eggs will let you know you've arrived. This particular trail goes on for another mile through a variety of terrain. Several trails branch off and connect to the Chesebro Trail. Pick up a trail map at PARAMOUNT RANCH, which is down the road a bit, or call to have one sent to you.

Hours: Open daily sunrise to sunset.
Admission: Free
Ages: 3 years and up (for shorter hikes).

CHEVIOT HILLS RECREATION AREA ☼
(310) 837-5186 - park; (310) 836-3365 - pool   !/$
Corner of Pico Boulevard and Motor Avenue
(GOING W. ON SANTA MONICA FWY [10], EXIT AT NATIONAL. DRIVE PAST NATIONAL, UP MANNING AND GO R. ON MOTOR AVE. GOING E. ON 10, EXIT N. ON OVERLAND, R. ON PICO. GOING S. ON SAN DIEGO FWY [405], EXIT E. ON PICO.)

This large park really fits the bill of a recreation area with its basketball courts, baseball diamonds, tennis courts, and nice playground. During the hot summer months, when kids have played hard and need to cool off, they can take a dip in the municipal swimming pool.

Hours: The park is open Mon. - Fri., 9am - 10pm; Sat. - Sun., 9am - 7pm. Summer sessions for the pool are Mon. - Fri., 10am - 1pm and 2pm - 5pm; Sat. - Sun., 1pm - 5pm.
Admission: The park is free. Each swim session costs $1.25 for adults; 75¢ for kids 17 years and under.
Ages: All

DENNIS THE MENACE PARK ☼
(562) 904-7127   !
9125 Arrington Avenue, Downey
(EXIT GOLDEN STATE FWY [5] S. ON LAKEWOOD BLVD., L. ON GALLATIN RD., L. ON ARRINGTON AVE.)

This park has nothing to do with the character, Dennis the Menace, but it has everything to do with fun, imagination, and Camelot. The age of chivalry is not dead as your kids become knights and ladies in King Arthur's court. A big cement castle is the main play structure, complete with an "upstairs," slides, and a wooden bridge for crossing over the pretend moat. Kids can also climb up a sea serpent, try pulling out the sword in the stone, or just play on the other equipment of slides and swings. Note: The play equipment here has not been updated for quite some time.

The front part of the park has huge shade trees and lots of grass. The community center building is open after school, and has board games and sports equipment to lend out. This park has readily become a favorite.

Hours: Gates are usually open Mon. - Fri., 10am - 5pm; Sat. - Sun., 10am - 6pm. The community center is open daily during the summer, and the rest of the year Mon. - Fri., 3pm - 5pm; Sat. - Sun., 10am - 6pm.

Admission: Free

Ages: All

DESCANSO GARDENS

(818) 952-4400   *$$*

1418 Descanso Drive, La Canada

(EXIT FOOTHILL FWY [210] S. ON ANGELES CREST HWY, R. ON FOOTHILL BLVD., L. ON VERDUGO BLVD., L. ON ALTA CANYADA RD., WHICH TURNS INTO DESCANSO DR.)

Descanso Gardens is over sixty acres of incredible beauty. It's not just a bed of roses here as lilacs, camellias, tulips, dogwood, etc., also bloom. Although flowers bloom here year round, you can also call for a specific bloom schedule. A network of stroller-friendly trails wind through the grounds. One trail that is particularly delightful goes through a forest of California oaks. There are also open grassy areas to run around.

The Japanese garden is intriguing because of its unique maze-like layout. It also has ponds and a stream. Be on the lookout for squirrels, and land and water birds, as this is a haven for more than 150 species.

Take the one-hour guided tram tour to see all of Descanso Gardens, or hop aboard the five-minute model train ride for a more kid-oriented trip. Either way, bring your camera and enjoy your fragrant outing. Food is available at a cafe daily from 9:30am - 3pm, at the Japanese Tea Garden on weekends, or bring your own and use the picnic grounds adjacent to the parking lot.

Hours: The gardens are open daily from 9am - 4:30pm. Closed Christmas. Tram tours are offered Tues. - Fri. at 1pm, 2pm, and 3pm; Sat. - Sun. at 11am, 1pm, 2pm, and 3pm. Train rides are available every Sat. and Sun.

Admission: $5 for adults; $3 for seniors; $1 for ages 5 - 12; children 4 years and under are free. On the third Tuesday of each month, admission is half price. The tram tour and train ride each cost $1.50 per person.

Ages: 2½ years and up.

DEVIL'S PUNCHBOWL

(805) 944-2743   *$*

28000 Devil's Punchbowl Road, Pearblossom

(EXIT ANTELOPE VALLEY FWY [14] E. ON AVE S., R. ON PEARBLOSSOM HWY [138], R. ON LONGVIEW, L. ON TUMBLEWEED RD. WHICH TURNS INTO DEVIL'S PUNCHBOWL RD.)

The "punchbowl" is a spectacular geological formation that looks like a huge jagged bowl created from rocks. The 1,310-acre park consists of rugged wilderness rock formations along the San Andreas Fault, and it has a seasonal stream. The hiking trails vary in degrees of difficulty. We hiked down into the punchbowl and back up along a looping trail which took about half an hour. The terrain is diverse, from desert plants to pine trees, as the elevation ranges between 4,200 feet to 6,500 feet. Rock climbing is a popular sport here, whether you want to climb on boulders or scale sheer rock walls.

The small nature center museum contains a few taxidermied animals and displays that pertain to this region. Outside the center, a few live birds, such as owls and hawks, live in cages. The park also offers picnic areas, equestrian trails, and many special events throughout the year.

Hours: Open sunrise to sunset.
Admission: $3 per vehicle.
Ages: 5 years and up.

EARL BURNS MILLER JAPANESE GARDENS
(562) 985-8885

Earl Warren Drive at California State Long Beach, Long Beach
(EXIT SAN DIEGO FWY [405] S. ON BELLFLOWER, L. ON STATE UNIVERSITY DR., OR TAKE GARDEN GROVE FWY [22] TO THE END, TURN R. ON BELLFLOWER, R. ON STATE UNIVERSITY DR. FROM STATE UNIVERSITY DR., GO THROUGH THE CAMPUS GATES, TURN L. ON EARL WARREN. THE GARDEN IS ON THE L.)

This one-acre, beautiful Japanese garden has two waterfalls, a meditation rock garden, a quaint teahouse (to look in), and a koi pond. Kids can help feed the koi weekdays at 8:30am and noon; Sundays at 12:30pm and 3pm. As you cross over the zig-zag bridge into the gardens, share with your kids that it was built in this shape to side-step spirits because, according to Japanese tradition, spirits can only travel in straight lines!

Hours: Open Tues - Fri., 8am - 3:30pm; Sun., noon - 4pm.
Admission: Free. There is metered parking (to your right) in Student Lot D on weekdays.
Ages: 3 years and up.

EATON CANYON COUNTY PARK
(818) 398-5420

1750 North Altadena Drive, Pasadena
(GOING W. ON FOOTHILL FWY [210], EXIT AT SIERRA MADRE BLVD.; THE OFF RAMP TURNS INTO MAPLE. STAY ON MAPLE AND TURN R. ON N. ALTADENA DR. OR, GOING E. ON 210, EXIT N. ON ALTADENA DR.)

Located in the foothills of the mountains, this 184-acre wilderness park has several rugged dirt trails leading up and into the mountains. For hardy hikers, Mt. Wilson is a "mere" ten-mile hike. Approximately two-thirds of this park was burned in a 1993 brush fire. As the slopes and flats continue to recover from the fire, new plant growth is restoring the park's beauty.

There are shorter trails around the immediate vicinity of the nature center, which is temporarily housed in an on-site trailer. One such trail is only a quarter of a mile and has a self-guiding pamphlet (pick it up from the nature center) that helps you identify the plants.The first plant to recognize, and this is an important one, is poison oak. The Eaton Canyon Wash (river bed) is filled with rocks and is fun to explore, when it's dry, of course. The Eaton Creek flows through the canyon, except during the summer months. Pretty, shaded, and almost hidden picnic areas are found just off the parking lot. Remember to B.Y.O.W. - Bring Your Own Water. The park offers many special events, such as free family nature walks which are given every Saturday from 9am to 11am.

Hours: Open daily sunrise to sunset.
Admission: Free, until the nature center is rebuilt.
Ages: 3 years and up

EL DORADO NATURE CENTER
(562) 570-1745

7550 East Spring Street, Long Beach
(EXIT THE 605 FWY W. ON SPRING ST. EL DORADO PARK IS ON THE N. SIDE, THE NATURE CENTER IS ON THE S. SIDE. IF GOING W. ON SPRING, USE THE PARK ENTRANCE AND DRIVE AROUND TO THE NATURE CENTER.)

The eighty-five-acre El Dorado Nature Center is part of the El Dorado East Regional Park. When crossing over the wooden bridge leading to the museum and trail-heads, look down to see the many ducks and turtles swimming in the water below.

The Nature Center Museum has skulls, antlers, and other artifacts to touch; bugs to look at through a magnifier; a few cases of live insects and reptiles; a display on feathers and wings; and a huge book depicting various animal habitats. Contact the Center for information on their many special programs, like the Turtle Show or summer camps.

Walk a short, quarter-mile paved trail, or hike a two-mile, stroller-friendly, dirt trail that goes under the pine trees. The longer trail winds around two lakes and a stream. I love being in God's beautiful creation! Picnicking is not allowed inside the Nature Center, but picnic tables and shade trees can be found outside the gates at the end of the parking lot. The Nature Center is truly "an oasis of greenery and woodland in the middle of Long Beach." (Also see EL DORADO REGIONAL PARK,)

Hours: The trails and park are open Tues. - Sun. from 8am - 5pm. The museum is open Tues. - Fri., 10am - 4pm; Sat. - Sun., 8:30am - 4pm. The Nature Center is closed on Christmas.

Admission: $3 per vehicle Tues. - Fri.; $5 on Sat. - Sun. and
holidays. (Entrance fee is good for a same-day visit to El
Dorado Regional Park.)
Ages: All

EL DORADO REGIONAL PARK ☿

(562) 570-1771 $

7500 East Spring Street, Long Beach
(EXIT THE 605 FWY, W. ON SPRING ST. EL DORADO PARK IS ON THE N. SIDE, THE
NATURE CENTER ON THE S. SIDE. IF GOING E. ON SPRING, USE THE NATURE CENTER
ENTRANCE AND DRIVE AROUND TO PARK.)

El Dorado has 450 acres of lush green park with lots for kids to do!
There are three fishing lakes, that have ducks clamoring for handouts;
pedal-boat rentals at $7 per half hour; an archery range (targets are
provided, but you must bring your own equipment); a model glider field;
several playgrounds; a Frisbee golf course; four-and-a-half miles of
biking trails, including access to the San Gabriel River cement
embankment; and a one-mile, steam train ride that runs in the summer,
Tuesday through Sunday from 11am to 7:30pm. The rest of the year it
runs Wednesday through Sunday and holidays from 10:30am to
4:30pm. The cost is $1.75 for ages 16 and up, $1.25 for ages 2 - 16.
Hayrides are also available in the park. Call (562) 865-3290 for
information and reservations. Organized youth groups are invited to
camp here overnight. You can be as active or relaxed as you want (or
as the kids let you!) at El Dorado Park. (Also see EL DORADO
NATURE CENTER.)
Hours: Open daily from 7am - dusk.
Admission: $3 per vehicle Mon. - Fri.; $5 on Sat. - Sun. and holidays.
(Entrance fee is good for a same-day visit to the Nature
Center.)
Ages: All

EXPOSITION PARK ☿

Exposition Park, Los Angeles   !
(EXIT THE HARBOR FWY [110] W. ON EXPOSITION BLVD., L. ON FLOWER, L. ON
FIGUEROA. OR, EXIT SANTA MONICA FWY [10] S. ON VERMONT, L. ON EXPOSITION,
R. ON FIGUEROA. PARKING IS AVAILABLE BY ENTERING THE FIRST DRIVEWAY ON THE
RIGHT.)

The expansive Exposition Park encompasses the AEROSPACE
MUSEUM, CALIFORNIA AFRO-AMERICAN MUSEUM, CALIFORNIA
SCIENCE CENTER, NATURAL HISTORY MUSEUM OF LOS
ANGELES, and 3-D IMAX THEATER, plus the L.A. Memorial Coliseum
and L.A. Sports Arena. Up until now, most of park has simply been
grassy areas surrounding these attractions. Exposition Park is currently
undergoing development that is transforming it into a more family-
oriented park. The perimeters of the park will be lined with trees and
each of the four corners of Exposition Park will become distinct parks in

their own right, with picnic table, barbecue grills, playgrounds, as well as open grassy areas. A Community Center, with recreational facilities, will be located in the Southwest quadrant of the park. While paved pedestrian areas will provide easy access to and from the Coliseum, spacious lawns will provide a great place for picnics and tailgate parties.

The sunken Rose Garden, adjacent to the California Science Center, has always been a *scent*ral part of the park. Enjoy its seven acres of beauty where 16,000 specimens of 190 varieties of roses are cultivated. (I bet your kids didn't know all that!) The gardens are wonderful for walking, smelling the perfumed air, and picture taking, plus it's stroller accessible. Often on Saturdays and Sundays people of various nationalities have their wedding ceremonies in the garden. (We like looking at the wedding attire.)

Hours: Open daily.
Admission: Free
Ages: 3 years and up.

FRANK B. BONELLI REGIONAL COUNTY PARK   ☼

(909) 599-8411- park information $$

120 East Via Verde, San Dimas
(TAKE SAN BERNARDINO FWY [10] OR ORANGE FWY [57] TO THE 210 FWY, EXIT ON RAGING WATERS DR. IT'S JUST S. OF RAGING WATERS.)

This sprawling park is centered around the huge Puddingstone Reservoir; an ideal water hole for all your fishing and boating desires. (A fishing license is required for those over 16 years old.) Boat rentals, (909) 599-2667, are available daily during the summer and on weekends the rest of the year. Rental prices start at $13 an hour for a four-passenger boat. Life jacket rentals are an additional $5. You can also launch your own boat here. Jet skiing, fast boating, and water skiing are allowed on alternate days. If the fish are biting, your kids can catch bass, catfish, and trout. They'll also enjoy feeding the ducks and observing the wildlife. (We saw a heron and a crane, which my kids thought was pretty cool.) Picnic areas are plentiful with tables, barbecue pits, and playgrounds, too.

There are a few walking paths here, but you can really rein your kids in with a horseback ride. Horse rentals are available Tuesday through Sunday from 9am to 4pm (later on weekends), for $20 an hour for adults; $15 for ages 7 - 12. Younger children can take a pony ride around the compound for $5. Call (909) 599-8830 for more information. The scenery along the equestrian trail changes and ranges from cacti to pine trees - only in California!

Just outside the park grounds, treat yourself and the kids to a relaxing time in a hot tub - choose from fifteen private, hilltop tubs. (Or just indulge yourself after spending a day with the kids!) Tub rentals are available daily from noon to midnight for $20 an hour. Celebrate "Happy Hour" from 5pm tp 7pm, when rentals are half price. Call Puddingstone

Hot Tubs Resort at (909) 592-2222 for reservations. To reach the hot tubs, exit the 10 Fwy at Fairplex Drive, turn left on Via Verde Drive, right on Camper View Drive.

Hours: Open daily March 1 through October 31 from 6am to 10pm. Open November 1 through February 28, sunrise to 7pm. Boat rentals are available Fri., 7am - 4pm; Sat. - Sun., 6:30am - 4pm.

Admission: $6 per vehicle; $6 for a daily boat permit.

Ages: All

FRANKLIN CANYON

(310) 858-3834

Franklin Canyon, Los Angeles

(FROM L.A., EXIT SAN DIEGO FWY [405] E. ON SUNSET BLVD., L. ON BEVERLY DR. (PAST BEVERLY GLEN BLVD.), FOLLOW SIGNS "TO COLDWATER CANYON DRIVE" TO THE STOPLIGHT AT BEVERLY HILLS FIRE STATION #2, TURN L. - STAYING ON BEVERLY DR. GO 1 MILE TO FRANKLIN CYN. DR., TURN R. AND GO 1½ MILES TO LAKE DR., AND FOLLOW SIGNS TO THE CANYON. FROM THE VALLEY, EXIT VENTURA FWY [101] S. ON COLDWATER CYN. DR., R. ON FRANKLIN CYN. DR. (CROSS OVER MULHOLLAND DR.) TO THE CANYON.)

Franklin Canyon, almost 600 acres large, proves that there is more to Los Angeles than just skyscrapers. The lower canyon is the site of an old ranch house, which is now an office. A big green lawn and a few picnic tables are all that's here. Follow the creek along the mile-and-a-half trail leading to the Upper Canyon, and the Nature Center. Inside the Sooky Goldman Nature Center are displays of animals that live in the canyon, a scale model of the Santa Monica Mountains, an interactive exhibit on Native Americans, and an exhibit on the importance of water conservation. For your tactile child, there are fossils, antlers, furs, bones, and even a few nests to touch.

This Center is also the headquarters of the William O. Douglas Outdoor Classroom, which is really the name for numerous, on-going, free nature programs. Docent-led tours are open for the general public on weekends, with titles like "Incredible Edibles." There are programs for all ages that range from "Babes in the Woods," which is a stroller-friendly walk on a paved trail, to "Full Moon Hikes," geared for older kids to have a howling good time. Tours are available for school groups Tuesday through Friday, between 10am and noon.

The canyon has a variety of trees such as California live oaks, black walnuts, and sycamores. Wildlife here includes deer, bobcats, coyotes, rabbits, etc. The Upper Reservoir has reverted to a natural lake, and is a wetland area for herons and other waterfowl. Enjoy your day in the wilds of L.A.!

Hours: The canyon entrance is open daily from dawn to dusk. The Nature Center is open daily from 10am - 4pm.

Admission: Free

Ages: All

GRIFFITH PARK ☼

(213) 665-5188　　　　　　　　　　　　　　　　　　　　　!/$

4730 Crystal Springs Drive, Los Angeles

(GOING N. ON GOLDEN STATE FWY [5] OR W. VENTURA FWY [134], EXIT AT ZOO DR. AND FOLLOW THE SIGNS. GOING E. ON 134 FWY, EXIT S. ON VICTORY BLVD., L. ON ZOO DR. ON 5, EXIT S. ON WESTERN, L. ON VICTORY BLVD. TO ZOO DR.)

The vast 4,200 acres of the eastern Santa Monica Mountains encompass wilderness areas, picnic areas, and children's attractions. There are numerous trails for hiking and horseback riding. Call or visit the Ranger's Station for trail information. One particularly interesting picnic area is the Old Zoo Picnic Area, on Griffith Park Drive, that has tables placed around obsolete animal cages from the original zoo. Another standout picnic area is Park Center, near the merry-go-round, because it has playground equipment as well as picnic tables.

The children's attractions include (from the northern end of the park to the southern end): (1) Los Angeles Live Steamers - located west of the Victory Boulevard entrance to the park. (Also see TRAVEL TOWN.) This club offers free twelve-minute, large scale model train rides on Sundays from 11am to 3pm. Call (213) 669-9729 for more information. (2) Merry-go-round - located off Griffith Park Drive, by the Park Ranger Headquarters. The antique carousel offers rides daily from 11am to 5pm ($1.25 per ride). (3) Pony rides and Stagecoach rides - located at the Los Feliz entrance to the park. Each ride is $1.50 and available Tuesday through Sunday from 10am to 4pm. (4) Train rides and Simulator - located at the Los Feliz entrance to the park. The eight-minute mini-train ride costs $1.25 for children and $1.75 for adults. The simulator (simulates bobsledding, riding a roller coaster, or being in an airplane) costs $1.25 for adults and children. Both are open daily from 10am to 5pm. (5) Tennis courts, a soccer field, and a swimming pool - located at the Los Feliz entrance to the park. (The cross street is Riverside.) Several tennis courts will put you in the swing of things, while the pool will put you in the swim of things. The pool is open mid-June to September, Monday through Friday, 11am to 3pm and 4pm to 7pm; Saturday through Sunday, noon to 3pm and 4pm to 7pm. Adults cost $1.35 per session, kids 17 years and under are 75¢. Call (213) 665-4372, seasonally, for pool information. (6) Bird Sanctuary - located on Vermont Canyon Road. This area simply has a wide variety of bird species living in their natural habitat. It's open daily from 10am to 5pm. (7) Ferndell - located near the Western Avenue entrance. This is a pretty spot to rest and picnic. Ferns and flowers growing along the brook make it an attractive, cool haven on hot days. A snack stand, open seasonally, is also available here.

There are refreshment stands located throughout the park, as well as two restaurants. Operating hours fluctuate. (For other kid-oriented activities located in Griffith Park, see AUTRY MUSEUM OF WESTERN HERITAGE, GRIFFITH OBSERVATORY AND PLANETARIUM, and LOS ANGELES ZOO.)

Hours: The park is open daily from 6am - 10pm.
Admission: Free
Ages: All

HERITAGE PARK (Cerritos)
(562) 916-8570

18600 Bloomfield, Cerritos
(EXIT SAN GABRIEL FWY [605] E. ON SOUTH ST., L. ON BLOOMFIELD.)

One if by land, two if by sea . . . The most unique feature of this favorite park is an island with a kid-size version of an old New England town. Cross the covered bridge and be transported back in time. (Not actually, it's just the atmosphere of the island.) This "town" has a replica of Paul Revere's house, a cemetery, and the North Church Tower, which has two slides coming out of it. (Creative parents can reinforce a Paul Revere history lesson here.) Next to the cement slide are rocks to climb up. Kids can take the challenge and pull themselves up through a short tunnel by using an anchored rope. A small replica of a British ship is harbored here, designed for small merchants to climb aboard. Other little buildings are open to climb into with firehouse-like poles to slide down, small cannons to sit on or "fire," and more slides. The island has a brook running through it and plenty of shade trees, so it is refreshingly cool even on hot days.

The ducks swimming in the "moat" surrounding the island are always looking for a handout, so make sure you bring old bread. Across the water are two wonderful play areas; one for slightly older kids, and one with scaled-down equipment for younger children. The park also has picnic tables, a few barbecues, basketball courts, large grass areas, climbing trees, and a baseball diamond with stadium-type benches.

Hours: The park is open daily sunrise to sunset. The island is open September through May, Mon. - Fri., 2pm - dusk; Sat. - Sun., 11am - 4pm. During the summer it's open daily from 11am - 5pm.
Admission: Free
Ages: All

HOPKINS WILDERNESS PARK
(310) 318-0668

1102 Camino Real, Redondo Beach
(EXIT HARBOR FWY [110] W. ON SEPULVEDA, WHICH TURNS INTO CAMINO REAL.)

Escape to the wilderness of Redondo Beach. This gated, eleven-acre, hilltop park has two streams running through it, two ponds, and a wonderful view of the city. Hike along the nature trail that will take you through trees such as California Redwoods and pine trees; through a meadow - be on the lookout for butterflies and lizards; and to the small waterfall and pond, where turtles, crayfish, and bullfrogs have made their homes. Wilderness Park is also a popular spot for local overnight camping. Note: Wilderness protection is strictly enforced here.

Hours: Open Thurs. - Tues. from 10am - 4:30pm. Closed New Year's Day, Thanksgiving, Christmas, and in bad weather.

Admission: The park is free. Tent camping is $4 a night for non-resident adults (residents are $3); $2 a night for non-resident kids 17 years and under (residents are $1). Picnic tables and BBQ pits are available for campers.

Ages: 3 years and up.

JOHNNY CARSON PARK

Bob Hope Drive and Parkside Avenue, Burbank   !

(GOING W. ON VENTURA FWY [134], EXIT N. AT HOLLYWOOD WY., GO RIGHT AT END OF OFF RAMP ON ALAMEDA AVE., R. ON BOB HOPE DR. GOING E. ON 132, EXIT N. ON BOB HOPE DR. ACROSS THE STREET FROM NBC STUDIO TOURS.)

Despite the proximity of the freeway, this pleasant park offers a refuge, of sorts, in downtown Burbank. Kids will enjoy the large grassy areas, small woods, climbing and shade trees, and stroller-friendly dirt pathways that run throughout the park. The Tonight Show Playground, for today's kids, has slides, swings, and a climbing apparatus. Picturesque bridges go over what I first thought was a seasonal stream, but it is only a drainage "creek." Come enjoy a picnic here after the NBC or WARNER BROTHERS STUDIO TOURS.

Hours: Open daily

Admission: Free

Ages: All

LIVE OAK PARK

(310) 545-5621   !

Valley Drive N. and 21st Street, Manhattan Beach
(EXIT SAN DIEGO FWY [405] W. ON ROSECRANS AVE., L. ON PACIFIC COAST HIGHWAY, NEXT R. ON VALLEY DR.)

This park is formed around a bend in the road and is divided into various, gated sections. The northern section has baseball diamonds, picnic tables, and some short, bent gnarled trees for climbing. One particular threesome of trees bends in and down so much that they form a kind of hideout.

Another section has playground equipment, while others have tennis courts (call [310] 545-0888 for reservations), a soccer field, and places just to run and play. Parking is plentiful here.

Hours: Open daily from dawn to dusk.

Admission: Free

Ages: All

LOS ANGELES STATE and COUNTY ARBORETUM ☼
(818) 821-3222 $$

301 N. Baldwin Avenue, Arcadia
(GOING W. ON FOOTHILL FWY [210], EXIT S. ON BALDWIN. GOING E. ON 210, EXIT E.
ON FOOTHILL BLVD., R. ON BALDWIN.)

Do you have a budding horticulturalist in your family? Come visit this awesome arboretum and explore the more than 127 acres of plants and trees from around the world. The blooming flowers and the variety of gardens is astounding. We walked along the southern (and most interesting) route first. There are numerous paved pathways as well as several dirt pathways leading through trees, bushes, and jungle-like landscape which makes the walk an adventure for kids. Ducks and geese loudly ask for handouts at Baldwin Lake. (Look for the turtles in the water.)

For your history lesson for the day, peek into the spacious Hugo Reid Adobe house where each room is furnished with period furniture. The adobe grounds are beautiful and reflective of the mid-1800's. Peer into the gracious Queen Anne "Cottage" for a glimpse of the past. You'll see mannequins dressed in old-fashioned clothes, elegantly furnished rooms, and a harp in the music room. The immaculate Coach Barn has stalls ornately decorated with wood paneling and iron grillwork. Instead of horses, they now display farm tools, blacksmith tools, and a coach. Also see the Santa Anita Depot with a train master's office and railroad paraphernalia.

The lush greenery around the waterfall makes it one of the most enchanting spots in the arboretum. Walk up the wooden stairs for a panoramic view and "discover" a lily pond. Back down on the Waterfall Walk you'll see a serene woodland area and rock-lined stream. I was utterly content to sit while the kids let their imaginations kick into gear and played. Colorful Koi fish are just around the "corner" at the Tule Pond.

The northern section has a few greenhouses with exotic flowers and plants. An African and Australian section at this end have an abundance of trees.

Peacocks are everywhere - strutting their stuff and calling out in plaintive-sounding wails. (Peacock feathers are available at the gift shop for $1 each.)

Picnicking is not allowed on the grounds, but there is a shaded, grassy area between the parking lots. Or, eat at the Peacock Cafe which has reasonably priced food. Tip #1: Tram rides around and through the extensive arboretum are available every twenty minutes for $1.50. Tip #2: It gets hot here during the summer, so bring water bottles and look for the sprinklers!

Wonderful family-geared events are held here several times throughout the year. In the summer, Science Adventure Day Camps (which include classes on space and rocketry, magic, etc.) are also available.

Hours: Open daily from 9am - 4:30pm. Closed Christmas.
Admission: $5 for adults; $3 for seniors, students with ID, and ages 13 - 17; $1 for ages 5 - 12; children 4 years and under are free. The third Tuesday of every month is free for everyone. Free parking. (Certain discounts for the arboretum are available through AAA.)
Ages: 2 years and up.

MADRONA MARSH

(310) 32 MARSH (6-2774)

!/$$

3201 Plaza Del Amo, Torrance
(FROM SAN DIEGO FWY [405], EXIT S. ON CRENSHAW BLVD., R. ON CARSON ST., L. ON MADRONA AVE., L. ON PLAZA DEL AMO. GOING S. ON HARBOR FWY [110], EXIT W. ON CARSON ST., L. ON MADRONA AVE., L. ON PLAZA DEL AMO. GOING N. ON 110, EXIT AT 220TH, L. ON FIGUROA ST., L. ON CARSON ST., L. ON MADRONA AVE., L. ON PLAZA DEL AMO.)

The Madrona Marsh hosts educational nature walks for kids (and adults) of all ages. During the hour, or so, guided tour, you'll see and learn mostly about birds, plus ground animals and several varieties of plant life. Summer field study tours are also given. A mobile trailer Nature Center holds a few displays, and is open during scheduled walks. The forty-three acre marsh is located in the middle of an industrial section. If it's not big enough to make you feel like you've gotten away from it all, it's at least big enough to make you feel like you've gotten away from some of it.

Hours: The marsh is open sunrise to sunset to explore on your own. Guided walks are given the fourth weekend of every month, and field study tours are given at various times. Call for details.
Admission: Free; donations gladly accepted. Summer field study tours are $5 per person or $10 per family.
Ages: 6 years and up.

MALIBU CREEK STATE PARK

(818) 880-0350 - park;

$

(800) 444-7275 - (Destinet) campground reservations
On Malibu Canyon Road, Calabasas
(EXIT VENTURA FWY [101] S. AT LAS VIRGENES RD. DRIVE 4 MILES DOWN THE ROAD UNTIL YOU GET TO THE PARK AT MALIBU CANYON RD. S. OF MULHOLLAND HWY.)

Of the many hiking trails to choose from in the Santa Monica Mountains, one of our favorites is the Malibu Creek Trail. Starting at the broad fire road, veer to the right as the trail forks onto Cragg Road. The scenery keeps getting better the further in you hike. Oak trees shade part of the trail as you follow the high road along the creek. Man-made Century Lake is a great place to stop for a picnic, take in the beauty of your surroundings, and/or fish. This spot marks a four-mile round trip.

Continue on an additional two miles (round trip) to the former M*A*S*H* set. Being here might not have any meaning for your kids, but they'll at least think the rock formation (named Goat Buttes and used in the opening scene of the show) is worth a "wow".

Malibu Creek Park has many other interesting things to see and do. A mile in from the parking lot is the Visitor's Center, which also has a small museum. Each room in the museum is different. One contains taxidermied animals, another contains M*A*S*H* memorabilia, and yet another is a room for school groups to work on craft projects.

Feel like taking a dip in cool, refreshing water? Just beyond the Visitor's Center, over the bridge and to the left, is a rock pool.

Take advantage of all that the park offers by spending a night or two here. Each of the sixty-two campsites, some of which are shaded, has a picnic table and charcoal-use fire pit. Eight people per campsite are allowed.

Hours: The park is open daily from 8am to sunset. The Visitor's Center is open Sat. - Sun. from noon - 3pm.

Admission: $5 per vehicle. Camping prices are seasonal, starting at $12.

Ages: 3 years and up.

MATHIAS BOTANICAL GARDEN / U.C.L.A.   ☼
(310) 825-3620 $
U.C.L.A. Campus, Westwood
(EXIT SAN DIEGO FWY [405] E. ON WILSHIRE BLVD., L. ON WESTWOOD BLVD. TO THE INFORMATION KIOSK. MAKE SURE YOU ASK FOR A MAP. PARKING LOT 9 IS THE CLOSEST TO THE GARDEN.)

Mathias Botanical Garden, located on the U.C.L.A. campus, gave us the feeling of being in a secret garden, with its stony pathways through a lush "forest" and a hidden dirt path along the small creek. Trails crisscross through cactus and various other plant sections, which are as interesting to study as they are beautiful.

We took a free shuttle to the north end of the campus to the Murphy Sculpture Garden, which has over sixty sculptures scattered around an open grassy area. My 10-year old summed it up best from a kid's perspective; "I thought this was supposed to be great art. How come it's just a bunch of naked people?"

The U.C.L.A. Fowler Museum of Cultural History is also on the north end of campus. The majority of the exhibits are sophisticated, but older kids might enjoy them. Call (310) 825-4361 for a current schedule of exhibits showing in the gallery rooms.

I hope walking around the classic campus, with its huge old brick buildings and stately trees, planted some dreams in my children's minds of going to college. There are several places to eat lunch or grab a snack on campus, and since you've paid for parking, you might as well make a day of it!

Hours: The Botanical Gardens are open Mon. - Fri., 8am - 5pm; Sat. - Sun., 8am - 4pm. The Fowler Museum is open Wed. - Sun., noon - 5pm; Thursday until 8pm. Both are usually closed on University holidays.

Admission: Free admission to the gardens. The Fowler Museum is $5 for adults; $3 for seniors; discounts are given to U.C.L.A. associated alumni; free to ages 17 and under. The museum is free every Thursday. Parking in U.C.L.A. is $5 for the day.

Ages: All for the Botanical Gardens; 8 years and up for the Fowler Museum.

MAYFAIR PARK   ☼

(562) 866-4776 - park; (562) 804-4256 - pool (in season)   !

5720 Clark Street, Lakewood

(EXIT ARTESIA FWY [91] S. ON LAKEWOOD BLVD., L. ON SOUTH ST. IT'S ON THE CORNER OF SOUTH AND CLARK.)

Mayfair Park is a very fair park indeed! The two enclosed playgrounds have fun equipment for younger children. The best attractions (judging by my kids playing on them for a long time) are the wooden train to climb on and in, and a sand play area that has buckets attached to pulleys on the outside of a small climbing structure. Open grassy fields are plentiful here, plus there are basketball courts, tennis courts, baseball diamonds with lights and stadium seating, barbecue pits, a swimming pool, a wading pool, and an Express McDonald's that is only open during special events.

Hours: The park is open daily. The pools are open mid-May through mid-June, weekends only; open daily in the summer. Swim sessions in the big pool are 1pm to 2:30pm and 2:45pm to 4:15pm. Call for extended nighttime hours.

Admission: Free to the park. Each pool session costs $1.25 for adults; 75¢ for children 8 years and under.

Ages: All

NEW OTANI HOTEL AND GARDENS   ☼

(213) 629-1200   !

120 S. Los Angeles Street, Los Angeles

(EXIT HARBOR FWY [110] E. ON 4TH ST., L. ON LOS ANGELES. OR, EXIT SANTA ANA FWY [101] S. ON ALAMEDA, R. ON 1ST ST., L. ON LOS ANGELES.)

Amid the hustle and bustle of downtown Los Angeles, take a quick breather at the New Otani Hotel gardens. Ride the elevator up to the small, but beautiful Japanese garden located just outside the Thousand Cranes Restaurant. The garden is serene with its waterfalls and uniqueness of location - on top of a roof! My kids thought this was really neat. Enjoy your short break from the busy world not far below.

Hours: Open daily - hotel hours.
Admission: Free; metered parking is available.
Ages: 2 years and up.

NORWALK PARK   ☼

(562) 929-2677   !

12203 Sproul Street, Norwalk
*(EXIT SANTA ANA FWY [5] S. ON PIONEER BLVD., L. ON FIRESTONE BLVD., L. ON
SAN ANTONIO DR., R. ON SPROUL.)*

This park has a Nature Center located in the back corner, near the
freeway. A little stream, plus benches and shade trees, make it a nice
place to visit some farm friends. The animals, all in pens, include
spotted goats, sheep, a donkey, pot-bellied pigs, geese, and steer.

The park itself is spacious with lots of open grassy areas, a
playground for younger kids, tennis courts, basketball courts, and a
pool with a shallow end and a diving board at the deep end. A snack
bar is in the pool area.

Hours: The park is open daily sunrise to sunset. The Nature
Center/mini-farm is open daily from noon - 3pm. It is
open during the week from 9am - 11am, by appointment,
for tours for younger children. The pool and snack bar
are usually open daily mid-June through August.
Admission: Free. Swim sessions are $1.25 for adults; 75¢ for kids 17
years and under.
Ages: All

PARAMOUNT RANCH   ☼

(818) 597-9192   !

On Cornell Road, Agoura Hills
*(EXIT THE VENTURA FWY [101] S. ON KANAN RD., GO ¾ OF A MILE AND TURN L. ON
CORNELL RD., DRIVE 2½ MILES TO THE RANCH.)*

Howdy partners! You've come to the right ranch if you're looking for
some action. Western Town in Paramount Ranch was once owned by
Paramount Studios and used as a western movie set. The "town" still
stands. In fact, the television show, "Dr. Quinn, Medicine Woman" is
filmed here and if you happen to come on the right day during the
week, you can watch the filming. On non-shooting days and on
weekends, come walk the dusty roads and inspect the town buildings,
from the outside. The town even has a train depot and a quarter-mile or
so of railroad track. It all looks so real! Dress up your cowboy or cowgirl
and bring your camera. Better yet, bring your video camera (and a
script) and do your own western mini-movie.

There is a huge meadow next to the main part of town with an old-
looking church building, and a schoolhouse on the perimeter. There are
a few picnic tables here, too. Guided tours, describing the set and
history of the area, are given on select weekends.

Down by the meadow a wonderful, wooded trail that follows along a creek, is only one-eighth of a mile round trip. If the kids are in the mood for hiking into the mountains, go up Coyote Canyon Trail, just behind Western Town. This uphill, three-quarters of a mile round-trip trail goes through green chaparral-covered canyons overlooking the valley. The picnic spot up here has a view that is worth the effort. The 5K Run Trail is longer, obviously. It traverses a variety of scenery from the Oak Restoration Area, through Western Town, and down near the creek. Ranger-led naturalist programs are also offered at the park. Call regarding the many special events that the ranch hosts.

Hours: Open daily 8am - sunset.
Admission: Free
Ages: All

PETER STRAUSS RANCH
(818) 597-1036

3000 Mulholland Highway, Agoura
(EXIT VENTURA FWY [101] S. ON KANAN RD., L. ON TROUTDALE DR., L. ON MULHOLLAND HWY.)

This sprawling park, once owned by actor Peter Strauss, goes for miles and miles, with great hiking trails amongst the chaparral and oak trees. One of the smaller trails is only a three-quarter-mile loop, but there are several other trails for more ambitious walkers.

Hours: Open daily from 8am - 5pm.
Admission: Free.
Ages: 4 years and up.

PLACERITA CANYON NATURE CENTER AND PARK
(805) 259-7721 $

19152 Placerita Canyon Road, Newhall
(EXIT GOLDEN STATE FWY [5] N. ON ANTELOPE VALLEY FWY [14], S. ON PLACERITA CANYON RD.)

Placerita Canyon was the site of one of the first gold discoveries, small though it was, in California. In fact, the famed oak tree where gold was first discovered, "Oak of the Golden Dream," is only a quarter-mile walk from the parking lot. There is a wealth of history and wilderness to be found at this Nature Center and park.

The Center has live animals such as snakes and lizards, on display outside. One of the rooms inside has exhibits regarding the circle of life (predators, prey, and plants); equipment that monitors weather conditions; dirt samples comparing texture and content; and taxidermied animals. Another room has live snakes and spiders (in glass cases), and a touch table with nests, pine cones, and bones.

The hiking is great here, especially for more experienced hikers. Canyon Trail is a gradual climb, following along a stream. The left fork leads to the scout campground. The right fork leads to the Waterfall

Trail, where yes, about two-thirds of a mile back, is a waterfall. Canyon Trail also hooks up to Los Pinetos Trail, which is a hardy, eight-mile hike.

The large picnic area on a hillside is in a huge grove of oak trees. Play equipment is here, although the main attraction is the beauty of the area, and a small hiking trail. Call to find out more about the Saturday nature hikes, animal demonstrations, and other special programs, like summer camps.

Hours: Open daily 9am - 5pm.
Admission: $3 per vehicle.
Ages: 2 years and up.

POINT FERMIN PARK

(310) 548-7756

807 S. Paseo del Mar, San Pedro
(EXIT HARBOR FWY [110] TO THE END, L. ON GAFFEY ST., L. ON 9TH ST., R. ON PACIFIC AVE. TO THE END, THEN R. ON PASEO DEL MAR.)

This corner park has lots of green grassy areas, shade trees, and a few play structures. Its two best features are the wonderful view of the California coastline and a nineteenth-century lighthouse. The lighthouse is not open for tours, but it is very picturesque, with a wide variety of flowers and other plants surrounding it. I mention this park mainly because of its large size, makes it ideal for picnicking, and its proximity to several fun places in San Pedro.

Hours: Open daily sunrise to sunset.
Admission: Free
Ages: All

POLLIWOG PARK

(310) 545-5621

Corner of Manhattan Beach Boulevard and Redondo Avenue, Manhattan Beach
(EXIT SAN DIEGO FWY [405] S. ON INGLEWOOD, R. ON MANHATTAN BEACH BLVD.)

This expansive park is wonderfully deceptive. The part seen from the street is beautiful, with a play area and lots of grass and trees. (Some of the trees have low branches that beckon to climbers.) There is also an exercise area, with wood benches and handles for pull-ups, sit-ups, etc. A huge portion of the lawn is graded for summer concerts in the park.

However, as you take the stroller-friendly pathway leading down toward the interior of the park, you'll discover some "hidden" delights, such as a pond where marshy reeds and ducks abound. (Signs ask that you don't feed the ducks.) Tip: Watch your children around the water - there are no guard rails. Kids, ages 6 - 12, have a play structure here that looks like Noah's Ark. This big boat was built with its middle pulled apart so kids can climb on it and slide down it, but hopefully not jump ship. Part of the ship was destroyed in a fire, but kids enjoy playing on it just the same. Younger kids, ages 2 - 5, have a playground designed especially for them with rope bridges, tires, slides, and swings.

Hours: Open daily from dawn to dusk.
Admission: Free
Ages: All

RANCHO SANTA ANA BOTANIC GARDEN   ☼

(909) 625-8767   !

1500 N. College Avenue, Claremont

(EXIT SAN BERNARDINO FWY [110] N. ON INDIAN HILL BLVD., R. ON FOOTHILL. GO 3 BLOCKS, THEN TURN L. ON COLLEGE AVE.)

This eighty-six-acre botanic garden is beautiful in scope and sequence, and abundant with plants native only to California. Thousands of different kinds of plants grow in our state, so this garden covers a lot of ground with giant sequoias, fan palms, California live oak, manzanitas, cacti, and wildflowers.

The numerous trails here afford good walking opportunities. Since the diverse vegetation attracts a wide variety of birds, bird lovers can pick up a bird check list at the gift shop, or join an organized bird walk on the first Sunday of each month. I don't know how much horticulture my kids take in when we go to botanic gardens, but it's a good introduction to the variety and importance of plant life, plus a beautiful walk is always enjoyable.

Hours: Open daily from 8am - 5pm. Closed New Year's Day,
Independence Day, Thanksgiving, and Christmas.
Admission: Free; donations encouraged.
Ages: 3 years and up.

ROXBURY PARK   ☼

(310) 550-4761   !

471 S. Roxbury Drive, Beverly Hills

(EXIT SANTA MONICA FWY [10] N. ON ROBERTSON, L. ON OLYMPIC. IT'S ON THE CORNER OF OLYMPIC AND ROXBURY.)

This beautiful park fits right in with its surroundings of well-manicured lawns and stately homes. Although it is off a main street, it still seems somewhat removed from city life. The park offers a wealth of activities to choose from, such as tennis (plus backboards for practice), grass volleyball, basketball, baseball, and soccer. Along with a few picnic tables, barbecue pits, and some large shaded grassy areas, there is a good-size playground. One of the wooden structures is designed for slightly older kids with a big slide to go down, bridges to cross, and ropes to climb. The other is designed with younger kids in mind with swings, slides, and fun cement shapes to crawl through.

Hours: Open daily from 7am - 11pm.
Admission: Free

Ages: All

RUNYON CANYON PARK

(213) 666-5004

Fuller Street, Hollywood

(EXIT HOLLYWOOD FWY [101] W. ON SUNSET BLVD., N. ON FRANKLIN ST. ALL THE WAY TO THE TOP.)

Hike the hills of Hollywood in the popular Runyon Canyon. The dirt trail starts off at an upward slant, leading past ruins where house foundations and a few chunks of wall still remain. We walked the scenic, mostly woodland, main trail all the way up the mountain, as it affords a spectacular view of the famed city. The hike is strenuous, going up and along the rim of the hills. The trail eventually levels off, then loops back down. Bring water! Guided hikes are given on the third weekend of each month. Inquire about the periodic full-moon hikes.

Hours: Open daily from dawn to dusk.
Admission: Free
Ages: 5 years and up.

SADDLEBACK BUTTE STATE PARK

(805) 942-0662

17102 Avenue "J" East, Lancaster

(GOING N. ON ANTELOPE VALLEY FWY [14] EXIT N. ON 20TH ST. WEST, N. TO AVE. "J." GOING S. ON ANTELOPE VALLEY FWY [14] EXIT E. ON AVE. "J." ABOUT 19 MILES TO THE PARK.)

This state park is 3,000 acres of desert landscape, with Joshua trees scattered throughout and a huge granite mountain top, Saddleback Butte, jutting up almost a 1,000 feet above the valley. Several hiking trails are available here, including a two-mile trail that leads to the top of the Butte, and a view that makes the hike worthwhile. Springtime is particularly beautiful at the park because the wildflowers are in bloom. Near the entrance and park headquarters are several covered picnic areas, complete with barbecues. Please remember that desert weather is hot in the summer and cold in the winter, so dress accordingly. Overnight camping is available here. Saddleback is located just a few miles down the road from the ANTELOPE VALLEY INDIAN MUSEUM.

Hours: Open sunrise to sunset.
Admission: $5 per vehicle for day use; camping is $10 per night.
Ages: 5 years and up.

SAND DUNE PARK

(310) 545-5621

At the corner of 33rd Street and Bell Avenue, Manhattan Beach

(EXIT SAN DIEGO FWY [405] W. ON ROSECRANS AVE., L. ON BELL.)

This little park has a big surprise. While there is a small play ground for younger children, the park is really beachy because of its steep wall of sand that is perfect for running, jumping, or rolling down. Here is a local's favorite tip: After it rains, take a snow sled down the hill!

Wooden steps lead to the top of the hill. Behind the steps is a short "trail" in a small wooded area. With a little imagination this section becomes a jungle, or a deserted island. Picnic tables and a few barbecue pits are also available. Parking is limited.

Hours: Open daily dawn to dusk.
Admission: Free
Ages: All

SANTA FE DAM RECREATIONAL AREA

(818) 334-1065 $$

15501 Arrow Highway, Irwindale
(FROM SAN GABRIEL RIVER FWY [605], EXIT E. ON LIVE OAK AVE. WHICH TURNS INTO ARROW HWY. FROM FOOTHILL FWY [210], EXIT S. ON IRWINDALE, R. ON ARROW HIGHWAY.)

Though located in the middle of an industrial section, city sounds fade away while at this enormous recreational area that sports a mountainous backdrop. Our first stop was at the nature center trail, at the northern end of the park. The rock-lined, three-quarter-mile looping trail is paved, level, and a delight to walk. Desert is the predominant theme here as we observed an abundance of cacti and other plant life, and animals such as jackrabbits, lizards, roadrunners, and hummingbirds.

The huge lake towards the entrance offers a nice-size beach and a lifeguarded swimming area that is open seasonally. Other attractions in the park include a playground; fishing - a California state license is required for those 16 years of age and older; quiet boating activities (no gasoline powered boats allowed), with rentals available; picnic facilities; and unpaved walking trails. This lakeside area, with its shade trees and acres of green grass, is vastly different from the northern desert area.

Ready for a bike ride? Choose your distance and route and go all the way north to San Gabriel Canyon or south to Long Beach on various trails that go through this park. Parts of the trail are paved while other parts are not.

Hours: Open sunrise to sunset.
Admission: $6 per vehicle; $3 for a senior citizen's or a disabled person's vehicle. There is no extra charge to use the swim beach.
Ages: All

SOUTH COAST BOTANICAL GARDENS

(310) 544-6815 $$
26300 S. Crenshaw Boulevard, Rolling Hills Estates

(EXIT SAN DIEGO FWY [405] S. ON CRENSHAW BLVD. IT'S SEVERAL MILES TO ROLLING HILLS ESTATES.)

This attractive, eighty-seven-acre garden is planted with exotic vegetation from Africa and New Zealand, as well as from other parts of the world. My kids love taking pictures of the roses here - such color and variety! Sometimes it just feels good to be surrounded by such beauty. There is a lake in the middle of the gardens where ducks are waiting to be fed. Enjoy a forty-five-minute tram tour on the weekend. A picnic area is just outside the gates.

Hours: Open daily from 9am - 4:30pm. The tram tour is available Sat. - Sun., at noon and 2pm. The Gardens are closed on Christmas.

Admission: $5 for adults; $3 for seniors and students; $1 for ages 5 - 12; children 4 years and under are free. The tram tour costs $1.50 per person.

Ages: 4 years and up.

STONEY POINT

Topanga Canyon Boulevard, Chatsworth

(EXIT SIMI VALLEY/SAN FERNANDO VALLEY FWY [118] S. ON TOPANGA CANYON BLVD. IT'S THE FIRST BIG ROCK ON YOUR LEFT.)

Do you have a rock-climber "wannabe" in your household? Stoney Point is a famous (at least locally) rock climbers' delight. Practice repelling on this small mountain of stone, or just hike the trail up to the top. Either way, it can be an exhilarating way to spend the day.

Hours: Open daily sunrise to sunset.

Admission: Free

Ages: 4 years and up to hike; your discretion about rock climbing.

VASQUEZ ROCKS

(805) 268-0840

10700 East Escondido Canyon Road, Agua Dulce

(EXIT ANTELOPE VALLEY FWY [14] N. ON AGUA DULCE CANYON RD., R. ON ESCONDIDO CANYON RD. FOLLOW THE SIGNS ALONG THE WAY.)

This park became an instant favorite with my boys. The Ranger Station, housed in a barn with corralled horses outside, sets the mood for this all-natural, rustic park. Some of the unusual rock formations are almost triangular in shape, jutting practically straight up from the ground. They have ridges along their sides making them moderately easy to climb. The kids can climb until their hearts' content, or until your heart can't take them going up to the tops anymore. For those who don't like heights, there are several smaller rocks to conquer, and plenty of walking trails.

If you experience "deja vu" while here, it's probably because this park has been used in commercials and numerous films, including westerns and science fiction thrillers. It was also the home of Bedrock in the movie, "The Flintstones." Tip: Call before you come because sections of the park are closed while filming is done.

Vasquez Rocks, named for an outlaw who hid among the rocks here, also contains Tatavian Indian sites and a seasonal stream, but beware - drinking water is not available in the park. Camping for organized youth groups is allowed.

Hours: Open daily sunrise to sunset.
Admission: $3 per vehicle.
Ages: 3 years and up.

VINCENT LUGO PARK
(818) 308-2875
Wells Street, San Gabriel
(EXIT SAN BERNARDINO FWY [10] N. ON RAMONA ST., R. ON WELLS ST.)

There are three great play areas immediately visible here: A small enclosed one for toddlers; one with a rocket structure to climb up and slide down; and another that is just fun. In the summertime a very small enclosed wading pool is open. A sand pit, lots of grassy running space, and picnic tables classify this park as a good one.

According to my "park-smart" kids, however, the best part of the park is across the service road and to the south, almost hidden from sight. Children can play on the oversized cement sea creatures that have surfaced here, such as an octopus and whale. Shouts of, "This is the best!" came from my kids as they slid down the sea serpent that is wrapped around a lighthouse. Another giant sea serpent is curled around a rocky hill, which has a huge shade tree growing from it, plus a slide to go down. This nautical park was a treasure of a find!

Hours: Open daily from 7:30am - 10pm.
Admission: Free
Ages: All

WHITTIER NARROWS RECREATION AREA
(818) 575-5526
Rosemead Boulevard and Santa Anita Avenue, South El Monte
(THERE ARE A FEW DIFFERENT ENTRANCES - EXIT POMONA FWY [60] N. ON ROSEMEAD BLVD. TO THE ATHLETIC FACILITIES; EXIT S. ON SANTA ANITA AVE. TO THE LAKE AND PARK; EXIT S. ON PECK, R. ON DURFEE TO THE NATURE CENTER.)

Whittier Narrows will broaden your horizons with the scope of its recreational activities. This expansive 1,100-acre park offers something for every age, interest, and activity level in your family. The section of park on the northern side of the freeway is for the sports-oriented with sixteen lighted tennis courts, six soccer fields, seven baseball diamonds, an archery range, a trap and skeet shooting range, a model plane airfield, a model car track, playgrounds, bike trails, and a bicycle motocross (BMX) track - (818) 331-3434!

Don't want to make waves? Visit Legg Lake, (562) 434-6121, which is south of the freeway. Pedal boat rentals are available here at $6 a half hour, or rent a rowboat for $9 a half hour. Boating activities are operational only on the weekends. Kids can have a "reel" fun time fishing here, too. The pretty parkland surrounding the lake has shade trees, large grass areas, and playgrounds.

For those who hear nature calling, the nature center is located at 1000 Durfee, (818) 575-5523. The center is small, but it has live frogs, snakes, and turtles and a few taxidermied animals. We saw cardinals and blue jays at the bird feeders just outside. There are miles of hiking and biking trails going through the trees, along a creek, and throughout the park. The particularly beautiful Lake Trail (three-and-a-half-miles long) loops around the lake and back towards the center. (Also see the AMERICAN HERITAGE PARK/MILITARY MUSEUM, located at the northeast section of the park.)

Hours: The park is open daily from sunrise - sunset. The nature center is usually open Mon. - Sun. from 9am - 4pm. Closed Christmas.

Admission: Parking is free on weekdays; $3 on weekends.

Ages: All

WILLIAM S. HART MUSEUM AND PARK   ☼

(805) 254-4584 - museum; (805) 259-0855 - park and camping   !

24151 San Fernando Road, Santa Clarita

See WILLIAM S. HART MUSEUM AND PARK under MUSEUMS.

WILL ROGERS STATE HISTORIC PARK   ☼

(310) 454-8212 $$

1501 Will Rogers State Park Road, Pacific Palisades

(FROM PACIFIC COAST HIGHWAY, EXIT N. ON SUNSET BLVD., L. ON WILL ROGERS STATE PARK RD. FROM SAN DIEGO FWY [405], EXIT W. ON SUNSET BLVD., R. ON WILL ROGERS STATE PARK RD.)

"I never met a man I didn't like." These famous words were spoken by the "cowboy philosopher," actor, columnist, humorist, philanthropist, etc. - Will Rogers. His ranch house was deeded to the state, and is now a museum. It has been left virtually unchanged from when he lived here in the late 1920's. The rustic, wood-beamed living room features many Indian blankets and rugs, saddles, animal skins, a longhorn steer head over the fireplace, a wagon wheel "chandelier," Western statues, Will's boots, and furniture. You'll also see his library/drawing room, upstairs bedrooms, and an office, which are all simply and comfortably furnished, and decorated with a western flair, of course.

The Visitors Center shows a free, continuously playing twelve-minute film on Will Rogers featuring some of his rope tricks. Also available at no cost is an audio wand tour. Borrow a wand and place it at the several designated locations throughout the park, and it will tell you information about that area.

Picnic tables are plentiful at the park. The huge grassy area is actually a polo field for weekend games. So come, have fun, learn a little history about a fascinating man, and if you feel like horsing around, watch a polo match.

There are several trails leading through the park that connect with its "backyard" neighbor, the huge Topanga State Park. One of the most popular hikes is the two-mile loop to Inspiration Point which, on a clear day, gives an inspirational, breathtaking view.

Hours: The park is open daily from 8am - 6pm. Tours of the house are available every hour from 11:30am - 4:30pm, staff and weather permitting.

Admission: $6 per vehicle. House tours and polo matches are free.

Ages: 5 years and up.

ADVENTURE PLAYGROUND (Huntington Beach)   ☼
(714) 376-1626 or (714) 536-5486 $

7111 Talbert, in Huntington Beach Central Park, Huntington Beach
(EXIT SAN DIEGO FWY [405] S. ON GOLDEN WEST. OR, EXIT 405 FWY, N. ON EUCLID, L. ON TALBERT. THE CROSS STREETS ARE GOLDEN WEST AND TALBERT, DIRECTLY BEHIND THE HUNTINGTON BEACH PUBLIC LIBRARY.)

The entire play area is exactly how a child would design it, if given free reign. Young Huck Finns can use a raft (push poles are provided) in the shallow, muddy waters of the small man-made lake. Tip: Wear shorts and shoes you don't care about so you can wade in next to your younger children. There is a slide (i.e. a tarp-covered hill with a hose) ending in a little mud pool; a rope bridge leading to a tire swing that kids sit on to slide down the mini-zip-line; and a big sand box for young castle-makers. Tip: Bring a change of clothing, at least for your child. An outdoor shower is available.

For children 7 years and up who want to practice their carpentry skills, there is a "city" always in the process of being built. (Actually, it's mostly shacks, but kids can pretend.) Lumber, hammers, nails, and saws are provided so they can work on the ground forts or climb up trees to work on clubhouses.

The best time to visit Adventure Playground is after 2pm on the weekdays and on Saturdays, as day camps often ~~invade~~ visit in the morning. Note: Close-toed shoes are required. (Also see HUNTINGTON BEACH CENTRAL LIBRARY)

Hours: Open mid-June through mid-August, usually Mon. - Sat. from 10am - 5pm. Closed July 4th.

Admission: $1 for kids who are Huntington Beach residents; $2 for non-resident children; free for adults.

Ages: 2 years and up.

ADVENTURE PLAYGROUND (Irvine)   ☼
(714) 786-0854   !

1 Beech Tree Lane, Irvine

(EXIT SAN DIEGO FWY [405] S. ON JEFFREY, WHICH TURNS INTO UNIVERSITY DR., R. ON BEECH TREE. IT'S IN THE UNIVERSITY COMMUNITY PARK.)

This park is a dream come true for children, as they are actually encouraged to play in the mud! They can go down a waterslide (i.e. a tarp-covered hill with a hose) into the mud, and ooze their way through an obstacle course. (Call to make sure that the water is being turned on the day you plan to come - no water, no mud.) Bring a change of clothes for the kids (and you). There is an outdoor shower.

Drier play equipment includes kid-size buildings (to climb through), a tire swing, a skateboard ramp, a few holes of miniature golf, and a big wooden climbing structure. Kids 6 years and older can add on to the little shanty town here. After completing a one-hour safety course (yea!) they are free to use the wood, hammer, and nails provided to build onto existing forts, clubhouses, castles, etc. - whatever they imagine the structures to be. If your child is a regular here, he/she can stake a plot of land and construct his/her own building.

Some of the special classes offered (for a small fee) include Basic and Advanced Carpentry, Pioneer Cooking (campfire cooking), Mechanical Gadgetry, Jr. Archaeologist, etc.

Shade is scarce in Adventure Playground, but fun is not. Bring a picnic lunch to enjoy either in here or just outside the gates at University Community Park. This spacious grassy park has non-muddy playgrounds, a Frisbee golf course, and open areas for field sports and roller hockey, which is offered a few days a week.

Note: Close-toed shoes are required at Adventure Playground. The best times to come are after 2pm during the week or on Saturdays, as day campers often ~~invade~~ come play at this unique play area.

Hours: Open in the summer Tues. - Sat. from 10am - 5pm. Open the rest of the year, Tues. - Fri., 2:30pm - 5pm; Sat., 10am - 5pm.

Admission: Free. Groups must call for reservations, and they are charged a minimal fee.

Ages: 5 years and up. Note: Kids under 6 years must be accompanied by an adult at every activity.

ALISO AND WOOD CANYONS REGIONAL PARK   ☼
(714) 831-2791   !

Alicia Parkway and Aliso Creek Road, Laguna Niguel
(EXIT SAN DIEGO FWY [5] W. ON CROWN VALLEY PKY., R. ON LA PAZ RD., L. ON ALISO CREEK RD., L. ON ALICIA PKY., R. ON AWMA. THE ENTRANCE IS 500 FT. S. OF ALICIA PKY. AND ALISO CREEK RD.)

This regional park has 3,400 acres of wilderness sanctuary to explore by hiking or biking. You and your child will see everything that patience allows - coastal sage, chaparral, oak woodlands, open grassland meadows, canyons, and creeks, plus wildlife such as deer, possums, coyotes, bobcats, etc.

This huge park is like life, offering many paths to choose from. Take a trail from here into the adjacent Laguna Niguel Regional Park; ride the twelve-mile Aliso Creek Bikeway, which basically follows along Alicia Parkway; or choose from several other paths. We walked the Aliso Trail. The first part is paved and rather bland, scenically speaking. As we reached the dirt pathway and went into the hills, the terrain and scenery became much more interesting. (Strollers can go here, but it does get a bit bumpy.) About a mile and half down the road is the Nature Center. It houses Indian artifacts, taxidermied animals, photographs of the wild flowers in bloom, and maps.

There are numerous caves, or overhangs, throughout the park. A few are open to the public. Past the Nature Center, or Gate 2, is Cave Rock. Kids enjoy climbing up into Cave Rock, and sliding back down. Further back on the trail, is Dripping Cave, also called (and this has much more kid-appeal) Robbers Cave. Legend has it that bandits used this cave as a hideout after a robbery! At one time the holes inside supposedly had wooden pegs to hold their saddle bags, and bags of booty. Tell this to your kids and let their imaginations take over.

If you have the time and energy, keep on going to Coyote Run, deeper into the heart of the park. Tip: Bring water!

Hours: The park is open 7am to sunset. The Nature Center is open sporadically, whenever staffing is available.

Admission: Free. Parking in the lot is $2 per car, or park across the street for free.

Ages: 2 years and up.

ATLANTIS PLAY CENTER   ☼

(714) 892-6015 $

9301 Atlantis Way, Garden Grove
(EXIT THE GARDEN GROVE FWY [22] S. ON MAGNOLIA, L. ON WESTMINSTER, L. ON ATLANTIS WAY. IT'S N. OF THE GARDEN GROVE PARK.)

This "lost island" park is quite a find. Atlantis Play Center is a wonderful, large, enclosed play area for kids of all ages. Several different playgrounds are scattered around the park featuring slides, tubes, swings, sand pits, etc., plus big, concrete aquatic creatures to play on. The sea-serpent slide is a favorite. The green rolling hills are perfect for picnicking. The numerous shade trees make it surprisingly cool, even in the heat of the summer. A full-service snack bar is open daily during the summer, and usually on the weekends the rest of the year.

One of my boys' favorite things to do is to play in and amongst the bushes that go around the perimeter of the park. The bushes become hideouts, forts, a pirate's landing, etc. - a little imagination goes a long way!

Just outside Atlantis is the Garden Grove Park, with more play equipment and wide open grassy areas.

Hours: Open Tues. - Fri., 11am - 4pm; Sat., 10am - 4pm; Sun.,
noon - 4pm.
Admission: $1 for ages 2 and older; children under 2 years are free.
Ages: 1½ - 12 years.

BOLSA CHICA ECOLOGICAL RESERVE ☼
(714) 897-7003   !
Warner Avenue, Huntington Beach
(EXIT SAN DIEGO FWY [405] S. ON BOLSA CHICA RD., R. ON WARNER AVE., L. ON
PACIFIC COAST HIGHWAY. THE RESERVE IS OPPOSITE BOLSA CHICA STATE BEACH.)

This 530-acre, saltwater wetland reserve supports waterfowl such
as avocets, egrets, plovers, and terns. We also saw herons, and a few
brown pelicans that swooped down to scoop up fish. Cross over the
bridge to walk on the easy mile-and-a-half trail that loops through the
reserve (and partially along the highway). There are several other trails
here too, mostly stroller-friendly. My little explorers especially liked
walking down, off the trail, to inspect the water and its inhabitants, up
closer than I felt comfortable with. BOLSA CHICA STATE BEACH is
directly across the street for more fun in the sun.

An Interpretative Center is housed in a trailer at 3842 Warner
Avenue. Inside, a laboratory does water analysis, while the rest of the
Center contains mostly information panels on the value of wetlands.
Call (714) 846-1114 to reach the Center.

Hours: The Reserve is open daily sunrise to sunset. The Center
is usually open Mon. - Fri., 1pm - 4pm; Sat. - Sun., 9am -
3pm.
Admission: Free
Ages: All

BROOKHURST COMMUNITY PARK ☼
2271 W. Crescent Avenue, Anaheim   !
(GOING S. ON SANTA ANA FWY [5], EXIT S. ON BROOKHURST ST., R. ON CRESCENT.
GOING N., EXIT W. ON LA PALMA AVE., L. ON BROOKHURST, R. ON CRESCENT.
FROM CRESCENT, TURN R. ON VENTURA, WHICH TURNS INTO GREEN ACRE. THE
PARK IS RIGHT THERE.)

Baseball diamonds, basketball courts, a few picnic tables, and
barbecue pits are here, but more importantly, your kids can come here
and walk on the moon! "Crater Park" (our nickname for it) resembles
the surface of the moon with play equipment inside crater-shaped
areas. There are slides, swings, climbing structures, a rocket ship (for
blasting off to parts unknown), and a big, white, cement walkway that
interconnects the play areas. Being here almost eclipses playing at
other parks.

Hours: Open daily sunrise to sunset.
Admission: Free
Ages: 2 years and up.

CARBON CANYON REGIONAL PARK   ☼
(714) 996-5252 $

4442 Carbon Canyon Road, Brea
(EXIT RIVERSIDE FWY [91] N. ON IMPERIAL HWY., R. ON VALENCIA AVE., R. ON CARBON CANYON RD.)

Talk about recreational opportunities! Carbon Canyon is 124 acres big and offers everything for the sports-minded and fun-loving family. There are tennis courts, volleyball courts, horseshoe pits, softball fields, a huge open field for whatever other sport you feel like playing, and five great playgrounds scattered throughout the park.

Other activities include taking a hike to the ten-acre Redwood Grove; cycling on the one-and-a-half-mile paved trail; or riding the equestrian trail that accesses to Chino Hills State Park. The beautiful four-acre lake in the middle of the park has two fishing piers, but it is not stocked. Bring suntan lotion and food, and have a great day.

Hours:	Open November 1 through March 31 from 7am - 6pm.
	Open April 1 through October 31 from 7am - 9pm.
Admission:	$2 vehicle entrance Mon. - Fri.; $4 on Sat. - Sun.; $5 on holidays.
Ages:	All

CARL THORNTON PARK   ☼
(714) 571-4200   !

1801 W. Segerstrom Avenue, Santa Ana
(GOING E. ON SAN DIEGO FWY [405], EXIT N. ON FAIRVIEW RD., L. ON SEGERSTROM AVE. GOING S. ON COSTA MESA FWY [55], EXIT E. ON DYER RD. WHICH TURNS INTO SEGERSTROM AVE.)

The front part of this park is a huge open area, great for kite flying because the trees are short (at least right now). A small creek runs through this area, ending in a big pond that attracts a lot of ducks and sea gulls. (Don't get goosed by the geese!) For your sporting pleasure, there are also two baseball diamonds.

At the northeast corner of the park, accessible by paved pathways, is an enclosed "barrier free" playground. This means that it has special apparatus designed for disabled children. One of the swings can hold a wheelchair-bound child. A sand play area, with water fountains to make sand castles, is elevated for kids in wheelchairs. Other play areas are great for all kinds of kids, as there are slides, tunnels, and things to climb. Stone turrets give the playground a castle-like setting. A large grassy area is inside the enclosure for safe, run-around play.

Hours:	Open daily from 8am - 10pm.
Admission:	Free
Ages:	All

CASTLE PARK (Irvine)
(714) 552-4352

Northwood Community Park, 4351 Bryan Avenue, Irvine
(EXIT SANTA ANA FWY [5] N. ON CULVER, R. ON BRYAN.)

The focal point of Castle Park is the big, castle-like structure which is great for climbing on and around. It has slides, steps, and a rocky wall that completes the fortress image. The playground also has tire swings, a balance beam, slides, a wooden and cement pirate ship, and sand box areas.

The surrounding park has soccer fields, tennis courts, a basketball court, shuffleboard, a handball court, and baseball diamonds. You can check out play equipment, free of charge, at the information building.

Hours: The park and information building are open Mon. - Sat., 9am - 9pm; Sun., noon - 6pm.
Admission: Free
Ages: All

CRAIG REGIONAL PARK
(714) 990-0271

3300 North State College Boulevard, Fullerton
(EXIT ORANGE FWY [57] W. ON IMPERIAL, L. ON STATE COLLEGE.)

124 acres and three separate playgrounds make this an ideal park for all ages. The upper area is hilly and woodsy, blessed with lots of pine trees. The lower slopes flatten out, with alder and willow trees. One of the playgrounds meets the ADA (Americans with Disabilities Act) Standards; one is geared towards little ones; and another is intended more for slightly older kids, as it has steeper slides.

There are picnic gazebos, baseball diamonds, volleyball courts, tennis courts, racquetball courts, and a lake. Fishing is allowed in the lake, but it isn't stocked - so bring your wiggliest worms. The Nature Center has dioramas depicting the changing environment of animals in Craig Park, and the surrounding areas.

Hours: Open daily April through October from 7am - 9pm. Open daily November through March from 7am - 6pm. The Nature Center is open Sat. - Sun. from 8am - 4pm.
Admission: $2 per vehicle Mon. - Fri., $4 Sat. - Sun.; $5 on holidays.
Ages: All

CRYSTAL COVE STATE PARK
(714) 494-3539

East Coast Highway, between Laguna Beach and Newport Beach.
(TAKE THE SAN DIEGO FWY [405] OR THE COSTA MESA FWY [55] TO THE CORONA DEL MAR FWY [73], WHICH TURNS INTO MACARTHUR BLVD. EXIT MACARTHUR BLVD. S. ON EAST COAST HIGHWAY. A GATED ENTRANCE IS JUST OPPOSITE NEWPORT COAST DR. THE VISITOR CENTER AND RANGER STATION ARE FARTHER DOWN ON COAST HWY., ON THE L.)

This 2,800-acre, largely undeveloped, state park encompasses everything from coastal and canyon areas to three-and-a-half miles of sandy beach. The size of the park allows a variety of programs and fun things to do, such as guided tidepool tours (when the tide is low), whale watching, fishing, hiking, camping, mountain biking, or just enjoying the beach!

Environmental camping (meaning whatever you backpack in you take out) is an adventure in the "back country" of the park. The closest campsite is a four-mile hike. No open fires are allowed. With twenty miles of trails on relatively untouched land, hiking and/or camping here is a real opportunity to commune with nature! Get a map at headquarters.

If you get hungry, the Crystal Cove Shake Shop, serving shakes (try their date shakes) and sandwiches, is across the way at 7408 Pacific Coast Highway, (714) 497-9666. It is open daily from 11am - 4pm.

Hours: Open daily from sunrise - sunset.
Admission: $6 per vehicle. Camping is $10 a night per person Mon. - Fri.; $11 a night Sat. - Sun.
Ages: All

EISENHOWER PARK   ☼

1045 E. Lincoln, Orange   !
(EXIT COSTA MESA FWY [55] W. ON LINCOLN, R. ON OCEANVIEW, R. AT MAIN TO THE PARK.)

Driving down Lincoln Boulevard, it's easy to miss Eisenhower Park, but it's worth looking for. This park has a stream running through it with almost irresistible stepping stones. The lake here is just right for fishing. There are two small play areas for slightly older kids. One area is especially "cool" with a rocket ship play structure, wavy slides, swings, and a big sand area. Along the west side of the park is a deer pen with quite a few of the en*deer*ing animals behind chain link fence.

This big park offers plenty of green, rolling hills, plus a few scattered picnic tables and barbecue pits to make your day picnic perfect. Cement pathways make the entire park stroller accessible.

Hours: Open daily sunrise to sunset.
Admission: Free
Ages: All

ENVIRONMENTAL NATURE CENTER   ☼

(714) 645-8489   !
1601 16ᵗʰ Street, Newport Beach
(TAKE COSTA MESA FWY S.W. TO END, CONTINUE ON NEWPORT BLVD., L. ON 17ᵀᴴ, R. ON IRVINE AVE., L. ON 16ᵀᴴ.)

This two-and-a-half acre nature center is an almost hidden gem that has been here for twenty-five years! Walking back to the trailhead, notice the rocks along the path containing fossilized shells imbedded in them. Although buildings are around the perimeters of this wooded area, you'll still feel like you're in the midst of nature while walking along the various cris-crossing trails. You'll see a cactus garden, pine trees, woodland trees, and a small rock-lined stream. You can purchase a pamphlet (25¢) at the center to help identify the various plants and animals found here.

The small nature center building has shelves and tables that contain rocks, shells, animals skins, turtle shells, skulls, feathers, and bird's nests, plus many nature-inspired, craft ideas. My boys also liked seeing the live snakes, crickets, and lizards in here.

Hours: Open during the school year Mon. - Sat. from 8am - 3pm; open in the summer Mon. - Sat. from 8am - 4pm. Closed Sundays and school holidays.

Admission: Free

Ages: 2½ years and up.

FULLERTON ARBORETUM ☼

(714) 278-3579 - arboretum; (714) 278-2843 - house/museum   !/$

1900 Associated Road, Fullerton

(EXIT ORANGE FWY [57] W. ON YORBA LINDA, L. ON ASSOCIATED RD. (OR CAMPUS DR.), ONTO CALIFORNIA STATE FULLERTON CAMPUS.)

This twenty-five-acre botanical garden is a delightful, verdant refuge, with flower-lined pathways, a small lake, a stream, and a few bridges. It's big enough to let the kids run loose a little. Take a whiff - the air is perfumed with the scent of roses, mint, and citrus. Garden benches offer a picturesque resting spot, underneath shade trees in the midst of the plants and flowers. (Idea: Have your kids dress up and bring your camera for some potentially great shots in a garden setting.)

An 1894 Victorian Heritage House, that was the home and office of the first physician in Orange County, is also on the grounds. Older kids will appreciate a tour through the house that has turn-of-the-century furnishings.

There are many special events going on at Fullerton Arboretum throughout the year, including Science Adventure programs, volunteering opportunities, and much more. Please call for details.

Hours: The Arboretum is open daily from 8am - 4:45pm. Closed New Year's Day, Thanksgiving, and Christmas. The house is open for tours Sunday from 2pm - 4pm. The house is closed for tours in January and August.

Admission: The Arboretum has a donation box by the entrance gate. The house tour is a $2 donation.

Ages: All

HART PARK ☼

(714) 744-7272   !

701 Glassell Street, Orange

(EXIT GARDEN GROVE FWY [22] N. ON GLASSELL.)

Stone walls add to the beauty of this spacious park. The northern
section has <u>lots</u> of picnic tables and barbecue pits, a playground, trees
to climb, a few tennis courts (although kids were roller skating on them
when we visited), a sand volleyball court (or a sandbox with a net), and
a swimming pool.

The southern section has a large open grassy area lined with trees,
plus soccer fields and a few baseball diamonds. One of the diamonds
has stadium seating and lights.

Hours: The park is open daily from 8am - 10pm. The pool is
open in the summer Mon. - Sun., with swim sessions
usually at 1pm - 2:30pm and 2:45pm - 4pm. Tues. and
Thurs. it's also open from 6:15pm - 8:15pm.

Admission: The park is free. Each swim session costs $1.25 for
adults; $1 for kids.

Ages: All

HERITAGE PARK (Irvine)
(714) 724-6750 - Youth services center;
(714) 559-0472 - Aquatics Complex
14301 Yale Avenue, Irvine
*(GOING S. ON SANTA ANA FWY [5], EXIT S.W. ON CULVER DR., L. ON WALNUT AVE.,
L. ON YALE AVE. GOING N. ON 5, EXIT S.W. ON JEFFREY RD., L. ON WALNUT AVE.,
R. ON YALE AVE.)*

Heritage Park is forty-five acres huge - the city's largest community
park. The wooden water tower slide is almost as tall as a real water
tower - whoosh on down!! There are two terrific playgrounds here. One
has a pirate-ship shaped area to play in with bridges, slides, and a
ropes obstacle course - kid heaven!

The center area has a beautiful lake to skate or stroller around, and
lots of grassy, gently rolling hills to play on. There are also basketball
courts, twelve lighted tennis courts, and four lighted fields for organized
sports play. The community youth services center, library, and the
IRVINE FINE ART CENTER are adjacent to the park. The Heritage
Park Aquatics Complex is just around the corner. Two of their pools are
open for recreational swim in the summer.

Hours: The park is open daily. The pools are open daily in the
summer, usually from 1pm - 3pm.

Admission: The park is free. Swimming costs $1.50 for adults; $1 for
ages 18 and under.

Ages: All

HILLCREST PARK
Brea Boulevard, Fullerton
*(EXIT THE RIVERSIDE FWY [91] N. ON HARBOR BLVD., R. ON BREA BLVD., R. INTO
THE PARK.)*

For some Fullerton fun, try Hillcrest Park. This huge hilly park has a winding road throughout, with parking lots in several different spots along the way. We saw some creative kids using cardboard to slide down a hill, which probably isn't great for the grass, but it looked like fun. Hillcrest has a few woodland areas with dirt paths for hiking. There are also some play areas, picnic tables, and barbecue pits. The wooden playground at the base of the hill, on Lemon Street, is in the shape of a ship.

Hours: Open daily.
Admission: Free
Ages: All

HUNTINGTON CENTRAL PARK / SHIPLEY'S ☼
NATURE CENTER
(714) 960-8847   !

Golden West Street, Huntington Beach
(EXIT SAN DIEGO FWY [405] S. ON GOLDEN WEST ST. IT'S BETWEEN SLATER AND ELLIS AVE.)

There are many options to lose yourself, temporarily of course, in this gigantic park: Fish at the un-stocked lake, which is tucked in the corner; let the kids go wild on the playgrounds; ride bikes along the cement pathways that crisscross all over; enjoy the sports fields; play the Frisbee golf course on the west side of Golden West Street; see a weekend polo match or horse show at the Equestrian Center, call (714) 848-6565 for details; check out books from the huge library off Talbert Street (see HUNTINGTON CENTRAL LIBRARY); see ADVENTURE PLAYGROUND for summertime fun; or go for a nature walk at Shipley's Nature Center at the northern end of the park.

We turned the easy, fifteen-minute walk around Shipley's Nature Center into over an hour of delightful exploration. The trail, which is not stroller-friendly, leads around a pond that supports diverse animal life - frogs, turtles, and butterflies. We hiked the trail through tall grass, to the pine trees, and looped back around to the small Nature Center building. Inside, are a few taxidermied animals and other natural exhibits.

If you'd like to have breakfast (or lunch) in the park, see ALICE'S BREAKFAST IN THE PARK.

Hours: The park is open daily. The Nature Center is open sporadically.
Admission: Free
Ages: All

IRVINE LAKE ☼
(714) 649-9111 $$$
4501 Santiago Canyon Road, Orange
(EXIT NEWPORT-COSTA MESA FWY [55] E. ON CHAPMAN, R. ON SANTIAGO CANYON RD.)

Casting around for fun places to go with your little fisherman? The huge Irvine Lake is stocked seasonally with a variety of fish such as bass, trout, catfish, crappie, and bluegill. (There is a five fish limit per person.) A smaller, almost-guarantee-you'll-catch-something Catch Out (trout) Pond is also here. Conveniently, a bait and tackle shop are also on the grounds. No fishing license is needed. Most boat rentals are available on the weekends only, including motorboats - $40 for the day, $27 after noon; rowboats - $25 for the day; pedalboats - $6 for a half hour, $10 for an hour; and kayaks - $8 a half hour, $12 an hour. Overnight camping for organized groups is available here. (It's ideal for those who enjoy fishing in the wee hours of the morning, but don't want to actually be on the road that early.) For those kids who get antsy after quietly fishing for a while, there is a three-a-half-mile nature trail that goes around the lake.

Hours: Open daily from 6am - 5pm. Summer twilight hours are Fri. - Sat., 2pm - 11pm. (Hours do fluctuate.)

Admission: Fishing is $12 for adults; $5 for ages 4 - 12. Call about twilight rates. Entrance other than fishing is $3 per person. Overnight camping is $3 per person, or $8 per person with fishing, too.

Ages: 4 years and up.

IRVINE REGIONAL PARK   ☼
(714) 633-8074 $

1 Irvine Park Road, Orange
(EXIT NEWPORT FWY [55] E. ON CHAPMAN, N. ON JAMBOREE, WHICH ENDS AT IRVINE REGIONAL PARK.)

Entire days can be spent exploring all there is to see and do at this 477-acre regional park. The middle area is "carved out" with lots of grass for picnic areas, playgrounds, and baseball diamonds. Toddlers through about 8 years old can ride ponies around a track that is open weekends from 10am to 4pm at $2.50 a ride. Kids 8 years and older can take a guided horseback ride inside the park, Wednesday through Sunday for $20 an hour. Call Country Trails at (714) 538-5860 for horse rental information. More fun can be had with pedal boat rentals, which are available weekends from 10am to 5pm at $7 per half hour. Bike rentals are available weekends from 10am to 5pm at $10 per hour for side-by-sides. Ten-minute, scale model train rides around the park are available daily, from 10am to 4pm at $2 per person. This is a fun little trip!

The Interpretive Center, (714) 289-9616, has taxidermied animals to look at; skulls, furs, and animal pelts to touch; a grinding rock to try out; plus displays and information about the wilderness part of the park. Biking, hiking, and equestrian trails are plentiful here with creeks, sagebrush, and animals throughout. Rangers are available for school and scout tours. (Also see ORANGE COUNTY ZOO - located inside the park.)

Hours: Irvine Park is open daily April through October from 7am - 8:45pm; it is open the rest of the year daily from 7am - 5:45pm. The Nature Center is usually open Sat. - Sun. from 11am - 3:45pm.

Admission: $2 per vehicle, Mon. - Fri., $4 on Sat. - Sun; $5 on holidays.

Ages: All

LAGUNA LAKE PARK   ☼

Lakeview Drive and Clarion, Fullerton   !
(EXIT RIVERSIDE FWY [91] N. ON EUCLID, R. ON LAKEVIEW DR.)

Leaping frogs! This lake is literally covered with large lily pads. In contrast to my earlier thinking, I now know that parks don't require a playground to make it "good." It simply must have kid-appeal, and this one does. The dirt path around the long lake is bike and stroller friendly. The marshy reeds are a great place for dragonfly hunting. Bring bread for the ducks, bait for your fishing pole, and enjoy this unusual park. Barbecue pits and picnic tables are here, too.

Hours: Open daily sunrise to sunset.

Admission: Free

Ages: All

LAGUNA NIGUEL REGIONAL PARK   ☼

(714) 831-2791 $

28241 La Paz Road, Laguna Niguel
(EXIT SAN DIEGO FWY [5] W. ON CROWN VALLEY PKY., R. ON LA PAZ.)

This park is 236 acres of adventures waiting to be had with volleyball courts, horseshoe pits, tennis courts, an area for flying remote-controlled airplanes, toddler-friendly playgrounds, open grass areas, barbecue pits, and picnic shelters, plus a forty-acre lake for fishing and boating. No fishing license is required. The park tends to get crowded on weekends and holidays, so get an early start!

Hours: Open daily November through March from 6am - 6pm. Open daily April through October from 6am - 9pm.

Admission: $2 per vehicle Mon. - Fri.; $4 on Sat. - Sun.; $5 on holidays. Fishing cost $10 for adults; $7 for kids.

Ages: All

MILE SQUARE PARK   ☼

(714) 962-5549 $

Warner Avenue and Euclid Street, Fountain Valley
(EXIT SAN DIEGO FWY [405] N. ON EUCLID ST.)

This park has everything you need for a full day of family fun. There are picnic areas with barbecue grills, bike trails, baseball fields, a hobby area for flying model planes and rockets, blacktop for racing cars, and four playgrounds. One of the playgrounds is on an island in one of the lakes. Kids can take the bridge across and have fun climbing up and down the tower. You may fish in the two man-made lakes - no license is needed unless your child is over 16 years old. Duck food is available to purchase for $1 a bag, in case you forgot to bring your own.

Get physical with various pleasure rentals - surrey bikes are between $12 - $22 an hour, depending on the number of passengers; peddle boats are $12 an hour; and funcycles or tandems are $6 an hour.

Hours: Open daily in the summer from 7am - 9pm. Open daily the rest of the year from 7am - 6pm.

Admission: $2 per vehicle Mon. - Fri; $4 on Sat. - Sun.; $5 on holidays.

Ages: All

OAK CANYON NATURE CENTER   ☿

(714) 998-8380   !

6700 Walnut Canyon Road, Anaheim

(EXIT RIVERSIDE FWY [91] S. ON IMPERIAL HWY, L. ON NOHL RANCH RD., L. ON WALNUT CANYON. IT'S NEXT TO THE ANAHEIM HILLS GOLF COURSE.)

This rustic Nature Center is a fifty-eight-acre natural park nestled in Anaheim Hills. Surrounded by such beauty, it doesn't seem possible that there is a city nearby. Take a delightful, easy hike along the wide pathways through the woods and along the stream. Or, opt for more strenuous hiking on the six miles of trails offered here. No bikes or picnicking are allowed so that the animals and plants that consider this canyon their home can continue to live here unharmed.

The good-size, Nature Center building houses live critters, plus several trays of mounted insects and butterflies. The small stage area is great for putting on shows using the animal puppets.

The Nature Center offers many different programs. One-hour programs for preschoolers like "Feed the Critters" or "Mudpies and Stone Soup" include a guided nature walk and related activities. The fee is $3 per child. For ages 4 to 6, "Tykes on the Go" is a once-a-month, two-hour program that may include a guided nature hike, live animal demonstrations, and/or a related craft. The fee is $5 per child. Every Saturday morning a family program is offered that incorporates learning about nature with doing a craft together. This program is usually free. On Wednesday evenings throughout the summer, "Nature Nights" for families begin at 7pm with a twilight walk through the canyon. A formal presentation is given at 7:30pm at the outdoor amphitheater.

Hours: The Center is open daily from 9am - 5pm.

Admission: Free

Ages: All

O'NEILL REGIONAL PARK ☼

(714) 858-9365 $

30892 Trabuco Canyon Road, Trabuco Canyon
(EXIT SANTA ANA FWY [5] N.E. ON EL TORO RD., R. ON LIVE OAK CANYON RD.,
WHICH TURNS INTO TRABUCO CANYON RD.)

As we explored parts of this over 2,000-acre park, I kept thinking of
how absolutely gorgeous it is. O'Neill Park is a canyon bottom and so
filled with trees, it's like being in a forest. A creek runs throughout,
creating lush greenery. The abundant nature trails are mostly hilly dirt
trails, though a few are paved "roads."

The playground has a log cabin-like building with slides and swings
and such around it. Inside the small Nature Center are taxidermied
animals around the perimeter of the room. A few tables in the middle
display skulls, furs, and rocks to touch.

The park also has beautiful campgrounds. Make your day or
overnight trip here more special by renting horses at Live Oak Canyon
Stables, directly across the road. Enjoy a guided ride on the scenic
trails inside the park. Call (714) 858-9922 for more information.

Hours: The park is open daily from 7am to sunset. The Nature
Center is open Sat. - Sun. from 2pm - 4pm.
Admission: $2 per vehicle on Mon. - Fri.; $4 on Sat. - Sun; $5 on
holidays. Camping starts at $12 a night.
Ages: All

PETERS CANYON REGIONAL PARK ☼

(714) 538-4400   !

Canyon View Avenue, Orange
(EXIT COSTA MESA FWY [55] E. ON CHAPMAN., R. ON JAMBOREE, R. ON CANYON
VIEW.)

My boys and I have decided that this huge 354-acre undeveloped
park is for rugged hikers. The lake by the parking lot is one of the most
scenic spots here. The narrow dirt trails are lined with sage scrub,
grassland areas, and willow and sycamore trees. The upper Lake View
Trail guides you through the reservoir, while the lower East Ridge Trail
provides a panoramic view of the canyon and the surrounding area.

Hours: Open daily from 7am - sunset.
Admission: Free
Ages: 5 years and up

RALPH B. CLARK REGIONAL PARK ☼

(714) 670-8045 $

8800 Rosecrans Avenue, Buena Park
(EXIT SANTA ANA FWY [5] N. ON BEACH BLVD., R. ON ROSECRANS.)

This sixty-five-acre park is one of the most aesthetically pleasing
parks we've seen. It has all the things that make a park great - a lake to
fish in, ducks to feed, tennis courts, horseshoe pits, three softball fields,

a baseball diamond, volleyball courts, and a few small playgrounds. Take a short hike around Camel Hill, or let the kids climb on the small (ironically named) Elephant Hill. Additionally, there is a paved bicycle trail all around the perimeter of the park.

The Interpretative Center has a working paleontology lab where kids can look through a big window and observe the detailed work being done. The Center also houses a twenty-six-foot Baleen whale fossil; a skeletal saber-tooth cat "attacking" a skeletal horse; fossils of a ground sloth and a mammoth; a model of a T. rex; shells; and more.

Kids really dig the marine fossil site across the street where a *bone*afide paleontologist conducts "Family Fossil Day" four times a year. This three-hour class is geared for youngsters 6 years and up. They can practice their ~~paleontologistical paleontologisting~~ bone-digging skills, bring the fossils back to the lab at the Interpretive Center to study and classify, and perhaps do a related craft. The price for the field trip is simply the price of admission to the park.

> **Hours:** The park is open November 1 to March 31 from 7am - 6pm; April 1 to October 31 from 7am to 9pm. The Interpretative Center is usually open Tues. - Fri., 12:30pm - 5pm; Sat. - Sun., 9am - 4:30pm.
>
> **Admission:** $2 vehicle entrance Mon. - Fri.; $4 on Sat. - Sun.; $5 on holidays.
>
> **Ages:** All

RANCHO MISSION VIEJO LAND CONSERVANCY

(714) 489-9778   !/$$

Ortega Highway, San Juan Capistrano
(EXIT SAN DIEGO FWY [5] E. ON ORTEGA HWY. [74], ABOUT 5.1 MILES.)

The Land Conservancy manages a 1,200 acre wilderness reserve in the coastal foothills. They offer an incredible array of special programs to the general public and to school groups that offer a glimpse into the wilderness of Orange County. Programs include guided nature walks, bird watching (and finding), wildlife workshops, astronomy nights, owl outings, bat walks, butterfly classes, and butterfly counting (for research purposes), trail maintenance, and much more. The programs are given by trained docents, or professionals in that field of study. What a wonderful opportunity for kids to become aware of wildlife, and what they can do to help protect it.

> **Hours:** Call for program hours or to receive a calendar of events.
>
> **Admission:** Depending on the program; free to $8.
>
> **Ages:** It varies, depending on the program.

RONALD W. CASPERS WILDERNESS PARK

(714) 728-0235 $

33401 Ortega Highway, San Juan Capistrano
(EXIT SAN DIEGO FWY [5] E. ON ORTEGA HWY. IT'S OVER 7 MILES DOWN THE ROAD.)

Orange County's largest park is massive, and mostly wilderness. The over thirty miles of hiking trails, ranging from an easy walk to strenuous, mountain-man hikes, are only available when hiking with a ranger or a park docent. (This really is a wilderness park, with all of the implied dangers, and beauty.) There is, however, plenty to do. For instance, enjoy a barbecue under shade trees; play on the large wooden playground with swings and slides, surrounded by trees; check out the Nature Center that has a few taxidermied animals and hands-on activities; hike the mile-and-a-half paved trail; and/or walk around the wooded day use area. There are numerous camp sites here.

Hours: Open daily sunrise to sunset. Rangers are available on the weekends at 9:30am and sometimes in the afternoon to hike the trails.

Admission: $2 per vehicle Mon. - Fri.; $4 Sat. - Sun; $5 on holidays. Camping is $12 a night.

Ages: All

SANTIAGO OAKS REGIONAL PARK ☼

(714) 538-4400 $

2145 North Windes Drive, Orange

(EXIT COSTA MESA FWY [55] E. ON KATELLA, WHICH TURNS INTO VILLA PARK, THEN INTO SANTIAGO CANYON RD., L. ON WINDES, TO THE END.)

Get back to nature at this 350-acre park that has beautiful hiking and equestrian trails that connect to the Anaheim Hills trail system. Take a short path along the creek leading to a waterfall at the dam, or travel more rugged terrain into the heart of the park. Be on the lookout for animals such as lizards, squirrels, deer, and birds. Mountain lions have been seen on rare occasion, too.

A favorite activity here is cooking breakfast over the charcoal barbecues early in the morning, while it's still quiet and cool. A small playground and a few horseshoe pits round out the facilities under a canopy of oak trees. The small Nature Center has taxidermied animals, pictures, and a few hands-on activities.

Hours: The park is open daily from 7am - sunset. The nature center is open daily from 8am - 4pm.

Admission: $2 per vehicle Mon. - Fri., $4 Sat. - Sun.; $5 on holidays.

Ages: All

TEWINKLE PARK ☼

(714) 754-5300   !

970 Arlington Drive, Costa Mesa

(EXIT SAN DIEGO FWY [405] S. ON FAIRVIEW, L. ON ARLINGTON.)

This fifty-acre park has something for everyone. There is a play area with a big tire to climb on, volleyball courts, baseball and softball fields, and a utility field.

I think nature-loving kids will enjoy this park most. A stream goes around a good portion of it, with ducks and geese having a swimmingly good time. They also populate the small lake. A hike up the hill yields the treasure of a pond in a small, forest-like setting. This park is cool, even on a hot day.

Hours: Open daily dawn to dusk.
Admission: Free
Ages: All

TUCKER WILDLIFE SANCTUARY

(714) 649-2760

29322 Modjeska Canyon Road, Modjeska
(EXIT COSTA MESA FWY [55] E. ON CHAPMAN, WHICH TURNS INTO SANTIAGO CANYON RD. TURN R. ON MODJESKA CANYON RD., DRIVE ABOUT 2 MILES, VEER TO THE RIGHT AT THE FORK.)

Tucker Wildlife Sanctuary is tucked in the mountainside at the end of a long and winding road. The Nature Center has a small, one-room museum with live snakes, lizards, and turtles. It also contains taxidermied animals and a touch table with skulls, fossils, and bird's nests.

There are several short (one-fifth or so of a mile) nature trails to walk. Along the Riparian Woodland Trail you'll find a small pond, a few caged animals, and an enclosed observation porch. The porch, located over a creek, has birdseed scattered on it so kids can sit and readily observe wild birds. The hummingbirds, attracted by the brightly-colored sugar water in their feeders, are our favorites. There are picnic tables along the trail.

Hours: Open daily from 9am - 4pm.
Admission: $1.50 donation requested.
Ages: All

TURTLE ROCK NATURE CENTER

(714) 854-8151

1 Sunnyhill Drive, Irvine
(EXIT CORONA DEL MAR FWY [73] S. ON JAMBOREE, L. ON UNIVERSITY DR., R. ON CULVER DR., L. ON BONITA CYN., L. ON SUNNYHILL.)

This small, five-acre nature preserve has both a desert habitat and pine trees, so the stroller-friendly trail is partially in the sun and partially in the shade. Going around a little pond, over a few bridges, and looping back around takes "ten minutes if you don't see anything, thirty minutes if you follow the trail guide. The longer you're here, the more you'll learn."

Inside the Center, a quiz board lights up if the right answer- button is pushed. Kids can also reach in discovery boxes to feel for animal pelts or bones. Visit the small Animal Room (50¢) to see live snakes, bunnies, turtles, crows, and a raccoon. (The animals on exhibit do change.) Find out why the animals are here and what we can do to take better care of their homes. The room is open every hour on the hour from 11am - 3pm.

The surrounding park has tennis courts, a basketball court, sand volleyball courts, and a playground, plus a nature trail that goes over a creek.

Hours: The nature center is open Mon. - Sat. from 10am - 4pm. In the summer, it is also open Sun., noon - 4pm. The park is open daily sunrise to sunset.
Admission: Free
Ages: 2 - 13 years

UPPER NEWPORT BAY ECOLOGICAL RESERVE   ☼
AND REGIONAL PARK
(714) 640-6746   !/$$

600 Shellmaker, Newport Beach
(TAKE NEWPORT FWY [55] S.W. TO END, TURNS INTO NEWPORT BLVD., L. ON W. COAST HWY., L. ON JAMBOREE RD., L. ON BACKBAY DR. TO SHELLMAKER. OR FROM CORONA DEL MAR FWY [73], EXIT S.W. ON JAMBOREE R., R. ON BACKBAY DR. TO SHELLMAKER.)

This reserve is part of an endeavor to conserve wildlife in the Upper Bay. Introduce your children to the valuable natural resources that God originally put on the earth by involving kids in a variety of interactive and interpretive programs. As you "Canoe the Back Bay," you'll see herons, egrets, and other waterfowl. This program is available every Saturday and costs $13 per person. Campfire Programs are offered the first, second, and third Saturday of each month at 7:30pm. This is a wonderful family time with skits, stories, a speaker, songs, and games. Free walking tours are given on the first and third Saturday of each month at 9am. All this is just a sampling of what the reserve has to offer.

Hours: Hours vary, depending on the program.
Admission: Prices vary, depending on the program.
Ages: 3½ years and up.

WHITING RANCH WILDERNESS PARK   ☼
(714) 589-4729 $

Santiago Canyon Road, Portola Hills
(EXIT SAN DIEGO FWY [5] E. ON LAKE FOREST, GO 5 MILES AND TURN L. ON PORTOLA PKY., R. ON MARKET, FIRST DRIVEWAY ON THE LEFT. OR, FROM LAKE FOREST, TURN R. ON PORTOLA PKY., L. ON GLENN RD. AND INTO THE LARGE DIRT PARKING AREA. THIS SECTION LEADS INTO SERRANO CANYON.)

"Real" hikers can explore the hills of Trabuco Canyon via Whiting Ranch Wilderness Park. Follow the trails through forested canyons, along streams, and past huge boulders. A moderate hike starts at the Borrego Trail and leads to the Red Rock Canyon trail, which is five miles round trip and loops back around. (This trail is more easily reached from the Market Street entrance.) The scenery is outstanding. The size and beauty of this park offers the opportunity to enjoy some good, back-to-nature time with your kids.

Hours: Open daily 7am - sunset.
Admission: $2 per vehicle.
Ages: 5 years and up.

WILLIAM R. MASON REGIONAL PARK ☼

(714) 854-2490 $

18712 University Drive, Irvine
(EXIT SAN DIEGO FWY [405] S. ON CULVER DR., WHICH TURNS INTO UNIVERSITY DR.)

This 350-acre park is great for children of all ages. There are three different playgrounds with modular plastic equipment like tunnels, slides, swings, forts, etc. Fishing is allowed in the lake, but be forewarned - it isn't stocked. Lots of ducks, geese, and other birds will vie for food, so bring those bread crumbs. Come enjoy the over two miles of paved bike and walking trails.

Hours: Open daily November through March from 7am - 6pm.
Open daily April through October from 7am - 9pm.
Admission: $2 per vehicle Mon. - Fri.; $4 Sat. - Sun.; $5 on holidays.
Ages: All

ARLINGTON PARK ☼

(909) 715-3440 !

Van Buren Boulevard, Riverside
(EXIT RIVERSIDE FWY [91] N. ON VAN BUREN BLVD. IT'S JUST PAST MAGNOLIA, ON THE W. SIDE OF THE STREET.)

This nice corner park has an older style playground and well-used shuffleboard courts. It also has basketball courts, tennis courts, barbecue pits, and a swimming pool.

Hours: The park is open daily. The pool is open in the summer Mon. - Sat. from 1pm - 5pm; plus Tues. and Thurs. from 6:30pm - 8:30pm.
Admission: Free to the park. Swim sessions are $2 for adults; $1 for ages 6 - 17; 50¢ for children 5 years and under.
Ages: All

CALIFORNIA CITRUS STATE HISTORIC PARK ☼

(909) 780-6222 !

Van Buren Boulevard at Dufferin Avenue, Riverside
(EXIT THE RIVERSIDE FWY [91] S. ON VAN BUREN BLVD., L. ON DUFFERIN AVE. INTO THE PARK.)

This park, with its acres of citrus groves, captures the spirit of Riverside's slogan, "The land of citrus and sunshine." The main section is beautifully landscaped, and has a big, grassy area for running around or for picnicking.

There are two, mile-long hiking trails. The Arroyo Trail goes through a wooded area and creek bed, up towards the dam. The Knolls Trail takes the high, non-shady road, past Grower's Mansion (the soon-to-be restaurant) towards the dam. Neither trail is very strenuous, just good, short nature hikes. Don't forget to stop and smell the oranges along the way!

Hours: The park is open daily from 8am - 5pm.
Admission: Free
Ages: 2 years and up.

FAIRMONT PARK   ☼
(909) 715-3440   !
Off Market Street Riverside
(EXIT POMONA FWY [60] S. ON MARKET ST., R. ON LOCUST ST.)

This lush park has a lot to offer. The huge playground has swings, slides, bridges, and lots of other fun things. The surrounding grassy area is large, with plenty of shade trees and picnic tables. With all this, plus tennis courts, basketball courts, and horseshoe pits, kids can play here all day!

Take a very windy drive around the enormous lake, and watch out for the ducks - they're everywhere! Don't forget your fishing poles as you can stop almost anywhere to fish, including from a small, horseshoe-shaped pier. A fishing permit is required.

The Information Center is open on weekends from 10am to 5pm and has exhibits of local history and environmental projects. You'll have a better than fair day at Fairmont Park!

Hours: Open daily sunrise to 10pm.
Admission: Free
Ages: All

HIDDEN VALLEY WILDLIFE AREA   ☼
(909) 785-7452 $
At the west end of Arlington Avenue, Riverside
(EXIT RIVERSIDE FWY [91] N. AT LA SIERRA, KEEPING L. AS IT TURNS IN TO ARLINGTON.)

Aptly named, this 1,300-acre wildlife area is indeed off the beaten path. There are several options to see at least parts of this "park": Drive along the ridge to see vast expanses of treeless stretches that are close to the road, and wooded areas that are further back into the park; hike along the numerous trails and view the wildlife closer up; or horseback ride, which is obviously a popular option judging from the number of horse trailers we observed.

A small Nature Center is up the road a bit. As Hidden Valley is located along the Santa Ana River, much of the wildlife encouraged and seen here are migratory birds. There are many ponds, too, as you'll discover if you hike into this sprawling park.

Hours: Open daily from 7am - 4:30pm. The Nature Center is open Tues. - Sat. by appointment.

Admission: $2 for adults; $1 for children 12 years and under. There is a box near the entrance, so admission is on the honor system.

Ages: 4 years and up.

HUNTER PARK

Corner of Columbia and Iowa, Riverside   !
(EXIT SAN BERNARDINO FWY [215] E. ON COLUMBIA AVE. IT'S JUST N. OF 91/60/216 JCT.)

Hunter Park is comprised mostly of unkempt playing fields. Its best feature occurs on the second and fourth Sunday of each month when scale model train rides are offered. Kids love taking a ride on the track that encircles the park.

Hours: Steam train rides are on the second and fourth Sunday, from 10am - 3pm.

Admission: Free

Ages: All

JENSEN- ALVARADO RANCH HISTORIC PARK

(909) 369-6055 $

4307 Briggs Street, Riverside
(EXIT POMONA FWY [60] S. ON RUBIDOUX BLVD., R. ON MISSION ST., L. ON RIVERVIEW DR., L ON 42ND ST., R. ON BRIGGS ST.)

This historic site brings the history of the 1880's to life. Costumed docents are on hand to demonstrate farm chores like butter churning, livestock care, and outdoor cooking. The front part of the park is a large, fairly treeless area, with picnic tables. Rusty old farm equipment lines the main pathway. The corral and animal pens, with a few horses, sheep, chicken, and other ranch animals, are located next to the Jensen-Alvarado Ranch House. Behind the house was a winery; it's now a small museum. Inside is period furniture, plus wine-making presses, barrels, and other equipment.

A two-and-a-half-hour school tour includes all of the above, plus hearing a living history presentation; participating in hands-on demonstrations such as making ice cream or tortillas; and maybe, feeding the animals. Tour reservations begin the first week of September; openings are usually filled by the end of the month. (Also, check the September CALENDAR section for the Cornelius Jenson Birthday Celebration.)

Hours: Open September 15 through June 30, Tues. - Fri. for school and large groups only, by reservation. Open to the public on Saturdays from 10am - 4pm. Closed holidays.

Admission: Saturday admission is $3 for adults; $1.50 for kids 12 years and under. School tours are $4 per child; adults are free.

Ages: 6 years and up.

LAKE PERRIS STATE RECREATION AREA   ☼
(909) 657-0676 - general info.; (909) 940-5603 - camping; $$
(909) 657-2179 - marina; (909) 657-8660 - waterslide
17801 Lake Perris Drive, Perris
(EXIT ESCONDIDO FWY [215] E. ON CAJALCO EXPRESSWAY/RAMONA EXPRESSWAY, L. ON LAKE PERRIS DR.)

Come for at least a day of play at the popular Lake Perris! This gigantic, man-made lake supports a multitude of water activities. (It's hot here, so you'll need them.) For your boating pleasure, choose from four- or six-passenger boats, ranging from $19 - $54, or pontoon boats, ranging from $40 - $180 a day. Waterskiing is available, if you bring your own boat. Fish at the lake and catch a big one (or at least try to); a license is required for those over 16 years. There are seven (!) swim beaches, each with a playground and barbecue pits. The three waterslides add a little zip to your day, at a cost of $5 an hour per person, or $10 for all-day water fun.

Drier activities include picnicking, hiking, biking (a nine-mile trail goes around the lake), rock climbing, and a visit to the small Regional Indian Museum. The museum contains stuffed animals, displays on native plant life, exhibits of Indian art, and a beautiful view of the lake out the glass windows. What more could nature-loving kids want?! Camping! There is so much to do at Lake Perris, that you'll want to spend a night, or two, here.

Hours: The recreation area is open in the summer, 6am - 10pm; open the rest of the year 6am - 8pm. The marina is open 6am - 8pm year round. The waterslides are open daily in the summer from 11am - 4pm; open weekends only in April through mid-June and September through October from 11am - 4pm. The museum is open Wed. from 10am - 2pm, and Sat. from 10am - 4pm.

Admission: $6 per vehicle. Tent camping is $15 a night; RV camping is $22 with hook-ups; prices include vehicle admission. Waterslides and boat rentals are priced above.

Ages: All

LAKE SKINNER COUNTY PARK   ☽
(909) 926-1505 - recorded info.; (909) 926-1541 - park ranger; $
(800) 444-7275 camping reservations, Destinet.
Rancho California Road, Riverside County

(EXIT TEMECULA VALLEY FWY [15] N.E. ON RANCHO CALIFORNIA RD.)

Here's the skinny on Lake Skinner: Its main attraction is fishing, either from a boat, or from the shore. A California state license is required. Day permits are $5 for adults; $4 for children 12 years and under. The well-equipped marina offers all sorts of fishing supplies as well as a cafe-restaurant (for those who didn't have much luck catching their own meal). Other activities include hiking, picnicking, playing on the small playground, overnight camping, and seasonal swimming in the pool.

Hours: The park is open daily 6am - 8pm. Fishing is available daily from 6am - dark. The pool is open daily in the summer.

Admission: $2 for adults; $1 for children 12 years and under. The pool is an additional $1 per person. Tent camping is $12 a night; RV camping is $17 a night.

Ages: All

LOUIS ROBIDOUX NATURE CENTER

(909) 683-4880

5370 Riverview Drive, Riverside
(EXIT THE POMONA FWY [60] S. ON RUBIDOUX BLVD., R. ON MISSION ST., L. ON RIVERVIEW DR. AS RIVERVIEW TURNS INTO LIMONITE AVE., TURN L., STAYING ON RIVERVIEW.)

This nature park is wonderful for kids who have an adventuresome spirit. A grouping of big rocks in front of the nature center is here for your climbers. A pond is at the trailhead of Willow Creek Trail, which is an easy, half-mile loop to walk around. Other pathways veer off in all directions, allowing some real hiking excursions. Walk along a tree-lined creek; explore the woodlands and water wildlife along the Santa Ana River; or go farther into the Regional Park system along the horse trail that has extensive chaparral. No biking is allowed, and only off-road strollers will make it. Pick up a self-guided trail map, which also has nature questions for kids to answer.

The main building, or Interpretive Center, houses live animals such as snakes, and taxidermied animals, plus an extensive butterfly and insect collection. Kids are welcome to touch the various animals pelts; use the discovery boxes that contain skulls, seeds, or feathers, etc.; or just play with the puzzles. As with most nature centers, special programs are offered throughout the year. Note: The trail by the parking lot leads into RANCHO JURUPA REGIONAL PARK.

Hours: The park and trails are open daily, sunrise to sunset. The Interpretive Center is open to the public on Sat. from 10am - 4pm. With advanced reservations, it is open Tues. - Fri. to school groups and other large groups.

Admission: Free

Ages: All

MOUNT RUBIDOUX   ☼

Off Buena Vista Drive, Riverside   !
(GOING S.W. ON RIVERSIDE FWY [91], EXIT W. ON 7ᵀᴴ ST. GOING N.W. ON 91, EXIT W. ON UNIVERSITY AVE., WHICH MERGES WITH 7ᵀᴴ ST. 7ᵀᴴ ST. TURNS INTO BUENA VISTA DR. JUST S. OF THE SANTA ANA RIVER, TURN IN WHERE YOU SEE A SMALL GREEN PICNIC AREA AND PARK AT THE BASE OF THE MOUNTAIN.)

For kids who enjoy a somewhat rugged hike, climbing Mount Rubidoux is a great adventure. The steep trail winds around the hill that is barren except for boulders and cacti. Reaching the top is a climax. There are rocks to climb on, and on a clear day, the panoramic view of the San Gabriel and San Bernardino Mountains is beautiful. Hiking here in the summer gets hot, so bring a water bottle. Plan on about an hour-and-a-half round trip. The bike trail at the base of the mountain goes a few miles back to Martha McClean/Anza Narrow Park.

Hours: Open daily.
Admission: Free
Ages: It depends how far up you want to hike!

RANCHO JURUPA REGIONAL PARK   ☼

(909) 684-7032 $
4800 Crestmore Road, Riverside
(EXIT POMONA FWY [60] S. ON RUBIDOUX BLVD., L. ON MISSION BLVD., R. ON CRESTMORE RD., ABOUT 1 MILE.)

This huge mountain-wilderness park, which is part of the even bigger Santa Ana River Regional Park system, provides a delightful escape from the city. The three-acre lake is beautiful. It is stocked with trout in the cooler months and catfish in the summertime. Fishermen (and women) 16 years and older must have a state fishing license. Near the lake is a big, wooden play structure with slides, swings, and monkey bars. Enjoy a day (or two or three) here by camping in one of the eighty camp sites that are slotted in a big, open space near one end of the lake. Horseshoe pits are located over here, too.

On the other side of the main lake are a few smaller lakes, big grassy open spaces for baseball or whatever, plenty of picnic tables, and barbecue pits. Enjoy an easy hike along the river trail to the adjoining LOUIS ROBIDOUX NATURE CENTER, where more trails, an Interpretive Center, and rocks to climb on await your kids.

Hours: Open daily from 8am - 8pm.
Admission: $2 per person for ages 13 and up; $1 per person for children 12 years and under. Dogs are $2 each. Fishing is $5 for ages 16 and older; $4 for ages 6 - 15. A campsite with one vehicle and two people costs $16. Each additional person is $1; up to six people allowed in one campsite. Group rates are available.
Ages: All

UNIVERSITY OF CALIFORNIA AT RIVERSIDE ☼
BOTANIC GARDENS
(909) 787- 4650   !

University of California, Campus Drive, Riverside
(EXIT MORENO VALLEY FWY [215] E. ON UNIVERSITY AVE. TO THE ENTRANCE OF THE
CAMPUS, FOLLOW CAMPUS DR. TO PARKING LOT 13.)

Riverside's climate ranges from subtropical to desert to mountains all within forty acres, and five miles of hilly trails! Explore the botanic gardens to see rose gardens, fruit trees, an herb garden, saguaros, barrel cacti, pine trees, giant sequoias, and so much more.

Besides the diverse plant life, numerous animals share this habitat. Be on the lookout for bunnies, lizards, squirrels, snakes, and coyotes, to name a few. A main trail loops around, and is walkable in forty-five minutes. At the far end of the trail is a pond supporting more wildlife such as frogs, turtles, dragonflies, and koi. A dome-shaped building made of cedar that houses a "living fossils" collection, and a greenhouse are more discoveries you'll make along the way.

Come with your kids to enjoy the beauty of the gardens, and/or come for an educational field trip. Ask for a self-guiding tour booklet, like "Outdoor Classroom" or "Deserts of the Southwest," which will greatly enrich your day of exploring and learning.

Hours: Open daily from 8am - 5pm. Closed New Year's Day, Independence Day, Thanksgiving, and Christmas.
Admission: Free; donations appreciated.
Ages: All

SANTEE LAKES REGIONAL PARK AND ☼
CAMPGROUND
(619) 448-2482 $

9040 Carlton Oaks Drive, Santee
(TAKE THE 52 FWY E. TO THE END, GO E. ON MISSION GORGE RD., L. ON CARLTON
HILLS BLVD., L. ON CARLTON OAKS DR. GOING N. ON SAN VICENTE FWY [67], EXIT
W. ON PROSPECT AVE., R. ON CUYAMACA ST., L. ON MISSION GORGE RD., R. ON
CARLTON HILLS BLVD., L. ON CARLTON OAKS DR. GOING S. ON 67, EXIT W. ON
WOODSIDE AVE., WHICH TURNS INTO MISSION GORGE RD., R. ON CARLTON HILLS
BLVD., L. ON CARLTON OAKS DR.)

This regional park is like a mini-resort. It has campgrounds, a swimming pool (for campers only), a general store, laundry facilities, a recreation center, playgrounds, and several lakes for boating and fishing. The lakes are seasonally stocked with trout, catfish, bluegill, and bass. A California state fishing license is required and are available to purchase at the park entrance. Full hook-up campgrounds are available for $20 a night for two people; $1 for each additional person. Primitive campgrounds are available for $14 a night for two people; $1 for each additional person. Each campsite has a picnic table and barbeque pit. It's a great day to get away to Santee!

Hours: The park and fishing are open Mon. - Thurs., 8am - sunset; Fri. - Sun., 6am - sunset. The pool is open seasonally.

Admission: $3 per vehicle during the week; $4 per vehicle on the weekends. Fishing permits are $4 for adults; $2 for ages 7 - 15; children 6 and under fish for free. Camping prices are listed above.

Ages: 2 years and up.

CUCAMONGA-GUASTI REGIONAL PARK

(909) 481-4205   *$$*

800 North Archibald Avenue, Ontario
(EXIT SAN BERNARDINO FWY [10] N. ON ARCHIBALD AVE.)

Guasti Regional Park offers seasonal catfish and trout fishing at its nice-sized lakes. The playground has a tire swing, monkey bars, and cement tubes with holes to climb through, plus open grassy areas for running around.

During the summer have some wet fun by going down the two waterslides and/or swimming in the pool. You can also just beach it on the sandy area around the pool and grassy area beyond that. Pedal boats are another fun way to cool off. The snack bar sells hot dogs, burritos, chips, ice cream, etc., and is located next to the bait shop - make sure you choose the right one!

Hours: The park is open Thurs. - Tues. from 7:30am - 5pm. (Closed on Wed.)

Admission: $5 per vehicle weekdays; $6 per vehicle on weekends and holidays. Pedestrians are $2. Fishing permits are $5 for ages 8 years and older; $2 for 7 years and under. Pedal boat rentals are $5 a half hour, and available in the summertime only. Swimming is $3 for 4 years and older, plus the entrance fee. An all-day swim and waterslide pass costs $8, plus the entrance fee.

Ages: All

GLEN HELEN REGIONAL PARK

(909) 880-2522   *$*

2555 Glen Helen Parkway, San Bernardino
(EXIT SAN BERNARDINO FWY [215] S. ON DEVORE RD., WHICH TURNS INTO GLEN HELEN PKY. OR, EXIT ONTARIO FWY [15] N.E. ON GLEN HELEN PKY.)

This 1,340-acre park is worth the drive. It offers an assortment of year-round fun, such as fishing in the sizeable lake (a license is needed for those over 16 years old), volleyball courts, playgrounds, campgrounds, and lots of trails for hiking up and down the mountain. Favorite summer activities include renting pedal boats, swimming in the half-acre lagoon, sunbathing on the surrounding beach area, and slip-sliding down the two waterslides. A snack bar is close by the activities so you can replenish your energy. Camping is available so you can enjoy the park longer.

Hours: Open Mon. - Fri., 7:30am - 5pm; Sat. - Sun., 7:30am - 6pm. Water activities are open Memorial Day through Labor Day.

Admission: $5 per vehicle, or $2 for pedestrians. All-day swimming is $2, plus the entrance fee. All-day swimming and use of waterslides is $8, plus the entrance fee. Pedal boat rentals are $5 for a half hour. Camping starts at $10 a night.

Ages: All

JURUPA HILLS REGIONAL PARK / MARTIN TUDOR ☼
(909) 428-8360 $

11660 Sierra, Fontana
(EXIT SAN BERNARDINO FWY [10] S. ON SIERRA AVE.)

Jurupa Hills is another terrific park nestled into a rocky mountainside. It has a great wooden playground for slightly older kids, with wavy slides, a big spiral slide, swaying bridges, and swings. The playground is just outside the water play area. A 418-foot long, gently winding waterslide helps cool off sweaty bodies during the hot summer months. There is also a pool with a small slide. The lower level of the park has a grassy picnic area, along with a baseball diamond, and a few swings.

Hours: The park is open daily 10am - dusk. The pool and slide are open weekends only May and September; daily in the summer.

Admission: $2 per vehicle. $3 for pool use; $5.50 for using the pool and the small slide; $2.50 for five rides on the waterslide (kids 30" and under are free); $8 for all-day pool and waterslide use. Add the entrance fee to all water activity fees.

Ages: All

MOUNT BALDY TROUT PONDS   ☼
(909) 982-4246 $$$

Monte Vista Avenue, Mount Baldy Village
(EXIT 10 FWY N. ON MONTE VISTA AVE. IT'S ABOUT 11 MILES PAST MONTCLAIR.)

No waders are needed to catch fish at this delightful fishing spot up in the mountains. The first pond stocks fish 13" through 18"; the second holds smaller fish, 9" through 13". The fish are abundant here, so chances are your young fisherboy/girl will make at least one catch of the day! All fish caught must be kept and paid for. After you've caught your fill, or the kids need more action, take a hike through the woods on the surrounding trails.

Hours: The ponds are open most of the year on Sat., Sun. and holidays only, 9am - 4:30pm; they are open in July and August Tues. - Fri., 10am - 4pm, as well as on the weekends. 9am - 4:30pm. Closed Thanksgiving and Christmas.

Admission: $1 if your bring your own pole; $2 to rent a pole. Price includes bait, cleaning, and packing fish in ice. You may share poles. Fish prices range from $1.95 for 9" to $14.95 for 18".

Ages: 3 years and up.

PRADO REGIONAL PARK   ☼

(909) 597-4260 for park information; $$
(909) 597-5757 for horse rentals.

16700 S. Euclid Avenue, Chino

(EXIT RIVERSIDE FWY [91] N. ON THE 71, N. ON EUCLID [OR THE 83], JUST SOUTH OF PINE AVE. FROM THE POMONA FWY [60] EXIT S. ON THE 83.)

This is another, has-it-all regional park! Besides the three softball diamonds, two soccer fields for tournament games or family fun, and year-round fishing at the huge lake (over 16 years old needs a license), there are four playground areas. One playground has assorted cement shapes to climb up and through, while the others have newer equipment with more traditional activities.

For those of you with delicate noses, you have correctly detected the presence of horses, cattle, and sheep, as this is farm country. There are herds and ranches all up and down Euclid Street. The Prado Equestrian Center is located at the northern end of the park. Children 7 years old and up can take a one-hour, or more, ride on a trail through the park and to the basin. Kids 2 - 7 years can be led inside the arena for a minimal charge.

Get physical in the summertime by renting a row boat, pedal boat, or aqua cycle. There is a special area for radio-controlled boats, too. A snack bar is also open in the summer. The paved street that winds all around the park will have to suffice for most skating or hiking desires. Across Euclid Street, the park also has trap and skeet fields.

If you like it here so much that you don't want to go home, camp. The campgrounds are at the far end of the park and are nice-looking. A few of the sites have small shade trees. All of the campsites are near completely barren, gently sloping hills.

Hours: The park is open daily from 7:30am - 5pm and open extended hours during the summer. Boat rentals are available in the summer only. Horseback riding is available Tues. - Sun. from 8am - 5pm.

Admission: $6 per vehicle or $2 for pedestrians. Boat launches are
$2. Fishing, ages 7 and older, is $5 a person; $2 for
children 6 years and under. Horseback riding is $20 an
hour for the first hour; $5 an hour for the second. Pedal
boats rentals are $5 for half hour; aqua boats are $6 for
half hour; and rowboats are $4 an hour Mon. - Fri., $7 an
hour Sat. - Sun., with minimum rental hours required.
Camping starts at $10 a campsite.

Ages: All

YUCAIPA REGIONAL PARK   ☼

(909) 790-3127   *$$*

33900 Oak Glen Road, Yucaipa
(EXIT SAN BERNARDINO FWY [10] N.E. ON YUCAIPA BLVD., L. ON OAK GLEN RD. IT'S
W. OF THE OAK GLEN APPLE ORCHARDS.)

Nestled in the rocky San Bernardino Mountains is this huge,
beautiful oasis of a park offering year round fun. Fish in any one of the
three, very large, picturesque lakes to catch seasonal bass, trout, or
catfish. A fishing license is required.

During the summer months, get in the swim of things in the one-
acre swim lagoon, and/or go for the two long waterslides! White sandy
beaches frame the water's edge, with grassy areas just beyond them. A
few steps away is a full-service snack bar, plus pedal boat and aqua
cycle rentals. A wonderful playground is right outside the swim area.
Another playground, designed specifically for disabled children, is
across the way.

RV and tent camping is available for those who really want to get
away from it all for a weekend or so. The grassy areas, trees, and
mountains are a scenic setting for the camp sites. There are plenty of
picnic tables and shelters, as well as barbecue pits. Hiking is
encouraged on either paved trails or along the few dirt pathways. (See
APPLE PICKING - OAK GLEN for nearby places to go.)

Hours: The park is open daily from 7:30am - 6pm. Swimming is
available Tues. - Sun. from 10am - 5pm in the summer.

Admission: $5 per vehicle Mon. - Fri.; $6 per vehicle Sat. - Sun. and
holidays. Pedestrians are $2. A fishing license is needed
for those over 16 years - available here for $9.20. Fishing
is $5 a day for ages 8 and older; $2 for ages 7 and under;
plus park admission. Entrance to the swim lagoon is $3
per person for kids 4 years and up, plus park admission.
An all-day waterslide and swim pass is $8 per person,
plus park admission. Pedal boat and aqua cycle rentals
are $5 for a half hour. Camping prices range from $10 to
$17 per night, for up to four people.

Ages: All

AGUA CALIENTE SPRINGS COUNTY PARK ☾

(619) 565-3600 $

39555 Great Southern Overland Stage Route of 1849, Agua Caliente
Hot Springs
(FROM 8 FWY HEAD EAST TO OCOTILLO, N. ON IMPERIAL HWY [S2]. IT'S ABOUT 25
MILES TO THE PARK. FROM ROUTE 78 HEAD EAST THROUGH JULIAN, S. ON S2.)

For a more therapeutic take on life, come visit Agua Caliente
Springs County Park. It features a big, glass-enclosed pool with water
temperature maintained at 102 degrees as it is fed by underground hot
mineral springs. Ahhhh - feels so good! This indoor pool is only for
adults, however. (There are permanent residents on the grounds for
health reasons). The fifteen-foot by thirty-foot shallow outdoor pool is
fun for children to use, though.

The park also has a general store, shuffleboard courts, horseshoe
pits, play areas, over 140 campsites, and hiking trails. There are
several trails to choose from including a half-mile loop called Ocotillo
Ridge Nature Trail and a more arduous two-and-a-half-mile trail called
Moonlight Canyon Trail. The park is pretty and parts of it are lush with
lots of plant and tree coverage because of the natural springs running
throughout. Look for the many species of birds, and other wildlife, that
call it home.

Hours:	The park is open Labor Day through Memorial Day (closed for the summer), Mon. - Thurs., 9:30am - 6pm; Fri. - Sun., 9:30am - 9pm. The indoor pool is open Sun. - Thurs., 8am - 5:30pm; Fri., Sat., and holidays, 8am - 8:30pm. The outdoor pool is open daily 8am - sunset.
Admission:	$2 per vehicle for day use. Camping costs between $10 (tents) - $14 (full hook-ups) a night. There is an additional $3 fee for camping reservations.
Ages:	3 years and up

ANZA BORREGO STATE PARK ☼

(760) 767-5311 $

Anza Borrego
(FROM SAN DIEGO - EXIT 8 FWY N. ON SAN VICENTE FWY [67], L. ON 79 (ABOUT 10
MILES), R. ON S-2, L. ON MONTEZUMA VALLEY RD. [S-22] INTO BORREGO SPRINGS,
L. AT FIRST STOP SIGN, PALM CYN DR., WHICH DEAD ENDS INTO THE VISITORS
CENTER. LOOK FOR THE FLAGPOLE AS THE VISITORS CENTER BUILDING IS HIDDEN.
FROM ESCONDIDO FWY [15] EXIT E. RT.79 THROUGH WARNER SPRINGS, S. ON S-2,
THEN LOOK AT THE DIRECTIONS FROM SAN DIEGO FOR THE PARK ENTRANCE. FROM
SAN DIEGO FWY [5], EXIT E. ON 78 FWY TO JULIAN. TAKE 78 E. OUT OF JULIAN, N.
ON YAQUI PASS RD. [S-3] INTO BORREGO SPRINGS, L. ON PALM CANYON DR. [S-
22], STAY ON PALM CANYON TO THE END.)

This massive state park is over 600,000 acres of living desert
which includes sand, rocks, mountains, palm trees, flowers, and oases.
The following description merely touches on a few of the activities and
places that this park has to offer. Remember that this is a desert and

the temperatures can reach over 125 degrees during the summer - always bring water!!! Nighttime temperatures can drop drastically, no matter what time of year, so be prepared for anything!

As with any major park, your best bet is to start at the Visitors Center. Get familiar with the park by watching the slide show that is presented upon request, and looking at the exhibits such as taxidermied animals and photographs. Be sure to pick up trail guides and a map.

Within the park, take your choice of hiking trails which range from easy loops to arduous "mountain man" trails. One of the most popular hikes is a one-and-a-half-mile nature trail from the Borrego Palm Canyon campground up through Borrego Palm Canyon. The end of the trail is a sight for sore eyes (and hot bodies) - a refreshing waterfall with a pool! Parking is available near the trail entrance for $5 per vehicle.

There are several campsites available in this gigantic park, including one for campers with horses. Tip: Try to choose a site that has some shelter from the desert winds that blow in seemingly at random. Prices for camping run the gamut from the $5 per vehicle entrance fee for back country camping to $22 a night, depending on location and facilities. For more information call the park office at the number above. For reservations call Destinet at (800) 444-7275. Also see AGUA CALIENTE SPRINGS COUNTY PARK, as it located at the southern part of Anza Borrego park.

Hours: The park is open 24 hours a day, 365 days a year. The Visitor's Center is open Labor Day through Memorial Day daily from 9am - 5pm. It is open in the summer on weekends and holidays only, from 9am - 5pm.

Admission: $5 per vehicle for day use. Camping prices range from $5 - $22 a night.

Ages: 3 years and up.

BALBOA PARK   ☼
(619) 239-0512 - This Visitors Center number gives a listing of   !
the museums and information about upcoming events.
Balboa Park on the Prado, San Diego
See BALBOA PARK under MUSEUMS.

CHULA VISTA NATURE CENTER   ☽
(619) 422-2473 $
1000 Gunpowder Point Drive, Chula Vista
(EXIT SAN DIEGO FWY [5] W. ON "E" ST. TO PARK, OR EXIT E. ON "E" ST, TO PARK AT THE VISITOR'S CENTER AND TAKE THE FREE TROLLEY INTO THE NATURE CENTER.)

Putting their hands in a pool of hungry sharks is only one of the special things that kids (and adults) are invited to do at the Chula Vista Nature Center, located in the Sweetwater Marsh National Wildlife Refuge. You'll start your visit by taking an old-fashioned trolley (free of charge) into the refuge - cars are not allowed. The medium-sized center is full of interactive exhibits such as pulling apart tabs with suction cups attached to them to experience the grip of an octopus; using a bioscanner (i.e. a mounted camera with a zoom lens) to see anemones close up on a monitor; and poking your head up into an (glassed enclosed) exhibit to watch mice run around. (Mice use the marsh as hunting grounds.) The touch table has pelican bones, bird skulls, whale vertebrae, and shells. There are several tanks with live sea creatures, such as seahorses, halibut, and lobsters. Listen for the snapping sounds of the snapping shrimp as they try to frighten predators away. Like a good mystery? Then try to find the California scorpionfish, who are hiding in plain sight.

My boys proudly boast that they've touched a shark, and lived! The outside petting pool contains Leopard and Horn sharks as well as Batrays, Stingrays, and the odd-looking Shovel-Nose Guitarfish. Join in the feeding fun, which usually takes place around 4pm.

An outside overlook affords an opportunity to observe terns, killdeer, plovers, sandpipers, and more wetlands wildlife. Stroller-friendly trails in front of the Center branch off in various directions and allow kids to get closer to the bay to see geese, egrets, or smaller water inhabitants. Look for other wildlife along the trail such as bunnies, turtles, and lizards.

The Nature Center offers a variety of on-site special programs, such as Make It-Take It craft workshops, for ages five and up, on Saturdays and Sundays from 1pm to 2pm (50¢); Raptor Rap, where visitors learn about birds of prey, or raptors, every Sunday from 1:30pm to 3:30pm (free); etc. Call to get a complete schedule, or to sign up for a guided group tour.

Hours: Open Tues. - Sun. from 10am - 5pm. Open the same hours on Mondays during the summer months. Trolleys run approximately every 25 minutes. The Nature Center is closed on Easter and most major holidays.

Admission: $3.50 for adults; $2.50 for seniors; $1 for ages 6 - 17; children 5 years and under are free. The first Tuesday of every month is free admission day.

Ages: 3 years and up.

CUYAMACA RANCHO STATE PARK / LAKE CUYAMACA
(760) 765-0755 $

12551 Highway 79, Descanso, San Diego County
(EXIT 8 FWY N. ON HWY. 79, ABOUT 9 ½ MILES UP; OR EXIT HWY 78 (FROM JULIAN) S. ON HWY. 79.)

Retreat from the buildings, noise, and general business of city life to this outstanding state park with its 25,000 acres of pristine wilderness - a balm to the mind and soul. Take in the forests, grassy meadows, streams, peaks, and valleys that this park has to offer. There are over 125 miles of hiking trails and forty miles of biking trails along the fire roads and access roads. As the terrain varies, hiking trails vary in their degree of difficulty. Be on the lookout for birds, mule deer, lizards, coyotes, etc. Pick up a trail map (50¢) at the park headquarters. While at the headquarters, go through the adjacent museum, which features Native American artifacts, and other exhibits regarding the history and the plant and animal life of this area. The once-prosperous Stonewall Mine site now has just a few pieces of mining equipment to see, and the opening to the shaft behind a fence. There are some photographs of the mine nearby.

Seasonal changes at this altitude of 4,000 feet are often drastic and beautiful. Autumn bursts on the scene with its rich colors of gold, red, and orange; winter brings a white blanket of snow; spring explodes with a profusion of brilliant wildflowers; and the summer is refreshing, as you sit by the stream, under a canopy of trees.

Want to go horseback riding through the mountainside, but don't own a horse? Call Holidays on Horseback riding stables, (619) 445-3997, and enjoy a one-and-a-half-hour ($25 per person) or two-hour ($35 per person) excursion. Rides are given between 9:30am to 2:30pm, and riders must be at least 6 years old. Call to make a reservation.

Beautiful campgrounds in the park are available for families, at either Paso Picacho or Green Valley (hike to waterfalls from here), for $12 per night, maximum eight people per campsite. Most of the camp grounds have picnic tables, fire rings, and heated showers for 25¢. Call Destinet at (800) 444-7275 to make a reservation.

Fishing or boating at Lake Cuyamaca, (760) 765-0515, is another way to enjoy this area. Motorboat rentals are $25 a day *oar* rent a row boat at $12 a day. Fishing permits are $4.75 for adults (a California license is also required); $2.75 for kids 8 to 15 years; children 7 years and under are free. Depending on the season (and your luck), you can catch trout, catfish, bass, bluegill, and crappie. The lake is at the northern end of the park.

Hours: The park is open daily sunrise to sunset. The gift shop and museum are open Fri. - Mon., 10am - 4pm. Fishing and boat rentals are available daily from 6am - 6:30pm.

Admission: $5 per vehicle for day use of the park; dogs are $1 each. There are several scenic turn-outs off Hwy. 79 that offer picnic tables and hiking trails, with no park fee.

Ages: 2 years and up.

KIT CARSON PARK / ESCONDIDO SPORTS CENTER
(760) 741-4691

Bear Valley Parkway, Escondido

(EXIT ESCONDIDO FWY [15] E. ON VIA RANCH PKY WHICH TURNS INTO BEAR VALLEY PKY.)

Come to where the action is! This "state-of-the-art" sports center, scheduled to open in September of '97, is located in the heart of Kit Carson Park. It will offer a soccer arena, a roller hockey arena, and a 20,000 square-foot skate park complete with ramps, etc., plus a pro shop and concession stand. Sign up for leagues, camp, and/or skate sessions, or just come to watch.

Kit Carson park is large, and very family-friendly with plenty of picnic tables, barbeque pits, green grassy areas for running around, and a few playgrounds.

Hours: The park is open daily from dawn to dusk. Call for details about the sports sessions.

Admission: The park is free. Call for details about the sports sessions, or membership.

Ages: All for the park. Call for details, and age recommendations, for the sports center.

LA JOLLA INDIAN RESERVATION CAMPGROUND / ☼
Tubing on San Luis Rey River
(760) 742-1297 $$$

Route 76, on the La Jolla Indian Reservation, Pauma Valley
(EXIT ESCONDIDO FWY [15] E. ON RT. 76 AND UP ABOUT 25 MOUNTAIN MILES, 100 YARDS N. OF SEGNME OAKS RD., R. AT THE TEXACO GAS STATION.)

Come to the campground just for the day, or spend a night or two here in the lush, semi-wilderness of the foothills of the beautiful Palomar Mountains. Hike amongst the beautiful foliage along the San Luis Rey River; climb the rocks on the river banks; try your luck at fishing; or wade in the river waters.

For more wet thrills, go inner tubing down the river. Cruise down the two mile stretch (which takes about an hour) as many times as you want throughout the day. Parts of the river are idyllic, while other parts are a bit more exciting (and bumpy). Old army troop transportation trucks will pick you up at the end of the run and bring your family back to the starting point. Be prepared for this adventure by wearing a hat, tee shirt, sunscreen, and sneakers (for painlessly stepping on the rocks on the river bottom). B.Y.O.T. (Bring Your Own Tube) or rent an inner tube here for $5. Tip: Tie your inner tube to your child's so you can stay together!

Almost all of the camping sites are located right by the river. (The water can be soothing or loud, depending on how you interpret its sound.) Chemical toilets are scattered throughout the camp, and hot showers are available at designated places. Campfires are allowed. Firewood, tackle, supplies, and food are available at the small Trading Post on the grounds.

Hours: Open sunrise to sunset.

Admission: $9 per vehicle for day use for up to four people. Additional passengers are $1 per person. River tubing is included in this price. Tube rentals are $5. Camping is $13 per vehicle for tents; $18 for R.V.s.

Ages: 4 years and up

LAKE POWAY RECREATION AREA / CLYDE E. REXRODE WILDERNESS AREA

(619) 679-5466

Lake Poway Road, Poway

(EXIT ESCONDIDO FWY [15] E. ON RANCHO BERNARDO RD. (GO ABOUT 4 MILES), L. ON LAKE POWAY RD., UP THE HILL.)

The fish are usually biting at the stocked Lake Poway. Depending on the season, reel in catfish or rainbow trout. Boat rentals are available here. Looking for something fun to tackle on summer nights? Try night fishing from Memorial Day through Labor Day on any Thursday, Friday, and/or Saturday night from 4pm to 11pm.

The 400 acres surrounding the lake are the Clyde Rexrode Wilderness Area, named after Poway's first mayor. There are miles of trails to choose from, including a scenic three-mile loop around the lake (which takes about an hour), or a more rugged two-and-a-half-mile hike to Mt. Woodson. Scenery ranges from sage bush to large trees. Be on the lookout for wildlife such as red-tail hawks, raccoons, and even deer. This wilderness area offers an escape from city life.

Hours: The park is open daily 7am - sunset. The lake is open for fishing and boating, Wed. - Sun. from sunrise to sunset.

Admission: Entrance to the park is free during the week. Sat., Sun., and holidays, non-residents pay $4 per vehicle. Daily fishing permits are $4.50 for adults; $2 for ages 8 -15 years; children 7 years and under may fish off an adult permit. Full-day boat rentals are $15 for a motorboat; $10 for a rowboat.

Ages: 3 years and up.

MISSION BAY PARK

San Diego

(EXIT SAN DIEGO FWY [5] W. ON CLAIREMONT DR. TO DRIVE THE MISSION BAY LOOP - GO S. ON E. MISSION BAY DR. TO SEA WORLD DR. TO MISSION BAY DR. (OR N. ON INGRAHAM ST.) TO GRAND AVE.)

Mission Bay Park is not a singular bay or park like the name implies - it is thousands of acres of incredibly beautiful vistas, and of beaches, water, pathways, playgrounds, grassy areas, and various attractions. Generic things to do include jogging, cycling, in-line skating, swimming, picnicking, fishing, kayaking, sailing, pedal boating, paddle boating, and camping. Park at any one of the scenic spots you see along Mission Bay Drive, or Ingraham Street, and enjoy. Hot spots include: Pacific

Beach, just north of Mission Beach on Mission Boulevard - a favorite hang out for surfers, swimmers, joggers, etc.; Fiesta Island, just northeast of Sea World, and Vacation Isle, on Ingraham Street north of Sea World Drive - both have numerous biking trails, delightful picnic areas, and a few playgrounds; South Mission Beach and North Mission Beach, both along Mission Boulevard - popular beaches for swimming and laying out; and De Anza Cove, on E. Mission Bay Drive - a nice area for swimming.

A few helpful names and phone numbers in the Mission Bay area include: Campland on the Bay, (619) 581-4200, for camping; Hamel's Action Sports Center, which is a building shaped like a castle, (619) 488-5050, for rentals of bikes, skates, boogie boards, etc.; San Diego Sailing Center, (619) 488-0651, for rentals of sailboards and kayaks; and Windsport Kayak & Windsurfing Center, (619) 488-4642, for kayak and windsurfing rentals.

Attractions listed separately in Mission Bay Park are: BELMONT PARK, SAN DIEGO VISITOR INFORMATION CENTER, SEA WORLD, and TECOLOTE SHORES PLAY AREA.

Hours: Open daily
Admission: Free
Ages: All

MISSION TRAILS REGIONAL PARK ☼
(619) 668-3275   !

One Father Junipero Serra Trail, San Diego
(THERE ARE SEVERAL ENTRANCES TO THE PARK. FROM MISSION VALLEY FWY [8], EXIT N. ON MISSION GORGE/FAIRMOUNT AND GO 4 MILES N. ON MISSION GORGE RD. THE VISITOR AND INTERPRETIVE CENTER ENTRANCE IS ON THE L. BETWEEN JACKSON DR. AND GOLFCREST DR., ON FATHER JUNIPERO SERRA TRAIL. FROM ROUTE 52, EXIT S. WHEN IT ENDS ON MISSION GORGE RD. IF VISITING THE OLD MISSION DAM AREA, THE OLD MISSION DAM ENTRANCE IS ABOUT ½ MILE DOWN MISSION GORGE RD. THE VISITOR AND INTERPRETIVE CENTER IS ABOUT 2 MILES FURTHER DOWN MISSION GORGE RD. SEE DIRECTIONS FROM FWY 8.)

This massive, almost 6,000 acre recreational area is comprised of several major areas and points of interest: 1) Lake Murray - At the southern part of the park is a beautiful, stocked lake that allows fishing and boating activities from 5:30am to 5pm on Wednesdays, Saturdays, and Sundays between November and Labor Day. A paved trail goes around the lake. Picnic tables are also available; 2) Cowles Mountain - Hiking is the main sport here. For an outstanding 360 degree view of the city, take the one-and-a-half-mile trail (about two hours) to the top of the mountain; 3) Old Mission Dam Historic Area - This is a starting point for several hikes. (Picnic tables are here, too.) People of all abilities can go on a self-guided paved pathway from the parking lot to the footbridge across the San Diego River, with its lush foliage. Further along is the gorge with rock cliffs. Press buttons along the trail, and listen to explanations of the area. Take a longer hike, too. So many trails - so little time!; 4) East Fortuna Mountain - This area offers some of the most diverse environments of the park. (Check out some of the canyons!) The smallish Kumeyaay Lake, accessible from Father Junipero Serra Trail, is fun for shoreline fishing. A relatively flat one-and-a-half-mile trail goes around the lake; 5) West Fortuna Mountain - You can hike or mountain bike up plateaus and series of canyons; 6) The Visitor and Interpretive Center - This architecturally beautiful building blends in with the natural rock setting of the park, and is a great starting place for an adventure. Pick up trail guides, program information, and/or enjoy some interactive exhibits inside. Kids gravitate to the Indian faces carved from "rocks." Several touch screens offer information about the park - where to go, the plants, the animals, etc. Every thirty minutes the small theater presents a film on the park. Walk to the upper story of the center amid bird and animal sounds. See ancient volcanic rock and a great view of the park. Outside the center is a small stage, and rocks that are almost irresistible for kids to climb. The kids sweated (I glowed) as we hiked on the moderate looping trail around the Visitors Center, which took us a good hour. Our mission is to come back to Mission Trails and experience more of what it has to offer!

Hours: The trails and park are open daily sunrise to sunset, although the car entry gates are open from 9am - 5pm. The Center is open daily from 9am - 5pm; closed on Christmas. See the above description for hours.

Admission: Free

Ages: 3 years and up.

OLD POWAY PARK   ☼

(619) 679-4313   !/$

14134 Midland Road, Poway

(EXIT ESCONDIDO FWY [15] E. ON CAMINO DEL NORTE, R. ON MIDLAND RD.)

This gracious park is set up like a small historic, western village, complete with its own train depot. The two-acre grassy park boasts of shade trees, a gazebo, picnic tables, barbeques, crisscrossing pathways, and bridges over the creek. Come during the week to simply enjoy the park. Come on a weekend, however, for some action, because that's when the "town" is open and everything comes to life! Regular weekend activities include a farmer's market on Saturday mornings, arts and crafts booths, tours through the museum and house, and train rides. The small Heritage Museum has glass-encased displays from olden times in Poway such as pictures, clothing, a guitar, glassware, a piano, etc. The small Nelson House contains a turn-of-the-century, fully furnished kitchen, living room, music room, and bedrooms. The blacksmith's shop puts on demonstrations of its craft on the third and fourth Saturdays of each month. Last, but not least, take a short ride around "town" on a genuine steam engine train, or one of the other train cars. Take a look into the train barn which houses the steam engine, a 1938 Fairmont Speeder, ore cars, and a 1894 Los Angeles Yellow Trolley. Don't forget to check out the many special events that go on here throughout the year!

Bring a picnic lunch, or enjoy good old American food at the Hamburger Factory. The Factory is wood-paneled and decorated with buffalo heads, steer skulls, etc., giving is a rustic ambiance. The restaurant is open daily for breakfast, lunch, and dinner.

Hours: The park is open daily. Rail cars operate Sat., 10am - 4pm; Sun., 11am - 2pm. - closed the second Sunday of each month. The museum and Nelson House are open Sat., 9am - 4pm; Sun., 11am - 2pm. Attractions are closed on Christmas.

Admission: The park is free. Train rides vary from $1 to $2 for adults depending on the rail car; children 12 years and under are 50¢. Donations are requested for the museum and Nelson House.

Ages: All

PALOMAR MOUNTAIN STATE PARK / PALOMAR ☼ OBSERVATORY

(760) 742-2119 - observatory; (760) 742-3462 - state park $

S6, Palomar Mountain

(EXIT ESCONDIDO FWY [15] E. ON PALA RD. [ROUTE 76], L. [N.E.] ON S6 ABOUT 26 MILES UP THE MOUNTAIN TO THE OBSERVATORY.)

Up in the Palomar Mountains, at the end of a long and winding road, is the Palomar Observatory. A short hike up to the observatory allows you to see the famed 200" Hale telescope. But forewarn your children - you can only look at the telescope which is housed behind glass panes; you cannot look through it. The telescope is magnificent in size and scope and almost worth the drive here! The small one-room museum displays outstanding photos of star clusters, galaxies, and clouds of glowing gas. It also shows a continuously running video about the workings of the telescope and about our universe.

Just a few miles down the road is Palomar Mountain State Park. If you're planning on coming to the observatory, I suggest making the park a destination, too, as just walking around the observatory and museum took us only half an hour. Palomar Mountain General Store, (760) 742-3496, is at the junction of S7 and S6, making it a natural stopping place before going on to the park. The store has a bit of everything, including fossils, gems, Indian jewelry, and artifacts.

Continue about three miles on S7 to reach the park. At 2,000 acres, this Sierra Nevada-like park is incredibly beautiful. You'll find several hiking trails through the scenic mountainside. The Boucher Hill Lookout trail, for instance, is a looping two-mile hike with marvelous vistas. Fishing is available at Doane Pond, which is stocked regularly. There is a five fish limit per day, and those 16 years old and older need a California state license. The park also provides areas for picnicking and overnight camping. The family campsites have fire rings, picnic tables, and coin-operated hot showers. Call the ranger station (park office) for more information.

Hours: The museum and the observatory are open daily 9am - 4pm. The state park is open sunrise to sunset.

Admission: Free to the observatory and museum; $5 vehicle entrance fee for day use of the park. Overnight camping is $15 weekdays, $16 on weekends for a maxiumum of 8 people, 1 vehicle. Additional vehicles are $5. Call Destinet at (800) 444-7275 to make reservations.

Ages: 8 years and up for the observatory and the museum; ages 3 and up for the park.

QUAIL BOTANICAL GARDENS

(760) 436-3036

230 Quail Gardens Drive, Encinitas
(EXIT SAN DIEGO FWY [5] E. ON ENCINITAS BLVD., L. ON QUAIL GARDENS DR. THERE ARE SIGNS ALONG THE WAY.)

We didn't see any quail on our visit to the Quail Botanical Gardens, but we did see (and hear) woodpeckers plus a variety of other birds such as wrens, finches, scrub jays, and hermit thrushes. The thirty landscaped acres here include desert, exotic tropical, palm, bamboo, and native California plants. The lush foliage; the incredible array of flowers; the meandering trails (some dirt, some paved); the beautiful waterfall; and the benches under shade trees, invoked the sensation of visiting a secret garden. Some of our highlights included seeing the Sausage Tree, with its large and very heavy pods that really do resemble sausages; walking up to the Overlook Pavilion for a 360-degree view of the gardens, mountains, ocean, and surrounding community; and taking pictures of the unique flowers. Our favorite flowers were the white and yellow upside-down bellflowers. Strolling around the botanical gardens is a delightful way to spend the day!

Hours: Open daily 9am - 5pm. Closed New Year's Day, Thanksgiving, and Christmas.

Admission: $3 for adults; $1.50 for ages 5 -12; children 4 years and under are free.

Ages: 2 years and up.

RANCHO VISTA SPORTS PARK AND COMMUNITY RECREATION CENTER

(909) 694-6410   !/$

30875 Rancho Vista, Temecula
(EXIT TEMECULA FWY [15] E. ON RANCHO CALIFORNIA RD., S. ON YNEZ RD., L. ON RANCHO VISTA)

Have a ball at this terrific sports park! It has twelve ball fields, seven soccer fields, lots of open grassy areas for running around, two great playgrounds, shade trees, picnic shelters, and barbecue grills. The one-acre, concrete skateboard park has ramps, rails, etc., which make it fun and challenging. The roller hockey rink has some open time, though it is used mostly by leagues. The indoor gym offers basketball, and can be set up for volleyball. Keep your cool in the twenty-five-meter outdoor swimming pool that has a diving board and a waterslide. There is also a shallow pool just for tots. The Teen Center is a great place for 12 - 18 year olds to hang out. It offers pool, air hockey, Carom, Nintendo, and more. This park offers everything active kids need - my boys would be very happy living there!

Hours: The park is open 6am - 10pm. Skateboard sessions are 2½ hours long: Mon. - Fri., between 1pm - 9pm; Sat., between 10am - 9:30pm; Sun., between 1pm - 6:30pm. The roller hockey rink is usually available for open play Mon. - Fri. before 4pm. After 4pm and on weekends, it is booked for leagues. The pool is open weekends only in April, May, September, and October from 1pm - 5pm. During summer months it is open Mon.- Fri., 1pm - 4pm; Sat. - Sun., 1pm - 5pm. The Teen Center is open Mon. - Fri., 2pm - 8:45pm during school hours. Weekends and off-school hours, it's open 10am - 8:45pm.

Admission: The park is free. Skateboard sessions cost $2 for residents, $5 for non-residents. Bring your own equipment, or rent everything needed for $5. Pool sessions for residents are $2.25 for adults; $1.75 for ages 8 - 17; $1 for kids 7 years and under. Pool rates for non-residents are $3 per person. The Teen Center asks that a resident card be purchased - $1 for a year's membership.

Ages: All ages for the park. Skateboarders under 7 years must be accompanied by an adult. Kids must be between 12 - 18 years to hang out inside the Teen Center.

SAN DIMAS COUNTY PARK ☼
(909) 599-7512					!
1628 Sycamore Canyon Road, San Dimas
(FROM THE 210 FWY, TAKE THE 30 FWY E. GO N.W. ON FOOTHILL BLVD., R. ON SAN DIMAS CANYON DR., UP THE HILL TO THE PARK OFFICE.)

Nestled in the foothills of the San Gabriel Mountains, adjacent to Angeles National Forest, is a wonderful county park, museum, and wildlife sanctuary. The nature museum is small but comprehensive. It has live snakes, such as rosy boas and rattlesnakes; taxidermied animals such as California gray squirrels, birds, and raccoons; and several small collections including rocks, arrowheads, insects, and butterflies.

The outside wildlife sanctuary offers a caged home to several injured or non-releasable native animals. Hawks, heart-faced barn owls, and great-horned owls are part of the bird rehabilitation area, not part of the bird "rebellion" area - my son misread the sign. Other live animals here include a deer, raccoon (his little paws were busily cleaning his food when we saw him), possum, (destunked) skunk, fox, pheasants, and tortoises, plus many squirrels running around freely.

A one-mile, self-guided nature trail, beginning in the oak woodland just behind the nature center building, loops around. There are several other trails to choose from that satisfy both novice and experienced hikers. There are plenty of picnic tables here under the cover of shady oak trees. Some of the picnic areas have barbeques. Come visit the park on your own, or with a Jr. Ranger Program, offered through the park system. The area below the museum has a baseball diamond, a few playgrounds, and large grassy areas. An equestrian center is next to the park, and a portion of a long bike route goes through part of the park. A visit to the San Dimas County Park is a great for temporarily escaping city life.

Hours: Open 8am - sunset.
Admission: Free
Ages: All

SAN PASQUAL BATTLEFIELD STATE HISTORIC �☀ PARK

(619) 220-5430   !

15808 San Pasqual Valley Road (SR78), San Pasqual
(GOING S. ON SAN DIEGO FWY [5], OR ESCONDIDO FWY [15], EXIT E. ON HWY 78, TURNS INTO SAN PASQUAL VALLEY RD. GOING N. ON 15, EXIT E. ON VIA RANCHO PKWY., TURNS INTO BEAR VALLEY RD., R. ON SAN PASQUAL RD., TURNS INTO VIA RANCHO PKWY., GO TO END, R. ON SAN PASQUAL VALLEY RD. IT IS JUST E. OF SAN DIEGO WILD ANIMAL PARK)

This is the site of the worst (i.e. bloodiest) battles in California in the Mexican-American War. (Kids need to know this fact for its historical signifigance, and because it will make their visit here more exciting.) The visitors center overlooks the battlefield, which is actually across the highway, on private land. The small center has interpretive panels, a few uniforms, weapons, and a ten-minute video entitled "Mr. Polk's War." A Living History Day is held here in June, and the battle is reenacted in December. The grounds have picnic tables, and a quarter-mile looping trail.

Hours: The park is open Sat. - Sun. and holidays, 10am - 5pm;
Tues., 10am - 4pm; and usually on Fri., 10am - 4pm.
Guided school tours are given during the week, by
appointment.
Admission: Free
Ages: 6 years and up.

SOUTH CLAIREMONT RECREATION CENTER /
POOL

(619) 581-9924 - recreation center; (619) 581-9923 - pool   !/$

3605 Clairemont Drive, Clairemont

(GOING N ON SAN DIEGO FWY [5], EXIT W. ON BALBOA AVE., L. ON CLAIREMONT AVE. GOING S. ON 5, EXIT S. ON MISSION BAY DR., L. ON GARNET, TURNS INTO BALBOA AVE., L ON CLAIREMONT AVE.)

This large community park offers various activities for families to enjoy. Green grassy areas and scattered picnic tables provide a picnic atmosphere, while the older-style playground, complete with hopscotch, slides, swings, and climbing apparatus, provides the fun. Check at the community center building for special classes, programs, and events. There are also two tennis courts and a good-sized, outdoor swimming pool that is open year round. During the week, only half of the pool is open for public use as the swim team uses the other half. On weekends, the whole pool is open for the public.

Hours: The park is open daily sunrise to sunset. The pool is open Mon. - Fri. noon - 2:30pm and 4:30pm - 7pm; Sat. - Sun., noon - 4pm.

Admission: The park is free. Swimming sessions cost $2 for adults; $1.50 for kids 15 years and under.

Ages: All

TECOLOTE SHORES PLAY AREA

West Mission Bay Drive, San Diego   !

(EXIT SAN DIEGO FWY [5] W. ON CLAIREMONT DR., L. ON E. MISSION BAY DR., PAST THE HILTON.)

Head for some big time fun at the large Tecolote Shores Play Area. This wonderful playground has a great combination of old and new equipment. In the huge sand area there are slides, swings, and cement turtles to climb on (and under). Other sections include aquatic cement creatures, a pirate ship, mini-obstacle ropes course, bridges, and various other climbing apparatus. There are plenty of picnic tables and grassy areas here, too. As the playground is right on the bay, the view is beautiful. Tip: There aren't many tall trees here, so this is a great place to fly a kite.

Hours: Open daily sunrise to sunset.

Admission: Free

Ages: All

TIJUANA ESTUARY and VISITORS CENTER /
BORDER FIELD STATE PARK

(619) 575-3613 - Estuary and Visitors Center;   !
(619) 424-3124 - Sandi's Rental Stables

301 Caspian Way, Imperial Beach

(Exit San Diego Fwy [5] W. on Coronado Ave., turns into Imperial Beach Blvd., L. on 3ʳᵈ St., L. on Caspian Wy.)

First things first - an estuary is: "The wide part of a river where it flows near the sea; where fresh water and salt water mix." (That's why this book is called "Fun and *Educational*...") The Visitors Center has several wonderful interactive exhibits. One of our favorite displays were ordinary-looking, black and white sketched pictures of habitats that magically revealed brightly colored birds, insects, fish, and other animals when viewed through a polarized filter. The touch table contains snake skin, nests, skulls, and a dead sea turtle. The food chain is portrayed through pictures and graphs. "Beneath the Sand" exhibit entails pressing the bill of bird puppet heads into holes in various levels of "sand." A light on the side panel displays what birds with shorter beaks, that reach only shallow levels, eat (insects and plant seed), compared to what birds with longer beaks, that can reach deeper levels, eat (crabs and worms). A small theater shows, upon request, films such as "Timeless River" and "Tide of the Heron."

Eight miles of walking trails are interspersed throughout the reserve. Ask for a map at the center, as there are different entrance points. Some of the trails follow along the streets, while others go deeper into the coastal dunes and near the Tijuana River. Be on the lookout for terns, egrets, herons, curlews, etc. and other wildlife. On a very short loop around the center, my boys and I saw interesting plants and birds, plus thirteen bunnies! Take a guided walking tour to learn more about the flora and fauna at the estuary, or sign the kids up for one of the numerous programs available. The Jr. Ranger Program, for students kindergarten through sixth grade (under 6 years old must be accompanied by a parent), is offered every Thursday from 3:15pm to 4:45pm. During the program kids will enjoy a walk, earn patches or buttons, and/or make a craft - all free of charge!

Just south of the estuary is Border Field State Park, which borders Mexico. A marker shows the United States - Mexico boundary. The cliffs provide an awesome view of the ocean, and of the whales during whale-watching season, which is January through March. You can even see some of Tijuana from here, including a bullfighting ring. Picnic tables are here, grassy areas for running around, and pathways for hiking into parts of the estuary. An exciting way to see more of the park is by taking a horseback ride on the beach. Wear long pants, a windbreaker, and close-toed shoes, and saddle up for a two or three-hour adventure. Sandi's Rental Stables, located at 2060 Hollister Street, also gives other rides, such as going on the wildlife trail in the estuary, or mounting up for a Chuckwagon Meal Ride. Younger children may take a pony ride around the parking lot.

Hours: The Visitors Center is open Wed. - Sun. from 10am - 5pm. Closed Thanksgiving and Christmas. The stables are open every day.

Admission: Free to the Visitors Center. Horseback riding starts at
$20 an hour; $10 for a half-hour pony ride around the
parking lot.
Ages: 3 years and up.

TORREY PINES STATE RESERVE

(619) 755-2063

Torrey Pines Park Road, La Jolla
(EXIT SAN DIEGO FWY [5] W. ON DEL MAR HEIGHTS RD., L. ON CAMINO DEL MAR,
TURNS INTO NORTH TORREY PINES RD., R. ON TORREY PINES PARK RD. PAST THE
BEACH AND UP THE HILL.)

The Torrey pine tree grows only in this reserve - no where else in
the whole world! My kids were impressed with this fact and by the
beauty of the park. Our favorite trail was the Guy Fleming Trail. It's an
easy loop, only two-thirds of a mile, and incredibly scenic through the
trees out to a cliff overlooking the ocean. Tip: Hold on to younger
children! Other trails include the half-mile Parry Grove looping trail; the
two-thirds-of-a-mile Razor Point Trail with dramatic views of gorges; the
steep, three-quarters-of-a-mile (one way) Beach Trail which ends at the
San Diego - La Jolla Underwater Park; and the two, demanding, Broken
Hill Trails.

The Visitors Center shows a short film that gives an overview of the
reserve - just ask to see it. The exhibits here offer good visual
information regarding the plants and animal wildlife of the reserve.
There are taxidermied raccoons, skunks, and birds; a pine cone
display; a pine needle display; and more. We appreciated Torrey Pines
Reserve for its glorious nature trails and its breath of fresh air! A
lifeguarded State Beach is right below the reserve for those who are
into sand and surf.

Hours: Open daily from 8am - sunset.
Admission: $4 per vehicle.
Ages: 3 years and up.

CHANNEL ISLANDS NATIONAL PARK

(805) 658-5730 - National Park; (805) 642-7688 - recorded   *$$$$$*
information for Island Packers; (805) 642-1393 - Island Packers
reservations

The park headquarters is at 1901 Spinnaker; Island Packers is at 1867
Spinnaker Dr., Ventura
(GOING S. ON VENTURA FWY [101], EXIT S. ON HARBOR BLVD. GOING W. ON 101,
EXIT S.W. ON SEAWARD AVE., L. ON HARBOR BLVD. FROM HARBOR, GO R. ON
SPINNAKER DR., ALL THE WAY TO THE END. ALSO SEE CHANNEL ISLANDS
NATIONAL PARK VISITOR CENTER.)

The Channel Islands comprise a chain of eight islands, five of
which make up Channel Islands National Park. Prepare your kids for a
half or whole day excursion to an island by first obtaining information

from the park service. The islands were originally the home of
Chumash Indians and the Gabrielino people. Then, hunters came and
killed certain otter, seal, and sea lion species almost to extinction.
Finally, ranchers settled here. Some parts of the islands are still
privately owned. It's important to emphasize to your child that Channel
Islands is a national preserve, so "take only memories, leave only
footprints".

Climate on the islands is different from mainland climate, even
during the summer. The harsher conditions have produced various
terrains within the relatively small parcels of land; from sandy beaches
to rocky hills. Bring jackets and your camera; wear sneakers; pack a
water bottle; and have a terrific outing!

Here is a very brief overview of the islands (enough to whet your
adventuring appetite), along with cruise prices from Island Packers:

Anacapa - This is the closest island to Ventura, only fourteen miles
away. It is five miles long. On East Anacapa, climb up the 154 steps to
the small visitor's center and hiking trails. There is no beach here, but
swimming is allowed at the landing cove on calm summer days, as is
scuba and skin diving. Picnicking is welcomed. This is one of the most
popular islands to visit. Round-trip takes about seven hours, including
about three hours on the island. Adult fare is $37; children 12 years and
under are $20. A half-day cruise around the island, with no island
landing, is about three-and-a-half hours long. Whale watching is offered
on this cruise from the end of December through the month of March.
Adult fare is $21; children 12 years and under are $14. Take an express
run - a five-hour day, including two hours on the island, for $32 for
adults; $20 for kids.

Santa Cruz - At twenty-four miles long, this is the largest island.
Topography varies from steep cliffs and caves, to green hills. Round-
trip takes eight to nine hours, including about three-and-a-half hours on
the island. Adult fare is $42; children 12 years and under are $25.
Overnight camping here is $54 for adults; $40 for children 12 years and
under.

Santa Rosa - This island is fifteen miles long and, although eighty-five
percent of it is grasslands, there are still canyons, volcanic formations,
and fossil beds to vary the landscape. There is plenty to see and do
here for those who thrive on being in the midst of nature. Round-trip
takes about twelve hours, including about four hours on the island.
Adult fare is $62; children 12 years and under are $45. Overnight
camping is $80 for adults; $70 for children 12 years and under.

San Miguel - This eight-mile-long island has beaches and an incredible
number of archeological sites. The most popular destination here is the
Caliche Forest (i.e. mineral sand castings), which is a three-and-a-half-
mile hike from the beach. Be prepared for strong winds, plus rain and
fog any time of the year. The varying island terrains reflect the assault
of weather upon San Miguel. Weekend camping and round-trip
transportation costs $90 for adults; $80 for children 12 years and under.

Day trips leave only from Santa Barbara, and entail spending the night before on the boat. San Miguel is recommended for hardier kids.

Santa Barbara - This is the smallest island, at only 640 acres, and is the farthest away from mainland Ventura. It has steep cliffs, a small "museum," and hiking trails. There are no shade trees on the island, so load up with sunscreen. Round-trip takes about twelve hours, including about three hours on the island. Adult fare is $49; children 12 years and under are $35. Camping is $75 for adults; $65 for children 12 years and under.

Cruise to the islands and explore nature at her best and wildest. Kids get especially excited about seeing the numerous seals and sea lions that are plentiful because they breed on many of the islands. Once on an island, be on the lookout for some unusual animals like the island fox and the brown pelican.

If you prefer to fly, check out Channel Islands Aviation, (805) 987-1301, located in the Camarillo Airport. Following a half-hour scenic flight over Anacapa and Santa Cruz Islands, you'll land on Santa Rosa Island. A tour guide will take you around the island where you'll see a century-old cattle ranch and other island highlights. You can hike around a bit, have a picnic lunch (which you supply), and explore more of the island before you fly back to Camarillo. Adult fare is $85 roundtrip; children 2 - 12 years cost $60.

Hours: Listed under each island.
Admission: Listed under each island.
Ages: 6 years and up.

CONEJO VALLEY COMMUNITY PARK and BOTANIC ☼ GARDEN

(805) 495-2163   !

1300 Hendrix Avenue, Thousand Oaks
(EXIT VENTURA FWY [101] N. ON LYNN RD., R. ON GAINSBOROUGH RD.)

This nature park is delightful in size and scope. There are acres and acres of green rolling hills, and a creek running throughout. The creek, by itself, is a major attraction. My boys loved looking for crawdads and, of course, stepping on the rocks, with the possible thrill of getting a bit wet. Almost a full day's adventure can be had by climbing the gnarled, old oak trees. There are cement pathways throughout the park making much of it stroller accessible. The ambiance here is peaceful, unless you bring your kids, of course!

The upper field sports a baseball diamond, while a basketball court is across the way. A playground is located in front of the community center building. A covered picnic area with barbecue pits is also available here.

The Botanic Garden is bigger than it first appears. One short path traverses through a variety of sceneries, looping around and covering most of the garden. Another nature trail goes up and around the hillside, following a creek through oak and willow trees before looping back around. I don't know how much actual plant knowledge my kids gained from our garden walk. I'm always hopeful, though, that just spending time in such an environment will help them develop an appreciation for the beautiful gift of nature.

Hours: The park is open daily from dawn to dusk. The community center is open Mon. - Fri., 9am - 7pm; Sat., 9am - 4pm; Sun., noon - 4pm.

Admission: Free

Ages: All

LIBBEY PARK   ☼

Ojai Avenue [or Highway 150]), Ojai !
(ENTER DIRECTLY OFF EITHER OJAI AVE. [150], WITH SIGNAL AS THE NEAREST CROSS STREET, OR FROM OJAI AVE. TURN S. ON MONTGOMERY ST.)

This sprawling park is a combination of several kinds of parks. The playground area, accessible from Ojai Avenue, is terrific with heavy-duty, plastic tubes to crawl through, suspension bridges to cross, plus slides and swings. Kids love squishing the wonderfully fine sand between their bare toes. A thirty-five-foot long talking tube is mostly underground, with just the funnel-shaped ends above ground, at kid-level. Have your child talk into one end while you listen at the other.

Tennis courts with stadium seating are abundant here, as this is the home of an annual spring tournament that attracts the country's top-ranked collegiate players. The half-dome-shaped Libbey Bowl has graded seating for concerts, or for your young stars to make their (pretend) debut.

Further back, or entering from Montgomery Street, is the nature section of the park. Kids naturally gravitate to the creek that is surrounded by glorious old oak and sycamore trees. For just a little while, you'll feel refreshingly removed from civilization. The OJAI VALLEY NATURE TRAIL also begins (or ends) here. Tip: Top off your time with a visit to the ice cream store across Ojai Street, in the Antique Mall.

Hours: The park is open daily from dawn to dusk.

Admission: Free

Ages: All

MORANDA PARK   ☼

(805) 986-6555 !
Moranda Parkway, Port Hueneme
(EXIT VENTURA FWY [101] S. ON VENTURA RD., L. ON PORT HUENEME RD., R. ON MORANDA PKY.)

This hilly green park is spread out, and diverse with eight tennis courts, two softball fields, horseshoe pits, a sand volleyball court, a basketball court, and a nice playground. A path goes around and through the park making it a great place to stroll, jog, or bike. Stop to play, or have a picnic while exploring Oxnard and Ventura!

Hours: Open daily from dawn to dusk.
Admission: Free
Ages: All

OJAI VALLEY NATURE TRAIL

(805) 654-3951

Ojai

(THE TRAIL BEGINS OR ENDS AT LIBBEY PARK OR FOSTER COUNTY PARK, WHICH IS ALONG VENTURA AVE., HWY. [33].)

This nine-mile paved trail is great for strollers, bikes, horses, or just walking. The pathway follows along the major street of Ventura Avenue, but the oak and sycamore trees make it pretty, while shading a good portion of it.

Ages: All

RANCHO SIERRA VISTA / SATWIWA INDIAN CULTURE CENTER

(818) 597-1036

Potrero Road, Newbury Park

(EXIT VENTURA FWY [101] S. ON CAMPINO DOS RIOS/WENDY DR. ABOUT THREE MILES, R. ON POTRERO ABOUT 1 MILE.)

The chaparral-covered hillsides and large grassy fields make this an ideal place for some great hiking and/or picnicking. Various trails hook up to the Pt. Mugu State Park.

Come on a Sunday to the Satwiwa Native American Culture Center, located in the park, to listen to a traditionally-dressed, Native American tell stories, or to watch a craft demonstration. The Center also has Chumash exhibits such as gourds, pictures, and text. Outside, there are picnic tables and a Chumash round dwelling.

Hours: The park is open daily from dawn to dusk. The Culture Center is only open on Sundays from 10am - 5pm.
Admission: Free
Ages: 8 years and up.

WILDWOOD REGIONAL PARK

(805) 381-2741

W. Avenue de los Arboles, Thousand Oaks

(EXIT VENTURA FWY [101] N. AT LYNN RD., L. AT AVENIDA DE LOS ARBOLES, ALL THE WAY TO THE END.)

Take a walk on the wild side at Wildwood Regional Park. The narrow, dirt trails and service roads are great for real hiking. There are two major trail heads that lead to an extensive trail system for hikers, bikers, and equestrians. Come prepared by bringing water bottles, sunscreen, and backpacks with food for designated picnic areas. Although hiking downhill is easy, plan twice as much time for the hike back up.

Some highlights along the somewhat shorter trails, which are still an almost all day event, include Indian Cave with re-created Indian rock drawings, the Nature Center, Little Falls, and Paradise Falls, which is a forty-foot waterfall that you'll hear before you actually reach it.

As you walk along the creek or throughout the chaparral and woodlands, be on the lookout for wildlife, such as mule deers or lizards.

Hike here during the spring months and you'll see an abundance of wildflowers. I encourage you to get a trail map as different routes have different highlights that you'll want to explore. The park offers wonderful, fun, and educational programs like Saturday Night S'Mores, Full Moon Hikes, and Outdoor Experiential Workshops. Enjoy nature, almost in your backyard!

Hours: Open daily from dawn to dusk.

Admission: Free. (Some of the programs cost between $3 - $4.)

Ages: 4 years and up. Kids will tire easily.

MALLS - Kid's Clubs

This section is not to tell you where to go shopping, but rather to inform you of free kid's clubs and programs that your local mall has to offer. Be entertained, enjoy, and create (and maybe get a little shopping in, too)!

THE GALLERIA, AT SOUTH BAY - KIDZ PLAY

(310) 371-7546

1815 Hawthorne Boulevard at Artesia Boulevard, Redondo Beach
(EXIT SAN DIEGO FWY [405] W. ON ARTESIA BLVD. THE SHOW IS HELD AT THE
PICNIC PLACE STAGE, LEVEL THREE.)

Twice a month kids can come to the Galleria and enjoy an hour of
entertainment such as stories, puppets, an animal show, or a sing-
along. Make new friends as you and your child become regulars!

Hours: The shows are presented the first and third Tuesdays of
each month at 10:30am.
Admission: Free
Ages: 1½ - 6 years.

LAKEWOOD CENTER MALL - A2Z KIDZ CLUB

(562) 531-6707

200 Lakewood Center Mall, Lakewood
(EXIT ARTESIA FWY [91] S. ON LAKEWOOD BLVD.)

The first 225 kids are invited to participate in a fun, usually seasonal
craft, like decorating a Father's Day barbecuing apron in June, or sand
buckets in August. It's a great club to belong to as kids love to make
projects, and all the materials are supplied for free! There are also
member discounts on various products and restaurants in the mall.

Hours: The club meets the second Tuesday of every month from
4pm - 7pm.
Admission: Free
Ages: 3 - 12 years.

NORTHRIDGE FASHION CENTER - NFC KIDS KLUB

(818) 885-9700

At Tampa Avenue and Nordhoff Street, Northridge
(FROM SAN DIEGO FWY [405], EXIT E. ON NORDHOFF ST. FROM VENTURA FWY
[101], EXIT N. ON TAMPA AVENUE.)

Become a NFC kid and get in on all the fun! Storytelling, singing,
dancing, or even short plays are on the morning's agenda. The Klub
also gives its young members discounts at participating mall stores,
and a free gift on their birthday.

Hours: The third Thurs. of each month at 10:30am in Bullock's
Court.
Admission: Free
Ages: 2 - 12 years.

SOUTHBAY PAVILION - LI'L SHOPPERS CLUB

(310) 327-4822

Avalon Boulevard, Carson
(EXIT THE 405 FWY AT AVALON BLVD. THE CLUB MEETS AT CENTER COURT.)

Encourage your little shoppers to join the Li'l Shoppers Club. Children enjoy the forty-five-minute shows put on by some great children's entertainers.

Hours: The first and third Thursday of every month at 6pm.
Admission: Free
Ages: 1½ - 8 years.

STONEWOOD MALL - KID'S CLUB   ☀
(562) 861-9233   !

251 Stonewood Street, Downey
(EXIT SAN GABRIEL FWY [605] W. ON FIRESTONE BLVD., R. ON LAKEWOOD BLVD., R. ON STONEWOOD ST.)

Join Kid's Club, held in the fountain court, for a half-hour of fun and entertainment. The shows feature singers, dancers, puppets, or magicians. What a great family outing!

Hours: Every Thursday at 6pm.
Admission: Free
Ages: 1½ - 8 years.

VALENCIA TOWN CENTER - KIDSTOWN   ☀
(805) 287-9050   !

24201 W. Valencia Boulevard, Valencia
(EXIT GOLDEN STATE FWY [5] E. ON VALENCIA BLVD. KIDSTOWN IS USUALLY HELD IN THE SEARS COURT.)

Kidstown comes to town every other Thursday morning. Join in the forty-five-minute show of puppetry or song and dance - it's all interactive fun for young kids.

Hours: Every other Thursday morning at 10:30am.
Admission: Free
Ages: 1½ - 6 years.

BREA MALL - KIDS & COMPANY   ☀
(714) 990-BREA (2732)   !

1065 Brea Mall, Brea
(EXIT ORANGE FWY [57] W. ON IMPERIAL HIGHWAY, AT STATE COLLEGE.)

Kids and Company presents a free, forty-five-minute show once a month that varies in context from storytelling to puppetry to singing, etc. This is a fun way to enjoy entertainment with your child.

Hours: Shows are the first Tuesday of every month at 10am.
Admission: Free
Ages: 1½ - 6 years.

MALL OF ORANGE - KIDS KORP
(714) 998-0440

2298 N. Orange Mall on Tustin Avenue, Orange
(EXIT COSTA MESA FWY [55] E. ON LINCOLN, L. ON TUSTIN AVE. OR, EXIT [55] FWY,
E. ON KATELLA, R. ON TUSTIN.)

Kids Korp. is a club where the first 300 kids can decorate themed crafts with their parents. It's designed for kids and parents to spend some fun time together, to encourage your child's creativity, and to take home a seasonal memento, like a Father's Day baseball cap or a Halloween tote bag. Members also receive coupons for special values on meals and merchandise at participating Mall of Orange stores.

Hours: The club is usually held on Tuesdays from 4pm - 7pm; call for dates.
Admission: Free
Ages: 3 - 12 years.

WESTMINSTER MALL - VIK (VERY IMPORTANT KID) CLUB
(714) 898-2550

Bolsa Avenue and Golden West Street, Westminster
(EXIT SAN DIEGO FWY [405] AT GOLDEN WEST ST.)

Calling all younger children - come and enjoy a forty-five-minute show of magic, storytelling, puppets, or sing-alongs. Afterwards, each child receives a small treat.

Hours: The show is presented on the first Thursday of every month at 5:30pm.
Admission: Free
Ages: 1½ - 8 years.

PLAZA BONITA KIDS CLUB
(619) 267-2850

3030 Plaza Bonita Road, National City
(EXIT JACOB DEKEMA FWY [805] E. ON BONITA RD., L. ON PLAZA BONITA RD.)

Have some fun while making new friends at the Kids Club at Plaza Bonita. Free weekly entertainment includes puppet shows, toe-tapping music, storytelling, and/or singing. Each club "meeting" starts with Kid Aerobics or jazzercise. Meet in the Center Court near J. C. Penney.

Hours: Every Wednesday at 3:30pm
Admission: Free
Ages: 1 -10 years.

PLAZA CAMINO REAL KID'S CLUB
(760) 729-7927

El Camino Real at the Plaza Camino Real Mall, Carlsbad
(EXIT SAN DIEGO FWY [5] E. ON 78 FWY, R. ON EL CAMINO REAL)

Come join in the Kid's Club fun at the Center Court, lower level, at Plaza Camino Real. Clubs usually begin with an action warm-up of Kid Aerobics or jazzercise. Free, half-hour, weekly entertainment includes laughing with kids' comedians, dancing, singing, storytelling, and general silliness.

Hours: Every Tuesday at 10am.
Admission: Free
Ages: 1 - 10 years.

MUSEUMS

When I was a child, the word "museum" conjured up images of quietly walking through rooms filled with great works of art (i.e. boring). While children are (almost) never too young to start appreciating art, there is a whole new world of kid-friendly museums that captivates their imaginations, hearts, and even their hands!

A few tips about museums:

• Exhibits rotate, so be flexible in your expectations.

• If you really like the museum, become a member. You'll reap benefits such as visiting the museum whenever you want during the course of a year; being invited to members-only events; receiving newsletters; etc.

• You can "$ee" L.A. or you can "¢.E.E." L.A.! The Cultural Entertainment Events card (C.E.E. L.A.) is an incredible way to explore twenty top museums, including Autry Museum, George C. Page Museum, Los Angeles Children's Museum, Kidseum, Natural History Museum of Los Angeles, the Richard Nixon Library and Birthplace, and more for only $40 a year for your family! (i.e. A family is defined as four to six members; up to three generations.) This card also offers 50% off major sporting events, and theater and concert venues - as often as you want to go. A minimum of 25% of every dollar spent on the card is donated directly to participating museums. So, support the arts and "C.E.E." them as often as you want! Call (818) 957-9400 for more details.

• If you're looking for a special gift, most museum gift shops carry unique merchandise that is geared towards their specialty. For instance, natural history museums have dinosaur paraphernalia; airplane museums carry everything relating to aviation; art museums carry books, puzzles, and crayon books pertaining to art; etc.

• It's an unusual place for a birthday party!

• Check each museum's calendar of special events. They'll include anything from making adobe bricks, celebrating heritage day, eating ice-cream at an old-fashioned social, creating seasonal crafts, etc.

• At some of the fine art museums, your kids will take more of an interest in the exhibits by participating in a children's tour, doing a paper treasure hunt, acting out the art-work, or drawing their favorite pieces (bring a clipboard, paper, and pencil).

• Most museums offer group discounts for ten or more people. School tours get a discount, and usually a more interactive tour than a general-public tour.

ADOBE DE PALOMARES

(909) 623-2198 $

491 East Arrow Highway, Pomona
(EXIT SAN BERNARDINO FWY [10] N. ON TOWNE AVE., L. ON ARROW HWY.)

This thirteen-room restored adobe was originally built in 1854. A guided tour of the house includes seeing authentic period furniture, as well as cooking utensils (how did they live without so many technical doohickeys?!), tools, antique clothing, and children's toys. The grounds are lovely. Adjacent to the Adobe is the Palomare Park, so bring a picnic lunch and enjoy some running around space.

Hours: Open Sundays from 2pm - 5pm
Admission: $2 for adults; $1 for children 12 years and under.
Ages: 6 years and up.

AEROSPACE MUSEUM

(213) 744-7400 $

Exposition Park, Los Angeles
(EXIT HARBOR FWY [110] W. ON EXPOSITION BLVD., L. ON FLOWER, L. ON FIGUEROA. OR, EXIT SANTA MONICA FWY [10] S. ON VERMONT, L. ON EXPOSITION, R. ON FIGUEROA.)

This building is hard to miss with a jet fighter perched precariously on its top! The atmosphere is uplifting with planes (such as the 1902 Wright Flyer), jets (such as the Northrop T-38 jet trainer), and a space capsule (the Gemini II) suspended from the ceiling in mock flight. Catwalk-like ramps add to the airy feeling. Educating the public on flight technology is accomplished through several interactive displays. Kids have hands-on fun designing their own computer-generated jet fighter, and learning the principles of aerodynamics using a control stick. Space Station Earth has video displays to monitor our weather, and the weather on Venus or Jupiter. A weather station on the roof of the museum shows the collected data, such as temperature, humidity, barometric pressure, etc., on the first floor in the museum.

There are many fascinating space exhibits here including a darkened room with a big screen movie that explains how we reach for the stars. Kids will glean even more information about our universe on a school tour here, plus they'll get a closer look at the DC-3 and DC-8 planes parked outside the museum.

A wonderful way to round out your day is to have a picnic and visit one of the other attractions in this complex - CALIFORNIA AFRO-AMERICAN MUSEUM, CALIFORNIA SCIENCE CENTER, EXPOSITION PARK, NATURAL HISTORY MUSEUM OF LOS ANGELES, and 3-D IMAX THEATER

Hours: Open daily from 10am - 5pm. Closed New Year's Day, Thanksgiving, and Christmas.
Admission: Free. Parking is $5.
Ages: 3 years and up.

AMERICAN HERITAGE PARK / MILITARY MUSEUM ☀
(818) 442-1776 $$

1918 N. Rosemead Boulevard, South El Monte
(EXIT POMONA FWY [60] N. AT ROSEMEAD BLVD. THE ENTRANCE IS ON THE R. SIDE
OF THE STREET, AT THE NORTHERN PART OF WHITTIER NARROWS
RECREATION AREA.)

Attention! Over 100 pieces of equipment, representing all branches of the United States Military, can be found at this outside museum. The collection contains vehicles and weapons from World War II, and the Korean and Vietnam wars. It includes Jeeps, amphibious trucks, ambulances, cannons, gun turrets, and thirty-ton Sherman tanks. The vehicles can be looked at, but not sat on or touched.

To the untrained eye it looks like a random compilation of old military equipment. And it is. However, some pieces are in the process of being restored, and some have been used in movies and T.V. shows. The volunteers are knowledgeable and know many of the "inside" stories about the vehicles. Idea: This is an ideal setting if your kids are studying any of the wars and want to make a video.

Hours: Open Sat. - Sun. from noon - 4:30pm; open Wed., Thurs., and Fri. for groups by appointment.

Admission: $4 for adults; $3 for seniors and military; $2 for ages 10 - 16; 50¢ for ages 5 - 9; children 4 years and under are free.

Ages: 4 years and up.

ANGELS ATTIC ☀
(310) 394-8331 $$

516 Colorado Avenue, Santa Monica
(EXIT SANTA MONICA FWY [10] N. ON 5ᵀᴴ ST., R. ON COLORADO AVE.)

Picture a quaint Victorian house filled with beautiful collectable dolls and doll houses; now add a warm, inviting atmosphere and you've got Angels Attic. This 1895 Queen Anne house/museum has antique toys, dolls, and over sixty doll houses. Each doll house is complete and the architectural style and furnishings reflect the times in which it was built (a mini-history lesson). Although little hands may not touch, little eyes will enjoy looking, especially since most exhibits are at eye level. Tea time, with homemade cake and cookies, is also available with advanced reservations and an additional $7.50 per person.

At Christmas time, the outside of Angels Attic is decorated and so is every doll house - truly a mini-extravaganza. Don't miss Santa's Workshop in miniature, with reindeer, Santa and Mrs. Claus, and over 130 elves completing the festive scene.

The small gift shop sells doll house accessories, and books and magazines related to collecting miniatures and dolls.

Hours: Open Thurs. - Sun. from 12:30pm - 4:30pm.

Admission: $6.50 for adults; $4 for seniors and students; $3.50 for
                 children 12 years and under.
Ages: 5 years old and up.

ANTELOPE VALLEY INDIAN MUSEUM   ☼
(805) 942-0662 $
Avenue "M", between 150ᵗʰ and 170ᵗʰ Streets East, Lancaster
*(EXIT ANTELOPE VALLEY FWY [14] E. ON AVE. "K", R. ON 150ᵀᴴ ST. EAST, L. ON
AVE. "M". OR EXIT PEARBLOSSOM HIGHWAY [138] N. ON 165ᵀᴴ ST. EAST, TURNS
INTO 170ᵀᴴ ST., TURN L. ON AVE. "M".)*

Built into and around rock formations of the Mojave Desert, the
outside of this Indian museum looks incongruously like a Swiss Chalet.
The inside is just as unique. Once the home of artist Howard Edward,
portions of the interior (i.e. walls, ceilings, and flooring) are composed
of boulders. My kids' reaction was simply "WOW!" The large, main
room is lined with Kachina dolls on the upper shelves and painted
panels of the dolls on the ceiling. (The Hopi People believed that
Kachina dolls brought rain.) The unusual furniture and the support
beams are made from the Joshua tree. A connecting room has several
glass-cased displays of pottery shards, once used for money and
jewelry; cradle-boards; baskets; and various plants and items made
from plants, such as yucca fiber sandals.

Kids love climbing up the narrow stony steps into a large display
room, also "carved out" of rock. Exhibits here include arrowheads,
whale bone tools, shells, whale ribs, harpoons, and weapons. Go back
down a few of the steps, stop, look up, and you'll see re-created cave
paintings and Indian dioramas.

Outside, you'll pass by a series of small cottages that were once
used as guest houses. Your destination is Joshua Cottage, a place that
has some hands-on activities for kids. They can grind corn with stone
mortars and pestles, try their hand at using a pump drill to drill holes,
and "saw" with a bow drill to create smoke. Kids can even learn how to
make a pine needle whisk broom. (The brooms may not much practical
use now-a-days, but it's a fun and educational project.) Docents will
gladly explain the usage of various seeds and other plant parts. The
small adjacent room is a gallery also used for educational programs.

The museum is part of the California Department of Parks and
Recreation. Enjoy an easy half-mile nature walk on the trails through
the buttes and desert just behind the Indian Museum. A guidebook
(50¢) explains the fourteen Native American symbols on the posts
along the trail.

Hours: Open from the middle of September through the middle
             of June on Sat. - Sun. from 11am - 4pm. Tours are
             available Tues., Wed., and Thurs. by appointment.
Admission: $3 for adults; $1.50 for ages 6 - 12; children 5 years and
                 under are free.
Ages: 5 years and up.

AUTRY MUSEUM OF WESTERN HERITAGE   ☼
(213) 667-2000 $$$
4700 Western Heritage Way, in Griffith Park, Los Angeles
(GOING N. ON GOLDEN STATE FWY [5] OR W. VENTURA FWY [134], EXIT AT ZOO DR.
AND FOLLOW THE SIGNS. GOING E. ON 134, EXIT S. ON VICTORY BLVD., L. ON ZOO
DR. GOING S. ON 5, EXIT S. ON WESTERN, L. ON VICTORY BLVD. TO ZOO DR. THE
MUSEUM IS ACROSS THE PARKING LOT FROM THE L. A. ZOO.)

The cowboy lifestyle lassos our imagination. Bryce, my middle son,
wants to become a cowboy missionary (yes, he is special), so this
museum really spurred on his desire, at least regarding the cowboy part
of his career choice. It will also delight fans of the Old West with its
complete array of paintings, clothing, tools, weapons, and interesting
artifacts. Movie clips and videos throughout the museum highlight
specific areas of this romanticized period. In the Spirit of Imagination
Hall, a big hit is sitting on a saddle and making riding motions to
become part of an old western movie showing on a screen behind the
rider.

My kids particularly enjoyed the small Children's Discovery Gallery,
where they dressed up like cowboys, played with toys in a re-created
town-home attic, "washed" clothes and put them through a wringer, and
sat on a lifelike horse statue. The entire museum is interesting and
stroller-friendly, but you do have to keep your kids corralled, as most of
the exhibits are not hands-on. Saturday programs, for ages 6 - 12, are
more interactive with storytelling, games, and even sing-alongs. Ask
about their weekly summer history classes for kids. A cafe is on the
grounds, as is a wonderful, grassy picnic area.

Hours: Open Tues. - Sun. from 10am - 5pm. Closed
            Thanksgiving and Christmas.
Admission: $7.50 for adults; $5 for seniors and ages 13 - 18; $3 for
            children 2 - 12 years old. (Certain discounts available
            through AAA.)
Ages: 4 years and up.

CALIFORNIA AFRO-AMERICAN MUSEUM   ☀
(213) 744-7432 $
600 State Drive, at Exposition Park, Los Angeles
(EXIT THE HARBOR FWY [110] W. ON EXPOSITION BLVD., L. ON FLOWER, L. ON
FIGUEROA. OR, EXIT SANTA MONICA FWY [10] S. ON VERMONT, L. ON EXPOSITION,
R. ON FIGUEROA. PARKING IS AVAILABLE THE FIRST DRIVEWAY ON THE R. IT'S
LOCATED IN THE SAME BUILDING COMPLEX AS THE CALIFORNIA SCIENCE
MUSEUM.)

This museum portrays the works of Afro-American artists
documenting the Afro-American experience in this country. The rotating
exhibits are interesting for kids of all races. The exhibits we saw were
various playhouse-size houses and work environments made from
recycled materials, along with photographs, and various sculptures.
Another room contained lots of Western artifacts, and the fascinating

history of James Beckwourth, an explorer, trapper, and businessman who lived from 1798 - 1866. (See the nearby AEROSPACE MUSEUM, CALIFORNIA SCIENCE CENTER, EXPOSITION PARK, NATURAL HISTORY MUSEUM OF LOS ANGELES, and 3-D IMAX THEATER.)

Hours: Open Tues. - Sun. from 10am - 5pm. Closed New Year's Day, Memorial Day, Thanksgiving, and Christmas.
Admission: Free. Parking costs $5.
Ages: 5 years and up.

CALIFORNIA HERITAGE MUSEUM

(310) 392-8537

2612 Main Street, Santa Monica
(TAKE SANTA MONICA FWY [10] E. ALMOST TO THE END. EXIT S. ON 4TH ST., R. ON PICO, L. ON MAIN.)

This two-story house/museum is hard to miss with its giant cowboy sign out front! A grassy lawn welcomes picnickers. Inside, the downstairs living room is cozy and rustic-looking. (I like the antler candelabras on the mantel). The dining room atmosphere is more elegant as the table is set with fine china. The restored kitchen is the one Merle Norman originally used to cook-up her cosmetic recipes. (From such humble beginnings . . .)

The upstairs is redecorated each time a new exhibit is installed. Often the exhibits are aimed at appealing to the younger generation. Past themes have included cowboys; guitars from all over the world; children's books and illustrations; and model trains. Call for information on the current display.

Hours: Open Wed. - Sat., 11am - 4pm; Sun., noon - 4pm.
Admission: $3 for adults; $2 for seniors and students; children 12 years and under are free.
Ages: 5 years and up.

CALIFORNIA SCIENCE CENTER

(213) 744-2533   n/a

700 State Drive, Exposition Park, Los Angeles
(EXIT HARBOR FWY [110] W. ON EXPOSITION BLVD., L. ON FLOWER, L. ON FIGUEROA. OR, EXIT SANTA MONICA FWY [10] S. ON VERMONT, L. ON EXPOSITION, R. ON FIGUEROA. PARKING IS AVAILABLE AT THE FIRST DRIVEWAY ON THE R.)

What a face lift! The former California Museum of Science and Industry is being transformed into an incredible state-of-the-art, interactive, math and science technological wonder. Phase I, of the three-phase rebuilding project, is scheduled to be completed by February, 1998. Along with the following exhibits, the facility will include a special exhibits gallery and food and retail shops. The outside courtyard will feature science-oriented art pieces, such as a giant sphere that represents the solar system and a visualization of a DNA spiral. Enter through the doors of the Center into the Science Court, which offers a preview and passageway to each of the four major exhibition areas. The twelve-story Court atrium will be an attraction in itself with a fifty-foot kinetic unfolding structure, created by an artist-engineer, that is suspended by cables; a visitor-propelled high-wire bicycle; and a yo-yo, with a six-foot translucent wheel, that travels the length of the Court.

The first exhibit area is called, "World of Life" and its purpose is to explore how living things function. The centerpiece will be Body Works, a fifty-foot long, prostrate, transparent human figure whose bones, muscles, and organ systems will be illuminated by fiber optics. Towards the head of the model, large screen images of real body organs, along with other footage, will explain how our body parts work together. The five exhibits surrounding Body Works are Energizing Life, Supplying Life, Creating Life, Controlling Life, and Defending Life. The displays will be comprised of live plants and animals, a huge model of the brain, preserved organs, hands-on activities to reinforce the concepts presented, computer touch screens, and more.

Another major exhibit area, "Creative World," will showcase the environment people have built to meet their needs for food, shelter, clothing, communication, and transportation. Children are challenged to construct a building, using scale model parts, that can stand up when subjected to an earthquake on a shake table. Then, they can actually feel an earthquake in a room that looks like part of a high-rise office tower. Still want to shake, rattle, and roll? Visit Technopolis, an interactive theater, and experience what an entire city goes through during an earthquake. Learn why some buildings collapse and others don't, and what difference soil can make. And this is only one aspect of Creative World! Kids can also play at virtual reality programs; whisper into a parabolic dish and have someone across the room hear; immerse themselves in Hollywood-type stage settings; interact with robotics; compare and contrast themselves with a mouse and other animals; play pinball to learn about math; etc.

Another component of each of the major exhibit areas will be a Discovery Room, containing a series of drawers with experiments, activities, or exercises that kids can delve into. Is science supposed to be this much fun?!

Future plans include a third major exhibit area, "World of the Pacific," an enormous aquarium. It will feature animals and eco systems ranging from the coral reef to the tropical rain forest. Walk underneath a glass tunnel while sharks and schools of fish swim above your head. Learn about tides, currents, islands, and ice formations in innovative ways. "World Beyond" will be the final major exhibit area. It has the small task of examining the universe utilizing models, equipment, instruments, and lots of visuals. Suspended air and space craft will provide a setting for conducting space mission simulations, including a flight training center. An on-site science and math public elementary school and an educational resource center are also in the works. Ask about the numerous special classes and programs being offered for adults and children. Don't forget about "Science Comes Alive," forty-five minute, audience participatory shows now held at the museum theater on weekends. In one show, for example, audiences became neurons sending messages to a six-foot stuffed brain. (This is more stimulating than it sounds.) Call (213) 744-7444 for booking a production for a group during the week, or for more information. Come encounter science in ways you never imagined, at the California Science Museum!

(Check out the nearby AEROSPACE MUSEUM, CALIFORNIA AFRO-AMERICAN MUSEUM, 3-D IMAX THEATER, and NATURAL HISTORY MUSEUM OF LOS ANGELES.)

Hours: To be announced.
Admission: To be announced.
Ages: 3 years and up

CAROLE & BARRY KAYE MUSEUM OF MINIATURES   ☼

(213) 937-6464 $$$

5900 Wilshire Boulevard, Los Angeles
(EXIT SANTA MONICA FWY [10] N. ON LA BREA, L. ON WILSHIRE.)

This building houses "the biggest little collection of miniatures in the world." The displays range from one-room dioramas to relatively huge houses and castles. Most of the exhibits have step-stools, so that children can see every little thing. The first floor gallery has a replica of Fontainebleau that has furnishings, wallpaper, chandeliers, silverware, etc., complete to the minutest detail. A bakery shop has tiny little cakes and other pastries so real looking that you can almost taste 'em. On a grand (but still small) scale is an exquisite Victorian village.

The second floor has a lot of kid-appeal. Ships, cars, airplanes, and trains each have a display area to themselves. For those who still think that miniatures are just for girls playing with doll houses, check out Old West Town with its cowboys and Indians. Action figures in other displays include samurai warriors, Batman, RoboCop, and more.

Carnival Nights depicts a pier scene, complete with a "big" Ferris wheel, and real fish swimming underneath it! A collection of First Ladies, from Martha Washington to Nancy Reagan, are in reproductions of their Inaugural Ball gowns. Just a few other highlights include: Knights in shining armor; a miniature violin workshop inside an actual violin; and an old-fashioned brass diving helmet with a diver and his equipment inside. There is too much to mention here because 14,000 square feet is maximum coverage for miniatures! If all this makes you long for a Lilliputian lifestyle, check out the gift shop. You'll find everything you need to furnish and decorate your miniature dream house - you can even buy the house.

Hours: Open Tues. - Sat., 10am - 5pm; Sun., 11am - 5pm.

Admission: $7.50 for adults; $6.50 for seniors; $5 for students (13 - 21 years); $3 for ages 3 - 12. Parking is 50¢ an hour on the street, $5 for the day at a lot across the street, or $1.20 an hour (which is the validated price) for parking under the Mutual Benefit building next to the museum.

Ages: 6 years and up.

CRAFT AND FOLK ART MUSEUM   ☼

(213) 937-5544 $

5814 Wilshire Boulevard, Los Angeles
(EXIT SANTA MONICA FWY [10] N. ON FAIRFAX, R. ON WILSHIRE BLVD. IT IS LOCATED ON MUSEUM ROW, WITH SEVERAL OTHER MUSEUMS CLOSE BY.)

This museum displays ethnic and folk art from all over the world. Since exhibits rotate, I advise calling before your visit to see if the current exhibit is one that would be interesting to your kids. My family has seen toys and dolls from around the world (which definitely qualifies as kid-friendly), and a colorful exhibit on masks.

Hours: Open Tues. - Sun. from 11am - 5pm.

Admission: $4 for adults; $2.50 for seniors and students; children 11 years and under are free.

Ages: 5 years and up.

THE DRUM BARRACKS CIVIL WAR MUSEUM   ☼

(310) 548-7509 $

1052 Banning Boulevard, Wilmington
(EXIT HARBOR FWY [110] E. ON PACIFIC COAST HIGHWAY, R. ON AVALON BLVD., L. ON "L" ST., R. ON BANNING BLVD.)

The year is 1861 and the Civil War has broken out. Although most of the fighting was done in the east, troops from Camp Drum, California fought on the Union side. Your forty-five-minute tour of the medium-size barracks/house/museum starts in the library research room. The first video is six minutes long and tells the history of Camp Drum through reenactments, with a costumed character narrating. Do your kids enjoy a good mystery? The second video features the Drum Barracks in an episode of "Unsolved Mysteries." Apparently, a few good ghosts from the Civil War still hang out here. Needless to say, my kids heard "ghostly" noises throughout the rest of our visit.

The parlor room is where the officers entertained. Besides period furniture, it also has a stereoscope, which is an early Viewmaster™, to look through. Q: Why didn't people smile for photographs back then? A: Many people had bad teeth, plus it took a half hour to take a picture.

The hallway shows a picture of the Camel Corps. which is a regiment that actually rode camels. It also has a flag from an 1863 battlefield - have your kids count the stars (states). Upstairs, the armory room has a few original weapons, like a musket and some swords. A rotating exhibit up here has displayed a hospital room with beds, old medical instruments, and a lifelike mannequin of a wounded soldier; a quarter master's quarters; etc. The officer's bedroom has furniture, personal effects, and old-fashioned clothing. Q: Why did women usually wear brown wedding dresses? A: You'll have to take the tour to find out!

Hours: Tours are given on the hour between 10am - 1pm, Tues. - Thurs.; and between 11:30am - 2:30pm, Sat. - Sun.
Admission: $2.50 per person.
Ages: 5 years and up.

EDWARDS AIR FORCE BASE / AIR FORCE FLIGHT ☼ TEST CENTER MUSEUM
(805) 277-8050   !

Edwards Air Force Base
(EXIT THE GOLDEN STATE FWY [5] N. ON THE ANTELOPE VALLEY FWY [14] FWY. EXIT [14] E. ON EDWARDS/ROSAMOND.)

Edwards Air Force Base is the premier site for flight research and flight testing. (On you're way into the base, you'll drive by a huge dry lake which is the main landing site.) The museum, at least for now, is located in two places on the base compound. Kids can walk around the fourteen or so aircraft on display on the corner of Rosamond Boulevard and Lancaster Boulevard. The planes vary in design, shape, size, and maneuverability. Some of the planes currently on display include A-12, B-52D, T-33A, and an F-104A. (Even if these names don't mean anything to you, the planes are still cool to look at.)

The small, indoor, storefront museum is temporarily located on Payne Avenue. A larger, permanent facility is being built where the planes now reside. The museum is packed with memorabilia fitting for the birthplace of supersonic flight. One section is dedicated to "Mach Busters," the men who broke sound barriers, including, of course, Chuck Yeager. It shows and tells how planes (and men) were tested for this significant breakthrough. The "First Flights Wall" is a model display of the more than 100 aircraft that completed their first flight at Edwards AFB. Other items on exhibit include aircraft propulsion systems, life support equipment, photographs, flight jackets, and personal memorabilia. Ask to see the film on the history of Edwards and on flight testing. Note: There is a Burger King and Baskin Robins just down the street. (Also see the NASA DRYDEN VISITORS CENTER.)

Hours: Open Tues. - Sat. from 9am - 5pm.
Admission: Free
Ages: 6 years and up.

EL MONTE HISTORICAL MUSEUM   ☼
(818) 580-2232   !
3150 North Tyler Avenue, El Monte

(EXIT SAN BERNARDINO FWY [10] S. ON SANTA ANITA, L. ON MILDRED ST., L. ON NORTH TYLER AVE. IT'S ON THE CORNER, NEXT TO EL MONTE SCHOOL.)

A visit to this adobe-style museum offers fascinating glimpses into the history of the United States, as well as the history of the pioneers of El Monte. There is plenty to see and learn to keep young people's interest peaked, even though no touching is allowed. Items in the numerous glass displays are labeled, making it easy to self-tour. However, I highly recommend taking a guided tour, given for groups of ten or more people, so your family doesn't miss out on the many details and explanations of the exhibits.

My kids were captivated by the hallway showcasing Gay's Lion Farm, a local training ground in the 1920's for lions used in motion pictures. The photos depict the large cats interacting with people in various circus-type acts. There are also several adorable shots of lion "kittens." A lion's tail and teeth are on display, too. The Heritage Room, towards the back, looks like an old-fashioned living room with antique furniture and a piano, plus cases of glassware, ladies' boots, and clothing. The walls are lined with pictures of walnut growers and other first-residents of El Monte.

The Pioneer Room has wonderful collections of typewriters, lamps/lanterns, dolls, toys, books, bells, quilts, army medals, and Bibles. It also contains ornate swords, a flag (with two bullet holes in it) from the battlefield at Gettysburg, a piece of the Berlin wall, George Washington's lantern, and an actual letter written by the Father of our Country who, by the way, had nice handwriting! The Frontier Room is equally interesting with early-day policeman and fireman hats; police badges and guns; a 1911 Model T; a wall of old tools; early Native American artifacts; and a re-created old-time law enforcement office.

The huge Lexington Room is sub-divided into smaller, themed "rooms" such as a turn-of-the-century schoolroom with desks, maps, and schoolwork; an old-time general store with shelf-loads of merchandise; a barber shop with a chair; a music shop with ukuleles, violins, a Victrola, and more; and a dressmaker's shop with beautiful dresses, sewing machines, elegant hair combs, and beaded handbags. Most of the rooms also have period-dressed mannequins. This section of the museum also contains re-created rooms that would have been found in a house of the early 1900's such as a parlor, bedroom, kitchen, and library. Each room is fully furnished and complete to the smallest detail. The El Monte Historic Museum - "The end of the Santa Fe Trail" - offers a window to the world!

For further study, or just for the joy of reading, the El Monte Public Library is only a few buildings down. Directly across the street from the museum is a park. This pleasant corner park offers plenty of picnic tables and shady oak trees, plus a few slides and some metal transportation vehicles to climb on.

Hours: Open Tues. - Fri., 10am - 4pm; Sun., 1pm - 3pm. Open on Sat. by appointment.

Admission: Free

Ages: 5 years and up.

FORT MACARTHUR MILITARY MUSEUM   ☼
(310) 548-2631- Museum; (310) 548-7705 - Angels Gate Park   !
3601 S. Gaffey Street, San Pedro
(*EXIT HARBOR FWY [110] S. ON GAFFEY ST. DR. ALMOST TO THE END OF GAFFEY,
THEN R. THROUGH THE GATES ON LEAVEN WORTH DR., PAST ANGELS GATE PARK.*)

This concrete World War II coastal defense battery building really
fires up kids' imaginations as they tour the grounds and the rooms filled
with big artillery guns, cannons, mines, uniforms, pictures, and other
war memorabilia. Military history is important to learn, but my boys
really loved just running through the underground corridors! Starting at
the Gun Pit, it's a (scary) thrill to run from one end of a long narrow
darkish tunnel to the other end, where they climb up stairs, through an
open trap door, and into the Plotting Room. Now this is adventure!

There is a sixteen-minute video that shows the history of this
museum and recoil guns shooting. In the small Decontamination Room
my kids pretended they had come in contact with poisonous gas and
stepped on an air pump to blow it off, just like the soldiers of old. Only
then could they enter the Communications Room. This special room
has fascinating old radios and transmitters, all behind glass. Store
Room 2 has riveting pictures of battleships being blown up. The
pictures also tell stories of soldiers' bravery and hardships. The
Barracks Display shows the inside of a soldier's small room and typical
army articles.

Talking through the elaborate speaking tube system keeps kids
busy for a long time as one speaks through an end while another tries
to find the receiving end. Don't forget to take the steps up to the top of
the defense building. One of the hideouts, where lookouts with guns
watched for incoming, attacking ships, is still open to spy from. There
are picnic tables on the rooftop of the small souvenir shop, making a
picnic here that much more special. (Check the July CALENDAR
section for "Old Fort MacArthur Days" re-enactments.)

Just east of the museum, on a hill in Angels Gate Park, sits the
seventeen-ton Korean Friendship Bell, set in a traditional, Korean-style
pagoda. Let the kids loose to run around and enjoy the grassy knolls.
Since it's a fairly treeless area, it's also ideal for kite flying. There are a
few pieces of climbing apparatus and a basketball court, too. On a clear
day the coastal view is gorgeous, and you can see Catalina Island.

Hours: The Museum is open Tues., Thurs., Sat. - Sun. from
noon - 5pm. Docent tours are offered Sat. - Sun. at 1pm
and 3pm. The park is open daily from sunrise to 6pm.
Admission: Free; donations gladly excepted.

Ages: 2 years and up, though younger ones will have to be careful not to yell in the corridors, where noise reverberates off the cement walls. The walls are marked "Quiet please" in an attempt to keep the noise level at a minimum.

GENERAL PHINEAS BANNING RESIDENCE MUSEUM AND PARK

(310) 548-7777 $

401 E. M Street, Wilmington

(EXIT HARBOR FWY [110] E. ON PACIFIC COAST HIGHWAY, R. ON AVALON BLVD., L. ON M ST.)

This huge, Victorian, residence museum, where the founder of Wilmington once lived, is reflective of the Banning family lifestyle in the 1800's. First, you'll watch a film that gives a history of the family and this era. Next, you'll tour through the photo gallery, and then into the house where the rooms are beautifully decorated with period furniture and eclectic art work. (Note: The house is completely decked out at Christmas time and looks particularly splendid.) Get the kids involved with the tour by asking them questions like, "What's missing from this office that modern offices have?" (Answer - a computer, a fax machine, etc. Surprisingly, a copy machine *is* here.) Check out the hoof inkwell in the General's office.

Other rooms of interest are the children's nursery, the bedrooms (one has a unique hat rack made of antlers), and the kitchen with all of its gadgets. (Obviously some things never change.) The one-room schoolhouse has definite kid-appeal with old-fashioned desks, slates, and McGuffy primers. School groups are given tours that include donning an apron or ascot, getting a math or English lesson from that time period, and playing games of yesteryear. The Stagecoach Barn has real stagecoaches, and is a fully-outfitted, nineteenth-century working barn. Ask your kids if they can figure out what some of the tools were used for.

The hour-and-a-half tours are best suited for older children, as there is much to see, but not to touch. The museum is situated in the middle of a pretty, twenty-acre park that has a small playground, a few picnic tables, and plenty of eucalyptus and giant bamboo trees.

Hours: Touring hours are Tues. - Thurs. at 12:30pm, 1:30pm, and 2:30pm; Sat. - Sun. at 12:30pm, 1:30pm, 2:30pm, and 3:30pm.

Admission: $2 per person.

Ages: 7 years and up.

GEORGE C. PAGE MUSEUM / LA BREA TAR PITS

(213) 857-6311 $$$

5801 Wilshire Boulevard, Los Angeles

(EXIT SANTA MONICA FWY [10] N. ON FAIRFAX, R. ON WILSHIRE BLVD, L. ON CURSON ST.)

Kids boning up on becoming paleontologists will really dig this place. First, take them to see the fifteen-minute movie, "Treasures of the Tar Pits." It's an interesting overview and explains that the fossils they'll see in the museum have been excavated from the pits, just outside.

The George C. Page Museum has over thirty different exhibits including saber-tooth cats, an imperial mammoth, dire wolves, mastodons, bison, giant ground sloths, and a variety of birds and plants. (Forewarn your kids that dinosaurs had been extinct for many years before the tar pit entrapments occurred, so the only thing here on dinosaurs is a short film.) The exhibits are comprised of fossils, skeletons, and lifelike murals, plus an animated model of a young mammoth. Kids can pit their strength against the force of asphalt by pulling on glass enclosed cylinders stuck in the sticky stuff. The futility of this effort makes it easier to understand why animals, of any size, couldn't escape the tar pits.

Other highlights include the La Brea Woman, whose image changes continuously, via optical illusion, from a skeleton to a fleshed-out figure; the wall display of over 400 dire wolf skulls; and watching through the huge windows of a working paleontologist's laboratory where cleaning, studying, and cataloging newly excavated fossils is an ongoing process. Kellan, my oldest son, wanted to become a paleontologist until he saw how tedious the work can be. I'm encouraging him to keep an open mind. Towards the exit is a room devoted to the theory of evolution.

Outside, enjoy a walk around the twenty-three acres of beautifully landscaped Hancock Park, otherwise known as the La Brea Tar Pits. Pits are comprised of asphalt that has seeped to the surface to form sticky pools in which the animals got trapped and died. There are several active tar pits in the park, with hundreds more having been dug out and filled in. For two months during the summer, you can see real excavation work going on at Pit 91. If all else fails, kids will have a great time rolling down the hills outside the museum and climbing on the statues!

Hours: Open daily in the summer from 10am - 5pm. Open the rest of the year Tues. - Sun. from 10am - 5pm. Closed New Year's Day, Thanksgiving, and Christmas.

Admission: $6 for adults; $3.50 for seniors and students with ID; $2 for ages 5 - 10; children 4 years and under are free. (Certain discounts available through AAA.) The museum is free to everyone on the first Tuesday of the month. Parking in the lot behind the museum is $5.50, with validation, or try parking on 6th Street directly behind the museum, for free.

Ages: 3½ years and up.

GORDON R. HOWARD MUSEUM / MENTZER ☼
HOUSE
(818) 841-6333 $

The Museum is located at 115 N. Lomita Street, Burbank; the Mentzer House is connected to the museum by a walkway, but its address is 1015 West Olive Avenue, Burbank

(EXIT VENTURA FWY [134] N. ON VICTORY BLVD., L. ON OLIVE AVE. OR, EXIT GOLDEN STATE FWY [5] W. ON OLIVE AVE. TO THE HOUSE: N. ON LOMITA ST. TO THE MUSEUM)

Make sure to save a Sunday afternoon to come and explore the Gordon Howard Museum. The hallway has old toys and dishes on display, plus a drawing room and a music room. The salon contains wedding dresses, stylish old dresses (that are now back in style), a stunning 1898 dress with both beads and lace, plus ladies boots, jeweled hat pins, and dolls.

The Historical Room is large, and filled with interesting slices from Burbank's past. Along one wall are glass-enclosed rooms, each one complete with furniture and period-dressed mannequins. Look into the rooms, pick up an old-fashioned telephone receiver, press a button, and listen to stories about Dr. Burbank (does that name ring a bell?), a family-owned winery, a 1920's hotel lobby (when $1 paid for a room!), a country store, and the "Jazz Singer," Al Jolson. Other exhibits in this room include military uniforms, flags, and other war memorabilia; a display devoted to Lockheed, comprised of numerous pictures and model airplanes; a tribute to Disney featuring animation cells, photographs, and posters; an ornate desk used by Spanish noblemen; and more.

The Vehicle Room is packed with lots of antique "stuff," such as an old switchboard, tools, parking meters, a huge Gramophone, a hotel telephone booth, fire hats, etc. It also showcases classic cars in mint condition, and several vintage vehicles including a 1922 Moreland Bus, a 1909 Ford horseless carriage with a crank, and a 1949 fire engine with a huge target net which my kids thought was a trampoline. The small upstairs gallery has pictures and paintings as well as a complete collection of old cameras. A video on the history of Lockheed is shown at 1:10pm and again at 2:30pm.

Follow the walkway from the museum courtyard to the reconstructed Mentzer House, which was originally built in 1870. On your walk-through tour you'll see two bedrooms, a dining room, and a living room containing period furniture, plus old-fashioned items such as a phonograph, an old telephone, a vacuum cleaner, etc. The kitchen has a beautiful coal stove, china dishes, and cooking gadgets.

Right next door is the Olive Recreation Center, easily identified by the model F-104 Starfighter in the front. The park has picnic tables and a playground, plus tennis and basketball courts.

Hours: Open Sundays from 1pm - 4pm
Admission: $1 donation per person is requested.

Ages: 5 years and up.

GRIFFITH OBSERVATORY AND PLANETARIUM ☼
(213) 664-1191   !

On the slope of Mount Hollywood, in Griffith Park, Los Angeles
(EXIT GOLDEN STATE FWY [5] W. ON LOS FELIZ BLVD., TAKE HILLHURST AVE. N.
PAST THE GREEK THEATER TO THE OBSERVATORY.)

The Observatory is one of the best places to get an overview of the
city on a cloudless day, and to view the city lights and stars on a clear
night. Coin-operated telescopes are here to get that "closer" look that
kids insist they need. The largest public telescope in California is
available to use (for free) every clear evening in the summer from dusk
- 9:45pm. It's available the rest of the year Tuesday to Sunday from
7am - 9:45pm. Call the Sky Report, (213) 663-8171, for twenty-four-
hour recorded information.

The Hall of Science in the Observatory has some fascinating and
interactive exhibits that explore astronomy and the physical sciences.
The West Hall emphasizes light and stars. The solar telescope allows
viewing of the sun, through filters, on clear days, so kids can actually
see sun spots or solar flares. Have the kids step on a scale and see
how much they would weigh on Mars or Jupiter. (The moon scale is my
personal favorite.) The computer terminals have astronomy quiz games
like astronomer's hangman, etc.

The East Hall's emphasis is on more down-to-earth sciences. The
weather exhibit has an earth and moon globe, plus a seismograph
exhibit where kids can stomp on the floor and measure their own
"earthquake." The space telescope here is one-fifth the size of the
Hubble. Out on the rotunda, kids enjoy the huge Foucault pendulum
that knocks big pegs over onto the floor, illustrating the rotation of the
earth. (See GRIFFITH PLANETARIUM AND LASER SHOWS for show
information.)

Hours: Open daily in the summer 12:30pm - 10pm. Open the
rest of the year Tues. - Fri., 2pm - 10pm; Sat. - Sun.,
12:30pm - 10pm.
Admission: Free
Ages: 4 years and up.

GUINNESS WORLD OF RECORDS MUSEUM ☼
(213) 463-6433 $$$

6764 Hollywood Boulevard, Hollywood
(EXIT HOLLYWOOD FWY [101] W. ON HOLLYWOOD BLVD.)

There are over 3,000 facts, feats, and world records told about and
shown at this very Hollywood museum, so there is something for all
ages to be astounded at. See life-size models, pictures, videos, and
special effects of the tallest, smallest, most tattooed, most anything,
and everything. (The kids should be great at Trivial Pursuit after this

visit.) We were enthralled with the domino exhibit, which shows a video of an incredible domino run!

Prep your children before their visit: Q. - Do you know who holds a record for the most fan mail in one day? (A. - Mickey Mouse. He received 800,000 letters one day in 1933.) Q. - What animal had the smallest brain in proportion to his body? (A. - Stegosaurus.) Q. - What was the longest length a human neck was stretched using copper coils? And why? (A. - Fifteen and three-quarter inches. I don't know why, though.) Watch some fascinating footage of intriguing and bizarre facts about our world and the people and animals in it: "The Human World," "The Animal World," "Planet Earth," "Structures and Machines," "Sports World," and a salute to "The World of Hollywood."

Hours: Open Sun. - Thurs., 10am - midnight; Fri. - Sat., 10am - 1:30am. Closed major holidays.

Admission: $8.95 for adults; $6.95 for ages 6 - 12; children 5 years and under are free. Combination tickets with HOLLYWOOD WAX MUSEUM are $12.95 for adults; $8.95 for ages 6 - 12.

Ages: 4½ years and up.

HACIENDA HEIGHTS YOUTH SCIENCE CENTER
(818) 854-9825   !

16949 Wedgeworth Drive, Hacienda Heights
(EXIT POMONA FWY [60] S. ON AZUSA, R. ON PEPPER BROOK, R. ON WEDGEWORTH.)

The Youth Science Center functions as a museum and a classroom. Actually, it's located in classroom 8 at Wedgeworth Elementary School. A lot of science is contained in this one room, such as a sand pendulum that creates patterns depending on how you swing it; a heat-sensitive, liquid crystal display that leaves colored impressions when touched; a fossil case; a fish tank; lots of little critters to look at; and computers. There is also a small store where kids can purchase rocks, shells, and science books.

For a minimal fee, children can attend classes like "The Great Paper Airplane Race," where they'll learn about aerodynamics and wind, while making and flying paper airplanes. Field trips, like a nature hike to Dripping Springs, are offered throughout the school year. A terrific array of science-related classes, from model rocket-building to hands-on, physical science, are available during the summer. Call for a schedule.

Hours: Open in the summer, Mon. - Fri. from 8am - noon. Open during the school year on Saturdays from 10am - 2pm.

Admission: Free

Ages: 4 years and up.

THE HATHAWAY RANCH MUSEUM   ☼

(310) 944-6563 $

11901 East Florence Avenue, Santa Fe Springs
(FROM SANTA ANA FWY [5] OR SAN GABRIEL RIVER FWY [605] EXIT E. ON
FLORENCE AVE. THE DRIVEWAY IS JUST EAST PIONEER BLVD.)

This museum is on a five-acre ranch. All of the antiques on display have been accumulated from three generations of Hathaways; things used until they couldn't be fixed, and kept because the family couldn't bear to throw anything away. (So, if I start saving all my "stuff" and my children's "stuff," someday their children could open up a museum!) Nadine Hathaway, a great grandmother now, still lives on the premises.

Drive up the driveway and into the past. Barking dogs will greet you at the Visitor's Center (i.e. sign-in room). Inside are saddles, old pictures, irons, etc. Check out the 1930's machine shop next door, filled with tools, tractor pistons, and even some working lathes.

The first room inside the house museum is a fully furnished living room. The kitchen contains a coal and a wood burning stove, ice box, old baby buggy, high chair, and a myriad of labeled gadgets such as butter molds, old graters, etc. A 1920's girl's bedroom holds dolls, pictures of movie stars from that era, tennis racquets, etc. Another bedroom displays Nadine's grandmother's wedding dress, feather boas, and more. Upstairs is an attic room, or hideaway room, that kids immediately want to duplicate in their own homes. The small "secret" room now holds model trains and old-fashioned toys. One room has dresses from different eras including a prom dress, plus fur coats, shoes, hats, and sewing machines. The hallway has a display of once-stylish hats and beaded handbags. The "military room" is packed with personal belongings from several wars, such as uniforms, medals, a forty-eight star flag, a Civil War hat, and a WWII helmet. See history close up!

The grounds are equally fascinating - so much machinery in one place! If your group is small, a golf cart is used to show you around. If your group is larger, or you come on a Sunday, a tractor wagon is used. You'll see and learn about old John Deeres, combines, numerous tractors, oil well engines, gas shovels, old trucks, farming equipment, a wagon originally used on the Oregon Trail, a steam roller, a filling station with gas pumps, and lots more. Though it may resemble a large junkyard, much of the machinery is in the process of being restored. There are other things to see while at the ranch, too, such as ducks and chickens, a garden growing of its own accord, and more old farm equipment.

Hours: The grounds are open Mon. - Tues., Thurs. - Fri., on a drop-in basis. The museum is open and a tour of the grounds is available the first Sunday of the month from 2pm - 4pm; call to make an appointment if you're interested in coming during the week.

Admission: A donation of $1 per person is appreciated.

Ages: 4 years and up.

HERITAGE PARK (Santa Fe Springs)   ☼

(562) 946-6476   !

12100 Mora Drive, Santa Fe Springs

(EXIT SAN GABRIEL RIVER FWY [605] E. ON TELEGRAPH RD., PAST PIONEER, R. ON HERITAGE PARK DR. TO THE END.)

Heritage Park is like a breath of fresh air among the historical parks. Its six acres of beautifully landscaped grounds make any length visit here a pleasure. The high- ceilinged, wood Carriage Barn, which holds turn-of-the-century exhibits, is a must-see. Two carriages from horse and buggy days take the center floor. Behind glass is a large display of period clothing, including a wedding dress, plus dolls, toys, and books. The small touch and play area has clothing to try on, an old telephone to dial (not touch tone), and a few other articles to play with. Inventing a Better Life display features old phonographs, typewriters, bikes, roller skates (not in-line skates), plus cameras and other equipment. It's interesting to see how the inventions of yesteryear benefit us today.

Grab a bite to eat at The Kitchen, an outside, full-service snack bar. It's open Monday through Friday from 8am - 3pm. The average cost of a sandwich or salad is $4. Or, bring your own lunch, and enjoy the garden setting with beautiful old shade trees and wooden picnic tables. A walk-through aviary has parakeets, canaries, etc. A small window to an archeological pit shows excavated trash like cattle bones, pottery, etc. There are remain sites marking original fireplace and basement foundations, but kids cannot go down to explore. There is a hedge around the beautiful formal gardens. Inside is an old fig tree with huge roots that are irresistible for kids to climb on. An immaculate wood-paneled tank house, with a windmill on top, is at the far end of the park. On a school tour, kids can go inside and walk up the crisscross stairs to the top, then go outside, and take in the view.

I can't emphasize the beauty of this park enough. It's clean, green, and the walkways throughout make every area accessible.

Just outside the park gates are three restored railroad cars on a track. Take a tour through the engine car and ring the bell, then go through the caboose and see where coal was stored.

Hours: The park is open daily 7am - 10pm. Railroad exhibit hours are Tues. - Sun., noon - 4pm. The Carriage Barn is open Fri. - Sun. and Tues., noon - 4pm; Wed. - Thurs., 9am - noon.

Admission: Free

Ages: All

HERITAGE SQUARE MUSEUM   ☼

(818) 796-2898 $$

3800 Homer Street, Highland Park

(Exit Pasadena Fwy [110] S. on Avenue 43. Take an immediate R. on Homer St.)

This little "town" behind a gate at the end of a residential street has eight houses, a carriage barn (used for storage), a church building, and a train depot. The elegant Victorian homes have been relocated here and are in the process of being restored. Each one has a different architectural style. One is white with columns, almost colonial-looking, while another is green, gingerbreadish in style, and has a brick chimney. The octagon-shaped house is the most unique house here. Its unusual configuration makes it interesting to look at as well as walk through.

Only on the one-hour guided tours can you go through the homes which are in various stages of restoration. Some are being plastered, some painted, and some have a long way to go! The last house on the tour is the only one furnished, making the tour a progression of restoration. The grassy grounds are ideal for picnicking.

Hours: Open Fri., 10am - 3pm; Sat. - Sun., 11:30am - 4:30pm. Tours are given Sat. and Sun. only, at noon, 1pm, 2pm, and 3pm.

Admission: $5 for adults; $4 for ages 13 - 17; $2 for ages 7 - 12; children 6 years and under are free.

Ages: 6 years and up.

HOLLYWOOD BOWL MUSEUM

(213) 850-2058

2301 N. Highland, Hollywood

(Exit Hollywood Fwy [101] at Highland and follow signs to Hollywood Bowl.)

While at the Hollywood Bowl for a concert, or if you're in the area, stop by the Hollywood Bowl Museum. This 3,000 square foot museum offers a history of the Bowl via displays of musical instruments and pictures of performers and conductors. Touch screens show concerts featured at the Bowl. The second story has rotating exhibits focusing on various aspects of music. A music education program is offered for school groups. Kids learn about music, as well as try their hands at playing some instruments. The program specifics change from season to season.

Hours: Open during the summer daily from 10am - 8:30pm; open the rest of the year Tues. - Sat. from 10am - 4:30pm. It's also open during intermission on concert evenings.

Admission: Free. Parking before 4pm is free.

Ages: 7 years and up.

HOLLYWOOD ENTERTAINMENT MUSEUM ☼
(213) 465-7900 $$$
7021 Hollywood Boulevard, Hollywood
(EXIT VENTURA FWY [101] E. ON HOLLYWOOD BLVD.)

The main room in this entertaining museum is done up dramatically
in true Hollywood style with movie posters, old movie cameras,
microphones, lighting equipment, a Hollywood time line, and video
screens that show the history and background information of particular
exhibits. Listen to Walt Disney talk about animation, or see Buster
Keaton in action. Other exhibits include the armor, sword, and helmet
from "Ben Hur"; a gown worn by Marilyn Monroe; a Max Factor display
showing stars at their most glamourous; and the opportunity to become
a Star Trek character, via a mirrored reflection. A central screen
intermittently shows a montage of film clips and/or a mini-documentary.
The stage below the screen has a model of the town of Hollywood built
into the floor and covered with plexiglass so you can walk on it.

Take the behind-the-scenes tours which are included in your
admission price. One enables you to see a prop room filled with masks,
desks, stuffed animals, clocks, sports equipment, musical instruments,
etc., plus closets stuffed with costumes and outfits that are categorized
by color and season. Star Trek fans (and others) can beam aboard the
Enterprise's deck, sit in the captain's chair, and watch clips from the
original and "Next Generation" series. Picard's ready room is also here.
Look closely at the diagrams and technical jargon on the display panel
in the hallway. You'll see a hamster on a wheel, "slippery when wet"
signs, and sayings such as, "In space no one can hear you scream."
The cameras never shot close enough to catch these details! Another
Trekker room follows, with masks and items that would be found on a
Klingon vessel. For a change of scenery, walk through the entire
original Cheers bar, where everybody knows your name.

The second tour is the fascinating Foley Room. Station one shows
how sound effects bring life to motion pictures. Horses clopping,
kissing, even putting on a leather jacket are all sounds later
incorporated into a film using a variety of creative props, such as trash
can lids, etc. Kids (and adults) can try out their new-found knowledge at
station two where a silent clip is shown once, and then again. The
second time the audience is invited to add dialog and use the doorbell,
typewriter, telephone, etc., at the proper spots. The clip is played for a
third time with the (hilarious) results recorded.

Other intriguing, interactive tours involve recording at the Recording
Studio, and editing film in the Editing Suite. The museum also offers
school programs to students who are interested in learning about the
entertainment industry. Note: Flash photography is not allowed in the
museum.

The museum is located in a complex with a theater and several
shops and restaurants. It is also in the heart of Hollywood's Walk of
Fame, so look down to see the stars' names adorning the sidewalks.
Just a few blocks down is Disney's El Capitan Theater, the famous

Mann's Chinese Theater (with stars' handprints and footprints), plus other Hollywood museums and activities.

Hours: Open Tues. - Sun. from 10am - 6pm. Closed most major holidays.

Admission: $7.50 for adults; $4.50 for seniors and students; $4 for ages 5 - 12; children 4 years and under are free. Metered parking is available wherever you can find it, or park for $2 around the corner on Sycamore Street.

Ages: 6 years and up.

HOLLYWOOD WAX MUSEUM   ☼

(213) 462-5991 $$$

6767 Hollywood Boulevard, Hollywood
(EXIT HOLLYWOOD FWY [101] W. ON HOLLYWOOD BLVD.)

Hundreds of celebrities from the world of television, movies, sports, politics, and religion are presented in waxy lifelikeness, surrounded by appropriate and realistic settings. Kids will enjoy "seeing" their favorite stars like Sylvester Stallone as Rambo, Clint Eastwood dressed in his "make my day" attire, Dorothy and her companions in the Wizard of Oz, Kareem Abdul Jabar, Elvis, and hundreds more. A permanent exhibit here includes over 100 original movie costumes such as Christopher Reeve's "Superman," Esther Williams' bathing suit, etc. A word of caution: There is a House of Horrors which might frighten younger children, though thankfully it has a separate loop.

Hours: Open Sun. - Thurs., 10am - midnight; Fri. - Sat., 10am - 2am. Closed major holidays.

Admission: $8.95 for adults; $7.50 for seniors; $6.95 for ages 6 - 12; children 5 years and under are free. Combination tickets with GUINNESS WORLD BOOK OF RECORDS are $12.95 for adults; $8.95 for ages 6 - 12.

Ages: 4 years and up.

HOLYLAND EXHIBITION   ☼

(213) 664-3162 $

2215 Lake View and Allesandro Way, Los Angeles
(EXIT GOLDEN STATE FWY [5] S.E. ON GLENDALE FWY [2]. GO TO END AND TURN R. ON GLENDALE BLVD., R. ON COVE AVE., TURNS INTO OAK VIEW, R. ON OAK GLEN, L. ON ALLESANDRO WY. AND GO TO THE END. THE HOUSE IS ON THE CORNER OF LAKE VIEW AND ALLESANDRO.)

Wow! I could take this tour at least three more times and still not see and learn everything this museum has to offer! The Holyland Exhibition is an inconspicuous two-story corner house that was built in the late 1920's. It contains an incredible collection of priceless Egyptian and biblical items. The two-hour tour is not hands on. It does involve, however, a lot of listening and learning. An incredibly well-informed, costumed docent will take you first to the tapestry-rich

Bethlehem/Egyptian room which, like all the rooms, is not large, but packed with artifacts. You'll feel transported to a different time and country. Some of the items explained in depth are the 2,600-year-old mummy case; the hand-made brass art pieces and plates; papyrus; shoes made of camel hide and ram skin; headdresses; and a lunch bag made of goat skin. Each item is presented with its history and its biblical connection. You'll also see jewelry, engraved leather goods, a 2,000-year-old lamp, and much more.

The Bible Art and Archaeology Room has stones, shells, pottery, spices, etc., from Nazareth, Bethlehem, the Jordan River, and surrounding areas. The Bible becomes real to kids (and adults) as they see the type of large thorns used in Christ's crown of thorns; a big chunk of salt called Madame Lot; a very comprehensive family tree detailing lineage from Adam to Jesus; the kind of stones crushed and used for pitch on Noah's ark; a picture of Mt. Ararat where *ark*eologists believe the ark landed; and a re-created Ark of the Covenant. Make sure your tour guide explains how Mr. Futterer, the museum founder, went on an expedition to find the ark and how this was the basis for the movie "Raiders of the Lost Ark." (This will definitely spark your children's interest.) Again, amazing amounts of Bible references are given with the presentation of each article.

While sitting on oriental rugs around low tables, you're served small samples of Holy Land refreshments - a taste of Israel. The Jerusalem Bazaar is a gift shop with souvenirs (and great teaching materials) made of olive wood, mother-of-pearl, etc., at bargain prices. The Damascus Room has an intricate game table inlaid with mother-of-pearl that took fifty man-years to make - kids may not play games on it! The room also contains beaded lamps, musical instruments, a camel saddle, animal skin (to write on), and many unique pieces of furniture. With all that I've just written, I've barely scratched the surface of what this museum features. So, come, take a trip to the middle east, via the Holyland Exhibition, and learn about its peoples and customs. The interdenominational museum is frequented by Christians, Jews, Muslims, and people of various other faiths.

Hours: The museum is open to tour 7 days a week, including holidays and evenings. Call at least a week ahead of time, and choose the most convenient time for your group of at least 10 or more.

Admission: $2.50 for adults; $2 for ages 2 - 16 years.

Ages: 6 years and up.

THE HOMESTEAD MUSEUM

(818) 968-8492

15415 E. Don Julian Road, City of Industry

(EXIT POMONA FWY [60] N. ON HACIENDA BLVD., L. ON DON JULIAN RD.)

The Homestead Museum resides on six acres of land. A major portion of the property is an open, grassy area between the main group of buildings and the old mausoleum. A shady picnic area is here, too. A one-hour guided tour, starting at the water tower, will take you behind the gates. Kids will see and learn about the history of the United States, and about California in particular. They'll learn, for instance, that our state was once Mexican territory, and how that influence has factored in the development of our culture. They will also learn about the art and architecture of the 1840's through the 1920's.

The tour goes into the two residences. The Workman adobe home has no furniture inside, but outside are a few artifacts that kids can touch. The Temple house is spacious with twenty-five rooms, mostly furnished in 1920's decor. Kids will also get information about the pump house, tepee, and mausoleum.

Hours: Open for tours Tues. - Fri., 1pm - 4pm; Sat. - Sun., 10am - 4pm. The tours are given on the hour. Closed major holidays and the fourth weekend of every month.

Admission: Free

Ages: 6 years and up.

HUNTINGTON LIBRARY, ART COLLECTIONS AND ☼ BOTANICAL GARDENS

(818) 405-2125   *$$*

1151 Oxford Road, San Marino

(EXIT FOOTHILL FWY [210] S. ON SIERRA MADRE BLVD., R. ON CALIFORNIA, L. ON ALLEN AVE. THE ENTRANCE IS AT ORLANDO RD. AND ALLEN AVE.)

The Library houses one of the world's greatest collections of rare books and manuscripts, including a Gutenberg Bible, the Ellesmere Chaucer, and Benjamin Franklin's autobiography, in his own handwriting. The Huntington Art Gallery contains Gainsborough's "Blue Boy" and other paintings, rare tapestries, miniatures, and period furniture. The Library and Art Gallery will probably interest only older children, unless you get the younger ones involved. Point out to them paintings that feature children, particularly ones with different styles of dress. Share the stories behind the pictures, allowing the subjects to become real to your kids. This is a gentle way to introduce children to some truly great works of art.

The botanical gardens are comprised of twelve separate amazing gardens that cover 150 acres of the 200-acre estate. As Lisa Blackburn, a museum associate says, "The gardens . . . have wide open spaces and vast rolling lawns; great for running, somersaulting, cartwheeling, shrieking, and releasing all that boundless energy that is sometimes stifled in traditional museum settings." The bamboo groves and jungle garden are big hits with little Tarzans. There are waterfalls, lily ponds, koi, ducks, turtles, and frogs to capture their attention - almost more than can be seen in one day. The Desert Garden has, again to quote Lisa, "twelve acres of some of the most bizarre, colorful, creepy-crawly plants that a child could imagine." Another favorite garden is the Japanese garden, which is a quarter-mile west of the main entrance. This has a traditionally furnished Japanese house, stone ornaments, an old temple bell, a moon bridge, and a bonsai court.

No picnicking is allowed on the grounds. However, a special treat for you and your daughter (as it's not really a boy's cup of tea) is to get dressed up and sip English tea in the Rose Garden Tea Room, (818) 683-8131. Prices for the variety of finger sandwiches and delightful English desserts are $11 for adults, $5.50 for children 9 years and under. A restaurant is on the grounds, too.

Hours: The Library and Gardens are open in the summer Tues. - Sun. from 10:30am - 4:30pm; open the rest of the year Tues. - Fri., noon - 4:30pm; Sat. - Sun., 10:30am - 4:30pm. Garden tours depart Tues. - Sun. at 1pm; self-guiding tour brochures are available. Closed major holidays.

Admission: $7.50 for adults; $6 for seniors; $4 for students with ID; children 12 years and under are free.

Ages: 4 years and up.

JAPANESE AMERICAN NATIONAL MUSEUM ☼
(213) 625-0414 $$
369 E. 1ˢᵗ Street, Los Angeles
(EXIT HARBOR FWY [110] E. ON 1ˢᵀ ST. OR, EXIT HOLLYWOOD FWY [101] S. ON ALAMEDA, R. ON 1ˢᵀ ST. IT'S ON THE CORNER OF 1ˢᵀ ST. AND CENTRAL AVE. IN LITTLE TOKYO.)

During World War II, more than 120,000 people of Japanese ancestry, most of whom were American citizens, were incarcerated in American relocation/concentration camps from 1941 - 1946. This museum is dedicated to preserving the memory of that time period, and learning from it.

The Legacy Room displays photographs of Japanese families, the Japanese-American time line, uniforms, and scale models of the layout of the camps. In addition, there are personal belongings and works of art, like wood carvings done while the carver was in a concentration camp. The second floor shows a forty-five-minute collage of homemade movies called "Something Strong Within." This film documents the harsh conditions of every day life in the camps. Across the street, fifty-year-old, renovated wooden barracks are open to tour through. There is also a twenty-six-foot replica of a guard tower.

The Japanese American Museum has computers for kids to play history games, or to learn how to compose a Haiku poem. A craft table is available, too, where volunteers show kids how to create origami art.

Hours: Open Tues. - Wed. and Fri. - Sun., 10am - 5pm; Thurs., 10am - 8pm. Closed New Year's Day, Thanksgiving, and Christmas.

Admission: $4 for adults; $3 for seniors, ages 6 - 17, and college students with ID; children 5 years and under are free.

Ages: 7 years and up.

KENNETH G. FISKE MUSICAL INSTRUMENT MUSEUM
(909) 621-8307   !

Fiske Museum, in Claremont College, Claremont
(EXIT SAN BERNARDINO FWY [10] N. ON INDIAN HILL BLVD., R. ON 4TH ST. THE
COLLEGE IS AT THE CORNER OF 4TH ST. AND COLLEGE WAY. THE MUSEUM IS ON THE
LOWER LEVEL OF THE BRIDGES AUDITORIUM.)

   This museum is like music to your ears. The three galleries contain
a comprehensive collection of over 400 rare, historic, and ethnic
musical instruments. The instruments on display range from the 1600's
to the twentieth century, from exotic drums to Civil War bugles to player
pianos. A half-hour tour consists of the curator explaining the various
instruments and even playing a few of them. So, this museum can be
instrumental in teaching your kids about music!

     Hours: Call for an appointment.
Admission: Free; donations accepted.
     Ages: 7 years and up.

KIDSPACE
(818) 449-9143 $$

390 S. El Molino Avenue, Pasadena
(TAKE PASADENA FWY [110] TO END, R. ON CALIFORNIA BLVD., L. ON EL MOLINO.
OR, EXIT FOOTHILL FWY [210] S. ON LAKE AVE., R. ON DEL MAR, L. ON EL MOLINO.)

   This is a great participatory museum for kids. Your children will
immediately get immersed in the professions and activities offered as
they sit behind the desk at a TV studio and become newscasters; dress
up as firefighters and man (or woman) the hoses and ladders (which
are attached to walls); learn how they get things letter-perfect at the
Post Office by playing Postmaster; get sand between their toes at the
beach play area; and play in, on, and under the indoor treehouse play
area, Critter Caverns. There is also a dress-up area, a Legos® area, a
computer room, and a small planetarium that shows the nighttime stars
on the inside ceiling. For your shoppers or cashiers-in-the-making,
there is a mini-market with baskets, food, and a (play) cash register.
The little ones have a wonderful area just for them where they can play
with and on large balls. The museum also offers many special
programs and workshops throughout the year. We thoroughly enjoyed
a school field trip here as the students learned about insects in depth,
completed a related craft project, and played.

     Hours: Open in the summer Sun. - Thurs., 1pm - 5pm; Fri. and
Sat., 10am - 5pm. Open the rest of the year Tues. -
Thurs., and Sun., 1:30pm - 5pm; Sat., 10am - 5pm. Open
for school tours during the week, with advanced
reservations.

Admission: $5 for ages 3 and up; $3.50 for seniors; $2.50 for
children 1 - 2 years old. (Certain discounts available
through AAA.) School tours are $2.50 per person. On the
last Monday of every month (except October), from 5pm
- 8pm, admission is free.

Ages: 1½ - 11 years old.

THE LEONIS ADOBE   ☼

(818) 222-6511   *!*

23537 Calabasas Road, Calabasas
(EXIT VENTURA FWY [101] S. ON VALLEY CIRCLE BLVD. AND TAKE A QUICK R. ONTO
CALABASAS RD.)

Step back in time over 100 years when you visit the Leonis Adobe.
The restored buildings help kids to picture the wealthy ranchero as it
once was. The rustic grounds, complete with grape arbors, old farm
equipment, windmills, and a corral containing longhorn cattle, horses,
sheep, and goats, enhance the yesteryear atmosphere. Officially Los
Angeles' Historic Cultural Monument No. 1, the adobe was once owned
by Miguel Leonis, a Basque who led a very colorful life, and Espiritu, his
Native American wife. Both the museum and its owners have a rich and
fascinating history that kids will enjoy hearing. The Visitor's Center has
a few glass-cased displays of mannequins dressed in period clothing.

Outside, a huge, 600-year-old oak tree dominates the grounds.
Penned turkeys, ducks, and chickens; a covered beehive oven which
was used for baking bread; and steps leading up to the tank house, or
worker's bedroom, are also part of the ranch. You are welcome to
explore the barn, complete with wagons and buggies; a blacksmith's
shop that is outfitted with saddles and tools; and the adobe. The bottom
story of the adobe has a kitchen with a wood-burning stove and other
old-fashioned kitchen implements; a pantry for preserving and drying
food (kids like the hanging cow with fake blood); and a dining room -
notice the dirt floors. Upstairs is the Leonis' elegant bedroom that has a
red velvet bedspread over the canopy bed, ladies' boots, and leather
trunks. You'll notice that the hallway floor tilts at a downward angle,
slanting it away from the house. It was built like that to ensure that rains
would run away from the walls, not seep into them. The Juan
Menendez (bed) Room has a ghost story associated with it. (Every
good historic building has one such story!) Also up here is an office,
complete with desk, ledger, and guitar. The Leonis Adobe is a classy
reminder of the brief, but pivotal Mexican/California era.

Just a short walk towards the east, past the Sagebrush Cantina
restaurant, is the small, but beautiful Calabasas Creek Park. With a
rose garden out front, wrought-iron benches throughout, massive
shade trees, and bridges over the duck pond, it offers a pleasant picnic
area and respite. The only drawback to this serene scene is the ever-
present freeway noise.

Hours: The Leonis Adobe is open Wed. - Sun. from 1pm - 4pm.

Admission: Free; donations are appreciated.
Ages: 4 years and up.

LOMITA RAILROAD MUSEUM
(310) 326-6255 $

250th Street and Woodward Avenue, Lomita
(EXIT HARBOR FWY [110] W. ON PACIFIC COAST HWY. TO WOODWARD AVE.)

This small, re-created, turn-of-the century train depot beckons the
engineer in everyone. Outside, on real train tracks, is a 1902 Southern
Pacific Steam locomotive with a cab that the kids can climb in and let
their imaginations go full steam ahead. (The valves and handles are
labeled with explanations for their use, but they are not for touching.)
There is also an all-wood, 1910 Union Pacific caboose to look around
in.

Inside the depot, kids can look through the window of an old-style
ticket office. They also enjoy seeing the model trains, telegraph
equipment, hand-lantern collection, and other train memorabilia. A
grassy picnic area, with a fountain and a boxcar, is across the way.
Hours: Open Wed. - Sun. from 10am - 5pm. Closed
Thanksgiving and Christmas.
Admission: $1 for adults; 50¢ for kids under 13 years.
Ages: 3 years and up.

LOS ANGELES CHILDREN'S MUSEUM
(213) 687-8800 $$$

310 N. Main Street, Los Angeles
*(EXIT HOLLYWOOD FWY [101] S. ON ALAMEDA, R. ON TEMPLE ST., R. ON LOS
ANGELES ST. IT'S IN THE LOS ANGELES MALL.)*

In the midst of skyscrapers, the city of angels has a very kid-
friendly building - the Los Angeles Children's Museum. City Streets will
rev up the engines of your child's imagination as he/she "drives" the
front end of a bus, "rides" on a real police motorcycle, and, for a really
hot time, dresses up in a firefighter's uniform. The Play Zone is a place
for family fun, with organized, non-competitive games such as playing
with a parachute, huge balls, or acting out theater games, etc. The
Recording Studio has real equipment for your child to showcase his/her
talent. (Buy a tape for blackmail, I mean to cherish, for $1.) My oldest
gleefully took the microphone in hand and proceeded to tell some really
bad knock-knock jokes, but he had a good time. The Videozone has
"blue screen" technology so kids can choose any back drop, from the
moon to the ocean, dress up, and act out stories (or whatever) and
have it taped for posterity. (Buy the tape if you want for $2.) Studio time
fills up fast, so sign your kids up as soon as you get to the museum. In
the H_2O area kids will get their hands wet, but it's O.K. - they're learning
about water! Shadow Box, where a light flashes and takes a "picture" of

your body (or body parts) against the wall, and the small Cave of the Dinosaurs are also terrific.

On the second floor, kids can create take-home treasures from the Loft and paper products from the Pulp Factory. Weekends are extra fun as different programs such as storytelling, mini-productions, etc., are offered. Don't be fooled by the name *Children's* Museum - adults have a great time here, too.

Hours: Open in the summer Mon. - Fri., 11:30am - 5pm; Sat. - Sun., 10am - 5pm. Open the rest of the year, Sat. - Sun. from 10am - 5pm. Reservations for groups of ten or more are also available at other times throughout the school year. Closed major holidays.

Admission: $5 for ages 2 and up; children under 2 years are free. Parking ranges from $5 - $15 and is available at the Los Angeles Mall (Los Angeles Street and Temple) daily; Lot 7 Municipal Parking (San Pedro Street and Temple) on Saturdays and Sundays only; and Lot 2 Municipal Parking (Temple and Alameda) weekdays only.

Ages: 2-13 years old.

LOS ANGELES COUNTY MUSEUM OF ART   ☼
(213) 857-6000 $$$
5905 Wilshire Boulevard, Los Angeles
(EXIT SANTA MONICA FWY [10] N. ON FAIRFAX AVE., R. ON WILSHIRE.)

Art, according to Webster, is: "The use of the imagination to make things of aesthetic significance; the technique involved; the theory involved." This leaves the interpretation of what constitutes art wide open! The Los Angeles County Museum of Art is composed of four buildings, plus the Bing Center of theater and movies for older audiences. Each building features a different style of art.

The Anderson building is a favorite with its twentieth-century art, which translates as "anything goes." We started in the "Garage," our title for it. Open the door to this walk-through exhibit, and it's like being in your grandfather's garage. It's crammed with old, rusted tools hanging up on the walls; other storage-type incidentals; and a car that needs more work than it will ever get. (I can now tell my husband that our garage is not a mess - it's art.) Throughout the Anderson building kids are attracted to and puzzled by the larger than life sculptures; abstract paintings on gigantic canvases; and common objects that express artistic creativity, like a kitchen sink, or an arrangement of cereal boxes. Two particularly eye-catching pieces are the life-size, faceless monks sitting around in a circle, and "The Black Planet," which is a huge black disc with long strands of black tubing (think Cajun spaghetti) coming out of it.

In contrast, the Ahmanson Building has more traditional works of art from Medieval European, the Romantic, and the Renaissance periods. Classic paintings and portraits hang in various galleries throughout the stately, three-story building. Gilbert gold and silver pieces, such as elaborate bowls, candelabras, etc., are on display here, as are incredibly detailed, inlaid stone pictures. Other exhibits include Korean, Chinese, and American art.

The Pavilion for Japanese Art is architecturally unique, inside and out. It houses mostly paintings and a few sculptures in a serene, natural light setting. The stairs spiral downward, toward the small waterfall and pond on the lowest level. The Samurai warrior statue dressed in eighteenth-century black chain mail armor gets our vote for the most interesting exhibit here.

The Hammer Building specializes in photography, impressionism, and prints. The permanent and temporary exhibits here portray another medium of artistic endeavor.

Although many docents are on hand to insure that nothing is touched, the atmosphere is not stifling. Contact the museum about educational and family tours, and art classes that are offered throughout the year. A cafe, serving great food, is in the courtyard.

Hours: Open Tues. - Thurs., 10am - 5pm; Fri., 10am - 9pm; Sat. - Sun., 11am - 6pm. Closed Thanksgiving and Christmas.

Admission: $6 for adults; $4 for students and seniors; $1 for ages 6 - 17; children 5 years and under are free. Parking costs $5 in the lot at the S.E. corner of Wilshire Blvd. and Spaulding, or at Hancock Park at Sixth St. and Curson Ave. Admission is free on the second Wednesday of each month, except for ticketed events.

Ages: 6 years and up.

LOS ANGELES MARITIME MUSEUM

(310) 548-7618 $

Berth 84, San Pedro

(TAKE HARBOR FWY [110] TO THE END. IT TURNS INTO GAFFEY ST., L. ON 9TH, L. ON HARBOR BLVD. IT'S AT THE FOOT OF 6TH ST.)

If you have older children who dream of sailing the oceans blue, they will enjoy walking through the six galleries of this maritime museum, which is housed in an old ferry building. There are hundreds of ship models to look at, ranging from real boats to ones inside a bottle. (How do they do that?) An impressive twenty-one-foot scale model of the Queen Mary and two cut-away models of the Titanic and Lusitania give your kids the inside scoop on ocean liners.

A highlight is the Amateur Radio Station where your child might be able to talk to someone on the other side of the world. (See SAN PEDRO for more things to do in this area.)

Hours: Open Tues. - Sun. from 10am - 5pm. Closed New Year's Day, Thanksgiving, and Christmas.

Admission: $1 donation for adults.

Ages: 5 years and up.

MISSION SAN FERNANDO REY DE ESPAÑA   ☀

(818) 361-0186   *$$*

15151 San Fernando Mission Boulevard, Mission Hills
(FROM SAN FERNANDO VALLEY FWY [118], EXIT N. ON SEPULVEDA BLVD., R. ON
SAN FERNANDO MISSION BLVD. GOING N. ON SAN DIEGO FWY [405], EXIT E. ON
SAN FERNANDO MISSION BLVD. GOING S. ON 405, EXIT E. ON RINALDI ST., R. ON
SEPULVEDA BLVD., L. ON SAN FERNANDO MISSION BLVD.)

This quaint mission shows visitors what life was like in the early days of California. Take a self-guided tour through the residence quarters, the church, and the gardens, while explaining each area and its importance to your kids. (Pick up an information pamphlet at the entrance.) Learn that the huge wine vats once produced a major source of income for the missions, etc. Seeing this historic site is one of the best ways to gain understanding about this time period, and the people that once dwelt here. Right across the street from the mission is Brand Park, so don't forget a picnic lunch!

Hours: Open daily from 9am - 4:15pm.
Admission: $4 for adults; $3 for ages 7 - 15; children 6 years and under are free.
Ages: 6 years and up.

MUSEUM OF CONTEMPORARY ART / TEMPORARY ☀
CONTEMPORARY

(213) 626-6222   *$$$*

250 South Grand Avenue, Los Angeles
(GOING W. ON SANTA ANA FWY [101], EXIT S. ON GRAND AVE. GOING E. ON 101,
EXIT E. ON TEMPLE ST., R. ON GRAND AVE.)

The elegant Museum of Contemporary Art is located on top of a plaza. As with any contemporary art museum, exhibits rotate a few times a year, and the paintings, sculptures, photos, and other art works are eclectic in nature. As we looked at the huge paintings on canvas, my boys and I took the liberty of renaming several pieces. (I think some of their title choices were more apropos than the ones the artists chose.) This got the kids more involved in studying the art and enhanced our visit here.

Downstairs is a reading room with several books, many geared for children, that pertain to the art and artists currently featured at the MOCA. A satellite building of MOCA, is the Temporary Contemporary located one mile away at 152 North Central Avenue, Los Angeles in Little Tokyo. The Museum of Contemporary Art is one museum in two buildings.

This type of museum is a fun one to bring kids to as an introduction to art because the pieces are unusual, imaginative, and sometimes puzzling. Idea: After visiting the museum, have the kids come home and create their own contemporary or abstract piece of art.

Hours: Open Tues. - Sun. from 11am - 5pm (Thurs. until 8pm).
Free public tours are given at noon, 1pm, and 2pm.
Closed New Year's Day, Thanksgiving, and Christmas.
Admission: $6 for adults; $4 for seniors and students with I.D.;
children 12 years and under are free. Thurs. from 5pm -
8pm is free admission. Paid admission is good for both
locations of the museum, if visited on the same day.
Parking in the plaza costs about $5.
Ages: 6 years and up.

MUSEUM OF FLYING   ☾
(310) 392-8822 $$
2722 Donald Douglas Loop, North, Santa Monica
(EXIT SANTA MONICA FWY [10] S. ON BUNDY DR., R. ON OCEAN PARK BLVD., L. ON
28TH ST. IT'S N. OF SANTA MONICA AIRPORT.)

Ready to take-off to a place where the sky is the limit? Look - it's a
bird, it's Superman - no, it's a plane (several of them) displayed
overhead! This airy museum has three stories of vintage aircraft,
models, and air-related exhibits. Take the catwalk-like stairs to the
second level, which has an observation window overlooking the airport.
Kids can listen to the control tower via the headphones. My boys also
liked the mock-up of a war-briefing room up here.

Some of the planes are maintained in flight-ready condition. In fact,
a hangar door is open for kids to watch WWII planes and other small
aircraft taxiing, flying, and landing on the runway. Want to feel the
jolting of a "real" flight? Take a simulator ride -$2. If you've always
wanted to be a tactical fighter (but have a real day job), then take
control of the gear for a half-hour simulated flight on a FA-16 - $20.

A replica of the Voyager, which flew non-stop around the world in
1986, is on display at the entrance to Airventure. So is a slightly older
flying model - a Pterodactyl. Airventure is designed just for kids. They
can sit in a real Vietnam War-era helicopter, pilot the controls at a real
cockpit, and play in various pretend planes. There are workshops for
kids ages 5 and older on the weekends. Call for specific times and
details.

Tip: Propel yourself over to the adjoining DC3 RESTAURANT for
their Jr. Jet program. It entails eating at a nice restaurant while the kids
eat, and then enjoy supervised play at the museum. (See DC3
RESTAURANT for more details.)
Hours: Open Wed. - Sun. from 10am - 5pm.
Admission: $7 for adults; $5 for seniors; $3 for ages 3 -17; children 2
years and under are free.
Ages: 3 years and up.

MUSEUM OF NEON ART   ☀
(213) 489-9918 $
501 W. Olympic, Los Angeles

*(EXIT HARBOR FWY [110] E. ON 9TH ST., R. ON HOPE. IT'S ON THE CORNER OF
OLYMPIC AND HOPE, WITH THE ENTRANCE ON HOPE. FREE UNDERGROUND PARKING
IS AVAILABLE AT THE RENAISSANCE TOWER ON GRAND AVE., JUST N. OF OLYMPIC
BLVD.)*

For an enlightening experience, bring the kids to the Museum of
Neon Art. Only here can you see Mona Lisa's smile really light up. Walk
through the rainbow arch and into the warehouse-like rooms that
display rotating exhibits of artists who use kinetic and electric art as an
outlet for their creative endeavors. In other words, there are some
funky-looking, 3-D reliefs and sculptures in here! Most of the pieces are
fragile, but some of them have buttons to push that make parts light up
or move around.

Just outside the museum is Hope Grant Park, which is the front
lawn to the Fashion Institute of Design and Merchandise. This haven of
greenery in the middle of downtown Los Angeles is a welcome respite.
It has a small playground, a mosaic clock tower, colorful mosaic art
forms, and a large fountain that kids love to climb on.

Hours: The museum is open Wed. - Sat., 11am - 6pm; Sun.,
            noon - 5pm. On the second Thurs. of each month, the
            museum is open until 8pm (and admission is free on this
            Thurs. from 5pm - 8pm.) The park is open daily from
            7am - 6pm.

Admission: $5 for adults; $3.50 for students; children 12 years and
            under are free. The park is free.

Ages: 4 years and up.

THE MUSEUM OF TELEVISION AND RADIO   ☼
(310) 786-1000 $$
465 N. Beverly Drive, Beverly Hills
*(EXIT SANTA MONICA FWY [10] N. ON ROBERTSON, L. ON WILSHIRE, R. ON BEVERLY
DR. OR, EXIT SAN DIEGO FWY [405] E. ON SANTA MONICA BLVD, R. ON BEVERLY
DR. TWO HOURS OF FREE VALET PARKING, WITH VALIDATION, IS AVAILABLE UNDER
THE MUSEUM, JUST OFF LITTLE SANTA MONICA BLVD.)*

Tune in to the Museum of Television and Radio, which houses the
ultimate collection of broadcasting programs. Inside the upscale,
contemporary-looking building are various rooms to watch and listen to
shows, with just the touch of a button. The lobby has rotating exhibits of
art, mementos, storyboards, costumes, sets, etc. The Radio Listening
Room is just what its name implies. The room is quiet as visitors use
headphones to choose from five preset radio channels. A sampling of
the rotating selections can include comedy, rock 'n roll, history of radio,
witness to history (e.g. historic speeches), etc. There is also a fully
equipped radio station in here to do live broadcasts. Next door, watch a
pre-selected show in the fifty-seat Screening Room, or watch a film in
the 150-seat Theater Room. Call to see what's playing.

Use the upstairs library to select your choice of radio or television
show. For example, key your television selection into the computer,

then view it in the adjacent Console Room. This room has individual monitors, and family consoles which accommodate up to four people. Your child is in couch potato heaven here, able to choose his own television programs from literally thousands of titles available.

Benefits of this museum include viewing (and listening to) historic shows both for school-aged children and for researchers. Ready access to programs is also great if you just want to choose a favorite show. Call for information on special children's events.

Hours: Open Wed. - Sun. from noon - 5pm; Thursdays until 9pm. Closed New Year's Day, Independence Day, Thanksgiving, and Christmas.

Admission: $6 for adults; $4 for seniors and students; $3 for children 12 years and under.

Ages: 6 years and up.

MUSEUM OF TOLERANCE / SIMON WEISENTHAL ◐ CENTER

(310) 553-8403 $$$

9786 W. Pico Boulevard, Los Angeles
(EXIT SAN DIEGO FWY [405] E. ON SANTA MONICA BLVD., R. ON GLEN BLVD., L. ON PICO.)

The Simon Wiesenthal Center's Beit Hashoah Museum of Tolerance is unique in its format of numerous technologically advanced, interactive major exhibits, and in its focus on personal prejudice, group intolerance, the struggle for civil rights in America, and the Holocaust. After orientation, enter through the door marked "Prejudiced" or the one marked "Unprejudiced" to begin your journey in the American Experience/Tolerancenter. A computer exhibit of the L.A. riots asks visitors for a personal profile - age, gender, ethnicity - then asks thought-provoking questions about social justice and responsibility. You'll be riveted and affected by the sixteen-screen video Civil Rights Wall, an interactive U.S. map that discloses 250 hate groups in America, an intense movie called "Genocide," and a short walk through the Whisper Gallery. Voices in here whisper racial slurs and derogatory remarks, and then encourage you to think twice about the words you use.

The Holocaust "tour" begins as you print out a child's passport. You then witness a series of chronological vignettes, while listening to narration that explains the events leading up to the Holocaust. This factual and emotional forty-five-minute tour is one of the most informative and visual ways to begin to understand what happened. After walking through a replica of the gates of Auschwitz, your tour culminates in the Hall of Testimony, where you'll discover the fate of the child whose passport you hold.

The second floor of the museum contains a Multimedia Learning Center with over thirty work stations. Housed here also, are original letters of Anne Frank, a bunkbed from a concentration camp, and medical instruments. Holocaust survivors speak here several times throughout the day. The third floor displays rotating exhibits. Call for a current schedule. The fourth floor has a cafeteria. Note: Cameras are not allowed in the museum.

On alternating Sundays at 2pm a one-hour musical and/or interactive play is presented for children 5 years and up. This is a lighter version of the museum's focus; encouraging kids to think about how they treat their friends, and other people. Admission to the show is $6 for adults, $4 for ages 5 - 12.

Hours: Open Mon. - Thurs., 10am - 4pm; Fri., 10am - 3pm; Sun., 10:30am - 5pm. Closed Saturdays, Thanksgiving, Christmas, and Jewish holidays.

Admission: $8 for adults; $6 for seniors; $5 for students with ID; $3 for children 12 years and under. Free validated underground parking is available on Pico Blvd.

Ages: 10 years and up - it is too intense for most younger children.

MY JEWISH DISCOVERY PLACE   ☼
(213) 857-0036, ext. 2257 $$
5870 W. Olympic Boulevard, West Los Angeles
(EXIT SANTA MONICA FWY [10] N. ON FAIRFAX AVE., R. ON OLYMPIC. IT'S IN THE WESTSIDE JEWISH COMMUNITY CENTER. PARKING IS AVAILABLE IN THE STRUCTURE BEHIND THE CENTER, ON OLYMPIC BLVD., AND ON SAN VICENTE.)

Shalom and welcome to this colorful and completely hands-on museum, developed for kids to have fun while learning about Jewish history, customs, values, holidays, folklore, traditions, heros, and music, as well as Shabbat, Israel, and the Hebrew language. Oy!

Some of the exhibits and things to do include boarding the Discovery Airplane, that has real cockpit controls, to watch a video of a flight to Israel; 3-2-1 Blast Off, a room with glow-in-the-dark stars, where black light is used to illuminate symbol puzzles (and white clothing), and the touch and feel objects in the discovery box; an activity center for arts and crafts; an Improv Theater, which is a stage and costume center; My Family Roots and Routes featuring a scaled-down Statue of Liberty, a map of the world, and other tools to trace your family's journey to America; a seven-foot by sixteen-foot Torah; a miniature model synagogue; a Jewish Artifact Rubbing Table; and lots of changing exhibits in playhouse-size rooms.

Hours: Open Tues - Thurs., 12:30pm - 4pm; Sun., 12:30pm - 5pm. Closed for national holidays and Jewish holidays.

Admission: $3 for adults; $2 for ages 3 - 7; children 2 years and under are free.

Ages: 2 - 12 years.

NATURAL HISTORY MUSEUM OF LOS ANGELES ☼ COUNTY

(213) 763-3466   *$$$*

900 Exposition Boulevard, Los Angeles
(EXIT THE HARBOR FWY [110] W. ON EXPOSITION BLVD., L. ON FLOWER, L. ON
FIGUEROA. OR, EXIT SANTA MONICA FWY [10] S. ON VERMONT, L. ON EXPOSITION,
R. ON FIGUEROA. METERED PARKING IS AVAILABLE ON THE STREET ACROSS FROM
U.S.C., OR PARK IN THE LOT ON MENLO BLVD.)

This museum has a lot of a little bit of everything. Four halls show North American, African, and exotic mammals mounted in a backdrop of their natural habitat (i.e. huge dioramas). The gigantic walrus, buffalo, and elephant were the most impressive. Take a walk through time in the American history rooms. They contain early vehicles, such as tractors, stagecoaches, and a streetcar; mannequins dressed in period clothing; early weapons; and other pioneer artifacts. The outstanding rock and mineral collection includes flourescent minerals (that shine neon colors under black light), and rocks that are so brilliant in color or so oddly shaped that they look unreal. Some of our favorite exhibits were the dinosaurs in the Din-O-Scovery room. On display in life-like poses are some of the massive animals in skeletal form, while others are fleshed out, so to speak. Other exhibits on this floor include a real mummy; a preserved, unusually long and flat-looking fish (the oarfish); a Megamouth shark; and a room devoted to pre-Columbian archaeology.

The second floor has an entire wing devoted to our fine feathered friends. There are taxidermied penguins, vultures, ostriches, ducks, turquoise cotingas (guess what color they are?), and more. Use the pull out drawers in the hallway to see a variety of feathers and bird eggs. A large part of the ornithology (study of birds) exhibit is interactive. Turn a disk to get a magnified view of wings, feathers, and bones. Step on a scale to see how much just your bones weigh - they make up 17% of your body weight. Exit through a dark rain forest that resounds with bird noises. Another room upstairs presents an in-depth look at marine life.

"Hands-on" is the motto at the wonderful Discovery Center. This includes putting on puppet shows; making rubbings from fossilized shells (you'll take home a lot of these papers); playing on computers; going for a fossil dig at the small sandpit; and touching rocks, shells, bones, and skulls of an alligator and polar bear. Kids can also touch (or wrap themselves in) skins of deer, fox, skunk, opossum, sheep, etc. There are live animals in here, too, such as iguanas, toads, a python (he gets fed once a week), and fish. Forty different Discovery Boxes offer different activities with varying degrees of difficulty such as "Sharks," which simply has shark teeth and fossil vertebrae to look at and study, plus books on sharks to read; "Native Games," which gives directions and materials to play with walnut shells, dice, Indian darts, etc.; and "Listen Up," a game where the same objects that are in clear jars are also in black jars. Shake them, listen, and then match the sounds and the jars.

Just up the stairs is the Insect Zoo, which has cases swarming with live insects! Show no fear (or disgust) in front of your kids - some of the little buggers are quite interesting. You'll see scorpions, millipedes, tarantulas, beetles, and more (than you've ever wanted!)

The museum also features wonderful rotating exhibits, usually downstairs. We saw "Cats, Mild to Wild," which featured housecats to lions in dramatic pictures, interactive animated figures, etc. Call to see what is currently showing. Picnic tables and lots of grassy area surrounds the museum. (Also see the nearby AEROSPACE MUSEUM, CALIFORNIA AFRO- AMERICAN MUSEUM, CALIFORNIA SCIENCE CENTER, EXPOSITION PARK, and 3-D IMAX THEATER)

Hours: Open Tues. - Sun. from 10am - 5pm. Closed New Year's Day, Thanksgiving, and Christmas.

Admission: $6 for adults; $3.50 for seniors and ages 12 - 18; $2 for ages 5 - 12; children 4 years and under are free. (Certain discounts are available through AAA.) The first Tuesday of every month is free admission day. Parking in the lot costs $5.

Ages: 2½ years and up.

NEWPORT HARBOR NAUTICAL MUSEUM

(714) 673-7863 $

151 East Coast Highway, Newport Beach
(TAKE COSTA MESA FWY [55] TO END, TURNS INTO NEWPORT BLVD., L. ON E. 17TH ST., R., AT END, ON DOVER DR., L ON E. COAST HWY., ON NEWPORT BAY)

This beautiful riverboat, now harbored in Newport Bay, looks like it just came down the Mississippi River. Our visit here wasn't long, but it was interesting. An upstairs room is devoted to glass-enclosed model ships. The huge (for a scale model) Fort Victoria is displayed in the center. The U.S.S. Missouri model, built in remembrance of the men who served on her and for the WWII peace treaty which was signed on board, is complete with men and little cannons, plus waves under the bow and stern. Other outstanding models were crafted from sterling silver, intricately carved wood, and bone. In the hallway is a captain's wheel with beautiful stained glass panels - spin it gently. Elegantly displayed exhibits in the other upstairs room consist of artifacts from early California. My boys particularly liked the bowl made from whale vertebrae and the necklace made from fish bones. Downstairs is a wall display of ships in a bottle and a small seashell exhibit. You can also watch a short, grainy, homemade video taken during a real hurricane in Newport Beach in 1939.

If you've worked up an appetite, try the classy Riverboat Cafe & Dinner House located on board. It's open Tuesday through Friday from 11am to 9pm,and weekends from 7am to 9pm, and offers good food at reasonable prices. For example, Chinese Chicken Salad is $7.25;

burgers, turkey and ham sandwiches average $6.50; Filet Mignon is $19.95; and Seafood Pasta is $17.95.

Hours: The museum is open Tues. - Sun. from 10am - 5pm.

Admission: $4 for adults; $1 for children 12 years and under.

Ages: 6 years and up.

PETERSEN AUTOMOTIVE MUSEUM   ☼

(213) 930-CARS (2277)   *$$$*

6060 Wilshire Boulevard, Los Angeles

(EXIT SANTA MONICA FWY [10] N. ON FAIRFAX, R. ON WILSHIRE.)

The driving force behind this 300,000 square foot, state-of-the-art museum is dedication to the art, culture, and history of the automobile. A visit here will definitely accelerate your child's interest in cars! Streetscape, on the first floor, displays classics and incredibly modern, almost futuristic cars. Each car is displayed in its own walk-through setting, complete with asphalt and manholes, or sidewalks and fake plants - whatever surroundings fit the car. Sounds, like birds chirping at "Stuck in the Mud," help kids enter into the spirit of the lifestyles represented here. Kids can climb aboard the trolley car used in Laurel and Hardy movies, although there are not many other cars that are hands-on. Take a chronological walk through time via cars, from horse and buggy to an exhibit of gas pumps to the fifties to solar-paneled cars.

The second floor has six galleries, including a terrific collection of hot rods, and the Hollywood Gallery that stars cars that were featured in movies and television shows, and/or that were owned by celebrities. However, the ultimate in kid-cool is putting on a helmet and getting behind the wheel of a real Indianapolis 500 race car! The Otis Chandler Motorcycle Gallery gets biking enthusiasts revved-up. The third floor showcases various artistic expressions centered around cars, such as pictures, sculptures, architecture, etc.

The Petersen Museum also offers special activities for kids such as Art Deco Days where kids paint a real car and/or decorate it with glued-on objects; a Kids' Pit Crew class in which the kids learn all about a drag race and then go to one; and a pencil Treasure Hunt which entails finding "mystery cars" by matching cars with line drawings and answering questions such as, "What was the speed limit in 1913?"

Stop in for a bite to eat at the AM/PM market (a clever tie-in), on the entrance level of the museum.

Hours: Open Tues. - Sun. from 10am - 6pm.

Admission: $7 for adults; $5 for seniors and students with ID; $3 for ages 5 - 12; children 4 years and under are free. Enter the museum parking structure from Fairfax - $4 for all-day parking.

Ages: 5 years and up.

POINT VINCENTE INTERPRETIVE CENTER AND PARK ☼
(310) 377-5370 $
31501 Palos Verdes Drive W., Rancho Palos Verdes
(FROM PACIFIC COAST HIGHWAY [1] IN REDONDO BEACH, TURN S. ON PALOS VERDES DR. W. AND DRIVE THE WINDING COASTAL ROAD JUST PAST HAWTHORNE BLVD., TURN R. INTO THE PARK. OR, EXIT HARBOR FWY [110] W. ON ANAHEIM, L. ON PALOS VERDES DR. N., L. ON CRENSHAW TO END, L. ON HAWTHORNE TO END, L. ON PALOS VERDES DR. W. OR, EXIT SAN DIEGO FWY [405] S. ON CRENSHAW, GO TO THE END, L. ON HAWTHORNE TO END, L. ON PALOS VERDES DR. W.)

This museum has a variety of natural wonders on display, such as fossils of ocean animals, a side-by-side comparison of fossilized shells with recent shells of the same type, and taxidermied animals such as the great horned owl, a gray fox, and a peacock.

Whales are the main focus here as this is a prime site for whale watching. The museum has an overhead model of a gray whale, a continuously running video on whales, and a telephone so kids can literally listen to the call of the whales. There is a small enclosed area upstairs and an outside area that are good spots to either watch the whales as they migrate, January through March, or just to see a terrific view of the coastline. The Point Vincente Lighthouse is close by and on foggy days, you'll hear the horn blast its warning signal.

A quarter-mile paved trail winds around the Interpretive Center, and the few picnic tables that are here. If you and the kids are in a hiking or biking mood, there is a three-mile, or so, narrow dirt trail leading from the Center and looping back around. This main pathway and its offshoots are alternately flat and hilly, so be prepared for some real exercise!

Have a whale of a time at this small museum and at the park.

Hours: The Center is open daily in the summer from 10am - dusk. It's open daily the rest of the year from 10am - 5pm. Closed New Year's Day, Thanksgiving, Christmas Eve, and Christmas Day. The park is open daily from dawn to dusk.

Admission: The museum is $2 for adults; $1 for seniors and ages 3 - 12; children 2 years and under are free.

Ages: 2½ years and up.

QUEEN MARY ☼
(562) 435-3511 $$$$
Pier J, Long Beach
(TAKE LONG BEACH FWY [710] TO THE END, R. ON QUEEN'S WAY BRIDGE AND FOLLOW SIGNS.)

Cruise over to Long Beach Harbor to see the Queen, Queen Mary, I mean, one of the largest luxury passenger liners ever built. Take a one-hour guided "Behind-the-Scenes" tour and learn about the ship's fascinating history. Only on this tour can you see the dining room/ballroom, boiler room, and an original First Class Suite. Younger children, however, will get antsy. We thoroughly enjoyed our self-guiding, "Shipwalk" tour. Starting on the lower decks, we watched a video called "The Queen Mary Story" about its construction, Maiden Voyage, and service during WWII. The Hall of Maritime Heritage (a small museum) displays navigating instruments, ship models, and pictures and stories of famous doomed ships, including the Titanic. Everything in the engine room is clearly marked, making it easy to explain the machinery's function. The last remaining propeller on the ship is in an open-top, propellor box in water. (It looks like a shark fin at first; and tell your kids that the life-size diver is just a model.) We toured the bridge, the wheel house where officers were quartered, and the state room exhibits.

The wooden upper decks are great for ~~running~~ strolling around. A highlight for the boys was playing on the gun turrets on the bow of the ship, as they fought off invisible enemies. For a real thrilling experience, bungee jump over the waters between the Queen Mary and dry land - $85 per jump. (I get a vicarious thrill just from watching!)

Queen Mary's Seaport, adjacent to the ship's berth, has the Queen's Marketplace for your shopping and dining pleasures. There are also several fine shops and restaurants on the ship. Tip: For a ~~cheap~~ inexpensive family date come on board after 6pm when there is no admission charge, only a parking fee. Although the stores and many parts of the ship are not available, the restaurants are open and it's fun for kids to walk around, plus the sunsets are beautiful.

Hours: Open daily from 10am - 6pm.

Admission: General admission is $11 for adults; $9 for seniors; $6 for ages 4 - 11; children 3 years and under are free. A combo, which includes general admission and the behind-the-scenes guided tour, is $15 for adults; $13 for seniors; $9 for children ages 4 - 11 years; children 3 years and under are free. (Ask about AAA discounts.) Parking is $2 for an hour; $5 for all day.

Ages: 3 years and up.

RANCHO LOS ALAMITOS   ☼

(562) 431-3541   !

6400 E. Bixby Hill Road, Long Beach

(EXIT SAN DIEGO FWY [405] S. ON PALO VERDE AVE. TO THE END. GO THROUGH THE GATED ENTRANCE [TELL THE GATE EMPLOYEE YOU ARE GOING TO THE MUSEUM], L. ON BIXBY HILL.)

This beautiful, historic ranch appeals to kids of various ages. The barn has several horse stalls, a few of which have been converted into small rooms (or self-contained history lessons). They display photographs, animal pelts, branding irons, and (our favorite) a suspended horse harness, showing how a horse was hooked up to help plow. Other buildings of particular interest, in this area, contain a blacksmith shop filled with old tools, and a room with lots of saddles and branding irons. A ranch is not complete without animals, so goats, sheep, chickens, ducks, and Shire horses are in outside pens.

An hour-long tour includes going inside the adobe ranch house. It's always fun to try to guess the name and use of gadgets in old kitchens. The bedroom, library, music, and billiards rooms are interesting to older kids.

The front of the house has a garden and two 150-year-old Moreton Bay fig trees with huge roots. An Artifacts Room is open at certain time where kids can touch - that's right - artifacts!

Hours: Open Wed. - Sun. from 1pm - 5pm. Tours are offered on the half hour. Closed holidays.

Admission: Donations are welcomed.

Ages: 3 years and up for the outside grounds; 6 years and up for a tour of the house.

RANCHO LOS CERRITOS

(562) 570-1755

4600 Virginia Road, Long Beach

(EXIT SAN DIEGO FWY [405] N. ON LONG BEACH BLVD., L. ON ROOSEVELT, THEN MAKE A QUICK R. ON VIRGINIA RD.)

This picturesque historic rancho is situated almost at the end of Virginia Road. The visitors center has a clever exhibit of big puzzle pieces representing different eras with pictures and information on them, that attempt to fit together pieces of our past. The information is interesting and some of the window-type "pieces" offer glimpses into the past by displaying old pottery, equipment, and other artifacts.

The perimeter gardens are beautifully landscaped around a grassy, center area. There is also a huge, old Moreton Bay fig tree with tremendous roots. A one-hour tour takes you through the house which is furnished as it was in the late 1870's. This is a terrific way to see and learn about our Mexican-California heritage. Kids can more easily relate to the bigger picture of state history when they explore a small part of it.

School groups experience hands-on fun, such as candle-dipping and playing old-fashioned games. They also have the opportunity to do chores, such as butter churning and washing clothes, the way they were done years ago. The tour might also include seeing a blacksmith's demonstration.

Ask for a Kid's Activity treasure hunt which uses pencil and paper to look for particular items throughout the museum - it makes the visit here that much more interesting. Bring a picnic lunch as there are tables on the grounds. Ask for a schedule of the Rancho's special family events - they are great!

Hours: Open Wed. - Sun. from 1pm - 5pm. Guided tours are given on the weekends only on the hour. School tours are given on Wed. and Thurs., from 9:30am - noon.

Admission: Free; donations appreciated.
    Ages: 7 years and up.

RAYMOND M. ALF MUSEUM   ☀
(909) 624-2798 $
1175 W. Baseline Road, Claremont
(EXIT THE SAN BERNARDINO FWY [10] N. ON TOWNE AVE., L. ON BASELINE RD., R.
UP THE HILL. IT IS PART OF THE WEBB SCHOOLS.)

Make no bones about it, this unique museum displays dinosaur skeletons and skulls, plus fossils and archaeological finds from all over the world. As you enter this circular museum you'll see "Footprints in the Sands of Time," an unusually large rock slab containing numerous reptile footprints that is reportedly 250 million years old. Kids can try the Indian stone mortar and pestles, used for grinding meal. Next to the display on Egyptology is a skull cast of a Purussaurus, an animal with jaws almost as big as the upper part of my body. The touch table has mastodon tusks, vertebrae, rocks, and a fossilized turtle shell, which is surprisingly heavy.

Good-sized rock and mineral specimens, like geodes and petrified wood, abound, as do fossils such as mammoth molars, and fern imbedded in rock. Have your kids look at the rocks on the table near the exit and take the "test" - do they know which is a fossil and which is a mineral?

Head towards the hallway to see quite a display of stuffed heads, including buffalo, mountain lions, and lots of members of the deer family. The exhibits downstairs consist mainly of trackways, which are rock slabs with castings of dinosaur, camel, horse, and bear-dog footprints. The trackways are displayed both on the walls and around the room, like glass-encased coffee tables (albeit priceless ones).

This museum is great for older kids who are interested in paleontology, or for younger ones to just see the sheer size of some of the animals from long ago. Month-long research expeditions, which combine fossil collecting and camping, are available for high school students during the summer.

    Hours: The museum is open Mon. - Thurs., 8am - noon and again from 1pm - 4pm; plus the first Sunday of each month from 1pm - 4pm. Closed June, July, August, and Webb School holidays.
Admission: $1 for ages 5 and up. On Wed. admission is free.
    Ages: 4 years and up.

RIPLEY'S BELIEVE IT OR NOT! MUSEUM   ☀
(Hollywood)
(213) 466-6335 $$$
6780 Hollywood Boulevard, Hollywood
(EXIT HOLLYWOOD FWY [101] W. ON HOLLYWOOD BLVD.)

See the description under RIPLEY'S BELIEVE IT OR NOT! MUSEUM (Buena Park). This museum displays nearly 300 unusual and amazing items and facts collected from around the world.

A few doors down is Mann's Chinese Theater, where many past and present stars have left their imprints in the concrete courtyard in front of the theater. See if your child can fill his favorite star's shoes!

Hours: Open Sun. - Thurs., 10am - 10pm; Fri. - Sat., 10am - 11pm.

Admission: $8.95 for adults; $6.95 for seniors; $5.95 for ages 5 - 11; children 4 years and under are free.

Ages: 5 years and up.

SHERIFFS TRAINING AND REGIONAL SERVICES (STARS) CENTER
(562) 946-7081   !

11515 South Colima Road, Whittier
(GOING N. ON SANTA ANA FWY [5], EXIT N. ON CARMENITA RD., R. ON LEFFINGWELL, L. ON COLIMA. GOING S. ON 5, EXIT E. ON IMPERIAL HWY., L. ON COLIMA.)

This 5,000 square foot museum depicts the history of the Los Angeles County Sheriffs Department from 1850 through present day. A 1938 Studebaker police car is a classic not to be touched, but kids can "ride" on the police motorcycle and push a button to make the red lights flash. (Hopefully, it won't bring back any bad memories for you who are reading this section.)

A westernized-room has a replica of a nineteenth-century sheriff's office, complete with a model sheriff, and a prisoner behind bars. The Vice Exhibit showcases how different carnival-type games can be a rip-off, as well as illegal. The back room, which can be bypassed, contains a gun case, gang weapons, and graphic scenes of some infamous cases.

Another room contains an entire helicopter, plus the side of a Search and Rescue helicopter mounted on the wall that has a child mannequin in a basket, being air-lifted. The live-video footage shows the awesome job that Search and Rescue teams do.

Hours: Open Mon. - Fri. from 9am - 4pm.

Admission: Free

Ages: 5 years and up.

SKIRBALL CULTURAL CENTER
(310) 440-4500 $$

2701 N. Sepulveda Boulevard, Los Angeles
(EXIT SAN DIEGO FWY [405] ON SKIRBALL CENTER DR.)

This Cultural Center tells the story of the Jewish people, from post-biblical days and journeys to present day life in America. The exhibits of Jewish heritage include ancient and modern artifacts, photographs, art,

and film and video screenings all housed in a building beautifully
designed with archways and high-ceilings. The variety of the unique
Torah mantles and Hanukkah lamps on display is outstanding. (One of
our favorites is the menorah with each of its eight branches fashioned
like the Statute of Liberty.)

The "Coming to America" room features a reproduction of the hand
and torch of the Statue of Liberty at seventy percent of full scale. It's
huge! This room also contains documents from past United States
Presidents that supported non-discrimination. The Lincoln display has
his face in life cast (i.e. a mold of his actual face), which is one of only
six ever made.

In the Discovery Center, geared for ages 8 and up, kids can
uncover the wonders of the archaeological world. Upstairs is a recreation of a dig site, a hands-on tool area, and a great computer game
called "Dig It." The stairway is lined with lamps behind glass displays.
The downstairs has a reproduction of a tomb in a rock; displays that
show the new condition of an animal or object, and then its remains
after years have gone by; and over twenty "discovery" games and
activities that reinforce the concepts presented. Kids can also learn
about the history of writing and try different forms of it at the rubbing
table. School tours will gain a tremendous amount of insight into the
archaeological world as docents teach and guide them through the
Discovery Center. Then, they'll go outside, where students can
excavate roads, walls, an alter, etc. at a small mock dig site.

As you enter and exit the Skirball Center, you'll see, etched in
stone, words fit for everyone, "Go forth . . . and be a blessing to the
world." (Genesis 12: 1 - 3)

Hours: Open Tues. - Fri., 10am - 4pm; Sat., noon - 5pm; Sun.,
10am - 5pm.

Admission: $7 for adults; $5 for seniors and students; children 11
years and under are free.

Ages: 7 years and up.

SOUTHWEST MUSEUM   ☼

(213) 221-2164 $$

234 Museum Drive, Highland Park

*(EXIT PASADENA FWY [110] N.E. ON AVENUE 43, R. ON FIGUEROA ST., L. ON AVE.
45, R. ON MARMION WAY, L. ON MUSEUM DR.)*

There are three ways to enter this museum on a hill. One is an
unadventurous walk up the driveway. Another is walking up the steep
Hopi trail, which is a stepping stone walkway. Catch your breath at the
top, and take a look at the view of the city and beyond. The third is
walking (running) through a 250-foot tunnel (which echos every footstep
and shout) burrowed into the museum hillside. It is lined with twenty
Indian dioramas. Take the elevator up into the museum.

The Southwest Museum collection represents Native American
cultures from Alaska to South America. The two-story building has

displays of Indian clothing, some decorated with elk's teeth or b
costumes; boots; beautifully beaded moccasins; an extensive co
of baskets; rabbit-skin blankets; weapons; turquoise and silver cr
jewelry; early baby snugglies (cradleboards); musical instruments such
as a flute, drum, and rattle; and Kachina dolls, which are supposedly
rain-bringing spiritual beings. The exhibits are mostly behind glass.

A rotating exhibit room currently has corralled Spirit Horses, the
entrance of which is a simulated cave, with horses painted on its walls.
The room itself, which doubles as an auditorium, has statues of horses,
paintings of horses, a mural of horses, beautiful saddles, etc. *Neigh*
doubt about it, this room embodies the American Indian legend that the
horse is a spiritual gift of the gods.

Another room has an eighteen-foot Cheyenne tepee (just to look
at), and a big rock with reproduced pictographs. Kids can crawl through
a doorway (think dog door) that has photographs on the other side. Also
on display here are headbands, arrowheads, bows, and rattles made of
cocoons and rattlesnakes. Outside, an archeological dig site is a bit
further up the hill. A small botanical garden is in the front of the
museum.

How do you learn more about Native Americans? An extensive
research library on the museum grounds is open to the public
Wednesday through Saturday, from 1pm to 5pm.

If you're looking for a place to picnic, Highland Park is just north, on
Figueroa Street.

Hours: Open Tues. - Sun. from 10am - 5pm. Closed major
holidays.
Admission: $5 for adults; $3 for seniors and students; $2 for ages 7 -
18; children 6 years and under are free.
Ages: 5 years and up.

S. S. LANE VICTORY ☼
(310) 519-9545 $
Berth 94, San Pedro
*(EXIT HARBOR FWY [110] OR VINCENT THOMAS BRIDGE ON HARBOR BLVD. CROSS
HARBOR BLVD. ONTO SWINFORD ST. AND FOLLOW SIGNS TO BERTH 94.)*

This forty-five-year-old ship served as a cargo ship during World
War II, the Korean War, and Vietnam War. The large Victory ship is not
only seaworthy, but it is a museum, with one-hour tours given by retired
merchant marines. We sensed adventure, though, and decided to
explore the ship unaccompanied.

You and your kids will get ship-shape by climbing up and down
ladders from the bridge and crew's quarters to the radio room, and into
the huge engine room. The multi-level engine room is a bit spooky, with
the noises and bulky machinery, but this added to the excitement of
being on our own.

Guns and superstructures make the decks interesting to
investigate. (Tell your kids that they are on a poop deck - it will make

your outing a big hit!) Below deck, the ship's museum room features memorabilia such as flags, whistles, photographs, and cannons. The Gift Shoppe sells wonderful nautical items from clothing to medals to model ship kits. Batten down the hatches and be sure to wear tennis shoes for your ship-to-shore adventure.

A few times a year, the S.S. Lane Victory hosts an all-day cruise to Catalina. A "Nazi spy" is discovered on board. Nazi fighters are soon attacking the ship, but American aircraft come to the rescue. The mock aerial dogfight uses blanks, but the World War II planes are real. This is more exciting than any Hollywood movie! The cruise also includes continental breakfast, live music, and a buffet luncheon. The cost is $100 for adults; $60 for kids under 15 years.

Hours: Open daily from 9am - 4pm.
Admission: $3 for adults; $1 for ages 5 - 15; children 4 years and under are free. Parking is free for the first two hours.
Ages: 5 years and up.

TOURNAMENT HOUSE and THE WRIGLEY GARDENS
(818) 449-4100

391 S. Orange Grove Boulevard, Pasadena
(TAKE PASADENA FWY [110] N. TO END, TURNS INTO ARROYO PKY., L. ON CALIFORNIA, R. ON ORANGE GROVE. GOING W. ON FOOTHILL FWY [210], EXIT S. ON FAIR OAKS, R. ON COLORADO, L. ON ORANGE GROVE. GOING E. ON 134, EXIT E. ON COLORADO, R. ON ORANGE GROVE.)

The Tournament House, more aptly referred to as a mansion, is used throughout the year as the meeting headquarters for committees, float sponsors, and practically everything else associated with the annual Tournament of Roses Parade. The rooms are elegantly furnished.

The second floor is interesting to kids who have some knowledge and interest in the parade and Rose Bowl games. Each former bedroom is dedicated to various elements of Tournament of Roses' traditions. The Rose Bowl Room showcases pennants and football helmets from Rose Bowl teams, plus photographs, trophies, and other memorabilia dating back to the first game in 1902. The Queen and Court Room is femininely decorated to allow the reigning Queen and her Court, who attend almost 100 events a year, a place to recuperate. A display case in here features past winners' crowns, tiaras, and jewelry. The Grand Marshall's Room shows photographs of past Grand Marshals like Bob Hope, Shirley Temple Black (do your kids know who she is?), Hank Aaron, Walt Disney, Charles Schultz, etc. Out in the hallway is an impressive 240-pound sterling silver saddle - heigh ho, Silver, away! The President's Room has pictures and other mementos of past presidents of the Rose Parade.

The beautifully-landscaped grounds have a fountain surrounded by a rose garden (surprise!). The huge rose garden at the north end also blooms seasonally.

Hours: Tours of the house are given February through August, on Thursdays from 2pm- 4pm. The grounds are open throughout the year except December 31 - January 2.

Admission: Free

Ages: 7 years and up.

TRAVEL TOWN ☿

(213) 662-5874

!

5200 Zoo Drive, Los Angeles

(GOING N. ON GOLDEN STATE FWY [5] OR W. ON VENTURA FWY [134] EXIT AT ZOO DR. AND FOLLOW THE SIGNS. GOING E. ON 134, EXIT AT FOREST LAWN DR., L. ON ZOO DR. GOING S. ON 5 EXIT S. ON WESTERN, L. ON VICTORY BLVD. TO ZOO DR. IT'S NEAR THE L. A. ZOO.)

"All aboarrrrrd!" This wonderful outdoor "town" has a "trainriffic" atmosphere. There are boxcars, a few cabooses, and steam locomotives to climb into (but not on top of). The grassy area invites you to rest (one can always hope), play, and/or picnic. A scaled model train take you for a ride around the small town - $1.75 for adults, $1 for seniors, $1.25 for kids 12 years and under.

Inside the buildings are old-fashioned carriages, wagons, period automobiles, and early fire-fighting equipment. It's tempting to touch the vehicles, but don't give in to temptation. Bring a few coins for the kids to put in the coin-operated player piano. If you are looking for more things to do in this immediate area, see GRIFFITH PARK. (Live Steamers, located just west of Travel Town, offers free, twelve-minute rides through Griffith Park on Sundays from 11am - 3pm.)

Hours: Open April through October, Mon. - Fri., 10am - 5pm; Sat. - Sun. and holidays, 10am - 6pm. Open November through March, Mon. - Fri., 10am - 4pm; Sat. - Sun. and holidays 10am - 5pm. Closed Christmas.

Admission: Donations

Ages: 2 years and up.

U.C.L.A. OCEAN DISCOVERY CENTER ☿

(310) 393-6149

$

1600 Ocean Front Walk, Santa Monica

(EXIT SANTA MONICA FWY [10] N. ON 4TH ST., L. ON COLORADO AVE. IT IS AT THE FOOT OF THE SANTA MONICA PIER.)

Discover what really lives in the Santa Monica Bay at the Discovery Center, located under the Santa Monica Pier. This small, but fascinating center has several tanks of live sea creatures to look at and touch. The changing exhibit is the open ocean tank. We saw Moon Jellies that were almost mesmerizing to watch as their milky white "bodies" floated gracefully around in their tank. Another large aquarium holds crabs, sea stars, and various fish. Use the flashlight provided to see the tiny swell sharks developing inside their hanging egg cases. Mature swell sharks, sand crabs, sand dollars, leopard sharks, and batrays are too fragile for fingers, but they are easily seen in shallow tanks placed at a child's eye level. Kids can, however, gently touch tidepool life such as sea stars, sea anemones, and sea slugs. A touch table displays a shark's jaw and individual teeth. It also has a microscope for closeup look at scales, shells, etc.

Another prime attraction in the center is the numerous Discovery boxes that are filled with age-appropriate activities, games, and/or books. Choose from Diving Deep, Knot Relay, Ocean Life Puzzles, Beach Bingo, and more. The beautiful marine-muraled classroom was designed for the instructional part of the school programs offered here. These informative and interactive one-hour programs are offered October through May. Various summer programs are also available.

Make a day of your visit to the Discovery Center by taking a walk on the pier, enjoying some rides at Pacific Park, or just playing at the beach! (See SANTA MONICA PIER for more information.)

Hours: Open Sat., 10am - 5pm; Sun., 11am - 5pm. School programs are currently offered Tues. - Fri. at 9am, 10:30am, and noon.

Admission: $3 for adults (or 2 adults for $5); $1 for students; children 4 years and under are free. School programs are currently $75 for up to 75 students.

Ages: 3 years and up.

VISTA DEL LAGO VISITORS CENTER   ☼
(805) 294-0219   !

Interstate 5, Vista del Lago
(EXIT GOLDEN STATE FWY [5] TO VISTA DEL LAGO. IT IS 20 MILES NORTH OF SANTA CLARITA VALLEY.)

Overlooking Pyramid Lake is a hexagon-shaped building showcasing California's liquid gold - water. This surprisingly interesting "museum" features many educational and interactive exhibits that show the water supply and delivery systems throughout California - the State Water Project. Step on special scales in the first room and find out how much of your body is comprised of water (and how much you weigh). Watch video presentations that point out that although water is abundant in the north, most of the population is in the south, so we need ways to transport it down. At the "Big Lift," visitors can turn a crank to lift up a full bucket of water; this translates into learning how much energy it takes for a pumping plant to lift water over the mountains. Learn how water is treated before it is delivered to homes, and how it is tested for quality. Thirsty yet? Go with the flow by playing the computer games and using the touch screens in each of the seven display rooms. The Visitors Center is a great place to quench your child's desire to learn about irrigation, flood control, and water conservation. Tip: After your visit here, enjoy the rest of the day at Pyramid Lake, where you can boat, fish, swim, picnic, hike, and even camp.

Hours: Open daily 9am - 5pm. Closed New Year's Day, Thanksgiving, and Christmas.

Admission: Free

Ages: 4 years and up.

WELLS FARGO HISTORY MUSEUM   ☀

(213) 253-7166 $

Wells Fargo Center, 333 S. Grand Avenue, Los Angeles
(EXIT HARBOR FWY [110] E. ON 3ᴿᴰ ST., R. ON GRAND.)

Discover the Old West in the middle of downtown Los Angeles. The history and development of the West (and of Wells Fargo) is laid out like booty in this museum. Highlights include an 100-year old stagecoach (which kids may not climb on); a replica stagecoach (that they are welcome to climb in); a replica of an 1850's agent's office; a mining display with yes, real gold; a gold miner's rocker; a telegraph machine to try out; photographs; and a twenty-minute film that depicts the hardships of a journey taken in 1852 from St. Louis to San Francisco. Buy a pan and some gold so kids can try their hand at working a claim in your backyard!

Hours: Open Mon. - Fri. from 9am - 5pm. Closed bank holidays. Tours are available with advanced reservations.

Admission: Free. Parking starts at $4 on Hope Street and 3ʳᵈ.

Ages: 4 years and up.

THE WESTERN HOTEL / MUSEUM   ☀

(805) 723-6250   !

557 W. Lancaster Boulevard, Lancaster
(GOING N. ON ANTELOPE VALLEY FWY [14] EXIT N. ON 20ᵀᴴ ST. WEST, R. ON AVE J,
L. ON 10ᵀᴴ ST., R. ON LANCASTER BLVD. GOING S. ON ANTELOPE VALLEY FWY [14]
EXIT E. ON AVE. J, L. ON 10ᵀᴴ ST., R. ON LANCASTER BLVD.)

This small, quaint Western Hotel/Museum has been restored to look like it did when it was originally built in the late 1800's, when room rentals were only $1 a day. The downstairs has a few bedrooms and a parlor that contains old furniture, a wheelchair, and a phonograph that belonged to the last owner, Myrtie Webber. Kids are interested in hearing some of the stories about her, and are impressed that she lived until she was 110 years old! (She doesn't look a day over 70 in her photographs.)

Upstairs is a dinosaur/fossil/artifacts room; a life-size diorama of early Antelope Valley residents and housing facilities, which translates as Native Americans and their huts; a furnished office; and Myrtie's bedroom, which displays some of her clothing and hats, along with her bedroom furniture. The highlight for my boys was seeing the vivid black-and-white pictures of jack rabbit hunts. The rabbits were hunted, corralled, and then clubbed to death. Although it is not a pretty sight, it is an interesting slice of Lancaster history.

Hours: Open Fri. - Sun. from noon - 4pm.
Admission: Free
Ages: 4 years and up.

WESTERN MUSEUM OF FLIGHT

(310) 332-6228 $

12016 S. Prairie Avenue, Hawthorne
(EXIT SAN DIEGO FWY [405] E. ON EL SEGUNDO, L. ON PRAIRIE. IT'S IN THE HAWTHORNE AIRPORT, ON THE CORNER OF PRAIRIE AND 120TH.)

A rendition of "Off we go, into the wild blue yonder, flying high into the sky. . ." goes through one's mind when visiting this museum. The Western Museum of Flight "houses" between twelve to fifteen rare planes like the YF23A, YF17, a flyable Freedom Fighter, and an exact replica of the first controlled aircraft, a 1883 glider. Most of the planes are outside, braving the elements, although several are inside the hanger. The ones inside are being restored, so kids have the opportunity to see this process. Also in the hanger are displays of engines, model planes, medals, leather helmets and jackets, and other memorabilia from WWI and WWII. This museum is for the more serious students of flight. For those interested in doing aeronautical research, an extensive library is available. Call for more details.

Hours: Open Tues. - Sat. from 10am - 3pm.
Admission: $3 for adults; $2 for kids 12 years and under.
Ages: 6 years and up.

THE WHITTIER MUSEUM

(562) 945-3871   !

6755 Newlin Avenue, Whittier
(EXIT SAN GABRIEL FWY [605] E. ON WHITTIER BLVD., L. ON PHILADELPHIA, L. ON NEWLIN. IT'S ON THE CORNER OF PHILADELPHIA AND NEWLIN.)

Journey back in time to the early days of Whittier, circa 1900. The first stop is a wonderfully re-created, full-sized Main Street. The Victorian style is predominate in both the store and home fronts, and in the fully-furnished, walk-through rooms. A stereoscope, an old-fashioned stove and bathtub are some of our favorite items. Authentically-dressed models all around make the kids feel even more a part of this era. The next few rooms feature an outhouse, a water pump that kids can actually try, photos, murals depicting early Whittier as a farming community, a tractor, old farm tools, and a big model of an oil derrick.

Sitting on old church pews, kids can watch a video that shows the history of Whittier. The transportation room has photos, an encased display of old medical instruments and medicine vials, plus a doctor's buggy, a racing plane, and a replicated front end of the historic Red Car.

Walk up through the Red Car and into the Children's Area to a room filled with hands-on delights, such as old typewriters, adding machines, telephones, and a switchboard. There are also old-fashioned toys to play with and clothes for dressing up.

The Library Room is an archival room on the history of Whittier. Upstairs is a large gallery room with changing exhibits, so call to see what's currently showing. Kids enjoy walking through history at this museum.

Hours: Open Sat. - Sun. from 1pm - 4pm. Group tours are also given Tues. - Fri., by appointment.
Admission: Free
Ages: 3½ years and up.

WILLIAM S. HART MUSEUM AND PARK ☼

(805) 254-4584 - museum; (805) 259-0855 - park and camping !

24151 San Fernando Road, Santa Clarita

(TAKE GOLDEN STATE FWY [5] N. TO THE ANTELOPE VALLEY FWY [HWY 14], W. ON SAN FERNANDO RD., APPROXIMATELY 1½ MILES TO THE PARK, AFTER THE RAILROAD TRACKS.)

The William S. Hart Museum and Park covers over 265 acres, with almost 110 acres set aside for wilderness area. The hiking and nature trails through chaparral and woodland, start behind the museum, and loop back around. There are herds of buffalo, separated from humans by a fence, and deer on the grounds. A large picnic area is next to the barracks, while another smaller one is behind the "farm." There are barnyard animals such as cows, horses, burros, ducks, and sheep in pens. Purchase some animal feed to entice them to come within petting distance. Primitive camping is available here, too. Call the park for more information.

William S. Hart was a famous western star of the silent films. His Spanish, colonial-style home is now a museum. It is a hike up a winding trail to reach the house/museum on the hill. (Seniors and physically disabled people can get a pass from the park ranger to drive up.) The half-hour tour through his home is interesting, as it is filled with western and Indian art. Kids can look at, but not touch, the saddles, guns and other weapons, forty-pound buffalo coat, bear skin rug, stuffed buffalo head, paintings, and western movie memorabilia.

Across the way from the park is the Historical Society of Saugus, which has a steam locomotive out front of its train station museum. Inside, the biggest draw is the model train. This museum is open Saturday through Sunday from 1pm to 4pm. Admission is free.

Hours: Hart park is open daily from 7am - sunset. The museum is open in the summer Wed. - Sun. from 11am - 3:30pm. The rest of the year, it's open Wed. - Fri., 10am - 12:30pm; Sat. - Sun., 11am - 3:30pm. Docent-led tours are given every half hour. The museum is closed New Year's Day, Thanksgiving, and Christmas.
Admission: Free
Ages: All

ANAHEIM MUSEUM   ☀
(714) 778-3301   !/$
241 S. Anaheim Boulevard, Anaheim
(EXIT SANTA ANA FWY [5] E. ON LINCOLN AVE., R. ON ANAHEIM BLVD.)

This small museum is housed in Anaheim's restored 1908 Carnegie Library building. The upstairs room shows the growth of Orange County's oldest city, from an orange grove and grapevine-producing society to the opening of Disneyland in 1955 and to the present. There are photos, a model of Disneyland, and a display of old tools and machines, as well as orange crate labels.

Downstairs is a small, children's gallery that features rotating, hands-on exhibits such as puppets, toys, musical instruments, and games. It reminds me of a culturally-aware kindergarten classroom, but there are also workshops for older kids.
Hours: Open Wed. - Fri., 10am - 4pm; Sat., noon - 4pm.
Admission: Donations appreciated.
Ages: 2 years and up.

BOWERS KIDSEUM   ☼
(714) 480-1520 $$
1802 N. Main Street, Santa Ana
(EXIT SANTA ANA FWY [5] S. ON MAIN ST. IT'S LOCATED ON THE CORNER OF MAIN AND 18TH ST., JUST SOUTH OF THE BOWERS MUSEUM OF CULTURAL ART. AND YES, THE BUILDING WAS A BANK AT ONE TIME.)

Kidseum is a hands-on, cultural center designed to assist kids, ages 6 to 12, develop an appreciation of art and the ways of life in African, Asian, and Native American cultures. Cross over the bridge into the main gallery. Your kids will love trying on unusual masks from around the world; playing unique musical instruments, like deer hoof shakers, African drums, and string instruments; and dressing up in a wide variety of ethnic costumes in the theater area.

The Time Vault, which was an actual bank vault, has an incredible mural on the wall. Kids can "saddle up" on the workbench horses in here or grind pretend corn with a stone mortar and pestle. Playing games from foreign lands; working on geography puzzles; and putting on your own puppet show at the small theater - all this is available at Kidseum!

Afternoons and weekends at the museum is a time for telling tales, storytelling that is. The storytelling room also brings to life Asian tales in January, to celebrate the Chinese New Year, African tales in February to celebrate Black History Month, etc. Stop by the Art Lab, which is usually open about the same hours as the museum, where kids paint, color, learn how to make Indian rain sticks, experiment with sand art, etc., for free. After school art classes ($10 per class) are offered for third through sixth graders to work on more involved projects that often tie into special programs. School tours here are my favorite combination of hands-on fun and learning. Kidseum proves that learning about other cultures can be exciting!

Note: The Bowers Museum is located just down the street at 2002 N. Main Street. It is the parent museum of Kidseum. It contains carvings, pictures, and other art work from African, Asian, and Native American cultures. Older kids might appreciate a walk through the galleries. As admission is reciprocal with Kidseum when visited on the same day, why not visit both?!

Hours: Open Thurs. - Fri., 2pm - 5pm; Sat. - Sun., 10am - 4pm. Tours are offered Tues. - Fri. at 9:30am and 11am.

Admission: $6 for adults; $4 for seniors and students; $2 for ages 5 - 12; children 4 years and under are free. Reciprocal admission with the Bowers Museum if both are visited on the same day.

Ages: 3 - 13 years. Young children will enjoy the hands-on quality of this museum, though signs do ask for a gentle touch.

CHILDREN'S MUSEUM AT LA HABRA ☼

(562) 905-9793 $$

301 S. Euclid Street, La Habra
(EXIT ARTESIA [91] FWY, N. ON EUCLID.)

This museum, housed in a renovated Union Pacific Railroad Depot, has a child's interest at heart. The small Science Station encourages hands-on exploration with a Dino dig, pendulum pictures, and various science experiments. The adjoining room has a carousel to ride, a mini-market for shopping, and the front end of an Orange County Transit bus to practice driving skills. Just outside, a train caboose is open to walk through at certain times. The next room has wonderful, interactive, changing exhibits. Past themes have included "Cowboys and the Wild West" which featured western gear to try on, a wooden horse with a saddle, and a guitar to strum on the range; and "Would You Look At That?" which featured fun with lenses, light, and optical equipment. This room is always enlightening! A connecting room, containing a big model train (do you hear it chugging, clanging, and whistling as it comes around the mountain?), leads you to the nature room. Listen to the sounds of nature (i.e. birds chirping, etc.) as you look at the taxidermied animals, a touch table, and observe a bee observatory, which gets the kids all a-buzz.

The dress-up area and stage are for inspired actors and actresses, while the lighting booth, with all of its working buttons, is perfect for aspiring directors. The playroom (for children 5 years and under only) has a fake tree to climb, a little puppet theater, a play castle, and a separate room for very little ones.

On Saturdays, the museum has special events like craft projects, a storyteller, or shows for kids to enjoy and participate in. Call for specific details.

Portola Park is located just behind the museum. Open daily, it features a playground, baseball fields, and tennis courts, plus picnic tables and barbecue grills.

Hours: Open Mon. - Sat., 10am - 5pm; Sun., 1pm - 5pm. Closed major holidays.

Admission: $4 for ages 2 years and up; children under 2 years are free.

Ages: 1½ - 12 years.

DISCOVERY MUSEUM   ☼
(714) 540-0404 $$
3101 W. Harvard Street, Santa Ana
(EXIT SAN DIEGO FWY [405] N.E. ON WARNER AVE., L. ON FAIRVIEW, L. ON HARVARD.)

Travel back to Victorian times as you visit the Kellogg House (i.e. Discovery Museum), built in 1898. Tours begin in the parlor where kids can play a pump organ, crank an old telephone, listen to music played on an Edison talking machine, and look through a stereoscope (an early version of the modern-day View Master™). The kitchen has wonderful gadgets that kids can learn about as well as touch. The wood dining room is oval-shaped with cabinets specially made to bend with the curves, like the inside of a ship. The twisted, wooden staircase got "cool" raves from all the kids.   Upstairs, children play a game that teaches them the parts of a Victorian house. The Master Bedroom is now a room to dress up in authentic Victorian clothing with beautiful dresses for the girls and dapper coats and vests for the boys. The hats are great, too. The Children's Room has old-fashioned toys to play with. Kids can sit at the one-room, schoolhouse desks and write with chalk on the slate boards.

On the back porch, children can practice *real* chores like "washing" clothes on a scrub board and drying them with the clothes wringer. Sometimes kids are invited to make their own butter or learn how to play Victorian-era games. After the official tour, kids are welcome to go back and explore their favorite rooms (with parental supervision, of course).

Towards the back of the property is a small nature trail, an interpretative center with a few live animals (i.e. snakes, insects, etc.), and a patio classroom with hands-on displays. Coming soon is a turn-of-the-century astronomical site with a 16" telescope built in 1908, star charts, and more interactive, heavenly exhibits. A wood-worker's shop is also in the works so kids can see, and maybe try their hand at making, wooden toys.

Enjoy a picnic lunch in the Gazebo area. A working blacksmith's shop is open on the third Sunday of the month and sometimes on Thursdays. Demonstrations are given such as crafting candlesticks out of iron. Once a month there are special events, such as American Indian Day, where kids are invited to make crafts and participate in theme-related programs.

Of all the historical homes we've toured, and we've been through quite a few, this one has earned one of the highest ratings from my boys. Most houses, while beautiful and worthy of a tour, are understandably hands off. The Discovery Museum has hands-on activities, plus the docents gear the tour towards youngsters, both in the tour length and the way the information is presented. Come here and let your kids touch history!

Hours: Open Wed. - Fri., 1pm - 5pm; Sun., 11am - 3pm. Open Saturdays for special events only.

Admission: $3.50 for adults; $2.50 for ages 3 - 12; children 2 years and under are free.

Ages: 3 years and up.

DISCOVERY SCIENCE CENTER ☼

(714) 540-2001   *n/a*

2522 Main St., Santa Ana

(EXIT COSTA MESA FWY [55] W. ON MACARTHUR BLVD., R. ON MAIN ST.)

The Discovery Science Center is scheduled to open in mid-1998. Go play at the LAUNCH PAD, in Costa Mesa, while you're waiting for the Center to open. It is a preview facility with terrific interactive activities that will whet your appetite for the full-fledged Science Center.

When it opens, the huge Center will have more than 100 hands-on exhibits that will open kid's minds to understand science and math in ways they've never before envisioned. The facility will encourage visitors to delve into the mysteries of "Human Perception," learn about the "Dynamic Earth," explore "Air and Space," and direct their own movie in "The Studio." Toddlers will have their own marine environment to play in at "Kidstation." In addition to the permanent exhibits, there will be traveling exhibits, live science shows, performances by top educational entertainers, a "Meet the Scientist" series, and special educational programs and workshops. The Launch Pad is currently one of our favorite places to go, so we can't wait for a science center of this caliber and size to open!

Hours: Hr: To be announced.

Admission: Ad: To be announced.

Ages: 2 years and up.

DOLL AND TOY MUSEUM

(714) 527-2323 $

1238 S. Beach Boulevard, Anaheim
(EXIT ARTESIA FWY [91] S. ON BEACH BLVD. OR, EXIT GARDEN GROVE FWY [22] N.
ON BEACH. THE MUSEUM IS IN HOBBY CITY, 2 MILES S. OF KNOTT'S BERRY FARM.)

Take a walk down memory lane as you go through this museum.
It's a personal collection of four to five thousand, rare and antique dolls
from around the world, all housed in a half-scale model of the White
House (making the museum easy to spot). There are Cupie dolls, Star
Wars figures, an extensive Barbie collection, etc. This small museum is
for the special child who can resist the touching urge. The attached
shop buys, sells, and repairs old and modern dolls. They also carry a
line of doll clothes, shoes, wigs, hats, and books. (Also see
ADVENTURE CITY and HOBBY CITY.)

Hours:　Open daily from 10am - 6pm.
Admission:　$1 for adults; 50¢ for senior citizens and children 11
　　　　　　　years and under.
Ages:　3 years and up.

FULLERTON MUSEUM CENTER

(714) 738-6545 $

301 N. Pomona Avenue, Fullerton
(EXIT RIVERSIDE FWY [91] N. ON HARBOR BLVD., R. ON COMMONWEALTH, L. ON
POMONA. IT'S ON THE CORNER OF WILSHIRE AND POMONA.)

This cultural museum has two small galleries with rotating exhibits
that usually have terrific kid-appeal. Past exhibits have included The
Nature of Collecting, which featured different collections ranging from "I
Love Lucy" paraphernalia to pencil sharpeners and old radios;
Touchable Sculptures, with over seventy touchable, lifecast sculptures
of contemporary and historic figures, such as George Bush, Clint
Eastwood, and Dizzy Gillespie; and Anne Frank, a re-creation of the life
and times of Anne Frank through photographs and facsimiles of her
diary, plus commentary.

Super Saturdays are offered one Saturday a month from 1:30pm to
3pm for kids ages 5 through 9. In the summer this becomes a weekly
event, and the day and the title changes to Super Tuesdays. These
culturally-themed workshops like Secrets of Pharaoh, International
Christmas Tree Ornaments, or Day of the Dead, include an interesting
lesson followed by a related craft. Reservations are needed.

Hours:　The museum is open Wed. - Sun. from noon - 4pm; open
　　　　　　　Thursdays until 8pm.
Admission:　$3 for adults; $2 for students; children 12 years and
　　　　　　　under are free. The "Super" days are $5 per participant,
　　　　　　　which does not cover the museum entrance.
Ages:　5 years and up.

HALL OF FAME MUSEUM   ☼
(714) 758-9882 $
2000 Gene Autry Way, Anaheim
(EXIT SANTA ANA FWY [5] N. ON STATE COLLEGE BLVD.)

Check out who's who in the Orange County Sports Hall of Fame, located at Gate 6 on the south side of the stadium. Come see the Mighty Ducks Wing, California Angels Wing, and Orange County Olympians. The sports world, including tennis, volleyball, off-road racing, football, basketball, boxing, baseball, golf, swimming, etc., is represented here in over 1,000 photographs and numerous displays of sports events and personalities. You'll see signed sports memorabilia including footballs, jerseys, hockey sticks, baseball bats, etc.; Olympic gold and silver medals; busts of baseball greats; trophies and awards such as Phil Neven's Golden Spike Award; autographed bowling pins; Gary Carter's shin guards; etc. This museum will score points with your young sports fan.

Hours: Open during Angel's games through the 7th inning, or by appointment.
Admission: $2 for adults; $1 for children. Parking is free (off of Orangewood).
Ages: 5 years and up.

HERITAGE HILL HISTORICAL PARK   ☼
(714) 855-2028 $
25151 Serrano Road, Lake Forest
(EXIT SAN DIEGO FWY [5] N.E. ON LAKE FOREST DR., L. ON SERRANO. IT'S ON THE CORNER, WITH PARKING IN THE SHOPPING CENTER.)

Heritage Hill consists of several restored historical buildings in a beautiful gated setting. Four buildings are open to tour through that reflect part of Orange County's heritage. The Serrano Adobe dates from 1863 and has furniture from the late nineteenth-century. The Bennet Ranch House, built in 1908, reflects a ranching family's lifestyle from the early twentieth century. St. George's Episcopal Mission, built in 1891, has many of its original interior furnishings. El Toro Grammar School was built in 1890. It is a favorite with kids because it has school books from that era, as well as desks and other school-related items. The Historical Park has a few picnic tables on the grounds.

One-and-a-half-hour tours are offered to school groups. The tours include hands-on, old-fashioned activities such as grinding corn, washing clothes by hand, going on a treasure hunt for "hidden" objects, etc. Reservations are required.

If your kids need more running around space, visit Serrano Creek Park, just behind Heritage Hill. Serrano is a long, narrow, wooded park with a paved walkway and a creek running through it. The big wooden play structure, which looks like a clubhouse, has a bridge, slides, and some huge tires to climb on.

Hours: Heritage Hill is open Wed. - Sun., 9am - 5pm. Guided tours are the only way to see the interior of the buildings. The tours are given Wed. - Fri. at 2pm; Sat. - Sun. at 11am and 2pm. School groups can make reservations for tours at other times throughout the week. Closed major holidays.

Admission: Donations. School tours are $2 a person.

Ages: 6 years and up.

HUNTINGTON BEACH INTERNATIONAL SURFING ☼ MUSEUM

(714) 960-3483 $

411 Olive Avenue, Huntington Beach

(EXIT SAN DIEGO FWY [405] S. ON ELLIS AVE., VEER L. PAST BEACH ONTO MAIN ST., R. ON OLIVE NEAR END OF MAIN.)

Surf's up at this small museum that celebrates surfing and surf culture, from its roots in Hawaii to the present day. Get in the mood with beach music playing in the background. Feel like catching a wave? Check out some of the famous and unique surfboards here, like the Batman board and a surfboard made in three pieces. There are also trophies, clothes, and photographs to look at. The Surfer's Walk of Fame (honoring eleven people) is just down the street.

Hours: Open daily, June through Labor Day, noon - 5pm. Open the rest of the year, Wed. - Sun. from noon - 5pm.

Admission: $2 for adults; $1 for school-aged children.

Ages: 6 years and up.

INDEPENDENCE HALL ☼

(714) 220-5244 - Adventures in Education tour information   !

Beach Blvd., Buena Park

(EXIT ARTESIA FWY [91] S. ON BEACH BLVD. IT'S RIGHT ACROSS THE STREET FROM KNOTT'S BERRY FARM.)

This full-size reproduction of Independence Hall houses a replica of the Liberty Bell. Press a button to hear a prerecorded history message about the bell. See the (replicated) room where the Declaration of Independence was signed. Every half hour, a twenty-minute "show" is presented. It consists of sitting in the darkened room while candle lights flicker, listening to voices debate the adoption of the Declaration of Independence.

Group tours are available, such as the half-hour, Adventures in History tour, or the two-hour, Our Early American Heritage tour, where a costumed docent explains the history of our revolutionary times. (Also check KNOTT'S BERRY FARM for historical tours.) The gift shop here has patriotic memorabilia to purchase. Tip: Bring a dime to put in the machine to watch the Spirit of '76 army (in miniature) march around.

The surrounding park has a pond with ducks, shade trees, and grass - perfect for picnicking.

Hours: Open daily from 9am - 5pm. Free parking is available by telling the attendant that you are here for Independence Hall.

Admission: Free. Various tours charge a minimal fee.

Ages: 5 years and up.

INTERNATIONAL PRINTING MUSEUM

(714) 523-2070   *n/a*

A visit to this museum helped kids to understand the importance of printed words and the history of how printing presses changed the world of reading. Unfortunately, as of June, 1997, this museum is looking for a new location. In the interim, traveling exhibits are available to come to classrooms. Call every now and then, though, to see when a new facility is found because this museum was one of the best. Kids became fascinated with the written word after a tour here, and the museum offered terrific character appearances of inventive geniuses such as Ben Franklin, Mark Twain, and Johann Gutenberg.

LAUNCH PAD   ☼

(714) 546-2061   *$*

3333 Bear Street, Suite 323, Costa Mesa
(EXIT SAN DIEGO FWY [405] N. ON BRISTOL ST., L. ON SUNFLOWER, L. ON BEAR ST. IT'S ON THE 3 RD FLOOR, CRYSTAL COURT AT SOUTH COAST PLAZA, NEXT TO MACYS.)

This small, hands-on, science museum for kids is a blast! (The Launch Pad is actually a preview facility for the gigantic and impressive DISCOVERY SCIENCE CENTER, scheduled to open in mid-1998). Some of the top attractions here are a Bubble Wall - a wall created out of dipping a long rod in bubble solution; a Gravity Well - drop balls in and watch as they go around; Pitch Speed - how fast do you throw a ball?; Muscle Coordination - help a mechanical man pedal a bicycle by manual manipulation; and Angular Momentum - where kids go around and around - this is not for those with a tendency towards motion sickness. Lasers, Lights, and Illusions is another exhibit section where you can watch live laser demonstrations; distort your image at a morphing station; walk into an eight-foot-tall kaleidoscope; and watch a sculpture change shapes via the magic of illusion. Younger kids will take particular delight in a room just for toddlers with soft foam blocks, bubbles and telephones that really work (inside the room only). Every hour, or so, a staff member conducts a fascinating show in the small theater room. We've learned about liquid nitrogen, snakes, the hair-raising qualities of electricity, and more.

The Launch Pad offers monthly events such as The Wonderful Circus of Science, and the Bubble Festival. Other special events include science camps, Mommy & Me classes, and birthday party packages. Call for more information. Tip: The gift store offers an terrific array of fun and educational experiments, toys, etc.

Hours: Open Mon. - Fri., 10am - 9pm; Sat., 10am - 7pm; Sun., 11am - 6pm.

Admission: $5 for ages 3 years and older; one adult is free with each paid child's admission.

Ages: 3 years and up.

MISSION SAN JUAN CAPISTRANO ☼

(714) 248-2048 $$

Between Camino Capistrano Street and El Camino Real, San Juan Capistrano

(EXIT SAN DIEGO FWY [5] W. ON ORTEGA HWY. [74], ON THE CORNER OF ORTEGA AND CAMINO CAPISTRANO.)

The Mission, founded in 1776, is thirteen acres of historic stone buildings and beautifully landscaped gardens, courtyards, and walkways. It's easy to see why the San Juan Mission was considered "The Jewel of the Missions." There are many "parts" to the Mission, so there is something to interest almost any age child. It's a history treat for school kids as they visit and "experience" the early Native American, Spanish, and Mexican lifestyles, depicted in separate rooms. Walk through rooms that contain murals such as Indians hunting, and artifacts such as like bone weapons. The Soldiers' Barracks room looks "lived in," just as it did many years ago. It contains life-size models of soldiers and their (few) possessions. Note: There are a few picnic tables behind the Barracks.

The extensive grounds are a maze of pathways. The Central Courtyard, the cemetery, the areas of on-going archaeological excavation, and the industrial center are all interesting. For instance, tanning vats in the industrial center were used to turn animal skin into sellable leather, while the ovens were used to turn animal fat into candles, soap, and ointments.

The Mission has two churches. One is the Serra Chapel, the oldest building in California, where mass is still regularly performed. The glittery baroque altar, made of gold leaf overlay, is eye-catching. The Great Stone Church, once a magnificent cathedral, was destroyed by an earthquake in 1812. Scaffolding is around the ruins, holding up the remaining walls while the church awaits restoration.

Mission San Juan Capistrano offers several special, educational activities such as Saturday at the Mission. This program is on the first Saturday of the month from 9am to 11:30am, geared for kids ages 6 to 12. A topic is introduced and then reinforced, either with a related craft, by playing games, or even by participating in a simulated, archaeological dig. Living History Day occurs on the last Saturday of each month from 10am to 2pm. Authentically costumed docents become living historians. Talk with them to find out about mission life "firsthand."

If you're looking for somewhere fun to eat, RUBY'S is across the street and up the stairs at the shopping district. This 1940's diner has a train going around overhead, red vinyl seats, and kids' meals that are served in a forties-style, cardboard car. Afterwards, take a walk around Camino Capistrano (street). It has many interesting stores with truly unique merchandise. Idea: Take a train into town and really make a day of your visit here! The train depot is only two blocks away from the Mission. (See the March CALENDAR section for the Festival of the Swallows. Also see CAPISTRANO DEPOT, which is another great place to eat, plus JONES MINI FARM, and the ORANGE COUNTY NATURAL HISTORY MUSEUM for other things to do and see in the immediate vicinity.)

Hours: Open daily from 8:30am - 5pm. Closed Good Friday afternoon, Thanksgiving, and Christmas.

Admission: $4 for adults; $3 for seniors and ages 3 - 12; children 2 years and under are free. Saturday at the Mission is $10 per participant.

Ages: 5 years and up.

MOVIELAND WAX MUSEUM   ☼
(714) 522-1154   *$$$*
7711 Beach Boulevard, Buena Park
(EXIT ARTESIA FWY [91] S. ON BEACH BLVD. IT'S 1 BLOCK N. OF KNOTT'S BERRY FARM.)

Over 400 movie and television celebrities are immortalized in wax, posed in the settings that made them famous. To insure authenticity, almost every measurement and picture angle imaginable is taken of the star before the sculptor begins his work. Often times the costumes and props adorning the wax figure, and its surroundings, are personally donated by the stars.

Kids who are film buffs will probably get more out of this museum, but almost any age child enjoys "seeing" Dorothy and the whole Wizard of Oz gang; Robin Williams as Mrs. Doubtfire; Michael Jackson dressed from his video "Bad"; as well as Whoopi Goldberg, Star Trek crew members, Superman, the Little Rascals, and many more. Special lighting, sound effects, and animation are also used throughout the museum to enhance the realism of the exhibits. Halfway through the museum, you are routed through a gift and candy shop and small arcade area. Here you have the choice of whether to go through the Chamber of Horrors or bypass it. (The Chamber of Horrors could frighten younger children.)

Hours: Open daily from 9am - 7pm.

Admission: $12.95 for adults; $10.55 for seniors; $6.95 for ages 4 - 11; children 3 years and under are free. (Certain discounts available through AAA.)

Ages: 4 years and up.

OLD COURTHOUSE MUSEUM   ☀

(714) 830-3703   !

211 Santa Ana Boulevard, Santa Ana

(EXIT SANTA ANA FWY [5] S. ON MAIN ST., R. ON CIVIC CENTER DR. ALTHOUGH THE ADDRESS IS ON SANTA ANA BLVD., METERED PARKING IS ON CIVIC CENTER DR.)

Order in the court! Older kids interested in the history of our legal system, or in seeing what an actual courtroom looks like, will enjoy visiting the oldest courtroom in Southern California. Built in 1901, this huge, red sandstone building contains three floors of Orange County history. The bottom floor has glass cases of archaeological artifacts, such as fossils and bones. The second floor, which is the entrance, has two displays containing information about the museum and the court of law.

The most interesting place is the third floor. It features a turn-of-the century courtroom, jury room, and judge's chambers, plus a court reporter's room that has original transcribing machines, a candlestick telephone, and an old roll-top desk. My boys and I role-played a bit here so they could get a feel for how the court system is set up. The museum, which is a room of changing exhibits, is across the way from the Superior Courtroom. Past exhibits have included a display of sheriff's badges, war posters, a mock-up of a 1940's living room, World War II artifacts from Orange County, etc. A visit to this museum is a good beginning for future lawyers. I rest my case.

Hours: Open Mon. - Fri. from 9am - 5pm. Tours are available Tuesdays from 10am - 2pm, and by appointment.

Admission: Free

Ages: 6 years and up.

ORANGE COUNTY MARINE INSTITUTE   ☀

(714) 496-2274 $

24200 Dana Point Harbor Drive, Dana Point

(EXIT SAN DIEGO FWY [5] S.W. ON CAMINO LAS RAMBLAS, WHICH TURNS INTO PACIFIC COAST HIGHWAY. GO N. ON P.C.H., L. ON DANA POINT HARBOR, ALL THE WAY TO THE END OF THE ROAD.)

The Orange County Marine Institute's main purposes are to teach about maritime history and about the marine environment. It offers wonderful classes and outings, such as the Bio-Luminescence cruise. This two-and-a-half-hour night cruise highlights glowing worms, glow fish, and plankton. The cost is $20 for adults, $14 for kids 12 years and under. (Children must be at least 4 years old for the cruises.) Other cruises include Let's Go Squidding, Marine Mammal Exploring, which includes whale watching in season, etc. Classes include tidepool hikes and more.

If, however, you are coming just to see the Institute, there are relatively few things here to look at besides the great gift shop that has educational toys, books, and games. One tank has an octopus. The back room has a touch tank, where a docent holds a starfish or a lobster for your child to touch. Overhead is a skeleton of a gray whale. Behind the Institute is a small park overlooking the harbor, with rock jetties and a few picnic tables. The historic Tallship, "Pilgrim," is moored in front of the building. (See the September CALENDAR, for the terrific annual Tallship Festival.) Make the Institute a stopping point during your visit to DANA POINT or better yet, go on an Institute outing.

Hours: The Institute is open daily from 10am - 4:30pm. The touch tank is open Sat. - Sun. from 10am - 4:30pm. Ship tours are given on Sundays from 11am - 2:30pm. Everything is closed on major holidays.

Admission: Donations

Ages: 3 years and up.

ORANGE COUNTY NATURAL HISTORY MUSEUM ☼
(714) 487-9155 $

31871 Camino Capistrano, Suite 101, in the Franciscan Plaza, San Juan Capistrano.

(EXIT SAN DIEGO FWY [5] W. ON ORTEGA HWY., L. ON CAMINO CAPISTRANO.)

This terrific storefront museum has exhibits of fossils and seashells, and an extensive butterfly and moth collection. It also has a skeleton of a dolphin, the tooth of a great white shark, whale bones, and Waldo, the remains of a walrus (or sea lion). Children may touch the animals bones and pelts. Taxidermied birds are captured in flight while live lizards, toads, and several kinds of snakes dwell in glass cases. Look for fossils in the pile of rocks here, and look at some of the shells recently gathered from Shellmaker Island and surrounding areas. Kids can take a pencil safari where they are given a list of things to find and check off.

Micropals is one of the many programs offered and sponsored through this museum. It is taught by a geologist and allows kids to extract specimens, process samples, and go on field trips while learning about the world of micropaleontology. Call for more information about this and other programs. (Also see CAPISTRANO DEPOT, JONES MINI FARM, and MISSION SAN JUAN CAPISTRANO for other things to do and see in this immediate vicinity.)

Hours: Open Wed. - Sun. from 11am- 6pm.

Admission: $1 for adults; 50¢ for children 15 years and under.

Ages: 3 years and up.

RICHARD NIXON LIBRARY AND BIRTHPLACE ☼
(714) 993-3393 $$

18001 Yorba Linda Boulevard, Yorba Linda

(EXIT ORANGE FWY [57] E. ON YORBA LINDA. OR, EXIT RIVERSIDE FWY [91] N. ON IMPERIAL HWY [90], L. ON YORBA LINDA.)

This museum/library/grave site/rose garden features nine acres of galleries and gardens, plus the restored birthplace of - here's a quiz - what number president? (The answer is at the end of this description.) Bring a pencil and request a Children's Treasure Hunt to encourage your kids to become more involved with the exhibits in the museum. They'll search for objects like the Presidential Seal, the Woody Station Wagon Nixon used for campaigning, and the piano he practiced on in his younger years.

The theater presents a twenty-eight-minute movie, documenting Richard Nixon's political career. It's a great introduction to who he was, both personally and presidentially. There are several videos and touch screens throughout the museum showing different aspects of his life, including the Kennedy/Nixon debates, footage from his speeches, a tribute to Pat Nixon, and a presidential forum with over 300 questions to choose from. I was surprised at how interested my kids were in all of this.

The exhibit of ten, life-size statues of world leaders (some of whom were very short) is impressive. Touch screens offer comments and biographical summaries on the leaders. Gifts of State are unique treasures to look at. My oldest son, however, thought the pistol from Elvis Presley was the coolest gift. Other pieces of history include a big chunk of the Berlin Wall; the presidential limo that at various times held Johnson, Ford, Carter, and Nixon; a re-creation of the White House's Lincoln Sitting Room; numerous photographs; Nixon's daughters' wedding dresses; and the Watergate Room. In the latter room, excerpts of the "smoking gun" tape can be heard through headsets. A pictorial and descriptive time line of this historic event takes up an entire wall. Tip: At the very least, know how to explain the term "impeach" to your kids. Free guided tours are given Monday through Friday for fourth through twelfth graders, with advanced reservations.

Walk outside, through the First Lady's beautiful rose gardens (which look prettier in bloom), to the home where Nixon was born. A tour through the small house only takes fifteen minutes. Richard Nixon was, by the way, our thirty-seventh President.

Hours: Open Mon. - Sat., 10am - 5pm; Sun., 11am - 5pm. Closed Thanksgiving and Christmas.

Admission: $5.95 for adults; $3.95 for seniors; $2 for ages 8 - 11; children 7 years and under are free. (Certain discounts are available through AAA.)

Ages: 6 years and up.

RIPLEY'S BELIEVE IT OR NOT! MUSEUM (Buena Park)

(714) 522-7045   *$$$*

7850 Beach Boulevard, Buena Park

(EXIT ARTESIA FWY [91] S. ON BEACH BLVD. IT'S JUST N. OF KNOTT'S BERRY FARM.)

As a reporter, Robert Ripley traveled all over the world visiting over 200 countries, and meeting with Kings and Queens, Cannibal Chieftains, and tribesmen to collect interesting, humorous, and bizarre items and facts. There are hundreds of pictures, life-sized models, special effects, statues, and assorted odd artifacts throughout the museum. My son, Bryce, summed up the exhibits best by saying, "They're kind of cool and kind of gross."

The "native" section is a little eerie and includes a real shrunken head. The Asian section contains a model of a Chinese man who had two sets of pupils in each eye, and a man who held a real burning candle *in* his head, among others exhibits. (Truth can definitely be stranger than fiction.)

The next section has unusual, rather than weird, displays, such as a sculpture of Marilyn Monroe made from over a quarter of a million "real" dollars (that will make your child's mouth drop open); a miniature violin - only five-and-a-half inches long yet it can actually be played; and a complete landscape scene painted on a potato chip. Two of my favorite exhibits here are a rendition of the Last Supper done with 260 pieces of toast (varying from barely toasted to burnt), and the huge portrait made out of dyed clothes dryer lint. How do people think of these things, and why?

Videos show amazing feats such as unusual body contortions, swallowing razor blades, etc. (Don't try these activities at home.) Trivia buffs can really study up here. Towards the end of the museum are a few graphically "bloody" exhibits to bypass. Word of warning: If you take an inquisitive child who can't read the explanations, be prepared to answer a lot of questions!

Hours: Open daily from 10am - 6pm.
Admission: $8.95 for adults; $6.95 for seniors; $5.25 for ages 4 - 11; children 3 years and under are free. (Certain discounts available through AAA.)
Ages: 5 years and up.

A SPECIAL PLACE

(909) 881-1201

1003 E. Highland Avenue, San Bernardino
(Exit Hwy 30 S. on Waterman, R. on Highland, R. into Harrison to park.)

A Special Place is very special for younger children who delight in this completely hands-on museum. Outside, a covered cement patio enhances disability awareness via a wheelchair maze (those corners are tough!); a swing for kids in wheelchairs; braces to try on; crutches to use; and even prostheses to touch. Let your kids get a feel for what it's like to be mobile in a different way. Also out here is western gear such as boots, cowboy hats, and a few saddles so kids can ride the range.

Inside, two rooms are divided into sections. The drama area has face painting and costumes. It's a hot time in the old town when kids dress up as firefighters and climb up (and down) the pole. The schoolroom area has a few old-fashioned school desks and a thirteen star flag. (See if your kids notice this and know how many stars are on our flag today.) There is also a working traffic light here to play "Red Light, Green Light."

Along the back wall is a wonderful aquatic mural, plus fish and turtle aquariums, and even a cage of birds. Kids can turn a handle at an Edison display to try to generate enough electricity to power a light bulb. At the puppet theater, children make the puppets come to life.

Another section is set-up like a mini-Kaiser clinic, with an X-ray machine, infant incubator, and blood pressure machine. Prepare your child to go to the doctor or to become one! The Shadow Room is always fun. When the light flashes, kids love posing to leave a temporary shadow of their body on the photo-sensitive wall.

The museum is small, but it has a great variety of interactive things to do, making it a special place, indeed.

Hours: Open Tues. - Fri., 9am - 1pm; Sat., 11am - 3pm. Call for extended summer hours.

Admission: $2 per person. The first Saturday of each month is free for grandparents who are accompanied by a paying child.

Ages: 6 months to 10 years.

CALIFORNIA MUSEUM OF PHOTOGRAPHY

(909) 787-4787

On Main Street, the pedestrian walkway, just west of the Riverside Visitor Center, Riverside

(*GOING S.W. ON RIVERSIDE FWY [91], EXIT W. ON 7ᵀᴴ ST./MISSION INN AVE., L. ON ORANGE ST., R. ON UNIVERSITY. GOING N.W. ON 91, EXIT W. ON UNIVERSITY AVE. PARK AND WALK TO THE PEDESTRIAN WALKWAY.*)

Expose your kids to the photographic arts at the unique, three-story California Museum of Photography. (What does the outside of the building remind you of?) The main level has rotating photo exhibits, with an emphasis on various photography styles or photographers, like Ansel Adams. The back area houses a collection of cameras, including working miniature cameras ("spy" cameras), old-fashioned cameras with the drape cloth, a Spiderman camera, and one that is part of a radio-controlled car! If you feel like taking up another sport, surf the Internet gallery for other museum sites.

Take the spiral stairs up to the mezzanine terrace, which is a catwalk-like hallway gallery. The top floor focuses on kids with its small, interactive gallery. Children can use the Zoetropes to draw pictures and spin them around in a drum, creating moving images - animation! The next exhibit proves that not all shadows are black as the images shadowed here produce a rainbow of colors. Use the next display to visually explain to kids how the aperture of a camera is similar to the pupils in their eyes. Have them look into a light and watch in the mirror as their pupils enlarge or contract, according to the amount of light entering in. The Shadows Room temporarily imprints body outlines on the photosensitive wall when a light flashes. Camera Obscura is a small, dark room with a tiny hole of light that projects an upside down image of the outside scene on its wall. This is a visual demonstration of how a camera lens works. Kids will get a wide angle view of photography at this Museum!

Hours: The museum is open Wed. - Sat., 11am - 5pm; Sun., noon - 5pm.

Admission: $2 for adults; $1 for seniors and students; children 12 years and under are free. Every Wednesday is free admission day. The first Sunday of every month from 1pm - 4pm during the months of September through May is free admission, too.

Ages: 3 years and up just to look at things; ages 5 and up will begin to really appreciate it.

GILMAN HISTORIC RANCH and WAGON MUSEUM ☼
(909) 922-9200 $

On Wilson Street and 16th Street, Banning
(Exit San Bernardino Fwy [10] N. on San Gorgonio, L. on Wilson, R. on 16TH.)

Wagons, ho! Take the dirt road back to the Gilman Historic Ranch and Wagon Museum, and explore life as it was over 150 years ago. Over fifteen wagons from yesteryear are inside the museum including chuckwagons, stagecoaches, and prairie schooners. (Some of the wagons are hitched to large wooden horses.) Learn how our pioneer ancestors traveled across the country, and hear about the hardships that they endured. Also on exhibit are saddles; a bedroom set with a ladies' riding habit and surrey; and Indian artifacts.

The adjacent ranch has a few historic buildings, shaded picnic grounds, and hiking trails. Some of the trails go across the creek and to the upper reservoir, while others go deeper into the canyons. Be on the lookout for rabbits, deer, and other wildlife.

School groups can take a forty-five-minute tour, which includes a tour of the museum and grounds, plus a choice of hearing stories of travelers and comparing wagons, or doing a museum paper treasure hunt. The latter entails learning about westward migration and encounters with Native Americans by finding objects throughout the museum. Three additional programs are available, at an additional $1.50 per person, and an extra half hour per activity: Learn about branding, then make your own rubber-stamp brand to take home; learn about the backbreaking, yet rewarding job of being a cowboy; and/or make the same kind of toy that children played with over 100 years ago. Enjoy your day reliving the past! (Look for Mountain Men Days under the October CALENDAR section.)

Hours: The museum and grounds are open Sundays, March through November, from 10am - 4pm. Tours for school groups can be made by reservation Mon. - Sat.
Admission: Call for the exact price of the minimal fee. School tours are currently $2.50 per person for the basic tour.
Ages: 5 years and up.

HERITAGE HOUSE

(909) 689-1333

8193 Magnolia Street, Riverside

(EXIT RIVERSIDE FWY [91] N. ON ADAMS ST., R. ON MAGNOLIA ST. IT'S ON THE N. SIDE OF THE STREET.)

Heritage House is a beautiful Victorian house built in 1892. It is fully restored and filled with elaborate, turn-of-the-century furniture. Adding to its charm is the wrought iron fence in front, the well-kept grounds, the backyard windmill, and the barn (with chickens clucking).

Your older children will appreciate the half-hour guided tour as they see a different era and style of living. The old music box is unique. Kids can look through the stereo-optic, which is an early version of today's View Master™. Explaining the Edison phonograph is a lot harder now that record players are also a thing of the past! The formal oak stairway leads upstairs to the master bedroom. You'll also find the office/library with trophy animal heads and bearskin rug, and the servant's quarters up here. Heritage House graciously displays the life of an affluent citrus grower. The last Sunday of every month is Living History Day, when the past comes to life in the present, as a docent dresses up the owner from 1892, gets ready for a party. Talk to the maid, cook, guests, and hostess to learn about customs from this time period. Call about other special events.

Hours: Open Thurs - Fri., noon - 3pm; Sun., noon - 3:30pm. Closed July through Labor Day, except for regular Sun. hours.
Admission: Suggested donations are $1 for adults; 50¢ for kids.
Ages: 7 years old and up.

JURUPA MOUNTAINS CULTURAL CENTER / EARTH SCIENCE MUSEUM

(909) 685-5818   *!/$$*

7621 Granite Hill Drive, Riverside

(EXIT POMONA FWY [60] S. ON PEDLEY RD., L. ON MISSION BLVD., L. ON CAMINO REAL, UNDER THE FREEWAY.)

This is a rock hound's paradise where kids can either start or add to their rock collection. The Center's main building is a gigantic warehouse with an incredible array of rocks, minerals, and fossils for display and purchase. There are dinosaur skeletons, fossils of all sizes and quality, and almost every kind of rock you've ever heard of, plus quite a few you might not have.

The adjacent Earth Science Museum has museum-quality rocks, minerals, fossils, and Indian artifacts displayed according to classification. The large crystals, geodes, carbons, etc. are worthy of a few "oohs" and "aahs." The collection of ancient and modern Native American artifacts includes tools, weapons, a wonderful arrowhead exhibit, a 1100 year-old corn cob, and costumes, in particular, a beautiful fringed and beaded wedding dress. Products, like Borax, are shown in their commercial form next to their original mineral form. Other unique exhibits are the florescent exhibit, which literally highlights rocks with luminescent characteristics; the space exhibit, which includes moon rocks; and the ivory exhibit, which has examples of intricately carved scrimshaw. Note: The outside of the building is comprised of petrified wood and fossils.

If your kids want to take home their own, hand-picked treasures, go "Rock Collecting at the Dinosaurs." This drop-in, family field trip starts at the magnetic rock, proceeds to the small petrified wood "forest," and has several other stops along the way, with kid-appropriate explanations about the fascinating plants and rocks you'll see. (I finally understand that fossil simply means, "something that was once living.") The destination, dinosaur mesa, has seven giant, kid-made dinosaurs. The highlight of the excursion is sorting through the huge spread of rocks and rock chips that are strewn at the dino's feet, and picking out twelve to take home! (Egg cartons are provided.) Crystals, jasper, malachite, petrified wood, amethyst, chrysocolla, etc., are some examples of what can be found here. Back at the store, we labeled each one of our treasures.

Another great drop-in field trip is "Kid's Fossil Shack," geared for ages 6 and up. Kids will learn about fossils, and then clean and prepare one to take home. This is, obviously, a more sit-down activity, but another great way to combine hands-on education and fun.

The Jurupa Cultural Center offers a wide variety of school-group programs such as gold panning, a tour of the Crestmore Mine tour, lapidary, making an Indian pictograph, and more. The Center also offers week-long classes of Nature School in the summer, ranging from hiking and survival, to dinosaurs and fossils.

Hours: The warehouse store and the Earth Science Museum are open Tues. - Sat. from 8:30am - 3:30pm. Closed national holidays. "Rock Collecting at the Dinosaurs" is held at 9am - 10:30am every Saturday. "Kid's Fossil Day" is held at 10:30am - noon every Saturday.

Admission: The warehouse store is free. The Earth Science Museum is $2 for adults; $1 for seniors and ages 2 - 12. "Rock Collecting at the Dinosaurs" and "Kid's Fossil Day" are $4 per person, each event. No reservations are needed. Call for school tour information and classes.

Ages: 3 years and up.

MARCH FIELD MUSEUM   ☼

(909) 697-6600 $

16222 Interstate 215, March Air Force Base
(EXIT MORENO VALLEY FWY [215] E. ON VAN BUREN BLVD.)

    A P-40 Warhawk stands guard at the entrance of March Air Force
Base, which is the proud home to one of the most extensive collection
of military aircraft and aviation artifacts in the United States. The
walkway is lined with airplane engines, plus a jeep that kids can get into
and "drive" around. Outside, over forty historic airplanes are on display,
from the smaller F-84 to the massive B-52 to the sleek SR-71. Kids are
welcome to look at the planes, but not to climb in them.

    Inside, the huge hanger displays everything possible pertaining to
the Air Force. Airplanes, such as a biplane trainer, have landed in here,
as have exhibits of flight uniforms, photographs, model planes,
engines, medals, weapons, and equipment from both World Wars,
Korea, Viet Nam, the Cold War, and Desert Storm. This museum
defines the word, "comprehensive"!

    "The March Field Story" and other informative movies are available
for viewing with prior notice. Although the only touchable activity for kids
is to strap themselves into a flight training chair, they really enjoy the
museum, particularly your pilots-in-training.

    Hours: Open daily from 10am - 4pm. Closed New Year's Day,
              Easter, Thanksgiving, and Christmas.
Admission: $3 for adults; $1 for ages 6 - 12 years; children 5 years
              and under are free. ($8 max per family.)
     Ages: 3 years and up.

MISSION INN AND MISSION INN MUSEUM   ☼

(909) 788-9556 $$

3696 Main Street, Riverside
(GOING S.W. ON RIVERSIDE FWY [91], EXIT W. ON 7TH ST./MISSION INN AVE. GOING
N.W. ON 91, EXIT W. ON UNIVERSITY AVE., R. ON ORANGE ST., L. ON 7TH
ST./MISSION INN AVE. 7TH ST. WAS RENAMED MISSION INN AVE. THE INN AND
MUSEUM ARE ON MISSION INN AVE.)

    This elegant, old, sprawling Inn is beautiful to look at and tour
through. The hour-and-a-half tour shows much of its eclectic
architecture and furnishings. Mediterranean style, emphasized in the
colorful tiles, spiral columns, and bells, is incorporated with an Oriental
influence, such as a hotel kitchen chimney in the shape of a pagoda,
plus other unique touches. Only through the tour can you see all four
wings of the hotel with highlights including the gilded eighteenth-century
altar in the wedding chapel; the music room; the Court of Birds (there
are no actual birds still here, but the stories about them capture the
imagination); the Taft Chair that seats up to five kids at one time; and
the open-air, five-story spiral staircase in the rotunda, which is quite
grand looking. If your kids are interested in architecture or hearing

about the Inn's history, they will enjoy the tour. If not, at least take a quick walk through the grounds.

The small museum is located on the pedestrian walkway, next to the Inn's gift shop. Frank Miller, the Inn's builder, had an international collection that reflected his tastes. Housed in the museum are a scale model of a pagoda, encased figurines, artifacts, and photos. The most appealing exhibit to kids has old-time barber shop chairs (not to sit in) with mirrors and hair cutting instruments. A tape of old-timers reminiscing adds to the display's atmosphere.

Hours: The Inn is a functioning Inn so it is open daily. Tours are given Mon. - Fri. at 10am, 10:30am, 1:30pm, and 2pm; Sat. - Sun. from 10am - 3pm, approximately every half hour. The Museum is open daily from 9:30am- 4pm.

Admission: You can walk around the hotel at no charge. The tour costs $8 for adults; children 11 years and under are free. Entrance to the Museum is a $1 donation for adults.

Ages: 8 years and up.

ORANGE EMPIRE RAILWAY MUSEUM   ☼
(909) 657-2605   !/$$
2201 South "A" Street, Perris
See ORANGE EMPIRE RAILWAY MUSEUM under TRANSPORTATION.

RIVERSIDE MUNICIPAL MUSEUM   ☼
(909) 782-5273   !
3580 Mission Inn Avenue, Riverside
(GOING S.W. ON RIVERSIDE FWY [91], EXIT W. ON 7ᵀᴴ ST./MISSION INN AVE. GOING N.W. ON 91, EXIT W. ON UNIVERSITY AVE., R. ON ORANGE ST., L. ON 7ᵀᴴ ST./MISSION INN AVE. 7ᵀᴴ ST. WAS RENAMED MISSION INN AVE.)

This museum contains a wealth of information and fun for both kids and adults. The Natural History exhibits are a natural place to start. Push a button and the taxidermied mountain lion crouched on the ledge "roars." Other stuffed animals are also posed in animated positions. For instance, a baby bobcat is batting at something and a skunk is doing a handstand on its front paws. The Geology area has a nice display of rocks and minerals, plus a section on earthquakes. The Paleontology exhibits have a saber-tooth tiger skeleton, some fossilized elephant tusks (they are huge!), and a few dinosaur bones. The Anthropology section has displays of Indian clothing, musical instruments, hunting weapons, and a few dioramas. The Local History display features Missions, cowboys, tools, and guns, plus machinery and crate labels of citrus growers.

The upstairs has rotating displays. We saw exhibits that emphasized Mexican heritage, with ethnic costumes, etc. The hallway is lined with small botanical dioramas. A favorite room is the small Nature Center Laboratory, which is usually only open on Saturdays from 1pm to 3pm. Kids can inspect shells and bugs under a microscope. They can also dissect owl droppings. (Watch their faces when you explain what the word "droppings" means.) There are live reptiles, and a small sea display with preserved sea horses. The entire museum rates high on kid-interest! Free arts and crafts activities are offered on the first Sunday of the month, from September through May, from 1pm to 4pm.

Hours: Open Mon., 9am - 1pm; Tues. - Fri., 9am - 5pm; Sat.,
10am - 5pm; Sun., 11pm - 5pm.

Admission: Free

Ages: 2 years and up.

WORLD MUSEUM OF NATURAL HISTORY ☼

(909) 785-2209   !

4700 Pierce Street in Cossentine Hall on the campus of La Sierra University, Riverside

(EXIT RIVERSIDE FWY [91] S.W. ON MAGNOLIA, R. ON PIERCE. ENTER ON CAMPUS DR. FROM THE INTERSECTION OF PIERCE ST. AND SIERRA VISTA AVE. PARK AT THE END OF CAMPUS DR. IN PARKING LOT F ON WEEKENDS. IF YOU'VE MADE ARRANGEMENTS FOR A SPECIAL TOUR, ASK THE CURATOR TO GET A PARKING PERMIT FOR YOU.)

This quality museum is tremendous in its comprehensive scope of minerals, and freeze-dried animals. Full-grown and young animals are displayed according to species. The old and new world primates - or monkeys, gorillas, and chimps - all look so life like! The size and variety of the Crocodiles of the World is impressive. We had not heard of at least half the ones featured here. The Indian Gavial is especially unique with a snout that resembles a long, thin saw blade. The numerous types of turtles were similarly astounding. They range from the very small to the gigantic alligator snapping turtle. Snakes of the World boasts another record-breaking variety, ranging from boas, pythons, and common garters, to venomous snakes and even a two-headed snake. Other reptiles, including a huge Komodo dragon, are also on display.

Birds from all over the world are represented here, such as pelicans, flamingoes, penguins, an imperial eagle, and a blue-hued hunting green magpie. Some of the more unusual animals on display are the flat-headed cat (which, not surprisingly, has a very flat head), bats (one is just the size of a pin), an armadillo, a kangaroo, and an Indian rhino.

A fine display of Indian artifacts, such as arrowheads and headdresses, is also noteworthy.

An outstanding collection of rocks and minerals are grouped, in one section, according to color. These include large specimens of amethyst, malachite, etc. Other groupings include meteorites, fluorescent minerals, geodes, and huge slabs of petrified wood. There is also a large display of sphere balls or, in kidspeak, "cool-looking bowling balls." Part of this display shows the progression of a chunk of raw rock to a cube and then to the finished, sphere product. The World Museum of Natural History is an gem of a place!

Hours: Open Sat. from 2pm - 5pm or weekdays by appointment. Tours are welcome.

Admission: Free; donations gladly accepted.

Ages: 2 years and up.

THE AIR MUSEUM "PLANES OF FAME" ☼

(909) 597-3722   *$$*

7000 Merrill Avenue, Chino
(EXIT RIVERSIDE FWY [91] N. ON THE 71, N. ON EUCLID [OR THE 83]. EXIT HWY 83 R. ON MERRILL AVE., R. ON AIRPORT WAY.)

For some *plane* old fun, come see the over 100 vintage aircraft (some are flyable) that have landed here, including the only air-worthy Japanese Zero in the world.

Outside the north hanger (Tom Friedkin Hanger) is the plane that crashed (and obviously never recovered) from the movie "Waterworld." Other planes, parts of planes, and military vehicles are stationed here. Inside the hanger are Japanese aircraft from WWII. Some of them are "flying" around overhead, while others are grounded. My boys were drawn to the "Wild Grinning Face of the Green Dragon Unit" - a nose of a plane that has machine guns and is decorated with a fire-breathing dragon painted on its side. This building also displays airplane engines and small models of Japanese army aircraft, plus news clippings regarding Pearl Harbor.

The Bob Pond Hanger has more colorful and historic aircraft to look at. In the midst of such classic planes, what really grabs my children's attention, however, is the cartoon characters on the sides of the planes (i.e. Goofy at bat).

Part of the Jim Maloney Display Hanger is a restoration work area. Kids who are aeronautically inclined will be in their element here, although they cannot touch anything. Children are welcome, however, to touch and play in the Hands-On Aviation room in this hanger. They can climb into three experimental planes and play pilot. They can also practice their mechanical skills by "using" rivet guns and drills, plus taking apart (and putting together) parts of an engine. This hanger also displays gun turrets, cockpit control panels, uniforms, and the most model aircraft we've ever seen in one place! To take care of that hands-on urge, every Saturday and Sunday there is a B-17 Bomber at the Air Museum that, for a $1 donation, your child can sit in and "fly".

It's a short drive around the corner to the Fighter Jets Museum and Space Exhibit. The Bell X-1 was used in the movie, "The Right Stuff," and was the first plane to break the sound barrier. Other planes here have descriptions that are equally informative, though some are a bit technical.

The Space Exhibit is preparing to launch a completely interactive space learning station. Plans include a walk-in space module, a cockpit with real control panels fueled by imagination, a walk on a simulated surface of Mars, and much more. Currently, it has a full-size model of the Apollo 13 capsule, along with posters, photos of astronauts, and rockets blasting off - all underneath a starry-night, painted ceiling.

The Air Museum is in the Chino airport, so kids can experience the thrill of seeing planes take off and land. If you get hungry, pilot your way to Flo's Cafe, which is also on airport grounds.

Hours: Open daily from 9am - 5pm. Closed Thanksgiving and Christmas.

Admission: $7.95 for adults; $1.95 for ages 5 - 11; children 4 years and under are free.

Ages: 3 years and up.

GRABER OLIVE HOUSE

(909) 983-1761

315 E. Fourth Street, Ontario

(EXIT SAN BERNARDINO FWY [10] S. ON EUCLID, L. ON FOURTH ST.)

This is an unusual pit stop for kids. On the grounds are a small museum, an olive processing plant, a gift shop, and the owner's house, whose Victorian-style living room doubles as a tea room and etiquette classroom for kids and adults. The one-room museum shows a pictorial history of olive processing. It also has an eclectic mix of antiques such as a big wooden olive grader, a Singer sewing machine, a sausage stuffer, etc.

Come during the off season (the on-season is mid-October through December) and take a short tour around the working olive plant. Walk into the grading room, where olives are sorted by size and quality, and peer into the enormous olive vats. The boiler room, where olives are sterilized, the canning machine, and the labeling machine are all interesting to look at. A ten-minute video, that shows the history of the packing plant, is also available to watch.

The gift shop is very classy with etiquette videos, stationery, delicious jams, and elegant candies. (The chocolate-covered cherries are to die for!) Kids can sample a Graber olive, which might mean more to them after a tour.

Hours: Open Mon. - Sat., 9am - 5:30pm; Sun., 9:30am - 6pm.

Admission: Free

Ages: 5 years and up.

JOHN RAINS HOUSE - CASA DE RANCHO CUCAMONGA

(909) 989-4970

8810 Hemlock Street, Rancho Cucamonga

(EXIT SAN BERNARDINO FWY [10] N. ON VINEYARD. IT'S 2 BLOCKS N. OF FOOTHILLS BLVD., ON THE CORNER OF VINEYARD AND HEMLOCK, IN A RESIDENTIAL AREA.)

Built with bricks in 1860, this restored rancho residence has an open courtyard. Tours are given of the beautiful grounds, and through the historical home to see period furniture in the bedrooms, living rooms, etc. Docents recount stories about the people who once lived here. Their lives were like soap operas, complete with affairs, murders, buried treasure, etc., - kids love this (and they are learning history!) Ask about the special events that the Rancho hosts, such as Old Rancho Days, etc.

Hours: Open Wed. - Sat., 10am - 5pm; Sun., 1pm - 5pm.
Admission: $1 donation per person.
Ages: 6 years and up.

MOHAVE RIVER VALLEY MUSEUM / DANA PARK ☼
(760) 256-5452 - museum; (760) 256-5661 - park   *!/$*
Corner of Barstow Road and Virginia Way, Barstow
(EXIT 15 FWY N. ON BARSTOW RD.)

This little museum is full of interesting artifacts and displays. My boys liked the story and seeing the bones of a headless horseman, found astride his horse. The rock and minerals on display include nice specimens of arrowheads, quartz, calate, and black and gold forms of chalocopyrite, plus flourescent minerals that glow neon colors under black light. Other glass-encased exhibits are an eclectic mixture, such as lanterns, irons, rug beaters, pottery, clothing, a collection of glass insulators used by telegraph companies, etc. Kids can try their hand at grinding corn with stone mortar and pestle. They can also touch various animal skins, a turtle shell, bones, pinecones, rocks, and cotton. Short nature films are available to watch upon request. Call to arrange a field trip, and students will not only learn a lot about local history, but they can pan for real gold (and keep it!). Classes are usually taught by Mr. Walker, an archeology instructor at the college. The outside of the museum has large mining equipment around its perimeters - ore carts, picks, etc. Across the street is the small Centennial Park, which is actually an extension of the museum. It has a caboose, an army tank, and a mining display; representative of the three industries that helped formed Barstow.

Dana Park is just across Virginia Way. It has picnic shelters, some grassy hills to roll down, a playground, and an indoor community swimming pool that is open year round. Call (760) 255-4431 for pool information.

Hours: The museum is open daily 11am - 4pm. The pool is open Mon. and Wed. from 6pm - 8pm; Sat. - Sun., noon - 4pm for family swim.
Admission: Free to the museum, though donations are appreciated. The pool is $2 per person, per session.
Ages: 3 years and up.

MUSEUM OF HISTORY AND ART, ONTARIO
(909) 983-3198

225 S. Euclid Avenue, Ontario
(EXIT THE SAN BERNARDINO FWY [10] S. ON EUCLID, L. ON TRANSIT. IT'S ON THE CORNER.)

The Museum of History and Art captures the flavor of historic Ontario. The hallway leading towards the history section is lined with local school children's art work. The small museum's history galleries feature artifacts from citrus groves and industry, such as a replica of a Graber olive grader and a citrus smudge pot (used to warm trees). Other displays, mostly behind glass, include an old-fashioned kitchen exhibit; an iron collection; a section of photographs, uniforms, and information on WWII; and old machinery such as a typewriter and switchboard.

The art rooms contain changing exhibits of local and regional artists, as well as student work. Set in a Mediterranean-style building with a big fountain out front, the museum is a pleasant way to learn more about local roots.

Hours: The museum is open Wed. - Sun. from noon - 4pm.
Admission: Free
Ages: 6 years and up.

ROY ROGERS - DALE EVANS MUSEUM
(760) 243-4547 $$

15650 Seneca Road, Victorville
(EXIT 15 FWY W. ON ROY ROGERS DR. AND CIRCLE 'ROUND TO THE MUSEUM. YOU'LL SEE IT FROM THE FREEWAY.)

The Roy Rogers - Dale Evans Museum is hard to miss from the freeway. It looks like a fort, and has a larger-than-life statue of Roy's horse, Trigger, out front. Step into the museum and step back in time, to a simpler time when cowboys were heroes and family morals were admired and desired. Although you, and certainly your kids, might be too young to remember when Roy Rogers and Dale Evans were household names and he reigned as "King of the Cowboys," this museum is fascinating to all ages. It is an extensive collection of personal memorabilia that is incredibly well-displayed and delightful to explore.

Roy saved a lifetime of things and turned them into a museum. Family albums and celebrity photos abound. There are also many cases of trinkets, letters, and other items sent by fans, including lots of signed sports paraphernalia. After the Roy Rogers Show went on the air, Roy's likeness began appearing on everything from cereal boxes to comic books, lunch boxes, etc. He endorsed almost every kind of child's toy imaginable from cap guns to lassos, rings, hobby horses, and more. A sample of these items are on display here. My middle son (and cowboy wanna-be) loved seeing all the guitars, glitzy saddles, spurs, Western statues, numerous pairs of boots, and the fancy western duds that both Roy and Dale wore. At the kiddie corral, three sturdy wooden horses and a blue sky backdrop make for a great "ride 'em, cowboy!" photo opportunity.

One of the most popular displays features the taxidermied Trigger (Roy's beloved horse), Buttermilk (Dale's horse), and Bullet (the wonder dog). There are many more stuffed animals on exhibit too, including an exotic black Russian Boar, a mountain lion, and an albino skunk and albino raccoon. Roy was a game hunter, at a time when it was politically acceptable. His collection also includes mounted baboons, a zebra leg stool, a monkey rug, and an elephant feet foot stool. He also amassed a number of guns, pistols, and rifles - some with extravagant handles.

We enjoyed the Story Theater which, several times a day, shows a film of the family sharing memories of growing up with Roy and Dale, plus movie clips. It's like watching a professional (and entertaining) home-video. The back room contains vehicles special to the family including a horse-drawn carriage, and a car with show guns mounted on the hood. The outside center courtyard has more displays of large game (an elephant's head, a polar bear, etc.), as well as Native American displays. The latter includes feather headdresses, beaded clothing, rugs, and more. I'll close this entry with an inevitable, "Happy Trails to you."

Hours: Open daily 9am - 5pm. Closed Thanksgiving and Christmas.

Admission: $6 for adults; $5 for seniors and ages 13 - 16; $4 for ages 6 - 12; children 5 years and under are free.

Ages: 3 years and up.

SAN BERNARDINO COUNTY MUSEUM ☼

(909) 798-8570 $$

2024 Orange Tree Lane, Redlands

(EXIT SAN BERNARDINO FWY [10] N. ON CALIFORNIA ST., R. ON ORANGE TREE LN.)

Spend a day at the incredible San Bernardino County Museum where the hallway exhibits are just as fine as the ones in the exhibit rooms! The distinctive half-dome attached to the main building is the Fisk Gallery of Fine Arts. The Hall of History and Anthropology is down the ramp from the main level. Here you'll find a covered wagon and a Wells Fargo stage coach, along with period clothing. The Anthropology section has Indian artifacts, such as arrowheads and painted rock art.

The hallway going to the Upper Level is lined with exhibits such as old-time medicine bottles, fossilized mammoth tusks, the bones of a ground sloth, and a saber-tooth tiger skull. The other side of the hallway is a wonderful prelude to the Upper Level, displaying taxidermied birds and bird eggs. The eggs vary in size from very large elephant bird eggs to very small hummingbird eggs.

If your kids show any interest in ornithology, the study of birds (calling each other bird brain doesn't count), they will be fascinated by the entire Upper Level. The Hall of Water Birds takes you on flights of fancy with taxidermied birds (although you wouldn't get very far). See if your kids can match the birds to their eggs, which are also on display throughout the room. The next wing, Hall of Land Birds, displays birds and eggs according to regional habitat. Look for the "awww, so cute" hatchling exhibit. I have never seen so many birds flocked together. A large stuffed California Condor guards the entrance to the Upper Dome Gallery. This gallery has rotating exhibits of art work.

An absolutely dazzling display of rocks, minerals, and gemstones line the hallway toward the Lower Level. The doors in the hallway lead out to the Discovery Hall, but we'll come back to that. Continue down the ramp into the Hall of Mammals. The walls in here are lined with fossilized animal bones, horns, and teeth. Bug collectors will be bug-eyed at the comprehensive collection of mounted insects of all sizes, shapes, and colors. Also along the walls are dioramas of smaller taxidermied animals and reptiles, such as spotted skunks, possums, and turtles. The Hall of Mammals is unique in that is also has exhibits of larger taxidermied animals, like a polar bear, an Alaskan brown bear, a mountain lion, a bison, and a gigantic moose. My kids were really impressed by the sheer size of some of the animals.

Outside, between the main building and the Discovery Hall, is a patio area designed just for kids. (Check out the F-105 jet just around the corner.) A mining car carrying "explosives" is on track towards a tunnel. A full-size caboose and steam engine are sometimes open to climb aboard. Picnic tables are here for snack attacks.

The Discovery Hall is a learning center that has small, live mammals, such as bunnies and bats, and reptiles, such as iguanas, a boa, and other snakes. Kids can touch fossils, animal furs, and casts of bones and dinosaur fossils. The hall also has aquariums.

The Elsie Munzig Special Exhibit Hall has terrific, changing, usually interactive displays. A past exhibit was rather batty - "Masters of the Night - The True Story of Bats." It included entering through the portals of a gothic castle, seeing videos, touching models of bats, and literally hanging around in a bat cave.

A one-hour, Saturday Morning Family Fun program is usually held every Saturday. It's designed to educate the entire family about a particular topic or animal in a fun, hands-on manner. The programs are free with general museum admission.

Hours: Open Tues. - Sun. from 9am - 5pm. Closed New Year's Day, Thanksgiving, and Christmas. The Discovery Hall is open Tues. - Thurs. from 10am - 1pm; Fri., 10am - 4pm; Sat. - Sun., 1pm - 4pm.

Admission: $4 for adults; $3 for seniors and students; $2 for ages 5 - 12; children 4 years and under are free. When the Special Exhibit Hall has a special exhibit, the admission price temporarily is raised: $7 for adults; $6 for seniors and students; $5 for ages 5 -12; children 4 years and under are free.

Ages: 2 years and up.

TEMECULA - OLD TOWN / TEMECULA MUSEUM   ☀
(909) 676-0021   !/$
Front Street and Moreno Street, Temecula
*(EXIT TEMECULA VALLEY FWY [15] W. ON RANCHO CALIFORNIA RD., L. ON FRONT
ST. TO OLD TOWN, OR L. ON MORENO ST. TO THE MUSEUM AT SAM HICKS PARK.)*

Mosey on over to Old Town Temecula and enjoy an hour or so on
Main Street. This western strip of town looks and feels authentic, right
down to its bootstraps. The many unique-looking stores and gift items
for sale make it an alluring place to shop, even with children.

The museum is located on a corner park - Sam Hicks Park - that
has a small playground, and a large rock inscribed with the names of
pioneers. The museum is an interesting glimpse into Temecula's past.
The tools, household goods, guns, saddles, army equipment, etc., on
display, portray life on the local ranches and frontier towns. A six-foot
by nine-foot diorama depicts the city of Temecula, circa 1914. There
are also Native American artifacts, plus memorabilia from Erle Stanley
Gardner, author of the Perry Mason stories and one-time resident of
Temecula.

Hours: Open Wed. - Sun. from 11am - 4pm
Admission: By donation
Ages: 5 years and up.

ANTIQUE GAS & STEAM ENGINE MUSEUM, INC.   ☽
(800) 5-TRACTOR (587-2286) or (760) 941-1791   !
2040 North Santa Fe Avenue, Vista
*(EXIT SAN DIEGO FWY [5] N. ON SAN LUIS REY MISSION EXWY [76], CONTINUE ON
MISSION AVE. OR, FROM ESCONDIDO FWY [15] EXIT W. ON PALA RD [76], WHICH
TURNS INTO MISSION AVE. FROM MISSION AVE. GO S. ON N. SANTA FE AVE. FROM
VISTA FWY [78] EXIT N. ON MELROSE DR., R. ON W. BOBIER AVE., L. ON SANTA FE
AVE.)*

This museum answers the age-old question, "Where do engines go
when they run out of gas (or steam)?" California has a museum for
almost any interest. This forty-acre, mostly outdoor museum, has
hundreds of tractors, combines, gas and steam engines (that's a given
from the name of the museum), horse-drawn carriages, and equipment
used in mining, oil drilling, construction, agriculture, and more. The
machines have been (or are in the process of being) restored to
working condition. In fact, some of the equipment is used to help farm
the adjacent lands. Walk around on your own; ask one of the
volunteers for a tour; or better yet, come to a
demonstration usually held on the third and fourth weekends of June
and October. At these Threshing Bees and Antique Engine & Tractor
Shows, watch or take part in planting, harvesting, household chores,
early American crafts, blacksmithing, log sawing, parades, square
dancing, etc. It's a good ol' time!

Some of the museum's collection are housed in structures resembling a small town. Featured buildings include a huge (and complete) blacksmith and wheelwright shop, a farm house with parlor, a sawmill, a one-third scale train with a telegraphers office, and a barn. There are picnic tables here and even a small playground with two small, stationary tractors to climb on. The museum is interesting to visit anytime, but it's exciting to visit at exhibition time!

Hours: Open daily from 10am - 4pm.
Admission: Free, except for special events that usually cost $5.
Ages: 4 years and up.

BALBOA PARK   ☼

(619) 239-0512 - This Visitors Center number gives a listing of $$
the museums and information about upcoming events.

Balboa Park on the Prado, San Diego
(GOING S. ON CABRILLO FWY [163], EXIT N. ON PARK BLVD. GOING S. ON SAN DIEGO FWY [5], EXIT AT ASH ST. / "A" ST., L. ON "A" ST., L. ON PARK BLVD. GOING N. ON 5, EXIT W. ON "B" ST., R. ON PARK BLVD. ONCE ON PARK BLVD. TURN L. ON PRESIDENTS WAY, TO GET TO THE MUSEUMS.)

This massive 1,158 acre park is the cultural and recreational heart of San Diego. Numerous programs and seasonal events are held here - see the CALENDAR section in the back of the book and/or call for a schedule of events. The park has shade trees, grassy areas, picnic areas, and playgrounds located at Pepper Grove Picnic Area on Park Boulevard, south of the San Diego Zoo, and another at the north end of Balboa Drive. Morley Field Sports Complex, located off Morely Field Drive in the northeastern section, has twenty-five public tennis courts available for $4 per person. Call (619) 295-2221 for reservations. It also has a fitness course; boccie ball courts, which is an Italian sport similar to lawn bowling; velodrome; fly-casting pool, with free lessons on Sunday mornings; an archery range; baseball diamonds; a frisbee golf course; playgrounds; picnic areas; and a swimming pool that is open seasonally. Swim sessions cost $2 for adults, $1.50 for seniors and children. Call (619) 692-4920 for more information. Call (619) 692-4919 for more information regarding the sports complex.

Balboa Park is home to a majority of the city's museums, as well as the world famous SAN DIEGO ZOO. Individual museum entries are found under the MUSEUM section, San Diego county, listed by their official titles: MINGEI INTERNATIONAL FOLK ART MUSEUM, MUSEUM OF PHOTOGRAPHIC ARTS, MUSEUM OF SAN DIEGO HISTORY, REUBEN H. FLEET SPACE THEATER AND SCIENCE CENTER, SAN DIEGO AEROSPACE MUSEUM, SAN DIEGO AUTOMOTIVE MUSEUM, SAN DIEGO HALL OF CHAMPIONS SPORTS MUSEUM, SAN DIEGO MODEL RAILROAD MUSEUM, SAN DIEGO MUSEUM OF ART, and SAN DIEGO NATURAL HISTORY MUSEUM. Passports can be purchased to visit eleven museums, plus the Omnimax Theater, for $19 for adults. Passes can be bought at the

Visitors Information Center and are good for one week from the date of purchase. Below is a list of which museums are free on particular Tuesdays: <u>First Tuesday</u>: S.D. Natural History, Reuben H. Fleet Science Center, and S.D. Model Railroad; <u>Second Tuesday</u>: Museum of Photographic Arts, Museum of S.D. History, and S.D. Hall of Champions Sports Museum; <u>Third Tuesday</u>: Japanese Friendship Garden, Mingei International Folk Art Museum, S.D. Museum of Art, and S.D. Museum of Man; <u>Fourth Tuesday</u>: Cottages and Hall of Nations films - "Children Around the World" (11am to 3pm), House of Pacific Relations International, S.D. Aerospace Museum, and S.D. Automotive Museum.

The park also offers many other attractions that are worthy of mention. The beautiful, latticed **Botanical Building** is located at the north end of the lily pond next to the San Diego Museum of Art. It has (labeled) tropical and subtropical plants on display. It is open Friday through Wednesday from 10am to 4pm. Admission is free. The **Timken Museum of Art** is located next to the Visitors Center. Housed here are collections of works by European Old Masters, eighteenth- and nineteenth-century American paintings, and Russian icons. It is open Tuesday through Saturday from 10am to 4:30pm; Sunday, 1:30pm to 4:30pm. Admission is free. The **Japanese Friendship Garden** is a Japanese-style house with a main room that has a traditional table set with (fake) Japanese food. Children must stay on the short path leading to the small garden. If you are interested in seeing this room and garden, come here when admission is free, on the third Tuesday of the month, as admission is otherwise $2. Free outdoor concerts are given every Sunday from 2pm to 3pm and on Mondays from 8pm to 9:30pm during July and August on the famous **Spreckels Pipe Organ**. It is located in an architecturally beautiful building set in a huge half circle. My kids think the steps are a great place for picnicking. The **Spanish Village Art Center**, (619) 233-9050, is just north of the San Diego Natural History Museum. The "village" has retained its old-world charm with its Spanish architecture and colorful courtyard tiles and flowers. The thirty-five art studios and galleries include woodcarvings, sculptures, and gems and minerals, for show and sale. Oftentimes, the artisans demonstrate their craft which makes the Spanish Village Center an intriguing stop for slightly older kids. The **House of Pacific Relations**, (619) 234-0739, is located behind the United Nations Building, across from the Spreckels Organ. The "House" is comprised of fifteen cottages representing thirty-one nationalities. Exhibits in each cottage pertain to specific ethnic groups. Music and dance programs are held on Sundays from 2pm to 3pm from mid-March through October 31. The cottages are open Sundays from 12:30pm to 4:30pm and on the fourth Tuesday from noon to 3pm. Admission is free. Two other kid-friendly attractions are the **miniature train ride** and the **merry-go-round.** Both rides are located south of the Zoo and north of the Spanish Village Center. They operate weekends and holidays only from 10:30am to 5:30pm. The train ride costs $1.25 per person. The old-fashioned carousel has horses and other animals to ride on, and offers a chance to grab at the gold ring. Rides cost $1 for all ages. There are many theaters and places to eat within Balboa Park, too.

At any time during your visit to the park, you are welcome to hop aboard the Balboa Park Tram. This free, intra-park transportation system can take you from Presidents Way and Park Boulevard, up to the carousel, through where the museums are, and up north to 6th Street and the Marston House. It makes several stops along the way, so you can catch it coming or going. It operates daily from 10am to 4pm, with extended hours in the summer. Plan to visit Balboa Park many times, as you obviously cannot see it all in one, two, or even three days!

> **Hours:** The park is open daily. The Visitors Center is open daily 9am - 4pm. Individual attractions are listed separately.
> **Admission:** Entrance to the park is free. Individual attractions are listed separately.
> **Ages:** All ages for the park. Individual attractions are listed separately.

BUENA VISTA AUDUBON NATURE CENTER

(760) 439-BIRD (2473)

2202 South Coast Highway, Oceanside

(EXIT SAN DIEGO FWY [5] W. ON VISTA WAY, L. ON SOUTH COAST HIGHWAY. IT IS JUST N. OF THE BUENA VISTA LAGOON.)

This museum is not just for the birds! The exhibits inside this small building consist mainly of taxidermied birds (some in flight) such as a pelican, a great blue heron, a red-tailed hawk, a colorful yellow western tanager, and more. A stuffed owl has a mouse in its beak and a pellet at its feet that contains partially digested animal parts. Other mounted animals on display include a bobcat and a possum. The touch table has a raccoon skin, petrified wood, and whale bones, among other things. Look through a kid-level window on the central display to see fish "swimming" underneath. A book corner for children has a nice selection of nature books to read. Other items of interest are the fish tank with catfish (it's easy to see where they got their name), a small rock and mineral display, and a live tarantula.

Outside, take a walk through the marshy reeds out to the lagoon. This area is home to a wide variety of birds. Guided field trips are one of the best ways to really learn about the abundant wildlife at Buena Vista. Migrate over to the picnic tables which are available to make your day just ducky!

> **Hours:** Open Tues. - Sat., 10am - 4pm; Sun., 1pm - 4pm.
> **Admission:** Free
> **Ages:** 3 years and up.

CALIFORNIA SURF MUSEUM   ☿

(760) 721-6876   !

223 North Coast Highway, Oceanside
(EXIT SAN DIEGO FWY [5] W. ON MISSION AVE., R. ON NORTH COAST HWY.)

Surfing is the heart of the Southern California beach culture. This small museum aims to preserve the history and lifestyle of surfing so it won't be wiped out. On display are a variety of surfboards, some looking (to the inexperienced eye) simply like thick boards. Other exhibits include lots of photographs and information, a tabletop wave machine, and an Hawaiian hut made of palm leaves that pays homage to surfing's roots.

Hours: Open Mon. - Fri., noon - 4pm; Sat. - Sun., 10am - 4pm.
Admission: Free; donations gladly accepted.
Ages: Surfer dudes 8 years and up.

CAMP PENDLETON   ☿

(760) 725-5569 - general information; (760) 725-5710 - rancho   !
tour information; (760) 725-2660 - amphibious museum
Oceanside
(EXIT SAN DIEGO FWY [5] W. AT HARBOR DR. / VANDEGRIFT BLVD. ONTO THE BASE.)

Driving on I-5 between Orange County and Oceanside, it's hard to miss the sprawling Camp Pendleton. This military training camp is one of the largest, especially for amphibious training. My boys like the thought of being on a real marine base, so taking a "windshield tour" (i.e. driving around in here) was a (quick) treat for them. Camp Pendleton is also on an historical site where early Spanish explorers traveled. For a more detailed understanding of this time period, Rancho Las Flores and the nineteenth-century Santa Margarita adobe ranch house are available to tour through, with advanced registration, for a group of twenty or more. The houses retain the essence of yesteryear in both landscaping and interior furnishings.

The Amphibious Vehicle Museum is located at the southern end of Camp Pendleton at the Del Mar basin. There are many military vehicles around the area, but the most interesting in the museum are the six L.V.T.'s (Land Vehicle Tracks) - amphibious vehicles used in combat. These relics from WWII are accompanied by war mementoes such as uniforms, weapons, personal artifacts, etc. You may ask to watch the video on the history of the L.V.T.'s. You'll need to show your driver's license and vehicle registration at the main gate.

Hours: Drive through Camp Pendleton Mon. - Fri. from 7:30am - 4:30pm. Call for rancho and adobe house tours. The Amphibious Museum is usually open Tues. - Sat. from 9am - 4pm.
Admission: Free
Ages: 6 years and up.

CARLSBAD CHILDREN'S MUSEUM   ☼

(760) 720-0737 $$

300 Carlsbad Village Drive, #102, Carlsbad
(EXIT SAN DIEGO FWY [5] W. ON CALSBAD VILLAGE DR.)

After my oldest son understood that we were not going to "Carl's Bad Children's Museum," his dread turned into anticipation and we all had a great time. Each room at the museum is themed, appealing to different aspects of your child's personality. Set sail for adventure and catch some pretend fish while skippering a real boat (at least the front end of one), surrounded by a wall with a sea mural. Use a cart to hold all your items while shopping at the well-stocked play market. The cashier can use the real cash register (with fake cash). Things are positively medieval when your kids play at the large replica castle. Girls dress up and turn into princesses (temporarily) while boys (and girls) suit up to become knights in shining (plastic) armor. My oldest son simply declared himself king and ordered everyone else around. Mirror Magic, a room with carnival-type "funny" mirrors, kept the kids busy for a long time. Who would have thought they could make that many faces?! Also, try playing mirror tic-tac-toe. On reflection, it's harder than it seems. Every week Creative Corner provides your child with a new project to create and take home. Aprons are available for those with messier instincts. At the science area, test a hand battery, watch a solar-powered train go around a track, and stand in the center of a bubble that's as tall as you are. There are a few computers in the museum and a small area for toddlers that has books, toys, and a puppet theater.

The Children's Museum is located in Villa Plaza, directly across from the Status Chocolates Shop. The fountain in the middle of the Plaza has reclining chairs around it making it a delightful place to rest, unless your child falls in the water!

Hours: Open Sun., Tues. - Thurs., noon - 5pm; Fri. - Sat., 10am
              - 5pm. It is open daily from 10am - 5pm in July and
              August.
Admission: $3.50 for ages 2 years and up.
Ages: 1½ years - 11 years.

CHILDREN'S MUSEUM SAN DIEGO / MUSEO DE   ☼
LOS NINOS

(619) 233-5437 $$

200 West Island Avenue, San Diego
(EXIT SAN DIEGO FWY [5] S. ON 1ˢᵀ ST., R. ON BROADWAY, L. ON STATE, L. ON ISLAND.)

The museum's emphasis is "to be a hands-on, minds-on experiential learning environment for people of all ages" and "to be truly bi-national, recognizing Tijuana and Mexico as neighbors."

There are very few permanent exhibits in this innovative children's museum that is housed in a warehouse. They include the Art Studio, which is a place to create wonderful art projects, plus it is the home of a 1952 Dodge pick-up truck that kids can paint, repaint, and paint again; the Improv Theater, which is a dress up and stage area; and Cora's Rain House, which is a giant tin house featuring a rain forest with recycling water. It is designed for kids to come in and express their thoughts or emotions by talking, drawing, or writing.

The temporary exhibits are all hands-on and great fun. Past exhibits have included building a prefab house with hammer and nails; the story of making candy told in pictorial renderings; a giant, floor checkerboard, played by using huge red and black foam pillows; and Pop Art featuring life-size super heroes and other cool guys. Call to see what is currently being featured, although kids will thoroughly enjoy whatever it is. A small park, good for picnicking, is located across the street, diagonally, from the museum.

Hours: Open Tues. - Sun. from 10am - 5pm.
Admission: $5 for ages 2 and up; $3 for seniors. There is limited free parking. Paid parking is available at Front and Island St. The trolley also stops at the museum.
Ages: 2 years and up.

CORONADO BEACH HISTORICAL MUSEUM

(619) 435-7242

1126 Loma Avenue, Coronado
(EXIT SAN DIEGO FWY [5] W. ON 75 AND CROSS OVER THE CORONADO BRIDGE, L. ON ORANGE AVE., R. ON LOMA AVE. THE TOLL IS $1 TO CORONADO AND THE RETURN TRIP IS FREE. IF YOU ARE CAR POOLING, CROSS THE BRIDGE USING THE RIGHT LANE, AT NO CHARGE.)

This quaint house contains exhibits depicting the early history of the seaside village of Coronado. Half of the downstairs displays rotate. A past favorite was "Toys and Treasures of a Coronado Childhood," which featured antique toys and furniture, books, games, clothing, and photographs from yesteryear. Note: The museum closes temporarily in between displays. The permanent exhibits include photographs and information on the Hotel Del Coronado, the Navy, the ferry, and tent city. There is also memorabilia such as vintage clothing, jewelry, and a few other items.

Hours: Open Wed. - Sat., 11am - 4pm; Sun., noon - 4pm.
Admission: Free
Ages: 7 years and up.

FIREHOUSE MUSEUM

(619) 232-3473
1572 Columbia Street, San Diego

(GOING N. ON SAN DIEGO FWY [5] EXIT AT THE FIRST EXIT AFTER CABRILLO FWY EXCHANGE, TURN L. ON 6TH ST. AT END OF OFF RAMP, R. ON ASH ST., R. ON STATE ST., L. ON DATE ST., L. ON COLUMBIA. GOING S. ON 5, EXIT AT ASH / "A" ST., GO R. AT END OF OFF RAMP ON ASH ST., R. ON STATE ST., L. ON DATE ST., L. ON COLUMBIA.)

Have a hot time in downtown San Diego by visiting the Firehouse Museum! Housed inside an old fire station, the museum displays several antique pieces of fire-fighting equipment such as a water pump and steamer, helmets, axes, and speaking trumpets through which chiefs would shout their orders, plus other items like a telephone switchboard, etc.

Hours: Open Thurs. - Fri., 10am - 2pm; Sat. - Sun., 10am - 4pm.
Admission: $2 for adults; children 12 years and under are free. The first Thursday of every month is free admission day.
Ages: 4 years and up.

GASKILL STONE STORE MUSEUM

(619) 478-5707

31330 Highway 94, around the corner from the San Diego Railroad Museum

(EXIT 8 FWY (45 MILES FROM DOWNTOWN SAN DIEGO) S. ON BUCKMAN SPRINGS RD., 10.5 MILES TO HWY. 94, BEAR RIGHT (1.5 MILES) TO THE STORE ON THE CORNER.)

This small museum is exactly as its name implies - a museum created from an old store built with stones in 1885. The exhibits in the room consist of a stocked, old-fashioned general store; a small, turn-of-the-century kitchen; tools; appliances; and lots of photographs and documents. The back room, once used for storing food and other items, is a cave that was blasted out of rock. Upstairs is a military room with mannequins in uniforms, plus photographs and information about this area's military region. A stream runs in front of the museum and a woods surrounds it. Just around the corner is the SAN DIEGO RAILROAD MUSEUM.

Hours: Open weekends and selected holidays from 11am - 5pm.
Admission: $2 for adults; children 12 years and under are free.
Ages: 7 years and up.

GUY B. WOODWARD MUSEUM OF HISTORY

(760) 789-7644

645 Main Street, Ramona

(FROM SAN DIEGO FWY [5] OR ESCONDIDO FWY [15], TAKE 78 FWY E. TO RAMONA, L. ON MAIN ST. (ALSO 78). FROM 8 FWY, TAKE SAN VICENTE FWY [67] N. STAY ON HWY 67 TO RAMONA, TURNS INTO MAIN ST.)

A complex of buildings make up this small, early western museum "town." The museum contains the heritage (and furnishings) of the older citizens of Ramona. The main house has roped-off rooms to look into including a turn-of-the-century doctor's office with a bloodied mannequin patient on the bed, and a collection of early medical instruments and bottles; a beautifully decorated parlor, which is a combination of living room and music room, with mannequins dressed in period clothing; a library; a bedroom; and a kitchen that is packed with irons, dishes, butter churns, and other implements. The screened in back porch is set up like a bedroom - my kids were ready to move in!

The downstairs of the house used to be a wine cellar, and the temperature is still cool here. The conglomeration of "stuff" now stored here includes Civil War artifacts such as uniforms and cannon balls; a collection of cameras; a turkey-feather cape; a six-foot long Red Diamond Rattlesnake skin; Native American artifacts such as stone mortar and pestle, and pottery; a hair perming machine that looks like something out of a science fiction film; a Casey Tibbs memorial exhibit dedicated to this World Champion rodeo rider; and more. Gift shop items can also be found down here.

The outside courtyard has a stage wagon - no springs makes for a bumpy ride! A red barn houses a medicine car (an RV prototype). The long garage contains a 1920 tractor, old buggies, an antique fire engine, fire fighting equipment, and lots of old tools, such as saws and wheat scythes, in neat rows on the walls. Just around the corner is a Honey House which contains beekeeping equipment. A narrow Millinery Shoppe features a doll collection, real mink stoles, outrageous feather hats, and a few beaded dresses. Other buildings here include a real jail; an outhouse; a re-created Post Office; a Hobby Room, which is really a catch-all room filled with old typewriters, bottles, and one of the first T.V. sets; a Bunkhouse where cowboys used to live; a Tack Room with dusty, rusty saddles; and a Blacksmith Shop complete with all the tools of the trade. Farm machinery is displayed all around the cluster of buildings. See if your kids can recognize washing machines, butter churns, the large incubator, a cream separator, a machine for bottling milk, etc.

This unique museum is more than a glimpse into the past - it is a good, long, and interesting look into our ancestors' way of life. While you're here, enjoy a stroll around historic Old Town Ramona, which is located on both sides and across the street from the museum.

Hours: Open Thurs. - Sun. from 1pm - 4pm.
Admission: $3 for adults; 50¢ for children 12 years and under.
Ages: 5 years and up.

HERITAGE OF THE AMERICAS MUSEUM   ☼
(619) 670-5194 $
2952 Jamacha Road, El Cajon

(GOING W. ON 8 FWY, EXIT S. ON 2ND ST./JAMACHA RD. [HWY 54], CONTINUE ON JAMACHA RD., R. ON CUYAMACA COLLEGE DR. W. GOING E. ON 8, EXIT S. ON FWY 125, EXIT S. ON SPRING ST., IMMEDIATELY GET ON 94 FWY E., CONTINUE ON TO END, TURNS INTO CAMPO RD., L. ON JAMACHA RD., L ON CUYAMACA COLLEGE DR. W. IT IS ON THE CUYAMACA COLLEGE CAMPUS.)

This museum makes learning about our heritage much more exciting than simply reading about it in a history book. Four different exhibit halls branch off diagonally from the reception desk. The <u>Natural History Hall</u> contains rocks and minerals, including a lodestone (i.e. a hunk of rock with a magnetic personality) with nails sticking out from it. The meteorite display is out of this world. Other favorite items in this wing include a fossilized turtle shell, a T-Rex tooth, an Allosaurus claw, trilobites, a rattlesnake skin, a and a prehistoric bee trapped in amber, plus shells, coral, and seahorses. The many taxidermied animals include a leopard, deer, coyote, and the head of a cape buffalo. The <u>Archaeology Hall</u> contains an incredible arrowhead collection, gathered from all over the world, and from different periods of time. Some of them are practical, while others are more ornamental. Other displays include stone artifacts, such as hoes and ax heads, in glass cases alongside Mayan treasures of stone and clay; necklaces made of jade, quartz, and amethyst; and various forms of money such as shells and copper. Weapons, of course, are always a hit with my boys. The <u>Anthropology Hall</u> showcases impressive Native American articles such as eagle feather headdresses, ceremonial costumes, and exquisitely beaded mocassins, gloves, and vests. More intriguing, however, are the elk tooth and eagle claw necklaces; the beaded mountain lion paw bag; tje knife made from a blackfoot bear jaw; the shark tooth sword that looks like a small chain saw; and dance rattles made out of turtle shells and trap door spiders' nests. This section also displays tomahawks, guns from the Old West, and a buffalo robe. The <u>Art Hall</u> has Western art featuring cowboys and Indians portrayed in drawings, paintings, photographs, and sculpture. Four different pamphlets are available that give details about exhibits in each of the halls. This hilltop museum also has two small gardens with picnic tables, plus a stunning 360-degree view.

Hours: Open Tues. - Fri., 10am - 4pm; Sat., 1pm - 5pm. Closed selected holidays.

Admission: $3 for adults; $2 for seniors; $1 for students with I.D.; children 12 years and under are free.

Ages: 5 years and up.

HERITAGE WALK / GRAPE DAY PARK
(760) 743-8207

321 North Broadway, Escondido
(EXIT ESCONDIDO FWY [15], E. ON HWY 78, R. ON BROADWAY)

Grape Day Park has a charming ambiance created by a rose garden, large grassy areas, shade trees, picnic tables, Victorian

buildings, a restored train depot, and a unique playground. The small
playground has colorful configurations that look like interlocking tree
branches to climb up, under, and through. It also has a small play
structure that resembles the top of a space ship, with enough room at
the flat top for just one person to sit - a natural setting to play "King of
the Hill." The park has horseshoe pits, too. Equipment can be checked
out weekdays from 8am to 4pm. (Parental supervision is required.)

The five buildings that comprise the museum complex of Heritage
Walk were relocated here in 1976, and are open to the public. They are:
1) Escondido's first library; 2) A quaint, completely furnished, two-story
1890's house with a living room, parlor, and kitchen, plus four small
bedrooms upstairs; 3) A 1900's barn with a wagon out front; 4) A
blacksmith's shop which holds demonstrations when it's open; and 5)
An 1888 Santa Fe Depot. The two-story depot building is nice-looking
and interesting to explore. Some highlights include a train master's
office, a working telegraph station (send a message to someone!), a
model train set that makes tracks around realistic looking landscape, a
stuffed grizzly bear, and displays of conductor's hats, dining plates once
used on trains, etc. The depot also has a real train car that can be
toured through. A tank house and a small herb garden can also be seen
on the short walk around around Heritage Walk. The park is a fun place
for kids to play, but bring them sometime to see the museum part of it,
also.

Hours: The park is open daily sunrise to sunset. The museum is
open Thurs - Sat. from 1pm - 4pm. It is closed
Thanksgiving weekend, and all major holidays.
Admission: Free; donations are appreciated.
Ages: All for the park; ages 5 and up for the museum.

JULIAN PIONEER MUSEUM
(760) 765-0227 $
2811 Washington Street, Julian
*(FROM SAN DIEGO FWY [5] OR ESCONDIDO FWY [15], TAKE 78 FWY E. TO JULIAN.
78 IS WASHINGTON ST. IN JULIAN. FROM THE 8 FWY, TAKE 79 N. TO JULIAN, AT 78
JCT. TURN LEFT ON MAIN ST., L. ON WASHINGTON ST.)*

If I were to clean out my grandparents' and great-grandparents'
attics, closets, garages, etc., I would probably find many articles similar
to what is inside this pioneer museum. The wide assortment of items
here include carriages, guns, saddles, tools, eyeglasses, mining
equipment, rocks, bottles, clothing, arrowheads, a ceremonial Indian
costume, kitchen implements, a metal bathtub, a pot-bellied stove, an
American flag (with forty-five stars), and lots of old, handmade lace. My
favorite exhibit was a machine from a 1930's beauty shop. It was
supposed to perm hair, but with the wires and rods sticking out all over
the mannequin's head, it looks more like something from a science
fiction film! Bring a lunch and enjoy a picnic on the tables outside this
quaint museum.

Julian is a quaint town with unique shops along Main Street. Your kids will enjoy a stop-off at the Julian Drugstore, at the corner of Main Street and Washington Street, to enjoy an ice cream at its old-fashioned soda counter. Also see EAGLE MINING COMPANY to take a tour of a real gold mine.

Hours: Open December - March, Sat. - Sun. from 10am - 4pm; open April - November, daily from 10am - 4pm. Closed New Year's Day, Thanksgiving, and Christmas.

Admission: $1 for adults; children are free.

Ages: 5 years and up.

MARINE CORPS RECRUIT DEPOT COMMAND ☼ MUSEUM

(619) 524-6038   !

In the Marine Corps Recruit Depot on Pacific Highway and Witherby Street, San Diego

(GOING S. ON SAN DIEGO FWY [5] EXIT AT OLD TOWN AVE., OFF THE OFF RAMP ONTO HANCOCK ST., R. ON WITHERBY ST. GOING N. ON 5 EXIT AT MOORE ST., L. ON OLD TOWN AVE, L. ON HANCOCK ST., R. ON WITHERBY ST. YOU MUST SHOW A VALID DRIVER'S LICENSE TO ENTER THE BASE. THE MUSEUM IS DIRECTLY ACROSS FROM THE GUARD ENTRANCE.)

The first thing my kids noticed were the Japanese 70mm Howitzers outside the museum. Inside, the downstairs California Room displays numerous paintings of war, including battles involving Native Americans, blue coats verses grey coats, etc. The hallway has photos of movies and television shows that have featured Marines. An on-going, twenty-minute narrated film is presented in the small theater. It shows all the different phases of Marine training, from boot camp to graduation. Naturally, the "coolest" parts of it, according to my boys, were the army maneuvers where rounds and rounds of ammunition were shot, and the nighttime target practice where spots of light were seen when the guns were fired. After the movie my youngest son, with shining eyes, said, "I want to be a Marine!" The Visitor's Lounge looks like a large living room with couches and chairs. Around the perimeter of the room are exhibits such as helicopter and ship models, various military hats, and models of physical fitness courses that make me tired just looking at them.

Upstairs are rooms filled with military memorabilia. The extensive exhibits include uniforms, swords, medals, grenades, posters, pictures, flags, mannequins dressed in camouflage, rocket launchers, jeeps, police motorcycles, a collection of knives (including machetes and bayonets), and a room devoted to guns and ammunition. The China Room focuses on American Marines in Peking. It contains a lot of documents and news articles from this time period, plus photos, traditional Chinese military dress, and a canon. The museum encompasses the history of the Marines from its inception 221 years ago, through WWI and WWII, and up to the present day. Always looking for "a few good men and women," the Marine Corps maintains a museum that is historically important, and that will enlist your child's attention.

Hours: Open Mon. - Fri., 0800 - 1600; Sat., 1000 - 1400.
Admission: Free
Ages: 5 years and up.

MARITIME MUSEUM (San Diego)   ☼

(619) 234-9153   *$$*

1306 North Harbor Drive, San Diego

(GOING N. ON SAN DIEGO FWY [5] EXIT AT THE FIRST EXIT AFTER CABRILLO FWY EXCHANGE, TURN L. ON 6TH ST. AT END OF OFF RAMP, R. ON ASH ST. GOING S. ON 5, EXIT AT ASH / "A" ST. GO W. ON ASH ST. THE MUSEUM IS AT THE END OF ASH ST., ON HARBOR DRIVE.)

"I saw a ship a-sailing, a-sailing on the sea; and, oh! it was all laden with pretty things for thee!" (An old rhyme.) The three historic ships that comprise the Maritime Museum; the Star of India, the Berkeley, and the Medea, are laden with wonderful nautical artifacts. The 1863 Star of India is beautiful to behold with its intricate-looking rigging, interesting figurehead, and polished wooden exterior. Inside, kids can look out the portholes; check out the very narrow bunks that once held emigrants; look at the old tools and display of knots; and marvel at the variations of ships in bottles. Not only are the ships unique, but the shapes of the bottles vary, too. Our favorite was the ship in a lightbulb. The fifteen-minute video "Around Cape Horn" is a bit dry, though it depicts action at sea. Top board is the captain's cabin (which is small enough to give me claustrophobia), a few passengers' cabins (which they had to furnish themselves), a dining room, and the chart room.

The 1898 ferryboat, Berkeley, contains a number of fascinating model ships and yachts. A model ship construction and repair shop is on board, and we watched a builder at work. He told us a model takes an average of five years to complete! Such detail work! One section of the Berkeley has a whaling gun on exhibit and displays of fish (mostly tuna) and fisheries. Downstairs is the engine room which you can explore on your own. The room is intriguing with its huge machinery and gears, narrow walkways, and slightly spooky ambiance. Also below deck is a room showcasing memorabilia from America's Cup. The triple expansion steam engine is put to work and demonstrated at various times throughout the day.

Cross over the bridge from the Berkeley to the 1904 steam yacht, Medea, which is a very small vessel. Peek into the elegant Edwardian-decorated smoking room and into the galley that contains a coal-burning stove, big copper pots, and a wooden ice box. All in all, we had a merry time at the Maritime Museum.

Hours: Open daily from 9am - 8pm.

Admission: Admission includes all three ships - $5 for adults; $4 for
                  seniors and ages 13 - 17; $2 for ages 6 - 12; children 5
                  years and under are free. (Ask about AAA discounts.)
                  Ask about the $12 family rate.
Ages: 5 years and up.

MARSTON HOUSE

(619) 298-3142 $

3525 7th Avenue, San Diego

*(GOING S. ON SAN DIEGO FWY [5], EXIT S. ON KETTNER BLVD., L. ON LAUREL ST., L.
ON 6TH AVE., R. ON UPAS ST. IT'S AT THE END OF UPAS ST. ON 7TH AVE. GOING N. ON
5, EXIT N. ON 6TH AVE., R. ON UPAS ST. GOING S. ON CABRILLO FWY [163], EXIT S.
ON 6TH AVE., L. ON UPAS ST.)*

This 1905 mansion was built to provide "function, simplicity and
good design." (For an interesting contrast, compare its practical exterior
and interior designs to the much more elaborate VILLA MONTEZUMA
JESSE SHEPARD HOUSE.) The various sixteen rooms, covering four
floors, are decorated in American Arts and Crafts, oriental, and Native
American styles. What a fun and different way to learn the many facets
of American history! This tour is better for older kids who can
appreciate the lifestyle changes that occurred during the early twentieth
century.

Hours: Open Fri. - Sun. from noon - 4:30pm
Admission: $3 for adults; children 12 years and under are free.
Ages: 8 years and up.

MINGEI INTERNATIONAL FOLK ART MUSEUM

(619) 239-0003 $$

Balboa Park, San Diego

*(GOING S. ON CABRILLO FWY [163], EXIT N. ON PARK BLVD. GOING S. ON SAN
DIEGO FWY [5], EXIT AT ASH ST. / "A" ST., L. ON "A" ST., L. ON PARK BLVD. GOING
N. ON 5, EXIT W. ON "B" ST., R. ON PARK BLVD. ONCE ON PARK BLVD. TURN L. ON
PRESIDENTS WAY TO GET TO THE MUSEUMS.)*

"Min" is the Japanese word for "all people"; "gei" means "art," so
mingei translates as "art of all people," or folk art. A child's enjoyment of
this folk art museum depends on the current exhibits. We saw many
tapestries, handcrafted furniture, and beautiful pieces of jewelry. Past
exhibits have included toys and dolls from around the world, Mexican
folk art, the horse in folk art, etc. Call first, or go on the third Tuesday of
the month when admission is free. The museum's gift shop offers
colorful and unique items. (See BALBOA PARK for a listing of all the
museums and attractions within walking distance.)

Hours: Open Tues. - Sun. from 10am - 4pm.

Admission: $5 for adults; $2 for ages 2 - 17. Admission on the third
Tuesday of every month is free. Passports for 11
museums in Balboa Park are available for $19 for adults
at the Visitors Center, and are good for one week from
the date of purchase.

Ages: 8 years and up.

MISSION BASILICA SAN DIEGO DE ALCALA   ☼

(619) 281-8449 $

10818 San Diego Mission Road, San Diego
*(GOING W. ON MISSION VALLEY FWY [8], EXIT N. ON MISSION GORGE RD., L. ON
TWAIN AVE., WHICH TURNS INTO SAN DIEGO MISSION RD. FROM ESCONDIDO FWY
[15], EXIT E. ON FRIARS RD., R. ON MISSION GORGE RD., R. ON TWAIN AVE., WHICH
TURNS INTO SAN DIEGO MISSION RD.)*

Father Junipero Serra came to California on a mission - to start
missions. The Mission San Diego de Alcala was the first church in
California, founded by the Padre in 1769. As with a visit to any of the
twenty-one missions, coming here brings the past vividly back to life.
The church is long and narrow and, of course, housed in an adobe
structure. The gardens here are very small, but pretty. The Padre Luis
Jayme Museum, named after the missionary who was killed here by an
Indian attack, contains some interesting excavated artifacts such as
flintlock pistols, swords, buttons, and pottery. Other exhibits here
include vestments, old photos, and small dioramas of all the missions.
The monastery ruins have partial walls and the outlines of where the
padres living quarters, the library, and other rooms once stood. Tip:
Read the pamphlet about the mission as you explore it, because
knowing its history makes it much more interesting for kids.

Hours: Open daily from 9am - 5pm. Closed Easter,
Thanksgiving, and Christmas.

Admission: $2 for adults; $1 for seniors and students over 12 years;
50¢ for children 11 years and under.

Ages: 7 years and up.

MISSION SAN ANTONIO DE PALA   ☼

(760) 742-3317 $

Pala Mission Road, Pala
*(EXIT ESCONDIDO FWY [15] E. ON PALA RD. [ROUTE 76], GO ABOUT 6 MILES, THEN
N. ON PALA MISSION RD. INTO THE TOWN OF PALA)*

This mission, founded in 1816, is the only remaining Spanish
California Mission to continue in its original purpose of proselytizing and
serving Native American Indians. The adjacent school is for Native
American children and the gift shop is run by Native Americans. The
small mission is located on an Indian Reservation, a fact that greatly
enhanced its value in my children's eyes.

The museum part of the mission consists of two small wings. One contains arrowheads, pottery, clothing with intricate beadwork, the Padre's small quarters, and an altar. Hand-carved religious figures and the Southwestern-style painted ceilings are eye-catching. The other wing is the Mineral Room, showcasing nice specimens of jasper, petrified wood slabs, and amethyst. The room also has a marine display that includes a stuffed puffer fish, corral, huge shells, and a giant clam shell.

The small back courtyard has a nicely landscaped garden, an altar, and a fountain with Koi fish. The old bell tower is around the side of the mission, next to the cemetery.

Hours: Open Tues. - Sun., 10am - 3:30pm. Closed most major holidays.
Admission: $2 for adults; $1 for children 12 years and under.
Ages: 6 years and up.

MISSION SAN GABRIEL ARCHANGEL   ☼
(818) 457-3048 $
537 West Mission Drive, San Gabriel
(EXIT SAN BERNARDINO FWY [10] N. ON DEL MAR AVE., L. ON WEST MISSION DR.)

Located in the Mission District, our fourth mission is aptly nicknamed "Queen of the Missions." The graceful buildings and pleasant grounds transport you back to 1771, when the mission was founded. They also offer a wonderfully visual way to learn about California's Spanish/Mexican heritage.

In the midst of the cactus garden are tanning vats, with a placard describing the tanning process. Walk up a few stone steps to see four large holes in the ground, which were once the soap and tallow vats. The San Gabriel Mission supplied soap and candles to most of the other missions. There are several fountains and statues distributed throughout the mission gardens. In the cemetery, for instance, is a life-size crucifix - a memorial to the 6,000 Indians buried here.

The Mission Church is still in use. The wall behind the altar is eye-catching as it is ornately decorated. The small baptismal room is equally impressive. Next to the church, the small and somewhat dark museum contains only a few articles that were of interest to my kids - big, old books covered in sheepskin dating from 1489 and 1588, and a Spanish bedroom set. Knowing that the museum was once a series of rooms, such as sleeping quarters, weaving rooms, and carpenter shops, made it a bit more interesting for my children.

Located in the center of the mission is the Court of the Missions. Models of each of California's twenty-one missions, varying in size and layout, but similar in style, are on display here. Vaya con Dios! (Go with God!)

Hours: Open daily from 9am - 5pm. Closed Easter, Thanksgiving, and Christmas.

Admission: $4 for adults; $3 for seniors; $1 for ages 6 - 12; children 5
years and under are free.
Ages: 5 years and up.

MISSION SAN LUIS REY DE FRANCA   ☼
(760) 757-3651 $
4050 Mission Avenue, Oceanside
*(EXIT SAN DIEGO FWY [5] N. ON SAN LUIS REY MISSION EXWY [76], CONTINUE ON
MISSION AVE. OR, FROM ESCONDIDO FWY [15] EXIT W. ON PALA RD [76], WHICH
TURNS INTO MISSION AVE.)*

Founded in 1798, this mission has been nicknamed "King of the
Missions" because it is the largest of the twenty-one missions. It is also
one of the most interesting. The extensive grounds cover nearly six and
a half acres, so wear your walking shoes. The first series of rooms
contain several glass-encased displays that document the history of the
mission. Next, is the Friar's small bedroom with a knotted rope bed, and
monks' robes. (Twenty-one Franciscan monks still live here in a
separate section of the mission.) The weavery and work rooms have a
loom, spinning wheel, and implements for leather tooling, respectively.
The kitchen contains pots, pans, a brick oven, and glassware typical of
the Mission period. The next few rooms display embroidered
vestments, statues of angels and the Madonna, and other religious art
work. The big Mission Church is gorgeous. Exit the church through the
Madonna Chapel into the cemetery which contains a large wooden
cross to commemorate the 3,000 Indians buried here.

The grounds are equally interesting to explore. Large grassy areas,
with plenty of picnic tables, are outside the mission's front doors. Just
past this area are ruins of soldiers' barracks. Further down, towards the
street, is an ornate stone arch and a tiled stairway that lead to an old
mission laundry area and large sunken garden. The garden looks like it
was left over from Babylonian times; once elegantly landscaped, but
now overgrown. Mission San Luis Rey de Franca is a great one to
cover for those fourth grade mission reports!
Hours: Open Mon. - Sat., 10am - 4:30pm; Sun., 11:30am -
4:30pm. Closed most major holidays.
Admission: $3 for adults; $1 for ages 8 - 14; children 7 years and
under are free.
Ages: 5 years and up.

MOTOR TRANSPORT MUSEUM   ☼
(619) 233-9707 or (619) 756-1543 $
31949 Highway 94, Campo
*(EXIT FWY 8 (45 MILES FROM DOWNTOWN SAN DIEGO) S. ON BUCKMAN SPRINGS
RD. 10.5 MILES, R. ON HWY. 94.)*

Museum is almost too formal a word for this truck yard, although it
is accurate in the sense that it holds a collection of over 150 antique

transportation vehicles. This museum-in-process is on the grounds of the historic Campo Feldspar Mill, which was built in 1929 to mill feldspar mined in nearby Hauser Canyon. (Feldspar was ground and processed into porcelain.) It displays mostly trucks and buses, plus a few fire-fighting vehicles. About fifteen of the vehicles are restored and inside the old nine-story building, while the others are outside. The few exhibits inside are photos, literature, and memorabilia relating to trucks. Ask about programs for older kids who like to work with their hands, and "keep on trucking."

Hours: Open April through November, on the second Sat. of each month from noon - 5pm. Call for more information, or to ask about other times to visit the museum.

Admission: Donations accepted.

Ages: 5 years and up.

MUSEUM OF CONTEMPORARY ART (La Jolla)   ☼

(619) 454-3541 $

700 Prospect Street, La Jolla

(EXIT SAN DIEGO FWY [5] W. ON LA JOLLA VILLAGE DR., L. ON TORREY PINES RD., R. ON PROSPECT PL., WHICH TURNS INTO PROSPECT ST.)

I admit two things about contemporary art museums: 1) I enjoy visiting them and 2) I don't always "get" the art on exhibit. I've learned not to step on things lying on the floor or to touch anything, even things as seemingly innocuous as a pole in the center of the room - it could be an exhibit. Displays here rotate quarterly, so there are new eclectic paintings, sculptures, photos, and other pieces to figure out every few months.

Our favorite exhibits included a room-size metal spider carrying a nest of eggs; toddler-size figures made out of wax in various stages of melting because of the heat lamps directed on them; the "Reason for the Neutron Bomb," which had 50,000 match tips glued onto nickels on the floor, each one representing a Russian tank; and a darkened room with a large church bell which, when my kids pulled on the rope, triggered a hologram of the Virgin Mary and baby Jesus to appear.

Rent, for free, an audio tape (and player) that explains the current exhibits. The M.C.A. offers free school group tours with titles such as "Meaning and Wonder of Art," "Art and Creative Writing," etc. Pick up a free children's guide (pamphlet) at the reception desk about discovering contemporary art. It asks thought-provoking questions, and gives kids things to do and look for. By the way, the view of the coastline from the museum is spectacular. Also see MUSEUM OF CONTEMPORARY, San Diego.

Hours: Open Tues. - Sat., 10am - 5pm, (Wed. until 8pm); Sun., noon - 5pm.

Admission: $4 for adults (also good for the downtown San Diego location for 3 days from date of purchase); $2 for seniors, military with I.D., and students; children 11 years and under are free. Admission on the first Tuesday of every month is free.

Ages: 6 years and up.

MUSEUM OF CONTEMPORARY ART (San Diego) ☀

(619) 234-1001 $

1001 Kettner Boulevard, San Diego

(GOING S. ON SAN DIEGO FWY [5], EXIT AT "A" ST. AND GO STRAIGHT OFF THE OFF RAMP ON 10TH ST., R. ON BROADWAY TO KETTNER. GOING N. ON 5, EXIT W. ON "J" ST., R. ON 12TH, L. ON BROADWAY TO KETTNER. IT'S AT BROADWAY, RIGHT BY THE METRO. PARKING IS HARD TO COME BY.)

This artsy-style building sets the right mood for your visit to San Diego's contemporary art museum. What kinds of materials are used in the art that you're looking at? Traditional materials, like paint? Or nuts, bolts, wires, or other improbable materials? These are a few of the questions listed in the (free) children's guide on discovering contemporary art, which is found at the reception desk. The guide helps your child become more involved with the art, and enables him/her to understand the artist's vision in creating their work. Contemporary art is fun because it is eclectic. Some art pieces might be as unusual as a box of cereal, while other paintings, sculptures, and/or photos are a more daring combination of design, light and texture. This small museum, which has quarterly rotating exhibits, is a branch of the main M.C.A. in La Jolla.

Hours: Open Tues. - Sat., 10am - 5pm (Friday until 8pm); Sun., noon - 5.

Admission: $3 for adults (good also for the La Jolla location for 3 days from the date of purchase), $1 for seniors, military with I.D., and students; children 12 years and under are free. Admission on the first Tuesday of every month is free.

Ages: 6 years and up.

MUSEUM OF CREATION AND EARTH HISTORY ☀

(619) 448-0900   !

10946 Woodside Avenue North, Santee

(TAKE THE 52 FWY E. TO THE END, GO E. ON MISSION GORGE RD, L. ON CARLTON HILLS BLVD., L. ON CARLTON OAKS DR. JUST PAST THE INTERSECTION AT MAGNOLIA, THE ROAD FORKS AT A STOP SIGN; GO L. ON WOODSIDE AVE. NORTH. THE MUSEUM IS ¼ MILE ON THE L. FROM SAN DIEGO - EXIT 8 FWY, N. ON SAN VICENTE FWY [HWY. 67], L. ON RIVERFORD RD., L. AT LIGHT, L. AGAIN UNDER FWY, L. ONTO WOODSIDE AVE. NORTH. THE MUSEUM IS ¼ MILE ON THE L.))

Genesis 1:1: "In the beginning, God created the heavens and the earth." This walk-through creation museum, a part of the Institute of

Creation Research, is a richly visual way of seeing how the earth and its inhabitants have developed. Each phase of the earth's history is graphically represented by murals, photographs, models, audio sounds, Biblical references, questions to ponder, and lots of technical information. Start at the beginning, of course, and proceed through to modern day. Day four (when the sun, moon, stars, and planets were created) is the first dramatic depiction of the unfolding wonders of our universe. This room is basically dark, with spotlights on stunning photos of the planets, constellations, and our sun. Each photograph is accompanied by factual explanations. Entering the room for days five and six is like entering a small jungle. Greenery abounds alongside a few cages of small live animals such as birds, fish, snakes, and mice. Accompanied by Psalm 139 ("I am fearfully and wonderfully made. . .") an entire wall shows models of man, his inner workings, diagrams, and pictures of families.

Continue on, and see the fall of man, illustrated by bones, decay, and the sound of crying; a wood-paneled room with a mural depicting Noah's ark, complete with storm sounds and lightening flashing; a room with touchable walls that are layers of the earth, plus a replicate of Mt. St. Helens' volcano that you can walk through; a blue hallway representing the Ice Age that has icicles hanging overhead, and models of woolly mammoths; an Egyptian room with a scale model of the enormous Tower of Babel taking center stage; the Stone Age room; the room of civilization immortalizing (so to speak) Greek and Roman cultures; and finally, the hallway of modern man, including pictures and philosophies of evolutionists and creationists. The Creation Museum is the ultimate interactive time line.

Each of the rooms offers various free pamphlets (to read later) that discuss the ideas and facts presented throughout the museum. Guided tours are available for groups, with reservations. Also available are classes for upper elementary students and older students who wish to delve into creation research and Biblical learning and understanding. The classes and the museum are geared for slightly older children as a lot of the information is very technical. However, the incredible visuals make quite an impact on any age.

Hours: Open Mon. - Sat. from 9am - 4pm. Closed holidays.
Admission: Free
Ages: 5 - 9 years for the visual enjoyment; 10 years old and up to understand the technical information.

MUSEUM OF PHOTOGRAPHIC ARTS
(619) 238-7559 $

Balboa Park, San Diego
(GOING S. ON CABRILLO FWY [163], EXIT N. ON PARK BLVD. GOING S. ON SAN DIEGO FWY [5], EXIT AT ASH ST. / "A" ST., L. ON "A" ST., L. ON PARK BLVD. GOING N. ON 5, EXIT W. ON "B" ST., R. ON PARK BLVD. ONCE ON PARK BLVD. TURN L. ON PRESIDENTS WAY TO GET TO THE MUSEUMS.)

Your shutterbugs will appreciate this large gallery that features changing exhibits of photographic works. Some exhibits zoom in on portraiture work or the history of American photography, while others focus more on pictures taken from all over the world. We enjoyed comparing styles and choice of subjects, as well as just the artistry in the pictures. (See BALBOA PARK for a listing of all the museums and attractions within walking distance.)

Hours: Open daily from 10am - 5pm.
Admission: $3.50 for adults; children 11 years and under are free. Admission on the second Tuesday of every month is free. Passports for 11 museums in Balboa Park are available for $19 for adults at the Visitors Center, and are good for one week from the date of purchase.
Ages: 7 years and up.

MUSEUM OF SAN DIEGO HISTORY

(619) 232-6203

Balboa Park, San Diego
(GOING S. ON CABRILLO FWY [163], EXIT N. ON PARK BLVD. GOING S. ON SAN DIEGO FWY [5], EXIT AT ASH ST. / "A" ST., L. ON "A" ST., L. ON PARK BLVD. GOING N. ON 5, EXIT W. ON "B" ST., R. ON PARK BLVD. ONCE ON PARK BLVD. TURN L. ON PRESIDENTS WAY TO GET TO THE MUSEUMS.)

This museum presents the history of San Diego, from the 1850's to the present, via numerous photographs, plus maps, works of art, costumes, household goods, furniture, and other artifacts. An authentic stagecoach is the first item you'll see and it sets the mood for your visit here. We always enjoy seeing history and understanding more about our ancestors' way of life. (See BALBOA PARK for a listing of all the museums and attractions within walking distance.)

Hours: Open Wed. - Sun. from 10am - 4:30pm. Open also the second Tuesday of each month.
Admission: $4 for adults; children 12 years and under are free. Admission the second Tuesday of every month is free. Passports for 11 museums in Balboa Park are available for $19 for adults at the Visitors Center, and are good for one week from the date of purchase.
Ages: 5 years and up.

NAVY SHIP'S OPEN HOUSE

(619) 532-1432;or (619) 437-2735;or (619) 556-7359
(619) 545-1133 - aircraft carriers; (619) 684-0166 - Kittyhawk;
(619) 553-8643 - submarines
U.S. Navy Pier of Harbor Drive, near Broadway on the Embarcadero, San Diego

*(GOING S. ON SAN DIEGO FWY [5], EXIT W. ON ASH ST., L. ON 4ᵀᴴ, R. ON
BROADWAY, L. ON HARBOR. GOING N. ON 5, EXIT S. ON 6ᵀᴴ AVE., R. ON BROADWAY,
L. ON HARBOR.)*

The Navy offers a unique opportunity for the public to tour a
destroyer, frigate, amphibious cruiser, submarine, aircraft carrier, and
other naval craft. The type of ship you actually see depends on what is
in the harbor on the day you plan to visit. A military tour guide will take
you through the ship and answer any questions, and we all know that
kids always have plenty of those. Please call first to make sure a ship is
available, and to find out which kind it is. Also be aware that phone
numbers might change, so be patient and persevere. Aircraft carriers
are often on deployment, so call for availability. Groups of ten or more
can schedule a tour on Tuesdays or Thursdays between 10am to 4pm.

Hours: General tours are available Sat. and Sun. from 1pm -
4pm.

Admission: Free

Ages: 5 years and up.

OCEANSIDE SEA CENTER

(760) 969-7102

221 North Coast Highway, Oceanside
*(EXIT SAN DIEGO FWY [5] W. ON MISSION AVE., R. ON NORTH COAST HWY./PIER
VIEW WAY)*

This small (800 square feet) Sea Center is big on learning about
local sea life, beaches, and geological and ecological variables that
influence the marine world at Oceanside's doorsteps. The wall exhibits
include a large Marlin, the one that didn't get away; a display on sand
movements; the life cycle of a sand dollar, with a sand dollar, photos,
and information; and a thirteen-foot by twenty-five foot undersea wall
mural that is a scientific piece of art. Kids can pick up rocks specimens;
look at the two aquariums that contain fish, seas stars, etc; and watch
continuously running short videos regarding the pier and surrounding
area.

Hours: Call for hours

Admission: Free; donations appreciated.

Ages: 3 years and up.

OLD TOWN SAN DIEGO AND STATE HISTORIC PARK

(619) 220-5422 - Robinson Rose House; (619) 298-9167 - park   *!/$$$*
rangers

San Diego

(GOING S. ON SAN DIEGO FWY [5] (JUST SOUTH OF INTERSTATE 8) EXIT E. (ACROSS THE BRIDGE) ON OLD TOWN AVE., L. ON SAN DIEGO AVE. OR L. ON CONGRESS ST. GOING N. ON 5, EXIT AT MOORE ST., R. ON OLD TOWN AVE., L. ON SAN DIEGO AVE. OR CONGRESS ST. PARKING IS AVAILABLE ON THE STREETS IF YOU ARRIVE EARLY, OR AT SEVERAL PARKING LOTS.)

Old Town is a six-block, closed-to-through-traffic area, bound by Taylor, Juan, Twiggs and Congress Streets. The places mentioned below encompass this area, plus the immediate (walkable) vicinity.

Old Town is a wonderful conglomeration of unique shops, scrumptious places to eat, vintage houses, museums, and a Mexican bazaar, all located along dirt "roads" that are closed to automotive traffic, and paved sidewalks. It's a town you'll want to revisit to make sure you experience all it has to offer. San Diego is the site of the first permanent Spanish settlement on the California coast, thus it shares a similar historical significance with Jamestown, the first English settlement on the East Coast. Old Town contains many original and restored buildings from San Diego's Mexican period before 1846, and the early California period. A day here is a combination of history lessons and fun shopping! The route for the attractions listed below starts at the Robinson Rose House - the park headquarters - then proceeds east, south, and north before looping back around. Most of the attractions are open daily from 10am to 5pm; shops are usually open until 9pm. Admission is free, unless otherwise noted. All historic buildings are closed on January 1, Thanksgiving, and Christmas. Free maps of the area are available at the park headquarters, many of the stores in Old Town, and local hotel lobbies. Free walking tours that cover all of the old buildings, not just the more kid-friendly ones I've listed here, are offered daily at 2pm beginning at Robinson Rose House.

ROBINSON ROSE HOUSE is located at 4002 Wallace Street, on the other side of the parking lot from Taylor Street. This 1853 adobe structure houses the park headquarters and has walking tour maps available for purchase. It also has a few exhibits, such as photo murals and a scale model of Old Town as it appeared in the mid 1870's.

OLD TOWN PLAZA is located directly in front of the Robinson Rose House. This area is essentially a large grassy area for kids to run around, with olive, fig, cork, and eucalyptus trees providing beauty and shade. A large fountain is in the middle of this park and there are plenty of benches for weary travelers (or shoppers).

The row of stores across from the Plaza are in reconstructed buildings dating from around 1830. Just a few of our favorite stores in Old Town include Miner's Gems and Minerals, Toler's Leather Depot, The Mexico Shop, and of course the ice cream and candy shops! Old Town is truly a shopper's delight.

COLORADO HOUSE/WELLS FARGO MUSEUM is located on San Diego Street in the heart of Old Town. This museum has the appeal of the Old West, with a Concord Stagecoach prominently displayed in the center. Other exhibits include a colorful wall display of Wells Fargo featured in comic books, trading cards, and even a board game; rocks with gold, gold coins, and bags of gold found in treasure boxes; mining tools; Old West posters; and more. A video shows and describes this time period and the history of Wells Fargo.

CASA DE MACHADO Y STEWART is located almost directly behind the Colorado House/Wells Fargo Museum. This plain-looking adobe is an exact replica of the original house, complete with a dirt walkway leading to it. The brick-floored house contains few furnishings; a dining table, shelves with dishes and pottery, a sparsely furnished bedroom, and some tools. Just beyond the front porch is a beehive oven and open fire stoves, evidence of the outdoor cooking that pioneers once employed.

MASON STREET SCHOOL is located on Mason Street, diagonal to the Casa de Machado y Stewart. This 1865 red schoolhouse is a child's favorite historical stop in Old Town. It was the first public schoolhouse in San Diego and retains its old-fashioned ambiance with twenty school desks, a school bell, flags, a chalkboard, a wood-burning stove, the dunce's corner (and cap), and old pictures and books. It's open daily from 10am to 4pm.

THE DENTAL MUSEUM is located on San Diego Avenue, in front of the schoolhouse. Kids will enjoy a quick peek at the past here as they see a dentist chair, instruments, and even some molds of teeth.

SAN DIEGO UNION BUILDING is located on San Diego Avenue. The first edition of the San Diego Union came off the presses here way back when. Now, kids can see an old Washington handpress (printing press), typeset letters and tools, and the adjacent small newspaper office.

WHALEY HOUSE, (619) 298-2482, is located at 2482 San Diego Avenue, with the cross street being Harvey Street. Built in 1847, this two-story brick house/museum is definitely worth touring. It has served in the community as a residence, store, theater, and courthouse, and is filled with numerous early California artifacts. The first room you're ushered into, the courthouse room, is fascinating. As you listen to the ten-minute tape explaining the history of the house and this time period, look around. Behind the railing is an old wooden judge's desk, and chairs for the jury. Along one wall is a bookshelf given to Ulysses S. Grant on his inauguration, and an 1860 lifemask (only one of six in existence) of Abraham Lincoln. Display cases in this room feature documents, spurs, pistols, Spanish helmets and swords, clothing, and ornate hair combs and fans. An early copy machine, a letter press, a handmade U.S. flag from 1864 (how many stars does it have?), plus pictures and portraits of Washington, Lincoln, Grant, and General Lee are also here.

The kitchen, with all of its gadgets, is downstairs, as is the beautifully decorated parlor, and a small music room that contains a spinet piano used in "Gone With the Wind." There are several bedrooms upstairs that can be viewed through the protective glass in the doorframes. The bedroom behind the staircase has a decorative wreath, framed on the far wall. It is made from the Whaley girls' hair gathered from hairbrushes and then braided - something to keep the family busy on pre-television nights. The children's bedroom has dolls and toys, while the other bedrooms contain a soldier's dress uniform, mannequins clothed in elegant, ladies' dresses, a lacy quilt covering a canopy bed, and period furniture. The Whaley House is also one of two authenticated haunted houses in California. I highly recommend taking a guided tour, so you don't miss out on any of the background information.

Exit through the backdoor into a small, picturesque, tree-shaded courtyard. A quick peek into the Old Town Drug Store Museum allows kids to see an old-time pharmacy containing bottles, patented medicines, and a mortar and pestle. Push a button to hear more of the building's history. The Whaley House is open daily from 10am to 4:15pm, and open until 5pm in the summer. Admission is $4 for adults; $3 for seniors; $2 for ages 5 to 17 years; children 4 years and under are free. Kids 7 years and up will enjoy this museum the most.

HERITAGE PARK, (619) 565-3600, is located north of the Whaley House, on Harvey and Juan Streets. This group of buildings is enchanting to simply look at. Each of the seven Victorian houses now serve other functions: The Sherman Gilbert house, our favorite, was built in 1887 and is now the "Old Doll Shoppe," offering dolls, dollhouses, miniatures, and ornaments for sale; the Christian House is now a bed and breakfast; etc.

THE MORMON BATTALION VISITOR CENTER, (619) 298-3317, is located on Juan Street. An informative tour guide will show your family around this small center. The first thing we noticed was a statue that is as tall as the biblical Goliath - he *really* was tall! Kids can hold a sun-baked adobe brick and learn its historical significance. They'll also learn how people placed copper pennies in an oven (an alternative way of baking bricks) until the pennies began to melt, at 2,000 degrees. This meant the oven was hot enough to bake bricks (and lots of other things, too!)

Although the 500 men (and women and children) of the Mormon Battalion never fought a battle, the 1846 volunteer unit marched 2,000 miles across country to San Diego to help fight in the Mexican/American war. Their arduous trail blazing efforts and accomplishments are re-enacted in an interesting fifteen-minute film. The diorama adjacent to the screen is occasionally spotlighted to emphasize portions of the movie. After the film, we were led into another room and shown huge paintings of Jesus during various times of his ministry. As our tour concluded, we were offered a Book of Mormon and asked if we could have someone call on us regarding the Mormon religion. The visitor center is open daily 9am to 9pm. Admission is free.

SEELEY STABLES is located on Calhoun Street. This huge, reconstructed barn contains several exhibit stalls. The saddles, bells, and harnesses, plus at least ten stagecoaches and carriages, are great visual aids for picturing the past. The upstairs loft has more exhibits of the wild, wild west, such as branding irons, spurs, more saddles, a Mexican cowboy hat, and furniture including an unusual chair made out of steers' horns. A native American display features Kachina dolls, a feather headdress, and baskets. Other exhibits up here include an old-fashioned slot machine, a roller organ, an antique telephone, a case of model horses, and a child's room with toys. Free slide shows are presented in the downstairs theater throughout the day, so come and rest, and learn a little history.

The backyard of the stables is an open courtyard with early farm equipment around its perimeters, plus several more carriages and stagecoaches in glass-cased enclosures. Also back here, or accessible from Mason Street, is THE BLACK HAWK LIVERY STABLE AND BLACKSMITH. This large blacksmith workshop holds demonstrations every Wednesday and Saturday from 10am to 2pm. Kids might see the hot fires help bend pieces of metal into horseshoes or heavy chains, or they might hear a hammer clank against the anvil to create a sword or branding iron. The stable room is filled with finished pieces, and tools.

GEORGE JOHNSON HOUSE is located on Calhoun Street, near Mason Street. This small building has a room to walk through - it took us about five minutes. It displays archaeological findings of the area such as bottles and pottery, plus tools of the trade and pictures showing the painstaking work of excavation and cleaning.

BAZAAR DEL MUNDO, (619) 296-3161, is located on the corner of Juan and Wallace Streets. This gaily decorated traditional Mexican courtyard is festive in appearance and atmosphere. Mariachi bands play, costumed dancers entertain occasionally, and the colorful storefronts and wares beckon shoppers of all ages. Our favorite shops here include Geppetto's, a wonderful toy store; Just Animals, for the wild (and tame) at heart; Creations and Confections, specializing in old-fashioned candies, chocolates, and party supplies; La Panadería, serving delectable Mexican breads and pastries, including churros; and Treasures, a store that carries gifts and crafts from exotic lands. If your tummy is saying, "Tengo hambre" (that's Spanish for "I'm hungry"), sample and savor some of the culinary delights at any one of the several restaurants here.

Look up PRESIDIO PARK, located just north of Old Town. The park also has the JUNIPERO SERRA MUSEUM on its grounds.

Hours: Most "attractions" open daily 10am - 5pm.
Admission: Free to most attractions, but bring spending money. See individual listings.
Ages: 4 years and up.

PRESIDIO PARK / JUNIPERO SERRA MUSEUM   ☼
(619) 297-3258 $
2727 Presidio Drive, San Diego
(GOING E. ON MISSION VALLEY FWY [8] EXIT S. ON TAYLOR ST., L. ON PRESIDIO DR., AND L. AGAIN TO STAY ON PRESIDIO DR. GOING W. ON 8, EXIT AT HOTEL CIRCLE/TAYLOR ST. (THE EXIT BEFORE MORENA BLVD.), GO STRAIGHT OFF THE OFF RAMP AND CURVE OVER FWY, R. ON TAYLOR ST., L. ON PRESIDIO DR., AND L. AGAIN TO STAY ON PRESIDIO DR.)

Located just above OLD TOWN SAN DIEOG AND STATE HISTORIC PARK, picturesque Presidio Park has green rolling hills and lots of old shade trees. Follow the signs and walk along the Old Presidio Historic Trail and you'll be walking in the footsteps of settlers from centuries ago.

On a hilltop in the park sits the mission-style Junipero Serra Museum. It was built in 1929 to commemorate the site where Father Junipero Serra and Captain Gaspar de Portola established California's very first mission and fortified settlement. Outside the museum is an old wine press. Inside, the first floor contains 400-year-old Spanish furniture, some of which is quite elegant. Second story exhibits include clothing, weapons (such as a cannon and cannon balls), art, and housewares that belonged to Native American and early Spanish/Mexican residents. There is also a room dedicated to the founder, Father Serra, that contains personal belongings and items given to him. A seven-minute video is shown throughout the day that describes San Diego's beginnings. Upstairs, in a bell-like tower, look through the windows for an unparalleled view of San Diego.

Can you dig it? During the summer, archaeological students work the site adjacent to the museum, unearthing artifacts and putting them on display. Several hundred people lived within the walls of the presidio during its sixty-year existence, so there are many "treasures" still left to uncover. The site is open year round to look at and into.

Hours: The park is open daily sunrise to sunset. The museum is open Tues. - Sat., 10am - 4pm; Sun., noon - 4pm.
Admission: The park is free. The museum is $3 for adults; children 12 years and under are free.
Ages: The museum is best suited for ages 7 and up.

RANCHO BUENA VISTA ADOBE

(760) 639-6164 $

640 Alta Vista Drive, Vista

(EXIT 78 FWY, N.E. ON SUNSET DR. / ESCONDIDO AVE., R. ON ALTA VISTA DR.)

Situated between residential homes is the Rancho Buena Vista, an historic adobe home built circa 1850. Take a forty-five minute tour of the gracious home to learn about this time period and the lifestyles of the rancheros. Part of the tour is a ten-minute video presentation, which helps present-day youth better understand the past. You'll see the living room, kitchen, bedrooms, etc., that contain period furniture, and other Mexican California memorabilia. Ask about "Adobe Days" (living history programs) for children as well as field trips, camps, and classes. Viva la historia!

Hours: Open Wed. - Sat., 10am - 3pm; Sun., 12:30pm - 3pm. Closed all major holidays, during inclement weather, and special events.

Admission: $3 for non-Vista resident adults; $2 for Vista resident adults and for seniors; $1 for students; 50¢ for children 12 years and under.

Ages: 7 years and up.

REUBEN H. FLEET SPACE THEATER AND SCIENCE CENTER

(619) 238-1233 $$

Balboa Park, San Diego

(GOING S. ON CABRILLO FWY [163], EXIT N. ON PARK BLVD. GOING S. ON SAN DIEGO FWY [5], EXIT AT ASH ST. / "A" ST., L. ON "A" ST., L. ON PARK BLVD. GOING N. ON 5, EXIT W. ON "B" ST., R. ON PARK BLVD. ONCE ON PARK BLVD. TURN L. ON PRESIDENTS WAY TO GET TO THE MUSEUMS.)

This huge Science Center is a fascinating place for hands-on exploration, experimentation, and discovery. There are numerous permanent exhibits, including a submarine periscope that literally goes through the roof to view the outside world; a fully operational amateur radio station; a build and play area for children ages 2 - 6; carnival-style "funny" mirrors; and experiments to try, such as testing one's reaction time, coordination, etc. Major theme exhibits usually change twice a year. We saw "Signals," which demonstrated the many ways that people transmit information. Kids practiced communication skills by sending Morse code messages, phone images, and the alphabet relayed via lights and then displayed digitally (i.e. just like the inner workings of a computer); sounds were transmitted through a microphone into wave forms displayed on a monitor; and flashing lights and/or symbolic flags were also used to send coded messages. The Science Center is currently in the midst of major expansion, slated to be completed in the beginning of 1998. Besides more interactive exhibits, a simulator ride is also being added.

The Omnimax theater screen looks like an inverted golf ball. One-hour films are shown that are ten times the size of those in regular movie theaters, therefore drawing you into the intense action on the screen, whether it's traveling to the ocean depths, through the human body, or hurtling down ski slopes. (Warning: For those prone to motion sickness, the swirling images can make your stomach queasy.) Past shows have also included a cosmic view of the universe in "Cosmic Voyage," and a behind-the-scenes tour of Hollywood's action films in "Special Effects." Other stellar productions include various planetarium shows where the stars, constellations, and planets can be seen, night or day.

Tip or warning: The gift shop appeals to all ages who are even slightly scientific or hands-on oriented. Star Trek fans, in particular, will have a field day here. (See BALBOA PARK for a listing of all the museums and attractions within walking distance.)

Hours: The Center and Omnimax theater (with shows almost hourly) are usually open daily 9:30am - 6pm. Hours will fluctuate with construction, so please call first.

Admission: The Science Center is currently $1 for adults; 50¢ for ages 5 - 15; children 4 years and under are free. Prices will change after renovations are completed. Admission on the first Tuesday of every month is free. Passports for 11 museums in Balboa Park are available for $19 for adults at the Visitors Center and are good for one week from the date of purchase. Admission to the Omnimax theater is currently $6.50 for adults; $5 for seniors; $3.50 for ages 5 - 15; children 4 years and under are free. Call before you go and ask about any show specials they might be offering.

Ages: 4 years and up.

SAN DIEGO AEROSPACE MUSEUM ☼

(619) 234-8291 $$

Balboa Park, San Diego

(GOING S. ON CABRILLO FWY [163], EXIT N. ON PARK BLVD. GOING S. ON SAN DIEGO FWY [5], EXIT AT ASH ST. / "A" ST., L. ON "A" ST., L. ON PARK BLVD. GOING N. ON 5, EXIT W. ON "B" ST., R. ON PARK BLVD. ONCE ON PARK BLVD. TURN L. ON PRESIDENTS WAY TO GET TO THE MUSEUMS.)

Take to the skies in this marvelous museum that visually chronicles the history of aviation from the dawn of flight through the age of space travel. The first few rooms, formally titled the International Aerospace Hall of Fame, give homage to the aero-engineers, pilots, and aviation founders that didn't fly off course in their vision for creating aircrafts and the aerospace industry. The hall is filled with photos, plaques, and medals of these aviation heroes. Portraits of Armstrong, Aldrich, and other astronauts, especially, caught my children's eyes. An Apollo XI display features a replica of the plaque left on the moon, the box used to collect lunar samples, and more.

The next rooms are packed with exhibits of early flying machines such as gliders, "birdmen" who used bicycle tires, bi-planes, and the Wright Brother's flyer, plus narrated videos that show pictures of early flying attempts. Consecutive eras are also well defined and enhanced with colorful wall murals, period-dressed mannequins, and other fine details. Wood-paneled rooms, complete with sandbags and army netting, house WWI and WWII planes and memorabilia such as helmets, goggles, and uniforms. The flying aces and the fighter planes that served them, including the Spad and the Nieuport, and the Spitfires, Hellcats, and Zeros, respectively, are well represented. In between wars, the U.S. Mail service was introduced. Displays here include a Curtiss JN-4 "Jenny," wall posters of stamps blown up that commemorate aviation, and a 1918 mail office. Kids love the next exhibits of barnstormers and pictures of daredevils using planes to entertain. These showmen of the air are doing headstands on wings, transferring from a plane to a speeding car, etc.

The next series of rooms honor women aviators, house engines and propellers, and display lots of model airplanes. Enter a pilot's ready room to watch the film "Sea Legs." The armed forces are saluted with their contributions and a scale model of the U.S.S. Yorktown, and the U.S.S. Langley - the Navy's first carrier.

Enter the Jet Age with the F-4 Phantom, and the spy plane, the Blackbird. This exciting time period is followed by the Space Age. This last set of rooms feature bulky astronaut uniforms, capsules, modules, a moon rock, and more. Soar to new heights as you and your children explore the Aerospace Museum! Tours of the aircraft restoration facility are available upon request. (See BALBOA PARK for a listing of all the museums and attractions within walking distance.)

Hours: Open daily from 10am - 4:30pm. Closed Thanksgiving and Christmas.

Admission: $6 for adults; $5 for seniors; $2.50 for ages 6 - 17; active duty military and children 5 years and under are free. Admission on the fourth Tuesday of every month is free. Passports for 11 museums in Balboa Park are available for $19 for adults from the Visitors Center, and are good for a week from the date of purchase.

Ages: 4 years and up.

SAN DIEGO AUTOMOTIVE MUSEUM   ☼

(619) 231-2886 $$

2080 Pan American Plaza, San Diego
(GOING S. ON CABRILLO FWY [163], EXIT N. ON PARK BLVD. GOING S. ON SAN DIEGO FWY [5], EXIT AT ASH ST. / "A" ST., L. ON "A" ST., L. ON PARK BLVD. GOING N. ON 5, EXIT W. ON "B" ST., R. ON PARK BLVD. ONCE ON PARK BLVD. TURN L. ON PRESIDENTS WAY TO GET TO THE MUSEUMS.)

Jump start your child's interest in automobiles at this museum that has more than eighty vehicles on display. Most of the gleaming cars are in a line and readily viewable. Some of the vintage automobiles are on display in appropriate settings, such as a fifties car in front of a backdrop of a drive-through. Classics here range from old-fashioned Model A's to futuristic-looking DeLoreans. Other favorites include a 1948 Tucker "Torpedo" (only fifty-one were ever built), a 1934 convertible Coupe Roadster, a 1955 Mercedes Benz (300SL Gullwing), a 1957 Chevrolet, and Packards from 1929-1936. Prototypes, model cars, a race car, a re-created mechanics shop complete with tools, and an engine room for those who want the inside scoop on cars, are also found at this museum. "Gentlemen, start your engines" applied to my boys as they raced over to see the over forty motorcycles on display. They were particularly elated by the Harley Davidsons, the Indian Chief, and an army cycle. (See BALBOA PARK for a listing of all the museums and attractions within walking distance.)

Hours: Open daily from 10am - 4:30pm.
Admission: $6 for adults; $2 for ages 6 - 15; children 5 years and under are free. Admission on the fourth Tuesday of every month is free. Passports for 11 museums in Balboa Park are available for $19 for adults at the Visitors Center, and are good for one week from the date of purchase.
Ages: 6 years and up.

SAN DIEGO HALL OF CHAMPIONS - SPORTS MUSEUM

(619) 234-2544 $

Balboa Park, San Diego

(GOING S. ON CABRILLO FWY [163], EXIT N. ON PARK BLVD. GOING S. ON SAN DIEGO FWY [5], EXIT AT ASH ST. / "A" ST., L. ON "A" ST., L. ON PARK BLVD. GOING N. ON 5, EXIT W. ON "B" ST., R. ON PARK BLVD. ONCE ON PARK BLVD. TURN L. ON PRESIDENTS WAY TO GET TO THE MUSEUMS.)

Give your sports fans something to cheer about by taking them to the Hall of Champions. Over forty different sports are represented in this eye-catching museum including baseball, basketball, hockey, boxing, table tennis, surfing, racing, boating, soapbox derby, and a beach game called over-the-line. The exhibits showcase athletes, like Ted Williams and Bill Walton, and teams, like the Padres, all associated with San Diego - what a winning city this is! You'll see photographs, statues outfitted in sports attire, videos, trophies, and lots of sports equipment such as uniforms, balls, and even a racing boat and a motorcycle. The theater presents continuously running sports films and clips, mostly bloopers, which kids love. (See BALBOA PARK for a listing of all the museums and attractions within walking distance.)

Hours: Open daily from 10am - 4:30pm.

Admission: $3 for adults; $2 for seniors; $1 for ages 6 - 17; children 5 years and under are free. Admission on the second Tuesday of every month is free. Passports to 11 museums in Balboa Park are available for $19 for adults at the Visitors Center, and are good for one week from the date of purchase.

Ages: 5 years and up.

SAN DIEGO MODEL RAILROAD MUSEUM   ☼

(619) 696-0199 $

Balboa Park, San Diego

(GOING S. ON CABRILLO FWY [163], EXIT N. ON PARK BLVD. GOING S. ON SAN DIEGO FWY [5], EXIT AT ASH ST. / "A" ST., L. ON "A" ST., L. ON PARK BLVD. GOING N. ON 5, EXIT W. ON "B" ST., R. ON PARK BLVD. ONCE ON PARK BLVD. TURN L. ON PRESIDENTS WAY TO GET TO THE MUSEUMS.)

You won't have to railroad your children into coming to this museum. Just one of the things I learned here was the difference between model trains and toy trains. (Hint: The way they operate and the way they look are very different.) The museum houses the largest operating model railroad exhibits in America. Kids (and short adults) can step up onto platforms to get a closer look at the several huge layouts. Watch scale model trains make tracks through and around authentically landscaped hillsides and miniature towns that are complete with scale cars, trees, and people. Some of the exhibits depicting the development of railroading in Southern California include the Tehachapi Pass, the Cabrillo and Southwestern, and a Civil War era live steam locomotive. One of our favorites is the Pacific Desert Line, which has a model train going through a town, citrus groves, and a gorge, all of which can be seen by looking through real train car windows!

Kids will have the most fun in the Toy Train Gallery, which features Lionel O Gauge trains and more. Turn knobs, push buttons, and pull back on throttles to operate trains and make signal crossers flash, windmills turn, and toy trucks haul "rocks" to a loading dock. A wooden Brio train set for younger children completes this interactive and at*track*ive room. As the railroad museum is always in the process of remodeling, it is fun and different every time you visit. (See BALBOA PARK for a listing of all the museums and attractions within walking distance.)

Hours: Open Tues. - Fri., 11am - 4pm; Sat. - Sun., 11am - 5pm.

Admission: $3 for adults; $2 for seniors and students; children 14 years and under are free. Admission on the first Tuesday of every month is free. Passports for 11 museums in Balboa Park are available for $19 for adults at the Visitors Center, and are good for one week from the date purchased.

Ages: 2 years and up.

SAN DIEGO MUSEUM OF ART
(619) 232-7931   *$$*

Balboa Park, San Diego

(GOING S. ON CABRILLO FWY [163], EXIT N. ON PARK BLVD. GOING S. ON SAN DIEGO FWY [5], EXIT AT ASH ST. / "A" ST., L. ON "A" ST., L. ON PARK BLVD. GOING N. ON 5, EXIT W. ON "B" ST., R. ON PARK BLVD. ONCE ON PARK BLVD. TURN L. ON PRESIDENTS WAY TO GET TO THE MUSEUMS.)

This ornately-edificed building primarily features European, American, Asian, and Twentieth-century art. Although the museum has more appeal for older children, Sunday Family Days are geared for ages 4 years and up. These programs focus on a particular aspect or image of art, (i.e. finding dogs in paintings), followed by a game and/or a related craft. Call for dates, times, and prices. As with any art museum, my children's interest was sparked by having them look for differences in artistic styles or color and looking at various choices of subject. Kids need to somehow participate with the art to enjoy their visit. They were mostly intrigued by the statues, especially the fighting Minotaur. The small Image Gallery room has touch screens that introduce and teach children (and adults) more about the paintings and sculptures throughout the museum. (Anything to do with computers draws this generation's interest!) Tip: If you're not sure your children will enjoy this museum, come on the third Tuesday of the month, when admission is free. (See BALBOA PARK for a listing of all the museums and attractions within walking distance.)

Hours: Open Tues. - Sun., 10am - 4:30pm. Closed Mondays, except Labor Day.

Admission: $7 for adults; $5 for seniors; $4 for military with I.D.; $2 for ages 6 - 17; children 5 years and under are free. Admission Fri. - Sun. is $1 more for all paying age groups. Admission on the third Tuesday of each month is free to view the permanent collection. Passports for 11 museums in Balboa Park are available for $19 for adults at the Visitors Center, and are good for one week from the date of purchase.

Ages: 8 years and up.

SAN DIEGO MUSEUM OF MAN
(619) 239-2001   *$$*

Balboa Park, San Diego

(GOING S. ON CABRILLO FWY [163], EXIT N. ON PARK BLVD. GOING S. ON SAN DIEGO FWY [5], EXIT AT ASH ST. / "A" ST., L. ON "A" ST., L. ON PARK BLVD. GOING N. ON 5, EXIT W. ON "B" ST., R. ON PARK BLVD. ONCE ON PARK BLVD. TURN L. ON PRESIDENTS WAY TO GET TO THE MUSEUMS.)

"You've come a long way, baby!" is the best way to rephrase this museum's theme of our ancestors' growth, change, and accomplishments into modern day man. The first floor exhibits that we saw (they do rotate) consisted of tapestry hangings, a weaving demonstration, and plaster casts of stone monuments engraved and dedicated to deities. Towards the stairs is a huge, stuffed mountain gorilla and displays on primate evolution. Upstairs, the theory of evolution theme continues with lots of visuals. There are skeletons of apes and man side by side to compare and contrast; a theoretical time line; and life-size models depicting what some scientists believe early man looked like. Warning: Many of the models are naked (and very hairy). Peoples of the Southwest are represented by displays of pottery, Kachina dolls, and jewelry. Hunters are represented by displays of weapons, tools, and foods. Our favorite exhibits, pertaining to this latter category, were the rabbit skin blanket, eagle feather skirt, shoes from fibers, and a quiver made out of a raccoon. Ancient Egypt was *tut*tilating with real mummies, dating from 332 to 330 B.C., coffin masks covered with symbols of Isis, etc., and exotic jewelry.

The hands-on Children's Discovery Center rotates its theme yearly. We "experienced" Ancient Egypt by dressing up in appropriate clothing and headwear, building pyramids with blocks, trying our hand at hieroglyphics, and playing ancient games - all in a replicated noble's home. On weekends, for a minimal fee, your children can also participate in a take-home, themed craft. (See BALBOA PARK for a listing of all the museums and attractions within walking distance.)

Hours: Open Mon. - Sat. from 10am - 4:30pm.

Admission: $5 for adults; $3 for ages 6 - 17; children 5 years and under are free. Admission on the third Tuesday of every month is free. Passports for 11 museums in Balboa Park are available for $19 for adults at the Visitors Center, and are good for one week from the date purchased.

Ages: 5 years and up.

SAN DIEGO NATURAL HISTORY MUSEUM ☼
(619) 232-3821   *$$$*

Balboa Park, San Diego
(GOING S. ON CABRILLO FWY [163], EXIT N. ON PARK BLVD. GOING S. ON SAN DIEGO FWY [5], EXIT AT ASH ST. / "A" ST., L. ON "A" ST., L. ON PARK BLVD. GOING N. ON 5, EXIT W. ON "B" ST., R. ON PARK BLVD. ONCE ON PARK BLVD. TURN L. ON PRESIDENTS WAY TO GET TO THE MUSEUMS.)

Naturally, this is a favorite museum for kids to visit! A good portion of the first floor of the museum features first class exhibits that are changed three times a year. We saw a wild and woolly exhibit with elephants, woolly mammoths, and mastodons. Knowing that elephants (and their ancestors) are the largest land animals still didn't quite prepare my kids for the impact of seeing the towering life-size models. Touching re-created hair, trunk, and feet was unique, as was seeing a live Asian elephant close up (outside, in the "backyard") and learning about its anatomy. A favorite past exhibit was on dinosaurs.

The Hall of Minerals has amazing specimens, including petrified logs, a huge jade boulder, and a gigantic amethyst geode. Walk through a re-created mine tunnel and see "holes" that showcase garnets, topaz, and other rocks and minerals. Try the crystal radio and hear how it works; touch a meteor that is out of this world; see flourescent rocks and glowing minerals; experiment with radioactive rock; see rainbows through special crystals using a polarizing filter; and don't let the earthquake exhibit shake you up!

Downstairs, a Discovery Lab allows kids to see and even touch live animals, such as snakes, as well as look through a microscope at animal fur, skin, etc. Huge walk-through dioramas with caves depict the southwestern desert. Some of the taxidermied animals in this exhibit and on this floor include cougars, coyotes, gold eagles, birds, and saber-toothed-tigers. One wall has a beautiful array of butterflies, some with fantastic flourescent colors. There are also numerous fossils, including those of dinosaurs. Dive into the next few rooms that contain models and stuffed sea creatures such as sea lions, stingrays, dolphins, sharks, and a pilot whale. Also on display are the menacing jaws of a shark, skeletons, a gigantic whale fin bone, and a whale skull.

The museum offers many classes, family programs, camp outs, and even camp-ins! Call for a schedule. (See BALBOA PARK for a lsiting of all the museums and attractions within walking distance.)

Hours: Open daily 9:30am - 4:30pm; open Thurs. until 6:30pm. Closed New Year's Day, Thanksgiving, and Christmas. During special exhibits, daily museum hours are extended - 9am - 6pm.

Admission: $7 for adults; $6 for seniors; $5 for ages 3 - 17; children 2 years and under are free. In between special exhibits, admission is half-price for all ages. Special exhibits cause prices and hours to fluctuate, even the free Tuesday admission, so always call first. Admission on the first Tuesday of every month is free. Passports for 11 museums in Balboa Park are available for $19 for adults at the Visitors Center, and are good for one week from date of purchase.

Ages: 3 years and up.

SAN DIEGO RAILROAD MUSEUM
(619) 595-3030 $$$
Highway 94, Campo
See SAN DIEGO RAILROAD MUSEUM under TRANSPORTATION.

STEPHEN BIRCH AQUARIUM-MUSEUM
(619) 534-3474 $$$
2300 Expedition Drive, San Diego

(EXIT SAN DIEGO FWY [405] W. ON LA JOLLA VILLAGE DR. STAY TO THE R. AS LA JOLLA VILLAGE DR. TURNS INTO N. TORREY PINES. TAKE THE NEXT L. ON LA JOLLA SHORES DR. AND FOLLOW IT TO SCRIPPS INSTITUTE OF OCEANOGRAPHY. STEPHEN BIRCH IS AT THE UNIVERSITY OF CALIFORNIA, SCRIPPS INSTITUTE OF OCEANOGRAPHY.)

Statues of leaping, large gray whales are in the fountain outside the entrance of the Stephen Birch Aquarium - Museum. This outstanding, sizable, aquarium-museum has three main exhibit areas. The aquarium section contains over thirty-three large tanks filled with an incredible variety of creatures found in the Earth's oceans; from eels to sharks to flashlight fish that glow in the dark. Just some of our favorite sea animals showcased here include the almost mesmerizing moon jellies; chocolate chip starfish; garden eels that look like hoses "standing" upright in the sand; bizarre-looking weedy sea dragons (related to the seahorse); the amazing giant octopus; and the beautiful, but venomous, striped lionfish. The largest tank has a huge kelp forest which makes it easy to view animals that are normally hidden on ocean floors. The fish are fed on Tuesdays and Thursdays, between noon and 1:30pm.

Outside, the rocky Tidepool Plaza connects the aquarium and the museum. A wave machine gently creates natural water motion in a simulated tidepool. Kids will see up close (and can gently touch) sea stars, sea urchins, sea cucumbers, etc. Also, take in the magnificent panoramic view of the La Jolla coastline (and the world famous Scripps Institute).

The museum features "Exploring the Blue Planet," a fantastic oceanographic exhibit with seven different, interactive display areas. Each area incorporates touch screens or an activity that shows and explains the integral part that oceans play in relation to how the Earth functions. Kids will learn about various aspects of ocean sciences from the displays on currents, tides, and waves; from earthquakes and plate tectonics; and as they experience a simulated, submersible ride to the ocean floor. My kids really enjoyed the "Ocean Supermarket," where they used scanners on common household products to see which ingredients came from the ocean. (Did you know that ice cream uses carrageenan - red seaweed - to make it smooth and creamy?!)

The above is a sampling of what the Stephen Birch Aquarium-Museum has to offer - come "sea" it for yourself! There is also an Aquarium Bookshop, and outdoor picnic areas that are stroller and wheelchair accessible. Call about the many special activities and programs offered through the aquarium-museum including tidepools tours, whale-watching cruises, grunion running, etc.

Hours: Open daily from 9am - 5pm. Closed Thanksgiving and Christmas.

Admission: $6.50 for adults; $5.50 for seniors; $4.50 for students; $3.50 for ages 3 - 12; children 2 years and under are free. Parking is $3

Ages: 3 years and up.

VILLA MONTEZUMA JESSE SHEPARD HOUSE ☼

(619) 239-2211 $

1925 "K" Street, San Diego

(GOING S. ON SAN DIEGO FWY [5], EXIT E. ON IMPERIAL AVE, L ON 20ᵀᴴ ST., L. ON "K" ST. GOING N ON 5, EXIT E. ON "J" ST., R. ON 20ᵀᴴ ST., R. ON "K" ST.)

Built and designed in 1887 for celebrated author, spiritualist, and musician, Jesse Shepard, this two-story house is by far one of the most interesting and ornamental Victorian houses we've ever seen. The outside is beautiful with its steep roofs, gables, turrets, and bay windows. The rooms inside are paneled with redwood and walnut, and are decorated with intricate wood carvings and moldings. The ceilings are elegantly embossed. There are numerous, gorgeous stained glass windows throughout that depict Beethoven, Mozart, a knight, the Greek poetess Sappho, and more. The furnishings are equally elaborate, and even though much of the furniture is not originally from this house, it is from the same time period. Older kids will enjoy the hour-and-a-half tour. They'll see the large music room, the drawing room, and the downstairs kitchen and laundry room which are filled with "labor saving" devices such as an early washing machine, vacuum cleaner, kitchen gadgets, etc. Upstairs are the bedrooms that, in keeping with the rest of the house, are also stylishly decorated. My 10-year old and I were fascinated by the house, but were bewildered as to why Jesse Shepard incurred the city's expense to construct it only to live in it for two years! Personally, I could live here for a lot longer.

Hours: Open Sat. - Sun. from noon - 4:30pm. Group tours are available Tues. - Sun. by reservation.

Admission: $3 for adults; free for children 12 years and under.

Ages: 8 years and up.

ALBINGER ARCHAEOLOGICAL MUSEUM ☼

(805) 648-5823   !

113 E. Main Street, Ventura

(GOING W. ON VENTURA FWY [101], EXIT N. ON CALIFORNIA AVE., L. ON MAIN ST. GOING S.E. ON 101, EXIT S. ON OLIVE, L. ON MAIN. IT'S ON THE N. SIDE OF THE STREET.)

This small, one-room museum has a collection of archaeological finds that have been uncovered from this site. Arrowheads, bottles, milling stones, bone whistles, and more are on display. When the kids have seen their fill, which was pretty immediate with my younger ones, head out the back door and look at the site of an actual dig. The foundations of an original Mission (church) are clearly marked here. My kids were more interested after I explained what we were looking at, and how archaeologists found the remains. (Digging in dirt is a popular pastime with our family, too.)

The enticing stone steps back here lead disappointingly, to a small street, but at least we got in some exercise.

Hours: Open June through August, Wed. - Sun., 10am - 4pm; open September through May, Wed. - Fri., 10am - 2pm; Sat. - Sun., 10am - 4pm. Closed New Year's Day, Easter, Thanksgiving, and Christmas.

Admission: Free; donations appreciated.

Ages: 6 years and up.

CARNEGIE ART MUSEUM

(805) 385-8157 - exhibit info.;

(805) 385-8179 - tour and class info.

424 South "C" Street, Oxnard

(EXIT VENTURA FWY [101] S. ON HWY 1 [OR OXNARD BLVD.], R. ON 4TH ST. IT'S ON THE S. SIDE OF THE STREET.)

I mention this small, beautiful museum mainly because of the kid-friendly workshops offered. (Tell your kids the building is done in neo-classical design, though they'll just think the columns look really neat.) I take my kids through art museums, explaining what I can and hoping that some understanding and appreciation for art will take root. However, I think the best way we can reach and teach our kids is through guided tours and hands-on workshops.

In a group tour here, kids learn about a particular style, artist, or medium. Then, they create their own art projects in a workshop taught by a local artist. Reservations are needed. Carnegie occasionally offers family classes, too.

Come see the permanent exhibits of paintings, photographs, and sculptures at this Museum. Have your children draw a picture of their outing!

Hours: Open Thurs. - Sat., 10am - 5pm; Sun., 1am - 5pm. (Call first as the museum is closed during installation of new exhibits.)

Admission: $3 for adults; $2 for seniors and students; $1 for ages 6 - 16; children 5 years and under are free. The museum is free from 3pm - 6pm on Fridays.

Ages: 6 years and up.

CEC-SEABEE MUSEUM

(805) 982-5163

Located on 23rd Street in the Naval Construction Battalion Center, Port Hueneme

(EXIT THE VENTURA FWY [101] S. ON VENTURA RD., THEN JUST S. OF CHANNEL ISLANDS BLVD. TURN R. ON 23RD AVE. THROUGH THE GATES OF THE MILITARY BASE. THE MUSEUM HAS A STATUE OF A HUGE BEE WITH A MACHINE GUN OUTSIDE THE ENTRANCE.)

This huge museum is dedicated to documenting, preserving, and maintaining public awareness of the contributions of the Seabees and Civil Engineer Corps. The mission statement is formal sounding, but the museum is incredibly rich with fascinating exhibits. There are life-size models and statues of men and women depicted in scenes of battle and peacetime, wearing authentic uniforms and costumes from around the world. There are displays of weapons, medals, banners, photos, and equipment (such as gas masks) from all facets of a Seabee's life in action.

Another wing has model boats, and an underwater diving exhibit with small, model scuba divers. Kids can touch a full-size, old-fashioned diving suit and helmet. Wonderful dioramas, such as a Seabee's amphibious landing and establishment of camp, can be easily seen, thanks to viewing platforms.

The Cultural Artifacts section is interesting because of the number of exhibits and international content. On display are unusual musical instruments; foreign currency and coins; tools; Indian weapons, beadwork, drums, and other artifacts; an Alaska exhibit; a China exhibit; and so much more! Although nothing here is hands-on, my kids were captivated by the variety and uniqueness of the items. Each exhibit brought a yell of, "Hey, come over here and check this out!" It's the kind of museum, because of its size and the scope of displays, that you can visit again and again.

Hours: The museum is open Mon. - Fri. , 0800 - 1630; Sat. 0900
                  - 1630; Sun., 1230 - 1630.
Admission: Free
Ages: 4 years and up.

CHANNEL ISLANDS NATIONAL PARK VISITOR CENTER

(805) 658-5730

1901 Spinnaker Way, Ventura

(GOING W. ON VENTURA FWY [101], EXIT S.W. ON SEAWARD AVE., L. ON HARBOR BLVD. GOING S.E. ON 101, EXIT S. ON HARBOR BLVD. FROM HARBOR, GO R. ON SPINNAKER DR., ALL THE WAY TO THE END.)

The Channel Islands Visitor Center is worthy of a trip in itself. You'll pass by beaches and stores (see VENTURA HARBOR), but pacify the kids with a, "We'll stop there on the way out." The Center is a great combination of museum, store, and resource center. The kids will head straight for the indoor tidepool (not a touch tank), which offers an up-close look at sea stars, anemones, and other small, ocean creatures. Other eye-catching displays are the taxidermied animals (some in flight), and a topographical model of the islands. My boys also enjoyed sifting sand in the mini-sand pit and grinding pretend meal with a Chumash Indian stone mortar and pestle.

The twenty-five-minute movie "A Treasure In the Sea" is shown throughout the day, and is a fun way to learn more about sea life. Tidepool talks are available on weekends as are free Ranger programs that offer an in-depth look at a particular animal or habitat.

Hours: Open Mon. - Fri., 8:30am - 4:30pm; Sat. - Sun., 8am -
5pm.
Admission: Free
Ages: 2 years and up.

CHUMASH INTERPRETATIVE CENTER /   ☀
OAKBROOK REGIONAL PARK
(805) 492-8076 $

3290 Lang Ranch Parkway, Thousand Oaks
(EXIT HWY 23 E. ON AVENIDA DE LOS ARBOLES, R. ON WESTLAKE, THEN THE FIRST
L. ON LANG RANCH PARKWAY.)

Long ago, the Chumash Indians occupied this area of land, which is
now Ventura County, and other surrounding areas. A small, one-room,
Interpretative Center features artifacts representative of the Chumash
way of life. Pictures and native paintings decorate the walls. Some local
plants, and the way they were used, are on display, such as yucca
fibers braided into ropes, and sticks fashioned into weapons. Rabbit
and bear furs can be touched, while other exhibits are behind glass. My
kids liked the musical instruments, such as drums and rattles, and I
admired the jewelry made out of beads. Outside, kids can see a
replicated Chumash village. If they can handle the one-and-a-half-mile
walk, hike back to see the centuries-old pictographs, or rock paintings,
visible from the caves/overhangs. (The pictographs might not look like
much to kids, but their symbolism and preservation is important to
Chumash heritage.) Sign up for a guided nature walk, given on
Saturdays at 1pm and Sundays at 2pm.

School or group tours are two hours long, very informative, and one
of the most effective ways to really see and understand what the Center
has to offer. The first hour consists of a slide presentation on the history
of the Chumash, making handcrafts to take home, and an explanation
of the exhibits. The second hour is a guided walk through the park and
archaeological preserve, from a Chumash perspective. You'll learn
about their way of life, and how different plants and trees were used. As
an alternative, the second hour could be a wildlife presentation, learning
about the native animals, and how to live with and respect them.

The park itself is beautiful, and can be visited without going into the
Interpretative Center. There are picnic tables, shady oak trees, and
miles of hiking trails.

Hours: The Center is open Tues. - Sat., 10am - 5pm; Sun., noon
- 5pm. The park is open daily from dawn to dusk.
Admission: $3 for adults; $2 for ages 5 - 12; children 4 years and
under are free. Tours are $3 per person. Entrance to the
park is free.
Ages: 7 years and up for the Center.

EARTH SCIENCE MUSEUM   ☀
(805) 646-5976 or (805) 642-3155   !
5019 Crooked Palm Road, Ventura
(EXIT OJAI FWY [33] R. ON SHELL RD., L. ON VENTURA AVE., L. ON CROOKED PALM
RD.)

   This small museum is run by the Gem and Mineral Society and is
open by appointment only. There are several displays here relating to
earth science, like rocks (volcanic ones are always interesting), lots of
minerals, and locally found fossils. The "dinosaur petting zoo" consists
of replicas of dinosaur bones that kids can touch. Tours are tailored
toward your children's ages and attention spans.
   Hours: By appointment.
Admission: Free
      Ages: 4 years and up.

GULL WINGS CHILDREN'S MUSEUM   ☀
(805) 483-3005 $$
418 W. Fourth Street, Oxnard
(EXIT THE VENTURA FWY [101] S. ON HWY 1 [OR OXNARD BLVD.], R. ON 4TH ST.)

   Children's museums strive for the right combination of fun and
education. Gull Wings has achieved a delightful balance of these goals.
The long building has sectioned off "rooms," each one focusing on a
different theme. The first room is a delightful toddler's play area. The
next one is for future geologists or paleontologists. It contains rocks,
fossils, and skulls to look at and/or touch. (The saber-tooth tiger is a
particular favorite). Kids can use a microscope to study other elements.
This room also teaches engineering principles through play with
wooden gears. Camping is next door with a tent to crawl into, and a
pretend campfire to cook over.
   My kids played doctor and patient in the next room for over an hour.
This complete medical room has gowns, a surgery table with play
instruments, an X-ray set up, wheelchairs, and crutches. For hands-on
health and science learning, there are plastic models of the body with
removeable parts, and cloth dolls that kids can unlayer to reveal
muscles, bones, and organs.
   Further back in the museum is an optical illusions room with
funhouse mirrors, etc. A mini-market has shopping carts, a cash
register, and bins of "food" for your little shoppers. The puppet theater
allows storytellers to express themselves in creative ways. For more
"let's pretend," kids can dress-up in elegant gowns, cowboy attire, or
firefighter's and sailor's uniforms, etc. Backdrops and props, like a fire
hydrant and a boat, help complete the scenes your kids act out. Enter
another dimension when you enter the Galaxy Room. This room is
black lit with painted stars on the ceiling and "Music of the Universe"
playing.

Other highlights include playing with a wooden train set, an attraction for kids of all ages, and "driving" a kid-proofed Saturn car. Young drivers can get behind the wheel, shift gears, turn on headlights and, via a plexiglass hood, see the inner workings of an engine. A side door panel is also clear.

Hours: Open Wed. - Sat. from 1pm - 5pm. Call first as hours fluctuate.
Admission: $3 per person; children under 2 years are free.
Ages: 1 to 13 years.

MARITIME MUSEUM (Oxnard)
(805) 984-6260
2731 South Victoria Avenue, Oxnard
(EXIT VENTURA FWY [101] S. ON VICTORIA ST. THE MUSEUM IS LOCATED AT CHANNEL ISLANDS HARBOR AT THE CORNER OF VICTORIA ST. AND CHANNEL ISLANDS BLVD.)

Explore the seas without leaving port! This good-sized, nautical museum has original paintings, and various sizes and styles of model ships behind glass cases. What detail! Marine artists from the 1700's to the present have their eye-catching work on display throughout the museum. If your child has the patience, or desire, a docent will gladly explain local nautical history, which gives more meaning to the exhibits.

Hours: Open Thurs. - Mon. from 11am - 5pm.
Admission: Free, but donations are appreciated.
Ages: 4 years and up.

OJAI VALLEY HISTORICAL SOCIETY AND MUSEUM
(805) 640-1390
130 W. Ojai Avenue, Ojai
(TAKE STATE HWY 150 INTO OJAI, TURNS INTO OJAI AVE.)

This museum recently relocated into an old chapel. Slowly, but surely all the exhibits are being moved into place. The museum's mission is dedication to keeping historic Ojai alive by preserving the valley's cultural and natural heritage. Since most of the exhibits are encased in glass, my kids did a lot of nose pressing. They smudged up the cases containing Chumash Indian artifacts such as arrowheads, beadwork, and rattles made from turtle shells and sea shells. The simulated archaeological pit was interesting, too. Another exhibit area with a lot of kid-appeal is the taxidermied animals, some of which can actually be touched. The stuffed animals on our hit parade include the black bear and the more unusual, platypus and bat. The museum also has a fine collection of taxidermied snakes.

Some of the fossils featured here include a big sea snail and an even bigger rock with at least a dozen sand dollars imbedded in it. (The buck stops here!) The museum has a fairly extensive shell collection, too. I only hope we can remember some of their names the next time we go to the beach.

Hours: Open Wed. - Sun. from 1pm - 4pm.
Admission: $2 for adults; children 12 years and under are free.
Ages: 3 years and up.

OLIVAS ADOBE HISTORICAL PARK
(805) 644-4346   !
4200 Olivas Park Drive, Ventura
(GOING S. ON VENTURA FWY [101], EXIT S. ON HARBOR BLVD., L. ON OLIVAS PARK DR. GOING N.W. ON 101, EXIT S. ON VICTORIA, R. ON OLIVAS PARK DR.)

The Olivas Adobe is a restored, two-story, adobe home built in 1847. It is representative of the rancho period in California's history. The residence has bedrooms, a living room, and a kitchen to look into that are furnished just as they were over 100 years ago. The grounds are beautifully landscaped, and the open courtyard, containing a Chumash Indian oven and some farming equipment, gives younger ones some running-around space. A small exhibit building, across from the rose garden, contains items that relate to this particular time period, such as saddles, pictures, and ranching equipment. While this is not an all day visit, kids enjoy the opportunity to "see" the past.

Hours: The grounds are open daily from 10am - 4pm. The Adobe, and tours of it, are available on Sat. and Sun., between 10am - 4pm.
Admission: Free
Ages: 6 years and up.

RONALD REAGAN PRESIDENTIAL LIBRARY AND MUSEUM
(805) 522-8444 $
40 Presidential Drive, Simi Valley
(EXIT THE SIMI VALLEY/SAN FERNANDO VALLEY FWY [118] S. ON MADERA RD., R. UP THE HILL ON PRESIDENTIAL DR.)

The massive, Spanish-style Ronald Reagan Library and Museum is alone on a hilltop. Remember those books that you read about kings and queens and their treasures? Walk down the hallway lined with incredible gifts from heads of states and feel like those storybook pages have come true. Treasures range from an exquisite hand-beaded blouse for the First Lady to an intricately carved, ivory-handled sword that has a gold sheath inlaid with jewels, for the President.

Reagan's heritage and love of the West is evident throughout the museum. One room, in particular, is dedicated to the American west with displays of elaborate saddles, boots, spurs, statues, and an eye-catching cowboy hat with a real rattlesnake head on the band. Even the full-size replica of the Oval Office, which reflects each President's personal style, is decorated with western art.

Two theaters show twenty-minute-plus videos of the Reagan years that include inauguration speeches, tearing down the Berlin wall, and a remembrance of the Challenger crew. My kids were thoroughly captivated by the footage.

The next few galleries depict Reagan's road to the presidency via movie posters, uniforms, costumes, documents, and lots of photos. My oldest child was also impressed by a nuclear cruise missile, once deployed in Europe. One room contains signed sports paraphernalia. Another displays gifts that range from the elegant to the homemade, such as a jellybean-painted cane, and the Presidential Seal crafted from 6,500 silver nails - what a great kid's project this would make! There are pictures of Nancy Reagan, some of her gowns, and a whole wall devoted to her "Just Say No" campaign.

There are numerous touch screens throughout the museum so kids can learn about Reagan's views on issues by letting their fingers "do the walking." Visitors can become members (albeit temporarily) of Reagan's cabinet while sitting around a table in a re-created White House Room. His image and responses are shown on a big screen in the room. Travel to the Geneva Convention and witness a historic meeting between Gorbachev and Reagan as their images are projected on the screen above the chateau's fireplace.

Out back is a huge, decoratively spray-painted, chunk of the Berlin wall. The gift shop has great aids for teaching history.

Hours: Open daily from 10am - 5pm. Closed New Year's Day, Thanksgiving, and Christmas.

Admission: $4 for adults; $2 for seniors; children 15 years and under are free.

Ages: 5 years and up.

SANTA PAULA UNION OIL MUSEUM   ☼
(805) 933-0076   !
1001 E. Main Street, Santa Paula
(EXIT THE 126 FWY, N. ON STATE ROUTE 150 [OR 10TH ST.]. THE MUSEUM IS ON THE N.E. CORNER OF 10TH AND MAIN ST.)

The Union Oil Museum is housed in the original headquarters of the Union Oil Company. The interior and exterior of the 1890 building has meticulously been restored to its original luster. Upon entering, kids can punch a keepsake time card in an old time card machine. The walls are covered with great pictures and murals regarding the history and technology of the oil industry.

Quite a few of the exhibits are interactive, such as the Lubricity Exhibit. Kids can turn the gears and see how much easier the figures on bicycles can pedal when the gears are oiled. They can push a button and watch a model rig "drill" for oil through the layers of the earth. With a touch of a button, the Centrifuge Exhibit spins to separate water and other substances from crude oil. A few touch screens are here that impart interesting information about how the oil industry affects so many aspects of our lives.

Since geology is vital to finding oil, several terrific geological displays are in the museum. Some of the fossils on display include shells, dinosaur bones, and shark teeth.

The upstairs, which can only be seen by a half-hour guided tour, is interesting to older kids. There are restored offices, bedrooms, a kitchen, and fireplaces with ornate tiles around them. The walk-in safe looks like a secret, hidden room.

Walk through the main building and outside to reach the Rig Room. Kids can see a huge cable rig in action as the engine turns the sand wheel that turns the band wheel that moves the wooden walking beam and the huge drill bits! I hope you feel like we did when we visited the museum - like we struck oil!

Hours: Open Thurs. - Sun. from 10am - 4pm. Tours of the upstairs are conducted only Fri. - Sun. from 11am - 3pm.

Admission: Free; donations appreciated.

Ages: 4 years and up.

STAGECOACH INN MUSEUM

(805) 498-9441

51 S. Ventu Park Road, Newbury Park
(EXIT THE VENTURA FWY [101] S. ON VENTU PARK RD.)

This beautiful 1870's hotel and stagecoach stop is both interesting and educational, and seen only by guided tour. The downstairs consists mainly of the parlor, dining room, and kitchen. The furniture, decor, and history are interesting to older kids, but younger kids get antsy.

Upstairs, however, it is a different story. A small "cowboy" bedroom has a saddle, bear skin rug, and other western paraphernalia. The Chumash Indian room has a collection of fossils, beadwork, and pictures. Another room has an extensive butterfly and bug collection in glass cases. The Music Room has an old-fashioned, elegant feel to it as antique violins, other instruments, and vintage clothing are fashionably displayed. A child's room is filled with toys of yesteryear (no Nintendo!), and a bed that Todd Lincoln slept in. (I hope kids won't ask, "Who's that?") Oooooh - a man named Pierre was supposedly shot here and his ghost still haunts the Inn. Now, the Inn becomes fascinating to kids!

Outside the hotel, take a short nature trail that leads to other historic points of interest. The Carriage House contains stagecoaches, while further around the bend are the Pioneer Newbury House and the Spanish Adobe House; both are open to tour through. The Chumash Indian Hut and a beehive oven are also interesting. Explain to your kids that the oven is named for its design, not for cooking bees.

When the kids have seen all that they want, head out to the small Stagecoach Park above the Inn. It's easier to drive to the park than to walk, as the entrance is on another street.

Hours: The Inn is open Wed. - Sun. from 1pm - 4pm. The
Carriage House is open only on Sundays from 1pm -
4pm.
Admission: $3 for adults; $2 for seniors; $1 for ages 5 - 12; children 4
years and under are free.
Ages: 5 years and up.

STRATHERN HISTORICAL PARK AND MUSEUM   ☼

(805) 526-6453 $

137 Strathern Place, Simi Valley
(EXIT SIMI VALLEY/SAN FERNANDO VALLEY FWY [118] S. ON MADERA RD., R. ON
STRATHERN PLACE.)

This outside museum is really several historical buildings inside a
gated, park-like setting. Start your one-hour guided tour at the Visitor's
Center. Learn about the early days of Simi by first watching a twenty-
minute tape about the Valley's history. Some of the exhibits in here
include maps and, a little more exciting, beekeeping equipment such as
smokers and hoods. Next, walk through one of the very first, local
colony houses. Though the inside decor is from the 1930's, the building
itself still retains its original charm. An adobe house, built in the early
1800's, displays a previous owner's furnishings, from the 1950's. The
Strathern House, which is a Victorian house built in 1893, has antique
treasures throughout including furniture, clothing, and a pump organ.

The library contains some fossils, as well as books. The enclosed
barn has eight stalls with different exhibits such as kitchen gadgets,
early laundry equipment, an old-fashioned switchboard, Chumash
Indian artifacts, farm machinery, and old automobiles such as a truck, a
tractor, and a Ford Model A. Another barn contains more farm
equipment such as hay wagons, etc. Around the perimeters of the
historical park are pieces of old (rusted) farming equipment, which adds
to the rustic ambiance.

Hours: Open Sat. - Sun., 1pm - 4pm and Wed. at 1pm for tours,
weather permitting.
Admission: $2 for adults; $1 for students.
Ages: 5 years and up.

VENTURA COUNTY MUSEUM OF HISTORY AND   ☼
ART

(805) 653-0323 $

100 E. Main Street, Ventura
(GOING W. ON VENTURA FWY [101], EXIT N. ON CALIFORNIA AVE., L. ON MAIN ST.
GOING S.E. ON 101, EXIT S. ON OLIVE, L. ON MAIN. IT'S ON THE S. SIDE OF STREET.)

This museum is a great introduction to art for children. The
paintings and dioramas are beautiful, and the variety of exhibits is even
better. As we followed along the building's circular layout, we saw a
wonderful display of fossilized shells and bones. The outside patio area

has an impressive collection of large farm machinery. Chumash Indian stone mortars and pestles are out here for kids to try. A section of the museum is set up chronologically, showing the beginnings of Ventura County, featuring Chumash artifacts, to the New West, represented by a 1910 car, an old vacuum cleaner, washer, etc.

The George Stuart Gallery room displays part of his over 200 historical figures. Marie Antoinette, American patriots, etc., are one-quarter life-size (three inches to the foot). The intricate art work and attention to detail makes the finished figures very lifelike. My kids were most intrigued with the models and pictures that explained how Mr. Stuart designs and constructs his figures. They now want to attempt to make similar figures at home.

The museum is well laid out and the kids enjoyed most of the exhibits - a good start for laying a foundation of art appreciation!

Hours: Open Tues. - Sun. from 10am - 5pm.
Admission: $3 for adults; children 16 years and under are free.
Ages: 4 years and up.

PIERS AND SEAPORTS

It ap*pier*s that walking around seaport villages, looking at boats, taking a cruise, and maybe going on some rides, is a delightful way to spend a few hours with your child!

FISHERMAN'S VILLAGE   ☼

(310) 823-5411   !/$

13755 Fiji Way, Marina Del Rey

(TAKE MARINA FWY [90] TO THE END, S. ON LINCOLN, R. ON FIJI)

This turn-of-the-century, New England-themed shopping and boating complex is located on the main channel of the Marina Del Rey harbor. It offers pier fishing, sail boat rentals, (see RENT-A-SAIL) and Hornblower dinner cruises. Cruises are $56.95 for adults, $28.50 for ages 3 to 12, are are available from 7:30pm to 10pm on the weekends. Call (310) 301-6000 to make reservations.

I still say the best things in life are free (or relatively inexpensive). It is fun just walking along the pier, looking at the boats, maybe grabbing a snack, and feeling the ocean breeze.

Hours: The Village is open Sun. - Thurs., 9am - 9pm; Fri. - Sat., 9am - 10pm.
Admission: Free
Ages: All

PORTS O' CALL VILLAGE   ☼

(310) 831-0287   !/$

Berth 77, San Pedro

(EXIT HARBOR FWY [110] S. ON HARBOR BLVD. AND FOLLOW THE SIGNS.)

This picturesque village with seventy-five shops and restaurants has cobblestone streets, making it an interesting stroll. Harbor tours are available (see TRANSPORTATION), as are Adventure Helicopter rides. Five-minute helicopter rides are $20, etc., and available on weekends and holidays. Call (310) 547-3419 for more information. (See SAN PEDRO for more things to do in this area.) Tip: The green, electric trolley has several stops in San Pedro, with Ports O' Call being one of them. Take the trolley to L.A. MARITIME MUSEUM, S.S. LANE VICTORY, or around town. At 25¢, this is a fun, mini-adventure.

Hours: Most shops and restaurants are open daily in the summer from 10am - 9pm; open the rest of the year daily from 11am - 8pm. Closed Christmas.
Ages: All

REDONDO BEACH INTERNATIONAL BOARDWALK / ☼ KING HARBOR

(310) 318-0648   !/$

Where Torrance Boulevard meets the sea, Redondo Beach

(EXIT SAN DIEGO FWY [405] S. ON WESTERN, R. ON 190TH ST. WHICH TURNS INTO ANITA ST., L ON PACIFIC COAST HIGHWAY, R. ON TORRANCE.)

This is no ordinary pier, but a fascinating place to explore with your family! Starting at the north end of the harbor, come hungry because enticing food smells waft through the air. Choose from egg rolls, gyros, hamburgers, or pizza as the international restaurants run the gamut from grab-a-bite to elegant. We munched as we watched the ducks and boats in the water, and soaked up the ambiance.

Stop off at Quality Seafood - it's like a mini-sea-zoo with tanks of live crabs, lobsters, shrimp, and shellfish. You cannot entirely avoid the Fun Factory which is a huge, under-the-boardwalk amusement center. It has over 200 video, arcade, and carnival-style games, plus kiddie rides, which adds up to a lot of noisy stimulus. Come up for a breather 'cause right next "door" is the Marina Boat Ride, open on weekends and holidays. Enjoy a half-hour boat ride for $3 for ages 4 and up, $1 for children 3 years and under, children 2 years and under are free. Look for the colony of sea lions that is usually hanging around.

Back on the cement, horse-shoe shaped pier, have your kids look down at the various sea etchings, including blue whales and sting rays. Try your luck at fishing off the pier! The gift shops on the older boardwalk offer a variety of merchandise for sale. Check out the store Shark Attack. Not only does it sell shark teeth, sea shells, etc., but for an additional $1.50 for adults, $1 for kids 10 years and under, you can go past the curtain and see a sixteen-and-a-half foot, taxidermied, great white shark.

Last, but not least, there are rock jetties here. Deeming them fairly safe for the kids to walk on, my husband and I won the coveted, "You guys are the greatest!" award. Ah, the simple pleasures.

Looking for other things to do and see in the immediate vicinity? Besides going to the beach, check out ISLE OF REDONDO (a deep-sea fishing barge) and look for the Whaling Wall. This incredible mural of the California gray whale, painted by marine artist, Wyland, decorates the massive wall of the Southern California Edison building located on Harbor Drive at Herondo Street. It's worth a drive by, or a stop and stare. For a tour of the Marine Research Laboratory, inside the Edison building, see SOUTHERN CALIFORNIA EDISON GENERATING STATION TOUR.

Hours: Most restaurants are open daily for breakfast, lunch, and dinner. Most of the stores, and such, are open daily from 10am - 6pm.

Admission: Parking is 50¢ for each 20 minutes; $5 maximum on weekdays; $10 maximum on weekends.

Ages: All

SANTA MONICA PIER

(310) 458-8900

Foot of Colorado Boulevard, Santa Monica

(EXIT SANTA MONICA FWY [10] N. ON 4TH ST., L. ON COLORADO BLVD.)

This renowned wooden pier offers a lot to do, as well as just soaking up the beach atmosphere. There are food stands, restaurants, and great shops that carry a little bit of everything. Peek in the fresh fish store as it has tanks of live lobsters, crabs, and other shellfish. Or, go fishing off the pier to catch your own fresh meal.

The major kid-attraction on the pier is Pacific Park. It has eleven family rides, including six kiddie rides. The rides include an eighty-five-foot Ferris wheel, a carousel, bumper boats, a swinging ship, and theater simulator ride. Tickets cost between $1 - $3 per ride. A food court is here to service your tummy. The Playland Arcade draws kids like a magnet with its video and arcade games. A friendly warning: Weekends can be almost overwhelmingly crowded here.

Discover a place where touchable tidepool life is teeming under the boardwalk. (See the U.C.L.A. DISCOVERY CENTER.) Santa Monica beach offers plenty of long stretches of beach, great surf, and several playgrounds.

Feel like going for a ride? A nineteen-mile bike path goes from Santa Monica to Torrance Beach. If you forget your wheels call Sea Mist Rentals at (310) 395-7076. They also have in-line skates and boogie boards for rent.

Hours: The stores are usually open 10am - 6pm year 'round. Pacific Park is open daily in the summer from 10am - 10pm; it is open the rest of the year, Fri. at 4pm, Sat. - Sun. at 10am.

Admission: Pacific Park unlimited rides pass cost $12 per person. Parking can be tough. On the pier parking is $3 for the first two hours with a vendor validation, or maximum $7.

Ages: 2 years and up.

SHORELINE VILLAGE

(562) 435-2668   *!/$*

407 Shoreline Drive, Long Beach

(Take Long Beach Fwy [710] to end, then proceed on Shoreline Dr.)

This turn-of-the-century coastal "village" has specialty shops and places to eat. Weekday mornings are a great time to stroll along here and enjoy the serenity.

Kids are mostly interested in watching the boats, eating ice cream, and riding the antique merry-go-round ($1 a ride).

Hours: The merry-go-round is usually open Mon. - Fri., 11am - 7pm; Sat. - Sun., 11am - 8pm. The stores are open daily, usually from 10am - 9pm.

Admission: Free

Ages: 2 years and up.

BALBOA PIER

400 E. Bay Street, Balboa Peninsula in Newport Beach   *!/$*

(Take Costa Mesa Fwy [55] to the end, which turns into Newport Blvd., which turns into Balboa Blvd., R. on Main St. to end for the pier; L. on Main St. for the Fun Zone.)

Enjoy the miles of sandy beach for sunning and surfing; fish from the pier just for the fun of it; or grab a bite to eat at the small RUBY'S Diner at the end of the pier. Peninsula Park is on the east side of the pier. This grassy park, shaded only by palm trees, has barbeques, picnic tables, and even a small playground. See BALBOA FUN ZONE, located just across the road, and combine both attractions for a full day of fun.

Hours: Open daily. Parking in the lot costs about $3.
Admission: Free
Ages: All

DANA POINT HARBOR - DANA WHARF / MARINER'S VILLAGE
(714) 496-1555   !/$

34675 Street of the Golden Lantern, Dana Point
(EXIT SAN DIEGO FWY [5] S.W. ON CAMINO LAS RAMBLAS, WHICH TURNS INTO PACIFIC COAST HIGHWAY. GO N. ON P.C.H., L. ON DANA POINT HARBOR DR./DEL OBISPO ST., L. ON ST. OF THE GOLDEN LANTERN.)

Dana Point Harbor has beaches, tidepools, a seaside shopping village, boat rentals, picnic areas, and more. Entering the Street of the Golden Lantern, Dana Wharf is to your left, and Mariner's Village is to your right. Activities on the Wharf side include shopping, whale-watching cruises, and boat fishing. Call Dana Wharf Sportfishing, (714) 496-5794 for more information. The Village offers many specialty shops, from Indian jewelry to seafaring items. Food choices range from the elegant to the quick bite, plus ice cream and candy shops, of course. Your young sailor can watch boats of all sizes, shapes, and colors sail in and out of the harbor and up and down the coast.

At the western end of the harbor, next to the Orange County Marine Institute, is Dana Cove Park, or "Baby Beach." There are a few picnic tables here overlooking the bluffs, rock jetties to climb on, and a waveless beach. Enjoy the day with your family day at Dana Point, whatever you choose to do! (See DOHENY STATE BEACH PARK and ORANGE COUNTY MARINE INSTITUTE for other things to do here.)

Hours: Most shops are open daily from 10am - 6pm.
Admission: Parking is free.
Ages: All

OCEANSIDE PIER AND HARBOR
(760) 721-1101 - Visitor's Information Center   !/$
At the end of Pier View Way at Pacific Street, Oceanside
(EXIT SAN DIEGO FWY [5] W. ON MISSION AVE., R. ON PACIFIC ST., L. ON PIER VIEW WY.)

The Ocean Beach Pier is the longest pier in San Diego County, and the majority of it is made from wood planks. It stretches out over the ocean almost 2,000 feet, or twenty minutes of walking, depending on the age of your youngest child. Don't want to walk? There is a Ruby's Scooby Doo golf-cart-like shuttle available for a mere 25¢ each way. The spacious Ruby's Diner at the end of the pier is a 40's diner serving great all-American food at good prices in a very kid-friendly atmosphere. Another pier-related activity is fishing. It doesn't require a license, so reel 'em in! The other end of the pier (the land end) offers a McDonald's restaurant, an outdoor amphitheater (used for in-line skating when concerts aren't in session), a playground with wooden, climbing structures, sand volleyball courts, and, of course, miles of surf and sand.

Breeze on over to the Oceanside Harbor, just a few streets north of the pier. The Harbor offers your choice of boat rentals at Harbor Paddle Sports, (760) 439-3050, including kayaks, jet skis, sailing, and sportfishing boats. Come on in, the water's fine for swimming and surfing. On the beach are sand volleyball courts, a playground for the younger set, and picnic areas with barbecues and covered cabanas. The Cape-Cod-like stores and restaurants entice the shoppers (and the hungry) to indulge.

I would be remiss if I didn't mention the famous Dog Beach, located a few miles south of the pier. Furry visitors from all over come to romp and play frisbee on this two-mile stretch of beach. Tip: Watch where you walk.

    Hours: Most stores are open daily 10am - 6pm.
Admission: Spending money.
     Ages: All

SEAPORT VILLAGE   ◑

(619) 235-4014 - information; (619) 235-4013 - special events   *$$*
800 West Harbor Drive at Kettner Boulevard, San Diego
(GOING S. ON SAN DIEGO FWY [5], EXIT W. ON ASH ST., L. ON 4TH, R. ON BROADWAY TO THE END, THEN L. ON HARBOR DR. GOING N. ON 5, EXIT S. ON 6TH AVE., R. ON BROADWAY TO THE END, THEN L. ON HARBOR DR.)

This delightful harbor-side shopping area is in an expansive, beautiful, park-like setting. There are three themed plazas here representing early California, a New England fishing village, and the Victorian era. There are several wonderful restaurants to choose from as well as numerous places for snackers to eat. Along its boardwalk and cobblestone "streets," the Village offers over sixty-five unique shops, including Magnet Max, Miner's Gems and Minerals, and Fantasy World of Toys. Kids will enjoy riding the 100-year-old carousel located in the West Plaza. The carousel is open daily from 10am - 9pm. Rides cost $1 each for ages 4 and up; children 3 years and under ride for free with a paid adult.

Admission: Technically free. Parking for two hours is validated with any purchase. Otherwise it is about $1.50 an hour.
     Ages: All

CHANNEL ISLANDS HARBOR VILLAGE   ☼

At the corner of Victoria Avenue and Channel Islands Boulevard,   !/$
Oxnard
(EXIT VENTURA FWY [101] S. ON VICTORIA AVE.)

    Stroll and shop the day away in this quaint-looking, Victorian harbor village. While some stores cater to your taste buds, others have great gift-giving items for sale. Kids enjoy walking the village "streets" and taking in the sights. Stop in at the MARITIME MUSEUM sometime before you ship out.

    Hours: Most stores are open daily from 10am - 6pm.
Admission: Free
     Ages: All

VENTURA HARBOR and VILLAGE   ☼
(805) 644-0169   !/$

1559 Spinnaker Way, Ventura
(GOING W. ON VENTURA FWY [101], EXIT S.W. ON SEAWARD AVE., L. ON HARBOR
BLVD. GOING S. ON 101, EXIT S. ON HARBOR BLVD. FROM HARBOR BLVD., GO R. ON
SPINNAKER DR.)

    This harbor has a lot to offer. The picturesque "village" has over thirty unusual gift shops and restaurants. Come for lunch, or just dessert! Enjoy a stroll around and look at the boats, or take a ride on the merry-go-round at $1 a ride.

    Your family can take a cruise (this is always such a treat for kids), play at the Marina Cove play area, and/or walk on the rock jetties down towards the Channel Islands Visitor Center. This last idea is not for the faint of heart or for really young kids, as part of the "walkway" on the rocks is washed away. Bring your fishing poles if you have the time and patience. The beach is here, too, of course, along with picnic areas and barbecues. Enjoy your day here with all there is to do and "sea"! (Also see CHANNEL ISLANDS NATIONAL PARK and CHANNEL ISLANDS VISITORS CENTER).

    For cruise information, call Bay Queen Harbor Cruise, (805) 642-7753 or Island Packers, (805) 642-1393. Both are located on Spinnaker Drive. If you want to experience the thrill of "really" flying like a bird, and you weigh at least 60 pounds, try parasailing, (805) 684-0022. The cost is $38 for a five-minute ride.

    Hours: Most stores are open daily from 10am - 6pm. The merry-go-round is open Mon. - Thurs., 10am - 7pm; Fri. - Sun., 10am - 9pm.
Admission: Free
     Ages: All

VENTURA PIER   ☼
Harbor Boulevard, Ventura   !

(GOING W. ON VENTURA FWY [101], EXIT S.W. ON SEAWARD AVE., L. ON HARBOR BLVD. GOING S. ON 101, EXIT S. ON HARBOR BLVD.)

The pier's real attraction is that it is the longest wooden pier in California, and the sunsets here are kid-approved! The playground and beautiful long stretch of sandy beach doesn't hurt, either.

Hours: Open daily.
Admission: Free
Ages: All

POTPOURRI

The dictionary defines potpourri as: "A miscellaneous mixture; a confused collection." This accurately defines this section!!! You'll find a little bit of everything here, so pick through and have fun.

CATALINA ISLAND   ☼
(310) 510-1520 - Visitors Bureau $$$$$

Catalina Island is a resort in the truest sense of the word. It's twenty-one miles long, eight miles wide, only twenty-two miles from the mainland, and packed with all sorts of things to see and do. The main town, Avalon, has an abundance of shops and restaurants along the beach and harbor. Come here to fish in the deep blue sea; take a glass bottom boat ride; go horse-back riding, hiking, or camping on the more untamed side of the island; take an Island safari where kids thrill at seeing real buffalo; or just enjoy the beach and all the water activities, such as swimming, snorkeling, canoeing, etc. Catalina has a quaint ambiance and is a wonderful family day trip or weekend excursion. I highly recommend ordering the 100-page Visitors Guide as it has *all* the information you could possibly want about Catalina. (Call the Visitors Bureau to order it.) The following are highlights and names and numbers to get you started.

How much time you have in Catalina will dictate what you should do. Consider taking a tour as you'll see more of the island. Both Catalina Adventure Tours, (310) 510-2888 and Discovery Tours, (310) 510-8687 offer numerous and diverse tours at comparable prices. (Prices quoted are from Adventure Tours.) Get acquainted with Catalina by taking a forty-five-minute, narrated city tour to see the Wrigley estate, the city streets, and an unparalleled view of the harbor while hearing about Catalina's history - $8 for adults, $6.50 for seniors, $4.25 for children ages 2 to 11. A longer city tour includes a stop at the Botanical Garden and Wrigley Memorial - a nice spot to walk along the pathways - about $15 for adults, $12 for seniors, $7.50 for children. The two-hour inner island tour is one of my favorites, although younger kids get antsy. You'll see canyons to coastlines; wild bison and maybe wild turkeys and foxes. A stop at Airport-in-the-Sky is good for stretching your legs, watching small planes land and take-off, and visiting the (free) Nature Center - $16.50 for adults, $14 for seniors, $8.75 for children. Adventure Tour offers a four-hour Land and Sea Tour that takes you all around the island by bus, including a stop over at the beach for an hour, then takes you back to Avalon by boat - $58 for adults, $50 for kids. Discovery Tours offers a narrated three-hour tour to see the Airport-in-the-Sky and to the Pacific side of Catalina where a visit to El Rancho Escondido, refreshments, and an Arabian horse performance are part of the deal - $29.50 for adults, $26 for seniors, $14.75 for kids. There are several cruise and water taxi options if you want to see Catalina from the water. (They usually run about $3 per person.)The two companies also offer forty-minute, narrated glass bottom boat rides, which are clearly one of the best ways to see the many varieties of fish and underwater gardens off the coast of Catalina. Aboard the Sea View, (Adventure Tours) you can even feed fish through specially designed tubes and watch the feeding frenzy. (It's just like the dinner table at home!) Night excursions are also available. Prices are about $8 for adults, $6.50 for seniors, and $4.25 for children.

The Undersea Tour (Discovery Tours) is given onboard a semi-submersible submarine - $21 for adults, $18 for seniors, $13 for children. Inquire about flying fish tours (yes, the fish really do fly) - and a cruise out to seal rock - each costing $8.50 for adults, $7.50 for seniors, $4.25 for children. Combo tour packages are available.

There are a myriad of water activities to choose, besides the obvious choice of swimming. Ocean Rafting Trips, (310) 510-0211, offers half-day and full-day voyages to explore coves, beaches, sea caves, and/or snorkeling, starting at $33 per person. (The raft ride itself is an adventure.) Take a guided kayak excursion with Catalina Island Expeditions, (310) 510-1226. A two-hour guided tour, which is really a natural history field trip, is two plus miles of kayaking - $34 for adults; $16.50 for children 11 years and under. Parasailing, (310) 510-1777, offers the thrill of flying (ten minutes air time) for $40 per person. The boat ride takes about an hour total and additional riders are $10 each.

Dryer, land activities are fun, too! Go on a guided horseback ride, via Catalina Stables, (310) 510-0478, through the mountains to see the unspoiled countryside, and a great view of Avalon. Children must have previous riding experience, and rides start at $20 for half-an-hour. Get it in gear and rent a bike at Brown's Bikes, (310) 510-0986, to explore the island. Take an open jeep tour, through the rugged inland, with Jeep Eco-Tours, (310) 510-2595, starting at $65 per person. Play a beautiful and challenging miniature golf course at (Miniature) Golf Gardens, (310) 510-1200 - $5.50 for adults; $3 for children 7 years and under. Arcade and video games can be found at Mardi Gras Arcade in the Metropole Market Place. They can also be found at Avalon Arcade, on the beach, along with pool and air hockey. There are two other noteworthy short stops: The small Catalina Island Interpretive Center, (310) 510-2514, which has mostly pictorial and informational displays, such as a marine mural with buttons to push to listen to whale sounds, a large kelp mural with text, and rocks that were found on the island. The Center is open daily 10am to 4pm, and admission is free. The Catalina Island Museum, (310) 510-2414, is located in the famous Casino building. (Take a tour of the building and admission to the museum is included). The museum has a wall with trophy fish such as Marlin; a few ship models; old operator switchboards; and informational and photographic displays of the island's history. It is open daily 10:30am to 4pm. Admission is $1.50 for adults; 50¢ for children 6 to 11 years old.

To really get away from it all, explore Catalina by hiking and/or camping. Seaside camp is at Two Harbors Campground, which is a quarter-mile from the small town of Two Harbors. The town is at the isthmus, down the coast quite a bit from Avalon. It's like being in another part of the world; a hidden paradise. This is one of the most popular camping sites because of its accessibility and water activities. Camping at a campsite is $8.50 per person; in a small cabin is $52 for four people; and inside a tepee is $66 for up to six people. Little Harbor Campground ($8.50 per person) is on the other side of the island from

Avalon. The campground is near two sandy beaches under small, but somewhat shady, palm trees. It is accessible by taking a shuttle bus. Blackjack Campground is situated among a grove of pine trees, away from the water, in the interior of the island. The surrounding area is great for hiking. Parson's Landing Campground is remote, located at the complete opposite end of the island from Avalon. Camping here costs $16.50 per person, and an additional $6 per person for water and firewood. It is beautiful, but mostly suitable for older kids who like to backpack. For more information and reservations regarding the above campgrounds, call Catalina Island Camping/Safari Shuttle service at (888) 510-7979. (The two-hour bus drive from Avalon to Two Harbors, for instance, is $18 one way.) Hermit Gulch Campground is the only campground in Avalon. Families can tent or tepee camp here. This is getting-away-from-it-all camping, but not too far away. With your own tent and other equipment, camping is $8.50 per person, per night. A six-person tepee or a small cabin is $25 a night, plus $8.50 per person. Reservations are always recommended, and are necessary in July and August. Call (310) 510-8368 for more information, and to make reservations.

Channel crossing time takes anywhere from one to two hours, depending on the point of departure and type of boat. Some places to call for cruise information, with various points of departure, are: *Catalina Channel Express*, (310) 519-1212, which departs from Long Beach Harbor and San Pedro. The just-over-one-hour cruise costs $36 for adults, $32 for seniors, $27 for ages 2 - 11. All-day parking is $7. *Catalina Cruises*, (213) 253-9800, departs from Long Beach Harbor. The hour-and-forty-five-minute cruise costs $25 for adults, $20 for ages 3 - 11, $2 for children 2 years and under. All-day parking is $7.50. *Catalina Passenger Service*, (714) 673-5245, departs from Balboa. The hour-and-fifteen-minute cruise costs $33 for adults, $30 for seniors, $16.50 for ages 3 - 12, $2 for children 2 years and under. All-day parking is $7. If time is of the essence, take a fifteen-minute helicopter ride with *Island Express Helicopter Service*, departing from Long Beach, (310) 510-2525 - $66 one way for all ages; or *Island Hopper/Catalina Airlines* airplane ride, departing from San Diego, (619) 279-4595 - $100 each way, with discounts offered for two or more people.

Admission: Prices given above.
   Ages: All

CLOSE ENCOUNTERS PAINT BALL   ☼
(213) 656-9179 - office; (805) 255-5332 - field   *$$$$$*
22400 The Old Road, Newhall

(EXIT GOLDEN STATE FWY [5] L. ON ROXFORD ST., UNDER THE FREEWAY TO THE DEAD END. TURN R. ON SEPULVEDA BLVD. AND FOLLOW IT ALONG THE FREEWAY FOR 1 MILE TO THE FIRST STOP SIGN. TURN L. ON SAN FERNANDO RD., WHICH TURNS INTO THE OLD ROAD. TRAVEL A LITTLE OVER 2 MILES AND ON THE RIGHT HAND SIDE ABOVE A RANCH, LOOK FOR IT, NOT NECESSARILY FOR THE ADDRESS. THE PLAYING FIELD IS ENCLOSED.)

Play this version of Capture the Flag while armed with markers (i.e. guns) filled with paint. This makes the game a bit more colorful! You'll be placed on one of two teams. A referee is on the playing field to help out. The object of the game is to get ther flag from your opponent's base, while dodging paintballs by hiding behind bunkers and trees. The mountainside is the perfect setting to play this rugged game. Each game lasts twenty minutes. After you're rested, go for another round. Food is available to purchase, or bring your own. Tip: Wear pants and other clothing you don't care about, and shoes with good traction. Getting hit stings, so wear a padded shirt or multiply layers to help absorb the hits.

Hours: Open Sat. - Sun., 8am - 4:30pm. to the general public. Groups of thirty or more can reserve play time during the week. All participating kids need a signed parental waiver.

Admission: $25 for all-day play, which includes a pistol, goggles, and face mask. There are two types of upgraded guns to rent - constant-air pump rifles at $20 a day or a semi-automatic, constant-air machine gun at $25, which includes free air refill. Paintballs cost $10 for 100 or $35 for 500. Call to inquire about discount packages for junior players, ages 10 - 15, such as a Ninja Special. This special includes all-day play, an air rifle, and 100 paintballs for $30.

Ages: 10 years and up.

EL PUEBLO DE LOS ANGELES HISTORICAL   ☼
MONUMENT (including OLVERA STREET)
(213) 628-1274 $$$
125 Paseo de la Plaza #400, Los Angeles
(GOING W. ON SANTA ANA FWY [101], EXIT N. ON ALAMEDA, L. ON PASEO DE LA PLAZA. GOING E. ON 101, EXIT N. ON LOS ANGELES ST., WHICH TURNS INTO PASEO DE LA PLAZA.)

This attraction is not a single monument, but the oldest part of the city of Los Angeles. It contains twenty-seven historic buildings, eleven of which are open to the public, (four are restored as museums), plus a traditional Mexican-style plaza, and Olvera Street. Tip: Read up a little on the history of this area, as it will make your visit here more meaningful.

The plaza is the central hub. Usually a docent is on hand giving out maps and other information. If not, check the Visitor's Center at

Sepulveda House, which is mentioned a few paragraphs down. The circular plaza has some interesting statues to look at. Across the way is the Firehouse Museum. Inside is a restored, old fire engine that was once hooked up to a horse. The walls are decorated with different fire hats. Next door is the Docent Center. This is the starting point for two free tours. One is a one-hour guided walking tour of the highlights of El Pueblo Monument. This is offered Tuesday through Saturday at 10am, 11am, noon, and 1pm. Reservations are required for groups, but not individuals. The second is a two-hour guided bus tour, for school-aged kids, covering the central city and points of historic interest. It starts at 10am on the first and third Wednesdays of each month. Reservations are required. Call (213) 628-1274 for more information, and to make reservations for tours.

Olvera Street is one of the oldest streets in Los Angeles. In 1930, it was closed to through traffic and reborn as a Mexican marketplace. It is very commercial and a definite tourist attraction, but it still conveys the flavor of old Mexico. Enjoy a walk down the brick-paved "street" to look at the colorful displays, watch a glassblower at work, see candles being dipped, hear strolling mariachi bands, and munch on bakery goods. There are inexpensive and expensive Mexican handicrafts to purchase both inside the stores and at the center stalls. Note: Kids love the variety of candy that is conveniently placed at their grabbing level.

Olvera Street offers four, full-service restaurants, a favorite one being La Luz del Dia located toward the entrance. Kids can climb the ornately tiled steps and peer into the kitchen to see tortillas being made by hand.

The Sepulveda House, which also houses the Visitor's Center, is a few doors down on the west side of Olvera Street. (You can also enter it from Main Street.) It has an encased display of Mrs. Sepulveda's bedroom and her kitchen as it appeared in the late 1800's. The small Visitors Center carries gift items, maps, etc. Inside a curtained room is an eighteen-minute film, "Pueblo of Promise" about the early history of Los Angeles. (My kids actually watched and enjoyed the movie.) The small gallery around the corner has some interesting artifacts from the area.

The Avila Adobe is located almost directly across from the Sepulveda House. This is the city's oldest building, constructed in 1818. It has rooms to walk through that reflect the style of a wealthy ranch owner in the 1840's. Some of the more interesting items include a child's bed that used rope and cowhide instead of box springs, a wooden bathtub, and a Chinese shawl that was used as a bedspread. The Courtyard, a packed-dirt patio, was used as a kitchen because most of the cooking was done outside. We enjoyed the side trip here, and learned a little along the way.

Enjoy soaking up the atmosphere of a different country while so close to home!

Hours: Olvera Street is open daily in the summer from 10am - 10pm; open the rest of the year from 10am - 7pm. The Sepulveda House is open Mon. - Sat. from 10am - 3pm. The Avila Adobe is open daily from 9am - 5pm. The Firehouse Museum is open Tues. - Sun., from 10am - 3pm.

Admission: The entrance to everything is free. Parking is available at a number of lots that charge between $5 - $10 for the day. The one on Main St., between Hope and Arcadia, charges $7.50 for the day. Some of them are quite a walk to the plaza.

Ages: 3 years and up in general; 7 years and up for the tours.

FOREST LAWN MEMORIAL PARK (Glendale)
(213) 254-3131   !

1712 South Glendale Avenue, Glendale
(FROM GLENDALE FWY [2], EXIT N. ON SAN FERNANDO RD, R. ON S. GLENDALE AVE. FROM GOLDEN STATE FWY [5], EXIT N. ON GLENDALE AVE, TURNS INTO BRAND BLVD., R. ON SAN FERNANDO RD., L. ON GLENDALE AVE.)

Most of the Forest Lawn Memorial Parks have outstanding works of art. This Forest Lawn features stained glass and oil paintings. The Hall of Crucifixion contains one of the largest religious oil painting ever created, 45-foot by 195-foot, titled "Crucifixion." The "Resurrection" painting is a close runner up for size, and impact, at fifty-one-feet by seventy-feet. The small, on-site museum contains stained glass pictures, coins mentioned in the Bible, and statues. Be sure to take your kids on a "tour" in the mausoleum to see a magnificent stained glass depiction of "The Last Supper."

Hours: The museum is open daily 10am - 5pm. The paintings and "The Last Supper" stained glass masterpiece can be seen on the half-hour and hour, respectively.

Admission: Free

Ages: 5 years and up.

FOREST LAWN MEMORIAL PARK (Hollywood Hills)
(818) 241-4151   !

6300 Forest Lawn Drive, Los Angeles
(EXIT VENTURA FWY [134] S. ON FOREST LAWN DR. IT'S W. OF GRIFFITH PARK.)

A cemetery might seem like an odd addition to this book, but Forest Lawn has several impressive art pieces and tributes to American history. There is a huge memorial and statue of George Washington, as well as larger-than-life commemorations of Abraham Lincoln and Thomas Jefferson. A 30-foot by 165-foot tiled mosaic graces the outside of the Hall of Liberty building. The colorful, chronological, mosaic scenes of freedom depict the surrender of General Cornwallis, the crossing of the Delaware, Betsy Ross making the flag, and the signing of the Declaration of Independence. Inside is a replica of the Liberty Bell, models of famous early Americans in period costumes, and a continuously running film regarding the founding of our country called "The Birth of Liberty." The small Museum of Mexican History is adjacent to the Hall of Liberty. It contains pictures, statues, models, clothing, and artifacts from Mayan, Aztec, and other Indian and Mexican cultures. (Check out FOREST LAWN, Glendale.)

Hours: Open daily from 9am - 6pm. It is closed during private services.

Admission: Free.

Ages: 6 years and up.

ISLE OF REDONDO   ☼

(310) 372-2111 - Redondo Sport Fishing $$$$

233 N. Harbor Drive, Redondo Beach

(EXIT SAN DIEGO FWY [405] S. ON WESTERN, R. ON 190TH ST., WHICH TURNS INTO ANITA ST., L. ON PACIFIC COAST HIGHWAY, R. ON TORRANCE BLVD TO THE END.)

This isle or island, located only a mile-and-a-half off Redondo Beach, is a 120-foot by 60-foot, deep sea fishing barge. It's anchored over two fishing reefs with a catamaran hull, and twin center wells for fishing in the middle of the barge, as well as around the sides. For those who like the gentle rocking motion of being on a boat, you'll feel it out here, too.

You supply the fishing pole (though rentals are available), sunscreen, a chair, and a cooler for your catches. The Isle will provide you with live bait and the twenty-minute boat ride out here and back.

The catch of the day (or night) could include mackerel, barracuda, bass, halibut, etc. If you're working up an appetite from reeling in all the fish, the Isle has a full galley that offers main meals and snack food. (And yes, there are bathrooms out here, too.) Night fishing is available during the balmy summer months. Bring your camera to capture your child's fishing endeavors and the spectacular sunsets.

Hours: Open mid-May through the end of October, daily from 7am - 4:30pm. Extended summer hours are 6pm - 4:30am. Boats leave from the fishing pier to the barge and back every hour. Closed November through mid-April, but call for information on whale-watching tours.

Admission: $17 for adults; $11 for kids 12 years and under. If you depart for the Isle in the late afternoon and want to stay for a night fishing session, it is an additional $10 fee.

Ages: 5 years and up.

MRS. NELSON'S TOY AND BOOK SHOP   ☼

(909) 599-4558   !/$

1030 Bonita Avenue, La Verne

(EXIT FOOTHILL FWY [210] E. ON BONITA AVE.)

Mrs. Nelson has a delightful selection of books, and educational toys, games, puzzles, tapes, and arts and craft supplies. Storytelling, followed by a related craft, is offered on Tuesdays at 10am, and again on Saturdays at 11am, unless a special program is going on. A few times a year, you are invited to bring your picnic blankets and enjoy a free sing-along or dance-along concert. Sign up to receive a quarterly newsletter that gives dates and times for these activities as well as workshop information, author book signings, etc.

Hours: Open Mon. - Thurs. and Sat., 9am - 6pm; Fri., 9am - 7pm; Sun., 11am - 5pm.

Ages: 2 years and up.

ROSE HILLS MEMORIAL PARK

(562) 699-0921

3900 S. Workman Mill Road, Whittier

(EXIT SAN GABRIEL RIVER FWY [605] E. ON ROSE HILLS RD., L. ON WORKMAN MILL RD. TO THE EAST PARK.)

This is one of the world's largest memorial parks. The east park features a three-and-a-half-acre Pageant of Roses Garden with more than 750 varieties. We enjoyed their fragrance as well as their names: Iceberg, The Doctor, Las Vegas, Confetti, Mister Lincoln, Summer Fashion, etc. The west park has a small traditional Japanese garden with a meditation house, lake, and a bridge that add to the serene beauty. Again, as with FOREST LAWN, perhaps this is an odd addition to this book, but it is an enjoyable (and different) place to go.

Hours: Open daily from 8am - 5pm.

Admission: Free

Ages: 4 years and up.

THE SEA

(310) 831-1694

305 N. Harbor Boulevard, San Pedro

(EXIT HARBOR FWY [110] S. ON HARBOR BLVD.)

Sally might sell seashells by the seashore, but this store, The Sea, sells seashells and then some! It rightly promotes itself as a museum-like store. Out front are giant wooden sailor figures and an upside down boat (part of the entrance sign), plus lots of other maritime artifacts.

Inside, a whale skeleton hangs overhead, as do other sea models. I almost lost the kids in the overwhelming array of nautical treasures to see and buy. There are all kinds of sea-oriented gifts, plus bins and bins of seashells, starfish, and beads to gently sort through. What do you do when your child wants to buy some of these items, but doesn't know what to do with them? Take a look at all of the sea "art" in the store, then purchase the shells, and such, to create his/her own masterpiece, or simply make a beach collage.

The Sea is a beachcomber's haven, without getting sandy!

Hours: Open Mon. - Fri., 9:30am - 5pm; Sat. - Sun., 9:30am - 6pm.
Admission: Free, but bring spending money.
Ages: 4 years and up.

STORYOPOLIS

(310) 358-2500   !/$

116 N. Robertson Boulevard, Plaza A, Los Angeles
(EXIT SANTA MONICA FWY [10] N. ON ROBERTSON. STORYOPOLIS IS ON THE E. SIDE
OF THE STREET, IN THE PLAZA, JUST N. OF 3ᴿᴰ ST.)

This unique store offers a perfect way to introduce children to art and to encourage a love of reading. Half of Storyopolis exhibits original art work by illustrators of children's books. The art is displayed at kids' eye level. Each book, from which the illustrations were inspired, is on a stand in front of its appropriate picture(s). My 7 year-old budding artist and I first read excerpts from the book and then matched the framed art work to illustrations in the book. He said it gave him the idea to write and illustrate his own book so that, "Maybe people can see my work here, too."

The other half of the medium-sized store has a cozy reading area and a terrific selection of children's books, with an emphasis on the arts. Storyopolis regularly hosts children's story-times, craft projects, author-signings, presentations, and special events. Call for a schedule of events.

Hours: Open Mon. - Sat., 10am - 6pm; Sun., 11am - 4pm.
Admission: Free
Ages: 4 years and up.

TREE PEOPLE / COLDWATER CANYON PARK

(818) 753-4600   !

12601 Mulholland Drive, Beverly Hills
(EXIT VENTURA FWY [101] S. ON COLDWATER CYN AVE., MERGES WITH
MULHOLLAND DR. NEAR PARK.)

Ever feel like our lease as earth's caretakers is up for renewal? And we might not get the contract because we haven't done a very good job? If you and your kids are concerned about environmental issues, come visit the Tree People. In a garage-type building, the Recycling Education Center shows how plastic, glass, and aluminum can be reused and recycled into clothing, fiberfill, etc. Kids can turn a crank to see a beautiful canyon transformed into a dirty landfill. Practical recycling tips are shown by neighbors Dirty and Desperate who create waste by throwing out everything, versus Clean and Cool who recycle everything possible and are earth-conscious shoppers. Visit the small garden and the next exhibit building to see an urban forest map, nests, eggs, a photo display on bees, and even a little stage for putting on *tree*mendous productions. The adjacent compost pile is smelly, but a fascinating resource tool. Guided tours include more in-depth information about conservation, as well as the importance of planting trees in areas damaged by pollution.

Coldwater Canyon Park is beautiful, with large oak and California Bay Laurel trees shading the meandering trails. Most of the five miles of hiking trails are covered with sawdust and small broken twigs (making it bumpy for strollers). Picnic tables are available towards the park entrance.

Hours: The park is open daily. Call to make a reservation for a Tree People tour.

Admission: The park is free, and the tours are usually free, too.

Ages: 6 years and up.

UNIVERSAL CITYWALK   ☼

(818) 622-4455 $$

Universal Center Drive, Universal City

(EXIT HOLLYWOOD FWY [101] N. AT UNIVERSAL CENTER DR. IT'S RIGHT NEXT TO UNIVERSAL STUDIOS.)

CityWalk is an outdoor mall built in theme-park style with fantastic stores, unique restaurants, and unusual entertainment. Everything here, from the larger-than-life neon signs to the oversized, Disneylandish-decorated storefronts is done with spectacular Hollywood flair, and that's just the outside of the buildings! On weekend nights, live entertainment, like jugglers and magicians, add to the carnival-like atmosphere.

Listed here are some of the outstanding attractions along the walkway: •Outside the **Hard Rock Cafe**, is a gigantic neon guitar. Inside this restaurant dedicated to the preservation of rock 'n roll, is a car spinning on a pedestal in the middle, while guitars, costumes, posters, and personal items from famed musicians decorate the walls. •Across the way from the Cafe is an eighteen-screen movie theater, which also has **Cinemania**, a simulator ride. Shake, rattle, and roll your way through a five-minute ride of Cosmic Pinball, the Devil's Mineride, etc. Cinemania is open during the week from 2pm to 11pm and on weekends from noon to 11pm. Kids must be 42", and each ride costs $5. •**Lighthouse Beach** is an outdoor snack bar (fish 'n chips - $9.95, cheeseburgers - $5.95, chili cheese fries - $3.95) with tables in the sand. Kick off your shoes 'cause "life's a beach." •**Sam Goody** has a giant neon gorilla (think King-Kong) hanging on its sign. Inside, kids like the constant music, the enormous wall posters, going up the grated stairs to the Coffee Cafe, walking over the bridge, and checking out the mini-museum that has signed Beatles photos, a Judy Garland letter, record plaques, and costumes of famous performers. •Look out for the water fountain in the center circle of CityWalk, where water descends from the roof as well as spouts up at unexpected times. •Two terrific kids' bookstores, **Upstart Crows Nest** and **Golden Showcase**, are decorated as you dream a (really large) children's room should look like. •**Hollywood Freez Way** draws people with Hagen Daz ice cream, and its entrance sign of a front end of a car crashed upside down through the wall. •**P. T. Copperpot** is an old-fashioned confectionery with everything sweet imaginable. •**Things From Another World** has the back half of a spaceship, which is emitting smoke, that has landed on its storefront. •Watch the ocean in motion outside **The Wave** store. Whew - the extravagant gimmicks alone are worth the price of parking! •An outdoor ice-skating rink is here November through February. Other months, concerts and other special events are offered. • See **COUNTRY STAR** restaurant, which is located at the end of CityWalk, under EDIBLE ADVENTURES.

You can experience practically all of Hollywood at CityWalk; all at one time! Note: Weekend nights are a bit overwhelming for younger children.

Hours: Most stores and restaurants are open Sun. - Thurs., 11am - 9pm; Fri. - Sat., 11am - 11pm.
Admission: Free. The parking lot, which is shared by Universal Studios, is $6.
Ages: 2 years and up.

WAYFARERS CHAPEL
(310) 377-1650
5755 Palos Verdes Drive South, Palos Verdes
(EXIT SAN DIEGO FWY [405] S. ON CRENSHAW BLVD., AND STAY ON THIS STREET INTO PALOS VERDES; TURN R. ON CREST RD., L. ON HAWTHORNE TO THE END, L. ON PALOS VERDES. IT'S ABOUT 2 MILES ON THE L.)

This unique, relatively small church, is nicknamed the "Glass Church" and built almost entirely of glass and stone. It is nestled in some overgrown trees and looks to be almost a part of them. It was designed by Lloyd Wright, son of Frank Lloyd Wright. The church is built on a bluff overlooking the Pacific Ocean, surrounded by redwoods and gardens. The chapel is unique and charming, and the landscaping is beautiful. (This is a short sto, so see POINT VINCENTE INTERPRETATIVE CENTER, REDONDO PIER, or SOUTH COAST BOTANICAL GARDENS for other things to do.)

Hours: Open daily from 9am - 5pm. (Church functions take precedence over tours.)
Admission: Free
Ages: 5 years and up.

WESTERN TOWN / SAN DIMAS ANTIQUE DISTRICT
(909) 592-8888 - Ghost Rider Trader Co.
235 W. Bonita Avenue, San Dimas
(GOING S. ON FOOTHILL FWY [210], EXIT E. ON ARROW, QUICK L. ON BONITA. GOING N. ON 210, EXIT E. ON BONITA. IT'S JUST N. OF FRANK G. BONELLI PARK.)

"Western Town" is not an official title of this area, but if the boot fits . . . . This small section of San Dimas, which encompasses twelve or so stores, looks like an old western town. The storefronts are done up "right fine" and the wooden sidewalk adds to the atmosphere.

One of our favorite stops here is the Ghost Rider Trading Co./ Wild West Museum. This small store sells a variety of authentic western wear and gear, from clothing and spur straps to badges and cowboy books. Judging by the people coming in here, I'd say it does a good job of catering to cowboys. The "museum" displays posters, guns, and other western items interspersed throughout the store. You can take an "old-time" photo of your family here, too.

Another fun place to check out at Western Town is the Train Stop. This huge store (the address is 211, 213, and 215 Bonita Ave.) is engineered to fulfill your every train need or want. A model train can be seen coming around the mountains from the street window. Western Town is not necessarily an ultimate destination, but it is a colorful side trip.

Hours: Most stores are open Mon. - Sat. from 10am - 5:30pm.
Admission: Free
Ages: 3 years and up.

DISNEYLAND HOTEL

(714) 956-6425

1150 W. Cerritos Avenue, Anaheim

(GOING S. ON SANTA ANA FWY [5], EXIT W. ON BALL RD., L. ON WEST ST., R. ON CERRITOS. GOING N. ON 5, EXIT W. ON KATELLA, R. ON WEST ST., L. ON CERRITOS. IT'S ACROSS THE STREET AND ON W. SIDE OF DISNEYLAND.)

If a day at the "Magic Kingdom" doesn't fit into your budget or energy level, come spend an hour or two at the magic hotel. One section of the lobby contains a collection of Disney memorabilia, while around the corner is a huge wall collage displaying trinkets from Disneyland's past. (Remember "E" ride tickets?)

A world of Disney delights are in the back courtyard, including pedal boat rentals at the Harbor Pavilion - $5 for a twenty-minute ride, open only during the day; a video arcade (underneath the Pavilion) that is open daily from 8am to midnight; remote-controlled boats for kids to steer around a replica of the Queen Mary - $2 a mini-voyage. (My kids, bless their inexpensive little hearts, had a good time just spinning the steering wheels around.) Further back, remote-controlled race cars are $2 a race. Want to indulge in the sweeter pleasures of life? Stop for an ice-cream cone at Castle Sundries - $1.75 for a single scoop.

The eastern part of the hotel complex has shops filled with every kind of Disney paraphernalia imaginable. A real treat for your kids is a meal at GOOFY'S KITCHEN, described under EDIBLE ADVENTURES. Enjoy a mini-adventure by taking the monorail round trip from the hotel through Tomorrowland and back, for $3 per person, kids under 2 years are free. Make sure to tell your children that you're not stopping in Disneyland.

Meander back to one of my favorite attractions on the hotel grounds - the waterfalls. Your kids will thrill at walking down the stony steps (this part is not stroller accessible), and going behind the waterfalls! It does get loud down here for younger ones because of the roar of the waterfall, and it is a little wet, as it's real water (not animated) that spritzes the pathways. After sunset, the underwater lights turn the waterfalls into a rainbow of cascading colors. Back on the surface, check out the koi pond. Call the hotel to find out what time the koi feedings are.

At 9pm and 10pm during the spring and summer, and usually at 7pm and 8pm the rest of the year (call to verify times), experience the highlight of a nocturnal visit to the hotel - a free, twenty-minute, Fantasy Water show, located by the fish pond. The dramatically lit water fountains dance, sway, and pulsate to classic and rock versions of Disney tunes. During summer nights, from this same spot, at 9:35pm, look between the hotel buildings to see a dazzling fireworks display put on by Disneyland Park; a terrific way to end your evening with a bang!

Hours: The hotel is open daily.
Admission: Parking is $2 per hour; $15 maximum. Validation at Goofy's Kitchen or other restaurants will save you a few dollars.
Ages: All

DOLL CITY U.S.A.
(714) 750-3585
2080 South Harbor Boulevard, Anaheim
(EXIT SANTA ANA FWY [5] S. ON HARBOR OR GARDEN GROVE FWY [22] N. ON HARBOR. IT IS THE 3RD SIGNAL S. OF DISNEYLAND.)

This is an interesting store and worth visiting if you have a doll buff in the family. There are hundreds of dolls and accessories here, ranging from $3.99 - $15,000. There are dolls for the serious collector, or for anyone who just needs "someone" to hug.

Hours: Open Mon. - Sat. from 10am - 6pm.
Ages: 2½ years and up.

HOBBY CITY
(714) 527-2323
1238 S. Beach Boulevard, Anaheim
(EXIT ARTESIA FWY [91] S. ON BEACH BLVD. OR EXIT GARDEN GROVE FWY [22] N. ON BEACH BLVD. IT'S 2 MILES S. OF KNOTT'S BERRY FARM.)

Twenty-three different hobby, craft, and collector's shops are located in this one area, along with a restaurant, a Doll Museum (see DOLL AND TOY MUSEUM) and an amusement park just for young kids (see ADVENTURE CITY). Hobby City is very kid-friendly - there is even a small picnic area here.

Some of the more kid-oriented shops include the Cabbage Patch Shop, The Bear Tree (in the shape of a tree trunk), Prestige Hobbies & Models (airplanes, ships, cars, etc.), The Little Depot (for all your model train needs and wants), The American Indian Store, Baseball Card Shop, Miniatures, Stamps, Coins, and Treasure Cove (for those hard to find craft supplies).

Hours: Most stores are open daily from 10am - 6pm.

Ages: 3 years and up.

HUNTINGTON BEACH CENTRAL LIBRARY and CULTURAL CENTER

(714) 842-4481

7111 Talbert Avenue, Huntington Beach

(GOING N. ON SAN DIEGO FWY [405] EXIT N. ON EUCLID ST., L. ON TALBERT AVE. GOING S. ON 405 EXIT S. ON BEACH BLVD, R. ON TALBERT AVE.)

When is a library more than just a place to peruse books? When it is the Huntington Beach Central Library! This multi-level facility is delightful to visit. Kids are captivated by the huge center fountain inside and the spiraling paved walkway that encircles it. The fountain is loud, especially on the lower level, in contrast to the normal quiet tones associated with a library. The bottom floor has vending machines and tables and chairs for eating, reading, and/or studying. Look up and see returned books being transferred to be re-shelved via a metal conveyor belt. (Only kids notice this sort of thing.)

One side of the main floor has an incredible number of books organized on several levels within the library. A map is available to help you find your topic of interest. There are even a few small art galleries in this wing.

Just outside the Children's Room is a circular aquarium (look for the eel). The Children's Room has a large selection of books. It also contains a reading area, a toddler's section, a wooden frame of a boat for tots to play in, and a big screen monitor that intermittently shows children's films. The adjacent Tabby Storytime Theater, which is used for storytelling events, and a media/computer room make this library complete. Pick up a calendar listing of children's events, or call (714) 375-5107 for children's programing information.

The Huntington Beach Playhouse, or Central Library Theater, is located on the lower level. Several performances throughout the year are given, such as marionette and puppet shows, and musicals. Call (714) 375-0696 for show information.

HUNTINGTON CENTRAL PARK surrounds the library. Directly behind the library is a trail leading down to a pond. Acres of trails, rolling green hills, shade trees, and picnic areas are all here to enhance your day. For summertime fun, check out ADVENTURE PLAYGROUND, just up the hill from the library.

Hours: The library is open Mon., 1pm - 9pm; Tues. - Thurs., 9am - 9pm; Fri - Sat., 9am - 5pm. Call for hours for special events, and for the shows.
Admission: Free to the library, although it is $25 a year if you are a non-resident and want to check books out. Ticket prices for shows vary; they are usually between $7 - $15.
Ages: All

RIVERSIDE VISITOR CENTER (and surrounding area)

(909) 684-4636   !

3720 Main Street, Riverside

(GOING S.W. ON RIVERSIDE FWY [91], EXIT W. ON 7TH ST./MISSION INN AVE. GOING N.W. ON 91, EXIT W. ON UNIVERSITY AVE., R. ON ORANGE ST., L. ON 7TH ST./MISSION INN AVE. 7TH ST. WAS RENAMED MISSION INN AVE. THE CENTER IS LOCATED ACROSS THE STREET FROM THE MISSION INN.)

The Visitor Center is a hub of information with maps, brochures, and special event listings. It also has some wonderful, rotating exhibits pertaining to local history. We saw "Centuries of Sunshine" which depicted citrus history through photographs, videos, a crate label display, the citrus time line, citrus genealogy, a Ford Huckster (which was used as a delivery truck), and, of course, lots of oranges. It was interesting as well as informative.

Just outside the Visitor Center is the pedestrian walkway, lined with shops and eateries. (We zeroed in on McDonald's, and then T.C.B.Y. for rainbow ice-cream.) Walk around here to begin your visit of the museums and other places of interest in Riverside. If you're looking for a fun, free way to get around downtown Riverside, hop aboard the old-time Orange Blossom Express trolley car. The cars run daily, every five minutes, along Main Street, Mission Inn Avenue, and Vine Street. You can pick up a route map at the Visitor Center, or just look for trolley stop signs. Call (909) 682-1234 for more information about the trolley.

Hours: Open Mon. - Fri., 9am - 5pm; Sat. - Sun., 10am - 5pm.
Admission: Free
Ages: 2 years and up.

CALICO GHOST TOWN

(800) TO CALICO (862-2542) $$$$

36600 Ghost Town Road, Yermo

(EXIT 15 N. ON GHOST TOWN RD (ABOUT 10 MILES E. OF BARSTOW). THERE ARE PLENTY OF SIGNS TO DIRECT YOU.)

Once upon a time, a rich vein of silver was found in a mine underneath some multi-colored mountains. Word about the strike spread like wildfire, and pretty soon there were 5,000 people, of twenty different nationalities, living in and around this mining town. The town was called "Calico" because the varied minerals that created the

different colors of the mountains were "purty as a gal's Calico skirt."
Between 1882 and 1907, the 500 mine claims produced eighty-six
million dollars worth of silver and forty-five million dollars worth of
borax. Then, the price of silver dropped. And the boom town went bust.
Thankfully, the story doesn't end here. In the 1950's, the town was
restored.

Nowadays, this authentic western town has twenty-three unique
shops and restaurants (including an ice cream parlor) on both sides of
the wide, dirt, main road that snakes up the mountain - put your walking
shoes on. Some of the current shops are even housed in original
buildings. Topping our list of favorite shops are the rock and fossil shop,
the leather works, and an 1890's general store.

There are several other attractions here. Shoot, gun fights break
out every hour on the half hour starting at 10:30am. Visit the re-created
schoolhouse at the end of the road and an authentically-dressed
schoolmarm will gladly teach your kids what going to school was like in
the olden days. There is a sturdy wooden teeter-totter and swing
outside the schoolhouse. If you want to know more about the town's
history, take a free guided tour offered daily at 10am, noon, and 2pm.
The Mystery Shack is a small house of optical illusions where water
rolls uphill, a broom stands up at an angle without falling over, etc.
before you walk through Maggie Mine, a real silver mine look at the
mining tools on display, such as a stamp mill, ore cart, re-created assay
office, and more. Just inside the mine is a display of rocks and minerals
mined from these parts, including flourescent ones that glow in neon
colors when the lights are turned off. Take a short walk through the
mine, which has mannequin miners in action and audio explanations of
the mining process. The Odessa Railroad is just an eight-minute train
ride on a narrow-gauge railcar that takes you around part of a mountain
where you'll see small cave-like openings that were front doors to
miners' homes. You'll learn that the huge pile of "tailing" from the Silver
King Mine still contains six million dollars worth of silver ore, but would
cost nine million dollars to process. Oh well! Sharpshooters can test
their skill at the shooting gallery, and gold diggers can pan for real gold.
Look at and into the house made of bottles - it's the ultimate in
recycling. Call for a schedule of special events, such as a Civil War
Reenactment (President's Day Weekend), Hullabaloo Festival (Palm
Sunday weekend), Calico Days (Columbus Day Weekend), etc. Oh,
and do explain to your kids that the term, "Ghost Town" doesn't mean
that there are ghosts here, simply that the town went from being
inhabited to being deserted.

Tent, RV, or cabin camping is available just below the town. The
sites are small, but the surrounding area makes it especially attractive
for kids because there are (small) caves all over. In fact, seeing and
even going into a few caves, was one of the things my children liked
best about Calico. If you have a four-wheel drive vehicle, head for the
hills to explore some of the hiking trails (and mineral deposits) in this
area.

Hours: Open daily from 9am - 5pm. Closed Christmas.
Admission: Entrance is $6 for adults; $3 for ages 6 - 15; children 5 years and under are free. Annual family passes are $20. The Mystery Shack and Odessa Railroad train ride are each $2.25 for adults; $1.25 for ages 6 - 15; children 5 years and under are free. A walking through Maggie's Mine is $1 per person. Gold panning is $1 per person. The Shooting Gallery is $1 for 20 shots. The schoolhouse, shootouts, guided tours, and tram ride up the hill from the parking lot, are free.
Ages: All

ARCO OLYMPIC TRAINING CENTER   ☼

(619) 482-6222   !

1750 Wueste Road, Chula Vista
(EXIT SAN DIEGO FWY [5] E. ON "L" ST., WHICH TURNS INTO TELEGRAPH CANYON RD., WHICH TURNS INTO OTAY LAKES RD. TURN S. ON WUESTE RD.)

This incredibly beautiful facility is nestled in a mountain range by the blue waters of Otay Lakes. The 150-acre campus is the training grounds for future Olympians (and other athletes) as they prepare for the thrill of victory. Throughout the day, the Visitor's Center shows a free six-minute video, plus a longer twenty-minute film titled "Once In A Lifetime." The movies are great motivators to get you in the spirit of the Olympic games! The gift shop is first class. Free guided tours of the facility are offered, or just take a detailed map and stroll along the paved Olympic Path on your own. The path slices through the center of the facility. It is elevated so you get a bird's eye view of the sports being played on both sides, including soccer, field hockey, tennis, track and field, cycling, and archery. Water sports, such as rowing, canoeing, and kayaking can also be observed from this vantage point. Visitors are asked to stay on the path, which is nine-tenths of a mile each way, as it winds through the training center.

Future sport venues in development are an aquatics center; a gymnasium for volleyball, basketball, and other indoor sports; and baseball diamonds. The facility also has athlete housing, an athlete dining area, a medical facility, etc. Call ahead to see what athletes are currently training here because seeing them in action makes the center come alive!

Hours: Open Mon. - Sat., 9am - 4pm; Sun., noon - 5pm.
Admission: Free
Ages: 6 years and up.

CABRILLO NATIONAL MONUMENT   ☼

(619) 557-5450 $

At the southern end of Point Loma on Cabrillo Memorial Dr., San Diego
(TAKE OCEAN BEACH FWY [8] TO THE END, L. ON SUNSET CLIFFS BLVD, L. ON NIMITZ BLVD., S. ON 209. FOLLOW THE SIGNS.)

In 1542 Juan Rodriguez Cabrillo sailed into San Diego Bay and claimed it for Spain. A huge statue of Cabrillo, commemorating his epic voyage along the western coast of the U.S., resides on the tip of the peninsula at this national park. Press the button near the monument to hear the history of Cabrillo and the bay area.

Older kids will appreciate the exhibit hall in the building behind the monument. Displays include maps and drawings of the areas Cabrillo and other explorers "discovered"; lots of written information; examples of food eaten on board ship like dried fish, hardtack, etc.; and ship models. The adjacent Visitor's Center offers pamphlets, film programs, and guided walks regarding this area, plus a book shop and an incredible view.

Before walking out to Point Loma Lighthouse, which was used from 1855 to 1891, listen to its history by pressing an outside storyboard button. (We listened to it in Japanese and German as well as English - just for the fun of it.) Kids think it's great to actually climb up the spiral staircase inside the refurbished lighthouse. The odd-shaped bedrooms are fully furnished with period furniture and knickknacks, as is the small living room, kitchen, and dining room. The entrance to the top floor is closed by a grate, but you can look through it and see the huge light that was a beacon to so many sailors.

Take the Bayside Trail, about three kilometers round trip, to walk further out to the point. Along the way look for remnants of a coastal artillery system used during both world wars. The trail goes down through a coastal sage scrub "forest." Topside of the trail, behind plexiglass, is a whale overlook. From late December through March, catch a glimpse of the gray whales during their annual migration southward. Audio information is, again, available at the touch of a button. (This time we listened to explanations in French and English.) Even if you don't see a whale, the view is spectacular.

From this viewpoint, look down to see the rocky marine environment of the tidepools. (There is a driveable road leading down to them.) Check with a park ranger for dates and times of low tides. Exploring tidepools is always a wondrous adventure for my kids. See and touch (but don't bring home) sea stars, anemones, limpets, and be on the lookout for crabs and even octopus. Tip: Be sure to bring your camera, wear rubber-soled shoes (the rocks get slippery), and keep a close eye on your little ones!

Hours: Open daily from 9am - 5:15pm.
Admission: $5 per vehicle; seniors are free.
Ages: 3 years and up.

GEMS OF PALA MINERAL SHOP ☀
(760) 742-1356 $$
Magee Road, Pala
(Exit Escondido Fwy [15] E. on Route 76, just past the cut-off to the town of Pala, L. on Magee Rd. Near corner of Pala & Magee.)

Located on the Pala Indian Reservation, the Gems of Pala offers a flawless selection of rocks and minerals. Both raw and polished emeralds, amethyst, opals, tourmaline, and more, can be found inside this small store. Outside, large bins hold chunks of rocks for sale. The gemstones come mostly from the nearby Stewart Mine, as well as from other mines all over the world. You can no longer go into the mine, but it is still worked regularly, and buckets of mine run are sold at the store. Purchase a two or five gallon bucket to dump and sift through on tables just outside the store, or at home. (First, watch a four-minute video that tells you how to do it, and what to look for.) Kids will be delighted with almost anything they find, although the "jackpot" is finding tourmaline. This precious stone comes in a rainbow of colors, with pink being the rarest, thus the most highly prized, color. The mine also produces kunzite, morganite, lepidolite, etc. (The store owners can answer any rock-related questions you may have.) Whether you come to browse or buy, your rock-lovers will appreciate the variety of minerals on display. Call first to make sure mine run is available, if this is your goal.

Hours: The store is open Thurs. - Sun. from 10am - 4pm.

Admission: Buckets of mine run cost $10, $25, or $50 per, depending on where it was extracted within the mine. Other rocks and minerals are sold at various prices.

Ages: 3 years and up.

HOTEL DEL CORONADO   ☽

(800) HOTEL DEL (468-3533) $$

1500 Orange Avenue, Coronado

(EXIT SAN DIEGO FWY [5] W. ON 75 AND CROSS OVER THE CORONADO BRIDGE, L. ON ORANGE AVE. THE TOLL IS $1 TO CORONADO AND THE RETURN TRIP IS FREE. IF YOU ARE CAR POOLING, CROSS THE BRIDGE USING THE RIGHT LANE, AT NO CHARGE.)

I don't normally mention hotels as an outing to take your children, but the "Hotel Del" is an exception. Just the outside of this architectural marvel will elicit a few "wows" from your family. Built in 1888, it is one of the most luxurious and celebrated buildings in the world, as well as one of the largest wooden structures in existence. The dark, wooden interior of the hotel is equally impressive and ornate. Tell your kids that this was the first hotel in the world to have electric lights. If that doesn't turn them on, be a name dropper and mention that none other than Thomas Edison supervised the installation of the lights.

You may walk around the elegant hotel completely on your own; take a forty-five minute, self-guided audio cassette tour for $5 (per person, as the tape player comes with headphones); or sign up for a one-hour guided tour at $10 per person. Your family will learn about the hotel's intriguing history, including the story of the haunted room. Note: Your children *will* ask if they can stay at the hotel. It's worth it if you can afford it, as each of the 692 rooms are unique, especially the 400 historic rooms. Rates start at $185 a night. The food is outstanding, the surroundings are lush, the pool is crystal clear, the stretch of beach is

incredibly beautiful, the tennis courts are great, etc. Also see
CORONADO BEACH HISTORICAL MUSEUM and HOTEL DEL
CORONADO - TEA TIME.

Hours: Come during the week if possible, as weekends are
crowded. Audio tape tours are available daily from 6am -
5pm. Guided tours are offered Thurs. - Sat. at 10am and
11am.

Admission: $5 per person for an audio tape tour; $10 per person
(ages 3 years and up) for a guided tour. Parking in the
hotel lot costs $2.50 per hour; street parking is free.

Ages: 6 years and up.

LA JOLLA CAVE AND SHELL SHOP

(619) 454-6080 $

1325 Coast Boulevard, La Jolla

*(EXIT SAN DIEGO FWY [5] W. ON LA JOLLA VILLAGE DR., L. ON TORREY PINES RD.,
R. ON PROSPECT PL., R. ON COAST BLVD.)*

The La Jolla Cave and Shell Shop has bins of sea treasures such
as sea stars, sea horses, sand dollars, and all different kinds, sizes,
and shapes of shells. The prices are conducive to purchasing the items
to make your own jewelry, an ocean collage, etc. There are also, of
course, "finished" items to buy.

One of the main attractions in the shop is the staircase in the center
that leads down to a cave. Once in the small cave, the only things to
see are a view of the ocean through the cave opening, and crabs
crawling around on the rocks below. The trip up and down the 145
wooden steps, which get slippery toward the bottom, was the primary
adventure. My boys were excited to tell everyone that they were inside
a real sea cave, though, so it was worth it.

Hours: The shop and cave are open Mon. - Sat., 10am - 5pm;
Sun., 11am - 5pm.

Admission: A walk down to the cave costs $1.50 for adults; 75¢ for
children 3 - 11 years.

Ages: 4 years and up.

LA JOLLA COVE

Coast Boulevard, La Jolla   !

*(EXIT SAN DIEGO FWY [5] W. ON LA JOLLA VILLAGE DR., L. ON TORREY PINES RD.,
R. ON PROSPECT PL., R. ON COAST BLVD.)*

In this beautiful seaside city is a wonderful cove, which is a favorite
spot for exploring tidepools, and watching or participating in some great
surfing, snorkeling, scuba diving, and swimming. The cove is located
near the LA JOLLA CAVE AND SHELL SHOP and the SEAL ROCK
MARINE MAMMAL RESERVE.

Hours: Open daily.

Admission: Free

Ages: All

SAN DIEGO BAY FERRY / OLD FERRY LANDING   ◑

(619) 234-4111 $$

1050 North Harbor Drive, Broadway Pier in downtown San Diego, and The Ferry Landing Marketplace, Coronado

(GOING S. ON SAN DIEGO FWY [5], EXIT W. ON ASH ST., L. ON 4TH, R. ON BROADWAY TO END. GOING N. ON 5, EXIT S. ON 6TH AVE., R. ON BROADWAY TO END.)

Take a fifteen-minute ride over to Coronado (and back) on the San Diego Bay Ferry. Enjoy the Ferry Landing Marketplace on the Coronado side with its Victorian-style shopping and eating complex. Bike, blade, or walk along the waterfront paved pathways. You can also romp in the grassy lawns along the pathways, or sunbathe on the beach. A farmer's market is held on the island on Tuesdays from 2:30pm to 6pm. See HOTEL DEL CORONADO for things to do on Coronado Island. If you want to go directly to the hotel, take the Coronado trolley, (619) 427-6438, from the landing. It runs approximately every hour from 9:20am to 6pm, with a few stops along the way. The trolley costs 50¢ a ride. Or, enjoy a scenic walk to the hotel (one-and-a-third miles), though it might get a little long for younger children. Also see SAN DIEGO HARBOR EXCURSION for longer, and more scenic, boat rides.

Hours: The ferry departs daily, approximately every 30 minutes from 9am - 9pm. It runs until 10pm on Fri. and Sat.

Admission: $2 for adults (one way); children 3 years and under are free; bikes are an additional 50¢ Parking at the Broadway pier is $1 per hour; $3 maximum.

Ages: All

SAN DIEGO VISITOR INFORMATION CENTER   ✸

(619) 276-8200   !

2688 East Mission Bay Drive, Mission Bay

(EXIT SAN DIEGO FWY [5] W. ON CLAIREMONT DR., INTO THE VISITOR CENTER.)

I don't normally mention visitor centers as attractions, although they are always a good source for maps and brochures. This one, however, is located right on the bay so both the scenery and the actual building are picturesque. There are basketball courts just outside the center, picnic tables, a small playground, and a paved biking/walking trail. Just down the street is the TECOLOTE SHORES PLAY AREA.

Inside the center you'll find a wealth of information on things to do in San Diego (actually it's all covered in this book!), plus maps, and discount coupons on attractions and hotels. Tip: Another San Diego Visitors Bureau carries a free coupon booklet titled, "VISA Preferred in San Diego For Super Savings" that offers discounts on hotels, main attractions around San Diego, harbor cruises, trolley rides, restaurants, and more when using your VISA. Call (619) 236-1212, Monday through

Saturday from 8:30am to 5pm for more information and/or to send for a copy of the booklet.

Hours: Open daily 9am - 5pm. Closed Thanksgiving and Christmas.

Admission: Free

Ages: All

SUMMERS PAST FARMS

(619) 390-1523   !/$

15602 Olde Highway 80, Flinn Springs

(EXIT 8 FWY N. ON DUNBAR LN., L. ON OLDE HWY. 80.)

Experience a genteel way of life (yes, even with kids) at Summers Past Farms. Although the Farm is not large, its beautifully-landscaped gardens, blooming with a variety of flowers and herbs, almost ensure a delightful (and fragrant) *thyme* here. The plants are both for show and sale. One of the small gardens has a little creek with a bridge over it. There is a grassy area with trees, trellises, and white wrought-iron benches.

One of the retail shops, housed in a big red barn, offers potpourri, wreaths, baskets, teas, essential oils, lotions, dried and fresh flowers, etc. Craft classes are available. The other shop is Ye Old Soap Shoppe offering a wide variety of *scent*sational herbal soaps. Pick up a free sample (I chose Lavender/French Vanilla), and maybe you'll even get to see (and smell) the owner mixing essences for his soaps. Pick up soap-making supplies, or a complete soap-making kit that includes everything you need to make twenty-eight aromatic bars for about $65.

Hours: Open Wed. - Sat., 8am - 5pm; Sun., 10am - 5pm.

Admission: Free

Ages: 5 years and up.

TIJUANA, MEXICO

$$$$

Hola - come spend the day in a foreign country without the European price tag (or luxuries, majestic sights, etc.). There are several ways you can arrive at and enter into Mexico: 1) Drive into Mexico; 2) Take a tram from downtown San Diego to the border, and then take a taxi or walk across; 3) Drive your own car, park on this side of the border, and then walk or take a shuttle across. The following is more details about the above options: Option 1 - If you drive into Mexico you must buy Mexican automobile insurance because American insurance doesn't mean anything over there. The border town of San Ysidro has several places to purchase Mexican insurance. The cost depends on the coverage you are buying and the value of your car. A few other things to take into account if you drive into Mexico: You will experience lines getting into and especially getting out of Mexico in the afternoon, no matter what mode of transportation - it's "rush hour" traffic; parking can be a problem (I mean challenge); and if you think that Los Angeles drivers are scarey - you ain't seen nothing yet! For those who like to live life on the edge - drive into Tijuana. Option 2 - Take a trolley into Mexico from downtown San Diego, which costs $1.75 one way for ages 6 years and older. Trolleys run every twenty minutes, from 5am - midnight. You can pick one up at the corner of First and Broadway at the Transit Store, or call (619) 233-3004 for more locations and information. There is paid parking available (about $6 for the day) at the downtown location; parking is free at Old Town San Diego. The trolley takes you to the border where you can walk across the bridge or take a taxi into Mexico. It is a long walk from the border, about a mile, to the main shopping area in Tijuana. Even if you walk into Tijuana, you might consider taking a cab or shuttle out because you'll be carrying shopping bags, and your children will be tired (and so will you!). Taxis are plentiful, but determine exactly where you are going first, and decide on a price before you get into the cab. The fare is usually $5 to Avenida Revolucion. Option 3 - This was our personal choice, and it was fairly hassle-free. We parked on this side of the border at Border Station Parking (you'll see signs off the freeway directing you to the huge parking lots), which was $6 for all-day parking, and attendants are on duty twenty-four hours. Tip: Just behind Border Parking are factory outlet stores. Then we took a Mexicoach shuttle ($1 per person), which runs every half hour, from the parking lot into the heart of the oldest Tijuana shopping district - Avenida Revolucion, which is seven blocks of tourist-shopping heaven. You may buy up to $400 of duty free goods in Tijuana.

Shopping along Avenida Revolucion is an experience. The numerous small shops have goods almost overflowing onto the sidewalks that practically scream at your children to buy them. And, the vendors are constantly hawking their wares, enticing you, begging you, to come into their store. Be tough. Tips to keep in mind when shopping: 1) Don't feel obligated to buy just because you asked the price; 2) I can almost guarantee that you will see that exact same item at least ten more times; 3) Never, under any circumstance, pay the original asking price. Bargaining is expected. As a rule of thumb, pay around half the asking price. Be willing to go higher if it's something you really want or can't live without. (Decide beforehand how much the item is worth to you.) Haggle if you want it, but be prepared to walk away in order to get a better price, or if it isn't the price you want; 4) Prepare your children, beforehand, that they won't always get the item being bargained for. And lastly, and most importantly; 5) Teach your children to not say, "I love it - I must have it!" Merchandise that appeals most to kids includes leather vests, hats, boots, purses, etc; gold and silver jewelry; kids' guitars; gaudy ceramic figurines; watches; blankets; ponchos; and knickknacks. (The more mature shopper will enjoy leather goods and jewelry, too as well as perfumes, pharmaceutical supplies, clothing, etc.) And yes, on every street corner you'll find the touristy-looking carts hooked up to donkeys, that are painted like zebras, along with gaudy sombreros available for you to wear while having your picture taken - $5 for a Polaroid, $1 with your own camera. I can't wait to see how our picture turns out!

There are other places to shop in Tijuana besides Avenida Revolucion, such as along Avenida Constitucion, which is the next street over, and Plaza Rio Tijuana Shopping Center, near the Cultural Center, which has a few major department stores and specialty shops. The latter is a long walk, or a short drive, from Avenida Revolucion.

We walked around downtown Tijuana, just beyond the shopping district. Tijuana has been cleaned up and renovated in certain areas, but we also saw a lot of poverty, broken sidewalks, and people setting up shop in much less healthy environments than would be allowed in the States. It was an eye-opener for my kids. And, since they couldn't read any of the signs, it gave them an understanding of how difficult it is for foreigners in America to get around. Tip: Bring your own water, still.

There are several attractions in Tijuana. (Note: The 01152 number designates making an international phone call; (66) is the area code; the other digits are the actual phone number.): • Bullfights, Plaza Monumental de Playas, near the border, and on Agua Caliente Blvd. Fourteen fights are held on Sunday afternoons, May through September. Tickets range from $15 - $38. Call 01152 (66) 80-1808 or (619) 232-5049 for more info. • Centro Cultural Tijuana, Paseo de los Heroes y Mina. The art gallery wasn't that exciting to my kids, but the Centro also has a planetarium/Omnimax theater. (The shows, of course, are in Spanish.) Call 01152 (66) 84-1111 for more info. • Hipodromo Caliente, Blvd. Agua Caliente y Tapachula. Greyhound races takes place here and there is a small zoo on the grounds. Call 01152 (66) 81-7811 for more info. • Jai Alai, Avenida Revolucion at Calle 7. The beautiful old building has a Jai Alai player out front, showing kids what to expect. The fast-moving court game is played with a ball and a long, curved wicker basket strapped to the player's wrist. Games are played on various days and at various times. Tickets range from $2 - $5. Call 01152 (66) 85-2524 or (619) 231-1910 for more info. • Mexitlan, Calle 2 and Avenida Ocampo. This city-block-long attraction houses about 200 scale models of Mexico's most important monuments, buildings, churches, plazas, archaeological sites, etc. This is a great way to get an overview of the country. Open May through October, Wed. - Fri., 10am - 6pm; Sat. - Sun., 9am - 9pm; open November through April daily 10am - 5pm. Admission is $3 for adults; children 11 years and under are free. Call 01152 (66) 38-4101 or (619) 531-1112 for more info. • Mundo Divertido (Family Entertainment Center), Paseo de los Heroes y Jose Ma. This Family Fun Center offers the same fun, and at comparable prices, as the Family Fun Centers in the States; miniature golf, batting cages, bumper boats, go karts, video and arcade games, and amusement rides such as a roller coaster and a kiddie train. Call 01152 (66) 34-3213 for more info. • State Park Jose Maria Morelos Y Pavon, Blvd. Insurgentes 16000. This state park has grassy lawns for picnicking and a Creative Center for children that offers an aquarium, a theater, and games. Call 01152 (66) 25-2469 for more info.● Q-Zar, at Via Oriente Local #9. This indoor laser tag arena is huge and located at the shopping Mall of Puerto Amigo. Phone 01152 (66) 83-6183 for more info. ● Wax Museum of Tijuana, Calle 1 near Avenida Revolucion. This museum is home to over sixty waxy, lifelike historical figures and movie stars such as Mikhail Gorbachev, Emiliano Zapata, and Pedro Infante. It is open daily from 10am - 10pm. Admission is $3 for adults, $2 for ages 6 - 12; children 5 years and under are free. Call 01152 (66) 88-2478 for more information.

   Hours: Most shops are open 10am - 8pm.
   Ages: 5 years and up.

BART'S BOOKS   ☀

(805) 646-3755   !/$
302 West Matilua, Ojai
(EXIT STATE HIGHWAY 150 [OR OJAI AVE.] N. ON CANADA, L. AT MATILUA. IT'S ON THE CORNER OF MATILUA AND CANADA.)

   This unique, outdoor, used bookstore is worth at least a browse-through, weather permitting. Your reader-child will delight in this big, Bohemian-style store. It's like exploring an old, comfortable (albeit roofless) house, except that most of the "rooms" are created by bookshelves. There are hundreds of books here on every subject, including a small, but packed, children's section. Sit down on assorted benches and chairs, or in a recliner by a fireplace, and peruse your purchase.

   Books that are on shelves facing the outside of the store are available for purchase any time of day or night. The trusting (or hopeful) store sign reads: "When closed please throw coins in slot in the door for the amount marked on the book. Thank you." The atmosphere here is worth the trip.

   Hours: Open Tues. - Sat. from 10am - 5:30pm.
   Admission: Free
   Ages: All readers.

SHOWS AND THEATERS

How about a day (or evening) at the theater? The listings here range from theaters that have productions specifically for children, to planetarium shows, to musical extravaganzas!

3-D IMAX THEATER

after 1:30 pm on weekdays because of school field trips

(213) 744-2014   *Tickets: (213) 744-2019*   **$$$**

M-F 9-9:00

Exposition Park, Los Angeles

(EXIT THE HARBOR FWY [110] W. ON EXPOSITION BLVD., L. ON FLOWER, L. ON FIGUEROA. OR, EXIT SANTA MONICA FWY [10] S. ON VERMONT, L. ON EXPOSITION, R. ON FIGUEROA. PARKING IS AVAILABLE THE FIRST DRIVEWAY ON THE RIGHT.)

Moviegoers can enjoy both traditional and 3-D films at this IMAX Theater. Note: 3-D films will be available for viewing after February, 1998. Until then, you may enjoy the "regular," spectacular films that IMAX is famous for showing. Using polarized glasses and a surround sound system, the seven-story high, ninety-foot-wide screen shows films that take you and your child on wonderful adventures. You'll fly around, up, and over Hawaii; river raft through the Grand Canyon; enter the world of outer space; etc., and feel like you've actually experience whatever is on the screen, without ever leaving your seat. "Edutainment" is what this theater all about! (The theater is in the CALIFORNIA SCIENCE CENTER complex. Also see nearby attractions such as the AEROSPACE MUSEUM, CALIFORNIA AFRO-AMERICAN MUSEUM, EXPOSITION PARK, and NATURAL HISTORY MUSEUM OF LOS ANGELES.)

Hours: Call for show titles and show times.

Admission: $6.25 for adults; $4.75 for seniors and ages 4 - 12; $3.75 for students 13 - 21; children 3 years and under are free. Parking is $5. Bring your parking stub for a $1 rebate for the theater.   *$1.00 price increase in '98*

Ages: 3 years and up.

BOB BAKER MARIONETTE THEATER

(213) 250-9995   **$$$**

1345 West 1st Street, Los Angeles

(EXIT HOLLYWOOD FWY [101] S. ON GLENDALE, L. ON 1ST ST., WHICH IS JUST BEFORE THE BRIDGE.)

The Bob Baker Marionette Theater has been around since 1963, proving its staying power in this ever-changing world. Interactive marionette performances are given while children sit on a horseshoe-shaped carpet around the stage, and parents sit in chairs behind them.

The musical revues feature marionettes (and some stuffed animals) that range in size from very small to some that are the size of a two-year-old! They "sing" and "dance" their way right into your child's heart. The puppeteers, dressed in black, become invisible to the audience as the kids get swept away in the magic of the show. The performance is done within touching distance of the kids, and sometimes the marionettes even sit in their laps! This is a great way to keep short attention spans riveted. If the story line seems a little thin to you and your attention drifts, watch the puppeteers manipulate the strings - it's a good show in itself. If it's your child's birthday, for an additional $6, he/she will get special recognition with a crown, a song just for him/her, and a little present.

After the forty-five-minute show, chat with the puppeteers, and enjoy a sack lunch (that you supply) at the picnic tables in the lobby. Reservations are required for all shows.

Hours: Performances are given Tues. - Fri. at 10:30am; Sat. - Sun. at 2:30pm. There are additional shows given during the month of December.

Admission: $10 for ages 3 years and up; $8 for seniors; children 2 years and under are free. Free parking next to the Theater.

Ages: 2½ - 11 years.

CERRITOS CENTER FOR THE PERFORMING ARTS ☼

(800) 300-4345 or (562) 916-8500 $$$$$

12700 Center Court Drive, Cerritos

(GOING E. ON ARTESIA FWY [91], EXIT W. ON ARTESIA, L. ON BLOOMFIELD. GOING W. ON 91, EXIT S. ON BLOOMFIELD. FROM BLOOMFIELD, L. ON TOWN CENTER DR., R. ON CENTER COURT DR.)

Every season this Center features four or five performances just for kids, like puppetry and dance. Call for times and dates.

Admission: Show prices usually range from $16 - $21.

Ages: 5 years and up.

CHILDREN'S THEATRE NETWORK (Northridge) ☼

(818) 706-9884 $$$$

California State University of Northridge, Northridge

See CHILDREN'S THEATRE NETWORK (San Diego) for a description.

CHILDREN'S THEATRE NETWORK (Torrance) ☼

(310) 376-1740 $$$$

Torrance Cultural Arts Center

See CHILDREN'S THEATRE NETWORK (San Diego) for a description.

DEAF WEST THEATER ☼

(213) 660-0877 $$$$

660 North Heliotrope Drive., Los Angeles

(GOING N. ON HOLLYWOOD FWY [101], EXIT N. ON VERMONT, L. ON MELROSE, L. ON HELIOTROPE. GOING S. ON 101, EXIT E. ON MELROSE, R. ON HELIOTROPE.)

A children's play is performed at this theater at least once a year. The hour-and-a-half show is performed in American Sign Language, while a spoken version can be heard through headsets. What a great opportunity for both hearing impaired and hearing children to enjoy a show together!

Hours: Call for show times.
Admission: $15 for adults; $12 for seniors, students, and kids high-school age and under.
Ages: 6 years and up.

EDWARDS IMAX 3D THEATER (Ontario)

(909) 476-1525   *$$$*

4900 E. 4ᵗʰ Street, Ontario

(EXIT 15 TO 4ᵀᴴ ST. IT IS JUST OUTSIDE THE ONTARIO MILLS MALL.)

Going to the movies is a lot more fun if you are part of the action, not just watching it happen. "Experience" a movie on this giant screen using lightweight headsets that create three-dimensional images. Objects will jump out at you, float around you, and seemingly become a part of your immediate surroundings. (Watch your kids try to reach out and touch the objects.) Live whatever adventure you see on the screen, whether it's underwater with fish, in the sky with birds, etc. Use your visit as an educational tool if you come with a group of students, and request a Teacher's Resource Guide, which are very well put together.

Hours: The first show starts at 10am.
Admission: $7 for adults; $6 for seniors; $5 for ages 2 - 12 years.
Ages: 4 years and up

THE ENCHANTED FOREST

(818) 716-7202   *$$$*

20929 Ventura Boulevard, Woodland Hills

(EXIT VENTURA FWY [101] S. AT DE SOTO AVE., R. ON VENTURA BLVD. AND INTO THE SHOPPING CENTER NEXT TO THE CORNER. PARKING CAN BE TIGHT.)

The Enchanted Forest magically touches kids' lives in a variety of ways. One-hour presentations of a fairy tale, or a musical-comedy, enchants and delights kids of all ages. In this eighty-seven-seat theater, villains might be bad, but they are never too scary or evil. Three or four new children's shows are produced each year. Nighttime productions, for older kids and adults, range from comedies to melodramatic spoofs to musicals. This is good, clean family entertainment.

Enchanting birthday parties can include magicians, marionettes, or karaoke. Costumes add to the fun of a theme party here at the Forest.

During the summer months, encourage your child's hidden talent to emerge by signing him/her up for classes. For instance, a class could include storytelling, a craft, dressing up, and putting on a little show. All of the activities center around a particular theme or character.

Hours: Call for show times and class schedules.
Admission: Usually $6 per person for the children's productions; $15 per person for the family/adult shows.
Ages: 3 years and up for the children's productions; 8 years and up for the family shows; 5 years and up for the classes.

GLENDALE CENTER THEATRE ☾

(818) 244-8481 $$$

324 North Orange Street, Glendale

(GOING E. ON VENTURA FWY [134], EXIT S. ON N. CENTRAL AVE., L. ON LEXINGTON DR., R. ON ORANGE ST. GOING W. ON 134, EXIT S. ON N. BRAND BLVD., R. ON LEXINGTON DR., L. ON ORANGE ST.)

This theater produces terrific, one-and-a-half-hour, family-oriented shows. Past productions have included "The Little Mermaid," "Sleeping Beauty," and "Hansel and Gretel." The season begins in March and ends in November.

Hours: Shows are given Sat. at 11am.
Admission: $9 for adults; $7 for children 12 years and under.
Ages: 3 - 13 years.

GRIFFITH PLANETARIUM AND LASERIUM SHOWS ☀

(213) 664-1191 - Planetarium; (818) 997-3624 - Laserium $$/$$$

On the slope of Mount Hollywood, in Griffith Park, Los Angeles

(EXIT GOLDEN STATE FWY [5] W. ON LOS FELIZ BLVD., TAKE HILLHURST AVE. N. PAST THE GREEK THEATER TO THE OBSERVATORY.)

The Planetarium has a gigantic projector that fills the dome ceiling with realistic views of the nighttime sky, even though you're inside and it might be daytime. The hour-long show is an eye-opener for citified kids (and adults) who have not seen starry wonders. Children 4 years and under are admitted only to the 1:30pm show on Saturdays and Sundays, but do take them then as the show, "Voyage to the Planets" is geared for young kids. A friendly, animated space alien is the tour guide, "talking" with the real-life lecturer, and taking the intrigued audience on a trip to different planets.

The Laserium shows are laser-beam concerts with rock, classical, or other music, and incredible special effects. Your audio, visual, and kinesthetic child will love this illuminating production. (See GRIFFITH OBSERVATORY AND PLANETARIUM for other things to do here.)

Hours: Planetarium shows in the summer are Mon. - Fri., 1:30pm, 3pm, and 7:30pm; Sat. - Sun., 1:30pm, 3pm, 4:30pm, and 7:30pm. Shows the rest of the year are Tues. - Fri., 3pm, and 7:30pm; Sat. - Sun., 1:30pm, 3pm, 4:30pm, and 7:30pm. Laserium shows are presented Tues. - Thurs. and Sun. at 6pm and 8:45pm; Fri. - Sat. and various holidays at 6pm, 8:45pm, and 9:45pm.
Admission: The Planetarium show is $4 for adults; $3 for seniors; $2 for ages 5 - 12. The Laserium show is $8 for adults; $7 for senior citizens and ages 5 - 12; children 4 years and under are not admitted. (Certain discounts are available through AAA.)
Ages: 3 years and up for the Saturday planetarium show; 5 years and up for all other shows.

L. A. CONNECTION COMEDY THEATER

(818) 710-1320   *$$$*

13442 Ventura Boulevard, Sherman Oaks
(EXIT VENTURA FWY [101] S. ON WOODMAN, L. ON VENTURA BLVD.)

Tickle your children's funnybones and bring them to the Comedy Theater for comedy improv performances by kids, for kids. The almost hour-long improvisational show is in a small room with tiered, theater-type seating. The performers consist of one adult and usually six kids that are between 5 - 14 years old. The kids are members of the Kids Repertory Company, trained in the L.A. Connection's Improv Workshops.

Audience participation is mandatory as the actors ask for help in creating characters, or supplying ideas to use in a skit. Your children love to see their suggestions acted out! Remember, the performers are kids, so there is a lot of kid humor. As with any improv show, the success of a skit depends on the improvisationalists and the audience. The L.A. Connection really connected with my kids!

If your child thinks the whole world is a stage, then maybe he should be on it! Sign him up for comedy improv classes and the next performance you see could be his.

Hours: Performances are Sundays at 3:30pm.
Admission: $7 per person.
Ages: 5 years and up - younger ones won't get the humor.

LOS ANGELES CENTRAL LIBRARY

(213) 228-7000 - Children's Literature Department   *$*

630 West Fifth Street, Los Angeles
(EXIT HARBOR FWY [110] E. ON 6ᵀᴴ ST., L. ON GRAND, L. ON 5ᵀᴴ. IT'S AT HOPE AND 5ᵀᴴ ST.)

On the second floor in the Children's Literacy Department, the KLOS Story Theater presents a free, one-hour show on Saturdays at 2pm. Various past shows have included magic, how to make a book (followed by actually making one), and storytelling with puppets. On Sundays at 2pm a free, one-hour children's video is shown. At least once a month, on the first floor of the library (at the Mark Taper Auditorium, which seats 225), a free, one-hour, usually culturally-themed performance such as folk-dancing, etc. is given. Call for specific themes and shows. Half-hour school tours are given Mondays, Thursdays, and Fridays, at 10am and 11am, which includes a story time, and sometimes making a craft. Call (213) 228-7055 to make a reservation.

Hours: The library is open Mon., Thurs. - Sat., 10am - 5:30pm; Tues. and Wed., noon - 8pm; Sun., 1pm - 5pm. Closed most major holidays.

Admission: Free. Enter the parking structure under the library on Flower St. - $1 for the first hour, $2.20 for the second hour - with validation.
Ages: 3 years and up.

LOS ANGELES PHILHARMONIC / TOYOTA SYMPHONIES FOR YOUTH and OPEN HOUSE SERIES

(213) 850-2000   *$$$*

Dorothy Chandler Pavilion in the Music Center, 135 North Grand Avenue, Los Angeles

(EXIT HARBOR FWY [110] E. ON TEMPLE, R. ON GRAND. OR, EXIT SANTA ANA FWY [101] S. ON GRAND.)

Five times a year the Los Angeles Philharmonic offers forty-five-minute concerts called Toyota Symphonies for Youth. They are designed to excite kids between the ages of 6 to 12 (and their parents) about the wonderful world of orchestral music. Meet in the lobby at 9:15am for pre-concert activities that can include arts and crafts, hands-on instrument stations, storytellers, dance and theater, and meeting the Philharmonic musicians who will demonstrate their instruments. All the activities help to introduce (and reinforce) the morning's theme. The concert begins at 10:15am at the Pavilion auditorium. Past concerts include "Magical Melodies," "Fun with Bach and Mozart," and "Peter and the Wolf." Performances are signed for people with a hearing impairment.

Open House is a fast-paced, entertaining introduction of classical music for kids ages 3 to 5. Children sit on the carpeted floor in the Grand Hall lobby of the Pavilion and surround the musicians. This half-hour, age-appropriate, mini-music fest follows the Symphonies for Youth. (Seating is very limited.)

Hours: Symphonies for Youth workshop begins at 9:15am; the concert begins at 10:15am. The Open House concert begins at 11:30am. The concerts are given on Saturdays, usually in the months of January, February, April, May, and December. Reserve your tickets as soon as possible.
Admission: Symphonies for Youth costs $6 - $10 per person, depending on your seat; Open House costs $6 per person. Parking is available in the Music Center Garage ($7); in the Mall Garage, across Grand Avenue ($6), and at the corner of Temple and Grand ($6).
Ages: Youth - ages 6 - 12; Open House - ages 3 - 5.

SANTA MONICA COLLEGE PLANETARIUM

(310) 452-9223   *$$*

1900 Pico Boulevard, Santa Monica

348 SHOWS AND THEATERS - LOS ANGELES COUNTY

(EXIT SANTA MONICA FWY [10] S. ON CLOVERFIELD, R. ON PICO BLVD.)
Do your kids have stars in their eyes? Bring them to the planetarium, then lean back, look up at the nighttime sky, and watch some of the mysteries of the heavens unfold. The lecture and shows (with titles like "Alien Skies") are presented in the Business Building, room 111.

Hours: Shows are every Friday night at 7pm and 8pm.
Admission: $4 for a single show; $7 for both shows (elementary-school-aged kids are half price).
Ages: 6 years and up.

SANTA MONICA PLAYHOUSE
(310) 394-9779   *$$$*
1211 4ᵗʰ Street, Santa Monica
(EXIT SANTA MONICA FWY [10] N. ON 4ᵀᴴ ST.)

This ninety-two seat Playhouse offers original, one-hour, family-style musicals every weekend. Most of the productions are based on well-known characters with titles like "Alice's Wonderful Teapot" and "Captain Jack and the Beanstalk." There is a cookies and punch intermission. Young and old will enjoy this theater experience. Ask about their special classes and workshops.

Hours: Every Sat. and Sun. at 1pm and 3pm.
Admission: $8 for ages 2 and up.
Ages: 3 years and up.

STORYBOOK THEATRE AT THEATRE WEST
(818) 761-2203   *$$$*
3333 Cahuenga Boulevard West, Los Angeles
(EXIT HOLLYWOOD FWY [101] AT LANKERSHIM BLVD., S. ON CAHUENGA. IF GOING N. ON 101 FWY, GO BACK OVER FWY ON LANKERSHIM, R. ON CAHUENGA.)

Every Saturday, Storybook Theatre presents a fun, musical, audience-participatory play geared for 3 - 8 year olds. Classics are re-done to appeal even more to children (with all the violence eliminated), like "Little Red Riding Hood" and "Jack In The Beanstalk." There is an apple juice intermission in this hour-long event. Afterwards, the cast is around to talk with the kids. What a wonderful, "first theater" experience! Call to find out what's playing.

Hours: Saturdays at 1pm.
Admission: $7 per person.
Ages: 3 - 8 years.

THE THIRD STAGE
(818) 842-4755   *$$$*
Third Stage Theater, 2811 W. Magnolia Blvd., Burbank
(EXIT VENTURA FWY [134] N. ON BUENA VISTA, L. ON MAGNOLIA BLVD.)

Mirror, mirror on the wall, what's the funnest show of all? The forty-eight seat Third Stage Theater presents the "Magic Mirror," a one-hour improvisational, fantasy show tailored for kids. Without the encumbrance of props, three adult actors work with an outline, but need your child's creative suggestions to flesh out the stories.

An imaginary mirror is "carried" on stage, but it's too heavy, so kids are asked to come and help out. They do and their imaginations are off and running! The silliness is contagious and everyone gets caught up in this magical world.

Some of the scenarios include: "Wishes Come True" - your child's wildest wish can come true, well, at least pantomimed on stage; "Storybook Characters" - actors improvise a character and freeze when the audience yells out who it is; Aesop's Fables - "The Ant and the Grasshopper" and "The Lion and the Mouse" are acted out; "Rap Song" - kids offer up subjects and themes and, together with the actors, a song is born; and "Opera" - kids become musical instruments on stage as an opera is created revolving around their parents' occupations.

This interactive play travels to schools; is wonderful for birthday parties; and is incorporated with workshops for kids through an after-school program called L. A.'s Best.

Hours: Performances are Sundays at noon.

Admission: $7 per ticket

Ages: 4 - 12 year olds will have the most fun here.

BALLET PACIFICA   ☼
(714) 851-9930   *$$$*

650 Laguna Canyon Road, Festival of Arts Forum Theater, Laguna Beach

(EXIT SAN DIEGO FWY [405] OR SANTA ANA FWY [5] S. ON LAGUNA CANYON RD. [HWY 133]. IT'S ON THE R., ON THE FESTIVAL OF THE ARTS GROUNDS.)

Ballet Pacifica has a Children's Series, consisting of four productions a year at the Forum Theater. The ballet productions are held in September, February, March, and April. Past performances include "The Emperor's New Clothes," "Winnie-the-Pooh," and "Puss in Boots." Each show is a winner for the whole family, especially your blossoming ballerina. A special showing of the Nutcracker is given in December. Check for time and location, as the company also performs at other locations such as the Irvine Barclay Theater.

Admission: Tickets are usually $11 for adults; $8 for children 12 years and under.

Ages: 5 years and up.

BROADWAY ON TOUR CHILDREN'S THEATER   ☼
(714) 282-8148   *$$$*

2190 Canal Street, Orange

(EXIT COSTA MESA FWY [55] W. ON LINCOLN/NOHL RD., L. ON TUSTIN, R. ON HEIM AVE., L. ON CANAL ST.)

This theater encourages an intimate feel by allowing only the first five rows of seating. Kids 10 to 18 years old put on presentations for younger children, who delight in seeing just slightly older versions of themselves on stage. The one-hour musicals are usually based on classic fairytales, and they run for six weeks. Broadway on Tour's motto is, "Children bringing theater to children." Call for show information, and to find out how your child could become a performer.

Hours: Shows are given Sat. - Sun. at 2pm.
Admission: $6 per person.
Ages: 4 - 12 years.

CALIFORNIA STATE FULLERTON PERFORMING ARTS
(714) 278-3371   *$$$*
Nutwood and State College, Fullerton
(EXIT ORANGE FWY [57] W. ON NUTWOOD.)

The Kaleidoscope Players put on special presentations every February, just for kids.
Ages: 5 years and up.

CURTIS THEATRE / CITY OF BREA GALLERY
(714) 990-7722 - theater; (714) 990-7730 - gallery   *$$$$*
1 Civic Center Circle, Brea
(EXIT ORANGE FWY [57] W. ON IMPERIAL, R. ON RANDOLF, R. ON BIRCH, R. ON CIVIC CENTER CIRCLE.)

Curtis Theatre boasts Brea's Youth Theatre and Kids Culture Club. The Youth Theatre is comprised of a talented cast of young actors and actresses (i.e. kids) who put on two musical extravaganzas a year. Last year's productions were "Peter Pan" and "Joseph and the Amazing Technicolor Dreamcoat." The Culture Club is comprised of six professional productions a year. Last year's forty-five-minute headliners included a music and laser show, a magic show, the "Nutcracker Suite," and Jim Gamble's puppets. Call for a current schedule.

Aross from the theater the Civic Center also has a small gallery called City of Brea Gallery. We saw an exhibit on Japanese dolls, but exhibits do change periodically. The gallery also has a Children's Art Space where young visitors may create their own masterpiece that is related to the current exhibit. The Brea Gallery is usually open on performance nights and gives kids something to do while waiting for the theater doors to open.

Hours: Call for a schedule of shows. The gallery is open Wed. - Sun., noon - 5pm; (open Thurs. and Fri. until 8pm). The Children's Art Space is open Wed. - Thurs., 3:30pm - 4:30pm; Sat. - Sun., 2:30pm - 3:30pm.

Admission: Tickets for the Youth Theatre usually run $9.50 for adults; $7.50 for children 12 years and under. Tickets for the Culture Club and other family shows generally run between $8 - $10 per person. The gallery is $1 for adults; free to youth 17 years and under.

Ages: 5 years and up.

EDWARDS IMAX 3D THEATER / IRVINE SPECTRUM ☼

(714) 832-IMAX (4629); or (714) 450-4900   *$$$*

At the junction of the 405 and 5 Fwy., at the Irvine Spectrum, Irvine

(GOING S. ON SANTA ANA FWY [5], EXIT W. ON ALTON PKY. AT THE END OF THE OFF RAMP, GO STRAIGHT INTO THE SPECTRUM. GOING N. ON 5, EXIT W. ON ALTON PKY. GOING S. ON SAN DIEGO FWY [405], EXIT N. ON IRVINE CENTER DR., R. ON PACIFICA.)

For your viewing pleasure, Edwards Theater has a twenty-one screen theater complex in the heart of the Irvine Spectrum entertainment center. The crown jewel of this Hollywood-looking building is the West Coast's first 3D IMAX theater. The giant screen is six stories high and ninety-feet wide. The lightweight headsets, which look like heavy duty sunglasses, help create three-dimensional images that look incredibly real. You become part of the forty-five-minute movie as you swim with fish, fly in an airplane, etc. You feel like you're really living the adventure! Watch your kids reach out to try to touch objects that seemingly jump right off the screen. The movies can be a terrific educational tool, too. If you make reservations to come on a class field trip, request a Teacher's Resource Guide for the group.

Some of the stores that comprise the Spectrum include a gigantic Barnes and Noble Bookstore; Out Takes, which takes your picture in your choice of computer-generated scenes; and a large Sega video arcade with simulator race cars and more. Hungry? Choose from four outstanding restaurants - Bertolini's, Champps Americana, P. F. Chang's China Bistro, and Wolfgang Puck. A wonderful food court is also here, complete with a Ben and Jerry's Ice Cream, and a sweet shop. As usual, kids also enjoy the simple pleasures, like playing on the turtle statues (and getting wet) in the fountain just outside the food court.

Hours: The first show starts at 10am.

Admission: The 3D IMAX is $8 for adults; $7 for seniors; $6 for ages 12 and under.

Ages: 4 years and up.

IRVINE BARCLAY THEATER   ☼

(714) 854-4646   *$$$*

4242 Campus Drive, Irvine

(EXIT SAN DIEGO FWY [405] S. ON CULVER DR., R. ON CAMPUS DR. TO BRIDGE RD.)

This theater offers four to five family-oriented shows a year, plus several touring shows geared for kids. The various types of shows include circus acts, folk singers, Indian dancers, acrobats, and the Nutcracker. Applause, applause - not a seat in the house is more than sixty feet away from the stage.

Admission: Tickets range from $5 - $50.
Ages: 5 years and up.

THE LAGUNA PLAYHOUSE   ☼
(714) 497-9244 $$$
606 Laguna Canyon Road, Laguna Beach
(EXIT SAN DIEGO FWY [405] OR SANTA ANA FWY [5] S. ON LAGUNA CANYON RD.
[HWY 133] IT'S ON THE R., IN THE LAGUNA MOULTON THEATER, ON THE FESTIVAL OF
THE ARTS GROUNDS.)

"Orange County's Award-Winning Theater for Young People and the Young at Heart!" Four great-for-the-kids plays are presented here each year. Call for dates and times.

Admission: Tickets are usually between $8 - $11.
Ages: 5 years and up.

LA MIRADA CENTER FOR THE PERFORMING ARTS   ☼
(562) 944-9801 $$$
14900 La Mirada Boulevard, La Mirada
(EXIT ARTESIA FWY [91] OR SANTA ANA FWY [5] N. ON VALLEY VIEW, R. ON
ROSECRANS, R. ON LA MIRADA.)

Golden State Children and Programs for Young Audiences are two production companies that present children's programs here three to five times a year.

Admission: Tickets are usually between $7 - $9.
Ages: 5 years and up.

MEDIEVAL TIMES   ☼
(714) 521-4740 $$$$$
7662 Beach Boulevard, Buena Park
(EXIT ARTESIA FWY [91] S. ON BEACH BLVD. IT'S N. OF KNOTT'S BERRY FARM.)

The sight of this eleventh-century-style castle sets the mood for a "knight to remember." Before entering the arena, the Museum of Torture welcomes visitors for $2 for adults, $1 for kids 12 years and under. This unusual museum displays over thirty reproductions of instruments of torture and ridicule, like "The Rack" and "The Stock and Pillories," used during the Middle Ages - a different kind of pre-dinner fare.

Wear the crowns to given ye, good Lords and Ladies, as the color designates which of the knights you'll cheer for. The Lord of the Castle has invited you, and 1,100 of your closest friends, neighbors, and foes to a two-hour royal tournament. First, silky-maned horses prance and high-step, delighting horse fans young and old. These elegant displays of horsemanship are the highlight of the pre-show activities.

Then comes the main event - the tournament. Six knights on horseback joust and perform feats of real skill. After every game the winning knight throws flowers out to his rooting section. The final battle looks real, with swords actually sparking as they strike each other. The knights fight on horseback, and then on foot, until there is just one victor. (Reassure younger kids that this is just a show.)

Throughout the evening serfs and wenches serve you a four-course feast, eaten without utensils, of course. The delicious meal consists of vegetable soup, whole roasted chicken, spare ribs, potatoes, pastries, and drink. We enjoyed the food and were riveted by the action! After the show, the gift shop selling medieval memorabilia is open, or dance the night away at the Knight Club.

One-hour, educational Castle Tours are offered for a minimum group of twenty students. Kids are guided by a costumed Master of Ceremonies through the decorated halls. Life in the Middle Ages is explained as they look at authentic Medieval artifacts, and learn about chivalry and knighthood. The highlights are meeting a "real" knight, and seeing demonstrations of horsemanship and actual Medieval weapons. Depending on the age of the children, a tour of the Museum of Torture might also be included. Tours are given Monday through Thursday at 10:30am and noon; call to make a reservation. The cost is $4 per person.

Student Matinees are offered January through August, on certain Tuesdays and Thursdays, from 11:30am to 1pm for grades Kindergarten through twelfth. A medieval history lesson is given, by a Master of Ceremonies on horseback, instead of some of the pageantry of a nighttime show. Kids still see, though, the knights engaging in sword fights and period games. This educational "tour" includes a lunch of chicken, apples, cookies, drink, etc. The cost is $15.95 per person. The castle is also open during the day for those who want to simply come in and look at the horses and the arena.

Hours: Call for times for the knightly performances and for the matinees on Sundays.

Admission: The price, including dinner, show, and tax, is $33.95 - $35.95 for adults; $22.95 for ages 12 and under. Reservations are required. (Certain discounts available through AAA, but not on Saturdays.)

Ages: 3 years and up.

ORANGE COAST COLLEGE   ☼
(714) 432-5880   *$$$$*
2701 Fairview Road, Costa Mesa
(EXIT SAN DIEGO FWY [405] S. ON FAIRVIEW.)

This college puts on <u>fourteen</u> children's productions throughout the year; that's two or three favorites for each person in my family.

Admission: Tickets range from $8 - $15; matinees are less expensive.

Ages: 5 years and up.

ORANGE COUNTY PERFORMING ARTS CENTER

(714) 556-2787   *$$$*

600 Town Center Drive, Costa Mesa
(EXIT SAN DIEGO FWY [405] N. ON BRISTOL ST., R. ON TOWN CENTER.)

Four to five Saturdays a year, Pacific Symphony puts on Mervyn's Musical Mornings, which are concerts geared for families. They vary in content, but are always fun for kids.

Admission: $11 for adults; $9 for children 12 years and under.

Ages: 5 years and up.

PAPER BAG PLAYERS

(714) 581-5402   *$$*

21801 Winding Way, Lake Forest
(EXIT SAN DIEGO FWY [5], N.E. ON LAKE FOREST DR., L. ON SERRANO RD., L. ON WINDING WAY. IT'S HELD ACROSS THE STREET FROM HERITAGE PARK AT RANCHO CANADA SCHOOL.)

The Paper Bag Players are sponsored by the Children's Theater Workshop. The Workshop teaches theater to children ages 7 to 16, who then put on a production. The Paper Bag Players are professional actors whose goal is to make theater accessible to children via interaction. Kids are invited to bring their own paper bag lunch (hence the name of the company) at 11:30am, and eat while watching the actors prepare for the performance. As the actors put on their make-up, children are invited to join in and also put on make-up (or face paint). During the show, kids are invited on stage to help tell the story. Afterward, the actors answer questions about scenes, scenery, costumes, technical equipment, or whatever other things kids wonder about. What a great way to encourage kids to be involved with theater! Past one-hour presentations have included "Tale of the Frog Prince" and "The Future of Maid Marion."

Hours: Each of the 3 yearly productions are put on for 3 consecutive weekends. Lunch is at 11:30am; the play starts at 12:30pm.

Admission: $5 per person.

Ages: 2 - 12 years.

RANCHO SANTIAGO COLLEGE PLANETARIUM

(714) 564-6600   *$*

West 17ᵗʰ Street and North Bristol, Santa Ana

(EXIT SANTA ANA FWY [5] W. ON 17TH ST. AT BRISTOL IN RANCHO SANTIAGO COLLEGE)

Twinkle, twinkle little star, how I wonder what you are? Your kids can begin to find the answers to this question in the 100-seat planetarium. The hour-long show during the week is a trip around the galaxy, seeing and learning about planets and constellations. The Sunday family show changes on a monthly basis, sometimes dealing with timely subject matters. Past shows include "Jupiter," "Stardust," and "E.T. - Searching for Extra Terrestrials." On the second Sunday of each month following the show narrated in English, a show is given that is narrated in Spanish. There is time after all the shows for questions and answers.

Hours: Shows are given mid-September through Mid-May, Mon. - Wed., and Fri. at 9:30am. A second show on Tuesday is offered at 11am. Reservations are needed. The Sunday showing is at 2pm, with the once-a-month Spanish show at 3pm. No reservations are required.

Admission: During the week, the shows are $2 per person. Sunday prices are $2 for adults; $1 for seniors and students; children 12 years and under are free.

Ages: 5 years and up.

SADDLEBACK CHILDREN'S FESTIVAL

(714) 364-ARTS (2787)   *$$$*

2700 Marguerite Parkway, Mission Viejo
(EXIT SAN DIEGO FWY [5], E. ON CROWN VALLEY PKY., L. ON MARGUERITE PKY. SECOND LEVEL OF MISSION VIEJO MALL, THE STOREFRONT THEATER NEXT TO MONTGOMERY WARD.)

Saddleback College is the proud sponsor of wonderful, year-round children's plays. One-hour plays are either musical or classic stories acted out. Past productions have included "A Tale of Peter Rabbit," "A Little Princess," and "Little Red Riding Hood and the Three Little Pigs." The theater location is great, especially if you want to go shopping at the mall or grab an ice-cream cone after a performance.

Hours: Performances are given Thurs. - Fri., 5pm and 7pm; Sat. - Sun., 1pm and 3pm during the school year. Summer performances are given Thurs. - Sun. at 11am and 1:30pm.

Admission: $6 per person

Ages: Plays are usually geared for children ages 4 -12.

SOUTH COAST REPERTORY

(714) 957-4033   *$$$*

655 Town Center Drive, Costa Mesa
(EXIT SAN DIEGO FWY [405] N. ON BRISTOL ST., R. ON TOWN CENTER.)

A few times a year, this theater offers productions for families. At least once a year, a performance is given by young actors. Kids get excited to see their peers on stage!

Ages:　5 years and up.

TIBBIE'S MUSIC HALL ☼

(714) 252-0834　　　　　　　　　　　　　　　　　　　*$$$$$*

4647 MacArthur Boulevard, Newport Beach
(EXIT SAN DIEGO FWY [405] S. ON MACARTHUR, JUST S. OF THE JOHN WAYNE AIRPORT.)

More than just dinner, and more than just a show - Tibbie's is a two-hour, dinner, musical song and dance revue. The waiters and waitresses are also the entertainers. They start the show by singing as they bring in the salad, and they entertain all the way through dessert. (Dinner choices include prime rib, salmon, and chicken entrees for adults; hamburger or chicken strips for kids.) They perform on the stage, as well as all around you. Audience participation, a code-word game, and other surprises throughout the evening add to your family's enjoyment.

If your child is celebrating a birthday, graduation, or other special occasion, be sure you tell Tibbie's beforehand so they will mention it sometime during the show. And don't tell the kids, but dessert is mud pie served in a flower pot, with a "real" flower! Enjoy this delightful night out on the town where the food is good and the entertainment is fun and clean. One to two week reservations are suggested. Call for particular show titles.

Hours:　Shows are Fri. at 7:30pm; Sat. at 7pm; and Sun. at 2pm and 5pm.

Admission:　Tickets, which include the show and dinner, are $27.95 - $28.95 for adults; $15.95 for ages 11 and under.

Ages:　6 years and up.

WILD BILL'S WILD WEST DINNER EXTRAVAGANZA ☼

(714) 522-6414　　　　　　　　　　　　　　　　　　　*$$$$$*

7600 Beach Boulevard, Buena Park
(EXIT THE ARTESIA FWY [91] S. ON BEACH BLVD. IT'S JUST N. OF KNOTT'S BERRY FARM.)

Put on your best cowboy or cowgirl duds and see how the West was fun! The atmosphere is rustic with stagecoaches outside, while posters, bandannas, and steer's horns decorate the inside.

Miss Annie and Wild Bill sing, talk, and cheer you through a two-hour, old-fashioned, Western-style extravaganza. The entertainment is constant with live music, outfits aimed towards pleasing older cowboys, cancan dancing, and Indian dancing like you've never seen. The specialty acts that we saw were exciting - lariat twirling, whip cracking, and Gauchos dancing with drums. The biggest hit was ropes that were twirled, while they were on fire! Audience participation (e.g. yahooing) is definitely part of the fun. (How often are your kids encouraged to yell at the top of their lungs in public?!) The show kept even my four-year old completely enthralled.

A four-course, all-American meal is served throughout the performance. The food includes chicken, salad, and apple pie. After the show, keep your cameras (no videos) out because the entertainers are ready to pose with you and your cowpokes. A gift shop is there if you want more tangible memories to take home. Yee-haa!

Hours: Shows are performed nightly, with matinees given on Saturdays and Sundays. Call for exact times.

Admission: Prices, including dinner and the show, are $33.95 - $35.95 for adults; $21.95 for ages 3 - 11. Reservations are required.

Ages: 3 years old and up.

RIVERSIDE COMMUNITY COLLEGE PLANETARIUM

(909) 222-8000 $

4800 Magnolia Avenue, Riverside
(EXIT RIVERSIDE FWY [91] W. ON 14TH ST., L. ON MARKET ST./MAGNOLIA AVE.)

Come see a truly star-studded show at the college planetarium! The theater seats sixty people and each presentation has a live narrator. Different shows study various aspects of astronomy such as constellations; revolutions (the earth's, not a country's); galaxies and measuring distances between them; lunar eclipses; and what makes the sun shine.

Hours: The shows are offered year round, usually on Friday nights at 7pm.

Admission: $3 for adults; $2.50 for students; $1.50 for children 11 years and under.

Ages: 6 years and up.

CALIFORNIA CENTER FOR THE ARTS

(800) 98-TICKETS (8-4253) $$$

340 N. Escondido Boulevard, Escondido
(EXIT ESCONDIDO FWY [15] E. ON VALLEY PARKWAY; TAKE THE EAST BOUND LANE
WHICH TURNS INTO GRAND AVE., L. ON ESCONDIDO BLVD.)

All the world's a stage and kids are invited to come watch the world, or at least a production or two. Several of the yearly performances given at the center are perfect for the entire family. Past productions have included "The Sound of Music," "The Magic Schoolbus," and "The Hobbit" which was performed with large puppets.

Hours: Call for the names and dates of productions.

Admission: Tickets are usually about $10 for children's productions.

Ages: 5 years and up

CHILDREN'S CLASSICS ☼
(619) 268-4494 $$
1540 Camino del Mar at the L'Auberge del Mar Garden Amphitheater,
Del Mar
(EXIT SAN DIEGO FWY [5] W. ON DEL MAR HEIGHTS RD., R. ON CAMINO DEL MAR.)
    An entertaining, thirty-five-minute presentation of classic children's
literature is performed by the San Diego Actors Theater a few times
each month. Past productions have included "The Giving Tree," "Snow
White and the Seven Dwarfs" (where kids came up on stage to help be
the dwarfs), "Hansel and Gretel," and "Goldilocks." These theater
presentations are great for the younger (and older) set! Sometimes
acting workshops are offered after the shows. They are geared for kids
4 - 9 years old and cost $10 per child.
    Hours: Performances are given the second and fourth Sat. of
                  each month at 11am.
Admission: $4 per person.
    Ages: 3 years and up.

CHILDREN'S THEATRE NETWORK (San Diego) ☼
(619) 238-8280 $$$$
Performed at Lyceum Theater at Horton Plaza, San Diego; and the
Center for Performing Arts, Poway
    This terrific, everyone-gets-a-role, theater group is comprised of
kids 4 years old through college-age, as well as a few adult performers.
What a great "first-theater" exposure for kids who are acting, and those
in the audience. (If your child is a thespian wanna-be, call about
enrolling him/her for the next production. The twelve-week Saturday
course costs $160 which includes rehearsal workshops, training, and
productions. Participants also have the opportunity to go abroad once a
year.) Past productions have included "Joseph and the Amazing
Technicolor Dreamcoat," "The Wiz," "Peter Pan," "Aladdin," and "Fiddler
on the Roof." (There are two other locations of the theatre network:
Northridge and Torrance.)
    Hours: Call for show locations, dates, and times.
Admission: Tickets are usually $15 for adults; $12 for children 4 - 12
                  years.
    Ages: 4 years on up to watch and participate.

CHRISTIAN YOUTH THEATER ☼
(800) 696-1929 or (619) 588-0206 $$$
San Diego
    Enjoy live musical theater, performed by students 8 through 18
years, and put on at six locations throughout San Diego County. Past
productions have included "Aladdin," "Jungle Book," "The Secret
Garden," "Tom Sawyer," "Willy Wonka & the Chocolate Factory," and

"Alice in Wonderland." The theater presents wholesome entertainment for the whole family!

Hours: Call for show locations, dates, and times.
Admission: Tickets usually cost about $7 for adults; $6 for children 12 years and under.
Ages: 4 years and up.

MARIE HITCHCOCK PUPPET THEATER
(619) 685-5045   *$*

Balboa Park, San Diego
(GOING S. ON CABRILLO FWY [163], EXIT N. ON PARK BLVD. GOING S. ON SAN DIEGO FWY [5], EXIT AT ASH ST. / "A" ST., L. ON "A" ST., L. ON PARK BLVD. GOING N. ON 5, EXIT W. ON "B" ST., R. ON PARK BLVD. ONCE ON PARK BLVD. TURN L. ON PRESIDENTS WAY TO GET TO THE MUSEUMS.)

This intimate theater, located behind the SAN DIEGO AUTOMOTIVE MUSEUM, presents kid-approved, half-hour, puppet shows. The type of puppets vary from show to show, and can include hand puppets, marionettes, dummies (for ventriloquists), and puppets made from anything and everything found around the house. The shows themselves are similar in that they never fail to capture a child's imagination. From "Cinderella" to "The Ugly Duckling" to "The Frog Prince," stories are told as only puppets can tell them! Shows change weekly so watch out - bringing the kids here can become habit forming. (See BALBOA PARK for a listing of all the museums and attractions within walking distance.)

Hours: Performances are usually given Wed., Thurs., and Fri. at 10am and 11:30am; Sat. - Sun. at 11am, 1pm, and 2:30pm.
Admission: $2 for adults; $1.50 for children 2-12 years.
Ages: 1½ - 10 years

POWAY CENTER FOR THE PERFORMING ARTS
(619) 748-0505   *$$$*

15498 Espola Road, Poway
(EXIT ESCONDIDO FWY [15], E. ON RANCHO BERNARDO RD., TURNS INTO ESPOLA RD., FOLLOW AS IT TURNS RIGHT.)

This Center offers a few outstanding children's programs a year. Last year's highlights included Jim Gamble puppets, and a troop that performed juggling, acrobatics, and comedy, combined with a laser light show.

Hours: Call for performance times.
Admission: Tickets usually run between $5 - $8.
Ages: 4 years and up.

SAN DIEGO JUNIOR THEATRE ☼

(619) 239-1311 or (619) 239-8355 $$$

Performed in Balboa Park Casa del Prado, San Diego

The San Diego Junior Theatre is a comprehensive workshop program for student 4 to 18 years old, who present six family-oriented shows a year. Past performances of the for-kids-by-kids group have included "Annie," "Master Prince and the Pauper," and "The Adventures of a Bear Named Paddington." Ask about special performances that are interpreted for the deaf.

Hours: Call for show dates and times.

Admission: Ticket prices usually range from $7 - $9.

Ages: 4 years and up.

THE MAGNIFICENT MOORPARK MELODRAMA AND ☼ VAUDEVILLE COMPANY

(800) 597-1210 or (805) 529-1212 $$$$

45 E. High Street, Moorpark

(EXIT THE SIMI VALLEY/SAN FERNANDO VALLEY FWY [23] E. ON NEW LOS ANGELES AVE. [23/118], N. ON THE MOORPARK AVE. [23], R. ON HIGH ST.)

This theater was built in 1928, and its antiqueness adds to its uniqueness. The stage, the velvet-like comfortable seats with wooden ledges in front for food or feet, and the old-time posters add to the old-fashioned ambiance.

"Camarillo Jones and the Search for Santa's Sleigh," "Cinderella Meets the Wolfman," and "Gone With the Gust" are some of the past musical melodramas presented here. The productions are very loosely based on other, more well-known shows. The Moorpark Theater presents seven different spoofs a year starring villains, heros, and assorted strange characters. Performances are rated "G", for Great family entertainment - acceptable for kids, sophisticated enough for adults, and highly enjoyable for everyone. The shows are contemporary in theme and humor, with old songs given new twists. My kids were thrilled to "boo," "hiss," and cheer, at appropriate times, of course. They might not have gotten all the jokes, but they thoroughly enjoyed the show. I didn't think my kids would last through the matinee, as they have a hard time sitting still through dinner, but they ate it up.

The melodrama is two hours long, followed by an hour-long vaudeville/variety act, which is a lot of show for your money. There is an intermission each hour, with a full-service snack bar available. Tip: If your child (or someone you are with) has a celebration of any kind, mention it at the box office so he/she will get special stage recognition.

Hours: Performances are given sometimes on Thurs. at 7pm; always on Fri. at 8pm; Sat. at 3pm and 8pm; Sun. at 3pm. Ask about special show schedules and prices for the holidays.

Admission: $12 for adults; $9.50 for seniors and children 11 years and under (except for Fri. and Sat. evening shows when all seats are $12). Reservations are recommended.

Ages: 5½ years and up.

TOURS

Insight into ordinary, and unique places, is what this section is all about. (There are many tours offered under MUSEUMS, and other sections, too.) Tip: See the IDEAS/RESOURCES section towards the back of the book for general tour ideas regarding a particular profession or subject.

CALIFORNIA INSTITUTE OF TECHNOLOGY - ☼
SEISMO TOUR
(818) 395-6811   !

1201 East California Boulevard, Pasadena
(EXIT FOOTHILL FWY [210] S. ON SOUTH LAKE AVE., L. ON CALIFORNIA BLVD.)

Too often in Southern California there is a whole lot of shakin' going on. What causes this? Find out by taking a Seismo Tour, offered periodically. Much of the information is technical, but older children can appreciate it. On the tour you can ask earthquake-related questions, visit the media center where press conferences are held after a quake, and see the seismographs and giant drums where seismic data are recorded.

Hours: Call for tour hours.
Admission: Free
Ages: 12 years and up

GUIDE DOGS OF AMERICA ☼
(818) 362-5834   !

13445 Glenoaks Boulevard, Sylmar
(GOING N. ON GOLDEN STATE FWY [5] EXIT N. ON ROXFORD ST., R. ON GLENOAKS BLVD. GOING E. ON FOOTHILL FWY [210] EXIT S. ON ROXFORD ST., L. ON GLENOAKS BLVD.)

Guide Dogs of America is a center that breeds, raises, and trains Labrador Retrievers, Golden Retrievers, and German Shepherds for the blind. It is also a school that teaches blind men and women how to use guide dogs. These services are offered free of charge. Free tours of the facility, which last about an hour and a half, consist of seeing a twenty-minute video; the administrative offices with photos of graduates; the dormitory where students stay for a month while receiving training; and (this is the best part, according to kids) the kennels, whelping bays, and future guide dogs. Tours are offered for groups of ten or more people with an advance registration of thirty days. "Walk in" tours, for individuals, are also available.

Have you ever thought about being a foster parent - for a dog? Guide puppies, or future guide dogs, need temporary homes for their first fifteen months of life. If you are willing to teach them basic obedience, love them, and encourage them to be well socialized (sort of like raising children), call for more information. The heartbreak of separation from your eighteen-month-old pup comes in the knowledge that your family enabled a blind person to be mobile and independent. You're invited to attend the graduation ceremony of your dog and the student you've helped.

Hours: Group tours are given Tues. and Wed. at 10am and 2pm, by appointment only. Tours are offered for individuals on the third Thursday of each month at 10am, with a seven-day advance notice.

Admission: Free
Ages: Fourth graders and up only.

JET PROPULSION LABORATORIES ☼

(818) 354-9314 !

4800 Oak Grove Drive, Pasadena
(GOING N.W. ON FOOTHILL FWY [210], EXIT S.E. ON FOOTHILL BLVD., GO TO END AND TURN LEFT ON OAK GROVE DR. GOING S.E. ON 210, EXIT S. ON GOULD AVE., L. ON FOOTHILL BLVD., GO TO END AND TURN LEFT ON OAK GROVE DR.)

"Space, the final frontier." JPL is a leading research and development center for NASA with 160 buildings on 177 acres of land. Its mission is to observe the earth, explore new worlds (via unmanned spacecraft), send back pictures, and ultimately, find the answer to the question, "Are we alone?" The twenty-minute film "Welcome to Outer Space," shows spectacular pictures of stars, moons, and various planet surfaces. It made my family aware of the incomprehensible vastness of our universe. My boys were awed by this realization - I just felt very small and insignificant. (Did you know that one light year is really six trillion miles?) The auditorium contains vivid photographs of star fields and pillars of gas; replica models of the Voyagers; and a Voyager gold record made for other intelligent life forms to listen to and learn about planet earth. Press the display button and listen to a sampling of the recording. The actual recording contains greetings in fifty-nine languages, photographs of our culture, and sounds of music, the rain forest, a heartbeat, and much more.

The adjacent museum has replicas of early and modern space craft including the 1958 Explorer, the Mars Pathfinder, the 1989 Galileo, and the Cassini, which is currently on its way to Saturn. Our tour guide talked extensively about the models and their actual missions. Although some of it was a bit too technical for my kids (and me - I guess I'm no rocket scientist), we learned a lot.

Trekking over to another building, we watched Mission Control in action. The viewing room allows you to see the Operations Chief tracking and (maybe) listen to him communicate with spacecraft - it depends on what's going on. The last stop is the assembly area where, again, depending on what is in process, you might see actual spacecraft being assembled. Maybe you'll see a piece of history in the making!

JPL facilities can only be seen on a tour. Presently only a limited number of tours are available. Call to find out the next date or ask about scheduling a tour for your own group of ten to forty people. Reservations are required. Also inquire about the monthly Sunday open houses that are in the process of being implemented. Tours are two hours long and require a lot of walking, although the center is also wheelchair accessible. You are welcome to take pictures. Bring your space cadets here and have a blast!

Hours: Call

Admission: Free
Ages: 7 years and up.

LONG BEACH AIRPORT TOUR   ☀
(562) 570-2611   !
4100 Donald Douglas Drive, Long Beach
(*EXIT SAN DIEGO FWY [405] N. ON LAKEWOOD, L. ON DONALD DOUGLAS DR.*)
   Invite your preschool-aged kids (and older) to come to the airport
and take a pretend trip. (No minimum group number is required.) A
customized forty-five to seventy-five-minute tour answers all their
questions about what goes on here. They'll see lots of different things,
depending on the business of the airport. Kids can talk to skycaps, go
to the boarding lounges, and walk through the screening area where
monitors show items going through the conveyor. Be prepared to
answer questions like, "How does it take pictures of the insides of
things?" and "Why?"
   The Observation Deck is great for, well, observing planes landing
and taking off. Your visit might include the baggage area (you just
never know what your child might find interesting), and for smaller
groups of older kids, the Control Tower, where air-traffic controllers are
at work.
   Kids might even see an Airport Fire and Rescue truck with all of its
heavy-duty equipment. Lastly, they'll board a mock-up wooden aircraft
and watch a video that simulates a flight. Afterwards, the kids are given
little souvenirs of their "trip." Flexibility is a key for this high-flying tour.
   Hours: Tours are available at your convenience, but preferably
             given Mon. - Fri. Two week reservations are needed.
Admission: Free
   Ages: 4 years old and up.

LONG BEACH PRESS-TELEGRAM TOUR   ☽
(562) 435-1161   !
604 Pine Avenue, Long Beach
(*EXIT LONG BEACH FWY [710] E. ON ANAHEIM, R. ON PINE.*)
   Children, at least 7 years of age, get a behind-the-scenes look at all
the different aspects of how a newspaper is put together. The one-hour
tour covers the telemarketing for the Classified Sections; the paper
storage area in the basement, where huge rolls of paper are ready for
print; the press room, where the very loud presses are usually running;
the mail room, where papers get bundled and put together; the
newsroom, where reporters are busy typing their stories; the photo
department; and the composing room, where the paper is pieced
together and made into plates for printing. Tours must have a minimum
of ten people and be booked one month in advance. Tip: Kids can
actually view the presses running through the huge glass windows on
Pine Street and 6th Street - kind of a mini-tour.

Hours: Tours are given Mon. - Fri. at 10am and 3pm.
Admission: Free. Pine Avenue has metered parking.
Ages: 7 years and up.

LOS ANGELES TIMES ☼

(213) 237-5757 !

202 W. 1st Street, Los Angeles

(EXIT HARBOR FWY [110] E. ON 4TH ST., L. ON MAIN ST., L. ON 1ST ST. OR, EXIT SANTA ANA FWY [101] S. ON ALAMEDA, R. ON 1ST ST.)

Children (who are at least 10 years old or in the fifth grade) with journalistic tendencies will enjoy seeing how a newspaper is put together. The forty-minute tour goes through the editorial offices, where news from all over the world is gathered, written, and edited; the composing room, where news stories and advertisements are put together in page format; the library; the photography department; and the test kitchen, where recipes are tested for the Times' Food Section.

If your group is between ten and thirty-five people, a tour can be arranged through the Olympic plant, too, where you'll pass through a pressroom, which is twice the size of a football field; the newsprint storage area, where robot-like automated vehicles carry rolls of newsprint weighing 2,500 pounds; the plate-making area, where newspaper pages go from photographic negatives to aluminum printing plates; and the mail room, where an automated distribution system takes newspapers from presses to the delivery trucks.

Kids (and adults) rarely realize what is takes, on a daily basis, to put together the internationally acclaimed newspaper that gets read with a cup of coffee every morning. Groups need to make reservations thirty days in advance.

Hours: Tours for individuals are available Mon. - Fri. at 11:15am. Tours for groups between ten and thirty-five people are given Mon. - Fri. at 10am or 1:15pm.
Admission: Free. Free parking at the Times garage at 213 S. Spring St.
Ages: 10 years and up.

NASA DRYDEN VISITOR CENTER ☼

(805) 258-3446 !

Lilly Avenue, Edwards Air Force Base

(EXIT THE GOLDEN STATE FWY [5] N. ON THE ANTELOPE VALLEY FWY [14] FWY. EXIT [14] E. ON EDWARDS/ROSAMOND., R. ON LILLY AVE., ALMOST TO HWY. 58)

A mural of twenty aircraft that reflect the aeronautical heritage of NASA Dryden dominates the lobby of the Visitor's Center. This is the primary research and test center for the space shuttle program, as well as a backup landing site. Your tour begins with a fifteen-minute video that gives insight to the importance and accomplishments of the space program. A ninety-minute guided tour, part-walking and part-bus tour, allows you to see past research aircraft, some of the current planes being tested, the control tower, and, time permitting, the fourteen aircraft on display on the base and the museum. (See EDWARDS AIR FORCE BASE / AIR FORCE FLIGHT TEST CENTER MUSEUM.) While some of the information is technical, the sights and the knowledge that does sink in make this a memorable tour for those who are air-bound.

> **Hours:** Tours of NASA are given Mon. - Fri. at 10:15am and 1:15pm.
> **Admission:** Free
> **Ages:** 8 years and up.

NBC STUDIO TOURS   ☼
(818) 840-4444 $$
3000 W. Alameda Avenue, Burbank
(GOING E. ON VENTURA FWY [134], EXIT S. ON PASS AVE., L. ON ALAMEDA. GOING W. ON 134, EXIT, AT HOLLYWOOD WAY, R. ON ALAMEDA.)

Take a seventy-minute walking tour of the NBC Studios and you might see (depending on availability) the Tonight Show set; the wardrobe department; a video demonstration of make-up; an NBC Sports Presentation; set construction; production studios; and maybe even a star or two. It's all contingent on what is going on at the studio that day, but it's usually a wonderful opportunity to see behind-the-scenes of a working studio. (See the JOHNNY CARSON PARK, right across the street.)

> **Hours:** Tours are given Mon. - Fri. from 9am - 3pm, every hour on the hour.
> **Admission:** $6 for adults; $3.75 for ages 5 - 12; children 4 years and under are free.
> **Ages:** 5 years and up.

PACIFIC STOCK EXCHANGE   ☾
(213) 977-4700 $
233 South Beaudry, Los Angeles
(EXIT HARBOR FWY [110] W. ON 3RD ST. IT'S AT THE CORNER OF 3RD AND BEAUDRY.)

Do you have older kids who are studying Wall Street's ups and downs? The twelfth floor offers a viewing gallery that will give them a first-hand look at the action that makes our financial world go 'round.

> **Hours:** The best time for watching the trading is between 7am and 1pm.
> **Admission:** Parking is available in the building - $1 for every twenty minutes, or behind the Stock Exchange - $3.25 for all day.
> **Ages:** 10 years and up.

PARAMOUNT PICTURES ☼

(213) 956-4848 $$$$

860 N. Gower Street, Hollywood
(EXIT HOLLYWOOD FWY [101] W. ON SANTA MONICA BLVD., L. ON GOWER.)

Paramount Pictures offers a two-hour, guided walking tour of its studio for ages 10 and up. This tour includes a historical and informative behind-the-scenes look of a major motion picture and television facility during its day-to-day operations. This is great insight for actor/director/producer "wannabes"!

Hours: Tours are given Mon. - Fri. from 9am - 2pm.
Admission: $15 per person.
Ages: 10 years and up.

SEBASTIAN INTERNATIONAL'S RAIN FOREST ☻

(800) 829-7322 !

6109 DeSoto Avenue, Woodland Hills
(EXIT VENTURA FWY [101] N. ON DESOTO AVE., L. ON ERWIN. IT'S ON THE CORNER.)

Sebastian International is a beauty care company that really cares about the environment and in particular, stopping the depletion of the rain forest. The corporate headquarters is in an angular, artsy building and has a room with displays pertaining to the rain forest. The Wall of Life has holes with objects in it, such as fake plants or animals, to pull out, look at, and read their descriptions. Its purpose is to demonstrate how species depend upon each other. Other exhibits include a big globe that shows how much of the earth used to be covered by rain forests, compared to now-a-days, and a wall-sized aquatic terrarium containing live fish and plants. Take the twenty-minute tour and use Sebastian's as a supplemental aid in teaching your kids about the rain forest.

Hours: Open to the public daily 9am - 3:30pm. Open for school tours Mon., Wed., and Fri. Call for an appointment.
Admission: Free
Ages: 6 years and up.

SOUTHERN CALIFORNIA EDISON GENERATING STATION TOUR ☼

(310) 318-7430 !

1100 Harbor Drive, Redondo Beach
(EXIT SAN DIEGO FWY [405] S. ON WESTERN, R. ON 190TH ST., WHICH TURNS INTO ANITA ST., THEN TURNS IN TO HERONDO, L. ON HARBOR.)

Wear long pants and closed-toed shoes (hard hats are provided) for your two-and-a-half-hour tour of the Edison plant. Kids will learn about the history of Redondo Beach, as well as how electricity is made, and how the ocean waters are a part of the process. They'll visit the control room, and the marine research laboratory where there is a small touch tank.

Hours: Tours are available for groups of fifteen - twenty-five people, Mon. - Thurs. between 8am - 3pm. Reservations are needed.

Admission: Free

Ages: Fifth graders and up.

VAN NUYS AIRPORT TOUR   ☼

(818) 785-8838   !

16700 Roscoe Boulevard, Van Nuys
(EXIT THE 405 FWY W. ON ROSCOE BLVD.)

Here's a way to stay grounded while touring an airport - take the one-and-a-half-hour bus tour of the Van Nuys airport. There are several stops along the way, depending on what's available on the day of your visit. The stops could include seeing the fire station, the helicopter pad, and several smaller aircraft. As the kids watch planes land and take-off, they'll learn the history of the airport and gain some high-flying knowledge.

Hours: Tours are offered for groups of fifteen or more people, Mon. - Fri. at 9:30am (the airport provides the bus for this tour), and 11am (groups provide their own bus for this tour). Reservations are required.

Admission: Free

Ages: 6 years and up.

WARNER BROTHERS, BURBANK   ☼

(818) 954-1744 $$$$$

4000 W. Warner Boulevard, Burbank
(GOING E. ON VENTURA FWY [134], EXIT S. ON PASS AVE., L. ON OLIVE/WARNER.
GOING W. ON 134, EXIT, AT HOLLYWOOD WAY, L. ON ALAMEDA., L. ON HOLLYWOOD
WAY TO WARNER.)

Kids must be at least 10 years-old to participate in this two-hour tour that gives an intimate and educational look at how a studio works. You'll see what is happening that day at the studio. This <u>could</u> mean seeing the wardrobe department, the building of a set, or filming in a sound studio. There are no guarantees as everything depends on the studio's schedule on that particular day, but what a great opportunity to see what actually goes go on behind-the-scenes. The tour will either take some of the romance out of picture-making, or make your child want to be involved in the process! Reservations are required.

Hours: Tours, for no more than 12 people at a time, are given Mon. - Fri. between 9am - 3pm.

Admission: $29 per person.

Ages: 10 years and up.

CRYSTAL CATHEDRAL OF THE REFORMED ☀
CHURCH IN AMERICA
(714) 971-4013   !
4201 Chapman Avenue, Garden Grove
(EXIT SANTA ANA FWY [5] E. ON CHAPMAN AVE.)

   This spectacular sanctuary, enclosed by 10,000 mirrored windows, is an impressive place to stop. Kids (and adults) look up and around in amazement at this church. Tour on your own, or take a forty-minute guided tour which goes through the church and around the other facilities. It will explain how and why it was built, plus offer information about the different ministries going on here. The tower of the Cathedral contains a fifty-two bell carillon that rings every fifteen minutes. (See CALENDAR for the incredible shows, "Glory of Christmas" in December, and "Glory of Easter" in March.)

   Hours: Tours are given Mon. - Sat. from 9am - 3:30pm. (Church functions affect tour times.) Closed major holidays.
   Admission: Donations are accepted.
   Ages: 6 years and up.

FULLERTON MUNICIPAL AIRPORT ☀
(714) 738-6323   !
4011 W. Commonwealth, Fullerton
(EXIT ARTESIA FWY [91] OR SANTA ANA FWY [5] N. ON MAGNOLIA TO END, L. ON COMMONWEALTH, 1 BLOCK TO THE TOWER.)

   Help navigate your kindergartner or older child on this one-hour walking tour. A docent, who is a member of the Fullerton's Pilot Association, will show your group of at least five people, around the airport.

   Tours are modified to fit your particular children's interests and questions. A highlight is sitting in a small Cessna plane and in a helicopter (owned by the Fire Department). Small groups of older kids can visit the Control Tower - depending on how busy the air traffic is. They'll get a bird's eye view of planes landing and taking off, and see how radar works. The tour ends on a high note as souvenirs like plastic wings for future pilots, or a fun facts work-sheet are given out.

   Hours: Hours and days are flexible, although Mon. - Fri. is preferred.
   Admission: Free
   Ages: 5 years and up.

GOODWILL INDUSTRIES ☀
(714) 547-6308   !
410 N. Fairview Street, Santa Ana
(GOING E. ON GARDEN GROVE FWY [22], EXIT S. ON FAIRVIEW ST. GOING W. ON 22, EXIT S. ON HASTER ST., L. ON GARDEN GROVE BLVD., R. ON FAIRVIEW ST. FROM THE SANTA ANA FWY [5], EXIT W. ON 1ST ST., R. ON FAIRVIEW ST.)

Learn how to spread goodwill as you accompany your kids on a half-hour tour of this facility. You'll get an overview of what Goodwill Industries does by watching people, including many disabled people, be trained to work in several different areas. Watching assemble-lines are interesting, as things are put together and packages are shrink-wrapped. Kids will also see recycling in action, as old stuffed animals and toys get fixed up for someone else to play with and love. Check out the receiving dock where the donations are piled. Idea: Clean out your closets and have your kids bring their old toys and clothes to Goodwill. Tip: Next door to the facility is a thrift store and an "as is" store where kids can hunt for treasure amidst the junk. There is no minimum number of people required for a tour, but a week's notice is requested. Goodwill facilities are also located in Long Beach and Los Angeles.

Hours: Tours are given Mon. - Fri. between 10am - 2pm.
Admission: Free
Ages: 5 years and up.

JOHN WAYNE AIRPORT TOUR

(714) 252-5219

3151 Airway Avenue, Costa Mesa
(EXIT SAN DIEGO FWY [405] S. ON BRISTOL, L. ON RED HILL, R. ON BAKER, L. ON AIRWAY.)

This one-hour tour is tailored towards the participants' ages. It shows how the airport is similar to a small city, with different people doing different jobs, each one making a contribution to the community. Kids get the opportunity (depending on the time of day and availability) to talk with pilots and flight attendants, as well as skycaps and airport security. They'll tour the departure and arrival levels, and see the various activities that happen at each one. There are huge windows all along the field, and a V-shape one jutting into it that offers a wonderful view of the planes landing and taking off, planes being serviced, and baggage being loaded and unloaded. A fun remembrance, like an airplane coloring book, is given out at the end of the tour - happy landings! A minimum of ten people are needed for a tour.

Hours: Tours are available 7 days a week, upon request.
Admission: Free
Ages: 5 years and up.

ORANGE COUNTY PERFORMING ARTS CENTER (tour)

(714) 556-2787

600 Town Center Drive, Costa Mesa
(EXIT SAN DIEGO FWY [405] N. ON BRISTOL ST., R. ON TOWN CENTER.)

All the world's a stage! Get a behind-the-scenes look at the 3,000-seat Segerstrom Hall, where major symphony concerts, operas, ballets, and Broadway musicals are presented. Take a tour, beginning at the ticket box office, through the theater, and finishing up backstage. Tour routes may vary due to rehearsal and performance schedules.

Hours: Guided tours are offered Mon., Wed., and Sat. at 10:30am. Reservations are required for a group of 10 or more people.

Admission: Free

Ages: 8 years and up.

THE ORANGE COUNTY REGISTER   ☼
(714) 835-1234   !/$

625 N. Grand Avenue, Santa Ana

(EXIT SANTA ANA FWY [5] S. ON GRAND AVE. IT'S JUST N. OF THE 55 FWY.)

The Register offers two tours of its facility for school groups, each with a slightly different technical and age emphasis. The Community Relation's one-hour tour is given once a month for kids that are at least 11 years old. The Customer Relation's one-hour tour prepares kids beforehand by sending each student five days worth of newspapers and several activity sheets. Both tours cover the newsroom - walking through it and seeing the reporters, editors, and photographers at work; circulation - which includes accounting and customer satisfaction; production - where composing, paste-ups, and plate-making takes place; and the pressroom - where students will see and hear the presses run.

Hours: The Community Relation's tour is offered on the first Wednesday of every month at 3:30pm. The Customer Relation's tour is offered Tues. - Thurs. at 10:30am. Please book tours a week-and-a-half in advance.

Admission: The Community Relation's tour is free. The Customer Relation's tour costs $20 per group of thirty.

Ages: 10 years and up.

ONTARIO INTERNATIONAL AIRPORT   ☼
(909) 988-2700 or (909) 988-2883   !

Vineyard Avenue, Ontario

(FROM THE SAN BERNARDINO FWY [10] EXIT S. ON VINEYARD AVE. FROM THE POMONA FWY [60] EXIT N. ON GROVE AVE., R. ON AIRPORT DR., R. ON VINEYARD AVE.)

Pretend to fly the friendly skies with your youngsters as you go on an hour-and-a-half to two-hour, guided tour of the airport. They will see the hustle and bustle as passengers arrive and depart; walk through a metal detector; see the baggage claim area and, find out, maybe, where luggage actually goes; learn about the people who work at an airport; watch planes land and take off; and more. If a school bus is used, the tour will incorporate a ride arond the airport perimeter, where kids will see and learn about other aspects of aviation.

Hours: Tours are given Mon. - Fri. from 9am - noon during the
school year. Reservations are needed.
Admission: Free
Ages: Kindergarten and up, only.

EAGLE MINING COMPANY   ☽

(760) 765-0036 $$

North end of "C" Street, Julian

*(FROM SAN DIEGO FWY [5] OR ESCONDIDO FWY [15], TAKE 78 FWY E. TO JULIAN.
78 IS WASHINGTON ST. IN JULIAN. FROM THE 8 FWY, TAKE 79 N. TO JULIAN, AT 78
JCT. TURN LEFT ON MAIN ST. GO N. ON "C" ST. FROM MAIN ST., IN THE HEART OF
JULIAN. FOLLOW THE SIGNS.)*

Eureka! There's gold in them thar hills! Original mining equipment
and a few old buildings make it look like time has stood still here. One
of the buildings is a small museum/store with rock specimens, mining
tools, and a glass-cased display of memorabilia from the early 1900's.

Trek through time on your one-hour, guided, walking tour through
two genuine gold mines that were founded in 1870: the Eagle Mine, and
the connecting High Peak Mine. My kids have studied about the Forty-
niners, but to actually go through a gold mine, walk on ore-cart tracks,
see stone tunnels hand-carved by picks, and learn the hardships of
mining, really made a lasting impact on them. We saw the vein that the
miners worked and realized, along with hundreds of other people both
past and present, that gold wasn't easily obtainable. It took one ton of
rock to yield a sugar-cube-size amount of gold! We went up two of the
eleven levels in the mines, saw the hoist room where ore buckets were
used as olden-day elevators, and experienced darkness so black that
we couldn't see our hands in front of our faces. I admire the fortitude of
our early engineers. It's interesting to note the difference between the
earlier smooth rock tunnels that were hand-drilled and the later jagged
edges left from blasting with charges. Don't forget to look up at the
amazing shaft tunnels (and duck your head)!

Outside, we saw the milling equipment used to crush rocks, and
learned the tedious process of extracting gold. Try your hand at
panning for gold (it's harder than it looks) in a "stocked" water trough on
the premises, but warn kids that they can't keep the gold. And just
remember: All that glitters isn't gold.

Julian is a quaint town with unique shops along Main Street. Your
kids will enjoy a stop-off at the Julian Drugstore, on the corner of Main
Street and Washington Street, to enjoy an ice cream at its old-
fashioned soda counter. Also see the JULIAN PIONEER MUSEUM.

Hours: Open daily from 9am - 4pm.
Admission: $7 for adults; $3 for ages 5 - 16; children 4 years and
under are free.
Ages: 4 years and up.

SAN DIEGO UNION-TRIBUNE

(619) 221-7215; or (619) 299-3131

350 Camino de la Reina, San Diego

(EXIT MISSION VALLEY FWY [8] - BETWEEN THE 5 AND 163 FWYS -)

Come and see for yourself how a newspaper is really put together - from stories-in-process to the printed page. The hour-and-fifteen-minute tour encompasses the editorial rooms all the way through to the press rooms, where you might have to cover your ears from the din of the presses. Group tours are given for a minimum of ten people, and a maxiumum of thirty-five people. If you, as an individual, would like to take the tour, you may join in with a pre-registered group tour; usually students.

Hours: Tours are usually given Tues., Wed., and Thurs. at 10:30am.

Admission: Free for an individual; call for group rates. (The fee covers materials sent to your school before your visit.)

Ages: Children must be at least 9 years old

ST. VINCENT DE PAUL VILLAGE

(619) 233-8500 ext. 1122 - tour information

1501 Imperial Avenue, San Diego

(GOING S. ON SAN DIEGO FWY [5], EXIT W. ON IMPERIAL AVE. GOING N. ON 5, EXIT N. ON CROSBY ST., L. ON 25TH ST., L. ON IMPERIAL AVE. FROM ESCONDIDO FWY [15], EXIT E. ON IMPERIAL AVE.)

". . . Give me your tired, your poor, your huddled masses yearning to be free. . ." (Part of a poem that is engraved on the pedestal of the Statue of Liberty.) St. Vincent's Village is a "network of residential centers providing a continuum of care to over 2,000 men, women, and children daily." This incredible, state-of-the-art, self-contained facility aids the poor and homeless in very practical ways. It offers them a new lease on life with homes, meals, life-skills programs, counseling, and medical programs.

A one-hour tour takes your group of ten people through most of the facility - lobby, office, kitchen courtyard, residential buildings, food storage, and medical buildings. This is quite an operation, so a behind-the-scenes tour is eye-opening. If you are seeking to instill compassion in your child and/or if your children are looking for a venue to help those less fortunate, a visit to this village is a good starting point as it sill make an indelible mark upon their hearts: The homeless will no longer be faceless or nameless, but real people with real needs.

Hours: Tours are offered Mon. - Fri. at 9am, 11am, 1pm and 3pm. Please call at least a week ahead of time to reserve a tour date and time.

Admission: Free

Ages: Tours are open to children 12 years and up.

WYCLIFFE BIBLE TRANSLATORS ☼

(714) 969-4630   !

19891 Beach Boulevard, Huntington Beach
(GOING S. ON SAN DIEGO FWY [405], EXIT S. ON BEACH BLVD. GOING N. ON 405,
EXIT S. ON HARBOR BLVD., R. ON ADAMS AVE., R. ON BEACH BLVD.)

"Then Jesus came to them and said, 'All authority in heaven and on earth has been given to me. Therefore go and make disciples of all nations. . .'" (Matthew 28: 18-19) In order to teach peoples around the world about Jesus and for them to have a New Testament, communication is necessary. For communication to happen, languages must be studied, learned, and translated into writing - hence, Cameron Townsend founded Wycliffe Bible Translators. Even with all the available technology, it takes, on the average, fifteen years for a two-person team to produce grammar, a dictionary, and a New Testament in a new language. There are over 6170 languages in the world today and less than half have God's written word!

Now that you know the mission, come explore the headquarters that enables linguists, missionaries, and countless helpers to spread the Good News - it's like taking a trip around the world! One of the second story windows is a huge "family" tree done in stained glass. Also in this immediate area is Martin Luther's impressive German Bible, printed in 1652. Other displays here include pictures of the founder in Guatemala and a bookshelf filled with New Testaments translated into various languages. The hallways are filled with fascinating exhibits such as primitive shields, dolls, bowls, clothing, drums, a necklace of monkey teeth feather headdresses, spears, baskets, statues, and pictures of tribal people from all parts of the earth. The artifacts are riveting, and introduce kids (and adults) to unknown cultures and customs. Downstairs is a life-size diorama, depicting a portion of a primitive village with a hut, large tree, canoe, and drum.

You are welcome to explore the Wycliffe building on your own. However, I highly recommend a tour because explanations about the exhibits are not readily available. Also, you'll want to see the eleven-minute movie in the uniquely decorated Visitors Center Room which shows the purpose and realities of Wycliffe. The tour lasts about an hour and a half. You are invited to attend chapel afterward where visiting missionaries speak. Interested in becoming a part of Wycliffe's vision? Kids can volunteer to do something as simple as stuffing envelopes and/or adopt a missionary by becoming a pen-pal.

Hours: Wycliffe is open Mon. - Fri. from 9am - 4pm. Tours are given Mon., Wed., and Fri. at 10am - no minimum number needed. Group tours are given by appointment.
Admission: Free
Ages: 6 years and up. (Tours are long, but interesting.)

TRANSPORTATION

Take a journey with your child via a plane, train, automobile, cruise, carriage ride, etc., for a truly "moving" experience together. Note: There are numerous boating companies up and down the coastline. I've mentioned only a few, giving just some pertinent facts. Anchors away!

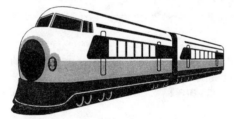

AMTRACK - ONE-DAY TRAIN RIDES

(800) 872-7245   *$$$$*

800 North Alameda Street, Union Passenger Station, Los Angeles
(EXIT SANTA ANA FWY [101] N. ON ALAMEDA.)

What a treat for any age child! The Union Station in Los Angeles is a wonderful starting place for this exciting journey. The station is grandly old and with its high ceiling, arched doorways, marble floors, and wood and leather seats (and a little imagination), it is a nostalgic and romantic reminder of the era when train travel was thee way to go. By incorporating a train trip into your day's excursion, whether it's simply to a park, to a special restaurant, or to a major destination, you make your outing and time together more memorable. The train cars have bathrooms and most have snack cars, too.

The prices quoted are for unreserved round trips; reserved seats are an additional $7. Summer rates are slightly higher. Always ask for special promotions. The age definition for children is 2 through 15 years. Listed below are six Amtrak destinations. Call for destinations closer to you, and please always call for current departure times and prices:

L. A. -   Fullerton; a thirty-three-minute ride that ends five miles north of Knott's Berry Farm.
Departs at 8:30, 10:30, etc. Adults are $12; children are $6.

L. A. -   Anaheim; a forty-two-minute ride, where you can walk across the street to Katella Street, and take a commuter rail to Disneyland, or the Disneyland hotel.
Departs at 8:45, 10:45, etc. Adults are $13; children are $6.50.

L. A. -   Santa Ana; a fifty-two-minute ride.
Departs at 6:45, 8:45, 10:45, etc. Adults are $15; children are $7.50.

L. A. -   San Juan Capistrano; a one-hour and fifteen-minute ride. (It lets off 2 blocks from Mission San Juan.)
Departs at 6:45, 8:45, 10:45, etc. Adults are $21; children are $10.

L. A. -   San Clemente; a one-hour and twenty-six-minute ride.
Departs at 8:45. Adults are $22; children are $12.

L. A. -   San Diego; a two-hour and forty-five-minute ride.
Departs at 8:45, 10:45, etc. Adults are $31; children are $15.50.
Tip: Call Great American Vacations, (800) 321- 9887, for a train ride and San Diego Zoo package.

Ages: All

BELMONT PIER

(562) 434-6781 $$$
29 39th Place, Long Beach
Take a whale-watching cruise, available January through March.
Admission: During the week, fare is $8 for adults for a three-hour
tour; $6.50 for children 12 years and under. On the
weekend, prices are $12 for adults; $7.50 for kids.

BEVERLY HILLS TROLLEY

(310) 271-8126 $
*Departs from the corner of Rodeo Drive and Brighton Way, and Rodeo
Drive and Dayton Drive, Beverly Hills*
(EXIT SAN DIEGO FWY [405] E. ON SANTA MONICA BLVD., R. ON RODEO DR.)
This is the best bargain in Beverly Hills! If you are in the area and
want to give your kids a taste of the posh lifestyle, at an affordable price
to you, hop on board the trolley for a mini-adventure. Take a forty-
minute narrated ride to see some of the most famous sights in Beverly
Hills, including a few celebrity homes, some of the high-priced
boutiques, and the elegant hotels.
Hours: The trolley runs July through September and in
December, Tues. - Sat. every half hour from 10:30am -
5:30pm, but not on rainy days or holidays.
Admission: $2 per person; children 11 years and under are free.
Ages: 5 years and up.

CALIFORNIA AQUATICS

(562) 431-6866 $$$
Bayshore Avenue and 2nd Street, Long Beach
Kayak rentals are $5 - $7 an hour, and peddle boats are $15 an
hour. California Aquatics also offers weekend water field trips for the
family. Another option is to sign up to become a member of the
Snorkeling By Kayak Club. The $35 membership fee is good for four
years, entitling the card bearer and family members (best suited for
junior high schoolers and up) to rent kayaks, peddle boats, wetsuits,
and skindiving equipment for only $10 per day! There is another
Aquatics location on Appian Way, by "Mother's Beach."
Hours: Call for hours.
Ages: 5 years and up.

GONDOLA GETAWAY

(562) 433-9595 $$$$$
5437 E. Ocean Boulevard, Long Beach
(EXIT SAN DIEGO FWY [405] S. ON CHERRY AVE., L. ON OCEAN BLVD.)
Long Beach, California is transformed into Venice, Italy when you
take your child on a gondola ride. I know this attraction is thought of as

a romantic excursion, and it is. It is also a wonderful treat for your child. Step into a Venetian gondola and for one hour, gently slip in and out through the waterways and canals of Naples. Your gondolier will serenade you with Italian music, regale you with interesting tales, or quietly leave you alone. After our kids plied my husband and I with questions about the possibility of sharks and whales, they settled down to enjoy the ride and look at the incredible homes. Christmas time is particularly spectacular, as many of the houses are decked out with lights, animated figures, etc. Make reservations for this time period far in advance.

Bread, cheese, salami, and a bucket of ice are provided, as is a blanket for the colder nights. Bring your own liquid refreshment. Your child will now be dreaming of visiting a tiny little town far away in a boot-shaped country. Ciao!

Hours: Open daily for cruises from 11am - 11pm. Suggested reservations are two weeks in advance.

Admission: Gondolas carry two to six people - $55 for the first two passengers; $10 for each additional person. Carolina carries eight to fourteen people - $17 per person. Fleet cruises carries twenty to fifty-six people - $15 per person.

Ages: 4 years and up.

HYDROSPHERE ☼
(310) 230-3334 $$$$

Long Beach

Looking for adventure with a bite to it? Hydrosphere was founded by a former Cousteau Society diver and documentary film producer. On board the *Pacific Explorer,* you have the opportunity to go on several expeditions, the most unique one being the Shark Tagging and Research Expedition, off the coast of Catalina Island. You are suited-up in a wetsuit and lowered into the ocean in a four-feet deep, open-top snorkel cage as a way of observing marine life while in a protected environment. The adventure takes a predatorial turn when blue, and sometimes mako sharks, drawn by chum, nudge the cages. They can't get to you, but that fact doesn't stop your heart from pounding wildly. Oftentimes, the sharks are brought on board for closer observation, an in-depth lesson, and tagging purposes. Other excursions, also educational in nature, include Sea Lion Observations, Catalina Island Adventure, etc.

Hours: Call for a schedule of dates and times.

Admission: Weekday prices for the Shark Expedition are $119 for adults; $99 for ages 8 - 18. The Sea Lion Observation is $79 for adults; $59 for ages 8 - 18. All weekend prices are higher. Rent a mask and snorkel for $5; a child's wetsuit for $3.

Ages: 9 years and up.

LONG BEACH MARINE INSTITUTE

(714) 540-5751   *$$$*

5857 Appian Way, Long Beach
(Exit Garden Grove Fwy [22] S. on Studebaker, R. on Westminster, R. on
Appian Way, near the bridge, first L. in the Marina lot parking, on the Sea
Explorer Base.)

"The Long Beach Marine Institute, formerly the Newport Institute of Oceanography, is an association of researchers and educators dedicated to bringing marine field research into the classroom and the classroom into the field." L.B.M.I. offers a myriad of different programs to encourage hands-on learning about marine life and their habitats. (Most programs are offered for groups of twenty-five or more. If your group number is smaller, the L.B.M.I. workers will hook you up with another group.) Besides going on the guided kayak tours, snorkeling excursions, and guided tidepool tours, being on board the *Conqueror* is a main attraction. This ninety-foot, ship-shape vessel is the host and means of transportation for several other field trips, too.

The three-hour Sea Creature Trawl is a popular expedition. After a slide presentation and boat orientation, set sail for adventure. Organisms from the sea floor are gathered (by use of a trawl) on board to be inspected and sorted through. Kids love being able to put their hands in this fascinating pile of gunk to find "treasures." They can also examine their findings under a microscope. Combine the Sea Creature Trawl with the Marine Mammal Safari (more than just a whale-watching cruise) for only a few dollars more. Another special outing combines a sleep-over on the boat, with the Sea Creature Trawl, and a morning kayak trip in the back bay. Life doesn't get any better than this!

Hours: Call for times for various excursions.
Admission: Prices range from $7 per person for a tidepool tour to $14 for a Sea Creature Trawl to $62 for the sleep over, etc.
Ages: 4 years and up.

LONG BEACH SPORT FISHING

(562) 432-8993   *$$$$*

555 Pico Avenue, Long Beach
Fishing and whale-watching cruises (January through March) are offered here.
Admission: $12 for adults for the two-and-a-half hour whale-watching cruise; $9 for children 12 years and under.

LOS ANGELES HARBOR CRUISES

(310) 831-0996   *$$$*

Ports O' Call Village, berth 78, San Pedro
Enjoy a one-hour cruise of the inner and outer harbor, past supertankers, cruise ships, a Coast Guard station, Terminal Island, a

Federal Prison, and Angels Gate Lighthouse. *Two-hour coastline cruises along the Palos Verdes Peninsula, and whale-watching cruises are also available.*
Hours: Depart from the Village Boat House Mon. - Fri., noon - 4pm; Sat. - Sun. and holidays, noon - 5pm. Closed Thanksgiving and Christmas.
Admission: $8 for adults for a one-hour cruise; $4 for ages 2 - 12. Two-hour cruises are $12 for adults; $5 for kids.

METRO RAIL
(213) 626-4455

Los Angeles
This rail mode of transportation is a work-in-progress, but the rail lines that are complete make going to a destination an adventure. The Blue Line runs north and south between Long Beach and downtown Los Angeles. Trains run every ten minutes. The Green Line runs east and west, connecting Norwalk, so far, to El Segundo. Trains run alongside, but separate from, the 105 freeway. The Red Line currently runs from Union Station in downtown Los Angeles to Wilshire/Alvarado. Eventually, it will go through Hollywood and out to the San Fernando Valley. The advantages of riding the rails are numerous, such as it's inexpensive, you don't have to fight traffic, you don't have to try to find a parking spot, and kids consider it a treat.
Hours: Trains usually run daily from 6am - 11pm.
Admission: $1.25 on up, depending on your route.
Ages: All

SHORELINE VILLAGE CRUISES
(562) 495-5884

401 East Shoreline Drive, Long Beach
Enjoy a forty-five-minute cruise through Queen's Way Bay, past the Queen Mary. Whale-watching cruises are also available the end of December through March.
Hours: Summertime departures are daily at 1pm, 2pm, 3pm, and 4pm. Wintertime departures are usually weekends only.
Admission: $6 for adults for the harbor cruise; $3 for children 12 years and under. $15 for adults for the two-and-a-half whale-watching cruise; $8 for children.
Ages: 4 years and up.

SPIRIT CRUISES
(310) 548-8080

Berth 77, Ports O' Call, San Pedro
A forty-five-minute cruise through the main channel is offered on Sat. and Sun. One-and-a-half-hour cruises are offered daily May

through October; weekends only the rest of the year. Reservations are suggested.

Admission: $6 for adults for a forty-five-minute cruise; $3 for children 12 years and under.

Ages: 5 years and up.

U.C.L.A. MARINA AQUATIC CENTER   ☼

(310) 823-0048 $$$

14001 Fiji Way, Marina Del Rey

(FROM SAN DIEGO FWY [405], EXIT W. ON THE MARINA [90] FWY, TURNS INTO THE MARIAN EXWY, L. AT THE SECOND STOPLIGHT, MINDANAO WY., L. ONTO ADMIRALTY WY., R. ON FIJI WY. FROM SANTA MONICA FWY [10] EXIT S. ON LINCOLN BLVD., R. ON MINDANAO WY., L. ON ADMIRALTY WY., R. ON FIJI WY.)

Chart your own course to explore the marina! Go windsurfing, kayaking, sailing, rowing, canoeing, etc., via the aquatic center. You can either rent a particular boat for an hour or so, or sign up for a class. At various times throughout the year, an experienced naturalist offers a four-hour natural history cruise on board the sixty-foot research vessel, *Sea World U.C.L.A.* Learn about the animals, and plants, that live in the Santa Monica Bay, and what can be done to take better care of them. Year-round classes are offered, such as oceanography, scuba diving, etc. The summer youth programs make a big splash with kids.

Hours: Hours vary, depending on the season, so please call ahead of time.

Admission: Windsurfing, kayaking, and canoeing rentals are $10 an hour; sailboats are $12; rowboats are $8. Become a member for $45 a year, which allows you discounts on rentals and access to any of the classes.

Ages: Most classes are geared for older children. Although kayaks are single-seaters, kids can join in on canoes, sailboats, and rowboats.

YOUNG EAGLES PROGRAM   ☼

(818) 725-4AIR (4247)   !

Whiteman Airport, Pacoima

(EXIT THE GOLDEN STATE FWY [5] E. ON OSBORNE, PAST SAN FERNANDO RD., TURN L.)

"They will soar on wings like eagles." (Isaiah 40:31) I think all kids (and adults) dream of flying, and the Young Eagles Program helps those dreams become a reality. Kids, ages 8 to 17, are invited to participate, one time only, in this unique flying experience that is offered one Saturday a month. Reservations are needed.

At the airport, after your child registers, he/she will (in no particular order):

• Participate in a pre-flight inspection training, which means looking over an airplane to make sure it's mechanically sound while learning some technical aspects of how to fly a plane.
• Fly! The flight is usually twenty minutes round trip, over Magic Mountain and back. What a thrill! If it becomes too thrilling for your child, airsick bags are provided. The planes are either two-seaters or four-seaters.
• Take a tour of the control tower. Kids will need to keep their voices low so they don't disturb the tower operators.

Two more wonderful freebies are a certificate upon completion of the flight, and a magazine called "Sport Aviation for Kids" that comes later in the mail. Plan on bringing something to munch on as picnic tables are available, and the entire program takes at least two hours. Please remember that everyone here is volunteering their time! Kids who are grounded will enjoy watching the planes take off and land.

Hours:　　One Saturday a month, starting at 10:30am. Call for specific dates.
Admission:　Free
Ages:　　8 - 17 years old.

AIR COMBAT USA, INC. ☿

(800) 522-7590　　　　　　　　　　　　　　　　　　*$$$$$$*

230 N. Dale Place, Fullerton

(EXIT ARTESIA FWY [91] OR N. SANTA ANA FWY [5] N. ON MAGNOLIA, L. ON COMMONWEALTH, R. ON DALE ST., VEER RIGHT FOR DALE PL. OR, EXIT S. ON THE SANTA ANA FWY [5], E. ON ARTESIA, R. ON DALE PL. (JUST AFTER DALE ST.). IT'S AT BEACH/AVIATION, ON THE N. SIDE OF AIRPORT.)

If being a Top Gun is your top dream, here's the opportunity to make it a reality. You, perhaps being an unlicenced pilot and leading an otherwise normal life, will actually fly and fight air-to-air combat. "The SIAI Marchetti SF260 is a current production, Italian-built, fighter aircraft. It has 260 horsepower, can fly at 270 MPH, FAA certified to +6 to -3 G's and can perform unlimited aerobatics. It was originally designed to transition student pilots to jet fighters. It is maneuvered by the stick grip complete with gun trigger, identical to the F4 Phantom. The pilot and guest pilot sit side-by-side with dual controls." If all this has your adrenaline pumping, go for it!

You'll be prepped for your flight in a one-hour ground school, which covers the basics, with emphasis on tactical maneuvers. After being fitted with a flight suit, helmet, and parachute, you'll soar for one hour with the birds over Catalina waters. You're actually in control of the aircraft 90% of the time, while receiving constant instruction on how to get the "enemy." After practicing maneuvers, you'll engage in six "g-pulling" (i.e. gut wrenching) dogfights against a real opponent (i.e. friend, spouse, etc.) A direct hit registers through an electronic tracking system, complete with sound effects and smoke trailing from the other aircraft. This is as close to the real thing as you can possible get without being in the military. I will confess that after a few "high/low yo-yos" and roll overs, I used that special white bag and became part of the 10% that share in this ritual.

After you've landed, and come down from your high, you can view the videos, complete with sound, that were simultaneously recorded from each aircraft. Relive your flight and your "hits" again and again on the copy you receive to take home. This is an unforgettable experience!

Hours: Four classes/flights that accommodate two people each, are offered every day. Class times are 7am, 9:30am, noon, and 2:30pm.

Admission: $695 a flight; $400 for ready/alert, which means they'll call you to come over A.S.A.P. if there is a cancellation.

Ages: 8 years old and up - large enough to wear a parachute and in good health.

BALBOA BOAT RENTALS ☽

(714) 673-7200 $$$

Balboa Peninsula, Balboa

Pontoons, kayaks (starting at $10 an hour), and motorboat rentals (starting at $50 an hour) are offered here.

CALIFORNIAN ☼

(714) 369-6773 $$$$$

Set sail on high seas adventures on the Tallship *Californian*, a full-scale (and impressive-looking) re-creation of the 1848 vintage Revenue Cutter. The purposes of these unique outings are to teach and train fourth grade students and older, the nearly forgotten art of sailing a Tallship, and to cultivate teamwork in an unusual setting. Various programs are offered throughout the year. The Sea Chest Program, for instance, is a three-hour class geared for thirty-five students in the fourth through eighth grades. Curriculum is sent beforehand containing students' shiplogs, a video tape of the *Californian*, a tape of sea chanteys, and a manual for tying knots. After a dock-side orientation, kids will help the crew actually sail the ship, and participate in numerous hands-on activities. What a memorable experience! The ship sails from Chula Vista, Long Beach, San Diego, and northern California, so call for a schedule and complete program information. Individuals are welcome on many of the programs.

Hours: Call for dates and times.

Admission: Starting at $38 per person, depending on the program.

Ages: 10 years old and up.

DAVEY'S LOCKER ☽

(714) 673-1434 $$$

400 Main Street, Balboa

Kayak rentals ($12 the first hour for a two-person craft), fishing, and whale-watching cruises (January through March) are offered here.

Admission: $12 for adults for the two-and-a-half whale-watching cruise; $8 for children 12 years and under.

NEWPORT HARBOR CRUISE, BALBOA PAVILION   ☼
(714) 673-5245 $$

400 Main Street, Balboa

Forty-five and ninety-minute cruises aboard the Pavilion Queen or Pavilion Paddy are available here. Depending on the length of your cruise, you'll see stars' homes such as George Burns and John Wayne; Pirate's Cove, where Gilligan's Island was filmed; and tour around six of the eight islands in the immediate area.

Hours: Daily departures are 11am - 5pm in the summer; 11am - 3pm the rest of the year. Closed Christmas.

Admission: $6 for adults for the forty-five-minute cruise; $1 for ages 5 - 12; children 4 years and under are free. $8 for adults for the ninety-minute cruise; $4 for seniors over 60; $1 for ages 5 - 12; children 4 years and under are free. (Certain discounts available through AAA.)

Ages: 4 years and up.

NEWPORT HARBOR SHOWBOAT CRUISE   ☼
(714) 673-0240 $$

700 E. Edgewater Avenue, Balboa

This forty-five-minute cruise is perfect for kids as they'll go around Balboa Island and, hopefully, see some sea lions. A ninety-minute cruise is also available. Seeing several star's homes and hearing the history of Balboa Island and Peninsula are interesting parts of the cruise.

Hours: Departures for the forty-five-minute cruise are daily at 11am, 1pm, and 3pm; for the ninety-minute cruise, daily on the hour 11am - 6pm in the summer; 11am - 3pm the rest of the year.

Admission: $6 for adults for the forty-five-minute cruise; $1 for ages 5 - 11; children 4 years and under are free. $8 for adults for the ninety-minute cruise; $1 for ages 5 - 11; children 4 years and under are free. Closed December 24 - 25.

Ages: 4 years and up.

NEWPORT LANDING SPORTFISHING   ☼
(714) 675-0550 $$$$

309 Palm, Suite F, Balboa

Whale-watching cruises from January through March are available here.

Admission: $14 for adults for the two-and-a-half hour cruise; $8 for children 12 years and under.

PADDLEPOWER
(714) 675-1215   *$$$*

500 West Balboa Boulevard, Balboa
Kayak rentals are available here.
Admission: Prices range from $9 an hour - $36 for the a day.

RESORT WATERSPORTS
(714) 729-1150   *$$$*

Newport Dunes Resort, Newport Beach
Located in NEWPORT DUNES RESORT, this rental facility has everything you need to make your day at the beach more exciting. Going rates are: $13 an hour for pedal boats, and $45 for electric-powered boats, plus bike rentals and skate rentals, starting at $5 an hour. They also offer kayak tours of a wildlife estuary reserve where you can see crabs, blue herons, snowy egrets, and other birds and animals in their natural habitat. We took a guided tour and learned why this reserve is becoming endangered, as well as some of the clean up projects that we can get involved with. A two-hour tour is $16 per person. What a work-out for those of us not physically fit! But it is also a fun and educational way to spend some family time together.

THE CARRIAGE HOUSE
(909) 781- 0780   *$$$*

Riverside
Take a ride in a beautiful horse-drawn carriage through the historic Mission Inn district. It holds four adults comfortably or two adults, three kids, etc. With horses named Cinderella and Belle, children feel like they are living out a storybook fantasy, if only for a short ride.

Tea parties are a perfect occasion to incorporate a carriage ride. Or, rent the wagon, which seats up to sixteen people, for a cowboy party. At Christmas time, even though there isn't any snow to glisten, the carriage sleigh bells ring, if you're listenin', plus Christmas lights are even more dazzling when seen from this old-fashioned vantage point.

Hours: Carriages can often be found along the Mission Inn district, but calling for reservations is your best bet.
Admission: A ten-minute ride is $10 for two people; twenty-minute rides are $20 for the entire carriage, and hour rides run $50.
Ages: All

CARRIAGES BY MARGARET
(909) 370-8691 or (909) 370-8691   *$$$*

Riverside

What Cinderella or Prince Charming child hasn't dreamed of riding in a horse drawn carriage, if only because of fairy tales? Take a ride in an immaculate white or black carriage pulled by a beautiful, silky horse that is gentle enough to pet. The carriages seat six people, four adults comfortably, while another person can ride up front with the driver. If you have a real party, reserve the horse-drawn trolley car that seats up to twenty people! Go down historic Magnolia Street or choose your own destination.

Hours: Although the carriages can be sometimes be found in front of Mission Inn, it's best to call for reservations.

Admission: Prices vary, depending on the length of the ride and the destination. A reserved carriage usually costs about $60 an hour if picked up at Mission Inn.

Ages: All

ORANGE EMPIRE RAILWAY MUSEUM   ☼
(909) 657-2605   !/$$
2201 South "A" Street, Perris
(EXIT ESCONDIDO FWY [215] W. ON 4TH ST. A MORE DIRECT ROUTE THAN FOLLOWING THE SIGNS IS TO TURN L. ON "A" ST., THEN GO DOWN A FEW MILES UNTIL YOU REACH THE MUSEUM ON THE LEFT.)

If you love trains, make tracks to the Orange Empire Railway Museum where you can really go full steam ahead! This huge, unique, outdoor museum is best described as a work-in-progress. Railcars from all over the country, in various states of disrepair, find their way here. Some are being restored while others are just stationed here. Walk around to see which railcars the volunteers are working on.

The museum is open daily, but weekends are the prime time to visit as this is the only time when train and trolley rides are available. Purchase an all-day ride ticket, which is good for rides on a locomotive, electric trolley, streetcar, freight car, and/or passenger car. (Usually three types of cars are running.) Each ride lasts about fifteen minutes, with a few stops along the way to explain the history of the vehicles and the museum, and the impact of train transportation in Southern California. The train's whistle, the clickety-clack of its wheels, and the clanging of streetcar bells add excitement to your adventure.

Walk through the several car houses (i.e. buildings that house railcars) to see historic "Yellow Cars" (which my kids thought looked like school buses); a San Francisco cable car; electric railway streetcars and locomotives dating from 1900; steam engines; and wood passenger cars. The car houses are usually open on weekends. They are open during the week whenever volunteer staff is available.

Check out the Middleton Collection that includes old toy and scale model railroad cars, etc. There is an ongoing video that shows how tracks are laid. We got derailed at the gift shop, which offers videos, books, and all sorts of train paraphernalia. There are also a few picnic tables and grassy areas here.

Hours: The grounds are open daily from 9am - 5pm. Train and trolley rides are available only on weekends and major holidays from 11am - 5pm. Closed Thanksgiving and Christmas.

Admission: The museum is free. All-day ride passes are $6 for adults; $4 for ages 6 - 11; children 5 years and under ride free.

Ages: All

BARNSTORMING ADVENTURES / AIR COMBAT ☼

(800) 759-5667 $$$$$

2198 Palomar Airport Road, McClellan Palomar Airport, Carlsbad
(EXIT SAN DIEGO FWY [5] E. ON PALOMAR AIRPORT RD.)

Flying in a restored open-cockpit biplane, wearing helmet, goggles, and a pilot scarf reminds me of another flying ace, Snoopy, and his adventures with the Red Baron. (Yes, I do know Snoopy is not real.) You'll be flying over the stunning San Diego coastline for twenty minutes, side-by-side with another passenger (your child), while the pilot is located behind you. It's like riding a motorcycle in the sky!

Another adventure offered is Air Combat. After a crash course, so to speak, on general aviation and specifically, tactical maneuvers during combat, you'll suit up and take off for the wild blue yonder. When you've gotten a feel for the controls, get ready for combat with a real "enemy." You'll fly for thirty minutes, experiencing "high low yo-yos" (which are as gut wrenching as they sound), and other maneuvers in your dogfight - let the fur fly! This exhilarating experience is one that you'll remember and talk about for the rest of your life.

Hours: Call to schedule a flight.

Admission: Barnstorming Adventures start at $49 per person for two people. Air Combat starts at $249 per person and a discount if you B.Y.O.E. (Bring Your Own Enemy). Ask about current specials.

Ages: 8 years and up.

CINDERELLA'S CARRIAGE ☼

(619) 239-8080 $$$$$

In front of the Harbor House Restaurant, Seaport Village or in front of Crowces Restaurant at 5ᵗʰ Avenue and "F" Street, Gaslamp Quarter, San Diego

(SEAPORT VILLAGE: GOING S. ON SAN DIEGO FWY [5], EXIT W. ON ASH ST., L. ON 4ᵀᴴ, R. ON BROADWAY TO END, L. ON HARBOR DR. GOING N. ON 5, EXIT S. ON 6ᵀᴴ AVE., R. ON BROADWAY TO END, L. ON HARBOR DR.
GASLAMP QUARTER: GOING S. ON SAN DIEGO FWY [5], EXIT W. ON ASH ST., L. ON 6ᵀᴴ AVE., R. ON "F" ST. GOING N. ON 5, EXIT S. ON 6ᵀᴴ AVE., R. ON "F" ST.)

The largest carriage company on the coast still makes every ride feel special and intimate. Enjoy the waterfront from a different vantage as you take a carriage around Seaport Village or explore the historic and romantic Gaslamp Quarter. The one-horse powered carriages are pulled by large draft horses (i.e. Clydesdale or Belgium horses). Kids (and adults) will get a thrill out of clip-clopping along the streets of downtown San Diego. And don't worry, your Cinderella's carriage won't turn into a pumpkin before your ride is over.

Hours: Carriages are available at Seaport Village on weekends from noon - 11pm and at the Gaslamp District on weekends from 6pm - 11pm. You may just show up, or you may make reservations for a ride.

Admission: Reserved rates for up to four people is $45 for a half-hour ride; unreserved rates are $40 for a half-hour ride.

Ages: All

H & M LANDING   ☀
(619) 222-0427 $$$$
2803 Emerson, San Diego
(GOING S. ON SAN DIEGO FWY [5], EXIT S. ON ROSECRANS ST., L. ON EMERSON. GOING N. ON 5, EXIT AT HAWTHORNE ST., GO STRAIGHT ON BRANT ST., L. ON LAUREL, R. ON N. HARBOR DR., L ON ROSECRANS ST., L. ON EMERSON.)

San Diego's oldest whale-watching expedition company offers two, three, and even five-hour cruises during whale-watching season, January through mid-March. Three-hour cruises depart at 10am and 1:30pm and head to the coastal waters of Point Loma. Five-hour trips depart at 10am and travel to the Coronado Islands and Mexico's marine wildlife sanctuary. Be on the lookout for whales, sea lions, dolphins, and elephant seals.

Hours: Stated above.

Admission: Whale watching is $17 for adults; $12 for children 12 years and under.

OCOTILLO WELLS STATE VEHICULAR   ☀
RECREATION AREA
(760) 767-5391   !
(TAKE 78 E. OUT OF JULIAN, BEYOND OCOTILLO WELLS.)

For a little off-roading fun, try Ocotillo Wells Recreation Area where you can go up hills, over sand dunes, and through dry washes! You must provide your own vehicles (and have them registered), but the entrance is free and so are primitive camping sites.

Hours: Open daily.

Admission: Free

Ages: 6 years and up.

OLD TOWN TROLLEY TOURS   ☀ - ☼
(610) 298-8687 $$$$
San Diego

Really get to know the city of San Diego by taking a narrated tour on board an old-fashioned looking trolley. The tour guide will tell you about the history of San Diego, plus lots of fun stories. One of the best features about this tour is that you can take a continuous two-hour tour, or jump off (so to speak) and rejoin the tour at any time throughout the day. There are nine locations covered on the loop, including Old Town, Seaport Village, Horton Plaza, San Diego Zoo, and Balboa Park. Appropriately nickname, "transportainment," we enjoyed the commentary, the freedom of stopping at attractions, staying for a bit, and getting back on board when we need were ready. Hassle-free parking is another plus. Ask about their specialty tours, such as the Military Tour, where you'll see various aspects of the military in San Diego.

Hours: Trolleys run daily from 9am - 5pm.

Admission: $20 for adults; $8 for ages 6 - 12; children 5 years and under are free.

Ages: 5 years and up.

SAN DIEGO HARBOR EXCURSION ☼

(619) 234-4111   *$$$*

1050 North Harbor Drive, Broadway Pier, San Diego

(GOING S. ON SAN DIEGO FWY [5], EXIT W. ON ASH ST., L. ON 4TH, R. ON BROADWAY TO END. GOING N. ON 5, EXIT S. ON 6TH AVE., R. ON BROADWAY TO END.)

Enjoy a one or two-hour narrated cruise along San Diego's coast in a nice excursion ship. A snack bar is on board. During a one-hour cruise, you'll see the Star of India, the Naval Air Station, and the San Diego shipyards that hold merchants' vessels, fishing boats, and more. During the two-hour cruise, you'll also travel by the Cabrillo National Monument. Whale-watching trips are given January through mid-March. Tip: Bring a jacket or sweater on any journey by sea! (Also see SAN DIEGO BAY FERRY.)

Hours: Cruises are available daily starting at 10am. Call for specific times.

Admission: One-hour cruises cost $12 for adults; $10 for seniors and military; $6 for ages 3 -12; children 2 years and under are free. Two-hour cruises are $17 for adults; $15 for seniors and military; $8.50 for ages 3 - 12 years. Parking at the Broadway pier is $1 per hour; $3 maximum.

Ages: 3 years and up

SAN DIEGO RAILROAD MUSEUM ☼

(619) 595-3030   *$$$*

Highway 94, Campo

(EXIT 8 FWY (45 MILES FROM DOWNTOWN) S. ON BUCKMAN SPRINGS RD., 10.5 MILES TO JUNCTION WITH HWY 94., BEAR RIGHT (1.5 MILES) TO OLD STONE STORE, L. AFTER RAILROAD TRACKS AND FOLLOW SIGNS TO THE MUSEUM.)

The sound of a train whistle blowing has always been a signal for adventure! Come abooooard the San Diego Railroad Museum train for an hour-and-a-half ride your children will never forget. You'll ride in restored classic steam or diesel locomotives, depending on what is available. My boys loved the freedom of moving about while traveling. They walked in between the cars (parents are asked to accompany minors); watched the scenic mountains and meadows roll past; saw a few cows; and played cards. Tip: We brought a picnic lunch, as only snack food is available for sale on the train. At the halfway point, kids can view (from the windows) the engine being switched around to pull you back the way you came. The conductors were friendly and shared a lot of information about railroads and the history of the area.

Free walking tours are offered at the end of the excursion. You'll see numerous old and restored rail cars such as passenger, Pullman, and freight cars; learn about the historical significance of the railways; and walk through a caboose. The forty-five minute tour leads you back to the Campo Depot.

At the Museum (Depot) there are a few stationary pull carts to climb on, a Box Car Theater that shows continuously running videos about the railway system, a gift shop, and picnic tables. In addition to weekly rides, special trips are arranged to Tecate, Mexico, and Jacumba, California.

Hours: The Museum hours are 9am - 5pm on weekends and holidays. Trains depart at noon and at 2:30pm on Sat., Sun., and most holidays. Closed Thanksgiving and Christmas.

Admission: To simply come and look at the trains is free. Train rides cost $10 for adults; $8 for seniors and active military; $3 for ages 6 - 12; children 5 years and under are free.

Ages: 3 years and up.

SAN DIEGO TROLLEY

(619) 685-4900 - 24-hour information express line;
(619) 233-3004 - office;
(619) 234-5005 - for persons with hearing impairments.

San Diego

The San Diego Trolley (and bus) line is a great way to get around San Diego. The North-South line extends from Old Town all the way down to San Ysidro. From this last stop at the border, you can either walk into Mexico, or take a cab. Park for free at the Old Town Transit Center, or all day at the MTS tower garage at 12th and Imperial for $6. The East line goes from Santee to Seaport Village. There are several places to catch the trolley line along the routes, with many of the stops being at major attractions. Part of the fun for a child is just the ride. (Also see OLD TOWN TROLLEY TOURS for another way to get around San Diego.)

Hours: It runs daily from 5am - 1am with service every fifteen minutes most of the day.

Admission: One-way fares range from $1 - $2.25, depending on how far you go. Children 4 years and under ride for free. Tickets are usually dispensed from machines.

Ages: All

TORREY PINES GLIDER PORT

(619) 452-9858

!

2800 Torrey Pines Scenic Drive, La Jolla

(EXIT SAN DIEGO FWY [5] W. ON GENESEE AVE., L. ON N. TORREY PINES RD., R. ON TORREY PINES SCENIC DR., TO THE END ONTO THE DIRT PARKING LOT.)

Man has had dreams and aspirations of flying since the beginning of time. Hang gliding and paragliding are the closest things we'll get to it in this lifetime (and they are much better than Icarus' attempt!) Kids may participate in this uplifting sport, or come to just watch. We brought a picnic lunch (there are tables at the cliff tops), although a full-service snack bar is here, too. Besides the exhilarating sight of gliders soaring and dipping along the coastline, there is a breathtaking view of the ocean and beach. And the small planes flying overhead are really remote control planes that have a take-off/landing site right next "door."

Hours: Flights are scheduled daily, although if you're coming to watch, you might want to call first to see if anyone is actually flying that day. Closed Christmas.

Admission: Free, unless you're flying! Tandem introductory lessons, starting at $125, usually take about an hour which includes ground school instruction and about 30 minutes of flight time. Solo lessons, starting at $125, can take all day with actual gliding practice done off "bunny slopes."

Ages: All to come and watch; 5 years and up for tandem; at least 100 pounds for solo flights.

FILLMORE & WESTERN RAILWAY

(805) 524-2546

$$$$

351 Santa Clara Avenue, Central Park Depot, Fillmore

(TO REACH THE CENTRAL PARK DEPOT IN FILLMORE: EXIT STATE ROUTE 126 N. ON CENTRAL AVE. AND PROCEED 1 BLOCK. TO REACH THE SANTA PAULA DEPOT: EXIT STATE ROUTE 126 N. ON STATE HIGHWAY 150 [OR 10TH ST.] AND PROCEED 3 BLOCKS.)

"More powerful than a locomotive"; "The Great Train Robbery"; "The Little Engine that Could" - What does this potpourri of things bring to mind? A train ride, of course! Riding on a train is a real adventure for children. The countryside is scenic along this route with citrus groves and beautiful landscapes. This railway line is also a favorite Hollywood location, so many of the trains you'll see and ride on have appeared in movies and television shows. Snacks are available on board.

There are several train rides offered. Hop on board for a two-hour, round-trip steam or diesel ride, between Fillmore and Santa Paula. You might have time to stop off at your destination city for a little while - check with the ticket agent about space availability for the return trip. Spirit of the West train rides include a stop at a private location for a barbecue dinner and musical entertainment. Other specialty rides are offered throughout the year.

Hours: Trains usually depart from Fillmore on Sat., 11:45am and 2:10pm; Sun., 10:30am, 11:45am, and 3:10pm.

Admission: Round-trip rides are $14 for adults; $12 for seniors; $8 for ages 4 - 12; children 3 years and under are free. Spirit of the West rides are $44.50 for adults; $40 for seniors; $37.50 for ages 8 - 12; $15 for children 7 years and under. Other specialty rides vary in price.

Ages: 3 years and up.

JIM HALL RACING SCHOOL ☼

(805) 654-1329 $$$$$

675 Harbor Boulevard, Ventura

(EXIT VENTURA FWY [101] L. ON VICTORIA, R. ON GONZALEZ, L. ON HARBOR BLVD.)

What child doesn't like racing around? Now he/she can learn how to do it in karts! Besides the adult classes, this racing school offers cadet classes, for kids 8 - 12 years old. Classes range from half-day instruction to a week, or more. On a modified course, the cadet group will learn safety (yea!), how to drive, braking techniques (this could be especially valuable in just a few years), and they'll even get timed. Watch out, Mario Andretti!

Hours: Call for class hours.

Admission: Varies, depending on the length of class. A half day for cadets, which is three hours of instruction and driving, starts at $95.

Ages: 8 years and up.

SANTA PAULA AIRPORT / CP AVIATION, INC. ☼

(805) 933-1155   !/$

830 E. Santa Maria Street, Santa Paula

(EXIT THE 126 FWY. N. ON STATE HIGHWAY 150 [OR 10TH ST.], L. ON HARVARD BLVD., L. ON 8TH ST., L. ON SANTA MARIA ST.)

This small airport is kid-friendly, partly because of its size, and partly because it's always fun to watch planes land and take off. Instead of just watching, however, why not take the kids up for a spin, literally! If your child is at least 12 years old (and doesn't get motion sickness), he/she can take an exhilarating twenty-minute aerobatic ride with loops, rolls, and G's (better than a roller coaster!) for $89. For those who enjoy a calmer, scenic ride, a Cessna 172, which seats three passengers, is only $39.50 (total) for a half-hour flight. Other aircraft are available for flights, too. Lunch at the airport restaurant will complete your lofty adventure.

One Sunday a month, take a free tour of the fifteen or so antique aircraft on display here. Depending on the docent, kids can look at and maybe touch these unique airplanes.

Hours: The airport is open daily. Call for hours for a flight. The antique aircraft and tour is only offered on the first Sunday of the month from 10am - 2pm.

Admission: Free, unless you are going to fly.

Ages: 4 years and up for a look around the airport and a scenic flight.

ZOOS AND ANIMALS

Kids and animals seem to go hand-in-hoof - both are adorable and neither is easy. Animal lovers - this section is for you! Tip: Take a trip to a pet shop. (See "Pets" in the IDEAS/RESOURCES section for some of our local favorites.)

CABRILLO MARINE AQUARIUM and BEACH   ☾
(310) 548-7562 $$
3720 Stephen M White Drive, San Pedro
(EXIT HARBOR FWY [110] TO THE END, L. ON GAFFEY ST., L. ON 9TH ST., R. ON PACIFIC AVE. ALMOST TO THE END, L. ON 36TH ST. WHICH TURNS INTO STEPHEN M WHITE.)

Explore the underwater treasures of Los Angeles Harbor without ever getting wet! Cabrillo Marine Aquarium specializes in the marine life of Southern California, and has quite a few tanks (mostly at kids' eye-level) filled with a wide variety of sea life.

The front Courtyard has full-sized killer whale, shark, and dolphin models. A full-grown gray whale is outlined on the cement - its size defines big! Kids are welcome to touch the whale bones in the Whale Graveyard.

The exhibit halls have tanks filled with live jellyfish, crustaceans, octopuses, fish, leopard sharks, moray eels, and other sea animals. There are numerous displays of preserved animals, like seals and sea lions; bones, skeletons, jaws and teeth of sharks and whales; pictures; and other models of sea life. My boys also liked pushing the button to hear the recording of a whale singing, although their renditions of it were more grating than musical. We also watched an angel shark blend into the sandy ocean floor; touched a sample of shark skin and compared it to a sample of sandpaper; and saw a slide show at the auditorium. Call to see what's currently showing.

As most kids have this inherent need to explore the world with their hands and not just their eyes, a definite favorite is the Tidepool Touch Tank. Kids can gently touch sea anemones, sea stars, etc.

The Cabrillo Aquarium offers seasonal events like grunion hunting (March through July), whale watching (January through April), and various workshops. At low tide (call for particular times and seasons), tidepool tours are given at the beach in an area called Pt. Fermin Marine Refuge.

Don't forget to pack your swimsuits and beach towels as CABRILLO BEACH is right outside the Aquarium. Wonderful sandy stretches and a play area await your children. For more adventuresome kids (or whosoever's parents will let them), there are rock jetties to explore. Enjoy your day playing by the ocean, and learning more about it.

Hours: The Aquarium is open Tues. - Fri., noon - 5pm; Sat. - Sun., 10am - 5pm. Closed Thanksgiving and Christmas. The Touch Tank doors open for twenty minutes at a time Tues. - Fri. at 1:30pm, 2:30pm, and 3:30pm; Sat. - Sun. at 11:30am, 1:30pm, 2:30pm, and 3:30pm. Slide shows are presented Tues. - Sun. at 11am and 2pm. The beach is open daily from 6am - 10pm.

Admission: The Aquarium is free. Parking, however, is $6.50 per car. If you get here early enough, you can park on the street and just walk through the beach/Aquarium entrance gate.

Ages: All

EXOTIC FELINE BREEDING COMPOUND   ◑

(805) 256-3793   !

Rhyolite Avenue, Rosamond

(EXIT ANTELOPE VALLEY FWY [14] W. ON ROSAMOND BLVD. (TO THE E. IS EDWARDS AIR FORCE BASE), R. ON MOJAVE-TROPICO RD., L. ON RHYOLITE AVE.)

This place is the cat's meow! There are fifty exotic wild cats living here, representing over fifteen different species. Since it is a breeding compound, you're almost guaranteed to see a few kittens, too. Unlike traditional zoos, the safety fences keep you only a few feet (not yards) away from the caged animals. This allows for plenty of up-close viewing. (Picture-taking, however, is not allowed unless you are an E.F.B.C. member.)

Strolling along the cement pathways, we saw jaguars, panthers, pumas, lynxes, fluffy Amur leopards, regal-looking servals, weasel-like jaguarundi, and lots of Chinese leopards. Do take a tour to see the cats in the back, where you'll see more leopards, plus three huge Siberian tigers that play with toys such as truck tires and bowling balls. You'll learn about the animals - what they eat, how much they weigh, their life span, etc., - and about the importance of this breeding compound. Tip: Hold on to young children while on the "back lot" tour. Cats tend to see them as potential meals, and although they are in cages (the cats, not the kids), only ropes further separate kids from cats who can stick their paws between the bars.

The gift shop has a few displays showing some of the reasons these cats are facing extinction - a fur coat made from fifteen bobcats, and another made from over fifty leopards. Tip: Late afternoon and cooler months are the best times to visit the compound as this is when the felines are more active. Please call if you want to schedule a tour for ten or more people. Educational outreach programs are also available.

Hours: Open Thurs. - Tues. from 10am - 4pm. Closed Christmas.

Admission: Free. Membership is $15 for an individual; $25 for a family.

Ages: 4 years and up.

THE FARM

(818) 341-6805 - recording; $$

(818) 885-6321 - The Farm on the weekends.

8101 Tampa Avenue, Reseda

(EXIT VENTURA FWY [101] N. ON TAMPA)

This Farm is like Old MacDonald's place in the song with all those vowels. There are over 100 animals to pet and feed (50¢), and even a few to hold. The llamas, cows, chickens, bunnies, turkeys, sheep, ducks, pigs, peacocks, and goats are readily accessible to pet through the fence pens. If you come at the right time of year, your children will also see baby animals and have the opportunity to cuddle a lamb or kid (i.e. baby goat). Old tractors and bales of hay (and aroma!) add to the farm atmosphere. Riding lessons and/or pony rides around a track are available, too. And yes, they do birthday parties.

Hours: Open Sat. - Sun. and holidays from 10am - 6pm, weather permitting.

Admission: $3 for ages 1 and up. Pony rides are an additional $2.50.

Ages: All

HOLLYWOOD PARK

(310) 419-1500   *$$*

1050 South Prairie Avenue, Inglewood

(EXIT SAN DIEGO FWY [405] E. ON CENTURY, L. ON PRAIRIE OR EXIT CENTURY FWY [105] N. ON PRAIRIE.)

Do your kids like horsing around? At Hollywood Park they can see thoroughbred horses, and enjoy a children's play area located at the north end of the park. Arcade games are also available here.

Hours: The season goes from April through July. Call for racing information and times.

Admission: $6 for adults (which includes parking and a program); children 16 years and under are free.

Ages: 4 years and up.

KELLOGG'S ARABIAN HORSE FARM

(909) 869-2224   *$*

Kellogg Drive, California State Polytechnic University, Pomona

(GOING E., EXIT SAN BERNARDINO FWY [10] S. ON KELLOGG DR. GOING N., EXIT ORANGE FWY [57] W. ON TEMPLE, R. ON S. CAMPUS DR., L. ON KELLOGG DR.)

Come see beautiful Arabian horses in an hour-long show. The horses demonstrate jumping, prancing, and some amazing tricks. Afterward, you're welcome to visit the horses. Students at the college use the horses to train and to study horse husbandry. The stables are open during the week throughout the year, but springtime is the best time to visit, as there are newborn colts to see.

Hours: The shows are offered October through June, on the first Sunday of each month at 2pm.

Admission: $3 for adults; $2 for ages 6 - 17; children 5 years and under are free.

Ages: 3 years and up.

LAKEWOOD PONY RIDES AND PETTING ZOO   ☀
(562) 860-1108 $
11369 E. Carson Street, Lakewood
(EXIT SAN GABRIEL RIVER FWY [605] W. ON CARSON. IT'S IN THE LAKEWOOD
EQUESTRIAN CENTER.)

If you're in the *neigh*borhood, saddle-up for a pony ride in this small park-like riding center. Choose from either a pony sweep, a parent-led walk around the track, or a trotting track (for ages 3 years and up). There is also a small petting zoo with a llama, a turkey, a pot belly pig, plus goats, rabbits, and sheep. Ponies are available to come to your house for a party, too!

Hours: Open Wed. - Sun. from 10am - 5pm.
Admission: Pony rides are $2. The petting zoo is 50¢ per person, or
$1 for the family.
Ages: Children 6 months (or able to sit up), and up to 100
pounds.

LONG BEACH AQUARIUM OF THE PACIFIC   ☼
(562) 590-3100   n/a
200 Shoreline Drive, Long Beach
(EXIT LONG BEACH FWY [710] E. ON SHORELINE DR.)

While the Pacific Ocean laps gently on the shores, just a few feet away a new aquarium is being built that will showcase the sea creatures living in these waters. Opening in summer, 1998, the multi-level Aquarium of the Pacific, encompassing more space than three football fields, will feature three main exhibit areas. The Southern California and Baja area will have octopus, leopard sharks, sea turtles, jellyfish, touch tanks, and a Kids Cove that can be reached by an underwater tunnel. Visitors can watch playful sea otters being fed at the Northern Pacific area. A short video will explain how otters eat, while a tank filled with live crabs and urchins (otter food) is nearby. Other animals in this exhibit area include diving birds, schools of fish, giant sea stars, and spider crabs. Tropical Pacific will be the most vibrant display area, with tanks containing brilliantly colored fish, and coral reef landscape. Here you'll see clownfish, seahorses, seasnakes, stinging catfish, and more. There will also be plenty of interactive exhibits at the Aquarium, as well as educational programs, and an outside viewing area where you'll be able to see seals. So much to look forward to!

Hours: To be announced.
Admission: To be announced
Ages: 2 years and up.

LOS ANGELES ZOO   ☼
(213) 666-4090 $$$
Griffith Park, Los Angeles

(GOING N. ON GOLDEN STATE FWY [5] OR W. VENTURA FWY [134], EXIT AT ZOO DR. AND FOLLOW THE SIGNS. GOING E. ON 134, EXIT S. ON VICTORY BLVD., L. ON ZOO DR. GOING S. ON 5, EXIT S. ON WESTERN, L. ON VICTORY BLVD. TO ZOO DR.)

All the big-name animals star at the Los Angeles Zoo - elephants, Siberian tigers, mountain lions, giraffes, bears, kangaroos, etc. Our favorites are the apes, chimps, and other primates - they provide entertainment that tops television any day! An aquatic area features otters and seals. The darkened Koala House has koalas and other nocturnal animals in their nighttime environment. Don't forget to ssssstop by the Reptile House.

Walk through a fun cave with interactive exhibits to get to Adventure Island, the children's zoo. Once in the kid's zoo, they can pet barnyard animals through the fence pens; learn more about various animals and their habitats by using touch screens; see baby animals in the nursery; and watch the "Animals and You" live demonstration/show that allows them to see, maybe touch, and definitely learn about an assortment of animals in a more intimate setting.

Come visit the prairie dogs for a fun photo opportunity. Kids can pop their heads up from underneath the ground into a plexiglass dome while real prairie dogs are looking at them! If you get tired of walking around this huge and hilly zoo, purchase an all-day shuttle pass for $3 for adults, $1 for seniors and ages 2 to 12. The shuttle goes around the perimeter of the zoo, and will drop you off or pick you up at various stops along the way.

Hours: Open daily from 10am - 5pm. Closed Christmas.
Admission: $8.25 for adults; $5.25 for seniors; $3.25 for ages 2 - 12. (Certain discounts are available through AAA.)
Ages: All

MARINE MAMMAL CARE CENTER AT FORT ☀ MACARTHUR

(310) 548-5677   !

3601 South Gaffey Street, San Pedro
(EXIT THE HARBOR FWY [110] S. ON GAFFEY ST. GO ALMOST TO THE END OF GAFFEY, TURN R. THROUGH THE GATES ON LEAVENWORTH DR., JUST PAST THE FORT MACARTHUR MUSEUM.)

Injured or sick marine mammals, like sea lions and seals, are brought here, doctored, and taken care of until they are able to be released back into the wild. Rehabilitation can take one to three months, depending on the case. We saw one seal that was severely underweight and another that had numerous shark bites. This small facility usually houses five to twelve marine mammals, outside in chain link fence pens. Your children have an opportunity to learn more about these animals as knowledgeable volunteers are on hand to answer any questions kids might ask. And they do ask! There are also classes offered through the school system that utilize the laboratory inside the adjacent building. (See FORT MACARTHUR MUSEUM, just across the street.)

Hours: Open daily from 8am to 4pm.

Admission: Free

Ages: All - younger ones will just enjoy seeing the animals, while older ones can learn about them, and appreciate what the Center does.

MONTEBELLO BARNYARD ZOO / GRANT REA PARK

(213) 887-4595 - park; (213) 727-0269 - pony and horse rides   !/$

600 Rea Drive (Grant Rea Park), Montebello

(EXIT SAN GABRIEL RIVER FWY [605] E. ON BEVERLY BLVD., R. ON REA DR.)

The small Barnyard Zoo is at one corner of the Grant Rea Park. This small "zoo" makes a stop at the park a little more special. It has goats, pigs, a cow, llamas, and sheep to pet through pens, plus an aviary with doves and peacocks. Younger children can take a pony ride around a track and/or join in taking a short hayride.

The surrounding, nice-sized park is pretty. It has baseball diamonds, a few pieces of metal climbing structures (for older kids), and bike trails along the river bed.

Hours: The zoo is open daily 9:30am - 5pm. The park is open daily from 7am - dusk. Pony rides are open zoo hours, except on Mondays, when it is closed.

Admission: Free to the park and zoo. Pony rides are $2 per ride, twice around the track; hayrides are $1 per person for a five-minute ride.

Ages: All

ROUNDHOUSE AQUARIUM

(310) 379-8117   !/$

Manhattan Beach Boulevard, at the end of Manhattan Beach Pier, Manhattan Beach

(EXIT SAN DIEGO FWY [405] W. ON ROSECRANS AVE., L. ON PACIFIC COAST HIGHWAY, TAKE THE NEXT R. ON VALLEY DR., R. ON MANHATTAN BEACH BLVD.)

Something's fishy at the Roundhouse Aquarium! On your way out to the Aquarium, which is located at the end of the concrete pier, check out all the beach activity. There is sand volleyball, surfing, swimming, and of course, sun bathing. You can also, ironically, fish from the pier.

This marine learning center is very small, but packed with information and exhibits. The various tanks contain leopard sharks and moray eels; a baby octopus; a fifty-year old, seventeen-pound spiny rock lobster (God definitely created some odd-looking creatures); giant bass; and a Touch Tank containing mostly sea stars. A few other tanks with tropical fish and local invertebrates round out the collection at

Roundhouse Aquarium. There are also whale bones and shark's teeth to examine.

Upstairs is a play and study center complete with sea animal puppets, books, and videos. It gets crowded quickly inside the Aquarium, but the outside beach and sidewalk shops are great side ventures.

The Aquarium also offers marine science programs and field trips for students. A one-hour "tour," for eight or more people of any age, includes the touch tanks, and learning about the marine environment. The cost is $4 per person. A three-hour class, given for kindergarteners through twelfth graders, includes a lot of fa*sea*nating information, as well as hands-on fun such as touching sea stars and even petting a shark. The cost is $150 for thirty-five students. "Sleeping with the Sharks" is an overnight field trip that includes a pizza party (i.e. similar to a shark feeding frenzy), touching sharks, shark teeth, dissecting parts of a shark, and more. The cost is $40 per person.

Hours: Open Mon. - Fri., 3pm to sunset; Sat. - Sun., 10am - sunset. Call for tour and program times.

Admission: Free entrance to the aquarium; donations encouraged. Tour prices are given above. Metered parking is available on Manhattan Beach Blvd. by the stores, or wherever you can find it!

Ages: 2 years and up.

SANTA ANITA PARK

(818) 574-7223

285 W. Huntington Drive, Arcadia

(EXIT FOOTHILL FWY [210] S. ON SANTA ANITA, R. ON E. HUNTINGTON, L. ON W. HUNTINGTON)

This is the home of one of the most famous thoroughbred horse racing parks in the United States. On Saturdays and Sundays, during the season (starting at 8am), you and your child can take a free, twenty-minute tram ride from the restaurant through the barn. You'll see horses here being put through their morning paces, or getting bathed.

On a daily basis, during the race season, you are welcome to come watch the morning workouts from 7:30am - 9:30am, for free. A playground and grassy picnic area are at the infield.

Hours: The season runs the month of October, and the end of December through April.

Admission: Free admission before 9:30am. Afterwards, it's $4 for adults; free for kids 17 years and under when accompanied by an adult. Parking is $3, after 9:30am.

Ages: 4 years and up.

SUNSET RANCH HOLLYWOOD STABLES

(213) 464-9612 $$$$$

3400 N. Beachwood Drive, Los Angeles

(EXIT THE VENTURA FWY [101] S. ON CAHUENGA BLVD., E. ON FRANKLIN AVE., N. ON BEACHWOOD DR., ALL THE WAY UP TO THE TOP.)

Many places offer scenic horseback riding, but this stable also offers guided, moonlit rides. You'll leave around 5:30pm and ride over the hills of Griffith Park. Parts of this trail are very secluded and beautiful. At 8pm or so, you'll arrive at Vivas Mexicas restaurant. After dinner, head back to arrive at the stables around 11pm. It's a long night, but a special one, too.

Hours: Friday nights from 5pm - 11pm.
Admission: $35 per person. Dinner costs extra.
Ages: 12 years and up.

TROUTDALE
(818) 889-9993 $$$

2468 Troutdale Drive, Agoura
(EXIT VENTURA FWY [101] S. ON KANAN RD., L. ON TROUTDALE DR.)

"Fishy, fishy in a brook/ Daddy caught him with a hook./ Mammy fried him in a pan/ And baby ate him like a man." (Childcraft, Poems and Rhymes, 1966)

Troutdale is in a woodsy setting with two small ponds to fish from - perfect for beginners. There are logs to sit on around the perimeter of the ponds. The entrance price includes a bamboo fishing pole and bait. For an extra 50¢, you can get your fish cleaned. Munch at the snack bar, or bring a picnic lunch to eat while you're catching dinner. Be sure to pick up a flyer that has some recipe ideas.

Hours: Open Mon. - Fri., 10am - 4pm; Sat. - Sun., 9am - 5pm. Weekend hours are extended during the summer.
Admission: $3 per person, fishing or not. Fish prices vary depending on its length. For instance, a rainbow trout that is 10" - 11" long costs $4.25.
Ages: 3 years and up.

WILDLIFE WAYSTATION
(818) 899-5201 $$$

14831 Little Tujunga Canyon Road, Angeles National Forest
(FROM GOLDEN STATE FWY [5], GO N.E. ON SAN FERNANDO FWY [118], E. ON FOOTHILL FWY [210], N.E. ON FOOTHILL BLVD., L. ON OSBORN, UP THE WINDING ROAD THAT TURNS INTO TUJUNGA CANYON RD. YOU'LL SEE THE SIGNS.)

This donor-supported waystation is in existence to help wild animals with the three "r's": rescue, rehabilitate, and refuge. (Our tour guide told us that they sometimes rehabilitate and release baby animals in the wild and, when appropriate, they release adults in the wild, too. My 7-year-old heard this, and with an incredulous look said, "They release adults in the wild?")

This can be a wonderful wildlife experience as long as you and your children follow the necessarily stringent rules. The shelters here provide homes to over 1,000 animals - like lions, tigers, the rare ligers (a cross between a lion and a tiger), bears, wolves, bobcats, jaguars, leopards, primates, etc. We were in awe of seeing so many "zoo" animals up close, separated by almost nothing more than a chain link fence. This is where the rules come in. Since carnivores tend to look at children as dinner, and the unpaved trails are narrow, parents must keep a really close eye, and/or hand on their kids.

We learned fascinating facts about the animals and their habitats on our forty-minute walking tour. The tour guides are committed and knowledgeable volunteers, but they do vary greatly in their ability and desire to relate to kids.

Feed the animals (for an additional 50¢) at the petting zoo, which is comprised of pigs, goats, llamas, and donkeys. Individual animals are brought out on a small stage, providing an opportunity to learn more about a particular species. Snacks are available for purchase, but bringing outside food is not allowed.

Hours: Tours are offered every hour between 10am - 5pm on the first and third Sunday of each month, weather permitting. Group tours can be arranged on other days. Reservations are required for all tours.

Admission: $9 for adults; $4 for ages 2 - 11. (Your "donation" is tax deductible.)

Ages: 3 years and up.

CASA DE TORTUGA   ☼

(714) 962- 0612   /

10455 Circulo de Zapata, Fountain Valley

(GOING N. ON SAN DIEGO FWY [405], EXIT N. ON BROOKHURST, R. ON SLATER, L. ON WARD, L. ON CIRCULO DE ZAPATA. GOING S. ON 405, EXIT E. ON WARNER. R. ON WARD, R. ON CIRCULO DE ZAPATA. CASA DE TORTUGA IS IN A RESIDENTIAL SECTION AND IS ACTUALLY OUTSIDE (AND INSIDE) A LARGE HOUSE.)

Come out of your shell to see the wonderful variety of turtle species (over 100) at this "House of Turtles." A favorite is the large Galapagos Island tortoise. In this one-hour, outdoor tour children walk around the turtle pens, within touching distance of the turtles. Kids will hear about what turtles like to eat, which are endangered species, what "endangered species" means, and the difference between a turtle and a tortoise. Docents welcome questions, which makes your curious child very happy.

We also loved the "really neat" pond in the backyard filled with turtles. If your child is interested in adopting a turtle, he/she will be given information to help make the best choice. Note: Pebbled walkways make strollers difficult to push.

Slow and steady might win the race, but tours here fill up almost a year in a advance, so hurry and make your reservation. (No more than twenty-five people in a group.) Casa De Tortuga has a free, annual open house, usually held the third weekend in August - no reservations are needed (or accepted).

Hours: Tours are given Mon. - Sat. at 10am.
Admission: Free
   Ages: 3 years and up.

CENTENNIAL FARM   ☼

(714) 708-1566   !

88 Fair Drive, Costa Mesa

(EXIT COSTA MESA FWY [55] S.W. ON NEWPORT BLVD., R. ON FAIR DR., THROUGH GATE #1. IT'S IN THE ORANGE COUNTY FAIR GROUNDS.)

This outdoor working farm has pigs, chickens, sheep, bunnies, ducks, Clydesdale horses, and a buffalo. During the springtime, in particular, be on the lookout for the many animal babies that are born here. The bee observatory is fascinating and with their nonstop motion, it's easy to see where the term "~~busy boys~~" oops, I mean "busy bees," came from.

Walk around the grounds to learn about other aspects of farming. Younger kids will probably be amazed to see vegetables such as carrots, zucchini, lettuce, and corn being grown, not already picked and packaged as in the grocery stores. (Please do not pick the vegetables or feed the animals.)

A one-and-a-half-hour free tour of the farm is available for groups of ten or more. This tour includes going into the main building and seeing chicks hatch in the incubator, planting a seed (and then taking it home), and learning about the food groups. Tuesday tours are best for preschoolers as the tour is conducted at a more relaxed pace than on other days. Reservations are needed.

A few picnic tables are here at the farm too, so pack a lunch. The huge parking lot is usually empty at this time, so bring skates or bikes.

Hours: The farm is open October through May, Mon. - Fri. from 8am - 5pm. Tours are available Tues. - Fri. at 9am and 11am. The farm is closed to the public in June; open in July only with a paid admission to the Orange County Fair (see the July CALENDAR section); closed August and September.
Admission: Free
   Ages: 2 years and up.

FRIENDS OF THE SEA LION MARINE MAMMAL   ☼
CENTER

(714) 494-3050   !

20612 Laguna Canyon Road, Laguna Beach

(EXIT SAN DIEGO FWY [405] OR SANTA ANA FWY [5] S. ON LAGUNA CANYON RD. [HWY 133]. IT'S JUST S. OF EL TORO RD.)

This Center is a small, safe harbor for sea lions and harbor seals that are abandoned, ailing, or in need of medical attention. The animals are kept outside in bathtub-like pens until they are ready to be released back into the wild. This is a good opportunity for kids to see these animals up-close, while learning more about them and the effect that we have on our oceans - their habitats. The volunteers are great at answering the numerous (and sometimes off-the-wall) questions they are asked.

Feeding time, usually around 3pm or 4pm, is lively as the sea lions go wild, barking in anticipation of a meal. (It sounds like mealtime at our house.) There are usually between five to twelve mammals here, but more arrive toward the end of pupping season, which is the end of March through July. (Also see LAGUNA KOI PONDS, located just north of the center.)

Hours: Open daily from 10am - 4pm.
Admission: Free; donations gladly accepted.
Ages: 3 years and up.

JONES FAMILY MINI FARM / LOS RIOS DISTRICT

(714) 831-6550

31791 Los Rios Street, San Juan Capistrano

(EXIT THE SAN DIEGO FWY [5] W. ON ORTEGA HWY [74]., L. AT CAMINO CAPISTRANO, R. ON VERDUGO. IT'S BEHIND THE AMTRACK STATION IN THE LOS RIOS HISTORIC SECTION.)

This working mini-farm will become a favorite mini stopping place whenever you visit San Juan Capistrano. Inside the barn is a small petting pen with goats, sheep, rabbits, and guinea pigs. The farm also has a few other animals to pet through the fence pens, like donkeys, horses, and a pot-bellied pig. Feed is available to purchase for the animals. Starting at 8 months old, kids up to eighty pounds can ride a pony around a track. For a birthday party with a real farm, or western flavor, rent the large outside picnic area.

Leave your car at the Mission or park by the Amtrack depot off Verdugo Street. Enjoy the short walk to the farm and around this quaint, historic area. In front of the farm is the 100-year-old Olivares Home, and next door is the O'Neil Historic Museum, (714) 493-8444. Older kids might enjoy a walk through these Victorian homes to see antique furniture and clothing. (See MISSION SAN JUAN CAPISTRANO for other things to see and do.)

Hours: The Farm is open Wed. - Sun. from 11am - 4pm. O'Neil Historic Museum is open Tues., 9am - noon; Fri., 1pm - 4pm; Sun., noon - 3pm.
Admission: Free to walk around the farm. It costs 50¢ per person to go inside the petting farm; 50¢ for feed. Pony rides are $2 per ride. O'Neil Museum costs $1 per person.
Ages: All

LAGUNA KOI PONDS ☼

(714) 494-5107 !

20452 Laguna Canyon Rd., Laguna Beach
(EXIT SANTA ANA FWY [5] S. ON LAGUNA CANYON RD. [HWY 133]. IT'S JUST S. OF EL TORO RD.)

This fun little stop off has several cement tanks filled with Koi fish, and a store carrying fish supplies. We enjoy just looking at these colorful fish with their beautiful patterns. Who knows, you may want to purchase a few to raise at home. You may also feed them for 25¢ for a handful of pellets. It's fun to watch their large mouths open and quickly bite at the food. Combine a trip here with a visit to the FRIENDS OF THE SEA LION MARINE MAMMAL CENTER, located just south of the ponds.

Hours: Open Mon. - Sat., 9am - 5pm; Sun., 11am - 5pm
Admission: Free
Ages: All

LOS ALAMITOS RACE COURSE ☼

(714) 995-1234 $

4961 E. Katella Avenue, Los Alamitos
(EXIT SAN GABRIEL RIVER FWY [605] E. ON WILLOW/KATELLA, OR GOING N. W., EXIT SAN DIEGO FWY [405] OR GARDEN GROVE FWY [22] N. ON VALLEY VIEW, L. ON KATELLA.)

Thoroughbreds, quarter horses, and harness racing are the attractions here. Have your child cheer for his favorites! Call for schedule information.

Admission: $3 for adults, or $5 for the clubhouse; kids 15 years and under are free. Free parking.
Ages: 4 years and up.

MAGNOLIA BIRD FARM (Anaheim) ☼

(714) 527-3387 !

8990 Cerritos, Anaheim
(EXIT THE SANTA ANA FWY [5] W. ON BALL RD., L. ON MAGNOLIA, R. ON CERRITOS. IT'S ON THE CORNER.)

Take your flock of kids to visit their fine feathered friends at the Magnolia Bird Farm pet shop. Birds here range from common doves and canaries to more exotic cockatoos and macaws. Upstairs is a small-bird aviary and a bird room with cement walls that echo their continuous squawking.

The Bird Farm has bird accessories, including a wide assortment of bird cages. Here's a craft idea: Buy a simple wooden cage for your kids to paint and decorate, then fill it with bird seed, and hang it up in your backyard. While you're here, have your kids take the bird challenge - see if they can get one of the talking birds to actually speak to them! (Also see MAGNOLIA BIRD FARM, La Sierra.)

Hours: Open Tues. - Sat. from 9am - 5pm.
Admission: Free
Ages: All

ORANGE COUNTY ZOO ☀
(714) 633-2022 $

1 Irvine Park Road, Orange

(EXIT NEWPORT FWY [55] E. ON CHAPMAN, N. ON JAMBOREE, ENDS AT IRVINE REGIONAL PARK.)

Take a trip to the zoo while you're in the park! Tucked away in the massive IRVINE REGIONAL PARK is the eight-acre Orange County Zoo. The zoo has barnyard animals like cows, sheep, goats, and pigs to pet through fence pens, and feed (food dispensers are available). The main section of the zoo features animals native to the Southwestern United States like mountain lions, bobcats, deer, coyotes, brown pelicans, a black bear, and a variety of birds.

Hours: Open daily from 10am - 3:30pm.
Admission: $1 for ages 6 and up; children 5 years and under are free, plus the vehicle entrance to the park.
Ages: All

SANTA ANA ZOO ☽
(714) 835-7484 $

1801 E. Chestnut Avenue, Santa Ana

(GOING S. ON SANTA ANA FWY [5], EXIT AT 4ᵀᴴ ST. GO STRAIGHT ON MABURY ST., WHICH TURNS INTO ELK LN., L. ON CHESTNUT. GOING N. ON 5, EXIT W. ON 1ˢᵀ ST., L. ON ELK LN., L. ON CHESTNUT. IT'S AT PRENTICE PARK.)

Lions and tigers and bears - not here! This small zoo, however, is perfect for young children. They can easily walk around it all, see everything, and still have of time to play on the playground. The Santa Ana Zoo houses llamas; cavies; small mammals such as porcupines; birds, including bald eagles; and a wide variety of monkeys - our personal favorites. Walk through the wonderful aviary where you can see beautiful and exotic birds close up. The Children's Zoo has pigs, goats, and sheep to pet through pens, plus reptiles and amphibians to look at. Kids can take a short elephant ride ($2.50 per person), between 11am to 3pm on most weekends. The playground is great, and the gift shop has a wonderful variety of animal-oriented merchandise. The snack bar is usually open, or you can enjoy a picnic right outside the zoo gates at the adjoining Prentice Park which offers picnic tables, grassy areas, and shade trees.

Once a month, or so, on a Saturday morning, "Breakfast with the Beasts" is offered for ages 3 and older. It includes a light breakfast, a guided tour, and a chance to feed some animals in the Children's Zoo. The fee is $15 for one parent and one child, $7.50 for each additional person. A variety of other educational and interactive programs for kids are also offered.

Hours: Open Mon. - Fri., 10am - 4pm; Sat. - Sun., 10am - 5pm. Closed New Year's Day and Christmas.

Admission: $3.50 for adults; $1.50 for seniors and ages 3 - 12; children 2 years and under and physically impaired people are free.(AAA discounts available.)

Ages: All

MAGNOLIA BIRD FARM (La Sierra)

(909) 278-0878

12200 Magnolia Avenue, La Sierra
(EXIT RIVERSIDE FWY [91] S.W. ON MAGNOLIA AVE.)

See MAGNOLIA BIRD FARM, Cerritos, for a fuller description of the bird farm. The main difference between the two is size, with the Riverside location being almost three times larger than the one in Cerritos. The aviary here includes parakeets, love birds, finches, and quail, as well as doves and pigeons.

As springtime brings the birth of new baby birds, kids can sometimes see them being hand fed through the glass walls. Tour groups, of at least ten or more people, will learn about seed, like which kind is best for what species; see and study a (live) white dove; and more.

Hours: Open Tues. - Sat. from 9am - 5pm. Reservations are needed for the half-hour tour.

Admission: Free

Ages: All

DEL MAR FAIRGROUNDS / RACETRACK

(619) 755-1141

Del Mar Fairgrounds, Del Mar
(EXIT SAN DIEGO FWY [5] W. ON VIA DE LA VALLE)

Horse racing season at the famous Del Mar Fairgrounds begins in July and runs through September. Kids have good horse sense - they aren't here to bet, but to enjoy the races. Also inquire about horse shows, rodeos, and polo games.

Hours: Gates are open Mon., Wed. - Fri. at noon; Sat. - Sun., 11:30am. Post time is usually 2pm, although it's at 4pm for the first five Fri.

Admission: General admission is $3 for adults; $6 for clubhouse; free for children 17 years and under.

Ages: 5 years and up.

SAN DIEGO WILD ANIMAL PARK

(800) 934-2267 or (619) 234-6541

15500 San Pasqual Valley Road, Escondido

(GOING S. ON SAN DIEGO FWY [5], OR ESCONDIDO FWY [15], EXIT E. ON HWY 78, WHICH TURNS INTO SAN PASQUAL VALLEY RD. GOING N. ON 15, EXIT E. ON VIA RANCHO PKWY., WHICH TURNS INTO BEAR VALLEY RD., R. ON SAN PASQUAL RD., WHICH TURNS INTO VIA RANCHO PKWY., GO TO END, R. ON SAN PASQUAL VALLEY RD.)

Go on a safari and see the exotic animals that live in the African Veldt and Asian plains, without ever leaving Southern California. The 2,000-acre San Diego Wild Animal Park has tigers, rhinos, elephants, giraffes, etc., in atypical zoo enclosures. The animals here roam the grasslands freely, in settings that resemble their natural habitats. The best way to see a majority of the animals is via the Wgasa Bush Line monorail, a five-mile, fifty-minute, narrated journey (tour). This ride is included in your admission price. I suggest going on the monorail first as the lines get longer later in the day.

The ride ends back at Nairobi Village, which is a great starting point for the rest of your wild animal adventure. From here you can walk through some of the thirty acres that comprise the "Heart of Africa." This circuitous path is three-quarters-of-a-mile long and takes about two hours. The trail will take you into the forest where antelope and okapi roam; along a stream (look for warthogs and foxes); near waterfalls; to a large watering hole where rhinos, waterbuck, etc., congregate. Cross to the one small island (out of five) that has a mock research station, along with a live aardvark and hornbill, and see lab equipment, dart guns, etc. The open plains are home to wildebeest, cheetahs, and even a station (open at designated times) to hand-feed giraffe. Back at Nairobi Village, head out to watch the antics of the monkeys and gorillas. The nearby Petting Kraal has small deer, goats, sheep, etc. to pet and feed. Check the time for the unusual animal shows performed here. I was enchanted by the Hidden Jungle. This "room" is filled with lush green plants and colorful butterflies fluttering all around. Hand-feeding rainbow lorikeets (they look like small parrots) is a thrill. Mombasa Lagoon is a terrific, interactive way to experience animal behavior "firsthand": Put on a furry pair of bat ears and look silly, but hear acutely; sit in a large turtle shell (and maybe hatch an idea or two); explore the inside of the weaver bird dwelling; climb a giant spider web; hop from one huge lily pad to another; and more! Enjoy all your travels through the animal kingdom.

Want to make your day picture perfect? The Photo Caravan (ages 12 and up) offers two photo opportunities to go on an open, flat-bed truck into some of the animal enclosures. The cost ranges from $65 to $89, depending on the length of the adventure. The Family Safari (ages 8 and up) is a two-hour, educational tour into the animal enclosures of rhinos, giraffes, and more. Your kids can feed some of the animals, take pictures of them, and learn all about them. You'll also come in closer-than-normal contact with water buffalo, zebras, camels, and flamingoes while learning their names in Swahili, or what their collective group name is (i.e. pride of lions), etc. These tours are offered Monday and Tuesday in the summer, and over most school breaks, starting at

5:30pm. The cost is $40 per person. Call (760) 738-5049 for more information. Roar and Snore overnight tent-camping safaris include nature hikes, a campfire and snacks, photo opportunities, and close-up encounters with wild beasts! The cost is $87.50 for adults; $67.50 for kids (who must be at least 8 years old). Call (760) 738-5022 for more information. These are just a few of the special programs offered - call for a complete schedule.

Hours: Open daily from 9am - 5pm.
Admission: $18.95 for adults; $17.05 for seniors; $11.95 for ages 3 - 11; children 2 years and under are free. Parking is $3. A combination ticket with the SAN DIEGO ZOO (to be used within five days) is $31.95 for adults; $18.35 for ages 3 - 11. Admission to the Wild Animal Park is free one day in May to celebrate Founder's Day.
Ages: All

SAN DIEGO ZOO   ☼
(619) 234-3153 $$$$
Park Boulevard in Balboa Park, San Diego
(Exit San Diego Fwy [5] to Pershing Dr., take Balboa Park exit and follow the signs.)

The world famous San Diego Zoo is home to some of the rarest animals in captivity, and almost every animal imaginable, at least that's what it seems like. Put your walking shoes on because this zoo covers a lot of ground! In fact, you'd be hard pressed to try to see all 4,000 animals in one day, at least with young children. The flamingos, just inside the entrance, are a colorful way to start your day. Tiger River, Elephant Mesa, the Horn and Hoof Mesa, Gorilla Tropics, and the Reptile House are just a few of the exhibit areas to visit. Be amazed at how enormous hippos really are and the size of polar bears in two underwater viewing exhibits - Hippo Beach and Polar Bear Plunge, respectively. Experience panda-monium and see the two giant pandas that are visiting from China - what unique-looking animals! Enjoy a walk through the bird aviary; watch the antics of the bears at Sun Bear Forest; see koalas in their trees; and take the opportunity to observe kangaroos, camels, primates, etc. in enclosures that simulate their natural habitat.

A thirty-five-minute, double-decker, narrated bus tour is not only fun and informative, but a great way to get a good overview of most of the animals here. The narrated Kangaroo bus tour also covers about seventy-five percent of the zoo, but you can hop on and hop off (hence the name) as often as you want throughout the day. The Skyfari Aerial Tram ride is another way to view a portion of the zoo at $1 per person, each way. For an educational twist, or to answer questions you usually answer with "I don't know," rent an audio tape and player for $4.

The Sea Lion Show and the Wild Ones show, presented twice daily, are an entertaining and interesting way to see some favorite animals close up. The Children's Zoo is always a highlight with animals to pet; mole-rats and other unique animals to look at; and an animal baby nursery that shows off the newest zoo additions. Ask about the many special programs the zoo offers during the year.

Hours: Open daily from 9am - 5pm.
Admission: $15 for adults; $6 for ages 3 - 11; children 2 and under area free. The bus tour is an additional $4 for adults; $3 for ages 3 - 11. The Kangaroo bus tour is $8 for adults; $5 for kids. A combination package with the SAN DIEGO WILD ANIMAL PARK (to be used within 5 days) is $31.95 for adults; $18.35 for children. Admission is free on the first Monday of October to celebrate Founder's Day.
Ages: All

SEAL ROCK MARINE MAMMAL RESERVE   ☀

Coast Boulevard, La Jolla   !
(EXIT SAN DIEGO FWY [5] W. ON LA JOLLA VILLAGE DR., L. ON TORREY PINES RD., R. ON PROSPECT PL., R. ON COAST BLVD.)

The reserve is within walking distance from the LA JOLLA CAVE AND SHELL SHOP. From a distance, we saw what looked like lumpy rocks on the beach. As we got closer, however, we could see that they were really numerous seals sprawling on the sand, and on the nearby rocks. My boys and I were thrilled that we were almost near enough to touch the seals, although doing so and getting too close is forbidden. (Even seals are protected by harassment laws!) A normal family might be here for just a few minutes; we were here for an hour because we were enthralled with seeing the seals so close up. Warning: Seals are not sunbathing here constantly, so whether you see them or not is a hit or miss deal.

Hours: ,Open daily.
Admission: Free
Ages: All

SEA WORLD   ☼
(619) 226-3901 $$$$$
Sea World Drive, San Diego
(EXIT SAN DIEGO FWY [5] W. ON SEA WORLD DR.)

Sea World entertains and educates people of all ages with its wide variety of sea animal exhibits. The dazzling dolphin and silly sea lion shows get top ratings. The killer-whale show, starring Shamu and friends, is a crowd-pleaser with its thrills (a trainer riding a whale gets catapulted) and chills (those sitting in the splash-zone bleachers get wet). Shamu Backstage allows visitors to wade into shallow water, reach over an acrylic panel, and touch the killer whales! Trainers also invite a few volunteers to help out and train the whales by holding targets, carrying food buckets, and rewarding the giant mammals for a behavior correctly performed. View the animals underwater at the viewing gallery.

Other unique attractions include: Shark Encounter, which culminates in a fifty-seven-foot-long enclosed people-mover tube that takes you through shark-infested waters(!); Rocky Point Preserve, where kids can actually touch and feed bottlenose dolphins (they feel rubbery); Forbidden Reef and the California Tide Pool, where you can touch bat rays and other marine animals if you stretch your arms far enough; Penguin exhibit, which also features the penguins' cousins, the very funny puffins who fly through the air and the sea; Sea Turtles and four other huge aquariums for kids to "oooh" and "aaah" at; and Wild Arctic, where a simulated helicopter ride lands you at a remote research station. Blasts of Arctic air greet you at the research station. (Actually, you're still at Sea World.) You have a great vantage point to see beluga whales, harbor seals, walruses, and polar bears. Kids will have an un*bear*ably good time playing in polar dens and using touch screens for more information on the animals they are observing.

Shamu's Happy Harbor is two acres of pure kid delight. This play area has tubes, slides, ropes, balls, a sandy beach, a moon bounce, an outdoor theater for kid-oriented entertainment, and a Funship for pretend pirates. For those who want (or are allowed) to get wet, there are a few water fountains to splash in, and water tubes to go through. Tip: Bring a towel or change of clothing.

For an additional $2 each, the Skytower (offering a panoramic view) and the Bayside Skyride (a gondola ride over Mission Bay) are fun treats. Sea World also offers various outstanding educational tours, such as the ninety-minute, behind-the-scenes tour. Or, sleep over with sharks or other animals. What fun! Call for information on the times, hours, and admission for these (and more) unique field trips. Although no outside food is allowed inside, a picnic area is set up just outside the park. Spending a day (or night) here is a great way for the whole family to "sea" the world!

Hours: Open daily from 10am - 6pm (check for seasonality).

Admission: $32.95 for adults; $24.95 for ages 3 - 11; children 2 years and under are free. Parking is $5.

Ages: All

STEPHEN BIRCH AQUARIUM-MUSEUM ☼
(619) 534-3474   *$$$*

2300 Expedition Drive, San Diego
    See STEPHEN BIRCH AQUARIUM-MUSEUM under MUSEUMS.

MOORPARK COLLEGE TEACHING ZOO ☽
(805) 378-1400   *$$*

7075 Campus Road, Moorpark

(EXIT SIMI VALLEY/SAN FERNANDO VALLEY FWY [118] N. ON COLLINS DR. CONTINUE ALL THE WAY UP COLLINS, BEHIND THE COLLEGE, R. INTO THE DIRT PARKING AREA WHERE YOU'LL SEE SIGNS FOR THE ZOO.)

Students attend this teaching zoo to become zoo keepers, veterinarians, animal trainers, etc. If your child aspires to one of these professions, or is just intrigued with animals, come visit. Picnic tables are here for your lunching pleasure.

Demonstrations feature three to five animals per show, such as primates, hoofed animals, or reptiles on a small, outdoor stage. The student trainers talk about the animal's habitats, nutrition, and training. Afterward, kids can come up and usually touch the animals and ask questions. One of the reptiles we saw and touched was a boa. We were amazed at its strength (and under-belly softness).

Don't miss the 3:45pm feeding of the carnivores! (Get there a little early and see animals being fed that aren't on the "scheduled program.") We saw a trainer go inside a cage to feed the tigers and to "show-off" their learned behavior. The trainers and students willingly answered all the questions they were asked. My kids learned so much here!

As this is a teaching zoo and not just here for public enjoyment, many of the caged animals are in rows, making it difficult, or impossible, to see a lot of them. However, the animals that are readily viewed can be seen more up close than at a typical zoo.

Watch out for a type of monkey called langurs. One growled and leapt at the bars towards my kids. We were told that this species considers eye contact to be a sign of aggression, and smiling children to be teeth-baring, aggressive adversaries. As parents, we often feel the same way.

Hours: The Zoo is open weekends only from 11am - 5pm. The demonstrations are every hour on the hour from noon - 3pm, weather permitting. You can call to see what animals will be shown. Feeding of the carnivores is at 3:45pm.

Admission: $4 for adults; $3 for seniors; $2 for children 12 years and under.

Ages: All

BIG BEAR

This four-season mountain resort is close enough to escape to for a day or a weekend, though it offers enough activities for at least a week's vacation. The pine trees and fresh air that beckon city-weary folks, plus all the things to do, make it an ideal family get-away. November through March (or so) the mountains become a winter wonderland with lot of opportunities for snow play and skiing. This section, however, covers a broader base of activities because Big Bear is great any time of year!

ALPINE SLIDE / MAGIC MOUNTAIN ☼

(909) 866-4626 - Alpine Slide $$$

Big Bear Boulevard, Magic Mountain Recreation Area, Big Bear
(EXIT BIG BEAR BLVD. IT'S ¼ MILE W. OF BIG BEAR LAKE VILLAGE.)

Alpine Slide lifts family fun to new heights! Take the chairlift up the mountain. Then, you and your child (he can go by himself if he's at least 7 years old) sit on a heavy-duty plastic sled and rip down the quarter-mile, cement, contoured slide. (It looks like a bobsled track.) Control your speed by pushing or pulling on the lever. Only on our first ride were we cautious.

If you don't succumb to motion sickness, take a whirl on the Orbitron. You'll be harnessed to the inside of this big sphere and spun around in all directions. Doesn't that sound like fun? The miniature golf course, Puttin' Around, doesn't have a lot of frills, but kids still enjoy puttin' around on it. Go karts are available to race around. Inside the main building are a few video games, of course, and a snack bar. That delicious food you smell is a burger or hot dog being barbecued right outside.

Summer play is enhanced by two zippy waterslides. You'll end with a splash in the three-and-a-half-feet deep pool, but it's not for swimming in. Winter allows you and the kids a chance to inner tube down the snow-covered hill, or cultivate the fine art of throwing snowballs. You'll have mountains of fun any season you come to Alpine Slide and Magic Mountain.

Hours: The Alpine Slide, Orbitron, miniature golf, and go karts are open mid-June through mid-September and November through Easter, daily 10am - 5pm (weather permitting). The rest of the year they are open the same hours, but on weekends only. The waterslide is open mid-June to mid-September, daily from 10am - 5pm. The snow play area is open as long as there is snow, daily from 10am - 4pm.

Admission: Alpine ride - $3 for one ride, $12 for a five-ride book; Orbitron - $4 a ride; miniature golf - $4 a round for adults; $3 for kids; go karts - $3.50 a single car, $5.50 a double car; waterslide - $1 for one ride, $7 for a ten-ride book, $10 for an unlimited day pass; snow play - $10 for an unlimited day-pass with a tube, $8 for an unlimited day-pass using your own tube. Children 6 years and under are free on the Alpine slide, waterslide, and snow play area, as long as they accompanied by an adult.

Ages: 3 years and up.

ALPINE TROUT LAKE ☼

(909) 866-4532 $$

Catalina Road, Big Bear
(EXIT BIG BEAR BLVD. S. ON CATALINA.)

This beautiful tree-lined lake is a restful place to fish. Chairs, picnic tables, and barbecue pits are around the perimeters of the stocked lake, so you can catch your meal and eat it, too.

Hours: Open Mon. - Fri., 10am - 5pm; Sat. - Sun., 9am - 6pm, weather permitting.

Admission: $5 for family entrance (or up to 6 people), with a rod rental, reel, and bait an additional $3.50 per. Fish cost $4.89 per pound.

Ages: 3 years and up.

BEAR MOUNTAIN RIDING STABLES

(909) 878-4677   *$$$$*

At the top of Lassen Drive, Big Bear

(EXIT BIG BEAR BLVD. S.E. AT MOONRIDGE RD. GO TO THE END OF MOONRIDGE AND TURN L. ON LASSEN DR. IT'S AT THE FOOT OF BEAR MOUNTAIN SKI RESORT.)

There is only so much you can see of Big Bear from the car! A horseback ride is an ideal way to experience the beauty of the mountains. Children 8 years and up can take a one or two-hour guided horseback ride through the pine trees and over mountain ridges. Back at the stables, younger children can take pony rides around the track.

Hours: Open daily 9am - 5pm, during good weather.

Admission: $20 per hour for horseback riding; $5 for 2 laps around the track on a pony.

Ages: 3 years and up.

BEAR MOUNTAIN TRADING CO.

(909) 585-9676   *!/$*

42646 Moonridge Road, Big Bear

(EXIT BIG BEAR BLVD. S.E. AT MOONRIDGE RD.)

This two-story trading company store is fun little stop off. There is a wonderful selection of old-fashioned gifts, including wooden toys, lots of candy favorites, and Indian accessories. Stop here on your way to or from MOONRIDGE ANIMAL PARK.

Hours: Open daily from 10am - 6pm.

Admission: Free

Ages: 4 years and up.

BIG BEAR HISTORICAL MUSEUM and CITY PARK

(909) 585-8100   *$*

Greenway Drive, Big Bear

(EXIT BIG BEAR BLVD. E. ON GREENWAY. THE MUSEUM IS IN THE N.E. PORTION OF THE BIG BEAR CITY PARK, E. OF THE AIRPORT.)

The past is definitely present at the Eleanor Abbott Big Bear Valley Historical Museum. The buildings that comprise the museum are very old (and old looking). The small main building contains a good assortment of taxidermied animals such as a golden eagle, skunk, red fox, badger, etc., displayed mostly behind glass in "natural" settings. Other exhibits include birds' nests, eggs, arrowheads, rocks, fossils, unique leather carvings, old photographs of old Big Bear, and old-fashioned toys. Outside on the porch are turn-of-the-century post office boxes, plus mining equipment and mining artifacts.

A furnished, 1875 one-room log cabin offers a real look into the pioneer lifestyle. The docents in here are wonderful at explaining to kids how pioneer families lived, and the uses of some of the household items. My boys couldn't believe that chamber pots were really used as portable potties. It finally dawned on them that entire families lived together in this one room; sleeping, cooking, eating, and playing together. I hope they'll be more thankful about their own living arrangements!

There is also an old barn, and lots of old, rusted agriculture equipment on the grounds.

The adjacent park has a few pieces of play equipment, and some old tennis courts. It's mostly good for running around in the overgrown fields. Shade is scarce, but there are a few picnic tables here.

Hours: Open May through September only, Sat. 10am - 4pm; Sun. and holidays, 11am - 2pm.
Admission: $1 per person donation.
Ages: 3 years and up.

BIG BEAR JEEP TOURS

(909) 878-5337 $$$$$

Stationed in Big Bear Village.

For rugged kids, who like bumpy adventures, jeep tours are the way to go. There are so many historical, beautiful places to explore in these mountains and some of them are only accessible via four-wheel drive. Take a one-hour trip to the top of the ridgeline, or explore Holcomb Valley where kids will learn about the Gold Rush, a ghost town, and gold mines. What a great way to see and experience a bit of golden history!

Hours: Call for tour times.
Admission: Prices range from $29.95 per person (one-hour tour) - $79.95 per person (four-hour tours).
Ages: 4 years and up.

BIG BEAR PARASAIL

(909) 866-IFLY (4359) $$$$$

At the north end of Pine Knott Boulevard, Big Bear
(EXIT BIG BEAR BLVD. S. ON PINE KNOTT BLVD.)

Ever had dreams where you can fly? Parasailing is the next best thing. Start off on dry land, attached by a harness to the parasail and by a tow rope to the boat. As the boat pulls away, you are lifted into the air, flying for ten minutes. You can stay dry if you want and if all goes well, or take a quick dip (more like a toe touch) in the lake before being airborne again. This is a thrill-seeking experience for kids and adults.

Hours: Seasonal only, Mon. - Fri., 9am - 5pm; Sat. - Sun., 8am - 6pm.
Admission: Single - $35 weekdays; $40 weekends. Tandem - $60 weekday; $70 weekends.
Ages: 90 pounds and up.

BIG BEAR SOLAR OBSERVATORY
(909) 866-5791 $

North Shore Lane, Big Bear
(EXIT NORTH SHORE DR. ON NORTH SHORE LN. IT'S PAST FAWNSKIN.)

The small, thirty-foot dome solar observatory offers a unique way to study the often sunny skies in Big Bear. Three telescopes monitor and record images of the sun, which are then displayed on video monitors. Cameras can show sharper details than the unaided eye can see. Take a twenty-minute tour, and get the hot facts about the sun.

Hours: Open July 4th through Labor Day, Saturdays only from 4pm - 6pm.
Admission: $1 donation per person.
Ages: 8 years and up.

BIG BEAR VISITOR CENTER
(909) 866-4608   !

Barlett Road, Big Bear
(LOCATED IN BIG BEAR VILLAGE ON BARLETT ROAD, JUST N. OF VILLAGE DR.)

Make this one of your first stops before exploring Big Bear. Pick up the maps and brochures you need so you can choose your adventures.

Hours: Open Mon. - Fri., 9am - 5pm; Sat. - Sun., 10am - 5pm.
Admission: Free

BLUE JAY ICE CASTLE
(909) 337-0802 $$$

27307 Highway 189, Blue Jay
(TAKE RIVERSIDE FWY [91] N.E. UNTIL IT TURNS INTO THE SAN BERNARDINO FWY [215]. STAY TO THE RIGHT AND TAKE THE 259/30 FWYS. STAY ON THE 30 THEN EXIT N. ON WATERMAN AVE. WATERMAN TURNS INTO HIGHWAY 18. GO PAST RIM FOREST, TURN L. ON DAILY CANYON WHICH TURNS INTO HWY. 189.)

Enjoy this open-air ice-skating rink all year round! Blue Jay Ice Castle has a roof overhead and is enclosed on three sides (one side has a lobby area), leaving the fourth side open to a great view of the surrounding pine trees. For the more adventuresome, try broom ball. This sport is played using brooms as hockey sticks, and wearing tennis shoes instead of ice skates. Yes, it's painful to fall on the ice, but what a fun, exhilarating game this is!

Hours: Open skating sessions are daily from 11am - 1pm and 3:30pm - 5:30pm. Fri. night sessions are 8pm to 10pm; Sat. night sessions are 8pm to midnight.

Admission: $6 for mountain residents; $7 for non-mountain residents; children 3 years and under are free.

Ages: 3 years and up.

HIKING   ☼

(909) 866-0130 or (909) 866-3437   !

There are many places to go hiking in the Big Bear area. The Ranger Station is the best place to call or visit for trail maps, camp sites, and specific information. I will share just two of the places my family has enjoyed trekking:

CASTLE ROCK:

(FROM HIGHWAY 18, THE TRAILHEAD IS ABOUT ONE MILE EAST PAST THE DAM.)

The trail is only eight-tenths of a mile, but it is an uphill walk over some rocky terrain. The destination is Castle Rock, a large rock that kids love to climb on. It's name gives lead to a lot of imaginative play time here. (All of my kids wanted to be king - what a surprise!) If everyone still has the energy, keep hiking back to the waterfalls, and/ or to Devil's woodpile. The scenery along the way is spectacular.

WOODLAND TRAIL

(ON HIGHWAY 38, PARKING IS ALMOST DIRECTLY ACROSS THE STREET FROM M.D. BOAT RAMP, JUST WEST OF THE STANFIELD CUTOFF ROAD.)

This one-and-a-half-mile loop is an easy walk, as the dirt trail follows more along the side of the mountain, rather than into the mountain. Although you can hear the traffic from certain sections of the trail, the changing landscape, from pine trees to coastal shrub to cactus, still offers the sense of being immersed in nature. An interpretative trail guide is available through the Ranger Station. Make it an educational field trip as well as a nice walk!

Admission: Free

Ages: 4 years and up.

THE HOT SHOT MINIATURE GOLF COURSE   ☀

Corner of Catalina and Big Bear Boulevard, Big Bear $$
(ON BIG BEAR BLVD., JUST N. OF MOONRIDGE.)

Putt around under shady pine trees at this basic, but fun miniature golf course. Encourage your kids to be hot shots here!

Hours: Open daily, weather permitting, from 10am - 6pm. Closed during the winter.

Admission: $4 for adults; $3 for kids 12 years and under. Replays are $1.

Ages: 3 years and up.

LAKE ARROWHEAD CHILDREN'S MUSEUM ☼

(909) 336-1332 - recorded information; $$
(909) 336-3093 - front desk
Highway 18, in the Village, Lake Arrowhead
(EXIT SAN BERNARDINO FWY [10] N. ON THE 215, E. ON THE 30. TAKE THE
WATERMAN AVE. [HWY 18] EXIT 'UP THE HILL' TO LAKE ARROWHEAD. THE MUSEUM
IS LOCATED IN THE LOWER LEVEL OF THE VILLAGE, AT THE END OF THE PENINSULA,
JUST PAST THE G.R. TOY SHOP AND ROCKY MT. CHOCOLATE FACTORY.)

(I know this is not in Big Bear, but it's close by and great fun for kids!) In the Lake Arrowhead Village shopping center, kids now have a place of their own to "shop" for fun. This museum is comprised of a large room, with beautiful nature murals, divided into interactive exhibit areas. Some of the permanent exhibits include the Ant Wall - where children are the ants, climbing up and down carpeted ramps and tunnels; Inventor's Workshop - where recyclable "trash" is crafted into take-home treasure; a Bubble Area - where bubbles can be kid-size; a Theater - with face paint and great costumes for dressing up and acting out; a Toddlers' Room - with several toys and Peter Pan's ship to climb aboard and sail off to Never Land; Science Stations - where kids can throw a ball and clock its speed, speak through tubes to each other, and experiment with magnets, hand batteries, etc.; and Village Merchants - with playhouse-size "stores" like a fire station, post office, photo shop (with a photosensitive shadow room), and Vet's office (with lots of stuffed animals). There is always something fun to do at the Children's Museum!

Hours: Open in the summer daily from 10am - 6pm; open the rest of the year Wed. - Mon. from 10am - 5pm.
Admission: $3.50 for ages 2 years and up; $2.50 for seniors.
Ages: 2 - 10 years.

MCDILL SWIM BEACH / MEADOW PARK ☼

(909) 866-0130 $
Park Avenue, Big Bear
(EXIT BIG BEAR BLVD. N. ON KNIGHT ST. TO THE END.)

This waveless lagoon, with a lifeguard on duty, offers a refreshing respite during the hot summer months. Kids can play in the water, or build castles on the sandy beach. Swimmers enjoy going beyond the roped area, out to the floating dock that they can lay out on or dive off. A small playground, a volleyball court, and a snack bar round out the facilities at this beach. And the view of the mountains is spectacular!

Meadow Park is just outside the Swim Beach gates. This large, grassy park has a small playground, nice tennis courts, volleyball courts, baseball diamonds, and horseshoe pits. Bring a picnic dinner to cook at the barbecue pits, and enjoy the sunset.

Hours: The swim beach is open seasonally, weekends from noon - 5pm, and daily in the summer from noon - 5pm. The park is open sunrise to sunset.

Admission: $2.50 for adults; $2 for ages 5 - 10; children 4 years and
under are free. The park is free.
Ages: All

MOONRIDGE ANIMAL PARK   ☼
(909) 866-0183 $
18012 Goldmine Drive, Big Bear
(EXIT BIG BEAR BLVD. S.E. ON MOONRIDGE RD. THE ANIMAL PARK IS TOWARDS THE
END OF THE ROAD, ON GOLDMINE DR.)

Get a little wild up in the mountains! Animals from the surrounding
mountains that need extra care, whether they are orphaned or hurt, find
sanctuary in this small animal park. A grizzly bear, a snow leopard,
Black bears, wolves, coyotes, bobcats, raccoons, deer, eagles, and
other animals and birds now consider the animal park their home. It's
just the right size for kids, and since the enclosures are not too large,
it's easy to see the animals up close here. Special daily events include
animal presentations at noon, where an animal is brought out and
talked about, and a feeding tour at 3pm (except on Wednesdays).
We've always found the docents and trainers willing, even eager, to
answer our kids' questions, so it makes our visit here more memorable.
A small education center has a few prepared specimens, such as a
snowy owl, and some hands-on exhibits. The Animal Park also offers
special programs, such as the tasty ice cream safari.
Hours: Open daily Memorial Day through October 10am - 5pm,
weather permitting. Open the rest of the year on the
weekends, 10am - 4pm, weather permitting. After a
snowfall, come take a guided "snow tour" through the
Animal Park from 11:30am - 1:30pm.
Admission: $2.50 for adults; $1.50 for ages 3 - 10; children 2 years
and under are free.
Ages: All

SCENIC SKY CHAIR   ☼
(909) 866-5766 $$
At Snow Summit ski area, Big Bear
(EXIT BIG BEAR BLVD., S. ON SUMMIT BLVD.)

Do your kids appreciate the awesome scenery of mountains, trees,
Big Bear Lake, and Big Bear Valley, plus breathing clean air? If not,
they'll still enjoy the mile-long, twenty-minute (each way) chair ride up to
the mountaintop. Once at the top, there is a picnic and barbecue area,
so you can bring your own food, or purchase a burger, chicken
sandwich, etc., from the snack bar. There are over forty miles of trails
through the forest and wilderness area up here, so hikers and biking
enthusiasts are in their element. The terrain varies, which means the
trails range from easy, wide, Forest Service roads to arduous, single-

track, dirt trails. What better way to spend a day than up here in a place readily described as "God's country."

Bike rentals are available at the base of Snow Summit at Team Big Bear Mountain Bikes, (909) 866-4565. The store has maps for all the Big Bear trails.

Hours: The sky chair operates May through mid-June and mid-September through October (or the beginning of ski season) on weekends only, 8am - 5pm. It's open daily, mid-June through mid-September, Mon. - Fri., 9am - 4pm; Sat., 8am - 5pm; Sun., 8am - 4pm, weather permitting.

Admission: One-way ride (no bike) - $5 for adults; $2 for ages 7 - 12; children 6 years and under are free when accompanied by a paying adult; one-way ride (with bike) or round trip (no bike) - $7 for adults; $3 for ages 7 - 12; all-day pass (with bike) - $19 for adults; $8 for kids. Ask about half-day prices.

Ages: 3 years and up.

SUGARLOAF CORDWOOD CO.   ☼

(909) 866-2220   !/$

42193 Big Bear Boulevard, Big Bear

(AT THE CORNER OF BIG BEAR BLVD. AND STANFIELD CUT-OFF)

The gigantic, wooden statues of bears, Indians, etc. (i.e. chain saw carvings), will attract your attention as you drive along Big Bear Boulevard. This unique store is worth a stop. Take a "tour" through the lot and inside the rooms to see smaller carvings and other unusual, artistic, gift items.

Hours: Usually open daily, from 10am - 5pm.

Admission: Free

Ages: 3 years and up.

SUGARLOAF PARK   ☼

Baldwin Lane, Big Bear   !

(EXIT BIG BEAR BLVD. [38] S. ON MAPLE LN., L. ON BALDWIN.)

It is a beautiful drive to this park, but where up here isn't the scenery beautiful? Sugarloaf Park has a softball field, a few tennis courts, a sand volleyball court, and older metal playground equipment, plus picnic shelters and barbecue pits. It also has a mini-forest; a small grouping of short trees that feels like the real thing to younger kids (but they won't get lost!).

Hours: Open daily, sunrise to sunset.

Admission: Free

Ages: All

SUNSET DINNER CRUISE

(909) 866-3218   *$$$$$*

Corner of Lakeview Drive and Paine Road, Big Bear Marina, Big Bear
(EXIT BIG BEAR BLVD. S. ON PAINE RD.)

Where can your family go for dinner that is a fun, kid-friendly treat
(and I don't mean McDonald's)?; somewhere that is exotic, yet cost
efficient?;different, but agreeable to all? - on a pontoon Sunset Dinner
Cruise! Pontoons are flat-bottomed boats and almost seasick proof.
Cruise around Big Bear Lake, in and out of the coves. Take a guided
tour, or rent a pontoon on your own, and even let the kids drive the
boat, but not too near the shore. Anytime during your cruise, pig out on
the delicious dinner supplied by Hall's which includes broasted chicken,
potatoes, coleslaw, and rolls. Bring dessert and drinks, and you are all
set to sail!

Hours: Open daily, seasonally (usually spring through November
1). Take the guided tour Mon., Tues., Thurs., and Fri,
from 6pm - 7:30pm. You must prepay by 3pm on the day
of your cruise. Dinner is provided. Or, rent your own
pontoon in the summer from 5pm - 8pm; other times
seasonally from 4pm - 7pm. You must prepay by 3pm on
the day of your cruise and don't forget to pick up your
dinner at Hall's beforehand. Reservations are strongly
suggested.

Admission: $15 per person for the guided tour; $75 for eight people,
or $100 for twelve people for your own pontoon rental.
Dinner is included in your admission price.

Ages: 3 years and up.

SUPER BEAR ARCADE

(909) 866-8620   *$*

Big Bear Boulevard, Big Bear
(LOCATED IN THE BIG BEAR VILLAGE.)

For those who need their video and arcade game fix, this arcade
center has a wide variety of games to choose from, plus a few kiddy
rides. It is conveniently located in Big Bear Village.

Hours: Open daily.
Admission: Token money.
Ages: 2½ years and up.

VICTORIA PARK CARRIAGES, LTD.

(909) 584-2277   *$$$$*

Big Bear

There is no more elegant, storybook way to explore Big Bear than
by horse and carriage. A carriage can usually be found in the heart of
the Village, across from Chad's, on the weekends. Take a fifteen- or

twenty-minute ride through the Village, and down to the lake. The
carriages seat between four to seven people.

Admission: $25 a couple during the day; no charge for small children.
Additional adults are half-price. ($30 a couple at
nighttime.)

Ages: 2 years and up.

PALM SPRINGS

A collage of words and images used to come to mind when I thought about Palm Springs - desert; hot; resort; homes of the rich and famous; golf; shopping Mecca; etc. Now that my family has thoroughly explored it, I can add to this list - kid-friendly; fun; beautiful; great hiking opportunities; and educational treasures. This area is one oasis that is no mirage!

Note: Although this section is titled PALM SPRINGS, it also includes attractions in the surrounding desert cities.

BIG MORONGO CANYON PRESERVE

(760) 363-7190

East Drive, Morongo Valley
(EXIT ROUTE 62 E. ON EAST DR.)

The quietness of this peaceful preserve was broken only by shouts from my kids whenever they spotted a lizard, bunny, roadrunner, or another animal. The trails are relatively easy to walk, and many of them go in and through the canyon and the fire-blackened trees. There are several short looping trails, as well as a longer hike of five-and-a-half miles along the Canyon Trail, which extends the length of the canyon. Fresh water marshes and a variety of trees and plants add to the otherwise more traditional desert landscape. Wildlife here includes Bighorn sheep, raccoons, coyotes, and so many species of birds that people come just to observe them. Bring binoculars!

Hours: Open daily from 7:30am - sunset.
Admission: Free
Ages: 3 years and up.

CAMELOT PARK FAMILY ENTERTAINMENT CENTER

(760) 321-9893   *$$$*

67-700 E. Palm Canyon Drive [111], Cathedral City
(EXIT INTERSTATE 10 S. ON GENE AUTRY TR., L. ON E. PALM CANYON DR. [HWY 111].)

In short, there's simply not a more congenial spot for happy ever aftering than here in Camelot! This huge family fun center (the first castle off Highway 111), offers a variety of entertainment for everyone. Choose from three themed **miniature golf** courses - $5.50 per round for ages 6 years and up, $4.25 for seniors, children 5 years and under are free; **go carts** - $4.75 a ride; **bumper boats** (avoid the shooting fountain or get refreshed) - $4 a ride; **laser tag** (a five-minute game of going through mazes in the dark, and zapping the other team with laser guns to score points) - $4; a **simulator** ride - $4; a castle **fun jump** (inflated bounce area) - $1 for ages 12 and under; **batting cages;** and over 200 video and sport games, plus a prize redemption center.

Hours: Open Mon. - Thurs., 11am - 10pm; Fri., 11am - midnight; Sat., 10am - midnight, Sun., 10am - 10pm.
Admission: Attractions are individually priced above, or purchase a super saver for $12.50, which includes a round of miniature golf, two attractions, and $2 worth of tokens.
Ages: 4 years and up.

CHILDREN'S DISCOVERY MUSEUM OF THE DESERT

(760) 321-0602 $

71-701 Gerald Ford Drive, Rancho Mirage

(Exit I-10 W. on Ramon, L. on Bob Hope Dr., R. on Gerald Ford Dr.)

The desert, known for golf and retirement living, will soon be able to boast of a terrific museum where children will enjoy hands-on fun. Scheduled to open in November, 1997 the plans for this beautifully designed, 8,000 square foot building include a rope maze; an archaeological dig (sand pit); a climbing wall; painting (and repainting) a Volkswagen car; playing police officer on a real CHP motorcycle; a workshop where busy hands can put together or take apart appliances; a theatrical section for kids to dress up in costumes, uniforms, etc.; a mini super market; a toddler area; an area to create Play-Doh™ pizzas and cook them in a pretend oven; and more! Call the museum for more information.

Hours: To be announced.

Admission: To be announced.

Ages: 9 months through 12 years.

COACHELLA VALLEY MUSEUM & CULTURAL CENTER

(760) 342-6651 $

82-616 Miles Avenue, Indio

(Exit Interstate 10 S. on Monroe, L. on Miles Ave.)

Each city desires to preserve its history and make it available for future generations. The Coachella Valley Museum has displays inside the small 1928 adobe home that reflect Indian and pioneer heritage. Some of the permanent displays include Indian pottery and arrowheads; dioramas of date picking and an interesting thirteen-minute video about growing dates; old-fashioned clothing; original kitchen appliances; and a large panel displaying various fire alarms.

Outside, on the beautiful grounds, are lots of old agricultural tools and machinery. Peek inside the blacksmith shop to see forges, anvils, tongs, etc. Take a guided tour to learn background information on the items here or, although nothing is hands-on, look around by yourself to get a rich, visual sampling of history.

Hours: Open October through May, Wed. - Sat., 10am - 4pm; Sun., 1pm - 4pm. Open weekends only in June and September. Closed July and August.

Admission: $1 for adults; 50¢ for seniors and ages 5 -1 4; children 4 years and under are free.

Ages: 5 years and up.

COACHELLA VALLEY PRESERVE   ☾
(760) 343-1234   !
Thousand Palms Canyon Road, Coachella
(EXIT INTERSTATE 10 N. ON RAMON RD., L. ON THOUSAND PALMS CANYON RD.)

This 18,000-acre preserve is not only immense, but it is diverse in topography and wildlife. The preserve straddles Indio Hills and the infamous San Andreas Fault. Thousand Palms Oasis (yes, it contains at least this many palm trees) is at the heart of the Coachella Valley Preserve. The oasis is supported by water constantly seeping along the fault line.

Kids begin to appreciate the many faces of the desert as they hike through here. It is sandy, dry, and rocky, and these elements create sand dunes, bluffs, and mesas. It is also mountainous, and interspersed with dense palm trees, cacti, and various other vegetation. Some of the trails are as short as one-quarter mile, while others are longer at one-and-a-half miles, and more.

Start at the rustic Visitors Center that has natural history exhibits behind glass. The displays include arrowheads, insects, birds' nests, and eggs. Grab a water bottle and/or a picnic lunch and have a delightful time exploring desert wilderness at its finest.

Hours: Open daily from sunset to sunrise.
Admission: Free
Ages: 4 years and up.

COVERED WAGON TOURS   ☾
(760) 347-2161 $$$$$
Ramon Road outside Thousand Palms
(FROM PALM SPRINGS, GO E. ON RAMON RD., OR GO N. ON WASHINGTON FROM LA QUINTA. IT'S ON THE E. SIDE OF RAMON RD.)

Travel in a mule-drawn, covered wagon for two hours through the Coachella Valley Preserve. You'll go along the San Andreas fault and see three oases, and lots of wildlife. The wagons are not the primitive ones your pioneer ancestors used, as these have padded seats, tires, etc., although part of the fun is the bumpiness of the ride. Take just the tour, or add on a chuckwagon cookout dinner and sing-a-long for the full western experience.

Hours: Call for tour times.
Admission: The tours are $30 for adults; $15 for ages 7 - 16; children 6 years and under are free. Tour and dinner costs $55 for adults; $27.50 for ages 7 - 16; children 6 years and under are free.
Ages: 5 years and up.

DESERT ADVENTURES   ☾
(760) 864-6530 $$$$$
Call for new location

Choose from three different tours to take your two-hour or four-hour jeep trip, and explore the wonders of the desert: Indian Canyon tour takes you through archaeology sites, two lush oases, and to a waterfall, while learning about the history of Palm Springs; Santa Rosa Mountains tour is a great combination of an off-road adventure, and a naturalist tour; Mystery Canyon Adventure tour goes through the Coachella Valley, across the San Andreas, and involves hiking around the area. Bighorn sheep, coyotes, and other wildlife are abundant along the back roads, so keep your eyes open. Jeeps seat up to seven people.

Hours: Two-hour tours leave at 8am, 10am, 1pm, and 3pm. Four-hour tours leave at 8am and 1pm. Ask about their sunset tours.

Admission: Two-hour tours cost $69 for adults; $64 for kids. Four-hour tours cost $99 for adults; $94 for kids.

Ages: 5 years and up.

DINOSAURS / SKYLINE AVIATION HELICOPTER RIDES / WHEEL INN RESTAURANT

(909) 849-8309 - dinos; (909) 699-3048 - helicopter rides;   !/$
(909) 849-7012 - restaurant.

Interstate 10, Cabazon

(GOING E., EXIT INTERSTATE 10 N. ON MAIN ST. IT'S E. OF HADLEYS; N.W. OF PALM SPRINGS.)

While cruising down the desert highway, looking out the window, your kids see the usual things, such as big trucks, cactus, and dinosaurs. Stop! The gigantic Brontosaurus, with fiery eyes, is almost triple the size of the actual dinosaur that roamed the earth long ago. The same goes for the Tyrannosaurus behind him.

Enter the steel and concrete Brontosaurus through its tail. Along the cave-like stairway are a few fossils and rocks behind glass displays, plus information and explanations regarding these two huge time travelers. Up in the Brontosaurus' belly is a gift shop, specializing in everything dinosaur. The fun for a child is simply being inside here. The T. rex, however, can just be looked at, but do look up at his mouth to see the remains of the last ~~victim~~ visitor.

Located behind the dinosaurs, Skyline Aviation helicopter rides take you to the skies on the weekends. Take a three or four-minute flight to see the great creatures from the sky, or go on a longer trip to see Whitewater Windmills, Palm Springs, etc.

Wheel Inn Restaurant is a folksy truck-stop cafe with merchandise for sale, like gift items, sculptures, etc., displayed throughout. Retail pictures on the walls range from Disney to the Southwest. (Note: There are pictures of scantily-clad women towards the back.)

All in all, it's a *dino*-mite little stop!

Hours: The dinosaur gift shop is usually open daily from 9am - 8pm. The restaurant is open twenty-four hours. The helicopter rides are on weekends only.

Admission: It's free to look and walk around the dinosaurs. The
                 helicopter rides start at $12.50 for two passengers for a
                 three - four-minute flight; $100 for two passengers for a
                 twenty-minute flight, etc.
Ages: All

GENERAL PATTON MEMORIAL MUSEUM   ◐

(760) 227-3483 $

Chiriaco, Chiriaco Summit

*(EXIT INTERSTATE 10 AT CHIRIACO. THE MUSEUM IS RIGHT OFF THE FREEWAY, 30
MILES EAST OF INDIO.)*

Any study of World War II includes at least one lesson on war hero,
General George Patton. Even if kids don't know who he is yet, they will
like all the "war stuff" at the museum. Outside the memorial building are
over a dozen tanks. Kids can't climb on them, but they can run around
and play army!

Inside, the front room is dominated by a five-ton relief map
depicting the Colorado River Aqueduct route and surrounding area. The
large back room is filled with General Patton's personal effects, and
WWII memorabilia such as uniforms, weapons, flags, and artillery. Our
favorite exhibits include a jeep, a lifelike statue of General Patton (who
looks amazingly like George C. Scott), and rounds of machine gun
bullets. Special displays showcase Nazi items taken from fallen Nazi
soldiers; a small, but powerful pictorial Holocaust display; and items
found on the battlefield of Gettysburg.

Over one million servicemen and women were trained at this huge
Desert Training Center site during WWII. If your child is especially
interested in this period of military history, take him to the remnants of
the training camps, accessible by four-wheel vehicles. Call the museum
for directions and more details.

Hours: Open daily from 9:30am - 4:30pm.
Admission: $4 for adults; $3.50 for seniors; children 12 years and
                 under are free.
Ages: 3 years and up.

HARD CLAY CAFE   ◐

(760) 341-3755 $$$$

Sage Street, Palm Desert

*(FROM HWY 111, HEADING TOWARD INDIAN WELLS, GO PAST MONTEREY, R. ON
SAGE ST.)*

An artist is defined as "a person who uses deliberate skill in making
things of beauty." I can, in all honesty, say that my children and I try to
be artists; we are deliberate in our attempts. Actually, I'm often
pleasantly surprised at how wonderful their creations turn out at paint-
your-own ceramic stores. Hard Clay Cafe offers a wide range of items
to artistically paint, including plates, picture frames, tiles, mugs, etc.

This is a great activity to share in together, and kids come home thrilled with their creations. (This is a great place to make gifts for hard-to-shop-for relatives!)

Hours: Open Tues. - Sun., 11am - 6pm.

Admission: The price of your item, ranging from $2.50 - $40, plus $6 an hour per painter which includes paints, brushes, glazing, and firing.

Ages: 4 years and up.

HEARTLAND (The California Museum of the Heart) ☼

(760) 32 - HEART (43278) $

39-600 Bob Hope Drive, Rancho Mirage

(EXIT INTERSTATE 10 W. ON RAMON, L. ON BOB HOPE DR. N. OF COUNTRY CLUB DR. IT'S IN THE HEART INSTITUTE.)

You'll receive a hearty welcome at this small, Smithsonian-quality museum that is in the Heart Institute. Listen - do you hear a heartbeat? The sound grows louder as you enter the museum through the pink plastic and white rubbery strands of a model heart valve. Stand in a pinkish tube, which is actually a replica of an artery, and touch the bumpy rubber walls. Look up to see how plaque attacks and constricts the function of this vessel. A video describes the process. The next display looks and feels like rubbery red doughnuts, but they're "actually" blood platelets. A video explains blood cells' relationship to the heart.

Kids won't draw a Valentine for heart after seeing the ten-foot model of a real heart, which isn't as cute looking. Different buttons either make the heart light up, tracing the circulatory system, or make this model seemingly come alive: moving, beating, pulsating. Another interactive display that got my kids really pumped was "Sound of the Heart." Place a stethoscope over your child's heart, record the heartbeat, and then play back the magnified version. Have your child jog in place, too, for a comparison. Listen to other recorded heartbeats to detect their irregularities, such as mitrostenosis.

No "butts" about it, the large, literally smoking cigarettes certainly drew my boys' attention. I hope that the cartoon about not smoking extinguished any desire to puff their lives away.

The 104-seat Happy Heart Theater shows any one of three films upon request. One is a fifteen-minute cartoon for young kids. Another is for school-aged kids called "I Am Joe's Heart." After this twenty-eight-minute film is shown, catch the three-minute "music video" - open heart surgery accompanied by jazz music. Reactions range from "cool" to "gross." The third film "How to Beat a Heart Attack" is geared for general viewing. Look for this theater to incorporate 3D and sensurround special effects in the near future.

Although the information in many of the exhibits is too technical for younger kids to fully digest, the hands-on features and outstanding visuals make an impact on the hearts and minds of all ages.

Hours: Operating hours are usually Mon. - Fri., 7:30am - 6pm -
              Summer hours may be shorter. It is also open
              September - May, Sat. from 7am - noon..
Admission: Suggested donations are $2 for adults; $1 for kids or
              students 6 - 17 years; children 5 years and under are
              free.
Ages: 4 years and up.

HI-DESERT NATURE MUSEUM   ☼

(760) 369-7212   !

57-116 Twentynine Palms Highway, Yucca Valley

(EXIT TWENTYNINE PALMS HIGHWAY [62] N. ON DUMOSA, JUST E. OF SAGE AVE.)

I highly recommend the Hi-Desert Nature Museum. It offers lots of
activity, and has fascinating exhibits on wildlife, geology, culture, and
science.

The rotating exhibits in the front room have included Wild on
Wildflowers; Shake, Rattle & Roll, Living With Earthquakes; Holiday
Traditions (from around the world); etc. We saw Black Widow.
Arachniphobia aside, the fantastic photographs, video, and information
combined with live and dead specimens made learning about this
feared insect interesting. The far wall in this room contains encased
displays of Indian baskets, arrowheads, pottery, and Kachina dolls.

Another section has taxidermied animals that are unique to the
desert such as mule deer, quail, roadrunners, jack rabbits, and coyotes.
A hands-on area in here has skulls and soft fur to match with the
stuffed animals.

Fossils, shells, and a wonderful rock and mineral collection
comprise the earth science room. The petrified logs are unusual, as are
the sphere balls. Rocks like amethyst and malachite are shown in their
rough, natural state, and also in a polished version. Original minerals
are shown next to their commercial counterpart such as fluorspar next
to toothpaste, and talc next to baby powder; this helps kids to make
connections and understand that man-made products were first God-
created resources.

A mini-zoo has live squirrels, lizards, snakes, and a tarantula. A
docent is often on hand to assist your child in holding one of the
animals. I'm proud to write that after recovering from my cold sweat, I
held the (large!) tarantula.

The Kid's Corner is action packed. There is a small sand pit (I
mean archaeological dig); animal puppets; a butterfly and insect
collection; stone mortar and pestles with corn kernels to grind;
discovery boxes to reach in and guess what you're touching; animal
tracks to match with animals; a touch table with whale bones, rocks,
shells, and a lightning ball; books; and containers of construction toys.
The Hi-Desert Nature Museum also offers themed traveling classroom
programs on recycling, insects, wildflowers, a particular animal, etc.

Opening an oyster and finding a pearl created by a grain of sand, is like opening the doors to this museum and finding a part of the sandy desert that has been transformed to a treasure of great worth.

Hours: Open Tues. - Sun. from 10am - 5pm. Closed major holidays.
Admission: Free
Ages: 2 years and up.

INDIAN CANYONS   ☽
(760) 325-5673   *$$*

S. Palm Canyon Drive, Palm Springs

(EXIT INTERSTATE 10 S. ON INDIAN CANYON DR., WHICH TURNS INTO PALM CANYON DR. KEEP GOING S. FOR A FEW MILES.)

Vast, spectacular, and awesome are three words that come to mind when exploring Indian Canyons. Long ago, ancestors of the Agua Caliente Cahuilla Indians made their homes in these canyons and the surrounding area. Today, a large number of Indians still reside on the reservation here. The Tribal Council has opened three out of four canyons for the public to explore.

A mile or so past the entrance gate is the trading post. Kids enjoy looking at the trinkets, jewelry, and Indian art work. Beyond the store are picnic grounds, and hiking and horse trails.

Palm Canyon is fifteen miles long and abundant with palm trees; a stark contrast to the surrounding rocky hills. The moderately-graded, paved walkway into this valley leads you along a stream, and to a picnic oasis. The scenery almost makes you forget that you're hiking! Andreas Canyon is unexpectedly lush with fan palms and more than 150 species of plants, all within a half-mile radius. Hike along a stream and see unusual rock formations. Challenge your kids to look for shapes or people in the rocks. There are also Indian caves back in the canyon and old grinding stones. You can hike to Murray Canyon from Andreas Canyon. Murray is smaller and less accessible, but no less beautiful. There are caves here also, which always sparks a child's imagination. Hiking in Indian Canyons is a wonderful opportunity to explore the desert wilderness surrounded by the stunning backdrop of the rocky mountains.

Hours: Open daily from 8am - 5pm. Summer schedule may vary.
Admission: $5 for adults; $3 for students; $2.50 for seniors (62 +); $1 for ages 6 - 12. Children 5 years and under are free.
Ages: All, but older kids for real hiking.

JOSHUA TREE AND SOUTHERN RAILROAD   ☀
MUSEUM
(760) 366-8503 - museum; (760) 363-6446 - tours   *$*
Willow Lane, Joshua Tree

(EXIT HIGHWAY 62 S. ON PARK BLVD., WHICH TURNS INTO QUAIL SPRINGS RD., S. ON WILLOW LANE.)

Both the Live Steam Club and the railroad museum are located here. Model railroad enthusiasts can not only work on their hobby, but some have engineered it so that they live here, too. The trains range from two-and-a-half-inch scale models to full-sized rail cars. If it's running, you're invited to ride on Uncle Bert's gasoline-powered model train, which covers about a mile of track. Take a tour through the full-sized cars including a diner, with its old-fashioned stove and icebox; a mail car, with small pigeonholes that are labeled with city names; a Pullman sleeping car, which always makes sleeping on a train seem romantic; and the grand finale - a caboose.

Inside the museum are model steam engines and lots of railroad memorabilia from Francis Moseley's collection. Ask to watch the video which shows how a model train operates. This site is great for those who are loco about trains!

Hours: Open to the public on the second and third Sat. - Sun. of the month from 10am - 4pm.
Admission: $1 donation.
Ages: 3 years and up.

JOSHUA TREE NATIONAL PARK / HEADQUARTERS ☼
(760) 367-7511 $

Joshua Tree

(THE SOUTH ENTRANCE: EXIT INTERSTATE 10 N. ON COTTONWOOD SPRINGS, 25 MILES EAST OF INDIO. THE NORTH ENTRANCE: EXIT TWENTYNINE PALMS HIGHWAY [62] BETWEEN THE TOWN OF JOSHUA TREE AND TWENTYNINE PALMS. THE WEST ENTRANCE: EXIT TWENTYNINE PALMS HIGHWAY [62] AT THE TOWN OF JOSHUA TREE. THIS IS THE BEST WAY TO REACH KEYS VIEW AND HIDDEN VALLEY.)

This 800,000-acre park gets its name from the unique Joshua trees that Mormon visitors likened to the biblical Joshua reaching up to God. Explore the riches of this national treasure by car, by foot, and/or by camping.

Entire books are written on Joshua Tree National Park, so consider the following information a very condensed version. "Wind-sculpted boulders"; "massive granite monoliths"; "five fan palm oases dotting the park"; "wildflowers and wildlife"; "mountainous"; and "rugged" are just a few phrases attributed to this enormous park. Start your visit at the main headquarters/Visitors Center in Oasis of Mara, located off the north entrance. You can get a map here, look at the botanical displays, and watch a slide show that gives a good overview of the park.

If you are automobile adventurers, which is a good way to get a lay of the land, there are many roads to travel. Keys View is the most popular destination because of its breathtaking view of the valley, mountains, and deserts. (Bring a panoramic camera.) If you don't mind a few bumps along the way, and kids usually don't, there are many dirt roads accessible only by four-wheel drive. Particularly outstanding is the eighteen-mile Geology Tour Road, which showcases some of the most incredible landscape the park offers.

Hiking runs the gamut from easy, one-tenth-of-a-mile trails, to strenuous, over thirteen-mile long trails. Three of the trails that offer fascinating terrain also lead to special destinations: The first one is Hidden Valley, with trails winding through massive boulders. It leads to and through legendary cattle rustlers' hideouts.The second is Barker Dam, which was built almost 100 years ago, and is now a reservoir that many desert animals frequent. Approach it in whispers, if possible, so as not to scare away any critters. Encourage your children to look for some of the "hidden" wildlife in the water. The third is Lost Horse Mine, which is a rugged one-and-a-half-mile hike. This mine was used for mining and prospecting gold. Maybe there still is gold in them thar hills! **Bring water** no matter which trail you take because it is not supplied in the park!!!

Rock climbing is a popular sport here. Even if your kids are too young to participate, they'll get a vicarious thrill at watching more experienced climbers. Boulder hopping is also fun, and that can be done by kids of all ages! Why do we have this urge to conquer inanimate rocky objects? (Because they are there.)

Camping is primitive at most of the 500 sites in Joshua Tree. Many campsites are located in the shelter of rocks, while others, at higher elevations, offer spots of shade. It is hot during the day, much cooler at night (even cold), and at times quite windy, but kids revel in it all. Water is only provided at Cottonwood and Black Rock Canyon campgrounds, so other sites are really back to basics.

National parks are sometimes called "universities of the outdoors." Joshua Tree National Park is an outstanding university to attend. Everyone will go home with a special memory, and a different reason for wanting to come back.

Hours: Open daily sunrise to sunset.
Admission: $5 per vehicle, which is good for a week's admittance. The Visitors Center is open daily from 8am - 5pm. Camping starts at $10 a night.
Ages: All

LAKE CAHUILLA   ◑

(760) 564-4712 - lake; (800) 234-park (7275) - camping $
reservations
58-075 Jefferson, La Quinta
(EXIT INTERSTATE 10 S. ON MONROE ST., R. ON AVENUE 58.)

Escape from the heat at Lake Cahuilla recreation park. The gigantic, stocked lake is a prime spot for fisherboys and girls to reel in the catch of the day. Kids over 16 years need a state fishing license. Night fishing is open Friday and Saturday during the summer. Although swimming in the lake is prohibited, there is a pool open for your aquatic pleasure. A wooden playground is located behind the pool - youngsters always have energy to play, no matter what temperature it is! The park is not abundantly blessed with shade trees, but there are large grassy areas and palm trees to enhance its beauty. Hiking trails traverse the park, so make sure you've got plenty of sunscreen and water. Over 150 campsites are available here, complete with barbecues and other amenities. Come escape the city life, if just for a day or night!

Hours: The park is open daily mid-October through April from sunrise to sunset, and May 1 through mid-October, Fri. - Mon., sunrise to sunset. The pool is open weekends only April through May, and September through October, 11am - 5:45pm. It is open during the summer Fri. - Mon. from 11am - 5:45pm.

Admission: $2 for adults; $1 for children 10 years and under. The swimming pool is an extra $1 per person. Primitive camping (space and a table - no shade trees) is $12 a site; an upgraded site is $16 a night. Fishing is $5 for ages 16 and up; $4 for ages 5 - 15; children 4 years and up are free.

Ages: All

LA QUINTA SCULPTURE PARK (SCULPTURELAND) ☼
(760) 564-6464 $$
57325 Madison Street, La Quinta
(EXIT INTERSTATE 10 S. AT JEFFERSON, L. ON 54TH ST., R. ON MADISON.)

Beauty is in the eye of the beholder. Sculpture is in the hands of the creator. This park is unique in the minds of children (and adults)! The setting is picturesque with twenty acres of gently rolling green hills and landscaped park, and a three-acre, man-made lake. There is an art gallery inside, but the main attraction is outside, where over 200 larger-than-life sculptures are on display (for sale or lease) throughout the park. They are made of various mediums such as bronze, stone, barbed wire, painted steel, etc., and are generally sold to public places, such as parks or shopping centers. Our favorite exhibit is "People Climbing on Air" (our title for it), which is comprised of pieces of automobile tires remade in the shape of people, and suspended by chains. Bryce, my middle child, is now saving all of his street-collected treasures to make his own abstract art sculpture.

Kids can walk through a sculpture rainbow, and maybe pose on an empty pedestal, but not climb on any of the exhibits, tempting though it may be. Golf cart rentals are available to drive around the park. If you want a closer look at the sculptures situated in the lake, rent a pedal boat. A picnic area makes your day here even more pleasant.

Hours: Open Tues. - Sun. from 9am - 5pm. Closed June 16 through August 31.

Admission: $5 for adults; $4 for seniors; $3 for ages 3 - 15; children 2
                years and under are free. Pedal boat rentals are $7; golf
                cart rentals are $9.
   Ages: 3 years and up.

LIVING DESERT WILDLIFE AND BOTANICAL   ☼
GARDEN PARK
(760) 346-5694   *$$$*
47-900 Portola Avenue, Palm Desert
(EXIT INTERSTATE 10 S. ON MONTEREY AVE., L. ON PALM CANYON, [HWY 111], R.
ON PORTOLA.)

Kids can experience a lot of living in the 1,200-acre Living Desert!
Choose one of three areas of interest - botanical gardens, wildlife, or
hiking - or partake in some of each.

The nocturnal (this can be your child's first new word of the day)
and small animals exhibit is to your immediate left through the entrance
gate. Bats are always a highlight in here. Behind this exhibit is the
Discovery Room. With the wonders a child can literally behold in here -
live snakes, turtles, and a big hairy tarantula, plus feathers, bones,
rocks, and fur - they can get a real "feel" for desert life. Kids can also
put on animal puppet shows at the box theater, or make crayon
rubbings of desert animals.

The northern section of this "like a zoo, only better" park is mostly
botanical. The pathways weave in and out amongst an incredible
variety of desert floral including saguaros, yuccas, and towering palm
trees. Caged bird life is abundant along the walkways, too. We took the
time to really watch our feathered friends' activities and learned quite a
bit.

Eagle Canyon houses twenty desert animal species living in their
natural element. Powerful mountain lions, Mexican wolves, and the
small fennec foxes dwell in their own craggy retreats that are easily
viewed through glass. Don't miss the tree-climbing coyote!

A trail system lies to the east, traversing through some of the
1,000-acre wilderness section of the park. Three loops offer something
for every level hiker: An easy three-quarter mile hike; a moderate one-
and-a-half-mile hike; and a strenuous five-mile, round-trip hike to the
base of Eisenhower Mountain. Don't get me wrong though, the walk
around the park is a hike in itself. If you get tired, take the fifty-minute
guided tram tour that goes all around the park.

Animals in the Living Desert dwell in outdoor enclosures that
resemble their natural habitat. A rocky mountain is home to the Bighorn
sheep. Look for them leaping among the boulders. Other exotic animals
include Arabian oryx, aardwolves, zebras, cheetahs, and small African
mammals and birds. We saw several other animals in the wild, too,
such as a snake slithering across our path and the ever-speedy
roadrunner darting out of the bushes. Seeing them authenticated the
unique setting of this park. Want to see more animals, more up close?

See Wildlife Wonders, a live animal presentation at the outdoor theater, featuring your favorite desert critters.

Visit here during the spring when the desert flowers and trees explode in a profusion of colors. Special events throughout the year include the winter WildLights. (See the November CALENDAR section for more information.) Anytime you come to the Living Desert will be a time of wonder, relaxation, and education.

Hours: Open October 1 through June 15 daily from 9am - 5pm. Open June 16 through July 31 and September daily from 8am - noon. Closed the month of August and on Christmas Day. The Children's Discovery Room is open daily 10am - 4pm, but closed the first Tuesday of the month. Times for weekend Wildlife Wonders show vary.

Admission: $7.50 for adults; $6.50 for seniors; $3.50 for ages 3 - 12; children 2 years and under are free. The tram tour is $4 a person. School groups, with reservations, are free, however, spaces fill up fast so make your reservation soon.

Ages: All

MOORTEN BOTANICAL GARDEN

(760) 327-6555 $

1701 S. Palm Canyon Drive, Palm Springs

(EXIT INTERSTATE 10 S. ON INDIAN CANYON, WHICH TURNS INTO PALM CANYON DR.)

This place has plenty of prickly plants along pleasurable pathways. In other words, this compact botanical garden, specializing in cacti, is a delightful stroll and an interesting way to study desert plant life. There are over 3,000 varieties of cacti, trees, birds, succulents, and flowers! You'll see giant saguaros, ocotillo, and grizzly bear cactus, plus you can walk through a greenhouse (or cactarium). Towards the entrance are petrified logs, and a few, small desert animals in cages. Enjoy this spot of greenery in the midst of the sandy, brown desert!

Hours: Open Mon. - Sat., 9am - 4:30pm; Sun., 10am - 4pm.

Admission: $2 for adults; 75¢ for ages 5 - 15; children 4 years and under are free.

Ages: All

OASIS WATERPARK

(760) 325 - SURF (7873) $$$$

1500 Gene Autry Trail, Palm Springs

(EXIT INTERSTATE 10 S. ON GENE AUTRY TRAIL. S. OF RAMON RD., N. OF PALM CANYON [HWY 111].)

This twenty-two-acre waterpark is truly an oasis in the desert. Built in and on top of a rocky hill, with an adjoining resort health club, the surroundings are luxurious. The over ten waterslides range from mild, uncovered slides, to enclosed forty-mph "Rattlers," to seventy-foot free

fall slides. Catch a wave, dude, in the wave pool where kids
or board surf. Get carried away in the gentle three-foot-deep
Whitewater River inner tube ride. Younger children can take the plun.
in their own small water play area. Oasis Waterpark also offers locker
rentals, private cabana rentals, and full-service snack bars for all your
creature comforts. (You cannot bring your own food inside the park.)
And yes, there is a video arcade here, too.

Tip: For a rocky mountain high in the desert, try your hand (and
foot) at the UPRISING ROCK CLIMBING CENTER, located right next
door.

Hours: Open daily, mid-March through Labor Day, plus
weekends through October, from 11am - 5:30pm.

Admission: $9 for local residents (bring proof of residency). For non-
residents - $17.95 for adults; $9.95 for seniors; $11.50
for kids 40" - 60" tall; kids under 40" are free. After 3pm,
admission is $12.50 for two residents; $17.95 for two
non-residents. Body boards rentals are $5. An additional
$5 will get you two climbs at the rock climbing center next
door. Parking is $3, or $5 for preferred (i.e. closer)
parking.

Ages: All

OFFROAD RENTALS

(760) 325-0376

Palm Springs

*(EXIT INTERSTATE 10 S. ON WHITE WATER, GO ONE MILE S. ON HWY. 111. IT'S 4
MILES N. OF THE PALM SPRINGS AERIAL TRAMWAY.)*

Come ride the sand dunes in Palm Springs! After watching a brief
instructional video, and getting safety equipment, go for an exhilarating
ride in an all-terrain Quad ATV. This is a wild and "radical" ride for you
and the kids! No reservations needed.

Hours: Open daily from 10am - sunset. Hours might vary during
the summer.

Admission: Half-hour rides start at $25.

Ages: 6 years and up.

PALM SPRINGS AERIAL TRAMWAY

(760) 325-1391

Valley Station is located on the north edge of Palm Springs
(TAKE TRAMWAY RD. OFF SR111, 3½ MILES UP THE HILL.)

In fourteen minutes an eighty-passenger, enclosed car, carries you
seemingly straight up the side of Mount San Jacinto. The scenery
change in this short amount of time is almost unbelievable - from
cactus and desert sand below, to the evergreen trees and cool air up
above. (Call ahead to see if there is snow.) The altitude up at Mount
San Jacinto State Park is 8,516 feet!

ountain Station has an Alpine Restaurant (which
nack bar, a game room, a gift shop, and
here you can see the entire valley, including the
forty-five miles away. The bottom floor of the
axidermied animals and an interesting twenty-two-
history of the tramway.

wn the Mountain Station building is Mount San
Jacinto Wilderness State Park, with fifty-four miles of great hiking trails,
campgrounds, and a ranger station. Though we just walked along the
easier trails, the mountain scenery anywhere up here is unbeatable!
Just remember that the trail you go down, you must also come back up
to catch the tram. Horse rentals are available for a guided tour. Snow
equipment rentals are available in the winter, as there are plenty of
areas to go sledding and cross country skiing. Snow rentals are
available November 15 through April 15, conditions permitting.

Catch the package deal called "Ride 'n' Dine," which includes tram
fare and dinner. The meal is your choice of prime rib or chicken served
from 4pm to 9pm at the Alpine Restaurant. Otherwise, the cost of a
buffet dinner is $9.95 for adults; $7.95 for children. The lunch menu is a
la carte. The tickets may be purchased after 2pm; no advanced
reservations are accepted. Tip: Bring jackets for everyone and wear
closed-toed shoes - it does get **really** cold up here!

Hours: Cars go up every half hour Mon. - Fri., starting at 10am;
Sat. - Sun., starting at 8am. The last car goes up at 8pm,
and the last car comes down at 9:45pm.

Admission: $16.95 for adults; $10.95 for ages 5 - 12; children 4 years
and old are free. Ride 'n' Dine costs $20.95 for adults;
$13.95 for ages 5 to 12.

Ages: 3 years and up.

PALM SPRINGS AIR MUSEUM

(760) 778-6262 $$$

745 Gene Autry Trail, Palm Springs
(EXIT INTERSTATE 10 S. ON GENE AUTRY TRAIL.)

Enjoy happy landings at this classy air museum, conveniently
located next to the Palm Springs Airport. Two hangers house between
fifteen to thirty vintage WWII aircraft that are being restored or are in
flight-ready condition. The collection includes Hellcats, Tomcats, B-17's,
a P-40 Warhawk, and more. The planes are not cordoned off, making it
easier to look at them close up, although touching is not allowed. Walk
under and look up into the belly of an A-26 "Invader" attack bomber. My
kids were thrilled to see the places where it actually held real bombs!
The planes are fascinating for the part they've played in history, and
visually exciting for kids because most have decorative emblems
painted on their sides. Bunkers and displays around the perimeter of
the airy hangers honor different eras of flight by featuring various
uniforms, flight jackets, photographs, patches, combat cameras, etc.

Other exhibits include gleaming antique cars, maps of missions, and touch screens. Tour the inside of a B-17 for $3 per person, or just admire it from the outside. Starting at 10am, the Wings Theater continuously shows war movies, combat videos, or interviews with war heroes. Kids always enjoy watching small planes land and take off at the adjacent runway. Free guided tours of the museum are conducted every Saturday and Sunday at noon and 2pm. For more entertainment with an altitude, come see fly-overs on Memorial Day, Veterans Day, Armed Forces Day, Pearl Harbor Day, etc. Call for a schedule and for more details.

Hours: Open daily 10am - 5pm.
Admission: $7.50 for adults; $6 for seniors and military with I.D.;
$3.50 for children under 12 years.
Ages: 4 years and up.

PALM SPRINGS DESERT MUSEUM ☼
(760) 325-7186   *$$*
101 Museum Drive, Palm Springs
(EXIT INTERSTATE 10 S. ON INDIAN CANYON DR., R. ON TAHQUITZ CANYON WAY, R. ON MUSEUM DR.)

There are many facets of this museum jewel. The Natural Science Wing has wall murals and life-size dioramas featuring taxidermied ice-age mammals and desert animals. Almost at floor level, in front of these dioramas, are displays of snakes and small desert creatures. Push a button to hear about their habits and habitats. Another room contains a replica skeleton of a saber-tooth tiger and the impressive giant ground sloth, plus other skulls. Live animals are always an attraction. Kids can see a variety of snakes, like sidewinders and kings, as well as gila monsters, scorpions, and kangaroo rats, displayed in glass cases along a wall.

The fine art gallery has permanent and changing exhibits of paintings, sculptures, and other forms of art. As the gallery is not overwhelmingly large, exploring the art world is a feasible journey for youngsters. My middle son has an artistic temperament, so I'm hoping art exposure will develop the talents, too!

The Steven Chase Art and Education Wing has galleries that exhibit modern and contemporary art; an enclosed sculpture garden; and the Denney Western American Art wing. The Denney wing features paintings, sculptures, and Native American art, plus miniature rooms that display a replica of the White House, colonial rooms, etc. A "living room," to read and view videos related to the exhibits, is also available.

The downstairs theater presents shows mostly for adult audiences, such as plays, ballets, and concerts. Even if you don't eat here, take a stroll through the Gallery Cafe to check out its colorful mobiles and funky decor.

The Palm Springs Desert Museum is an interesting way to learn about natural history and different art styles, plus it's a respite from the heat!

Hours: Open Tues. - Thurs., Sat. - Sun., 10am - 5pm; Fri., 10am - 8pm. Closed major holidays.

Admission: $6 for adults; $5 for seniors; $4 for ages 6 - 17; children 5 years and under are free. The first Friday of each month is free admission day.

Ages: 3 years and up.

PALM SPRINGS VILLAGEFEST   ☼

(760) 323-8274   !/$

Palm Canyon Drive, Palm Springs
(EXIT INTERSTATE 10 S. ON PALM CANYON DR.)

It's Thursday night and you're in Palm Springs with the kids, wondering what to do. You pick up this terrific book called Fun and Educational Places to go With Kids and read about VillageFest - problem solved! The VillageFest, or international street fair, is held along several blocks on Palm Canyon Drive in the heart of Palm Springs. There is food, arts and crafts vendors, boutiques, cafes, and entertainment such as live music. For kids, there are various attractions such as pony rides, magic shows, a party bouncer, a gyroscope, school band competitions, and a stage for children's productions.

Hours: Thursday nights from 6pm - 10pm. It is usually not open during July and August.

Admission: Free, though certain attractions cost $.

Ages: 4 years and up.

PIONEERTOWN / RUNNING DEER THEME PARK   ☼

(760) 228-1209 $

On Running Deer Tail, just off Pioneer Town Road, Pioneertown
(EXIT TWENTYNINE PALMS HIGHWAY [62] N. ON PIONEERTOWN RD., TRAVEL 4 MILES BACK TO PIONEERTOWN.)

Down a winding road, past boulders that line the sides of the street, is a town where time has stood still. Pioneertown was built in 1947 by Roy Rogers and Gene Autry as a permanent Old West movie and television set. Nothing much has changed in this small town, although real people now inhabit the railroad-tie and adobe buildings. The flavor of the Old West permeates every structure, such as the old-fashioned post office, the church, and the O.K. Corral. It is even evident in the motel (which looks like a [short] row of log cabins), bowling alley, and family restaurant that has live country music.

Running Deer Theme Park is an old, medium-sized ranch that has an eclectic mixture of things to do and see. There are reindeer, ducks, a bison, and a turkey in separate pens, as well as chickens, peacocks, cats, and dogs running around. Old farm equipment, like wagons, wheels, and some machinery, is scattered throughout. A small, one-room museum displays the kind of things that might once have belonged to your grandparents.

Other things to do here include dressing up in old-fashioned clothes for a photo; taking a pony ride; renting the one-room bunkhouse for an overnighter; or camping outside here in the dirt stretch between the animals and the picnic area. Picnic tables are set up among the desert plants in a small garden setting.

Hours: Both the town and park are open daily from morning 'til dark.

Admission: Admission to the town is free. Admission to the park is $2 for adults; $1 for kids. Pony rides are an additional $3. The bunkhouse room rents for $50 a night. Camping is $10 a tent, per night.

Ages: All

SUNRISE PARK / SWIM CENTER

(760) 323-8278   !/$

On Sunrise Way and Ramon Road, Palm Springs

(EXIT INTERSTATE 10 S. ON INDIAN CANYON DR., L. ON RAMON RD., L. ON SUNRISE WAY.)

This park has activities that will keep your family busy and refreshed from sunrise to sunset. Besides the wonderful grassy areas and big playground with bridges, slides, and swings, the most important feature here is the Olympic-sized swimming pool. It has a shallow end for younger kids to cool off, too. The deck has lawn chairs to relax in, plus a picnic area.

After spending a day at the park, take your kids out to the ball game next door. The baseball stadium has night lights.

Hours: The park is open daily from sunrise to sunset. The pool is open year-round, daily from 11am - 5pm. Night swimming is available in the summer.

Admission: The park is free. Swimming is $3 for adults; $2 for ages 4 - 12; children 3 years and under are free with a paid adult. Such a deal - pay $20 for a card worth twenty-five swims!

Ages: All

TOMMY JACOB'S BEL AIR MINIATURE GOLF GREENS

(760) 322-6062 $$

1001 South El Cielo Road, Palm Springs

(EXIT INTERSTATE 10 S. ON GENE AUTRY TR., R. ON RAMON, L. ON EL CIELO RD.)

This deluxe miniature golf course might not have the bells and whistles, or castles and windmills, that others have, but it is a beautiful course. Located next to the real golf course, it has shade trees and stone walls surrounding the "greens." The course itself is just difficult enough to make it fun, and it's lighted at night.

Hours: Open daily from 7am - 7pm.
Admission: $5 per round for adults; $3 for ages 17 and under.
Ages: 4 years and up.

UPRISING ROCK CLIMBING CENTER   ☼
(760) 320-6630 $$$
1500 S. Gene Autry Trail, Palm Springs
(EXIT INTERSTATE 10 S. ON GENE AUTRY TRAIL. S. OF RAMON RD., N. OF PALM CANYON [HWY 111]. IT'S IN THE SAME COMPLEX AS OASIS WATERPARK.)

Do your kids have you climbing the walls? Then you'll feel right at home at Uprising Rock Climbing Center. The three, outdoor climbing structures have micro mists systems and are covered with an awning to block out direct sunlight. Kids can test their rock climbing skills here and train to reach new heights. The tallest wall is forty feet high while another, connected structure, has a thirty foot repelling tower. There are forty top ropes in all. All climbers are belayed and wear harnesses, although lead climbing for advanced climbers is available. The twenty-foot "teaching" wall might not look that high, but it seemed tall to me when I was at the top! It's a great spot for beginners to get a grip on this sport. A small bouldering area (i.e. no ropes needed) is also here.

Rental gear is available, or you can bring your own. Climb once or twice during your visit, or make it an all-day workout. To stay for the day, you must pass a climbing test. If you don't pass, you may sign up for a class. Ask about climbing excursions to Joshua Tree, Idyllwild, and out-of-state sites.

Hours: Usually open Mon. - Fri., 9am - 8pm; Sat. - Sun., 9am - 6pm.
Admission: Climbs starting at $6, which includes the use of a harness, shoes, helmet, and chalk bag. It costs $5 to take the test to stay for the day; $15 for an all-day pass; $8 to rent the above mentioned equipment for the day. Staff members are willing to work out rates according to what you want to do. Ask about a combination pass to Oasis Waterpark.
Ages: 6 years and up.

WHITEWATER TROUT CO. / RAINBOW RANCHO   ☀
TROUT FISHING
(760) 325-5570 $
Whitewater Canyon Road, Whitewater
(EXIT INTERSTATE 10 N. ON WHITEWATER CANYON RD. IT'S LOCATED 5 MILES BACK.)

Grilled, baked, and fried are just a few savory suggestions as to how you can fix the trout lunch or dinner that you'll catch. Bring your fishing poles, or rent them here, to use in the two ponds surrounded by shade trees. Tip: Bring your own cooler for your fish. No outside food is allowed in.

Hours: Open Wed. - Sun. from 10am - 5pm.

Admission: 50¢ a person entrance; $2.50 per person fishing fee to rent a pole, bait, and tackle. (No state license is required.) Fish cost $2.72 per pound and 25¢ (per fish) for cleaning.

Ages: 3 years and up.

CALENDAR
(A Listing of Annual Events)

Many places listed in the main section of this book offer special events throughout the year. Below is a Calendar listing of other annual stand outs. If you are looking for more local events, like fairs, etc., call the Recreation Department of your City Hall; call your Chamber of Commerce; or check the front pages of your local phone book. The prices given here are from 1996/1997 and are quoted to give you a general idea of the cost. Please call an event a month in advance as dates sometimes vary.

JANUARY:

CHINESE NEW YEAR CELEBRATION, Los Angeles. (213) 617-0396, Chinatown. Starting off with the elaborate Golden Dragon Parade with floats, bands, dragon dancers (wonderful costumes), the Little King and Queen contest, and the Children's Lantern Procession, this month-long celebration might spill into February, depending on the Lunar Year. Other activities include arts, crafts, and music. Admission is free, although there are various prices for other events. "Gung Hay Fat Choy." (Happy New Year.)

TOURNAMENT OF ROSES PARADE, Pasadena. (818) 449-7673, Pasadena City Hall. This two-hour, world-famous parade of elegantly, fancifully, decorated floral floats, plus bands and equestrian units, is held on New Year's Day. Camp out on the streets to guarantee a viewing spot, or call Sharp Seating Company (818) 795-4171 if you are interested in grandstand seating. Prices for seats range from $27 - $45. Please make reservations at least two months in advance.

TOURNAMENT OF ROSES FLOATS VIEWING, Pasadena. (Along Sierra Madre Blvd., between Paloma St. and Sierra Madre Villa Ave.) The floats can be viewed up close for a few days after the parade. Let your kids "oooh" and "aaah" at the intricate workmanship, and bring your camera!

WHALE WATCHING. See TRANSPORTATION in the main section of the book for ideas on who to call for whale-watching cruises. The season goes from the end of December through March. The cruises are usually two-and-a-half-hours of looking for (and finding!) gray whales as they migrate to Baja. Be on the lookout also, for dolphins, pilot whales, and sea lions. Dress warmly!

FEBRUARY:

CAMELLIA FESTIVAL, Temple City. (818) 287-9150, Temple City Park, corner of Las Tunas Dr. and Golden West Ave. The festival is held the last weekend in February, with carnival rides and an art show on Sunday. The highlight, the Festival Parade, is held on Saturday. Camellia-covered floats (and they must be finished with parts of just camellias - no other materials), are designed and made by youth groups, with prizes, including a Sweepstakes Trophy, given out. Over twenty marching bands and drill teams, plus other organizations that promote the welfare of children, like Brownies and Cub Scouts, participate.

FESTIVAL OF THE WHALES, Dana Point. (714) 496-2274, 24200 Dana Point Harbor Drive, Orange County Marine Institute. This twenty-three day festival celebrates the California Gray Whales, as they migrate south. The whole family can enjoy a variety of events offered throughout Dana Point, such as parades, art shows, flying kites, sand castle workshops, tidepool explorations, street fairs, kids coloring contests, film festivals, and whale-watching excursions. Prices vary according to the event. Have a whale of a time!

FRONTIER 101 PRODUCTIONS INVITATIONAL RODEO - Burbank. (213) 733-1230, Los Angeles Equestrian Center. This unusual rodeo runs for two days. It starts off with a fifteen-minute history lesson about various Afro-Americans people and their contributions to America. The rodeo is geared for children, and even has kids participate as riders and ropers. The two-hour rodeo also has adult bull riding and ropers, featuring "cowboys of color." Shows are from 11pm - 1pm and cost $5 per person.

INDIAN VILLAGE, Orange. (800) 393-3276, 1 Irvine Blvd., in Irvine Regional Park. For two weeks, preschool-aged children and older have fun learning about and exploring Indian Village, which is presented by Green Meadows. The two-hour tour includes real tepees to go in; a thirty-minute Indian variety show with costumed dancers, singers, and a cowboy who does amazing rope tricks; various Indian artifacts to look at and touch, such as weapons and furs; animals to see, such as bison and goat; sand painting; face painting; demonstrations; an opportunity to talk with Indians and learn about their customs and their religion; and more! Open Mon. - Fri., 9:30am - 12:30pm (last tour); Sat., 10am - 2pm (last tour). General admission is $8 for ages 2 and up. Admission for groups of twenty is $6.50 per person. Reservations are required for groups.

NATIONAL DATE FESTIVAL and CAMEL RACES, Indio. (619) 347-0676, 46350 Arabia St. at the Desert Expo Center. This ten-day event usually begins the Friday proceeding President's Day. There are thousands of exhibits and activities! Some with particular kid-appeal include the gem and mineral show; carnival-type rides; a model railroad; a livestock show; a petting zoo; elephant rides; camel rides; pony rides; virtual reality rides; a spectacular laser show; a Mexican village; and a Renaissance Village. Another highlight is the camel and ostrich races. These races take place twice a day, and you just never know what is going to happen with two such stubborn species of animals. (There is a $1 additional charge to see the races.) On President's Day Monday there is an Arabian Nights pageant and parade - don't miss this! Open daily from 10am - 10pm. The cost is $6 for adults; $3 for children 11 years and under; rides and some attractions are additional fees. Parking on the fairgrounds is $3.

WINTER WONDERLAND, Glendale. (818) 548-2000, 1601 W. Mountain St., Brand Park. Kids can play in loads of man-made snow brought in for one day only. Admission is free.

MARCH:

BLESSING OF THE ANIMALS, Los Angeles. (213) 628-1274, El Pueblo de Los Angeles State Historic Park. This event is held on the Saturday before Easter. Children can dress up their pets (all domestic animals welcome) and bring them to the Plaza Church to be blessed by priests. This is done to honor the animal's contributions to the world. It gets wild with all different kinds of animals "held" in children's arms!

EASTER BUNNY CARNIVAL AND EGG HUNT, Mission Viejo. (714) 589-4272, Trabuco Mesa Park, Antonio Parkway and Las Flores. Usually held the Saturday before Easter, this event (with over 2,000 participants last year and 17,000 plastic eggs!) is really *egg*citing. Start your morning off at 7am with a pancake breakfast - $3 for adults; $2.50 for kids 7 to 12. Then join in the Easter egg hunt for children 2 to 10 years. (Each age group is given a different starting time.) Don't forget your Easter basket. Visit Mr. and Mrs. Bunny, the petting zoo, and the bounce house, plus make and decorate a child-size kite - all for free! There are also arts and crafts booths. At the Baby Goods Swapmeet you can buy good quality, used baby and children's old clothes and toys. Hours for the *egg*stra special carnival and hunt are 9am - noon.

EASTER EGG HUNTS. Many parks and schools put on free Easter egg hunts and/or Easter craft activities the weekend or Saturday before Easter. Call the Recreation Department at your local City Hall for more information.

FIESTA DE LAS GOLONDRINAS (Festival of the Swallows), San Juan Capistrano. (714) 493-1976. This week-long festival celebrating the return of the swallows from their annual migration to Argentina, takes place in different areas throughout San Juan Capistrano, including the

Mission. The swallows actually return every year on March 19th, so all of the festivities happen around this date. Some of the festivities include parades (like a children's pet parade); pageants; petting zoo; carousel; pony rides; carnival rides and games; a kid's hat contest; arts and crafts; music; and more! Free admission and parking, though certain activities and attractions cost. Call the Mission (714) 248-2048 to find out what special activities they have planned.

FLOWER FIELDS, Carlsbad. (619) 431-0352, 5802 Paseo del Norte, off Palomar Airport Rd. Walk through fifty acres of rows of blooming ranunculus March through April. The colors are amazing, and the trails lead to bluffs overlooking the shoreline. Call first to make sure the flowers are in full bloom. Open daily 9am - dusk. Admission is $1 for ages 4 and up.

GREEN MEADOWS FARM, Orange. (800) 393-3276, 1 Irvine Rd., in Irvine Regional Park. From mid-March through mid-April take a two-hour, guided, walk-around (tour sounds too formal) of this unique, completely hands-on, petting farm. There are over 500 animals to see, touch, snuggle, and sometimes feed, such as rabbits, cows, pigs, sheep, goats, turkeys, and a buffalo. Spring is in the air, so kids are almost assured of seeing many new animal babies. Your admission price also includes milking a cow, a pony ride, and a tractor driven hayride! All of this is a wonderful, informative, and memorable experience for kids and adults. There is a nice gift shop here, too. Open Mon. - Fri., 9:30am - noon (last tour); Sat., 10am - 2pm (last tour). General admission is $8 for ages 2 and up. Admission for groups of twenty or more is $6.50 per person. Reservations for groups are required.

GRUNION RUNS, up and down the coast. Call beaches, such as Cabrillo Marine Aquarium, the Orange County Marine Institute, or Stephen Birch Aquarium Museum for more details, dates, and times. Grunions are small, silvery fish that venture out of the waters from March to August to lay their eggs on sandy beaches. They are very particular about when they do this - after every full and new moon, and usually around midnight. No nets or gloves are allowed; only bare hands. (Did I mention that the fish are slippery?) Eat what you catch, and enjoy a unique night of grunion hunting.

OCEAN BEACH KITE FESTIVAL, Ocean Beach. (619) 531-1527, between Santa Monica and Newport Streets at Ocean Beach Elementary School and across the street at Ocean Beach Recreation Center. The first Saturday of the month offers a colorful, high-flying festival celebrating the joy of kites by building, decorating, and flying them. There are contests for all ages, and a parade. There is no charge for admission or for materials for kite-making.

POPPY RESERVE and FESTIVAL, Lancaster. (805) 942-0662 - state park; (805) 724-1180 - recorded info from the poppy reserve - 15101 W. Lancaster Rd., located 13 miles west of the Antelope Valley Fwy (14), off West Avenue I. As the wicked witch said in *The Wizard of Oz,* "poppies, poppies." They bloom in a profusion of colors on this massive reserve during the months of March and April. (Call first to see how rains have affected the bloom schedule.) Parking during poppy season is $5 a vehicle. Hike along the trails through the extensive 1800-acre reserve, and don't forget your camera!! The poppy festival is usually held for a weekend in April at Lancaster City Park, which is fifteen miles away from the reserve. The festival is complete with carnival rides, a twenty-minute helicopter ride over the reserve ($30 for adults, $25 for children), craft workshops, environmental displays, etc. Call (805) 723-6077 for information on the festival. Admission is $4 for adults; $2 for ages 6 - 12; children 5 years and under are free; parking is $2. The hours are 9am - 5pm.

POWWOW, Indio. (619) 342-2593, 84245 Indio Springs Drive at Fantasy Springs Casino. This Powwow brings together Native Americans and non-Indians in a celebration of music, dance, food and arts, and crafts. The powwow is usually held Fri. - Sun. from 11am - 11pm. Admission is $2 for adults; $1 for ages 6 - 12; children 5 years and under are free.

ST. PATRICK'S DAY PARADE, San Diego. (619) 239-0512, Balboa Park. Be sure to wear green so you won't get pinched! Celebrate the luck 'o the Irish by coming to this parade. (Make sure your kids eat some corned beef and cabbage sometime today!) Admission is free.

APRIL:

CIRCUS VARGAS, San Diego. (619) 239-0512, Balboa Park, the lower level off Park Blvd. For one week Circus Vargas, one of the largest circuses under the big top, presents everything a child dreams about in a circus. The animal acts; the atmosphere; the daring acrobatics; and the talented clowns are all part of this extravaganza. Tickets usually range from $6 for children to $8 for adults.

EARTH DAY, San Diego. (619) 239-0512, Balboa Park. Celebrate the environment along with several hundred organizations that host booths and exhibits on organic materials; alternatives to lighting, power, and energy; etc. Hopefully, kids (and parents) who attend Earth Day will become more planet smart. Activities begin at 10am and end at 6pm. Admission is free.

GLORY OF EASTER, Garden Grove. (714) 54-GLORY (4-5679), Crystal Cathedral, 12141 Lewis St. (Chapman Ave. and Lewis St.) This hour-long, spectacular production with live animals and actors celebrates the resurrection of Jesus Christ in a powerful way. The last days of his life; the events leading up to his death, including the crucifixion; and his glorious resurrection are presented in a dramatic and realistic re-enactment. The shows run for about ten nights with the curtain rising at 6:30pm and at 8pm. Tickets are $20 - $30 for adults; $2 less for children and seniors. Ask about family days discounts, when tickets are $15 per person.

GRAND PRIX RACE, Long Beach. (562) 981-2600, streets of downtown Long Beach. This three-day event includes pre-qualifying runs on Friday, celebrity racing, and final qualifying runs on Saturday, and final Indy races on Sunday. Reserved grandstand seats are $48 for adults on Sunday; $33 for kids. General admission is $22 for Fri. and Saturday for adults, and $22 - $35 on Sunday for adults; kids 11 years and under are free. See you at the races!

IMAGINATION CELEBRATION, Orange County. (714) 833-8500. The Orange County Performing Arts Center hosts this fifteen-day event held during the latter part of April, spilling into May. Fifty of Orange County's artistic and educational organizations bring performances, workshops, and exhibitions to over seventy locations. This festival of arts for families takes place at malls, museums, parks, schools, etc. Some of the activities include puppet making, family art day, folk tales, band and theater performances, and dancing. Almost every event is free in this county wide celebration of imagination! Call for a schedule of events.

KALEIDOSCOPE, Long Beach. (562) 985-2288, Bellflower and Atherton at California State Long Beach campus. This open house for the different departments of California State Long Beach is a wonderful one-day community event. There is face painting, carnival rides, cultural dances, an African marketplace, a Powwow, a solar car (from the Engineering Dept.), a Renaissance faire, and more. The hours are from 11am - 5pm and it is free!

KID'S STUFF EXPO, Anaheim. (714) 999-8900, at the Anaheim Convention Center. This two-day event is usually held in April (sometimes in March). Over 100 exhibitors feature the latest and greatest in products and services for kids. The activities vary from year to year, but usually include a moon bounce, a petting zoo, a bungee trampoline, a skating area, bowling, pog tournaments, laser tag, a free CHOC teddy bear clinic, educational toys, books, games, rides, and hands-on science experiments. There are a lot of fun things for kids to do here (and to buy), but it does get very crowded, so plan accordingly. Open Sat. - Sun. from 10am - 5pm. Admission is $8 for adults; $6 for ages 3 - 16. Parking is $5, and some of the activities cost extra.

OLD TOWN DAYS CELEBRATION, Newhall. (805) 254-1275, 24101 San Fernando Rd., enter through the William S. Hart Park. (I -15, N. on the 14, W. on San Fernando Rd.) This day-long, old-fashioned festival celebrates historic times in a variety of ways such as demonstrations of steam engines (you can blow the whistle of a locomotive); a tour through historic buildings that are normally closed to the public; pony rides; gold panning; a petting zoo; and demonstrations of sheep shearing, wood carving, spinning, and quilting. There are also crafts, music, and sometimes hayrides. The night before is a post Civil War encampment, where kids can talk to soldiers and see demonstrations. The cost for visiting the encampment is $10 for adults; $5 for kids, and includes entrance to the next day events. Old Town Days is celebrated from 10am - 4pm. Admission to the celebration is $1.99 for adults; 99¢ for ages 4 - 12; children 3 years and under are free.

POPPY RESERVE and FESTIVAL, Lancaster. (See **MARCH**, POPPY RESERVE and FESTIVAL for description.)

RAMONA PAGEANT, Hemet. (800) 645-4465, 27400 Ramona Bowl Road. Using an entire mountainside as a stage, a cast of over 350 people, and quite a few horses, tells the romantic story of Spanish Ramona and her Indian hero, Alessandro. This is also a tale reflecting our early California heritage. Going into its 74th year, this epic is performed for three weekends. Tickets range from $8 - $19. Bring a blanket and picnic dinner.

RENAISSANCE PLEASURE FAIRE, San Bernardino. (800) 523-2473, 2555 Glen Helen Parkway, Glen Helen Regional Park at the intersection of Interstate 15 and Interstate 215. Heare ye, heare ye, this annual faire runs for nine weekends from April to June, bringing the renaissance time to life. Eat, drink, and be merry as you cheer on knights; play challenging games from times of yor; be entertained by juggling, dancing, and singing; and enjoy the delicious food and faire! Open Sat. - Sun. from 10am - 6pm. Admission is $17.50 for adults; $15 for seniors and students; $7.50 for ages 5 - 11; children 4 years and under are free. Parking is $6.

SPEEDWAY, Orange County. (714) 708-3247, 88 Fairview Drive at the Orange County Fairgrounds. The Speedway roars to life every Saturday night (some years it's Friday night) from April through September. This spectator sport of motorcycle racing can include sidecars; go karts; Quads; a kid's class (ages 6 to 12); and more. After the two-hour show (which can get long for younger ones), take the kids into the pits to get racer's autographs, or, when the bikes cool down, to sit on a cycle or two. Wear jeans and t-shirt (and sweatshirt) as dirt tracks aren't noted for cleanliness. Gates open at 6:30pm; races start at 7:30pm. Admission is $9 for adults; $5 for ages 13 - 17; $2 for ages 6 - 12; children 5 years and under are free. Parking is free.

SPRING DINGER, Santa Fe Springs. (310) 946-6476, 12100 Mora Drive. This day of old-fashioned fun is held around Easter. Kids can ride on a fire engine; pet animals in the petting zoo; pump water from a well; dress-up in old-fashioned clothing; hunt for Easter eggs; listen to story-tellers; try square dancing; churn butter; crank ice-cream; and play turn-of-the-century games - all for free!! The hours are noon - 4pm.

SUNKIST ORANGE BLOSSOM FESTIVAL, Riverside. (800) 382-8202, historic downtown Riverside. Orange you glad you came to this weekend festival? Celebrate life as it was in Riverside over 100 years ago with a parade featuring floats, marching bands, and equestrian units; tasty orange treats; cooking demonstrations; live entertainment; magic shows; circus acts; carnival rides; a living history town recreated; a children's grove with crafts, petting zoo, and elephant rides; steam train engine rides; a fireworks display on Saturday night; and arts and crafts booths. Admission is free. The hours are Sat., 10am - 8:30pm; Sun., 10am - 6pm.

TEMECULA BALLOON AND WINE FESTIVAL, Temecula. (909) 676-4713, Temecula Valley. Rise and shine for this colorful weekend festival. The balloons are filled with hot air starting at 6am, an event that is fascinating to watch. Lift-off is around 7am with numerous balloons filling the sky with a kaleidoscope of color. Other, less lofty, activities include live entertainment, arts and craft, and a kid's faire with kiddie rides, pony rides, a petting zoo, etc. General admission is $15 for adults; $5 for ages 7 - 12; children 6 years and under are free.

WEEK OF THE YOUNG CHILD. Various parks in the Southland and San Diego participate in celebrating kids by hosting different events. Some of the activities include arts and crafts, hands-on science fun, blowing bubbles, family entertainment, and sometimes a petting zoo. Preschools, Y.M.C.A.s, Scout troops, etc., are on hand to provide a resource for parents to get information about education and services for kids. Check your local newspaper for a listing of events or call your local city hall. In San Diego, call (619) 239-0512 for information on this event held at Balboa Park.

MAY:

BULL FIGHT, Artesia. (562) 865-4693, 11903 E. Ashworth Ave. in the Artesia DES. Once a year a bloodless bull fight is put on here complete with professional matadors and their capes. The action happens here when celebrating a religious festival. Call to see which of the four festivals this year (it rotates) features the bull fight.

CHILDREN'S DAY, Los Angeles. (213) 628-2725, Little Tokyo. This two-day traditional Japanese celebration is for families, particularly children ages 4 - 12. They are invited to participate in a running race, as well as arts and crafts. Other attractions include magic shows, dancing, fine arts exhibits, etc. Admission is free.

CINCO DE MAYO CELEBRATION - Mexican Independence Day is celebrated throughout Southern California. For instance, in Los Angeles, (213) 628-1274, at El Pueblo de Los Angeles State Historic Park in downtown Los Angeles. The festival celebrates this Mexican holiday with several days of Mexican folk dancing, mariachi music, parades, puppet shows, booths, piñatas, and fun! Also call Bazaar del Mundo in Old Town San Diego, (619) 296-3161; Old Town State Historic Park in San Diego, (619) 220-5422; Borrego Springs, (619) 767-5555; or Oceanside, (760) 471-6549.

GREEN MEADOWS FARM, Los Angeles. (800) 393-3276, 4235 Monterey Rd., Ernest Debs Regional Park. The Farm is open May - June. (See **MARCH**, GREEN MEADOWS FARM for a description.)

INDIAN CULTURAL DAYS, San Diego. (619) 239-0512, Balboa Park. This weekend cultural event includes incredible Native American dancing, singing, tapestry displays, bead work, and crafts for kids to watch and/or make. Admission is free.

INSECT FAIR, Arcadia. (818) 821-3222, Los Angeles State and County Arboretum. (See the entry for the Arboretum in the main section of the book for directions and a description of the beautiful grounds.) Kids go buggy at this event where every kind of creepy crawly insect is here to look at and/or to purchase. Collectors bring both live and mounted insects. The fair includes educational programs for kids (and adults) as well as hands-on activities. Admission to the fair is included in regular admission to the Arboretum - $5 for adults; $3 for seniors; $1 for ages 5 - 12; children 4 years and under are free.

INTERNATIONAL MUSEUM DAY. Here is a little known fact - May 18 is International Museum Day. Many museums offer free admission, while others sponsor a family day of art and craft activities, storytelling, entertainment, celebrity appearances, or other special programs. Call your local (or favorite) museum and see what they have to offer.

JET PROPULSION LABORATORY, Pasadena. (818) 354-9314, 4800 Oak Grove Dr. This annual open house is out of this world. The space research center offers a glimpse into outer space with over 30 exhibits ranging from planetary imaging to spacecraft tracking; presentations; commercial technology booths that display state-of-the-art instruments and products; robotic demonstrations; thinking games for kids; and more. Open Sat. - Sun., 9am - 5pm. Admission is free.

MIRAMAR NAVAL AIR STATION FESTIVAL, Miramar. (619) 537-6289, Miramar Naval Air Station. This one-day event has a little of something for everyone including a car show, craft fair, kiddie rides, Native American Pow Wow, and military static displays such as planes, jets, helicopters, tanks, etc. The Festival usually runs from 10am - 6pm and admission is free.

PAN AMERICAN FESTIVAL, Lakewood. (562) 866-9771, Mayfair Park at the corner of South St. and Clark St. This two-day festival, usually held on Mother's Day weekend, features carnival rides for younger kids and older ones, carnival games, arts and crafts booths, and exhibitions, plus there is a great children's playground across the lawn. Free admission.

RAMONA RODEO, Ramona. (619) 789-1311, 5th St. and Aqua Ln. Kick up your heels 'cause the rodeo's in town! Activities start Friday night, while the weekend brings rodeo shows, a parade, and carnival-like atmosphere. Rodeo admission is usually $8 for adults; $5 for kids 12 years and under. Reserved seating is $2 more, but worth it since the shows can sell out.

RANCHO SANTA MARGARITA FIESTA RODEO, Rancho Santa Margarita. (714) 589-4272, corner of Santa Margarita Parkway and Los Flores St., next to Target. Yipee-aye-ay! This five-day fiesta begins on Thursday night with family activities. Friday starts with a cattle drive from Casper Wilderness Park ending at the rodeo grounds. Friday night is team-roping competition. Professional rodeos are held on the weekend. The two-hour shows (which seat 5,000) include bull riding, calf roping, womens' barrel racing, kids' rodeos, bronco riding, bareback riding, and rodeo clowns. There are also carnival rides for kids, game booths, pony rides, and lots of arts and crafts booths. The nights bring country western dancing and more fun. The rodeo grounds are open Fri., 3pm - 11pm; Sat., 10am - midnight; Sun., 10am - 6pm. Admission to the grounds is $2 for adults; $1 for kids. Tickets for the rodeo are $12 for adults in advance ($2 more at the gate); $10 for kids 3 - 12 years ($2 more at the gate). Parking is $3.

RENAISSANCE PLEASURE FAIRE, San Bernardino. (See **APRIL**, RENAISSANCE PLEASURE FAIRE.)

SAN BERNARDINO COUNTY FAIR, Victorville. (619) 951-2200, 7th St. (In years past, the fair has been held in July and August, so call to find out this years time frame.) For nine days, the desert really heats up with excitement when the county fair comes to town. 86 acres of rides, attractions, farm animals, Destruction Derby, a rodeo, entertainment, and more fun. Open Mon. - Fri., 4pm - midnight; Sat. - Sun., noon - midnight. General admission is $5 for adults; $3 for seniors; $2 for ages 6 - 12; children 5 years and under are free.

SAN DIEGO WILD ANIMAL PARK, San Diego. (619) 234-6541. Get a little wild in the beginning of May as the Wild Animal Park celebrates founder's day and admission is free! Call for the exact date.

SCOTTISH FESTIVAL AND HIGHLAND GATHERING, Costa Mesa. (714) 998-7857, 88 Fair Drive, Orange County Fairgrounds. This Memorial weekend festival features everything Scottish - tossing the caber, hammer throws, shot put, sheepdog herding, good food, and a lot of tartan. Bagpipes and highland and country dancing also entertain you and the kids throughout the day. The cost is $13 for adults; $3 for ages 5 - 12; children 4 years and under are free.

STRAWBERRY FESTIVAL, Garden Grove. (714) 638-7950. This four-day event features amusement rides, parades, arts and crafts booths, a pie eating contest, and lots and lots of strawberries! Free admission.

STRAWBERRY FESTIVAL, Oxnard. (805) 385-7578 at College Park at Rose Ave. and Channel Island Blvd. This big, juicy festival offers unique strawberry culinary delights, and a strawberry shortcake contest. Kids enjoy Strawberryland, in particular, because it has a petting zoo, puppet shows, arts and crafts, and carnival rides. Have a berry good time here! Admission is $7 for adults; $4 for seniors and ages 2 - 12.

YOUTH EXPO, Orange County. (714) 708-3247, 88 Fairview Drive, Orange County Fairgrounds. This giant, three-day expo highlights the talents of kids from elementary through high school age. Their artistic endeavors are showcased in different buildings according to age groups and categories such as fine arts, photography, woodworking, and ceramics. 4-H Club members also have a wonderful exhibit. The Science Fair is a highlight which draws people from all over the United States who offer money and/or scholarships to students whose experimentally based research designs are outstanding. The Expo is great for admiring other kids' works, and for sparking the creative genius in your child. Hours are Frid., 9am - 3pm (this can get crowded with school tours); Sat. - Sun., 9am - 5pm. Free admission.

JUNE:

CHERRY FESTIVAL and CHERRY PICKING, Cherry Valley. (909) 845-9541 - Beaumont Chamber of Commerce or (909) 845-3628 - Cherry Growers Association. I tell you no lie - the month of June is ripe for cherry picking. The three-week season starts with a festival that includes a parade, carnival-type rides, and a lot of family fun and entertainment. One of the places to pick cherries is Wohlgemuth Orchard (909) 845-1548, 1106 E. 11th St. in Beaumont. Older kids can put cans around their necks, and pick cherries with both hands, working from the ground (i.e. not using ladders). Per pound prices vary according to market value. Dowling Orchard, (909) 845-1217, is not a

U-Pic, but it does offer just-picked cherries and a year-round produce market.

COLORADO LAGOON MODEL BOAT SHOP, Long Beach. (562) 570-1719, at Colorado Lagoon. The shop is open mid-June through the summer. Kids 7 years and up can learn how to build model boats and sail them in the lagoon. Store hours are Mon. - Fri. from 10am - 4pm. Materials are available to purchase starting at $15.

DEL MAR FAIR, Del Mar. (619) 793-5555 - recording; (619) 755-1161 - fairgrounds, Del Mar Fairgrounds. The 3-week long major event features everything wonderful in a county fair - carnival rides, flower and garden shows, gem and minerals exhibits, farm animals, livestock judging, food, craft booths, and a festive atmosphere. Call for a schedule of events. General admission is $8 for adults; $3 for ages 6 - 12 years; children 5 years and under are free.

FORD FAMILY FUN SUMMER NIGHTS, Hollywood. (213) 256-7828, 2580 Cahuenga Blvd. E., at the John Anson Ford Amphitheater, located just N. of the Hollywood Bowl. This outdoor amphitheater presents wonderful, one-hour family performances almost every Saturday in July and August, along with a few Sunday afternoon shows. Bring a picnic lunch and enjoy an intimate setting with shows that feature top-name entertainment in magic, puppetry, storytelling, music, dance, or plays designed for children to enjoy. Saturday shows starts at 10am; Sundays shows at 4:30pm. Seats cost $7 per person, though discounts are offered of five admissions for $25. Parking on site costs $5. Shuttle services from the Hanna Barbera parking lot costs $1.

IRISH FAIR AND MUSIC FESTIVAL, Arcadia. (818) 574-7223, 285 W. Huntington Drive, at the Santa Anita Race Track infield. Top o' the mornin' to ye. This weekend Irish fair has featured top-name entertainment, like Clancy, and Hal Roach; parades; traditional contests such as fiddle playing and dancing; sheep-herding demonstrations; a dog show featuring Irish breeds; bagpipe music; vendors of Irish wares; and Leprechaun Kingdom for kids. The kingdom features storytelling, jugglers, pony rides, carnival rides, etc. Another favorite at the festival is a recreation of a medieval Irish village, Tara, where sword-yielding performers recount the Island's legends and history. The festival runs from 10am - 6pm. Admission is $12.50 for adults; $9.50 for students and seniors; children 12 years and under are free.

OUTDOOR FAMILY FILM FESTIVALS. Call your local park or Chamber of Commerce and ask for information about the many parks that offer free, nighttime, out-door family entertainment such as concerts, G, or PG movies. Bring a blanket, picnic dinner, and enjoy a show together!

PEARSON PARK AMPHITHEATER, Anaheim. (714) 254-5274, Lemon and Sycamore Streets. The terrific programs put on here throughout the summer are geared for kids in the K - 6th grades. They vary in length from one to three hours. Past programs have included Make-a-Circus and magic shows, plus audience participation shows with songs or a storyteller. The shows are on Friday night and usually start at 7:30pm. Tickets usually cost $3 for adults; children 10 years and under are free. Call for specific show information.

SAN DIEGO SCOTTISH HIGHLAND GAMES, San Diego. (619) 645-8080, Rancho Santa Fe Park. A weekend of Scottish merrymaking includes highland dancing, Celtic harping, a bagpipe competition (this is special), sheep dog herding trials, athletic competitions, and lots of good food. Call about the entrance fee.

SAWDUST FESTIVAL, Laguna Beach. (714) 494-3030, 935 Laguna Canyon Rd. This three-acre, outdoor arts and crafts festival, with over 200 artisans, goes from the end of June through August (almost simultaneous with the Festival of Arts). There are on-going demonstrations of ceramics such as throwing pots (so to speak), etching, glass blowing, etc. The Children's Art booth is for kids to create art projects - for free! Family-oriented daytime entertainment includes storytelling and juggling. Nighttime entertainment includes dancing and listening to bands. Tram service is available for a nominal fee. Hours are daily from 10am - 10pm. Admission is $5 for adults; kids 12 years and under are free.

THRESHING BEE AND ANTIQUE ENGINE SHOW, Vista. (619) 941-1791, Antique Gas & Steam Engine Museum. (See ANTIQUE GAS & STEAM ENGINE MUSEUM for directions and a description of the museum.) This show is held on two consecutive weekends in June, and again in October. There are demonstrations of American crafts, farming, log sawing, blacksmithing, and many of the restored tractors are put in a parade, making it an unusual-looking parade! Join in some of the activities and try some good, home-cooked food. Admission is usually $5 for adults; $3 for children 12 years and under.

JULY:

CORN FESTIVAL, Norwalk. (562) 863-4567, Paddison Farm at 11951 Imperial Hwy. Corny though it might be, this one-day festival, usually held the last weekend in July, includes hayrides ($1), pony rides ($2), a petting farm, mountain clogging, country-western dance demonstrations, antique farm equipment displays, carnival booths, and old-fashioned contests like corn-shucking, hog-calling, frog-jumping, and turtle racing. Adults are $6; children 12 years and under are $4.

CYPRESS COMMUNITY FESTIVAL, Cypress. (714) 827-2430, Brethren Christian High School. This one-day event gets bigger and better every year. There are kiddie rides, a moon bounce, carnival-like games, crafts to make, and family entertainment throughout the day. In addition, there are lots of food booths, craft booths, and a business expo. Put on the sunscreen and enjoy the day. Free admission. Various activities have a minimal cost.

FESTIVAL OF ARTS AND PAGEANT OF THE MASTERS, Laguna Beach. (714) 494-1145, 650 Laguna Canyon Rd. at Irvine Bowl Park. This annual event, from July through August, draws thousands of visitors. More than 150 artisans and craftsmen display their work - jewelry, wood crafts, paintings, etc. - here and at the nearby Sawdust Festival. Kids will be particularly drawn to the ongoing demonstrations such as glass blowing, print making, water color, Japanese pottery making, etc. For aspiring artists, the Art Workshop (open daily from 11am - 5pm) supplies free materials for paintings, paper hat making, etc. The Jr. Art Gallery is juried art work of over 150 school children from Orange County. Kids love looking at other kids' work. Bands play continuously, adding to the festive atmosphere. Call for a schedule of special events. Pageant of the Masters is live recreations of well-known art works, both classical and contemporary. Each ninety-second "picture" is accompanied by a narration and full orchestral music. This one-and-a-half-hour production (with over 250 participants) is staged nightly at 8:30pm. The cost ranges between $15 - $40 per person. The festival is open daily from 10am - 11:30pm. Entrance cost for the festival is $3 for adults; kids 12 years and under are free. Metered parking is available on the streets.

FIREWORKS and 4TH OF JULY SHOWS - Call your local parks or City Hall for information.

FORD FAMILY FUN SUMMER NIGHTS, Hollywood. (See **JUNE**, FORD FAMILY FUN for description.)

OLD FORT MACARTHUR DAYS, San Pedro. (310) 548-7705, 3601 S. Gaffey St., in Angels Gate Park. For two days, military encampments and re-enactments, from the time periods of 1876 through present day, are usually performed on the weekend following the 4th of July. There are military drills throughout the day and at least three shows (reenactments) that can include the Indian wars, the Calvary, both World Wars, and the Korean War. The productions are complete with shooting cannons, muskets, and other wartime artillery, plus uniformed riders and fighters. Open 9am - 4pm with shows usually at 11am, 1pm, and 3pm. Admission is $5 for adults; $3 for kids. (Your paid admission stub from Saturday allows you free entrance on Sunday.)

OPEN HOUSE AT THE HOLLYWOOD BOWL, Hollywood. (213) 850-2000. 2301 N. Highland. For six musically hot weeks, multi-cultural performances, incorporating dance and music, are given at the Bowl. A craft workshop for kids, ages 3 - 12, pertaining to the theme, follows each performance. Shows are Mon. - Fri. at 10am and 11:15am and the workshops are at 11am and 12:15pm. Adjacent to the Open House is the Hollywood Bowl, where the L.A. Philharmonic and other orchestras hold rehearsals from 9:30am - noon Tues., Thurs., and Fri. Open House participants are welcome to come and observe. Tickets for Open House are $3 per person, plus $1 workshop materials fee for each participating child. Parking is free.

ORANGE COUNTY FAIR, Costa Mesa. (714) 751-3247, Orange County Marketplace. (Off the Newport Freeway [55] and Fairview St.) This huge ten-day event is held at the Orange County Fairgrounds and is great fun for the whole family. There are lots of carnival rides and games; rodeos (that last a few hours); speedway racing; farm animals (featured in shows and races, and to pet); craft booths; acrobats; exhibits; demonstrations (such as a firefighter combat challenge, etc.); great food; and top-name entertainment. Each day brings new attractions and events. There is so much to see and do that one day might just not be enough! Call for discount days and the calendar of special events. Adults are $6; ages 13 - 17 are $5; ages 6 - 12 are $2; children 5 years and under.

PEARSON PARK AMPHITHEATER, Anaheim. (See **JUNE**, PEARSON PARK AMPHITHEATER for description.)

RINGLING BROS. & BARNUM AND BAILEY CIRCUS, Anaheim. (714) 704-2500, Arrowhead Pond. "The Greatest Show on Earth" comes to town for a little over a week at the end of July. Catch some of the most amazing animal and acrobatic acts ever performed!! Tickets range from $9 - $25, depending on performance date and time.

U.S. OPEN SANDCASTLE COMPETITION, Imperial Beach. (619) 424-6663, Imperial Beach Pier. This terrific, three-day sandcastle competition and parade is fun to either sign up as a competitor, as there are various age categories, or just watch other creative people at work. We are amazed at the fantastic designs the sand sculpturers dream up. Free admission.

AUGUST:

AIR SHOW, Miramar. (619) 527-6289, Miramar Naval Air Station. This two-day air show features the Blue Angels, civilian pilots, etc., performing thrilling aviation stunts and maneuvers. On the ground are over 200 displays of airplanes, helicopters, and military equipment. Admission and parking are free.

ANIFEST, Los Angeles area. (818) 842-8330. The International Animated Film Association brings together professional animators, collectors, and fans for this animated event. Exhibits include cels, movies, figurines, and other memorabilia. Activities throughout the day include cartoon voice shows, seminars, etc. What a fun family outing! Call for current admission prices - tickets for past shows have been between $5 - $10.

CASA DE TORTUGA, Fountain Valley. (714) 962-0612, 10455 Circulo de Zapata. One weekend a year, this "House of Turtles" hosts an open-house. They are normally booked a year in advance for their tours of this wonderful turtle place, so this is a great opportunity to bring your 3-year-old and up child! There is no admission charge.

FORD FAMILY FUN SUMMER NIGHTS, Hollywood. (See **JUNE**, FORD FAMILY FUN for description.)

LONG BEACH SEA FESTIVAL, Long Beach. (562) 570-3100. This month long festival occurs on the weekend at various locations throughout Long Beach. Join the fun with boat races, swimming contests, a fishing rodeo, and a sand sculpture contest.

OLD MINERS DAYS, Big Bear. (909) 866-4607, on Big Bear Blvd. This three-weekend event features a logger's jubilee with tree cutting and log rolling contests; arts and crafts booths; a doo dah parade; and a grand finale parade. Parade entries range from elegant equestrian units to floats to old wagons (old flatbed wagons and the red Radio Flyer types, too), and clowns. Admission is free.

OPEN HOUSE AT THE HOLLYWOOD BOWL, Hollywood. (See **JULY**, OPEN HOUSE AT THE HOLLYWOOD BOWL for description.)

PEARSON PARK AMPHITHEATER, Anaheim. (See **JUNE**, PEARSON PARK AMPHITHEATER for description.)

RENAISSANCE ART FESTIVAL, Long Beach. (562) 438-9903 at Rainbow Lagoon. Heralding all Lords and Ladies who wish to participate in two days of festivities that harken back to days of old! Renaissance period events include jugglers, magicians, children's games, hands-on exhibits, fencing instructions, and musical entertainment. Admission is $10 for adults; $4 for ages 5 - 12; children 4 years and under are free. Tickets bought in advance are less expensive.

SOUTHERN CALIFORNIA INDIAN CENTER'S ANNUAL POWWOW, Costa Mesa. (714) 530-0225, Orange County Fairgrounds. Come see spectacular traditional Native American dancing. (The hoop dance is our favorite.) Also enjoy handcrafted arts and crafts, and food. Call for admission fees.

TALLSHIPS FESTIVAL, Dana Point. (714) 496-2274, 24200 Dana Point Harbor Dr. at the Orange County Marine Institute. The three-day festival begins as the majestic tall ships sail into port. Tour the ships, enjoy demonstrations of the sailing arts, and see "Pirates of Penzance" performed on board ship. Pirates and sailors everywhere. Music, crafts, and food make this festival worth *sea*ing. Free admission. The one-hour play is $15 - $20 per person.

VENTURA COUNTY FAIR, Ventura. (805) 648-3376 at Seaside Park. This major event is a week and a half long. The fair offers lots of carnival rides, plus rodeos, pig races, a petting zoo, pony rides, on-going entertainment, and several buildings that have arts and crafts for sale as well as vendor demonstrations. Whew! Fireworks go off every night at 9pm. Admission is $6 for adults; $3 ages 6 - 12; children 5 years and under are free. The fair is open daily from 10am - midnight.

SEPTEMBER:

CALIFORNIA AMERICAN INDIAN DAYS CELEBRATION, San Diego. (619) 281-5964, Balboa Park. Usually held on the third weekend of the month, the Celebration showcases American Indian singers and (fantastic) dancers, as well as tribal arts and crafts to purchase or try making yourself. Open from 10am - 4pm; admission is free.

CORNELIUS JENSEN BIRTHDAY CELEBRATION, Riverside. (909) 369-6055, 4307 Briggs St. The Jensen-Alvarado Ranch Historic Park celebrates Cornelius's birthday on the last Saturday in September with a lot of hoopla. Watch and/or join in the gold panning, soap making, sheep shearing, branding, and spinning and weaving demonstrations. Kick up your heels to fun country music. The party goes from 10am - 4pm, and costs $3 for adults; $1.50 for kids 12 years and under.

GREEN MEADOW FARM, Los Angeles. (800) 393-3276, 4235 Monterey Rd., Ernest Debs Regional Park. The Farm is here from the end of September through October. (See **MARCH**, GREEN MEADOWS FARM for a description.)

LONDON BRASS RUBBING CENTER, Long Beach. (562) 436-4047, 525 E. 7th Street at St. Luke's Episcopal Church. Your child will thoroughly enjoy making medieval brass rubbings offered on Saturdays and Sundays from September through November. He/she can choose a white or black wax background paper, and colors like gold and silver for the intricate designs. Using the facsimiles of tombstones from England knights, ladies in fancy dresses, Shakespeare, etc. will be recreated. Small groups can have a twenty-minute "tour" and learn a little more about the stories behind some of the facsimiles. The Rubbing Center is open on weekends from 10am - 5pm. The cost per rubbing starts at about $3.

LOS ANGELES COUNTY FAIR, Pomona. (909) 623-3111, off the 10 Fwy. at Fairplex. Billed as the world's largest county fair, this three-week event is wonderful (and exhausting). It has carnival rides and games, livestock shows, horse-racing, flower and garden shows, booths, and several buildings of exhibits that display and sell truly unique items and products. Come early and plan to spend the whole day - there is a lot to see and do (and buy!). Admission is $9 for adults; $7 for seniors; $5 for ages 6 to 12; children 5 years and under are free. Parking is $4.

POWAY DAYS COMMUNITY CELEBRATION AND RODEO, Poway. (619) 748-0016 - parade info; (619) 748-0022 - rodeo info, held at the PRCA Arena on Tierra Bonita Rd. This is definitely a reason to come to Poway! The multi-day event kicks off with a parade that will have your kids hootin and hollerin'. PRCA rodeos (i.e. Professional Rodeo Cowboys Association) are one of the best in the nation with cowboys competing in several categories. See a show and stay for the entertainment, food, and booths. Tickets range from $8 - $14.

POW WOW, Newhall. (805) 259-0855, 24151 San Fernando Road at the William S. Hart Park. This celebration of Native Americans, usually held the last weekend in September, includes a dance contest (not disco), craft fair, mountain men, exhibits, tours, and great food.

SEAFEST, Corona del Mar. (714) 729-4400. This two-weekend fest has twelve different events including a sand castle and sand sculpting contest. Call about participating in this event and come down to "sea" the most imaginative things created with sand.

OCTOBER:

ARBORFEST, Fullerton. (714) 773-3579, 1900 Associated Rd. at Fullerton Arboretum. Pumpkins and bales of hay add to the atmosphere of celebrating harvest time here in early October. There's an apple press to make juice, and an opportunity to make butter, to "wash" clothes the old-fashioned way, and watch lace being made. The Heritage House is open and becomes a part of this harvest festival. Minimal fee.

EDWARDS AIR FORCE BASE. (805) 277-8050. Come see an outstanding air show put on by the air force. Watch acrobatic teams, biplanes, wing-walking, military air-ground task force demonstrations, and more. Bring sunscreen and hearing protection because some of the planes are loud!

FALL HALLOWEEN FAIR AND CELEBRATION, Fullerton. (714) 738-6595, 1201 W. Malvern Ave. at the Muckenthaler Cultural Center Foundation. This one-day affair offers face-painting, pumpkin decorating, games, and yummy cookies, followed by two concert performances. In the past, the Irvine Youth Orchestra has performed "Phantom of the Opera," with an intermission of a costume parade on stage, followed by "Carnival of the Animals," a reading accompanied by music. A fun, cultural way to celebrate fall. Call for hours. Admission is $3 per person.

FAULKNER FARM, Santa Paula. (805) 525-9293, 14292 W. Telegraph Rd., off Briggs Rd. This seven-acre pumpkin farm, part of a larger working farm, offers a month of family fun in the country. The Fall Festival is a major attraction featuring pumpkins ranging in size from mini up to 200 pounds, farm animals, and hayrides pulled by Clydesdale horses ($2). Afternoon weekday hayrides are 50¢ and operate 1:30pm - 5pm. Weekends also offer Grandpa's Model T rides ($2); pumpkin painting; face painting; western dancing; farm demonstrations; craft booths; and a variety of fresh foods to purchase, such as jams and squash. Bring your own little punkins here, and have a picnic, too! Call to reserve special school-group "tours," which includes hayrides, a pumpkin, and other goodies for $2.50 per person. The farm is open daily from the first Saturday in October through October 30 from 10am - 5:30pm. Admission is free.

HALLOWEEN ALTERNATIVES - For alternatives to door-to-door trick or treating, check your local park or church as many of them offer carnival-type of fun, a safer atmosphere, and still plenty of candy!

HARVEST FESTIVAL, Anaheim. (714) 999-8900, 800 W. Katella Ave., Anaheim Convention Center. This three-day event is the place to go for all your shopping needs and desires. Life in the nineteenth-century is the theme here, so an old-fashioned ambiance is prevalent through the Harvest Festival. Over 1,400 craftsman and artisans sell unique items, from hand-carved train whistles to elegant jewelry, and everything in between. There is on-going entertainment of craft demonstrations (which keeps kids intrigued) and live bands. Admission is $5 for adults; $3 for children.

HARVEST FESTIVAL, San Diego. (619) 236-6500, San Diego Concourse. (See above HARVEST FESTIVAL entry for a description.)

INTERNATIONAL FESTIVAL OF MASKS, Los Angeles. (213) 937-5544, Hancock Park (corner of Wilshire and Curson). Folkloric dance from all over the world, ethnic music, theater, storytelling, mask makers, and mask vendors contribute to this unusual weekend festival. Sunday's huge mask parade is an absolute hit with kids. The festival runs from 11am - dusk on both days. Admission is free.

KIDSARTZ FESTIVAL, San Diego. (619) 239-0512, Balboa Park. This one-day event is designed just for kids to create, have fun, and take home a special craft. Some workshop activities and performances include hat-making, face painting, storytelling, etc. The festival runs from 10am - 6pm. Admission is free.

LEGO CONSTRUCTION ZONE, San Diego. (619) 239-8180, Horton Plaza on the Sportsdeck. Everyone likes Legos™! Each participant is given a certain number of Legos™ and an assignment to make a unique design within a certain time limit. The competition is fun and creative, and who knows - your child might be an engineering genius! Free admission.

LONDON BRASS RUBBING CENTER, Long Beach. (See **SEPTEMBER**, LONDON BRASS RUBBING CENTER for a description.)

MOUNTAIN MAN DAYS (RENDEZVOUS), Banning. (909) 922-9200, 16th and Wilson at Gilman Historic Ranch and Wagon Museum. From Wed. - Sun. meet the trappers, mountain men, and cowboys of the Old West. Visit an 1700-1800's era living history encampment and see clothing, tools, and equipment as this time period is re-created. Bring your gold dust ($) to use at the trading posts. Food and drink is available. School tours are by reservation during the week. Public parking is $4. Call for school tour fees.

NATIONAL FIRE PREVENTION WEEK, all over. Call your local fire station to see if they are doing something special this week. Many offer tours of the fire engines and station houses, and sometimes kids can even dress up like a fireman. The safety tips are invaluable.

PUMPKIN CITY'S PUMPKIN FARM, Laguna Hills. 24203 Avenue De La Carlota, Laguna Hills Mall. This one-acre, fenced-in farm takes over part of the Mall parking lot for the month of October. The ground is covered with hay, while tractors, cornstalks and bales of hay all around help enhance the autumn mood. There are Indian tepees to go in; straw horses to "ride"; real ponies to ride ($3); a child's-size train to ride ($1.25); elephant rides on the weekends; and a few kiddie rides. There is also entertainment - costumed characters and country bands. Group reservations are offered that include special rates on pumpkins and pony rides. And oh yes - there are thousands of pumpkins here of all shapes and sizes - mini pumpkins to ones that weigh up to 200 pounds! The farm is open daily from 9:30am - 9pm. Free admission.

PUMPKIN PATCHES - Many offer hayrides and other special activities, so that looking for the Great Pumpkin is a lot of fun.

SAN DIEGO ZOO, San Diego. (619) 234-3153, Park Blvd. in Balboa Park. The world-famous zoo is usually free on the first Monday of October in celebration of Founder's Day. What a way to celebrate!

STORYTELLING FESTIVAL, San Juan Capistrano. (714) 768-1916. Enjoy a weekend of tall tales and some great storytelling. Learn fundamentals of storytelling from masters, or come to just be entertained. Your kids might even get their fill of stories, for a day or two at least. Sessions range from free to $4 and $10 per.

THRESHING BEE AND ANTIQUE ENGINE SHOW, Vista. (619) 941-1791, Antique Gas & Steam Engine Museum. (See **JUNE** THRESHING BEE AND ANTIQUE ENGINE SHOW for details.)

NOVEMBER:

DOO DAH PARADE, Pasadena. (818) 795-3355, near the heart of Old Town in downtown Pasadena. The spoof of parades is held the Sunday before Thanksgiving. There are no actual rules regarding the parade or the participants, but the wackier the groups or presentation, the better. Kids laugh it up as they see some of the funkiest outfits and most unique dance routines ever performed. Everyone may act up and act out! The parade goes from 11am - 1pm. Admission is free.

FAULKNER FARM, Santa Paula. (See **DECEMBER**, FAULKNER FARM for a description.)

GARDEN GROVE WINTERFEST CARNIVAL, Garden Grove. (714) 741-5200, 11300 Stanford Ave. at the H. Louis Senior Center. A lot of holiday fun is packed into this one day! There is a snow play area, pictures with Santa, games, and a crafts area where kids can make a variety of projects like ornaments, wrapping paper, Christmas cards, etc. Each activity takes one to two tickets, and tickets are only 25¢ each!

HOLLYWOOD CHRISTMAS PARADE, Hollywood. (213) 469-2337, starting at Gower St. and Sunset Blvd. All the stars come out at night - I mean the stars of Hollywood - for this annual celebrity-packed parade that is put on the Sunday after Thanksgiving. There are fantastic floats, live bands, equestrian units, and of course, Santa Claus. The two-hour parade goes along a three-mile course through the streets of Hollywood. Reserved grandstand seating is $30 - $40 per person. (Standing room is free, but it does get crowded, so get here early.) The parade goes from 6pm to 8pm. All-day parking in nearby lots is $5 - $15.

INDIAN VILLAGE, Los Angeles. (800) 393-3276, 4235 Monterey Rd., Ernest Debs Regional Park. The Indian Village is here mid-November through December. (See **FEBRUARY**, INDIAN VILLAGE for a description.)

LOGANS CANDY, Ontario. (909) 984-5410, 125 W. "B" St. This small retail candy store makes candy canes starting in November. A limited number of tours are given to watch the striped candy become a sweet reality. During the twenty-minute tour, the process is first described, then kids see it being made, and afterwards there is time for questions. The cost is $2.25 per person and includes a small bag of candy.

LONDON BRASS RUBBING CENTER, Long Beach. (See **SEPTEMBER**, LONDON BRASS RUBBING CENTER for a description.)

MOTHER GOOSE PARADE, (619) 444-8712. This parade has been going strong and gaining momentum since 1946. It features over 5,000 participants - bands, equestrian units, clown acts, and the best part of all - lots of floats depicting Mother Goose rhymes and fairy tales. The parade takes place the Sunday before Thanksgiving. Admission is free.

PILGRIM PLACE FESTIVAL, Claremont. (909) 621-9581, 660 Avery Road. This timely festival takes place on the second Friday and Saturday in November. Thanksgiving is a time to be thankful (and to eat), but do you know how it all began? Find out by watching the educational highlight here, an hour-long, live re-enactment called, "The Pilgrim Story." This play is put on at 1pm each day by the retired church professionals who live at this center. Call for special school performances. Other activities (50¢ each) include riding the Mayflower-on-Wheels, taking a mini-train ride, and visiting the Wampanoag Indian Village for story time, games, etc. A favorite activity here is called the Glue In. Tables full of recycled items are available for kids to glue onto a piece of cardboard to create a masterpiece (50¢). The festival runs from 10am - 4pm. Free admission and free, but hard-to-find, parking.

POWWOW, Indio. (See **MARCH**, POWWOW for description.)

SAWDUST WINTER FANTASY, Laguna Beach. (714) 494-3030, 935 Laguna Canyon Rd. Three acres of fun in the snow and other cool activities are offered for nine days. Real snow is brought in daily so you can teach your little angels how to make snow angels. Family entertainment includes jugglers and carolers. Children's art activities, like mask making, are different each day and are free! Over 150 artists have booths here, with on-going crafting demonstration. Get your holiday shopping done and keep the kids happy; all at the same time! To complete the fantasy, Santa Claus makes his rounds. Open from 11am - 7pm. Admission is $5 for adults; kids 11 years and under are free. There is metered parking and $5-a-day parking lots available.

STRICTLY DISNEY SHOW AND SALE, San Diego. (619) 747-2990, 1895 Camino del Rio at the Scottish Rite Center. Old and new Disney collectables are available to look at and purchase, such as animation cels, drawings, books, buttons, ornaments, cast member items, and more. Prices range from inexpensive to practically buying a piece of the Matterhorn. Call for dates and hours. Admission is $4 for adults; kids 12 years and under are free.

DECEMBER:

CHRISTMAS BOAT PARADE OF LIGHTS, Newport Beach. (714) 729-4400, Newport Beach Harbor. The largest and oldest boat parade, with more than 200 participants, sets sail December 17 through December 23. Consider taking the kids on a cruise for a closer look at the beautiful boats. The ideal location for viewing is Balboa Island, but you should arrive before 5:30 as parking is limited. If you are going to have dinner here, be sure to make reservations. The parade hours are from 6:30pm - 8:45pm.

CHRISTMAS BOAT PARADE OF LIGHTS, San Diego. (619) 488-0501, Mission Bay/San Diego; (619) 722-5751, Oceanside. Call these numbers to find out when and where, specifically, the boat parades will be held this year. The parades are a highlight of the season for my kids.

CHRISTMAS OPEN HOUSE AND PARADE, San Diego. (619) 435-8896 or (619) 437-8788, Ferry Landing Marketplace on Coronado. Start off your holiday season with a bang as this one-day event concludes with a fireworks display. During the day, kids will enjoy a parade along Orange Avenue, entertainment, and Santa's arrival by ferry (the reindeer are taking a rest). Admission is free.

CRUISE OF LIGHTS, Huntington Beach. (714) 840-7542, Peter's Landing. The Huntington Harbor Philharmonic Committee sponsors this event, raising money to donate to the youth music programs in Orange County. From December 13 through December 21 or so, forty-five-minute boat tours are given around the decorated homes of the harbor area. These homes have entered a competition, so you will see the creme de la creme, like the Sweepstakes winner, the Most Beautiful, the Most Traditional, etc. You'll also hear interesting commentary. Some boats along the way are also decked out in their Christmas best. Tours are offered from 5:30pm - 8:30pm. Tickets Mon. - Thurs. are $8.50 for adults, $5 for ages 2 to 12; Fri. - Sun., $9.50 for adults, $5 for ages 2 to 12. Book early!

FAULKNER FARM, Santa Paula. (805) 525-9293, 14292 W. Telegraph Rd., off Briggs Rd. Give your family an early Christmas present by spending a day at Christmas Forest, open daily, starting the day after Thanksgiving through December 23. This twelve-acre tree farm, part of a larger working farm, offers hundreds of trees to choose from to cut (saw, gloves, and tree carts are available), or purchase one pre-cut. Be on the lookout for deer and bunnies. Ask about the family tree decorating contest that includes receiving a free tree and decorating it for cash prizes. Also offered are train rides ($2); free horse-drawn hayrides; a fire pit; snack bar (weekends only); carolers; and craft booths. Admission is free. Morning school groups with a reservation includes a train ride and seedling for $2 per person.

FIRST NIGHT, Fullerton. (714) 738-6545, bordered by Lemon, Malden, Chapman, and Commonwealth. Bring in the New Year all night long! Activities include entrance to the Fullerton Museum Center; music and dancing in the streets; and a fun zone for kids that includes kid's karaoke, face painting, a petting zoo, and rides. Fireworks light up your life at midnight! First Night fun happens between 7pm - midnight. Tickets are $12 for adults; $6 for kids 12 years and under.

FLOATING PARADE OF 1,000 LIGHTS, Long Beach Harbor. (562) 435-4093. Come enjoy the boats on parade that are adorned with Christmas lights and decorations. Prizes are awarded in several categories. The best views are from Shoreline Village or Parkers Lighthouse.

GLORY OF CHRISTMAS, Garden Grove. (714) 54-GLORY (4-5679), Crystal Cathedral, 12141 Lewis St. (Chapman Ave. and Lewis St.) Come see this one-hour, spectacular, musical production that is a re-enactment of the miraculous birth of Jesus Christ. It's complete with live animals and angels soaring overhead. (Arrive a little early and see the animals in a farm enclosure towards the back of the parking lot.) Tickets are $20 - $30 for adults; $2 less for kids and seniors. Ask about family discount days, when tickets are $15 per person.

HOLIDAY BOWL PARADE, San Diego. (619) 283-5808, Harbor Drive. Although football is the focal point for this one-day event, the colorful parade is also a highlight. Floats, inflatable balloons, numerous bands, and other entertainment await sports fans of all ages. Admission is free.

LIGHTED STREETS. Is there a street or two in your neighborhood that the owners have gone all out to decorate every year? One of our family traditions is to choose one special night during the Christmas season, go out to a restaurant, and walk up and down the festive streets to enjoy the lights and displays.

LONG BEACH CHRISTMAS WATER PARADE, Long Beach. (562) 436-3645, Naples Canals. Boat-owners cover their boats with Christmas lights and parade past decorated homes along Naples canals. If you miss the boat parade, just seeing the homes along here is a special treat.

LOS ANGELES HARBOR CHRISTMAS BOAT PARADE, San Pedro. (310) 832-7272, Ports O' Call. Owners go all out to decorate their boats and compete for the best in a wonderful parade that is put on the second weekend of December.

MARINA DEL REY CHRISTMAS BOAT PARADE, Marina del Rey. (310) 821-7614. On the second Saturday of December over eighty boats decorated to the hilt with Christmas lights and decorations sail around the marina's main channel. The parade is exciting with winners chosen for Best Theme, Best Humor, Best Music, etc. The best views are from Burton Chase Park or Fisherman's Village.

MUSEUMS, all over. Many of your favorite museums get all decked out for the holidays, especially the historical homes. Many also offer holiday programs with special family activities.

PARADE OF LIGHTS, Ventura. (805) 642-7753, at the Ventura Village. This festive boat parade is usually held the first or second weekend in December. Call for specific dates. Take the Bay Queen for an hour-and-a-half cruise, as it goes around the harbor and to see homes that are decorated for the holidays. Also, call for the dates when a white Christmas is celebrated at the Village with snow that is brought in specially for kids.

STAR OF BETHLEHEM, Santa Ana. (714) 564-6600, W. 17th St. and North Bristol at Rancho Santiago College Planetarium. For the first three Thursday nights in December, the planetarium sky is reset to the time of Jesus' birth. This is a scientific look at the configurations and causal effect of this miraculous star. The show starts at 7:30pm and costs $2 per person.

VICTORIAN CHRISTMAS, El Toro. (714) 855-2028, 25151 Serrano Rd., Heritage Hill Historical Park. On the first Saturday in December, experience Christmas during the turn-of-the century. Walk through these four historic buildings, which are festooned with old-fashioned decorations. Over fifty exhibits display and demonstrate homemade handicrafts like wooden carvings and lace making. A popular display is on antique engines that includes a milking machine, a corn husker, and a corn grinder. A free children's crafts area is available for kids to make their own special creations. Genteel entertainment is provided, and Saint Nicholas also pays a visit. Open from 10am - 4pm. Admission is $3 for adults; $2 for kids.

VIEWING TOURNAMENT OF ROSES FLOATS, Pasadena. Rosemont Pavilion - 700 Seco St. (Exit Foothill Freeway [210] at Seco St., E. to Pavilion at the corner of Rosemont Ave.) Rose Palace - 835 S. Raymond Ave. (Exit Pasadena Freeway [110] N. at Fair Oaks Ave., N. to Glenarm St., R. to Raymond, L. to Palace.) Come see the famous floats as they are being made, from December 28 through December 31. Workers spend days meticulously decorating them using plants, seeds, tree bark, flowers, and single petals. Viewing times are from 9am - 9pm. Minimal fee.

WILDLIGHTS, Palm Desert. (760) 346-5694, 47900 Portola Ave., at the Living Desert Wildlife and Botanical Park. This six-week display features nearly a dozen, larger-than-life animals illuminated in lights, sometimes including a thirty-foot snowman, a gigantic teddy bear, assorted desert critters, and a golfing Santa. Live entertainment, good food, and a visit from Santa Claus (bring your own camera) add to the holiday festivities. The park reopens at 6pm and stays open until 9pm for these wild nights. (The animals are put to bed - it's just a people party.) Admission is $4 for adults; $2.50 for children 11 years and under.

WINTER WONDERLAND, Corona del Mar. (714) 644-3151, Grant Howald Park, between Iris and 5th Ave. If you don't feel like driving a few hours to the snow, just drive to Corona del Mar for this one-day event. Bring your mittens and have a great time building a snowman or starting having a snow ball fight with your 6 to 13 year olds. Food and beverages are available for purchase. The hours are 10am - 1pm and it's free!

IDEAS / RESOURCES

(General ideas of where else to go and what to do, plus where to find specific resource information.)

AIRPLANE or HELICOPTER RIDES -
Look in the phone book or call small, local airports for flight information.

ANIMALS -
AA Laboratories, (714) 893-5675, located in Westminster, sells fertilized eggs ($5 for a dozen chick eggs; $12.50 for a dozen chick embryos) and rents incubators ($10 a week) for home births without the labor pains! Be forewarned, however - very little instruction comes with your eggs and incubator. Tip #1 - Go to the library to research the process (check out picture books of developing chicks and ducks, etc.); # 2 - Pick up an information sheet (and feed) at Blacksmith's Corner, (562) 531-0386 in Bellflower, or at a similar pet store near you. And yes, if you do not want to raise the birds, AA Labs will (usually) take them back and donate them to farms, zoos, etc.
Insect Lore, (800) LIVE BUG (548-3284). This catalog offers living science, giving families the opportunity to observe insects transforming and growing. Our favorites are the Butterfly Kits (which includes caterpillars, food, and information); Earthworms and Compost Kit; Praying Mantis (egg case and info); Silkworm (eggs); Ladybird Beetles (i.e. ladybugs, to lay people); and Frog Hatchery Kits. It also offers owl pellet (kits), plus other science experiments, books, and visual aids.

ARTS AND CRAFTS -
Many places offer free or minimal fee classes/workshops for kids. Check out your local craft stores, such as Michaels (ask about Kids Club Saturdays); Ben Franklin Crafts; Lakeshore Learning Materials store; or The Bead Boutique in Irvine, (714) 725-0468. Also, look under "Arts and Crafts" in the main section of the book.

AUDIO TAPES -
The following are just a few of our favorite, non-musical, tapes:
Adventures in Odyssey, (800) A-FAMILY (232-6459) - 6 tapes for about $25.Focus on the Family puts out this tape series consisting of 12 half-hour- long, Biblically-based, radio dramas. The stories are centered around a fictional soda shop/Bible Room/Imagination Station/kid's hang-out called Whit's End, and the people that live in the small (made-up) town of Odyssey. Each episode involves kids, families, dilemmas, solutions, morals, wit, and wisdom. I can't recommend these adventures highly enough!

Boomerang, (800) 333-7858 - $7.95 per tape; $43.95 for 12 tapes. This audio magazine is filled with 70 minutes of stories of famous people, jokes, mysteries to solve, current events, and fun and factual information about the various states. Each issue is presented by kids, for kids; designed for ages 6 and up.

Classical Kids Series, retails for about $10.98 per tape. The tapes can be found in most larger retail record stores or ordered through catalogs such as Rainbow Re-Source Center, (800) 705-8809. Each tape in this wonderful series tells the story of a famous composer, told in play format, while the composer's music plays in the background. Titles include, "Beethoven Lives Upstairs," "Mozart's Magical Fantasy," etc.

Greathall Productions, (800) 477-6234 - about $9.95 per tape. Be enthralled by award-winning storyteller, Jim Weiss. Kids (and adults) of all ages will enjoy the masterful retelling of (mostly) classic stories. Tape titles include "Arabian Nights," "Sherlock Holmes for Children," "Three Musketeers," "Giants!," "Greek Myths," "Shakespeare for Children," "Animal Tales," etc.

BASEBALL -
Angels at Anaheim Stadium, (714) 663-9000.
Dodgers at Dodger Stadium, (213) 224-1400.
Padres at Jack Murphy Stadium, (619) 283-4494.
Minor league games can be major league fun. Check out teams such as Bakersfield Blaze, (805) 322-1363; High Desert Mavericks, (619) 246-6287; Lake Elsinore Storm, (909) 245-4487; Lancaster Jethawks, (805) 726-5400; Mission Viejo Vigilantes, (714) 699-1616; Rancho Cucamonga Quakes, (909) 481-5000; and San Bernardino Stampede, (909) 888-9922. High school and college games are fun, too.

BASKETBALL -
Clippers at L.A. Memorial Coliseum and Sports Arena, (213) 748-6136.
Lakers at Great Western Forum, (310) 419-3100.
Also check out high school and college games.

BATTING CAGES -
"Hey batter, batter" - great for hitting practice, in season or out.

BILLIARDS -
Several billiard parlors offer a family-friendly atmosphere.

BOOKS -
Many book stores have story times and/or craft times. Some of the bigger book stores, such as Barnes and Noble, Borders, and Crown have a huge children's selection, as well as a children's reading

area. Many smaller bookstores cater specifically to kids and are delightful to browse in. Also see "Educational Toys, Books, and Games" in this section.
Used book stores are a terrific bargain. To name just a few, try:
Acres of Books in Long Beach, (562) 437-6980.
Book Baron in Anaheim, (714) 527-7022 (vintage books and used books)
Book City, (213) 466-2525 in Hollywood, (818) 848-4417 in Burbank - specializing both in new and used books.
Brindles in Tustin, (714) 731-5773 (new and used).
Thrift stores and garage sales are another great resource for used books.

BOWLING -
Many alleys offer bumper bowling for kids, where the gutters are covered so kids always hit the pins.

CAMPING -
Campgrounds mentioned in this book are usually listed under the "Great Outdoors" or "Beaches" sections. Call Destinet at (800) 444-7275 to make camping reservations at any California State Park. Check your library or local book store for books written just on camping, too.

CELEBRITIES -
Call the Walk of Fame at Hollywood Chamber of Commerce, (213) 469-8311, to find out when the next celebrity will be honored with a ceremony dedicating his/her star along this famous "walk." Ceremonies occur almost monthly.

CIRCUS -
Check sports arenas, or newspapers for (as examples):
Circus Vargas
Cirque Du Solei
Ringling Bros. & Barnum and Bailey Circus

CONSTRUCTION SITES -
If you're toolin' around, these sites can give your youngster constructive ideas to build on.

CONVENTION CENTERS -
They host a multitude of activities, many of them geared for children, such as Kid's Stuff Expo, toy shows, circuses, etc. Call them intermittently to see what's going on:
Anaheim, (714) 999-8925 ext. 9888 - recorded info; (714) 999-8999 - real person info.
Long Beach, (562) 436-3661.
Los Angeles, (213) 741-1151.

San Diego, (619) 525-5000.

COUPONS -
Call the Visitors Center of the city you are planning to visit as they often offer coupons (and tour booklets) for attractions. For instance "The Family Values Coupon Book," for Orange County, features savings at over 50 area attractions, hotels, restaurants, and shops. Call (714) 999-8999 for information. The San Diego Visitors Center, (619) 236-1212, offers a free "VISA Preferred in San Diego for Super Savings" coupon booklet that saves on main attractions, harbor cruises, restaurants, and more.

CPR CLASSES -
Call your local Red Cross or hospital for class information. (This is a great idea for babysitters, too!)

DESERT -
The California Desert Information Center in Barstow, (619) 255-8769, is the contact place for people exploring the deserts from Mexico to the Mojave. Find out about off-roading, camping, sight seeing, hiking, etc. The Center itself is a mini attraction. Open daily 9am - 5pm; closed New Year's Day and Christmas.

EDUCATIONAL TOYS, BOOKS, and GAMES -
There are numerous stores and catalogs out there offering good quality, educational items. Some of our favorite toy stores include F.A.O. Schwartz, Imaginarium, Lakeshore Learning, and Learning Express. Many museum gift shops offer a terrific line of (fun and) educational supplies. Look in your telephone directory for two other great resources - teacher supply stores and, specifically, children's bookstores. Also check out the following companies that offer catalogs and/or home workshops for their products:

Discovery Toys, (800) 426-4777 - carries a fantastic line of toys, books, games, and computer software.

Dorling Kindersley Books, (800) 652-3551, Orlando office, or (888) 225-3535 (Ellen Knowles, independent consultant) - offers outstanding books.

Usborne Books, (800) 474-1828 or (714) 828-6664 (Debra Nunnally, independent consultant) - offers top-quality books for all interests and ages.

EQUESTRIAN SHOWS -
English and Western riding, jumping, prancing, etc., are all part of seeing a horse show. Call your local equestrian center for dates and times.

FARMER'S MARKETS -

See "Edible Adventures" in the main section of the book for details.

FOOTBALL -
Chargers at Jack Murphy Stadium, (619) 280-2121.
High school and college games are fun, too.

GYM CLASSES FOR KIDS -
Some suggestions are:
Gymboree - Check your local phone book for listings. Classes are offered for parents and their children - newborns through 4 years old - that can include easy exercise, songs, bubbles, and visits from Gymbo, the clown.
My Gym - Classes are offered for the younger set. In Newport Beach, call (714) 261-5252; in Aliso Viejo, call (714) 360-4668.
Y.M.C.A. - They offer fun fitness programs for kids.

HOBBIES AND MODELS -
Kids like to collect - anything! For example - bottlecaps, dolls, miniatures (dollhouses), postcards, rocks, sports cards, stamps, etc. Other hobby ideas include model-making (i.e. cars, planes, rockets, and trains), creating jewelry, sewing, etc.

HOCKEY -
Ice Dogs at Long Beach Arena in Long Beach, (562) 423-3647.
Kings at Great Western Forum in Inglewood, (310) 419-3100.
Mighty Ducks at Arrowhead Pond in Anaheim, (714) 704-2400.
San Diego Gulls at the Sports Arena in San Diego, (619) 688-1800

HORSEBACK RIDING -
Neigh doubt about it, this is a terrific family outing!

HOT AIR BALLOON RIDES -
Up, up and away! Hot air balloon rides are recommended for ages 10 and over, as younger children might get scared of the flames shooting out (i.e. the "hot air"); they might get bored; and they can't see very well over the basket. Kids, however, are enthralled by watching the balloon being inflated! Inquire about Hot Air Balloon Festivals for a real colorful outing. Most of the companies listed fly over Del Mar, Palm Springs, and Temecula. Flights are about an hour and include a champagne breakfast. Prices are per person. Here are just a few names and numbers to get you started:
American Balloon Charters, (800) FLY OVER (359-6837) - about $165.
Fantasy Balloon Flights, (800) GO ABOVE (462-2683) - about $135.
Sunrise Balloons, (800) 548-9912 - between $125 - $140.

ICE SKATING -
   For instance, Glacial Garden Skating Arena, (562) 429-1805, in
   Lakewood has three rinks - two for the ice and one for in-line
   skating. They also offer broomball which is *fun*tastic! Disney Ice,
   (714) 535-7465, is the rink where the Mighty Ducks practice!

JUNKYARDS -
   For kids who like to take things apart and make new creations,
   these are wonderful places to visit.

KITE FLYING -
   Go fly a kite! Call the San Diego Kite Club, (619) 685-2885,
   which is affiliated with the American Kite Association, for
   information on membership and activities.

LIBRARIES -
   Your local library has a lot to offer! Besides book, video, and
   cassette lending, many offer free storytelling on a regular basis
   and/or finger plays, puppet shows, and crafts. Some libraries
   also encourage your bookworms by offering summer reading
   programs.

MAGAZINES -
   If you only receive one magazine, make it "Family Fun." Put out
   by Disney, each edition is packed with do-able crafts, snacks,
   party ideas, games, activities, and family-friendly places to travel.
   Pick it up at the newsstand or call (800) 289-4849 for
   subscription information. (Currently, $14.95 for 10 issues.)

MALLS -
   Going to the mall can be a fun excursion with kids, especially if the
   mall has "extra" features like a merry-go-round or fountains; or, if it
   is spectacular in design, has unique shops and restaurants, etc. Just
   a few of our top picks include :
      Fashion Island, (714) 721-2000, Newport Center Dr., Newport
         Beach.
      Horton Plaza, (619) 238-1596, between Broadway and G St. and
         First and Fourth Ave., San Diego.
      South Coast Plaza and Crystal Court, (714) 435-2000, Bristol St.
         off the 405 Fwy., Costa Mesa.

MOVIE THEATERS -
   An obvious choice, but matinees can be an inexpensive and fun
   treat. Check theaters for summertime savings. For instance,
   Super Saver Theater in Seal Beach, (310) 594-9411, and in
   Norwalk, (310) 868-9694, sometimes offer summer movies for
   $1; AMC Theaters in Long Beach, (562) 435-4262, sometimes
   offer a book of 10 movies for $7.50.

PARKS -

Almost every local park offers classes or programs for free or at a minimal cost, such as a Saturday kid's cooking class, sidewalk chalk art day, etc.

PET STORES -

This is a fun mini-outing. (Ask about tours.) Cuddly puppies and adorable rabbits are great, but so are some of the stores listed below that offer more unusual animals:

Blacksmith's Corner in Bellflower, (562) 531-0386 - It's like visiting a mini-farm.

Last Straw Feed Store in Fallbrook, (760) 728-6482 - The animals are mostly outdoors; see a llama, camel, goats, turkeys, chickens, a gigantic Burmese python, etc.

Prehistoric Pets in Fountain Valley, (714) 964-3525 - Incredible! Exotic snakes (some 20ft. long) and monitor lizards from all over the world, plus a small fish pond in the middle of the store, and more.

Reptile Show in Fullerton, (714) 446-0470 - Iguanas, turtles, frogs, snakes, and more. They also offer educational assemblies.

Super Pets - It is a chain store, so look in your local phone book - fish, snakes, bunnies, iguanas, turtles, and birds.

PHOTO ALBUMS -

Tapped dry for ideas on just how to put together a creative and memorable photo album (using acid-free products, of course) for or with your kids:

"Creative Keepsakes" magazine, (888) 247-5282 - Browse through and implement the many ideas given here. Current subscription price is $19.95 for 6 issues.

Creative Memories, (800) 468-9335 - Call for information on purchasing craft scissors, and acid-free pages, stickers, cut outs, etc. Or, learn artistic techniques to organize and crop your photos by hosting or attending a workshop for you and your friends.

"Memory Maker" magazine, (303) 452-0048 - Pick up a copy of this beautifully laid out and inspirational magazine. Current subscription price is $24.95 for 4 issues.

PLAYGROUPS/TOT LOT -

Check local parks, newspapers, and "Parenting" magazine to hook up with a playgroup. This is a great way to share the joys and trials of raising children. For example:

MOPS (Mothers Of Preschooler), (303) 733-5353, is an international organization that has local meetings in almost every city. Moms usually meet at a church and talk, eat, listen to a speaker, and make a craft while their preschoolers are

being cared for by a Moppet. Great organization! Call the headquarters to find a MOPS near you.
Tot Lot is a playgroup designed for preschoolers (and their parents) to meet and play together at parks on a regular basis during the week, building those all-important socialization skills. Registration fees go towards crafts, snacks, and even field trips. Call, for example, Lakewood Recreation and Community Services, (562) 866-9771 for information on Tot Lot at Biscailuz, Bolivar, Boyar, Del Valle, and Mayfair parks.

RESTAURANTS -
See "Edible Adventures" in the main section of this book. Try eating at some unusual locations, such as airports, on boats (like the Queen Mary), etc. Take your kids out for ethnic foods, too.

ROLLER HOCKEY -
Blades at Great Western Forum in Inglewood, (310) 419-3100.
Bullfrogs at Arrowhead Pond in Anaheim, (714) 704-2400.

ROLLER SKATING -
On the sidewalks, around parks, etc. Fountain Valley Skating Center in Fountain Valley, (714) 847-6300, also offers stroller skating (skating around a rink while pushing your baby in a stroller) on Thurs. from 1pm - 2pm for $4 an hour per mother/child pair. Surf City Skatezone in Huntington Beach, (714) 842-9143, offers roller skating and ice skating under one roof!

SAN DIEGO THEATRE -
The San Diego Performing Arts League puts out a bimonthly booklet called "What's Playing?" has a complete listing of the music, dance, theater groups, specific show, dates, prices, etc., in the San Diego area. $10 for a year's subscription. Call (619) 238-0700 for more information.

SCIENCE PROGRAMS -
Check science museums for programs and workshops, including traveling programs that come to you. Inside the Outdoors, (714) 548-1175, sponsored by the Orange County Dept. of Ed., is just one example. Their traveling programs range from 45-minutes to all-day long, and start at $100 for up to 24 students. Launch Pad, (714) 546-2061, offers outstanding on-site and traveling programs.

SPORTS ARENAS -
Many special events are held at sports arenas including sporting events, concerts, Walt Disney's World on Ice, circuses, etc.:
Anaheim - Arrowhead Pond, (714) 704-2400.
Inglewood - Great Western Forum, (310) 419-3100.

Long Beach - Long Beach Arena, (562) 423-3647.
Los Angeles - L.A. Memorial Coliseum and Sports Arena, (213)
    748-6136.
San Diego - Sports Arena, (619) 688-1800.

SPORTING EVENTS -
Check out high school and college events. These local games
are a fun, inexpensive introduction to sports.

SWAP MEETS -
Give your kids a dollar or two to call their own as there are a lot
of inexpensive toys or jewelry items for them to choose from.
Everyone goes home happy with their treasures! Here's a list of
just a few good swap meets:
Alpine Village (indoor/outdoor) in Torrance, (213) 770-1961.
    Open Tues. - Sun., 8am - 2pm. Admission is 50¢.
Anaheim Marketplace (indoor) in Anaheim, (714) 999-0888. Over
    250 variety shops and a food court. They also have adjacent
    batting cages and arcade games. Open Wed. - Mon. from
    10am - 7pm. Free admission.
Kobey's Swap Meet (outdoor) at the sports arena parking lot in
    San Diego, (619) 226-0650. Taking up the equivalent of 12
    footballs fields, this swap meet offers bargains on everything
    under the sun. Open Thurs. - Sun., 7am - 3pm. Admission is
    50¢ on Thurs. and Fri.; $1 on Sat. and Sun. No charge for
    children 11 years and under.
Orange County Marketplace (outdoor) in Costa Mesa, (714) 723-
    6616. One of the best, with over 1,200 vendors, plus a food
    court. Open weekends only, from 8am - 3pm. Admission is $1
    for adults; children 12 years and under are free.
Rosebowl Flea Mart (outdoor) in Pasadena, (818) 577-3100.
    Held the second Sunday of each month. Admission is $15
    from 6am - 7:30am; $10 from 7:30am - 9am; $5 from 9am
    until it closes. Parking is $2.
Saugus Speedway Swapmeet (outdoor) in Saugus, (805) 259-
    3886. With over 700 vendors, this huge swap meet is held
    every Sunday from 8am - 3pm. Admission is $1 for adults;
    children 11 years and under are free.
Tip: Also check out 99¢ stores, which are along the same lines as
swap meets.

SWIMMING and WADING POOLS -
Community pools are open seasonally; call your local park or city
hall for information.

THRIFT STORES -

Teach your children the gift of thrift! Give them a few dollars to buy a "new" article of clothing, a toy, or a book. Tip: Main Street in the city of Ventura has 10 thrift stores in a row.

TICKETS -

Audiences Unlimited, (818) 506-0067, offers free tickets to watch the filming of almost all of the network television shows and many of their specials. For some shows, the minimum age for kids is 12 years old; for some, it's 21 years old.

Times ArtsTix, (619) 497-5000, located in San Diego next to Horton Plaza has half-price, day-of-performance, theater tickets available on a first-come, first-served, cash-only basis. Call for a listing of the day's half-price shows.

TOURS -

Also see "Tours" in the main section of the book. The following are general ideas of where you can go for group tours:

Animal Shelter
Airport
Bakery
Bank
Chiropractor
College/University
Dairy
Dentist
Factory
Fire Station
Florist
Grocery Store
Hospital
Hotel
Newspaper Office
Police Station
Post Office
Printer
Restaurant

TOYS -

Look in this section under "Educational Toys, Books, and Games." Two other listings worth mentioning are:

Constructive Playthings, (714) 636-7831 - Call for a catalog or visit their store in Garden Grove. They offer top-of-the-line toys, books, games, puzzles, etc., as well as lower priced, carnival-type prizes.

Oriental Trading Company, (800) 228-2269 - This catalog company offers bulk and individual novelty items, usually priced at the lower end of the scale.

VOLUNTEERING -
Volunteering is a terrific way to spend time with your children while teaching them the real values of life by giving and serving. Check with local churches and temples, as many have regular times when they go to help feed the homeless. Here are a few other volunteer agencies:

Fullerton Arboretum, (714) 278-3404. They encourage family participation in nursery projects (propagation, transplanting, weeding, etc.).

Green Networking for Orange County, (714) 449-9037. If you're concerned about the environment and don't know how to help or where to find information, this group provides you with names and numbers of more than 200 environmental groups, businesses, and agencies in Orange County.

Habitat For Humanity, (714) 895-4331. A non-profit organization committed to providing low-income, owner-occupied housing by utilizing volunteer labor and donated materials. (Former President Jimmy Carter is one of the more prominent members.) Volunteers are needed to build homes and serve on committees such as finance, construction, and public relations. Kids must be at least 16 years old to work on construction sites, but younger children can help with off-site activities such as registration, making lunches, etc.

St. Vincent de Paul - (619) 233-8500, ext. 1122. See the main section of the book under "Tours."

Volunteer Center of Greater Orange County, (714) 953-5757. A clearinghouse for a huge variety of age-appropriate opportunities, from feeding the homeless and visiting the elderly to planting trees, cleaning up parks, and removing graffiti. They even have a guide book on family volunteer activities.

ALPHABETICAL INDEX

INDEX BY CITY

INDEX BY PRICE

Free Occasionally - The following attractions have special days when there is no admission charged:

Los Angeles County

Fowler Museum - Every Thursday (located under MATHIAS BOTANICAL GARDEN), however parking is still $5.

George C. Page Museum - First Tuesday of each month.

Kidspace - Last Monday of each month (except October) from 5pm - 8pm.

Los Angeles County Museum of Art - Second Wednesday of each month.

Los Angeles State and County Arboretum - Third Tuesday of each month.

Natural History Museum of Los Angeles County - First Tuesday of each month.

Raymond M. Alf Museum - Every Wednesday.

Riverside County

California Museum of Photography - Every Wednesday.

San Diego County

Balboa Park Museums - See BALBOA PARK, as the museums vary in their "free day."

San Diego Zoo - First Monday in October.

San Diego Wild Animal Park - One day in early May, call for date.

Ventura County

Carnegie Art Museum - Fridays from 3pm - 6pm.

Palm Springs

Palm Springs Desert Museum - First Friday of every month.

- Free (!) -

ABOUT THE AUTHOR:

Fun and education are key words in our home. I enjoy home schooling my children; speaking to various groups; writing a weekly column for the Long Beach Press Telegram; writing other, soon-to-be-released books; and whatever else God brings my family's way!

I would appreciate your ideas about this book. Do you have a wonderful place to go with kids that wasn't included in this edition? Please let me know and I'll share it in the next one. You can write to me at:

FUN PLACES TO GO WITH KIDS
P.O. Box 376
Lakewood, CA 90714 - 0376

Fün Places to go With Kids
and educational

$14.95 plus tax and shipping

Please send copy(s) of this wonderful, innovative, well-written, absolutely fantastic, fun book to . . .

NAME _____

ADDRESS _____ CITY _____

STATE _____ ZIP _____ PHONE _____

ENCLOSED IS MY CHECK FOR $ _____ ($17.95 per book, includes tax and $2.00 for shipping.)

Make check payable to: **Fun Places**. Send to: **Fun Places Publishing, P.O. Box 376, Lakewood, CA 90714-0376**

--------✂--

Fün Places to go With Kids
and educational

$14.95 plus tax and shipping

Please send copy(s) of this wonderful, innovative, well-written, absolutely fantastic, fun book to . . .

NAME _____

ADDRESS _____ CITY _____

STATE _____ ZIP _____ PHONE _____

ENCLOSED IS MY CHECK FOR $ _____ ($17.95 per book, includes tax and $2.00 for shipping.)

Make check payable to: **Fun Places**. Send to: **Fun Places Publishing, P.O. Box 376, Lakewood, CA 90714-0376**

Fün Places to go With Kids
and educational

$14.95 plus tax and shipping

Please send copy(s) of this wonderful, innovative, well-written, absolutely fantastic, fun book to . . .

NAME _____

ADDRESS _____ CITY _____

STATE _____ ZIP _____ PHONE _____

ENCLOSED IS MY CHECK FOR $ _____ ($17.95 per book, includes tax and $2.00 for shipping.)

Make check payable to: **Fun Places**. Send to: **Fun Places Publishing, P.O. Box 376, Lakewood, CA 90714-0376**

- - - - - - ✂ -

Fün Places to go With Kids
and educational

$14.95 plus tax and shipping

Please send copy(s) of this wonderful, innovative, well-written, absolutely fantastic, fun book to . . .

NAME _____

ADDRESS _____ CITY _____

STATE _____ ZIP _____ PHONE _____

ENCLOSED IS MY CHECK FOR $ _____ ($17.95 per book, includes tax and $2.00 for shipping.)

Make check payable to: **Fun Places**. Send to: **Fun Places Publishing, P.O. Box 376, Lakewood, CA 90714-0376**